The Hardy Review

Volume IV   Winter 2001

THE THOMAS HARDY ASSOCIATION

The Hardy Review

*Edited
by
Rosemarie Morgan*

VOLUME IV   WINTER 2001

The Hardy Association Press
ISBN 0-9669176-7-7

First published in the United States in 2001
by The Hardy Association Press
124 Bishop Street, New Haven, CT 06511

© Copyright for the collection is retained by the Hardy Association Press. Copyright for individual essays is retained by the author.

All rights reserved. No part of this publication
may be reproduced, stored in a retrieval system,
or transmitted in any form or by any means,
electronic, mechanical, photocopying,
recording or otherwise without the
prior permission of the Copyright holders.

ISBN 0-9669176-7-7

Typesetting & cover design by Rosemarie Morgan.
Designed and originated in-house.
Printed by Goodcopy Inc, NewHaven

THE THOMAS HARDY ASSOCIATION

PRESIDENT:
ROSEMARIE MORGAN
www.yale.edu/hardysoc

Editorial Board

James Gibson	Ex, Christchurch Coll. Canterbury
Rosemarie Morgan	Yale University
William W. Morgan	Illinois State University
Richard Nemesvari	St Francis Xavier University
Linda Peterson	Yale University
Martin Ray	Aberdeen University
Robert Schweik	State University of N.Y at Fredonia
Keith Wilson	University of Ottawa

The Hardy Review
Editor: Rosemarie Morgan

Volume IV   Winter 2001

Copyright is retained by TTHA. Individual items will not be reproduced without the author's permission.
Contributors may reclaim their work for inclusion in book publication

CONTENTS

List of Illustrations	i
Editorial Column by Rosemarie Morgan	ii
TTHA FORUM: Hardy's Beliefs	2
TTHA POTM: Hardy and the Nature of Nature	38
➤ "Nature's Questioning"	39
➤ "The Mother Mourns"	44
➤ "The Subalterns"	46
➤ "The Lacking Sense"	49
➤ "In a Wood"	54
➤ "To Outer Nature," "June Leaves and Autumn"	60
➤ "Wagtail and Baby"; "On a Midsummer Eve"	63
➤ "Afterwards"	64
➤ "Shut Out That Moon"	71
➤ "Once at Swanage"	81
➤ "The Last Chrysanthemum"	85
➤ "The Year's Awakening"	85
➤ "The Night of the Dance"	88
TTHA FORUM: Hardy, Drama and Movies	91
➤ "The Claim"	94
➤ "Far From the Madding Crowd"	98
➤ A&E "Tess"	105
➤ "Jude"	115
TTHA FORUM: Notes and Queries	118
TTHA: "Checklist" by Robert Schweik	123
TTHA: Collation of the Gibson and Hynes Editions of Hardy's Poetry by Martin Ray	127
"The Excavating Consciousnsess in Hardy's *Two on a Tower*," by Andrew Radford.	141
"'A Complete Diorama': The Art of Restoration in Hardy's *The Return of the Native*," by Charles Lowe	148
Notes on Contributors	158
TTHA information and membership	159

Illustrations

Thomas Hardy, 1923, sketch by Augustus John	1
Stinsford Church, photograph by Dave Sands	7
Broken Key, drawing by Thomas Hardy	37
Wilted Vase, drawing by Thomas Hardy	59
Wagtails, by John Gould	63
Moon and Sea-Storm, photo-image by Roy Buckle	81
Robins, painting by Terence Lambert	87
Movie poster of *Jude*	116
"Is the Resemblance Strong?" by George du Maurier	120
Thomas Hardy, 1880	140
Bockhampton Cottage, photograph by Terry Linee	156

Editor's Column

ROSEMARIE MORGAN

WELCOME to the fourth volume in The Thomas Hardy Association's series of annual publications: *The Hardy Review*. In the period which has elapsed since Volume III appeared on the scene in the summer of 2000 TTHA has enjoyed, as ever, a year of intense literary activity.

Early in the spring of 2001, Professor Richard Nemesvari (Dept., of English, St. Francis Xavier University, Nova Scotia, Canada) was appointed to the Association's Council of Directors. Within a matter of weeks Richard had inaugurated a new TTHA "*Life*" page[1] which features

> information on Hardy's life and on the numerous biographies which have explored it. As well, the site lists resources such as letters, essays, notebooks, and interviews which contribute to our understanding of the relationship between his achievement as a writer and his personal experience (RN).

Also at this time, in mid-March, 2001, Professor Robert Schweik, TTHA's Vice President and "*Links*"director, was busy setting up an innovative "*Checklist*" page[2] which provides an up-to-the-minute listing of Hardy's works and works published on Hardy. The exceptional service provided by the "*Checklist*" is not only that of immediacy but also of comprehensiveness: relevant publications of all kinds are listed on this page as they come out – in the very moment of their emergence on the world literary market. In order to maximise the success of this ambitious project Bob recruited a group of 16 professors and Hardy scholars from across the globe, and conjoined them to the task of scanning assigned periodicals and publisher's lists in order to to document the relevant Hardy titles as and when these appeared in print publication or on the World Wide Web. The result is a unique and extensive bibliography which remains matchless in its scope and punctuality, within or beyond the internet.

---

[1] <http://www.yale.edu/hardysoc/LIFE/life.htm>
[2] <http://www.yale.edu/hardysoc/Members/MRRHome.htm>

In the hope of encouraging new membership in the Association the "*Checklist*" has been placed on yet another newly-established page. This is the "*Members' Research and Resources*"[3] page. Inaugurated in April 2001, this newest TTHA archive is available to members only (by means of a one-time annual entry by password), and will eventually be expanded to hold the full collection of Hardy's poetry, the Gerber-Davis bibliography, the Ottakers' bibliography, and the poetry archives of the Hardy Association's poetry discussion group on the "*Poem of the Month*" page.

TTHA has at all times, since its inception in 1997, striven to avoid exclusivity. Our policy has only ever been to share the professional skills and resources of our team and its associates freely with all-comers. The recent decision to create a "*Members' Only*" page, in the hope of increasing TTHA membership, was prompted by a universal desire, on the part of TTHA's international team of scholars, to keep *The Hardy Review* and its allied publications in print. Membership fees remain the only funding agency of this enterprise. All else – every other single professsionally-managed online service and resource, from *Drama* through *Links* to *Book Reviews* and onward – operates on a purely voluntary basis with each TTHA director managing the sundry expenses connected her or his website maintenance and page production.

There is one small but important exception to this entrepreneurial self-funding. A generous donor who wishes to remain anonymous was solely responsible for funding the "prizes" awarded for the Seasonal Frivolities of Christmas 2001. This was a heartwarming gesture and our thanks to "anon" are reciprocally heartfelt.

Returning to the year's literary events: with the summer of 2001 came the arrival of the second volume of TTHA's *Occasional Series*. Professor William W. Morgan (Executive VP and Director of TTHA's "*Poetry*" page) and I were exerting ourselves during these palmy days to no small degree. Together we selected, compiled and edited the dialogues from the *Poem of the Month's* discussion group and produced what we have chosen to call, in TTHA's *Occasional Series:*, *Hardy's Emma Poems*. Focussing specifically on a selection of these "love" poems, discussed over a period of several months, scholars from all corners of the earth conversed openly and freely[4] not only on formal issues such as metrics and poesis, form and meaning, but also on such sensitive topics as loss, death, bereavement and grieving. Hence

---

[3] TTHA is indebted to Seth Lachterman for his invaluable technical aid in establishing the "Members" page.
[4] TTHA's Poetry Forum is neither mediated nor moderated.

the printed version of these conversations is unique in its disarming spontaneity and intellectual verve, not to mention the erudition of its scholar-contributors. Speakers who remained strangers, geographically speaking, and who see each other rarely, met throughout the months of debate at these unique round-table talks in intellectual encounters not often found in conventional essay publications.

Finally, the most recent development on the Hardy Association's front is to be found in Professor Shannon Rogers' new *"Book Reviews"* page. Professor Rogers (Dept. of History, St Joseph's University, Philadelphia) was appointed as a VP to TTHA's team in the summer of 2001 and has since embarked upon the directorship of a *"Book Reviews"* page which will feature critical reviews of works on Thomas Hardy. To date, this new site is still under construction but should be up and going by the time this book emerges from the press.

A small sample of the intellectual energy that characterises the TTHA website will be found in the modest pages of this volume — notably in the sections featuring some of TTHA's *"Forum"* and *"POTM"*[5] debates, selected and edited here for print publication. These debates are launched by a lively exchange on "Hardy's Beliefs" — sparked into action by one lone student's breaching of the *"Forum"* for the very first time, and positing an innocent question about Hardy's agnosticism/atheism/churchiness. The resulting "take-off" was instantaneous and edifying.

These debates then move on to embrace topics as demotic as "Hardy on Film" or as elevated as the philosophical dimensions of Hardy's "Nature" poetry. They conclude with a "Notes and Queries" section containing the few questions put to the *Forum* panel which remain unanswered. Readers with responses to the queries are invited to write to the editor; their letters will be published in the next volume in the *Hardy Review* series.

Succeeding the online seminars Robert Schweik presents a brief report on his year's work on TTHA's *"Links"* and *"Checklist"* pages, and Martin Ray follows this succinct account with a remarkably detailed collation of the Gibson and Hynes editions of Hardy's poetry. The essay section of this *Review* concludes the volume with Andrew Radford's fine critical foray entitled, "The Excavating Consciousness in Hardy's *Two on a Tower*," and Charles Lowe's closely-focussed "A

---

[5] **Poem Of The Month**

Complete Diorama: The Art of Restoration in Hardy's *The Return of the Native*."

As to the editorial process itself, I have, in this volume, privileged, in terms of the selection of items for publication, TTHA's own online debates. I had hoped, in fact, to retain the "Hardy and Nature" dialogues for inclusion in an *Occasional Series* edition devoted to them alone. Due to lack of funding this could not be. Hence the originals have been pruned down for inclusion in the annual *Hardy Review* instead. Shorn as they are, they remain substantial. Consequently, conventional essays have been kept to a minimum to allow them sufficient space.

In matter taken from the TTHA *Forum* and *POTM* debates I have kept as close as possible to the original exchanges – allowing for an occasional idiosyncrasy or verbal mannerism. I have also retained invidual styles of spelling, punctuation and phraseology. In some instances, however, I have omitted repetitious material; this is indicated within the text by means of ellipses. I have also, in true Hardyan tradition, inserted illustrations as and when I could find appropriate images. Since the "finding" was not easy there are not many. Footnotes and bibliographical information have been added where and when I deemed they might be helpful. Otherwise all contributions are reproduced as in the original including individual variations of speech, spelling, forms of expression and the occasional *ad hoc* flight of fancy.

The only uniformity I have imposed on the book throughout is to format the dialogues in closely patterned contiguity to each other in an attempt to mirror, as nearly as possible, their conversational ebb and flow through space and time on The Hardy Association's online discussion groups. Finally, in this edition I have omitted the street addresses of the contributors. E-mail addresses alone, should suffice.

I wish to thank Martin Ray for his invaluable editorial aid and advice. And to all our other loyal members I wish to extend the deepest gratitude for their support and generous contributions to TTHA's debates and subject areas of research and information[6]. TTHA would not have achieved the outstanding success that has brought it countless followers and triumphal accolades without this generosity and support. Thank you, friends, one and all!

---

[6] Needless to say, all and any suggestions for improvement would be most welcome: <rm82@pantheon.yale.edu>

Hardy in 1923, by Augustus John

Hardy's Beliefs

INTRODUCTION

Some time ago a student preparing a report on Hardy, but puzzled about the exact nature of his religious beliefs, appealed to *Forum* members for help in clearing up his confusion. Little could he have anticipated at the time that this seemingly simple request would initiate a debate that could well constitute the most protracted, thought-provoking, and exhaustive examination of this subject to date.

Although a number of *Forum* members participated in the discussion two major contenders emerged. One of them proved to be less intent upon labeling Hardy a Christian in the strictly orthodox sense of the word than in defending him against the charge of atheism. The other, while conceding the strong appeal the church held for Hardy throughout his life, and acknowledging that many of the virtues he espoused were commonly associated with Christianity, maintained that the evidence overwhelmingly demonstrates that Hardy was "at least an agnostic and arguably an atheist."

Other contributors enriched the discussion with observations about Hardy's close involvement with folklore, rural superstition, and the irrational, drawing parallels between these subjects and religion. Commendably, the fervor of the debaters remained at all times tempered by civility and restraint in a subject area that, as Rosemarie Morgan has pointed out, traditionally has generated "more war than peace."

Above all, the fact that strong arguments can be extracted from the facts of Hardy's life and from his work to support different, even antithetical, points of view attests to the breadth, depth, and subtle complexity of his understanding of the truth.   Betty Cortus

Sun, 26 Mar 2000 18:59:54 EST
MRNYCEGUY@aol.com
Subject: Thomas Hardy's Beliefs

Hello to all. This is my first time at the Hardy Discussion group. I am a student and am doing a report on Thomas Hardy. I find him to be quite interesting but in my readings I am unclear about what his religious beliefs are. I have been led to believe that he is an atheist, but I am uncertain. I would appreciate it very much if anyone could tell me. I look forward to reading several of his works.

Tue, 28 Mar 2000 07:13:07 –0500
SHERRY STONE <smstone@neocom.net>
Subject: RE: Thomas Hardy's Beliefs

I am doing a term paper on *The Return of the Native* and in the process have consulted about eighteen different sources so far. Those sources have led me to believe that Hardy was more a believer in Darwinism. As near as I can see, his life and that of his ancestors seemed to tell him over and over that they could not fight their fate. To believe in God would have meant they had options in life and he didn't seem to think so. His philosophy was, 'You might as well expect the worst because that's what's going to happen.' If by chance something good did occur - you better enjoy it and it won't last long.

Several, if not all of his novels, employ the "teachings" of the Greek tragedies. If you end up deciding to read *The Return of the Native* the first few chapters deal with Egdon Heath (the setting) and have the tendency to bore one to tears. Plow through that section because the setting affects the actions of the characters and the rest of the book is quite interesting. I plan to read *Tess* once I finish this term paper and another that I am working on for my New Testament class. Good luck in your studies. Let me know your future perceptions on the man and his works. Sherry

Wed, 29 Mar 2000 22:58:23 +0100
ARTHUR F. JONES <afjones@sol.co.uk>
Subject: Thomas Hardy's Beliefs

Greetings to recent inquirers, and to all.

I would agree with C S. Lewis's summing-up of Thomas Hardy's philosophy of life as a form of "Heroic Pessimism" ("De Futilitate" *Christian Reflections*: Collins: Fount Paperbacks, UK, 1981). Here he is referring to Swinburne and to Shelley's "Prometheus" also. The exact nature of this heroism would make an interesting study in relation to male and female characters: Giles, Jude and Tess are the obvious ones. Hardy is, of course, largely metaphorical with regard to that against which the heroic battle is being waged - the ending of *Tess*, *The Dynasts* - and it is not always clear that the struggle is with fate itself or with feckless/cruel agencies, rather than with conventional attitudes spread throughout the mass of the people by earth-bound agencies such as the church, and often encapsulated in superstitions.

Interestingly, there is much evidence of Hardy's liking for churches, and not least for church music. There is also evidence of his reluctance to abandon conventional Christian belief, of his considerable knowledge of the Bible, and of a child-like part of his personality "wishing" that the simple Faith could be sustained.

I have also noted that there are quite a number of Christians who like Thomas Hardy's work – even feel uplifted by it: a far cry from the incident where the clergyman reported that he had burned his copy of *Jude*! It has to be remembered, I think, that the argument between religion and science in Victorian/Edwardian times was carrried out from entrenched positions which would not be recognised by most thinkers today as presenting a conceptually satisfactory conflict.

A very useful summary of Hardy's religious and philosophical standpoint, or standpoints (for Hardy denied that he had any systematic philosophy), can be found in F B. Pinion: *A Hardy Companion* (London: Macmillan/New York: St. Martin's Press, 1968), in which there is a chapter entitled "Christianity, Scientific Philosophy, and Politics". The subsection on "God" is an excellent starting point for studying his attitude to Christian theology, with many references to individual poems. I'm sorry this message has turned out so long.

Best wishes to all, Arthur Jones

Thu, 30 Mar 2000 09:31:37 +0100
ALAN SHELSTON <alan@shelston.freeserve.co.uk>
Subject: Thomas Hardy's Beliefs

Could I endorse the detailed content of Arthur Jones's message: Hardy's 'pessimism', 'atheism' etc., are at best simplifications of his very carefully thought-out views. In particular, as Arthur says, one must never forget Hardy's affiliations with the Christian - and specifically Anglican - church. Trevor Johnson recently worked with me on an outstanding PhD thesis - short title "A Churchy Hardy" - in which he investigated the ways in which Hardy's familiarity with the liturgy is ever-present in his work.   Alan Shelston

Thu, 30 Mar 2000 12:23:10 -0400
RICHARD NEMESVARI <rnemesva@stfx.ca>
Subject: Thomas Hardy's Beliefs

I am all in favour of recognizing Hardy's complex relationship with Christianity, and acknowledging that he held an eclectic and indeed unique mixture of beliefs. Two more recent works which I would recommend on this issue are Robert Schweik's "The influence of religion, science, and philosophy on Hardy's writings" which appears in *The Cambridge Companion to Thomas Hardy* (editor, Dale Kramer, 1999), and Jan Jedrzejewski's *Thomas Hardy and the Church* (St. Martin's, 1996). However, I also think that we do well to remember his challenge to Christian theology. His famous statement,

> I have been looking for God for 50 years, and I think that if he had existed I should have discovered him. As an external personality, of course - the only true meaning of the word,

demonstrates his rejection of a providential and anthropomorphic deity in a way which is fairly absolute. Or again, this declaration,

> The old theologies may or may not have worked for good in their time. But they will not bear stretching further in epic or dramatic art. The Greeks used up theirs: the Jews used up theirs: the Christians have used up theirs. So that one must make an independent plunge, embodying the real, if only temporary, thought of the age.

That "may or may not have worked for good" is rather telling, and this statement clearly suggests that Christianity, as it stood in Hardy's perception, no longer embodied the "thought of the age," at least as far as art was concerned.

Hardy's knowledge of the Bible, attachment to church ceremony and music, and use of biblical allusions cannot be denied, but that doesn't mean that his unbelief (if we want to avoid the word atheism) in certain crucial elements of Christianity was any less real.

Richard Nemesvari

Thu, 30 Mar 2000 13:15:40 -0500 (EST)
KEITH WILSON <kgwilson@aix1.uottawa.ca>
Subject: Thomas Hardy's Beliefs

I would like to endorse Richard's observations here, particularly since I have noticed an occasional desire in commentary on Hardy to rescue him for orthodoxy by translating constitutional churchiness (born, presumably, of various things, but perhaps especially dominant socio-cultural influences in formative years, and therefore shared by a great many, if not most, unbelieving Victorians) into some kind of vaguely Christian belief.

It seems to me clear from virtually everything that Hardy ever wrote that he was unequivocally an agnostic, and arguably – despite his own distinction between the two terms and location of himself as a "harmless agnostic"rather than a "clamorous atheist" (17th October 1896, included in *The Life and Work*, ed. Millgate, p. 302) –an atheist.

The poem "Hap" seems to me unambiguously to sum up (despite its earliness of composition) a position on the principles that govern the universe to which Hardy remained essentially committed throughout his life. He eventually posits the more complicated model of the "Immanent Will," on which he elaborates in *The Dynasts* (his most philosophically ambitious work), which gives, by viewing activity retroactively from a distance in time and space, the illusion of design/pattern to events. But that more complex model in no way contradicts anything in the relative conceptual simplicity of "Hap"; it merely engages with the possibility of complexly interacting contingencies assuming, from certain retroactive perspectives, the appearance of design, just as in "The Convergence of the Twain" accident (a maritime disaster) is turned into design by adopting the distanced view that can see iceberg and ship building to their point of "consummation."

In *The Dynasts* he takes the extra step of speculating, via the terminal Chorus of Pities, that consciousness of the kind that distinguishes the human part of the universe might evolve further to inform the whole Will, but this still has nothing to do with a possible divinity, or a divinely-sanctioned process (and in any case, Hardy observed that he would not have ended *The Dynasts* as he did had he written it after rather than before the First World War).

At no point is there any suggestion that such design is the fulfilment of some transcendental plan conceived by a divine mind. At no point is there any indication of actual belief in a divinity, Christian or otherwise. As an article of faith, or a serious intellectual/conceptual possibility, a Christian God would seem to have had no more meaning for Hardy himself (although he could acknowledge its meaning for others, and feel himself denied their good fortune in having faith: see "The Impercipient"), than that other imaginative/rhetorical convenience, the "President of the Immortals" (and surely no-one is going to suggest that because he invokes such a being, Hardy actually believed in Him/Her/It).

When Hardy toys, as he does in some of the "philosophical" poems, with a notion of divinity, he adopts it as an imaginative/argumentative convenience, as a way of putting a name to an essentially unconscious force that he can contrast with human consciousness. Under those circumstances, it doesn't matter whether he calls that unconscious force God, or Doom, or the Spinner/Spirit of the Years (i.e. undifferentiated temporal process), or – if he is thinking of the combined action of all the wills immanent in the physical universe – the Immanent Will. It is still a notion premised on the unconsciousness/moral unawareness of everything except humanity, and the non-existence of any transcendental force beyond that amalgamation of all that exists physically.

Given those assumptions, I don't see how Hardy can be reclaimed for anything even remotely resembling Christian faith, however instinctively churchy he remained, however able to see the consolations of faith for those who have it, and however uplifting some of his insights about the power of human consciousness.   Keith Wilson

STINSFORD CHURCH: photograph courtesy Dave Sands

Thu, 30 Mar 2000 15:38:39 –0600
MARK BROWN <brown@jc.edu>
Subject: Thomas Hardy's Beliefs

Keith Wilson wrote:
> I have noticed an occasional desire in commentary on Hardy to rescue him for orthodoxy by translating constitutional churchiness . . . into some kind of vaguely Christian belief.

Several years ago I attended a Christmas Eve service at an Episcopal church in Birmingham, Alabama, in which a musical setting of "The Oxen" was performed as an anthem. Several years before that, I attended a Sunday morning service at an Anglican church in Winnipeg,

Manitoba, on an interior wall of which was hung a banner depicting Blake's Urizen with the compasses ("The Ancient of Days"). And there's the well known case of Parry's "Jerusalem." Beside Hardy's "constitutional churchiness," Kipling's freemasonry and Yeats's theosophy read like the Thirty-Nine Articles. Mark Brown

Thu, 30 Mar 2000 22:43:14 -0500
ROSEMARIE MORGAN <rosemarie.morgan@yale.edu>
Subject: Thomas Hardy's Beliefs

Well said, Mark! Rosemarie Morgan

Fri, 31 Mar 2000 09:47:17 +0100
ALAN SHELSTON <alan@shelston.freeserve.co.uk>
Subject: Thomas Hardy's Beliefs

Full circle – my references to Hardy's churchiness seem to have started something. But in self-defence could I say that I had absolutely no intention of reclaiming Hardy for church-goers. My comments were perhaps in reaction to the opposite simplifications, which I still get from very intelligent students, that he was all of a piece fatalistically atheistic, pessimistic, inhuman, etc, etc.

As someone who left the C of E. at about the same age as Hardy was when he did I like to think that the pattern was rather more complicated than that. One other point: "Hap" is one of 900+ poems, although of course there are others like it.

It's splendid to get so much evidence of Hardy's popularity with students in these messages. Greetings to all, Alan Shelston

Fri, 31 Mar 2000 07:00:05 -0500 (EST)
KEITH WILSON <kgwilson@aix1.uottawa.ca>
Subject: Thomas Hardy's Beliefs

Absolutely no need for self-defence Alan – you certainly weren't one of those in my mind when I spoke of attempts to reclaim Hardy for Christianity, and your original posting was careful to indicate that you weren't implying this. I was merely confirming the suggestion of Richard's message that this does indeed happen, and that it is problematic when it does. I think you and I are responding to different but complementary simplifications about Hardy's beliefs, and they are not only found among students. Along with the, Hardy-was-a-pessimist-who believed-everything-is-directed-by-Fate, line (which I completely agree is the more common one), I recurrently encounter, Hardy-invokes-God-in-his-poetry-and-uses-a-lot-of-church-imagery-and-therefore-must-be-a-Christian-after-all.

Interestingly they both come from a similar source – the assumption that Hardy believes in some kind of conscious external (i.e. non-immanent) force that is influencing, usually malignantly, human circumstance.

I suspect that this comes about because people treat Hardy's figurative rhetorical conveniences – "President of the Immortals," "God" etc. – as literal articles of faith, and don't read the works—particularly *The Dynasts*—that give the most complex access to his beliefs, or rather ideas.

In fact, it may be the unhelpful resonance of the term "beliefs" that is causing the problem. Keith Wilson

Fri, 31 Mar 2000 06:00:56 -0800 (PST)
ANDREW HEWITT <aghewitt@yahoo.com>
Subject: Thomas Hardy's Beliefs

As I recall from looking at successive editions of *Origin of Species* Darwin worked at eliminating upper-case usages such as "Nature" from his text, presumably to avoid giving readers the impression that he was personifying an impersonal force?

Best wishes, Andrew Hewitt

Fri, 31 Mar 2000 16:05:04 +0100
JAMES WHITEHEAD <jamesswhitehead@hotmail.com>
Subject: Hardy's Beliefs

"Hardy's Beliefs" – where do we begin? Hardy and Religion, Hardy and the Church of England, Hardy and Agnosticism etc.,– these are all complex subjects, and require separate (albeit perhaps parallel) investigation. There is no doubt that Hardy was—as he famously described himself, in reaction to the strictures of the likes of Bishop Walsham How—"a harmless agnostic," but what often distinguishes agnostics from atheists is open-mindedness on matters of belief, a capacity to be betwixt doubt and faith – aware of the inner yearning for spiritual and religious truth while nevertheless deeply imbued with scepticism. Profoundly aware of Darwinism, Comtean Positivism and the work of continental philosophers such as Nietzsche and Schopenhauer, Hardy's work reveals a rich blend of contemporary philosophical and scientific thought. Given the complexity of his thinking on matters pertaining to philosophy, science and religion, we need to ensure that Hardy is not appropriated by cultural materialists while similarly ensuring that he is not appropriated for religious orthodoxy.

One thing that strikes me, in particular, is the way in which, so very often in Hardy's work, at key moments when thematic or psychological issues are clearly fore-grounded, there is an obvious recourse to religious language as a means of providing appropriate comment on behalf of character, narrator, or speaker. The re-iterative reference to the psalmic word-phrase "loving-kindness" in the fiction, the poetry and the 'Apology' to *Late Lyrics and Earlier* indicates what lies at the heart of Hardy's value-system. I am thinking here, for example, of the "loving-kindness" between Giles and Grace in *The Woodlanders* (Ch. 36), and that recommended by Tess in conversation with Alec in *Tess of the d'Urbervilles* (Ch 47): "Why, you can have the religion of loving-kindness and purity at least, if you can't have - what do you call it - dogma." We see in the following transcription from Hardy's notebook in the *Life,* Vol.1,[1] a fundamental Christian ethic lay at the heart of his message:

> Altruism, or The Golden Rule, whatever 'Love Your Neighbour as Yourself' may be called, will ultimately be brought about I think by the pain we see in others reacting on ourselves, as if we or they were a part of one body. Mankind, in fact, may be and possibly will be viewed as members of one corporeal frame.

While the latter part of this statement might well be fanciful aspiration, the idea of "loving-kindness" is essential to Hardy's understanding of the slow progress of "evolutionary meliorism" (see the 'Apology' to *Late Lyrics*, 1922). The way in which the Immanent Will functions in *The Dynasts*, affecting all and curiously somehow incorporating all, demonstrates a working model "one corporeal frame."

At the risk of being annoyingly self-referential, in my *TLS* article of 24 Dec 1999 ('Puzzled Phantoms'), I tried to illustrate how Hardy uses Christian moral argument to undermine the grotesque misuse of religious language in contemporary literary rhetoric at the turn of the century with regard to imperialist endeavour (see the poem, 'A Christmas Ghost-Story').

There are plenty of examples of wrong-headed clerical types in Hardy's fiction (eg. Alec d'Urberville during his religious phase, and Angel Clare's father and brothers), but it is probably also worth noting the positive, specifically Christian attributes of other characters;

---

[1] Florence Emily Hardy, *The Life of Thomas Hardy: 1840-1928* (The Macmillan Press Ltd, London and Basingstoke, 1962), hereafter the *Life.*

for example, the protagonist of the powerfully moving short story 'A Changed Man' (1900). Another story, 'Old Mrs Chundle,' shows more whimsical treatment of approximately the same subject; ie. the Clergy's dealings with the poor and the excluded.

Trevor Johnson's superb Ph.D. thesis 'Churchy Hardy: A Study of The Influence of the Anglican Liturgy on Hardy', together with other recent work on Hardy's engagement with religion – for example, Richard Nemesvari's excellent recent article "Appropriating the Word: *Jude the Obscure* as Subversive Apochrypha' in *Victorian Review* – demonstrate the depth and range of Hardy's often highly subversive but also often genuinely sympathetic (in a truly religious sense) engagement with the Bible and the Anglican Liturgy. James Gibson's enthralling volume *Thomas Hardy: Interviews and Recollections* quotes (from Edmund Blunden's *Thomas Hardy*, 1967), a conversation between Hardy and Brigadier Morgan (October 1922:

> I believe in going to Church. It is a moral drill, and people must have something. If there is no church in a country village, there is nothing ... I believe in reformation coming from within the Church. The clergy are growing more rationalist, and that is the best way of changing.

Pressed to charge the clergy, in that case, with casuistry in subscribing to articles in which they did not believe, Hardy would have nothing of it. He looked on it as a necessity in practical reform.

As he laid his flowers on the grave of his first wife, he began a long talk on the theme:

> The liturgy of the Church of England is a noble thing. So are Tate and Brady's psalms. These are things that people need and should have (p.178).

While we should perhaps retain a strong sense of the flavour of Hardy's doubt, of his criticism of orthodox dogma and of church morality, we should balance this with an equally strong awareness of the true Christian morality inherent in his work. Christ was probably just an exceptional human being for Hardy (see 'Panthera' and 'An Evening in Galilee'); the basic ideas (Tess refers to the Sermon on the Mount) and the self-sacrificial moral example are the primary elements still worth attention .... no doubt Hardy would have been cheered by much that is happening in the Church of England and the Episcopalian churches at the present time, where a non-theistic, largely non-dogmatic idea of Christian religion is gaining popularity (see, for example, the work of controversial Bishop John Shelby Spong, author of *Why Christianity Must Change or Die*.)   James Whitehead

P. S. Apologies if this is a controversial comment –
in addition to being too long!

Fri, 31 Mar 2000 11:25:47 -0500 (EST)
KEITH WILSON <kgwilson@aix1.uottawa.ca>
Subject: Hardy's Beliefs

All this is true, but doesn't seem to me to speak much to the question of "belief," as opposed to moral/temperamental inclination. The reason I make that distinction is in part to avoid the implication that Hardy's great humaneness – as manifest in the importance for him of the human capacity for altruism or pity, his recurrent use of such terms as "loving-kindness," and his patent sensitivity and humanitarianism (in short, many of those things that make him such a moving writer) – are specifically Christian: i.e. that that subset of people who would call themselves Christians in the sense of possessing a Christian faith particularly display these characteristics to a greater degree than any other subset of humanity.

I see little evidence for this in either the 19th or 20th centuries, and little evidence that Hardy saw any either, which explains why so many fictional clergymen receive such short shrift at his hands. Yet, many Christians display these humane capacities, and in some of them such capacities may well be related to their faiths (in Hardy's own experience, the Rev. Moule would have been an outstanding example of one of them). But do actual believing Christians in Hardy's fiction display these capacities to any greater degree than, say, Tess or Jude Fawley?

At this level – i.e. when such terms are being used to indicate sympathy with broadly humane impulses – aren't such responses simply humanitarian? If anything, they may be termable small 'c' christian, given the traditional tendency in Christian cultures – both nominal ones and actual ones – for such humanitarian impulses to be appropriated as specifically "christian" virtues, often with the regrettable implication that non-Christians don't and cannot possess them. And how is suggesting that Hardy does not have Christian belief and is in no meaningful sense a Christian allowing him to be appropriated by "cultural materialists"?

Surely no-one would suggest that "cultural materialists" by definition lack such humane qualities, or fail to appreciate them in Hardy? So the question then becomes whether the morality in his work is indeed "true Christian morality" (which sounds a little as if it might be intended to suggest morality deriving from a true Christian, or morality which is more truly Christian than, say, humanist) or simply morality/humanitarianism, manifest in someone who, as we have all been saying, is sympathetic to Christian liturgy, has an exhaustive knowledge of the Bible (both Testaments I hasten to add), was shaped by a Christian culture, emotionally attached to the church etc., but in no meaningful sense possesses Christian faith/belief?

All the best, Keith

Fri, 31 Mar 2000 12:58:02 -0500 (EST)
MEG CRONIN <mgcronin@anselm.edu>
Subject: Hardy's Beliefs

Hi there. I don't submit to the discussion very often, so you may not know me (though several of you helped me with a question about the Thomas Hardy yearbook last year). I want to take the discussion of Hardy's beliefs to a different topic, which you may find in-teresting. My work on Hardy is about superstition and folklore (in fact, I always meant to respond to Joan Sheski's point about Hardy and the folktale last year, but I had a baby instead).

I have claimed in the past that Hardy offers in some of the novels a "faith in the irrational" – which is not to say that he – Hardy the man – believes in the irrational or superstition. But the novels suggest that certain ways of seeing open up rather than close down possibility. At the same time, truly wrong-headed superstitious characters like Christian Cantle in *The Return of the Native* are clearly limited by their beliefs. (He says, "No moon, no man" to explain his lack of confidence).

There's an ambivalence about the irrational in general. Eustacia is not a witch and the people who persecute her are portrayed as backward and unthinking. But she is witchy, deific, goddess-like, "the raw material of a divinity." Think of Diggory Venn, too, who isn't entirely of this world, figuratively. Sure he's practical and knows that "hoptoads don't jump in ponds this time of year," but he's also seeming master of light and moths and glow-worms and heath ponies, and of course, the dice.

The list has also talked about *A Pair of Blue Eyes* in the past, and whether we agree with Millgate about its flaws. Millgate thinks the jewels and graves don't really form a pattern or sensical set of motifs. I disagree, and I think lore and superstition provide the coherence Millgate was looking for.

So, I'm trying to relate our discussion of (un)orthodox belief to a similar "agnosticism"... [or] irrational belief. Hardy of course entrenched himself in rural lore, nearly an amateur antiquarian, and his notebooks show as much.

My last comment isn't really connected, but I'm struck by my memory of a remark Hardy made in the interview with William

Archer. Archer asked him, "Have you ever seen a ghost?" and Hardy replied (I'm paraphrasing from memory), something like:

> Never the ghost of a ghost. But my will to believe is present. My imagination is keen; my nerves vibrate readily. If ever a ghost wanted to make himself known, I am the very man he should apply to.

My memory of this quotation is not precise, but the first and last lines are almost exactly right. I'm really interested in the will to believe and how it is frustrated in Hardy and Victorians and Modernists.

Thanks for a great discussion,

Meg Cronin

Fri, 31 Mar 2000 14:41:52 -0500
ROSEMARIE MORGAN <rosemarie.morgan@yale.edu>
Subject: Hardy's Beliefs

James writes: that it is "also worth noting the positive, specifically Christian attributes of other characters." Question 1: what *are* "specifically Christian attributes"? James also cites examples of "Christian" references to things biblical. Question 2: How does this "Christian" element tally with "things biblical" when these last are placed in the mouths of the rustics who openly misuse and abuse them? In fact, they abuse them to such an extent that contemporary critics accused Hardy of profanity and sacrilege, and this despite the fact that, in *Far From the Madding Crowd*, for example, editor Leslie Stephen had removed several of these "things biblical" prior to publication.

Cheers, Rosemarie

Fri, 31 Mar 2000 16:26:15 -0400
RICHARD NEMESVARI <rnemesva@stfx.ca>
Subject: Hardy's Beliefs

James Whitehead and I have had a private correspondence on this topic (thanks for the plug for the article James!), and as often happens Keith's comments below present my position more clearly than I could have myself. Hardy's endorsement of "loving-kindness," which finds (for me) its most moving evocation in *Jude*, is a powerful embodiment of what could be called Christian ideals, but there needs to be more than this for me to accept it as approaching Christian belief. Here is a (perhaps oversimplified) list of three questions, all of which I believe Hardy would have answered in the negative.
1. Does a providential, conscious, anthropomorphic God exist?
2. Is Christ a divine manifestation of that God?
3. Did Christ achieve an actual, physical resurrection from the dead?

If I'm right, and as a product of his Victorian culture Hardy (like so many others) simply could not accept the religious principles implicit in these questions, then as far as I can tell he could not be considered even remotely Christian in the terms of that culture.

That certain late-twentieth-century denominations are moving towards something like Hardy's "position" (using that term loosely), and that their answers to these questions might be qualified in certain telling ways, may be encouraging. But teaching as I do at a university with (in the carefully chosen words of our Calendar) "a Catholic character," I can assure the list that the priests on campus are quite clear that "that's not Christianity."

They may be wrong, but I'm pretty sure the majority of Hardy's contemporaries, and probably most Christians still today, would agree with them. Richard Nemesvari

Fri, 31 Mar 2000 21:21:38 –0500
ROSEMARIE MORGAN rosemarie.morgan@yale.edu
Subject: Beliefs

Hardy's life's work of creating and re-creating incarnations (incarnations which extend beyond birthplaces and the ancestral village) rarely encompasses the traditional concept of the (Christian) "ghost." Such phenomena more often manifest themselves pluralistically as "voices," "spirits," "presences," and even shadows on stones. This "Buddhistic" leaning seems almost an inevitable "turn" for Hardy, especially given its emphasis upon the inanimate, as well as the animate, spirit of things, upon compassion, non-aggressive seeking and acceptance (how many wars are fought in the name of Buddha?).

The greatest doubt I have (along with Keith and others), is that such attributes as "humanitarianism" and "loving kindness" are necessarily "Christian." Moreover, the Christian emphasis on self-salvation seems to leave less room for pure acts of altruism (though Gide would argue there is no such thing!) than might be found in belief systems fostering the idea of corporate identities, pluralistic existence and reincarnation. Cheers, Rosemarie

Sat, 1 Apr 2000 01:10:45 +0100
JAMES WHITEHEAD <jamesswhitehead@hotmail.com>
Subject: Beliefs etc

Some brief-ish responses to several questions:
1. What *are* specifically Christian attributes?

Well, I suppose, in the case of the characters I was thinking of, their determination to act out their faith by means of charity, in helping the community. In terms of the protagonist of 'A Changed Man', a willingness to sacrifice his own life for others. Obviously, these are humanitarian acts which might have been informed by other religious influences—religions generally share such core moral values. But I suppose what may be interesting is the idea that in Hardy's work positive moral action is described in biblical religious language in many key instances; in the case of these two minor examples, the protagonists consciously attempt to live in accordance with Christian example – and wear clerical garb! In both stories, there is a curious and fascinating balance struck between narrative irony and pathos. The potential groundlessness of the characters' individual belief-systems perhaps makes the effect of positive moral example appear all the more poignant to the reader in these instances.

2. How does this tally with "things biblical" being placed in the mouths of the rustics who openly misuse and abuse them? – to such an extent that contemporary critics accused Hardy of profanity and sacrilege (despite the fact that, in *FFMC*, Leslie Stephen had removed several of these "things biblical" prior to publication).

I think that as an agnostic Hardy was quite happy for the biblical texts to be represented in any way people saw fit, so long as "vaingloriousness" was avoided and so long as harm was not done to others through ideological manipulation. In his response to militaristic religious rhetoric in his war poetry and in his fictional responses to religious hypocrisy, Hardy showed a determination to contend with ideological manipulation.

Richard Nemesvari's article is particularly informative on the way in which Hardy was himself happy to negotiate with the issue of textual authority *per se* by drastically revising elements of narrative from the Apochrypha. Hardy was not, of course, afraid of being unorthodox and subversive. One other aspect of Hardy's religious interest that also perhaps needs noting is, of course, his interest in Buddhism, as revealed in several of the letters that he wrote at the time of the South African War, and evidenced by passages in the Literary Notebooks. Similarly, the fact that so many of the poems represent spirit interventions of one kind or another, the interesting use of the supernatural in *Return of the Native* and his own self-confessed desire (partly ironical) to see a ghost, may all point to an ongoing quest for all kinds of spiritual meaning and experience. "Beliefs" – well perhaps, as an agnostic, there were no concrete religious or spiritual beliefs (although arguably there were moral beliefs), but there were spheres

of reference, which provide us, as researchers, with subjects for investigation.
3. re. Keith's Question: "And how is suggesting that Hardy does not have Christian beliefs and is in no meaningful sense a Christian allowing him to be appropriated by 'cultural materialists'?

Surely no-one would suggest that "cultural materialists" by definition lack such humane qualities, or fail to appreciate them in Hardy?"

It would of course be very wrong for anyone to suggest that the representatives of any school of critical thought lacked any humane qualities or any capacity for understanding, or indeed, had any superiority in either of these respects to any other critical or social grouping. Cultural materialism as a critical tool for tackling texts recommends itself for a number of reasons, particularly in relation to investigation of the social dynamics of a text and of its critical/social history. But, speaking generally for the sake of concision, consideration of the complexities of an author's religious thinking (an important part of Hardy's intellectual development) is rarely high on the list of objectives for any such critical exposition, in my experience. No doubt there are exceptions ....

With regard to some of the points made by Richard, it is certainly the case that Hardy does not fit into any kind of orthodox model of belief, as would be indicated by a positive response to the three questions posed – I think that in many ways this makes his use of the Bible and other religious texts even more intriguing in terms of the way in which it reveals his negotiation with contemporary and past ideology, and his movement beyond any restrictions imposed

Best wishes to all, James Whitehead

Sat, 1 Apr 2000 09:34:28 +0100
ALAN SHELSTON <alan@shelston.freeserve.co.uk>
Subject: Hardy's Beliefs

Dear Meg, could I say how much I am in agreement with your phrase about Hardy's novels opening up rather than closing down possibility. And also the related 'will to believe'.

It's remarkable how many of the poems, when touching on matters of belief - spiritual, mythical, folk-loric, circumstantial – close in terms of rhetorical questions, implicit or explicit. To take an obvious example, that 'I *could* think' at the conclusion of 'The Darkling Thrush'. 'It was possible for me, just at that moment to think'? or, more firmly 'I was then enabled to think'? Marvellously ambivalent. Alan Shelston

Sun, 2 Apr 2000 12:11:32 -0400 (EDT)
KEITH WILSON <kgwilson@aix1.uottawa.ca>
Subject: Beliefs etc

No disagreement with this (above), James – it simply shifts the grounds of the discussion. Obviously to suggest the value of considering "the complexities of an author's religious thinking" (which noone has thus far in this discussion objected to doing – indeed, I thought that is what we had all been engaged in), is not at all the same thing as suggesting, as you did, that to dispute his possession of anything resembling Christian faith is to allow him to be appropriated by cultural materialists. And surely, as soon as we invoke, as you did in your earlier posting, contemporary (to us) "non-theistic" views of Christianity, we are invoking not only something that Hardy himself would not recognise as being in any meaningful sense Christian faith but which most of us wouldn't recognise as being in any meaningful sense "faith" (as opposed to well-meaning subscription to a desirable value system) either. Remove the Christian God from account (or read Him/Her/It simply as metaphor), remove any question of the divinity of Christ, and found faith in the general desirability of those small 'c' christian virtues (however appropriative some of us see that adjective as being), and surely most vaguely speculative, vaguely humane, vaguely socially well-adjusted people can be spuriously reclaimed for Christianity. By those lights Hardy (and probably most of *us*) can be made to appear practically as orthodox as the Archbishop of Canterbury.

I think we have probably all by now encountered, for example, perfectly well-intentioned, probably socially useful, Anglican clergymen who don't actually believe in the existence of a deity, don't believe in the divinity of Christ, don't believe in the immortality of the soul or the resurrection of the body or the existence of an after-life (except, as Hardy believed in it, as memory of the dead in the minds of the living, which memory therefore progressively dies with their own deaths). My suspicion is that were Hardy to encounter such clergy, he would find them perfectly amiable kindred spirits but feel that honesty should really require them to consider taking up a different line of work, or a similar line of work under frankly-declared secular auspices. In fact, one could say that far from Hardy being in any genuine sense reclaimable for Christianity, such clergy have themselves defected from what he would understand by the Christian faith and converted to something akin to Hardy's secular humanism, but without his intellectual courage in declaring their apostasy.

All the best, Keith

Sun, 2 Apr 2000 21:28:45 +0100
JAMES WHITEHEAD <jamesswhitehead@hotmail.com>
Subject: Beliefs etc.

My main point was that just as Hardy should not be appropriated by orthodox Christianity, he should not be regarded either as that entity so appealing to the Marxist Critic or Cultural Materialist, i.e. an atheist. He was an agnostic whose work engages with Christianity in a manner that is often critical, yet is not always wholly negative. In fact, when he comes to points in his writing where his "beliefs" (e.g. evolutionary meliorism) are highlighted, it is interesting that he uses biblical language to denote what are, to his way of thinking, the most valuable forms of human behaviour (e.g. "loving-kindness"). That he was, to use his own description, "churchy; not in an intellectual sense, but in so far as instincts and emotions ruled", should also be borne in mind when we conduct discussion of his treatment of religion in his writing. It could be argued – although, at present, I am not sure I would push the argument too far – that Hardy seems to be arguing in favour of a kind of humanistic, reformulated Christianity (in a manner that could be seen to resemble the theory, for example, of present day British Unitarianism or the more radical sections of the Church of England).

In the poetry we discover religious analogies (for example, the use of the "Pentecost Wind" to represent the kindly as opposed to the militaristic soldier spirits in 'The Souls of the Slain') which suggests that Hardy's engagement with Christian spirituality was long-term, complex and at times (in certain respects) sympathetic. To state this is not, of course, to avoid the implications of his fictional portraits of unsympathetic clergy, nor to ignore his various statements of disbelief in an occasionally interventionist, omnipotent deity....Hardy insisted upon the need for Christianity to accommodate rationalism. As stated in the *Life*,

> His vision had often been that of so many people brought up under Church of England influences, a giving of liturgical form to modern ideas, and expressing them in the same old buildings that had already seen previous reforms successfully carried out. He would say this to his friends, the Warden of Keble, Arthur Benson, and others, that if the bishops only had a little courage, and would modify the liturgy by dropping preternatural assumptions out of it, few churchgoers would object to the change for long, and congregations would be trebled in a brief time. The idea was

clearly expressed in the 'Apology' prefixed to *Late Lyrics and Earlier*.[2]

Personally, I can't see Hardy ever being inclined to point the finger at those whose ideas placed them in an awkward position with authority, while striving to do good in their communities and working to further a general sense of spirituality. He was more concerned that the Church hierarchy ("the bishops") should come to terms with modern rationalism. The groupings in the present day Anglican Church such as the 'Sea of Faith' organization, which explore a form of reformulated Christianity that accommodates rationalism and even postmodernism, would probably receive his approval. As the quotation from my previous posting illustrates, Hardy had no sympathy with those who accused individual reforming clergy of casuistry.

Whether or not the kind of congregational activity Hardy envisaged could, or should, be called "Christianity," or indeed whether or not the belief-system of many of the more radical, modern (non-evangelical, non-fundamentalist) clergy should be called "Christianity" is a difficult question. Speaking as a questing agnostic, I would be inclined to say "yes," for this means that Christianity (in an ultimately humanistic form; recalling the personal example of Christ but perhaps believing in the Resurrection in a spiritual rather than a physical sense) is being reclaimed from the realm of antiquated dogma. To re-quote Tess, "Why, you can have the religion of loving-kindness and purity at least, if you can't have - what do you call it - dogma."

Best wishes, James Whitehead

Sun, 2 Apr 2000 17:36:22 EDT
KEITH VAN ALLEN KVANART@aol.com
Subject: Beliefs etc.

Hardy was an artist, a true artist, which indicates often , and surely in his case, a calling higher than the priesthood. That is to say he is a seeker of truth, an observer of life, and a lover of the life which he observes. Finally, he is a communicator of this life and sought-for-truth. The greatest truth is to be gained this way, in reaching for God and loving the creation simultaneously (look at Robert Frost). Religion is part and parcel of the lives of Hardy's people, indeed of himself who also sprang from them. To eschew religion from one's subject or inner being, when one's subject is Devon, would be poor art indeed, and would not transcend, as great art should, even the teachings of the Church if it did not as well embrace the Church

---

[2] *Life*, 376

however critically or non-critically. The Church, after all, is a large enough microcosm unto itself to embrace the fullest range of good and evil.   Keith Van Allen

Sun, 2 Apr 2000 22:33:11 -0400 (EDT)
KEITH WILSON <kgwilson@aix1.uottawa.ca>
Subject: Beliefs etc.

Well, James, I think we are probably going round in circles on this one. Perhaps I should just close my end of the exchange by saying – again – that I never did suggest that Hardy is always negative towards Christianity (indeed, I pointed out how his own responses had in all sorts of ways been shaped by it, unable as he was to accept intellectually its main articles of faith), and I agree that some of his best friends were Christian. But (my main and fairly uncontentious point, I once thought!) that doesn't make him one. And if we have indeed moved into an intellectual/philosophical/theological world where Christians, in order to be Christians, no longer have to believe in God, or the divinity of Christ, or the Resurrection, or the notion of a soul, or an afterlife etc, but can instead rely for their articles of faith simply on the integrity of being "in an awkward position with authority, while striving to do good in their communities and working to further a general sense of spirituality," I would say that most of the nicest people I know are, by those flexible definitions, as Christian as Hardy. This is regardless of whether they are Hindus, Moslems, Jews, agnostics or atheists, although I doubt that many of them would be very grateful for having their conversion effected so effortlessly.

I suspect that they would also argue with the notion that Tess is any kind of Christian merely for wanting "loving-kindness" and "purity" without the dogma. That makes her humane, compassionate, sensitive, thoughtful – all sorts of wonderfully positive things – but not Christian. Of course, Christians, too, are as capable as anyone else of displaying these virtues.   All the best, Keith

Mon, 3 Apr 2000 17:35:42 +0100
JAMES WHITEHEAD <jamesswhitehead@hotmail.com>
Subject: Beliefs - A Last Word

A final word on a debate that may have run its course for the present: re. Keith's last comment: .... It is distorting my argument to use a reference to the activity of local clergy as a supposedly inclusive definition of avant-garde Christianity. Nowadays, it is in fact possible for people who have dispensed with the old-fashioned idea of a patriarchal interventionist deity but who believe in the individual soul or spirit, who venerate Christ's example as unique and seek a transcendent spiritual reality (however indefinable) in part through worship within a church framework, to be regarded as Christians.

Hardy was not far from this position; his general approach, I would suggest, is not dissimilar (even if it is in some respects different) from that of the more radical clergy of the present day. It is self-evident that Jews, Hindus, Muslims and others worship within the framework of their own faiths, disciplines and services. The genuinely positive human qualities demonstrated by all people of good will (including, of course, atheists) are not in dispute. While I would not suggest that Hardy was "a Christian" within the restrictive definitions offered by certain of the more conservative Churchmen of his day (e.g. Bishop William Walsham How) or of this, in his work you discover a profound, long-term engagement with Christian literature and thought, as most readers are aware. While he investigated other religious traditions such as Buddhism, his primary association (however critical) was with Anglicanism. That he was a "churchy" agnostic (not a determined atheist) with a particular fascination with certain aspects of Christian practice and literature seems undeniable. At the time of his death, when the Dean of Westminster made inquiries to the Vicar of Stinsford about Hardy's respectability and church-going, he was assured that Hardy's record in this respect passed muster. Church attendance remained meaningful to a degree for Hardy, even if it was in large part because of the aesthetic nature of the experience. Neither a religious conservative nor a determinedly anti-religious atheist, in his agnosticism Hardy is like many of those in late nineteenth- and early twentieth-century Britain who remained deeply attached to key aspects of their own early religious experience while resolving, through the influence of modern scepticism and awareness of a newly historcized Jesus (Strauss, Haeckel etc.), to adopt radical new formulas (e.g. the "Immanent Will") to express their views.

Best wishes to all, James Whitehead

Mon, 3 Apr 2000 16:27:12 -0400 (EDT)
KEITH WILSON <kgwilson@aix1.uottawa.ca>
Subject: Beliefs - A Last Word (fwd)

Well I thought the debate had probably run its course until I saw your latest, James!

1. It may be possible in their own eyes for people who do not believe in God, do not believe in the divinity of Christ, do not believe in the Resurrection, but who "venerate Christ's example"

and "seek a transcendent spiritual reality" to be regarded as Christians, but it is obviously quite difficult for many of the rest of us so to regard them.

2. It is even more difficult to watch Thomas Hardy being summarily enlisted in their ranks retroactively, especially since the very notion of an "*Immanent* Will" (which you invoke later as one of the "radical new formulas" adopted by sceptics "who remained deeply attached to key aspects of their own early religious experience") is that it is indeed premised on immanence, *not* transcendence.

But to go back to contemporary structures of faith. No doubt people of the kind you describe can regard themselves as what they want. The key is surely whether they can convince dispassionate observers that that is what they are, or that that is what Hardy was.

3 I can think of virtually no major 19th century English writer, and fewer 20th century ones than one might suppose, about whom one could not say that his/her work reveals a "long-term engagement with Christian literature and thought" (the profundity of it may vary).

Being a thinking person who had undergone any kind of education in England necessarily generated such an engagement. Indeed, most educated, and not so educated, English people brought up before the educational and demographic changes that were established by the late-1960s, were brought up in a notionally Christian culture.

In this, there were mandatory school-assemblies (where they would listen to Bible readings, worship from the Book of Common Prayer, sing hymns etc.), on the BBC ("Sunday Half Hour," "The Epilogue," "Five to Ten," etc., not to mention Christmas broadcasting), in the local churches that they might attend at least at Christmas and Easter. Similarly at the local church fêtes they might patronise, as an integral part of community life.

"Engagement" inhered in the very texture of their culture, and most especially in their reading of English Literature: even in the example provided by the (at least lip-service) attestation that their parents would have made to being Christian on the myriad of official government forms that required one to indicate religious allegiances (and tacitly discouraged one from denying the possession of any), they would willy-nilly "engage with Christian literature and thought."

Many if not most of them would retain a nostalgic attachment to this formative experience and environment. And this is the merest shadow of the rural-based Christian culture by which Hardy was surrounded in his formative years in the mid-19th century.

By such standards I would say that most English people of my, let alone Hardy's, generation might be termed Christian. If to be informed about and show an interest in Christianity is immediately to be enlisted for the cause, few of us will escape impressment.

4   If the claim on behalf of Hardy's belief (again, the point from which this thread started) is reliant on supposed support from the Vicar of Stinsford's attesting to Hardy's "respectability and church-going" as "passing muster" (meagre phrasing which surely gives a new spin to Laodicean motifs in Hardy), at a time when the push to have Hardy interred in Westminster Abbey was well under way for a myriad of institutional rather than religious/devotional reasons, the pass has already been sold.

5   Church attendance remaining "meaningful to a degree ... even if it was in large part because of the aesthetic nature of the experience" to people like Hardy "who remained deeply attached to key aspects of their own early religious experience" is a very familiar phenomenon – practically definitional of the experience of large numbers of non-believing Victorian intellectuals. It does not attest to latent structures of "belief."

I think we wholeheartedly agree on Hardy's interest in/emotional attachment to the Christian tradition that shaped him and most of his contemporaries. In fact, it would have been quite surprising if he didn't have such an attachment.

Our disagreement is on how much of a Christian he can be made to seem, even in the reduced terms of certain subdivisions of contemporary Anglicanism. That is to say, "subdivisions" which, from what you are saying, and certainly from my limited experience, don't seem to require much in the way of what most of us understand to be the non-negotiable tenets of Christian faith – tenets that distinguish it from all other faiths on the one hand and well-meaning liberal humanism on the other.

On the evidence you have so far adduced, the claim advanced on Hardy's behalf to any genuine credentials as a Christian believer, of however lukewarm a kind, seems tendentious in the extreme.

All the best, Keith

Sun, 4 Apr 2000 16:12:01 -0600
JOAN SHESKI <harrys@cnetco.com>
Subject: Re: Thomas Hardy's Beliefs

Thanks, Meg, for noticing the folklore connection of Hardy – by the way I hope you and your baby are fine.

Few men or women seem to have been as well informed about so many religions, including paganism and Greek mythology, as Hardy. It occurs to me that the sheer variety of knowledge he encompassed from the perspective of observation rather than participation kept him in a kind of exile from any one belief system. The loneliness of such a state is palpable in his work.

To assign "atheist" to him seems out of place because of his gift for humility — one doesn't get the impression that he was an arrogant naysayer, or someone overly impressed with his own cleverness. Throughout *Tess*, one can see natural elements of paganism aligned with birth and life being overrun by Christian writings and attitudes. Whether or not he "belonged" to one side or the other of that dichotomy, he saw it getting out of balance and wrote that reality — to us.

That is the thing which amazes me – his view, broad, panoramic, saw many many sides to humanity as if from a far distance, and yet with tremendous love and identific-ation. He was given the eyes of an eagle with the heart of a mouse, and so maybe he hunted himself through all his works.

Regards to all, Joan Sheski

Tue, 04 Apr 2000 19:06:11 +1000
DAVID CORNELIUS <dcorney@midcoast.com.au>
Subject: Hardy's Beliefs

Thank you for the interesting and lively discussion on Hardy's beliefs. May I say something after 'the final words' and throw in my thripence worth. I thought a bit of a look at the *Life* might be a little enlightening. Hardy tells us in the *Life* of his long and close association with the Church. As a child he played at being a parson. He also talks of his lengthy reading of religious books, particularly the Bible, and he was interested in the music of the church. Throughout his life he regularly attended church services. His work in church restoration and his marriage to Emma who was deeply religious very likely added to his attitudes towards organised religion. As a young man he says that he began reading for Cambridge with a view to taking Orders,[3] and considered 'the idea of combining poetry and the Church – towards which he had long had a leaning.'[4]

I don't know of anywhere that Hardy says he believes in God or a god. We are not privy to any information as to his loss of faith, though he did later write that

> I have been looking for God for 50 years, and I think that if he existed I should have discovered him. As an external personality, of course – the only true meaning of the word.[5]

He clearly stated that his 'philosophy' did not include a belief in God in the traditional Christian sense stating that the only 'reasonable meaning' of God was 'the Cause of Things, whatever that cause may be.'[6] In writing to a Dr Cervesato in Rome Hardy stated that he didn't think that there would be any permanent revival in what he called the 'old transcendental ideals.'[7]

While he concedes an ultimate 'Prime Cause or Invariable Antedent,' which he called 'It,'[8] he is critical of those 'dogmatic superstitions read every Sunday.'[9] In fact, much of what he says (on p. 333) supports what Keith has written. Although he does not deny a Christian God he is concerned to replace the old concept of God as all powerful by a new notion of universal consciousness, the 'Unconscious Will of the Universe' which gradually becomes conscious of itself and 'ultimately, it is to be hoped, sympathetic.'[10]

In the 'Apology' to *Late Lyrics and Earlier* he wrote,

> poetry, pure literature in general, religion – I include religion, in its essential and undogmatic sense, because poetry and religion touch each other, or rather modulate into each other; are, indeed, often but different names for the same thing .... It may indeed be a forlorn hope, a mere dream, that of an alliance between religion, which must be retained unless the world is to perish, and complete rationality, which must come, unless also the world is to perish, by means of the interfusing effect of poetry – "the breath and

---

[3] *Life*, 376
[4] ibid, 50
[5] ibid, 224
[6] ibid, 376
[7] ibid, 310
[8] ibid, 225
[9] ibid, 333
[10] ibid 335

finer spirit of all knowledge; the impassioned expression of science."[11]

It seems that he wanted this undogmatic religion of loving-kindness, a sort of bourgeois liberal-humanism, to replace the organisation which he felt had become flawed. However, whichever view one espouses Hardy is concerned with some form of moral system that took heed of one's fellow beings and the environment in which we live.

I'm sorry to have got carried away.

Regards, David Cornelius

Tue, 4 Apr 2000 02:07:06 -0700 (PDT)
ANDREW HEWITT <aghewitt@yahoo.com>
Subject: Re: Beliefs - A Last Word (fwd)

"Dispassionate observers"? I don't think so ... Hardy's beliefs and attachments are compared to those of "most educated, and not so educated, English people" of his time and found to be not so very different, as if no other reaction to the Anglican heritage was possible. But Dickens, George Eliot, George Meredith, Richard Jeffries, Trollope, et al, all made different use of their Christian heritage, rejecting or transmuting it in quite different ways to arrive at a set of beliefs held and expressed through actions and words during their adulthood.

Hardy's engagement with the Christian church, its history, dogma, folklore, culture etc., seems to have continued right to the end of his life. This does seem to set him apart from other writers/thinkers of the day, without of course making him a Christian in the sense of someone who is able to recite the Nicene Creed (though as a staunch church-goer he must have hypocritically done just that for many years).

The question "was Meredith (for example) a Christian?" is simply not as resonant as "was Hardy?" George Eliot's work reveals a "long-term engagement with Christian literature and thought", but the rules of that engagement, and its outcome, are quite different than in Hardy. "If to be informed about and show an interest in Christianity is immediately to be enlisted for the cause, few of us will escape impressment."

I think the irony here is a bit too heavy; there are huge differences in the quality and depth of the interest, and the extent of the information, between Hardy and, say, the columnist Julie Burchill, who had the sort of pre-late-1960s upbringing described.   Andrew

---

[11] Harold, Orel, ed, *Thomas Hardy's Personal Writings* (London, 1976), 567.

Tue, 4 Apr 2000 07:08:47 -0400 (EDT)
KEITH WILSON <kgwilson@aix1.uottawa.ca>
Subject: Re: Beliefs

I agree entirely (see above). Everything you say (like, I thought, everything I have been saying) confirms Hardy's detailed knowledge of/emotional attachment to the Christian tradition/culture/nexus of ideas that shaped him. I also agree (in fact I specifically said) that the 20th century Christian culture that most people brought up in England experienced – even Julie Burchill if you say so, though I wouldn't myself have thought of mentioning her in the same breath as Hardy – was the "merest shadow" of what Thomas Hardy experienced and remained in all sorts of ways attached to.

And obviously it is possible, as you are saying here, to be shaped by a Christian culture and have a very different, and far less sympathetic, response to that shaping than Hardy had (if we want a more modern version of this, Jeanette Winterson might be a better bet than Julie Burchill). This still has nothing to do with "belief" or Hardy's possible qualified status as a Christian, which is what this thread has been addressing. Neither sympathy, interest, nor emotional attachment is belief.

Since you imply doubt that I am a "dispassionate observer," let me assure you that I have no vested interest at all in enlisting Hardy for evangelical unbelief. I think "The Impercipient" one of the most poignant and moving poems in the English language. Were there the slightest evidence that in belief he was any kind of Christian other than a lapsed one, I would be delighted to acknowledge it.

It even seems to me entirely appropriate that his ashes were interred in Westminster Abbey and his heart in Stinsford churchyard – there is a national institutional rightness on the one hand and affectional/contextual/familial rightness on the other about both gestures, however macabre the process required to bring them about.

But I suppose lying behind my whole contribution to this discussion is something analogous to the response of T E. Lawrence, who *did* somewhat resent the Westminster Abbey end of things:

> I regret Hardy's funeral service. So little of it suited the old man's nature. He would have smiled, tolerantly, at it all: but I grow indignant for him, knowing that these sleek Deans and Canons were acting a lie behind his name. Hardy was too great to be suffered as an enemy of the faith: so he must be redeemed.[12]

---

[12] Quoted in Michael Millgate, Thomas Hardy: A Biography (Oxford University Press)

As we have all been indicating, Hardy was not really "an enemy of the faith," but he was certainly not a possessor of it. Which is why I have been so tediously resistant to apparent attempts to redeem him for some late-twentieth/early-twenty-first century diluted version of Christian witness.   All best wishes, Keith

Tue, 4 Apr 2000 07:24:56 -0700 (PDT)
ANDREW HEWITT <aghewitt@yahoo.com>
Subject: Beliefs

Not vested interest, no – just a "passionate" observer (if that's possible) ... it's the passion that keeps it going!   Andrew

Tue, 4 Apr 2000 16:44:23 +0100
JAMES WHITEHEAD <jamesswhitehead@hotmail.com>
Subject: Final Reply

Keith's opening remarks:
> It seems to me clear from virtually everything that Hardy ever wrote that he was unequivocally an agnostic, and arguably – despite his own distinction between the two terms and location of himself as a "harmless agnostic" rather than a "clamorous atheist"... an atheist.

My last word: No one, so far as I can tell, is enlisting Hardy in anything, or involving anyone in "impressment," unless it is for some kind of spurious atheism. A writer cannot, so far as I am aware, be both "unequivocally an agnostic" and also "an atheist." The fact that I have noted briefly – with relevant qualifications – certain similarities between the ideas expressed by a writer who died in 1928 with those expressed by unorthodox reforming clergy of the present day (with whom I have no personal association) is not to appropriate Hardy. Similarly, blithe characterization of the ideas of reformist clergy can be reductive. J. S. Spong, for example, would definitely argue in favour of belief in God, just not the old-fashioned, interventionist deity that is so obviously out of date. To call Hardy an atheist (in Hardy's sense of the term) is, however, to be "tendentious," to appropriate him for a negative position he explicitly rejected. It is as silly an academic exercise as it would be to appropriate him for Church orthodoxy, as a supposed paid-up member of the determined Christian faithful. To state that Hardy often attended Church is simply to give the facts, as far as biography establishes them. He was an occasionally subversive "Churchy" agnostic whose views were often expressed by means of biblical or liturgical language and metaphor; moreover, in his work those consciously attempting to live in accordance with fundamental Christian precepts are portrayed positively (e.g. 'A Changed Man'). Regards to all, James Whitehead

P. S. Perhaps Keith and I can continue discussion by means of personal e-mail - I'm sure that people must be getting bored by now!

Tue, 4 Apr 2000 13:24:39 -0400 (EDT)
KEITH WILSON <kgwilson@aix1.uottawa.ca>
Subject: Final Reply

The last thing I would want is to place myself in what the old "Beyond the Fringe" crew once termed a semantic cleft-stick. I am happy to change my phrasing to "at the very least an agnostic." But it still seems to me pretty unequivocal that Hardy was at least an agnostic and arguably an atheist.

The clearest indication in your latest posting as to the probable source of our disagreement is surely the statement that

> To call Hardy an atheist . . . is . . . to appropriate him for a negative position he explicitly rejected.

The tacit (indeed the explicit) assumption here is very telling, and takes us straight back to some of the assumptions lying behind the tenor of the attacks made on Hardy as an atheist in his own life-time (particularly around the time of the publication of *Jude*), which caused him by their judgemental manner such pain. Why on earth is atheism a "negative" position? It is neutrally definitional (i.e. descriptive of non-belief in God) not judgementally inflected, as "negative" suggests. By the same token, belief in God is not a "positive" position – it is a choice, a gift, a conclusion, all sorts of possible things, but not *per se* a more positive or moral or better position.

In fact, as Hardy observed, if a "Supreme Mover or Movers" did exist it/they "must be either limited in power, unknowing, or cruel – which is obvious enough, and has been for centuries." Nothing too "positive" here relative to "negative" atheism.

The Hardy who wrote,

> I have been looking for God for fifty years, and I think that if he existed I should have discovered him. As an external personality, of course, the only true meaning of the word,

seems to me a Hardy who is "arguably" (in fact at this point "unequivocally") articulating the view of an atheist – i.e. not "I see no evidence for God," but "am leaving open the possibility of his existence" (agnosticism) – "had he existed I should have discovered him, and therefore it is logical to deduce that he doesn't exist" (atheism).

Incidentally, I suspect that his reservation about being defined as "a clamorous atheist" rather than "a harmless agnostic" in the comment I quoted in my first posting is as much related to the adjectives he chooses to associate with the nouns as to the distinction between the nouns.

In the turn to poetry after the hysterical controversy surrounding *Jude* (which is the context for his comment), he wishes to appear harmless and not clamorous, so that, like Galileo had he seen fit to write in verse, he might both articulate unorthodox/heretical positions *and* be let alone. But clearly he is not going to be.

All the best, Keith

Wed, 5 Apr 2000 09:35:51 +0100
ALAN SHELSTON <alan@shelston.freeserve.co.uk>
Subject: Thomas Hardy's Beliefs

Yes, I think this one should cease. But surely the key issue would be whether or not Hardy took the sacrament – and I would assume he didn't after his early life. Certainly Dr Johnson – another troubled member of the established church – saw this as the crux.

Alan Shelston

Wed, 05 Apr 2000 20:28:41 -0400
ROSEMARIE MORGAN <rosemarie.morgan@yale.edu>
Subject: Thomas Hardy's Beliefs

Since our two great debaters have given of their "last word" I'd like to thank them both for their forbearance and patience in what, topically speaking – not to mention historically (over 2000 years of Christianity) – generates more war than peace. I doubt if anyone could summarise the opposing points made in the aforegoing debate on Hardy's beliefs without risking re-ignition, but it strikes me as singularly apt that we should conclude (almost!) with the words of One Who Knew (quoted by Keith) – T. E. Lawrence:

> I regret Hardy's funeral service. So little of it suited the old man's nature. He would have smiled, tolerantly, at it all: but I grow indignant for him, knowing that these sleek Deans and Canons were acting a lie behind his name. Hardy was too great to be suffered as an enemy of the faith: so he must be redeemed.

Unlike ourselves, T.E Lawrence knew Hardy intimately. On the other hand it seems singularly inapt to visit upon Hardy's head the very hypocritical stance he abhorred to the end of his life as made manifest by the Vicars of Christ's church (cited by James):

> At the time of his death, when the Dean of Westminster made inquiries to the Vicar of Stinsford about Hardy's respectability and church-going, he was assured that Hardy's record in this respect passed muster.

I think one of the more resounding points that has emerged over the last day or so is that Hardy, like other Victorians, lived in a Christianity-saturated society. So we are talking more *acculturation* than belief, in respect of "churchiness." Christian belief and church-going are two separable issues. I think that point has now been well-made.

When my father died a very thoughtful, very candid minister from the local parish church visited our family home and asked what to do about burial. My father's ancestors lay in the nearby village churchyard; where should my father lie and by what means? After all, as the minister noted, he was rarely a churchgoer (except at Christmas as part of the ritualised festivities), but on the other hand there is no adequate burial ritual in Britain comparable to the beautiful Christian service.

It was a dilemma. We spent two days discussing it. On the minister's recommendation we finally chose – with her aid and advice – a church service, but a revised version featuring some lines from the poets, some from the bible, some folk-songs which the children would sing and dance, and those pieces from the hymnal my father had, on occasion, enjoyed bellowing out at the top of his voice, and finally, some Requiem pieces on the organ. There probably wasn't a single "believer" among us. But there were plenty of music lovers, literature lovers and many a "religious" type who, like my agnostic self, visits sacred places of worship across the world for sheer love of the culture. Despite the "non-belief" of most I would call this particular funeral a "churchy" occasion for all of us – my absent father included.

Finally, with Meg and Joan, I too find Hardy's folkloric legacy marvellously enriching and (in the current context) enlightening. Highly illustrative is his juxtaposition of things folkloric with things biblical which frequently results in the latter being subverted by the former. A good example is Mark Clark's (churchy) allusion to Judas Iscariot – "Joey Iscariot" in this instance – which instantly evokes in the minds of his fellow workers a whole host of superstitions, from putting bellows on the table to finding "coffin-handles" on candles and seeing the new moon through glass. The implications of this narrative device of invoking things "churchy" in order to reveal, by association, what this actually means in terms of non-Christian belief systems (among the rustics), is instructive at this juncture. In terms of signification, it does not do simply to note the religiosity of the words – those that Hardy puts into the mouths of his characters. Context is all! And iconoclasm is the name of the game.

I would like to leave you with one of Hardy's greatest coups – this time, regarding the closure of *Far From the Madding Crowd*. And it is this: that in invoking the biblical words from *The Song of Solomon* which appear to give a semblance of respectable religiosity to this (dubious) "Happy Ending," this love "which many waters cannot quench," Hardy was well aware that the original words celebrate not the spiritual life at all but the carnal – a woman's lust for the male body! Cheers, Rosemarie

Thu, 6 Apr 2000 13:48:00 +0100
JAMES WHITEHEAD <jamesswhitehead@hotmail.com>
Subject: response/not re-ignition

Re. Rosemarie's point:

> On the other hand it seems singularly inapt to visit upon Hardy's head the very hypocritical stance he abhorred to the end of his life as made manifest by the Vicars of Christ's church (cited by James): "At the time of his death when the Dean of Westminster ..." etc.

This was not to equate Hardy's belief system with any particular putative "hypocritical stance" of the "Vicars of Christ's Church" but simply to draw attention to his "churchy"-ness, as noticed by contemporaries.

It reflected a lack of probity among those investigating Hardy's "beliefs" at the time of his death that "churchy"-ness and general "respectability" were seen as sufficient justification for an inappropriate Westminster ceremony. As Rosemarie is aware from her knowledge of my Ph.D. thesis (in which I explored in detail Hardy's relationship with T.E. Lawrence among others), I have investigated elsewhere the ideological implications of the appropriation of Hardy's body at his death by those keen to recover him for orthodoxy and the nation; a wholly regrettable episode all round, for which much of the blame attaches to Sydney Cockerell and J. M. Barrie.

Hardy's agnosticism did not make him a paid-up believer – critical /biographical reference to his church-going and to his spiritual questing does not mean that he should be in any way appropriated for Christian orthodoxy. In his poetry and prose Hardy explores a wide range of religious and non-religious perspectives (some of which have been cited by Keith – there are others). In many instances he is entirely subversive in his approach, incorporating in his writing "irreverent" reference to biblical/liturgical material, as Rosemarie's reference to *Far From the Madding Crowd* clearly illustrates. 'The Song of Solomon' is, of course, one of the most wonderful poems about love ever written, appreciated by atheists, agnostic and believers alike.

Nevertheless, in the key autobiographical entry in the *Life*, Hardy refers to himself as an agnostic (neither atheist nor believer). No amount of tangential debate should ignore this salient fact. More importantly, however, the central point that should be noted in relation to Hardy's "belief" system is that pertaining to "loving-kindness." Whatever the resonance of the biblical/Judao-Christian nature of the language and/or metaphor in a given passage may be, it probably doesn't matter. As many contributors to this discussion have noted and reflected in the open-mindedness of their comments, the key thing is the idea. Regards to all, James Whitehead

Thu, 6 Apr 2000 11:30:23 -0400 (EDT)
KEITH WILSON<kgwilson@aix1.uottawa.ca>
Subject:: response/not re-ignition

Absolutely not (see quoted material above), and that's why nobody *has* ignored this fact. They have simply found it relevant to a discussion of Thomas Hardy's belief that at other times in his life he adopted positions, and made overt declarations, that, in seeming to deny the existence of a God "as an external personality" (what Hardy himself defined as "the only true meaning of the word"), would make him "arguably" definable as an atheist. This assumes, of course (and perhaps this is where we are still not understanding each other), a definition of "atheist" as meaning *not* someone *hostile* to the idea of a God's existence, or anxiously desirous for a God *not* to exist, or contemptuous of those who believe God does exist, but merely someone who does not himself/herself believe a God exists and bears absolutely no ill-will to those who do.

As some contributors to this discussion have indicated in relation to their own experiences, and as the evidence of Hardy's comments certainly indicates in relation to his own, people define, when forced to put a specific (and therefore sometimes rather inadequately restrictive) name on things, their philosophical/theological positions differently on different occasions. This is why it is useful to speculate about Hardy's assumptions from the copious evidence of his philosophical/literary/epistolary/diary ruminations rather than merely from what he happened to term himself on a particular occasion with a particular, almost defensively situated, context (the shift to poetry), in a culture that (as he knew to his cost, since he was frequently on the receiving end of them) threw insults at those it assumed to be "atheistic."

Of course he would prefer, I think fairly routinely, the term "agnostic." If someone in 1950s Washington who, on significant objective evidence might "arguably" have been termed a communist, chose to say he/she wasn't—as so many did – would we in the present (who have no axe to grind pro- or con-communists but are simply speculating about whether this putative person may have been one or not) necessarily take this as the last possible word on the subject? Presumably not, but then nor would we dismiss it as irrelevant. We would add it to the whole body of evidence that was available for examination. That is all anyone is suggesting be done in relation to the question of Hardy's beliefs. 1890s England was not 1950s America. But atheism, as Hardy knew to his cost, was not exactly a socially/intellectually advantageous position to adopt, particularly for someone who is in the process of effecting a generic revolution in his writing career, almost entirely deserting the genre that had thus far defined him and on which his reputation was based, and deserting it in part because he had come close to being traumatised by what he saw – accurately or not – as vitriolic attacks on him, both publicly and domestically, for being an atheist.

Do be assured that finally I couldn't care less whether Hardy was an agnostic, an atheist, a seventh-day adventist, or a moony, if any of them can be proved. I am simply arguing what seems to me a vitally important intellectual and critical point. That *all* evidence needs to be taken into consideration, and intellectually flexible conclusions be drawn from that complex of materials.   All the best, Keith

Thu, 6 Apr 20
00 00:53:39 +0100
ARTHUR F. JONES afjones@sol.co.uk
Subject: Beliefs - a conclusion?

Greetings to all — A number of people, I'm sure, think this thread has unravelled far enough. As an early contributor who has been greatly impressed by the depth of knowledge and the strength of feeling contained in the correspondence which followed, I thought I might try to share in its ending. This message is just a personal statement. I do not intend to provide a lengthy summary of the

conflicting view-points which have emerged, though I suppose they might be very roughly divided between:
1. An emphasis on Hardy's undoubted intellectual rejection of core Christian theological statements of belief; an understanding of his churchiness purely on the basis of personal response to his cultural and social environment; and a strong resistance to the notion that his kind of heart-felt humanitarianism might be considered as some kind of modern liberal non-theologically-heavy spiritualist "christianity", much less its preserve.
2. An emphasis on Hardy's immense concern for the plight of human beings, his fellow-feeling for them, his positive acquiescence in the concept of "loving-kindness," and his ever-recurring Biblical references at key moments as evidence of his spiritual kinship with non-theologically-heavy "christianity"; resistance to describing him as an atheist rather than an agnostic; and a belief that many of the modernising trends of the Church (particularly of his own, the Anglican), would have met with his approval.

I don't know what the general outlook for Christianity is in other countries, but as a Scot brought up in the Presbyterian tradition, who rejected it in his late teens, came back into line in his mid-thirties only to fall away again in his late forties (and still remain fallen in his fifties), I am one of countless in this country feeling spiritually bemused and looking for something deep and meaningful to believe in.

Those who profess to be "humanists" seem to be obsessed with rejecting religion more than with promoting a positive vision for improving humanity's lot. One thing which has remained constant since my teens is an almost painfully appreciative response to the writings of Thomas Hardy. They seem to be able to make readers "go out into the world" (to use a churchy phrase) and engage more sympathetically and caringly with other people (and animals). It is almost a kind of sacrilege not to.

This is not an inevitable outcome of reading tragic literature. Hardy's is not a lofty or scornful depiction of human folly or misfortune, but a tender one — sometimes an angry one – a Job-like shaking of the fist at the sky. If there is a God, then Job is closer than his comforters.

I honestly believe, if I may skew the angle of approach to this discussion, that unless Christians and "christians" (or indeed the adherents or fellow travellers of any religion) can involve more of the kind of loving compassion for others which illuminates the work of Hardy (and others, no doubt) in the living of their public and private lives, then professions of faith, acceptance of key theological statements and the like are empty and useless.

I think I can unblasphemously say that Jesus was/is more for the former than the latter. This doesn't resolve anything, of course, as far as the group discussion goes – thankfully! All the most interesting things last for ever.

On a lighter note, I felt there was something ironically Hardy-esque in the fact that parallel to the Hardy's Beliefs discussion, there ran a detailed investigation into the meaning of one word in one of Hardy's poems. Great stuff! What a group - keep it up!

With every best wish to all from beautiful Scotland!   Arthur

"Broken Key":
Hardy's Illustration to "Nature's Questioning" in *Wessex Poems*, 1898

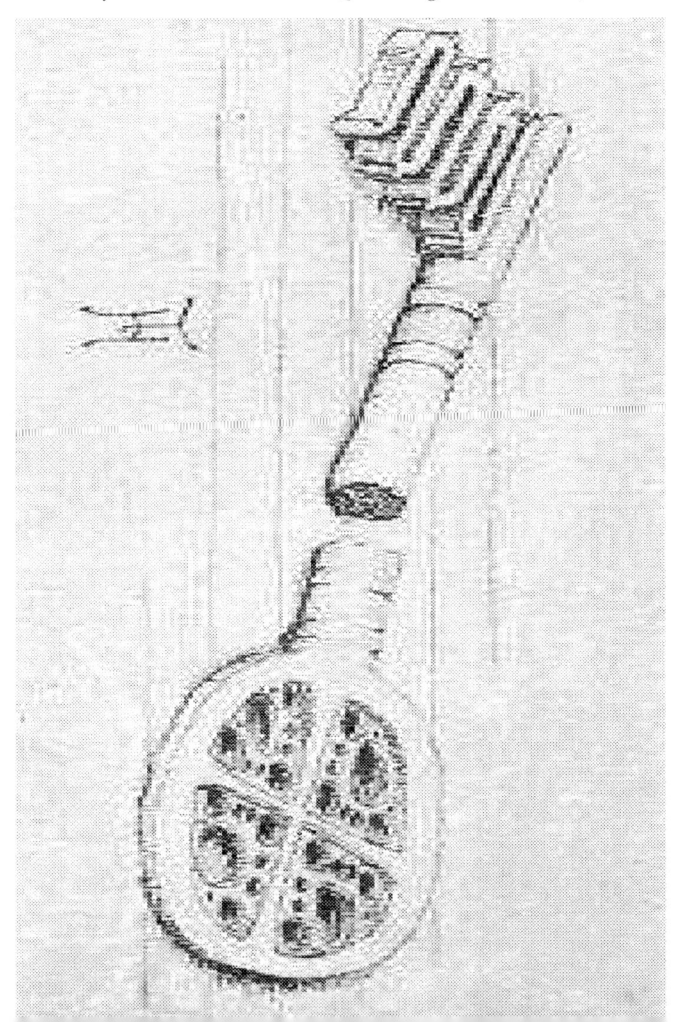

THE THOMAS HARDY ASSOCIATION POTM[1] DISCUSSION GROUP

Hardy & the Nature of Nature

INTRODUCTION

In preparing these discussions for publication, I have tried (as I usually do) to preserve something of the character of the original on-line interactions while bringing the texts just a little closer to the kind of finish and clarity that one might expect in published scholarly writing. Thus I have silently corrected obvious errors in spelling, punctuation, and the like and have omitted such extraneous matter as personal greetings. Occasionally I have omitted an entire posting if it did not seem to contribute materially to the discussion. But even as I have trimmed and corrected, I have also tried to preserve the character – or voice – of the original postings and hence have not imposed uniform styling on them: if the poster prefers single quotes and uses abbreviations, for example, I have left his or her styling intact. I hope that readers of the *Hardy Review* will find in the discussions below the vigor of informal intellectual conversation and the linear clarity of edited professional prose.

To my mind, the signal feature of these discussions (originally carried out at the TTHA Poem of the Month site, Jan-Nov 2000) is to be found in the closeness with which the participants have *listened* to Hardy's poems about the natural world – and to each other's comments on those poems. In the following pages you will find remarkably exact observation, rigorous analysis, rhetorically astute argument, and generous enthusiasm – all in the service of illuminating Hardy's ideas about the natural world, his sense of the relation of human endeavor to that world, his narrative and lyric technique, his command of diction, meter, and form; and the relation of his individual poems to the larger groupings within which they appear or may reasonably be read. And you will find 20 or so scholars, critics, students, and enthusiasts engaged in genuine dialogue with each other as they carry out and describe the joyful work of reading. In short, you will find the best intellectual and aesthetic pleasures of literary conversation and criticism.   Bill Morgan

---

[1] POTM: Poem Of The Month

Nature's Questioning

Sun Jan 30 13:07:43 US/Central 2000
BILL MORGAN (wwmorgan@ilstu.edu)
Subject: Introducing "Nature's Questioning"[2]

We begin the new century with "Nature's Questioning," one of Hardy's better-known poems and the first in a series of texts chosen to elicit discussion about his poetic examinations of nature, the natural world, and the mystery of things. "Nature's Questioning" is undated. It first appeared in *Wessex Poems*, 1898, but whether it belongs to, say, the 1860s along with "Hap" or whether it was written as late as the late 1890s it stands more or less at the beginning of a stream of such poems in Hardy's published work.

There are eighteen or twenty poems scattered all through his volumes of verse in which his narrators search for the meaning of (and for meaning in) the outer world – and this total does not include the more explicitly philosophical or theological poems such as "A Philosophical Fantasy" that try to address the meaning of life but do so without directly citing the natural world as a source of their musings. I am thinking of "In a Wood," "To Outer Nature," "The Mother Mourns," "The Lacking Sense," "The Subalterns," and "The Sleep-Worker," for example – and I want to invite commentary on any and all of these related poems during this month's discussion.

Here are a few specific questions to get us started:
1. What does Hardy's narrator mean by "Nature" in this poem, given that it includes a "field" and a "flock," which might reasonably be associated with the human world?
2. Does the device of making the narrator a passive reader and the outer world a "talking text" work successfully, or does it too obviously allow the narrator to evade responsibility for his or her interpretations?
3. Are we justified in treating the narrator as a version of Hardy himself? Is, for instance, this passage from the *Life* relevant to this poem: "In spite of myself I cannot help noticing countenances & tempers in objects of scenery: e.g., trees, hills, houses."[3]

---

[2] *The Complete Poems of Thomas Hardy*, edited by James Gibson (Macmillan, 1976), 43 – hereafter *CP*

[3] *The Life and Work of Thomas Hardy by Thomas Hardy*, ed. Michael Millgate, p.302

4. Does Hardy's own illustration of the broken key that first appeared in *Wessex Poems* accompanying "Nature's Questioning" seem appropriate and contribute legitimately to our understanding of the poem? Bill Morgan

Mon Jan 3 16:56:06 US/Central 2000
TOM SMITH (trs8@psu.edu)
Subject: Hardy's Idea of Nature

Having just discovered the TTHA site, I'd like to check in with a comment on this month's poem. Nature in "Nature's Questioning" appears to be everything not human.

As Bill Morgan points out, Hardy includes "field" and "flock" — aspects of the natural world shaped by human efforts — but they seem to the speaker not distinguished from the "pool" and "lonely tree." I'd add that the pool and tree may also be results of human activity, say, a farm pond and a tree planted by someone. But we have no way of knowing that for sure, unless someone has identified the setting of the poem. Hardy seems unconcerned with such distinctions in the poem, the fun of which is, I think, watching the ventriloquism in action.

I don't think the device allows the speaker to "evade" responsibility for his ideas, for I don't agree with the assumption that asking questions requires answering them. The speaker has "nature" ask the questions, and at the end, admits he has no answers to them. Is a poet – or anyone, like the speaker here – obligated to have answers to any question he or she raises? If so, many fewer people would raise Hardy's large questions than they do.

I think the device of projecting questions onto nature works as a poetic technique; of course I do not believe that nature speaks, but I accept the device as a poetic way of speaking, albeit now dated.

An indication of Hardy's relation to more "modern" poets might be suggested by comparing this poem to some by Robert Frost – "Design" comes to mind immediately – in which Frost raises the kinds of issues about the meaning of existence that Hardy does, but reflects on the implications of having done so in ways that constitute the poem. Here Hardy raises issues but doesn't attempt to come to grips with them, nor is he required to as a poet.

Finally, notice the sharp shift of tone and perhaps tense or mode in the last stanza, as in "The Voice," and indicated in both poems by "Thus." Tom Smith

Thu Jan 6 22:50:37 US/Central 2000
PHILIP ALLINGHAM (apalling@rockies.net)
Subject: "Nature's Questioning"— Schoolroom and Key

Those who have suffered continual, severe disappointments in life must inevitably (but probably only occasionally) feel like Victor Frankenstein's creature or Thomas Hardy's persona in "Hap," "Neutral Tones," and "Nature's Questioning": "Why has a supposedly benign Creator abandoned me in this cruel, blighted universe?" Of course, it is not the natural scene which does the questioning: "terrestrial things afar or nigh around" (as Hardy calls the environment in "The Darkling Thrush") are a collective personification and reflexion of the viewer's thoughts. The persona appears to be passive – a solitary walker, an objective commentator – but in fact he is a ventriloquist, projecting his own skepticism and pessimism onto fauna and (somewhat awkwardly in "Nature's Questioning") flora. "Nature" means both these things in Hardy, of course, but Nature is always more than a backdrop; rather, it is a person in the picture, a voice that anticipates and counteracts that of human optimism, a presence like Egdon in *The Return of the Native*.

In "Nature's Questioning," we would probably have to extend that definition to include the nature (personality, disposition, and views) of the persona himself. In other words, the poem is Expressionist in the same sense that Van Gogh's paintings are: every object, animate or inanimate, inside the frame is a manifestation of the artist's state of mind. Thus, "flock, field, and lonely tree" are personified: they "gaze," are "like chastened children," and possess careworn "faces." In "The Darkling Thrush" such projection is so subtly and gradually communicated that we accept it; here the controlling simile "Like chastened children" exposes the puppetmaster's strings.

Having turned Hardy's illustration over in my mind, I have concluded that the broken key is not to a schoolhouse, despite the central metaphor of the poem. So ornate a key is hardly suitable for so mundane a location. Rather, it appears to be the key to a portal – of a castle, of the gates of paradise, of Romance, perhaps? Like Jekyll's key to his laboratory, the key has been broken so that retreat is impossible: there is no going back (one wonders who has broken the key and how the damage occurred). Certainly that interpretation allows us to classify the poem under the same heading as A. E. Housman's "Into My Heart an Air That Kills," for "Nature's Questioning" is about loss of innocence. Hardy's Nature, like the narrator in "The Oxen," has lost childlike faith in the inherent goodness of creation and in the benign Creator, here merely a callous schoolmaster (being one myself

– well, not entirely callous perhaps – I am sure that most students regard their instructors as "Vast Imbecilities" and "Automatons").

Philip Allingham

Fri Jan 7 4:28:36 US/Central 2000
ALAN SHELSTON (alan.shelston@man.ac.uk)
Subject: "Nature's Questionings"

A few observations from a newcomer. What strikes me as remarkable, reading the poem again, is the way in which the extended simile of the children in the schoolroom takes over from the subject of the comparison. The surroundings are indeed inhuman, but the children, with "brain and eye" and above all voice, do more than anthropomorphise them – they effectively become the subject of the poem. A related point is the question of the separateness implied by the gaze. Hardy, of course, was a great 'gazer' and gaze implies speculation rather than understanding. Like Yeats, in "Among School Children" the speaker of the poem observes them but can only speculate about what is in their heads. Hardy frequently uses the device of a 'second speaker' in his poetry (e.g. "The Haunter," "Men Who March Away") and it invariably leaves him as "no answerer." But Hardy's poems are always about questions, never about answers. Alan Shelston

Sun Jan 30 13:03:58 US/Central 2000
BILL MORGAN (wwmorgan@ilstu.edu)
Subject: The Broken Key Illustration

It occurs to me that another possible symbolic meaning of the broken key that Hardy drew to illustrate this poem might simply be that the "key" to understanding the natural world is broken, leaving humanity with no access to the inner meaning of the world it inhabits. Perhaps more specifically the key represents older explanations of the meaning of the world – such as those offered by religious narratives – and that now are "broken" (i.e., inadequate). Bill Morgan

Tue Feb 1 10:47:19 US/Central 2000
MARK BROWN (brown@jc.edu)
Subject: Hardy's illustration

Before we learn by whom and how exactly it has become broken, the key in Stevenson's novel first presents itself as a baffling mystery ("This is beyond me, Poole," says Jekyll's lawyer to Jekyll's butler). I confess that I have similar feelings regarding Hardy's illustration.

Could it not just as easily accompany "To an Orphan [later "Motherless"] Child," which precedes "Nature's Questioning" in *Wessex Poems*? In the prior poem, the speaker complains of "niggard Nature's trick of birth," which "Bars, lest she overjoy, / Renewal of the loved on earth / Save with alloy." In other words, the speaker wishes that the child could be "wholly" the offspring of the dead mother, whom he loved, and not of the dead mother and her husband. But the "mechanic artistry" of "[t]he Dame" (Nature) does not allow the mother to "relive" in this way (cloning is not permitted). It is as though Nature herself had locked up that secret and broken the key. No doubt the connection I'm proposing here is only approximate, but is the connection between the illustration and "Nature's Questioning" any more precise? We may be grateful that for his own "song of experience" Hardy did not attempt a more literal rendering of "pool, / Field, flock, and lonely tree," let alone of the "chastened children" with whom they are compared (though Blake's illustrations aren't always so literal either). But a broken key seems little more than a conventional emblem for an unsolved mystery, an unanswered question. Since Hardy's poem poses a series of such questions, perhaps a more fitting emblem would have been a padlock together with a bunch of different keys – none broken, but none clearly seen to fit the lock.

Bill Morgan has noted that field and flock "might reasonably be associated with the human world," and Tom Smith adds that pool and tree "may also be results of human activity" (a farm pond, a planted tree). I would agree (though to my mind a solitary tree, especially in conjunction with domesticated animals and enclosed or cultivated land, sounds more like one that has been left standing after others have been felled). But if each of these things is in some way a human artifact, does it follow that Hardy is "unconcerned with such distinctions in the poem"? Do these objects merely represent "everything not human"? Given the questions that the "children" are made to ask, I don't think so.

Philip Allingham, commenting upon what he calls "the controlling simile," "the central metaphor" of the poem, identifies the school-children with creation and their "master" with the creator; and Alan Shelston says that "the extended simile of the children in the school-room takes over from the subject of the comparison," that "the children. . . effectively become the subject of the poem." But the schoolmaster who has "cowed" these children seems far more attentive than the negligent "Imbecility" of stanza 4, who behaves rather like the drunken Mr. Jones in Orwell's *Animal Farm*. Does stanza 1 in fact depict a derelict farmstead? Probably not (the "lonely tree" notwithstanding); but the sense of dereliction expressed in stanzas 4-6 is meaningful only if we posit a caretaker who has abandoned his charge. Insofar as the poem depicts a world seemingly deprived of divine attention, it is appropriate that "pool, / Field, flock, and lonely tree" be natural objects that show at least vestiges of human attention. Mark Brown

Sun Mar 4 14:08:21 US/Central 2001
ANN DUELL (ahd@duell.freeserve.co.uk)
Subject: "Nature's Questioning"

Given that Hardy usually seems to find solace and comfort in "nature"— this poem seems to me a mirror for the desolation he was feeling within himself at the time of its writing. For some reason his view has been tarnished and when he looks out all he sees is his unanswered questions staring back at him. Sometimes Hardy seems to find some hope within nature, but not this time. Ann Duell

The Mother Mourns

Tue Feb 1 13:01:35 US/Central 2000
BILL MORGAN (wwmorgan@ilstu.edu)
Subject: Introducing "The Mother Mourns"[4]

In last month's poem, "Nature's Questioning," Nature seems to be a collection of puzzled "things around" best understood (as Tom Smith succinctly puts it) as "everything not human." In this month's poem, however, the not-human has found a unitary voice and personality that is, if not literally human, then at least metaphorically so. Nature in this poem is a Mother capable of speech, a range of human emotions, and complex argument. Hence my first question for this month's discussion:
1. What is the relationship of Hardy's view of Nature in this poem to the view of John Stuart Mill in his famous essay "On Nature"? Mill, we might recall, argues that Nature is at best amoral and often distinctly cruel – and that hence the doctrine that one ought to follow Nature is moral nonsense and dangerous.

---
[4] *CP*,111-113

2. And whether Hardy's Nature resembles Mill's or not, just what is "her" argument in this poem? "She" seems to see in humankind an example of evolution gone awry, and in scientific and material progress she sees a threat to her own domain (was Hardy an early environmentalist?). But just as the poem suggests that Nature is in some sense human, is it also suggesting that humanity is an overdeveloped, over-evolved *part of* Nature rather than something separate?
3. The poem is a *tour de force* variation on the "ghazal stanza," a form Hardy used at least three more times.[5] In this case, Hardy makes the form more difficult than it usually is by replacing the variable refrain with a single terminal rhyming sound, repeated 22 times without any repetition of words! What is the relationship of theme to form in this instance?
4. In this poem as in many of his poems which address the mystery of things, Hardy's diction becomes particularly heavy: "old inadvertence," "potent appraisements," "to mechanize skywards," "mountings of mind-sight," "a Sanct-shape," etc. Does he perhaps believe that such poems require a special kind of diction and, more importantly, do we find such diction artistically effective? Bill Morgan

Sun Feb 6 19:28:12 US/Central 2000
PHILIP ALLINGHAM (apalling@rockies.net)
Subject: Hardy's Conception of Nature

Certainly, with genetic engineering and cloning every day in the news, Hardy's caution that man would one day believe that his "brain could evolve a creation / More seemly, more sane" seems eerily prophetic. ...Hardy's attitude seems more akin to Ruskin's than that of today's eco-terrorists, however. While "The Mother Mourns" seems alien to the pantheistic spirit of Wordsworth, it has echoes of Ruskin's notion that nature is an essentially benign system (what we have termed "ecology") that man tinkers with at his peril.

When Hardy has Mother Nature lament that "My children have aped mine own slaughters / To quicken my wane" we understand far better than early twentieth-century readers what he was getting at: the total annihilation of species that sit below us on the food chain, everything from whales to passenger pigeons. Tennyson may have

---

[5] See Dennis Taylor, *Hardy's Metres and Victorian Prosody* (Oxford: Clarendon, 1988), 233

seen Nature as "red in tooth and claw," but Hardy sees "her" as a pathetic mother whose brightest child seems bent on matricide, a child whose rank reason and undisciplined vision are restructuring the environment to serve his [sic] own ends. . . .

Throughout his works, Hardy as a countryman shows an awareness of both aspects of nature, the cruel and the nurturing; certainly such poems as "The Convergence of the Twain" reflect his view that nature is insentient – unaware of human aspirations and miseries, and such novels as *Tess* and *Jude* show human instinct to be capricious and destructive. Yet *Under the Greenwood Tree* and parts of other novels show nature as a positive and rejuvenating force. Hardy, then, seems more ambivalent about Mother Nature than Mill as he has been represented by Bill Morgan; at least, in "The Mother Mourns" Hardy is far more positive about nature than he is about the destruction of the habitat, an aspect of the spirit of the age which has possessed his contemporaries. The poem's surprising diction, full of coined words and archaisms, forces the reader to see Mother Nature both as indignant and poetic, and certainly as a life-force to be reckoned with.

Philip Allingham

The Subalterns

Wed Mar 1 11:23:40 US/Central 2000
BILL MORGAN (wwmorgan@ilstu.edu)
Subject: Introducing "The Subalterns"[6]

I offer four general questions as starting points for this month's discussion of "The Subalterns."

1. This poem, like those above, personifies Nature; do we detect interesting or important differences in Hardy's use of the technique in the three instances?
2. The poem appears in *Poems of the Past and the Present* (1901)[7]– does it gain from being read as part of a group or series?
3. "The Subalterns" is composed in Common Measure, one of the two most typical meters for hymns in the Christian church (think of "Oh God, our help in ages past, / Our hope for years to come, / Our shelter from the stormy blast, / And our eternal home!" or almost any Emily Dickinson poem!) and employs quasi-Biblical diction ("wanderer," "shorn one," "little ark," "pilgrimage," etc.); is there some complex system of allusion to Christian doctrine and practice at work in the poem?

---

[6] *CP*, 120-121
[7] *CP*, 84-187

4. In the British military, a subaltern is a commissioned officer below the rank of Captain, but in recent Post-Colonial theory[8] the term has come to mean a member of the native population who works for the Colonial power – or sometimes just any member of a colonized population; are there resonances in either the military or the political meaning of the term that enrich the poem for readers today? Bill Morgan

Fri Mar 3 17:35:48 US/Central 2000
BETTY CORTUS (hardycor@mailhost2.csusm.edu)
Subject: Nature of Nature

In response to Bill's first question as to whether there are differences in the way Hardy personifies Nature in "The Mother Mourns," "Nature's Questioning," and "The Subalterns," I find that, not only are there significant differences, but that these variations tend to bear out in part Hardy's contention, both in the *Life* and the "Apology" to *Late Lyrics and Earlier* (1922) that he never attempted to set forth a consistent "scientific system of philosophy" claiming further that his views were "really a series of fugitive impressions" which he had "never tried to coordinate." In each of these poems the role and status of Nature differ. "The Mother Mourns" depicts Nature as the creator; in "Nature's Questioning" it is the thing created; and in "The Subalterns" it is an intermediary figure between the creator and humankind. However, in each case Nature is presented as being ineffectual or flawed in some way.

In the first of these three poems Nature, as creator, has formed a creature having intellectual powers superior to those of her earlier creations. But this experiment has backfired. Instead of basking in the adulation she expected to receive from this privileged being, it mocks her achievements as "inept . . . ill-timed and inane." Not only has the gift of reason opened this upstart creature's eyes to the mistakes of its creator, it has corrupted it into a destroyer of Nature's flora and fauna, the "guileless forerunners" which were brought into being before it. If Nature appears fallible in the role of creator, in "Nature's Questioning" it is even more defenseless as the creation – an entity brought into existence and then neglected by an absent, unknown creator whose reasons for forming it in the first place seem unfathomable. Finally, in "The Subalterns," Nature is portrayed once again as impotent. Here, however, it is a benign intermediary doomed

---

[8] See the work, for example, of Gayatri Spivak

by a nameless but malign higher power to visit evil on humankind against its own inclinations. In view of the fact that the speaker seems to be utterly at the mercy of a vaguely defined higher power, his seeming resignation to his lot upon learning that Nature is carrying out its orders with a degree of reluctance, seems a little ironic, if not improbable. Although Nature's role varies from poem to poem, its limitations and imperfections, and by extension those of human beings, do seem to remain consistent throughout the three.   Betty

Sat Mar 4 22:27:12 US/Central 2000
PHILIP ALLINGAM (apalling@rockies.net)
Subject: "The Subalterns"

Although once again Nature is personified, in "The Subalterns" "she" is offstage; further, "she" is no longer a grieving mother, but a military commander, sending out against the persona, a lone human, her deadly agents: inimicable weather, the north wind, sickness, and death.

All the poems in this sequence are definitely variations on a common theme. What distinguishes "The Subalterns" from the others is the "I-am-only-following-orders," Nuremberg-like plea of Nature's agents. One can appreciate the poem's wry humour, despite its gloomy inevitability, by reading it as part of the sequence from "The Lacking Sense," which introduces the series, to "To An Unborn Pauper Child," which sums up the points Hardy makes throughout, about the fragility and vulnerability of the individual human life: "No man can change the common lot to rare"(l. 30). In essence, in "The Subalterns," he shows us that all creation is merely following Nature's orders – that we are all her "subalterns."

The bullfinches in the next poem sing so blissfully, implies Hardy, because they, unlike man, have no awareness of their own mortality:

> For we know not that we go not
>   When to-day's pale pinions fold
>   Where they be that sang of old (lines 3-5).

The mediaeval question rings through the verse: "Where are the snows of yesteryear? Where are the girls of yesterday?" Or, as Pete Seeger put it, "Where Have All the Flowers Gone?"

Common Measure produces a wonderfully ironic tone in each successive enemy's voice when one reads the poem aloud. Unlike Joyce's Little Chandler, I summoned up enough nerve to read it to my wife; in performance, one becomes aware of the incremental nature of each threat, and of the growing empathy of each agent toward his hapless victim, man. The archaic, hymn-like diction underscores this irony; indeed, the hymn form is an appropriate analogue, for in a hymn each successive stanza explores a new aspect of the general theme before leading the congregation to an affirmation of God's love, but here, of course, Hardy leads us to the best we can expect of our natural foes: passivity, indifference, insentience. "The Book of Ecclesiastes" comes to mind as a source for the diction, although certainly the "little ark" recalls Noah trying to escape the flood in "Genesis," while "Poor wanderer" suggests the afflictions of Job and Cain's becoming an outcast.

.... Finally, the fashionable nature of Post-Colonial theory notwithstanding, the military sense of "subalterns," uniformed lackeys who will always plead the necessity of "following orders," produces a more useful image in the mind's eye than native quislings and collaborators, concentration camp kapos who turn against their own for the occasional favour of the despot   Philip Allingham

The Lacking Sense

Sat Apr 1 22:22:11 US/Central 2000
BILL MORGAN (wwmorgan@ilstu.edu)
Subject: Introducing "The Lacking Sense"[9]

As I read it, this month's poem makes two broad points – that nature (or Nature) is limited in its (or her) beneficence by its blindness and that we humans, being one with nature ("of her clay," l. 30) have an obligation – or is it an opportunity instead? – to try to "Assist her" where we "can or may" (l. 29). Both of these ideas have been seen to be present in other poems in previous discussions this year.
1. Why does Hardy choose the sense of vision as the fundamental limitation of nature? (Note that the poem praises nature's tactile skills in lines 24-5.)
2. Exactly what would it mean to do as the poem says and "Assist her where thy creaturely dependence can or may"; what is the ethical imperative being recommended to us?
3. What is the significance of the poem's subscription, which names a specific setting and calls it "sad-coloured" (Waddon Vale is not, in my experience, particularly "sad-coloured")?

Bill

---

[9] *CP*, 116-118

Mon Apr 3 10:44:53 US/Central 2000
BOB SCHWEIK (schweik@ait.fredonia.edu)
Subject: Assisting Nature

About the lines,
> Assist her where thy creaturely dependence can or may,
> For thou art of her clay,

the writings of T. H. Huxley – e.g., *Man's Place in Nature* – and J. S.. Mill – e.g., "Nature" – are relevant parts of the context within which Hardy was writing. Both emphasized that nature was morally indifferent and that it was man's responsibility to alter it in ways consistent with his own ethic. But, as in so many other cases, Hardy gives that rather common contemporary idea his own special twist by at the same time stressing how very much a part of nature man is in the phrase "creaturely dependence." This is stresssed even more emphatically in the last line, so that the injunction "Assist her where thy creaturely dependence can or may" carries perhaps a somewhat greater suggestion that – in such circumstances – "can or may" may not be possible. A curious – and possibly momentarily misleading – feature of the poem is the use of dashes at the beginnings of stanzas II, III, and IV. They mark shifts from one speaker to another – from the speaker who begins the poem to "Time" in the second stanza, to the speaker again in the third, and, finally, back to "Time" who speaks from the fourth onward. I suppose Hardy was concerned that the reader would not catch the shift from speaker to speaker in those stanzas and, so, thought that beginning them with dashes would help call attention to the shift. But, grouped as they are at the beginning of only three stanzas, they can also have the effect of misleadingly setting them off as in some other way commonly related. Do other readers have the same impression, and are there other poems where Hardy also uses dashes in such apparently eccentric ways?   Bob

Sun Apr 9 20:37:05 US/Central 2000
PHILIP ALLINGHAM (apalling@rockies.net)
Subject: "The Lacking Sense" – Edgar or Lear upon the Heath? – Complaining of Nature's Ways

The dashes do indeed call attention to the dramatic nature of the poem. In "The Lacking Sense," the first of the speakers on this Shakespearean stage ("Scene – A sad-coloured landscape, Waddon Vale" seems almost out of *King Lear*) in stanzas one and three is unidentified; the second, in stanzas two, four, five, and six may be Time or an aged traveler, the archetypal sage whose age confers upon him a certain worldly wisdom; this second speaker is referred to by the first speaker as "thy Ancient Mind" (l. 11) in stanza three.

Who, then, is the complainant, and of what is he or she complaining? The "Mother" we may assume is Nature, the significant goddess of two aspects and two dispositions in *Lear*. However, Hardy speaks of her neither as a sprightly young goddess (Persephone) nor as a dignified and powerful matron (Demeter or Ceres, Magna Mater), but rather as an old crone who,

> all unwittingly has wounded where she loves?
> . . . . As of angel fallen from grace?

(in other words, like Satan, cause of our mortality and presider over a world enmeshed in sin).

The initial speaker laments that this witch – or Fate-like creature – does not weave "her world-webs to according lutes and tabors," that is, according to those musical instruments traditionally associated with the wedding feast, as in Coleridge's "The Rime of the Ancient Mariner." The nature of the initial speaker's complaint is therefore two-fold: that Nature clumsily hurts those whom she cares about, and that Nature does not work with the young, the vigorous, the fruitful, the live-giving, and the joyful end, in mind.

The initial speaker is a kind of chorus, a figure representing mankind, clear-sighted but pessimistic, for he realizes that all life tends towards the misery and pains of age:

> Into her would-be perfect motions, modes, effects, and features
> Admitting cramps, black humours, wan decay, and baleful blights,
> Distress into delights (13-15).

Why does Hardy choose the sense of vision as the fundamental limitation of nature? The answer is that she is blind or purblind; certainly, limited vision would account for her clumsiness; the speaker makes it clear that we cannot attribute her "unwittingly wounding" to conscious design or malevolent intent. Like some Cumæan sibyll's, "sightless are those orbs of hers." All creation groans because she, the initiator of all life, lacks the omniscience to guide it wisely towards the joy and fulfillment she perhaps intended (certainly those desirable ends are implied in "those fearful unfulfilments" (l. 19).

Exactly what would it mean to do as the poem says and "Assist her [nature] where thy creaturely dependence can or may" (l. 29): what is the ethical imperative being recommended to us? Since Nature can guide creation towards the useful and the good but "gropingly," we who can see (even if our vision, being mortal, is limited in time and place) must assist her when we see the opportunity, as we would assist a blind (visually impaired) person across a crowded thoroughfare, especially if that handicapped person were our relative. .... The implication is that we are of her make and mould, and that we therefore are also groping our way down the road of life most of the time. Philip

Fri Apr 14 22:15:30 US/Central 2000
ROSEMARIE MORGAN (rm82@pantheon.yale.edu)
Subject: "The Lacking Sense"

I'm prompted by the *Lear* associations to say that what strikes me about "The Lacking Sense" is not that it has Shakespearian elements but, rather, the weighty apparatus of metaphysical poetry. The speakers' archaisms help to point in this direction with "whence," "knowest," "thou" and "thy," although the ancient instruments, "lutes," and "tabors," are more precise signs. Not only are these early instruments beautifully designed for medieval stage-drama, but lute and tabor are illfitted to later performance works because they lack the resonance of their modern-day counterparts, the guitar, say, and the pitched drum.

And this, I think, adds force to the scene-setting of "A sad-coloured landscape," which purposefully sets the stage for the two spectators while accentuating the theatricality (artificiality?) of the metaphysical mode (structure flirting with content, you might say). For, implicitly placing the spectators at one step removed from nature, that is, as observers of a "Scene" which, in fact, they reflect upon, not with the eyes or mental attitudes of those born into the age of Darwin and what Victorians called "scientifics," but as play-goers of a kind endowed with "Ancient Mind" and a kind of post-lapsarian consciousness ("angel fallen from grace," "fallings from her fair beginnings"), the ancient instruments mirror the thoughts of the interlocutor who expects to hear sounds that are not present – musical sounds of a medieval kind – not in keeping with nature but rather with his own predispositions and his "Ancient Mind."

The poem's central irony informs the observers' perception of nature as groping and blind (akin to the imperceptient "God" of some of Hardy's poems). "Irony", because it is clear that neither of them, neither "Time" nor "Time's" Companion/Shadow/Conscience (?), has untainted vision. In their pursuit of truth – the truth of the nature of nature – each personifies it, anthropomorphises it, in effect deifies it even if demonising it (fallen angel). None of this helps them to understand it! But it does help them to blame it. And perhaps it helps all the more, in this postlapsarian world, to genderise this fault in nature as female. The irony (the blind leading the blind?) comes full circle in the last line: for, being "of her clay" these personifiers, these re-creators of natural phenomena do not escape "her" legacy as they have defined it – they too are afflicted by "The Lacking Sense." RM

Sun Apr 16 9:57:19 US/Central 2000
BOB SCHWEIK (schweik@ait.fredonia.edu)
Subject: Assisting Nature – Ambivalence

In my earlier message I noted that in "The Lacking Sense" the last two lines,

> Assist her where thy creaturely dependence can or may,
> For thou art of her clay

put such emphasis on the identity of humanity and nature as to suggest that – in such circumstances – "can or may" may not be possible. In a recent posting, Rosemarie Morgan has emphasized the irony in that reading:

> The irony (the blind leading the blind?) comes full circle in the last line: for, being "of her clay" these personifiers, these re-creators of natural phenomena do not escape "her" legacy as they have defined it – they too are afflicted by "The Lacking Sense."

But, it may be worth noting that, characteristic of so many of the poems Hardy wrote on "Nature," those last two lines are ambivalent. On the one hand, by closely identifying humanity with nature those lines can suggest that humanity may be less able to do much to assist her. On the other hand, that close identification of nature with humanity may also imply that we should have a very strong motive to improve where we can, for – being of her clay – we would be improving ourselves as well. Hardy's poem is certainly relatable to the discussion of "man's place in nature" in his day, but his use of personae, dialogue, and other poetic devices allows for, and heightens, ambivalences at best only implicit in the prose of writers such as Mill and Huxley. Bob

Sun Apr 16 20:56:45 US/Central 2000
ROSEMARIE MORGAN (rm82@pantheon.yale.edu)
Subject: "The Lacking Sense"

I didn't mean to suggest, Bob, that there is no ambiguity in these lines. I know Hardy would be the first to call for good husbandry. The question arises, why then treat such a topic (as, say, "cultivate your garden") in such an obscure manner, with an odd dramaturgy, archaisms ill-fitting to a Darwinian topic, and an unidentifiable interlocutor, if simply to follow Mill and Huxley's highly popularised dictates? (Not to mention an earlier influence invoked by Jude in his attack on Sue as "Voltairean"). The puzzle of the poem overall seems to be why the title, "The Lacking Sense," if it doesn't apply to the two speakers? After all, the blind old crone they assume to be "Mother Nature" is also deficient in her other senses: she can't hear the groans of creation, she can't speak except in whispers, she apparently feels nothing of pain and suffering – in sum, of all the five senses known to mankind there appears to be only one which the speakers are able to "see" in her and that is her touch, and her blighting touch at that. It seems clear that the last lines call for humanity to improve nature, or improve upon nature, but can we overlook the fact that the entire poem has been given over to delineating the subjectivity of the speakers' view of the "Scene" (as I outlined in my previous note), so to what extent can we trust their final "pulpit" judgement? If the speaker sees only what he wishes to see (in nature) might he then remain blind to the irony (and arrogance) of his own preacherly words? Moreover, "assisting" nature blindly (of her "clay") not only seems "salvationist" in tone but may well be the prelude (and the poet's cautionary note) to ecological disaster. Rosemarie

In A Wood

Mon May 1 16:14:00 US/Central 2000
BILL MORGAN (wwmorgan@ilstu.edu)
Subject: Introducing "In a Wood"[10]

Honoring the direction given by the headnote to "In a Wood," I begin my introduction of the poem with the most nearly parallel passage I can think of from *The Woodlanders* (1887):

> They went noiselessly over mats of starry moss, rustled through interspersed tracts of leaves, skirted trunks with spreading roots whose mossed rinds made them like hands wearing green gloves; elbowed old elms and ashes with great forks, in which stood pools of water that overflowed on rainy days and ran down their stems in green cascades. On older trees still than these huge lobes of fungi grew like lungs. Here, as everywhere, the Unfulfilled Intention, which makes life what it is, was as obvious as it could be among the depraved crowds of a city slum. The leaf was deformed,

---

[10] *CP*, 64-65

the curve was crippled, the taper was interrupted; the lichen ate the vigour of the stalk, and the ivy slowly strangled to death the promising sapling.[11]

1. Both this passage from *The Woodlanders* and earlier works in our series of Hardy poems about the nature of Nature imply a continuity between the natural and the human world. "The Lacking Sense" says that we humans are "of her clay" whereas "In a Wood" seems to argue for some kind of human superiority to Nature: what is the basis of that superiority?
2. Is it useful to read the poem – its second stanza in particular – as a reply to Wordsworth's view of Nature as a source of moral guidance and spiritual strength?
3. J. O. Bailey hears in this poem's meter something resembling the dactyls of Tennyson's "Charge of the Light Brigade"; I hear instead a combination of more ordinary poetic feet – iambs, trochees, and anapests; anyone care to offer a scansion or a commentary on the poem's meter?   Bill Morgan

Tue May 2 15:27:58 US/Central 2000
PATRICK ROPER (proper@dial.pipex.com)
Subject: "In a Wood"

Some readers of "In a Wood" might not be aware that, in Dorset, both the pine (Scot's Pine) and the Sycamore are alien trees. The pine has been widely planted, but mixes badly with other trees and, because it is quick growing, often overtops and kills them. I would certainly regard beech and pine as an uncomfortable combination. The Sycamore is a "weed tree". It produces huge quantities of seed and often takes over entire woods to the detriment of native species. Being an alien very little eats it so it flourishes, but does not carry the huge biodiversity of the oak or other species. It would appear that Hardy may have known these things when he wrote the poem and, consciously or subconsciously, be reflecting that knowledge.   Patrick

Wed May 3 22:11:03 US/Central 2000
WILEY CLEMENTS (jwcxxx@jdweb.com)
Subject: "In a Wood"

I think I see a possible rhythmic link to the Tennyson poem, provided one adjusts the reading to produce dactyls. "**Pale** beech and/**Pine** so blue/," corresponds to "**half** a league/**half** a league/". Of course the rhythm varies differently. Tennyson uses a trochee ("**half** a league

---

[11] *The Woodlanders*, Wessex Edition, Ch VIII

/**on** ward/") for the second foot in the 4th and 9th lines, whereas Hardy's poem can be read to hear a caesura ("**set** in one/**clay**/") in the 2nd, 4th and 8th lines of each stanza. I'd say Hardy's rhythm (if one reads for dactyls) is more like that of Hood in *Bridge of Sighs* which goes: "**one** more un-/**for**-tun-ate// **wear**-y of/ **breath**;// **rash**-ly im-/**por**-tun-ate// **gone** to her/ **death**." This is like Hardy's: "since then no/**grace** I find// **taught** me of/**trees**// **turn** I back/ **to** my kind// **worth**-y as/these." But whatever the rhythm, this one does not strike me as a very good poem. Patrick Roper

Fri May 5 19:36:03 US/Central 2000
HERMAN BOELEN (herman.boelen@hotmail.com)
Subject: "In a wood"

I often feel like Hardy, going into the woods to find some rest from life's hustle and bustle. Unlike Hardy though, I don't choose to go back finding the same things in nature as in my fellow men. On the contrary, experiencing nature as it is, I cry deep inside because of what mankind does to it. Spots to experience nature are getting rare as mankind grows, cities grow, mankind looking for places to live, destroying nature. Hardy, living in a time when there was still enough nature to turn to, could easily choose to go back. For modern man it is hard to find a place to rest. Herman Boelen

Sat May 6 9:32:59 US/Central 2000
PHILIP ALLINGHAM (apalling@rockies.net)
Subject: "In a Wood" – Definitely Not Wordsworth

Housman's "Loveliest of trees" or Wordsworth's "The Rainbow" the passage from chapter vii of *The Woodlanders* is definitely not – yet that is clearly where Hardy wants us to look for a context. The passage occurs just after Giles Winterborne begins to stalk Grace Melbury and her father through the woods, shadowing their movements and successfully avoiding being detected. The allusion to "Jarnvid wood" gives the forest a sense of the numinous; the references to "the depraved crowds of a city slum" and to "deformed" and "crippled" features convey a sense of the kind of unease that an upper-middle-class passenger might experience in Dickens' "Seven Dials" or Hardy's "Mixen Lane." As human society has produced pockets of contagion and crime, so nature has its less wholesome aspect.

Having re-read the pertinent passage from *The Woodlanders*, we return to Hardy's lyric with a sense of apprehension that Nature may mean much, but that it does not necessarily mean good. In "In a Wood," Hardy flatly rejects the notion of natural cooperation ("helpfulness") which Ruskin so praised in the raw and in Turner's paintings; in Hardy's wood, there is neither cooperation nor "comradeship"; rather, each tree species does its best to blight all others. While Wordsworth returned from the political bloodbath of the French Revolution to renew his youthful associations with nurturing nature, Hardy, adopting a similar rhetorical stance ("City-opprest, / Unto this wood I came / As to a nest") finds greater "unrest" among the Darwinian trees which compete with one another for light, soil, and water, than among the "getting and spending" of human society. "In a Wood" is not merely a rebuttal of Wordsworth, but of all those jolly Pantheists who insist they are closer to the spirit of the Gospels "in a vernal wood" than in the nave of a cathedral or the discords of the madding crowd.

Hardy's arboreal visitant can learn much about natural selection from nature, but far more about sentiment, comfort, and compassion from his fellow man. Our basest instincts – evidenced by the growing militarism characterizing the relations between the great European powers when Hardy revised the poem for publication – are what connect us with the vegetable life of the passage from *The Woodlanders* and "In a Wood." Mankind may have its baser motives and moods (especially collectively, as in 1914's "Channel Firing": "All nations striving strong to make / Red war yet redder" [lines 13-14]), but, unlike Tennyson's vision of "nature red in tooth and claw," Hardy's vision of human nature here occasionally offers the solace of emotional and intellectual communication ("smiles abound" and "discourse trills"), and even the promise (to be sure, not always fulfilled, as Hardy himself would readily have conceded) of "Life-loyalties." Philip Allingham

Tue May 23 22:29:49 US/Central 2000
MARK BROWN (brown@jc.edu)
Subject: Meter

Kipling composed many of his poems with hymn tunes in mind, the most notable instance being "Recessional," which may be sung to the same tune as "Eternal Father, strong to save" ("Melita"). Did Hardy ever do this? Yes, "In a Wood" sounds rather like "The Charge of the Light Brigade," and, in the main, I would concur with Wiley Clements's scansion (and evaluation). But a quick syllable count shows the meter of Hardy's poem to be 6.4.6.4.6.6.6.4 – the same as that of "Nearer, my God, to Thee" (tune "Bethany").

Unlike Bill Morgan, I don't detect any anapests, but whether the lines consist of iambs and trochees or of dactyls and monosyllabic feet (Wiley Clements uses the term "caesura" erroneously, I think), the correspondence between "In a Wood" and certain hymns ("Nearer, my God, to Thee" being one of several I found written in the same meter) is undeniable, if not intentional and (as with Dickinson and maybe even Kipling) subversive.   Mark Brown

Fri May 26 20:38:24 US/Central 2000
WILEY CLEMENTS (jwcxxx@jdweb.com)
Subject: Meter

Mr. Brown thinks I am "in error" in my use of the term *caesura*. In fact, I believe he has in mind a natural pause which may occur in a line and may, in scanning, be indicated by doubled vertical lines or by a double slash mark. I, on the other hand, refer to the foot consisting of a single stressed syllable – of which Poe, in his great essay *The Rationale of Verse* says, after giving an example:

> The caesura . . . is a perfect foot – the most important in all verse – and consists of a single long syllable; but the length of this syllable varies.[12]

All depends on which definition one chooses. Neither of us is "in error," in the sense of being in ignorance.   Wiley Clements

Sat May 27 7:19:04 US/Central 2000
MARK BROWN (brown@jc.edu)
Subject: Caesura

Many thanks to Mr. Clements for the clarification.   Mark Brown

Fri Oct 13 14:21:38 US/Central 2000
CHRISTINE HARRIS & REBECCA MACLEOD
(chris2620@hotmail.com; maybel14@hotmail.com)
Subject: Nature vs. Man?

We apologize for the lack of scholarly content. This is an assignment for a class; however, we will do our best to adequately answer the questions posed above. We would definitely agree that man is presented in such a way as to assume that we (man) have superiority.

---

[12] According to *The Bedford Glossary of Critical and Literary Terms*, caesura "is a pause in a line of poetry. The caesura is dictated not by meter but by natural speaking rhythm. Sometimes it coincides with the poet's punctuation, but occasionally it occurs where some pause in speech is inevitable" (Bedford Books: Boston, New York, 1997), 37

As the poem states the trees are "set in one clay" (l. 2) so this could be viewed as the trees are all on the same level – metaphorically speaking. They occupy the same space —and are unable to move away; they cannot intermingle without a fight or a struggle.

Lines 23-24 exemplify the ivy choking out the elm. There is a constant struggle going on in an environment that is supposed to be seen as a refuge. In response to the second question, both Wordsworth and Hardy believed that the city diminished all moral guidances and spiritual beliefs. As seen in this poem and "Tintern Abbey", it is the woods that re-instill morality and spirituality into humans. It is a place of emotional cleansing. Neither of us has had the opportunity to read "Charge of the Light Brigade"; however, the metre of this poem is fairly simple, and complements the content of the poem. Its simple and uncluttered rhythm reflects the mesmerizing effects of Nature that are presented in the poem. The rhythm does not bring a climax to the poem, but rather, carries it along.

Christine Harris & Rebecca MacLeod

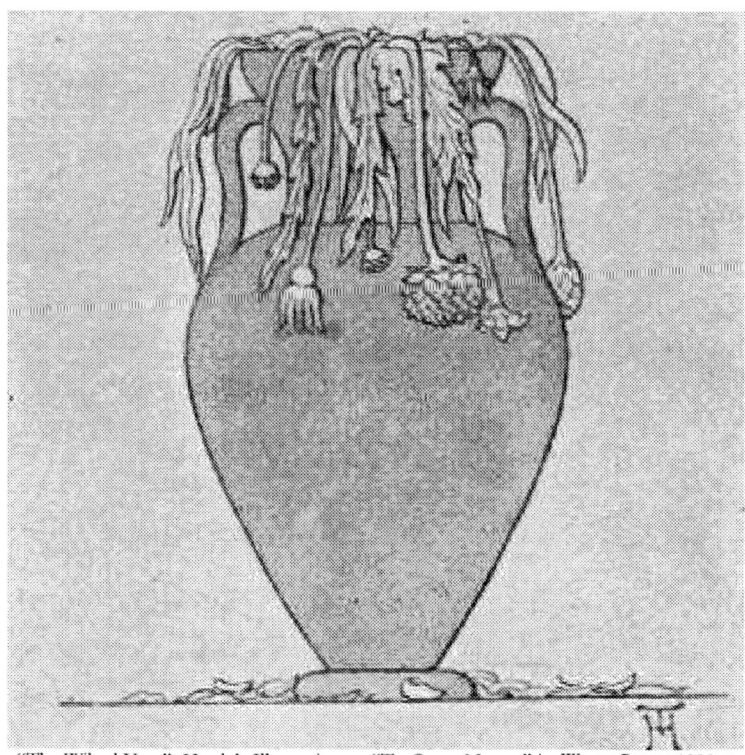

"The Wilted Vase": Hardy's Illustration to "To Outer Nature" in *Wessex Poems*, 1898

"To Outer Nature" and "June Leaves and Autumn"

Thu Jun 1 22:32:12 US/Central 2000
BILL MORGAN (wwmorgan@ilstu.edu)
Subject: Introducing 'To Outer Nature"[15] and "June Leaves and Autumn"[16]

I am hoping that this month's discussion will effect an interesting transition between our recent series of five poems theorizing about Nature – or the nature of Nature – and another kind of Hardy lyric in which Nature makes less theoretical and more concrete kinds of appearances. There are, of course, many more of the latter than of the former. As I understand the two poems I've chosen, "To Outer Nature" asserts certain general claims about Nature and thus bears a family likeness to the poems we've been looking at (though it differs in that it is presented in the form of a first-person human lament), whereas "June Leaves and Autumn" works with concrete details that tell a story and that allow the *reader* to draw theoretical inferences. Here are two general questions suggested to me by the contrasts between the two pieces:

1. Does the knowledge we might have gained from Hardy's theoretical poems about Nature serve us usefully when we come to read a more concrete poem about the natural world? Is he consistent as he moves from the theoretical level to specific observations? Does consistency matter?
2. How can we describe the language in the more theoretical poems, and is the language different in the more concrete ones (assuming for the moment that "To Outer Nature" and "June Leaves and Autumn" are typical of the two categories)? What does any difference we might detect tell us about Hardy's approach and attitude towards the two kinds of poems?   Bill

Sun Jun 4 16:29:51 US/Central 2000
PHILIP ALLINGHAM (apalling@rockies.net)
Subject: Literary vs. Colloquial Styles in Hardy Lyrics

At a first reading of each poem, it is difficult to believe that the same hand penned both, for the style of "To Outer Nature" is so "literary"

---

[15] *CP*, 61
[16] *CP*, 910-911

and that of "June Leaves and Autumn" so much more colloquial. All the characteristics of Hardy's later verse are present in "To Outer Nature": awkward syntax, experimental stanza form, short and medium-length lines intermingled, and unusual ("Omen-scouting") and even coined diction ("sempiternal" and "hodiernal"). Although the poem suggests by its title that it is a direct address to the outward aspects of Nature, the figure addressed quickly becomes a personification, namely the persona's beloved whom he is parted from by another personification, the adversarial Time. She is Eos, Goddess of the Dawn; he Tithonus, the mortal who cannot choose but age. Hence, the persona's seeing "Outer Nature" as fading, as "Darkness-overtaken," is highly ironic, for it is he and not she who cannot 'outleap' time and remain "sempiternal" with her. Aside from that ironic reversal, however, the inner significance of "Outer Nature" is quite apparent in the tone of the closing rhetorical question: "Why not sempiternal / Thou and I?"

The thematic significance of the prematurely lopped boughs in "June Leaves and Autumn" is not nearly so apparent, although the scenes of summer and autumn at the same location are more prosaically recorded and juxtaposed. The hewn boughs are less obviously personified than the subject of the apostrophe in "To Outer Nature." The leaves do not so much die as "rust" and "decay," and it is their "fate" and not they themselves that are "melancholy." The observer returns physically (rather than mentally, as in "To Outer Nature") to the earlier scene, leaving the reader to draw the moral – namely that death is a great leveller, so that those of a species who died early through untimely happenstance cannot be distinguished from those who have but lately passed away: the youth of spring are alike swallowed by the oblivion of autumn. Philip Allingham

Mon Jun 26 15:21:03 US/Central 2000
MARK BROWN (brown@jc.edu)
Subject: Style

Do the poems really differ that much in style? Granted, the syntax of the first is more awkward than that of the second; trochaic meter less natural, more forced (especially in lines 10, 20, and 23) than iambic; feminine rhyme more ostentatious than masculine. The shorter lines (three and two feet instead of four and three) also contribute to the difficulty and tax the poet's ingenuity to no small degree. But if one reads the third and fourth lines of each stanza of "To Outer Nature" as halves of a single line, the form may be seen to resemble that of "I Look Into My Glass," the last of the *Wessex Poems*, which is written in what the hymn books call short meter (a variant of the old "poulter's measure"). Not that "June Leaves and Autumn" is any more experimental in form. After all, the combination of four- and three-foot iambic lines sounds not too different from "common meter" (8.6.8.6). Moreover, what appear to be, improbably enough, two eleven-line stanzas are actually four stanzas, the odd ones consisting of five lines, the even of six, the true divisions dictated not by Hardy's Roman numerals but by the rhyme scheme and sentence breaks. Even so, the poem does exhibit a level of stylistic sophistication perhaps too easily overlooked. For instance, like "To Outer Nature," "June Leaves and Autumn" consists of "short and medium-length lines intermingled," and the rhyme scheme of the second poem is no less intricate than that of the first. What's more, the second poem exploits more thoroughly the resources of consonance, assonance, and alliteration (see especially lines 1, 7, 17, and 19). As for the diction, though "June Leaves and Autumn" contains nothing comparable to "Omen-scouting," "glow-forsaken," or "Darkness-overtaken," there is considerable self-consciousness in the choice of vocabulary. While some words and phrases ("hard by," "autumn-end") sound colloquial enough, others ("festal mien," "on high," "dun and sere") sound very "literary" indeed. Or consider the curious case of "fore-hewn." This sounds like a Hardy coinage, and so, apparently, it is; but it is something more than that. According to the *O.E.D*[17] "forehew" is an "erron[eous] form" of "forhew," an obsolete word meaning "To hew or cut to pieces," but which in its past participial form Hardy has used to mean "cut down beforehand." Hence the hyphenated "fore-hewn" constitutes a kind of pun, as does "quickened fall" and possibly even "Leaves" in the title. Though prefixing *fore-*[18] was common enough in the sixteenth and seventeenth centuries, such use as Hardy has made of the prefix "is felt to be somewhat archaistic or affected." The closest thing to "fore-hewn" in "To Outer Nature" may well be "embowment," an obsolete achitectural term meaning "Vaulting," here used metaphorically in conjunction with "Iris-hued" to mean "rainbow."

In any case, the stilted and Latinate "Sempiternal"[19] and "hodiernal"[20] are neither Hardy coinages nor even especially archaic. Though they call attention to themselves more than anything in "June Leaves and Autumn," upon closer examination neither these words (which only sound more recherché than the Saxon "fore-hewn") nor the

---

[17] 1933 edition
[18] Prefixed to verbs it gives the additional sense of 'before' (either in time, position, order, or rank.).
[19] *OED:* Enduring constantly and continually; everlasting, eternal
[20] *OED*: Of or belonging to the present day

other devices employed in "To Outer Nature" sharply distinguish the poems in terms of style. Clearly "the same hand penned both." Mark

Wagtail and Baby & On a Midsummer Eve

Sun Jul 2 12:19:23 US/Central 2000
BILL MORGAN (wwmorgan@ilstu.edu)
Introducing "Wagtail and Baby"[21] and "On a Midsummer Eve"[22]

"Wagtail and Baby" is a rather arch little narrative that seems to set forth a claim about the relationship of humanity to the rest of Nature, whereas "On a Midsummer Eve" uses imagery drawn from the natural world to make other (sometimes teasingly obscure) points.
1. Is Hardy a better poet when he works with natural particulars to make other kinds of points, or when he theorizes about the nature of Nature – or is it possible to generalize?
2. Both poems are written in quatrains (though the first alternates tetrameter and trimeter lines, whereas the second is all tetrameter); can we learn anything about Hardy's sense of line and form by comparing the two pieces?
3. The first of the two lyrics is fairly easy to interpret (non-human nature knows somehow that humans are different and dangerous, and the poem's "baby" seems on the point of learning this lesson for him or herself), but the second one is elusive; do we expect Hardy to be fairly straightforward about the meaning of his poems, and if so, is that a fair expectation?   Bill Morgan

There were no responses to these two poems – ed.

Wagtails: John Gould, *The Birds of Great Britain* (1862-1873)

---

[21] *CP*, 296
[22] *CP*, 443

Afterwards

Sun Jul 2 13:13:07 US/Central 2000
BILL MORGAN (wwmorgan@ilstu.edu)
Subject: Introducing "Afterwards"[23]

1. The natural world in this lyric serves almost purely as a source of descriptive imagery; is there any sense in which the poem develops a theoretical point about the nature of Nature?
2. This poem appears as the last piece in *Moments of Vision* (1917) and seems to be a kind of valediction (in case Hardy doesn't live to finish another volume of verse?); how does it compare to others of his valedictory poems, such as "I Look Into My Glass" (*Wessex Poems*, 1898), "Surview" (*Late Lyrics*, 1923), or "He Resolves to Say No More" (*Winter Words*, 1928)?   Bill

Thu Aug 3 14:26:40 US/Central 2000
PHILIP. V ALLINGHAM (apalling@rockies.net)
Subject: Hardy's Response to Gray's "Elegy"

I have always felt that this poem is Hardy's (less maudlin) response to Thomas Gray's "Elegy Written in a Country Churchyard" because the rhetorical stance is so similar: Hardy imagines not merely that he is dead (a circumstance difficult enough for most of us to confront so concretely in a lyric), but that others in his native place will recall him vividly when they note the natural sights and environmental details that he would have appreciated and to which he would have responded with such generous empathy. The "glad green leaves," the "dewfall hawk," "the wind-warped upland thorn," the "furtive hedgehog," "the full-starred heavens that winter sees," at first glance mark stages in a ramble over the moors.

However, the "bell of quittance" in the last stanza invests these signs with a greater significance than mere sights on a walk in the countryside, which begins on an exuberant May morning and ends on a clear winter's night. As in "The Five Students," the poem's valedictory quality is enhanced by the simultaneous movements of day and season. Hardy communicates his acceptance of departing from this scene by the undercurrent of humour in the opening line's periphrasis for death: "latched its postern behind my tremulous stay" seems

---

[23] *CP*, 553

self-deprecatory and quaint in its archaism; he never thought of himself as a permanent resident ("tremulous" in addition to the point about "vibrating" above is also suggestive of "tenuous" and "impermanent"). In contrast, there is a note of despair at having to confront the ravages of time on a regular basis in "I Look into My Glass" for his outward wasting is all too consistent with "hearts grown cold to me" (line 6). But what makes his "wasting skin" and social isolation worse is that he is still experiencing "throbbings of noontide" (line 12). In short, still wracked by youthful desires, his mind cannot accept any aspect of aging – he does not even confront the issue of his eventual death. In terms of its detailed analysis of what he loves in nature, "Afterwards" is a more engaging and far less despondent valediction, a genial wave rather than a stern nod of departure.

Similarly, the ironic dialogue with his conscience in "Surview" is self-critical and desponding; one is left with the persona's sense of utter failure in life because he feels he has been so unfaithful to his values and his calling as a writer. In "He Resolves to Say No More," Hardy (or, at least, Hardy's persona) seems to have arisen from the deep melancholy that enshrouds him in "Surview," but there remains the sense that his work serves to "load men's minds with more to bear" (line 6), and therefore that he should cease to write, because to do so entails expressing so bleak a vision, one apart from the norm, one that has ranged "beyond / The blinkered sight of souls in bond" (lines 16-17). Unlike "Afterwards," then, both later valedictory addresses are overwhelmed by self-pity and self-reproach.

.... The average length of a line in this poem confirms that the foot is not a standard iamb or trochee, and that the meter is neither of the standards of English lyric verse, tetrameter and pentameter (the mean of 13.05 syllables per line also rules out regular hexameter); in fact this line and many others feature the dactyl and the spondee, classical epic feet appropriate to an elegy. What Hardy seems to be striving for is flexibility suggestive of ordinary speech rather than the more rigid, short lines of "Surview" and "I Look into My Glass," since the longer lines enable him to describe scenes in a breath while alternating between the personal, subjective voice of the poet and the more detached, prosaic chorus of villagers whom he knew in life.

This alternation combined with the detailed scenes of nature and a total lack of the kind of self-pity with which Gray's "Elegy" drips ("Now drooping, woeful wan, like one forlorn," line 107, is a prime example) makes "Afterwards" a superior poem, an elegy celebrating not the passing of an imaginative voice unrecognized by and alienated from his fellow peasants, but an elegy celebrating the movement into nature, into what he loved ("If I pass during some nocturnal blackness, mothy and warm," line 9), into what endures forever, of a countryman born and bred, only secondarily a poet, but an observer of the scene who has no time for the conventional urban pieties with which Gray closes his epitaph and his poem. Hardy does not pass into "The bosom of his Father and his God" but into the natural mysteries of his native Wessex, and into the minds of those who remain to ponder and enjoy those mysteries.   Philip Allingham

Sat Aug 12 13:20:05 US/Central 2000
BETTY CORTUS (hardycor@mailhost2.csusm.edu)
Subject: "Afterwards" as Afterlife

For Hardy, being remembered after one's death by others is the equivalent of enjoying an afterlife of sorts, and in "Afterwards," a poem of great sensitivity and beauty, he leaves us in no doubt about how he wishes to be remembered himself. His description of his long life of successful achievement as a "tremulous stay" is disarming in its modesty. He does not ask to be known to posterity as a great man of letters, but rather as someone who closely observes and cares about the subtle beauties of nature and the welfare of the vulnerable creatures of the world.

The sensory imagery, aural and visual, in the poem underscores his alertness to the natural world. He notices minute phenomena such as the barely perceptible alighting of the hawk, soundless as the blink of an eyelid, just as clearly as he observes nature on the grand scale watching the mysterious starry panorama of the winter sky at night. But with the unclouded eye of a post-Romantic poet he sees nature in all its ugliness as well as its beauty. The "glad green leaves" of May might be as delicate as "new-spun silk," but the "upland thorn" is "wind-warped." Springtime's warmth and light is counterbalanced by the blackness and gloom of winter. Above all, one man striving to protect innocent creatures from the perils facing them in the wild is virtually powerless against the inexorable forces of nature.

Viewed as a poet's requiem for himself, this poem bears distinguishable resemblances, particularly in the closing stanza, to Tennyson's lines: "Twilight and evening bell / And after that the dark! / And may there be no sadness of farewell, / When I embark."

Yet, unlike "Crossing the Bar," Hardy's poem offers no hope of a union with the Divine after death. The only immortality he seeks is to be remembered as one observant of, and concerned about, the external world and its most humble inhabitants.   Betty

Sun May 6 20:03:13 US/Central 2001
SULEIMAN M. AHMAD (smahmad@mail.sy)
Subject: "Afterwards" and Hardy's Other Finales

Of the finales of Hardy's eight collections of poetry, "Afterwards" is the only one about how the poet wants to be remembered. In "I Look Into My Glass," the last piece in *Wessex Poems* (1898), it grieves the speaker to view his "wasting skin" "at eve" while his heart is still subject to "throbbings of noontide." "To the Unknown God", which closes *Poems of the Past and the Present* (1901), is one of many poems (e.g. "God-Forgotten," "The Impercipient," "The Oxen," etc.) that show Hardy's struggle, throughout his adult life, to regain his lost childhood's faith by coming to terms with God.

"A Young Man's Epigram on Existence," at the end of *Time's Laughingstocks* (1909), is "an amusing instance of early cynicism," as Hardy himself describes it (*Life and Work*, 440). "In the Moonlight," the 15th "Glimpse"of *Satires of Circumstance* (1914), presents one of life's little ironies: a workman discovering too late that he wronged his dead wife by not loving her in life as he had loved others.

The poet in "Surview," at the end of the 1922 volume of *Late Lyrics and Earlier*, judges his life by the standard of Charity (caritas), the greatest of the three Christian virtues. In the last poem of *Human Shows*, the speaker asks, "Why do I go on doing these things? / Why not cease [writing poetry]?" His resolution to stop, in "He Resolves to Say No More," concludes the posthumously published *Winter Words*. Thus, "Afterwards" seems to stand apart as a valedictory poem.

It is not easy to tell why Hardy wrote this valedictory poem in 1917, his 77th year. Longevity was common in his immediate family. Both his parents lived beyond the biblical life-span of threescore and ten. His father died at 81, his mother at 91. Perhaps it was the death of his sister Mary (1841-1915) that made him imagine his own end.

"Afterwards" is the poet's epitaph. In writing it, Hardy seems to have been influenced by Gray's "Elegy Written in a Country Churchyard." Both writers use the same tradition of a poet's writing his own valediction. The speaker in each poem can be described as an educated countryman in close communion with nature. In each, he imagines how others may remember him after his passing away.

The implied aim in both seems to be the same: to keep away what is called the "second death" in "The To-Be-Forgotten": "When, with the living, memory of us numbs, / And blank oblivion comes!"

Suleiman

Divertissement

At this point I'd like to switch channels and move over to The Thomas Hardy Association's **Forum** *discussion-group where, by happy coincidence, a spontaneous "Afterwards" debate arose a few months ago.*
Ed.

Tue, 2 Nov 1999 14:49:33 -0600 (CST)
DAVID HAVIRD <dhavird@centenary.edu>
Subject: "Afterwards"

I have a technical question. Brodsky,. in his introduction to *The Essential Hardy*, identifies the meter of "Afterwards" as hexameter and characterizes those "twenty hexameter lines" as "the glory of English poetry, and they owe all that they've got precisely to hexameter" (57).

My ear tells me that the first and third lines of the stanzas have six beats, while the second and fourth lines have five. The one exception, which has always puzzled me, comes in the last stanza, whose third line has five rather than six beats: "Till they rise" (an anapest) "again" (an iamb) "as they were" (an anapest) "a new" (an iamb) "bell's boom" (an iamb). Any thoughts?
David

Fri, 5 Nov 1999 09:12:30 EST
WALLY KERRIGAN <WWKerrigan@aol.com>
Subject: "Afterwards"

Prof. Havird's scansion of "Afterwards" seems right to me. Hexameter lines alternate with pentameter lines. But that scheme does render the penultimate line of the poem problematic: "Till they rise again, as they were a new bell's boom." This ought to be hexameter, but sure sounds like pentameter. We have three possibilities.
1. Preserve the norm and somehow scan it as hexameter, perhaps in the process learning how to say the line aloud. Maybe "Till they" (iamb) "rise a-" (near spondee) "-gain as" (trochee), "they were" (iamb) "a new" (iamb) "bell's boom" (spondee).
2. Hardy broke the norm on purpose. One could get fancy in talking about pauses and renewals of sound here.
3. Hardy just bungled it.
   I prefer the first possibility.
Wally Kerrigan

Fri, 5 Nov 1999 08:28:11 -0800
BOB SCHWEIK <schweik@oak.ait.fredonia.edu >
Subject: "Afterwards"

I have not yet seen Brodsky's *The Essential Hardy*, but I do hope there are not many more comments in that book as queer as the hyperbole that "Afterwards" is the "glory of English poetry" precisely because it consists of "twenty hexameter lines"! The comment would be odd even if the poem *did* consist of twenty hexameters,* but as David Havird and Wally Kerrigan point out in their scansion of "Afterwards," most of the stanzas would normally be read as having alternately six and five stresses, in feet varying between anapests and iambs, and with such ambiguities as to whether one should construe the penultimate line's "bell's boom" to be an iamb or a spondee.

But the comments on that penultimate line by both David and Wally – who both quote it as reading, "Till they rise again, as they were a new bell's boom" – reminded me once more how differences between the Gibson and the Hynes edition (or the underlying differences between readings in the *Collected Poems* and the Wessex Edition, which, in this case as in so many others they reflect) can make significant differences in the poems they reproduce. Those lines in the Gibson and Hynes editions differ in this way: Gibson has, "Till they rise again, as they were a new bell's boom." Hynes has "Till they swell again, as they were a new bell's boom." Hardy originally used "rise" in his manuscript and continued that wording into the *Collected Poems*; "swell" came about when he revised the poem for the Wessex Edition. It's not hard to guess why Hardy made that revision. The change to "swell" had the effect of creating a pronounced alliteration of el's – Till/swell/ bell – and a rhyme of "swell" and "bell." "Swell" had, too, perhaps, the additional advantage of being, at least to my ear, more idiomatic and psychologically precise: bell booms seem to, and I think are more often said to, "swell" than to "rise." For me, "swell" is a small but significant improvement. In any case, the difference gives us one more reminder of why Bill Morgan is so careful to call attention to such variants in presenting his texts for the Poem of the Month.   Bob Schweik

---

* It also seems slightly odd because the use of the unqualified term "hexameters" for 19th and early 20th century English poetry brings first to my mind – and I think to that of many others – poetry written in 5 dactyls plus one iamb or spondee, such as Hardy used in "In Tenebris III" and Longfellow is particularly associated with.

Fri, 05 Nov 1999 15:10:37 -0400 (EDT)
DENNIS TAYLOR < TAYLOR@bcaxp1.bc.edu>
Subject: "Afterwards"

My sense of the penultimate line of "Afterwards", indeed an interesting line, is that to get that extra accent in there, you have to accent as follows: "Till they **rise** a**gain** as they **were** a **new bell's boom**," – "Bell's Boom" serving as two monosyllabic feet, in sprung rhythm style (though the 1918 Hopkins edn. had not yet been published).

A rather unusual liberty in Hardy (I forget where the others are – does anyone know?), but the effect is, of course, to emphasize that big booming of the bell. The revision to "swell" might have been an attempt, through assonance, to raise "bell" into prominence, and alert the reader about that sprung foot. Dennis Taylor

Sat, 6 Nov 1999 15:25:04 -0600 (CST)
DAVID HAVIRD <dhavird@centenary.edu>
Subject: Re: "Afterwards"

Thanks very much to Bob Schweik for pointing out the difference between the Gibson version of "Afterwards" and the Hynes version. In fact, I've used Hynes's Oxford Poetry Library paperback in at least one course – I notice now that it has "swell" instead of "rise." But I don't typically keep this selection at hand. Am I alone in finding the selection unsatisfactory – despite its ampleness?

At one time I went through the table of contents and wrote out the titles of omitted poems that I considered essential, among them "A Sign-Seeker," "His Immortality," "A Wasted Illness," "To Meet, or Otherwise" (which hardly anyone else seems to consider essential, except for Hardy in his *Chosen Poems*), "The Schreckhorn," "Afternoon Service at Mellstock," "The Pedigree," "He Prefers Her Earthly," "Molly Gone," "'A Man Was Drawing Near to Me,'" "A Woman Driving."

Anyhow, I do agree that the change from "rise" to "swell" represents an improvement. I like the suggestion (by Dennis Taylor as well as Bob Schweik) that this alteration may encourage readers to hear "bell's boom" as a spondee, though this means that we have three stresses in a row. I wonder which text Robert Mezey has relied on for his new Penguin selection? I've ordered it sight-unseen for a course this spring.

As regards scansion of Hardy's poems, the most challenging for me is "After a Journey" – at least this one springs immediately to mind. David Havird

Sat, 6 Nov 1999 18:14:35 -0800
WALLY KERRIGAN <WWKerrigan@aol.com>
Subject: "Afterwards"

But our little problem with the apparently awkward line in "Afterwards" remains with us. If I read the Hynes apparatus correctly, Hardy went with "rise" for all impressions of *Moments of Vision* and *Collected Poems*, then switched to "swell" for the Wessex Edition. Hynes also reports holograph support for "rise." I do agree with Bob Schweik that "swell" is an improvement: you can hear the bell sound resume its full force in the progression of "Till ... swell ... bell." But leaving all this aside, it is clear that Hardy did not consider this much-pondered line metrically defective; he simply wavered between two monosyllables.

Dennis Taylor's suggestion that Hardy scanned "bell's boom" à la Hopkins as two feet seems highly improbable. The evidence suggests that the author thought the line passably hexameter. And I think the scansion I suggested is probably right. I certainly won't apologize for Brodsky's errors, though native Russians, even if Nobel Prize winners, might well have trouble scanning Hardy; we all do, apparently. But when Brodsky's good, he's very very good.

Wally Kerrigan

Shut Out That Moon

Fri Sep 1 9:00.39 US/Central 2000
BILL MORGAN (wwmorgan@ilstu.edu)
Subject: Introducing "Shut Out That Moon"[24]

Here are two broad questions – one each about form and theme – to initiate this month's discussion:
1. What can we say about the sound, rhythm, and shape of the poem? The rhythms, for instance, are to my ear more insistent than is usual with Hardy; there is something driving and incantatory about the lines (and of course about the poem's diction and syntax as well). And the rhyming pattern in the odd-numbered lines seems to take three stanzas to resolve itself into ababab – why?
2. Nature in this piece is associated with love and the fulfillment of desire, and the poem's insistent negatives seem to be meant to

---

[24] *CP*, 216

drive the narrator (and the reader) further and further away from that fulfillment and towards the "common lamp-lit room" of the last stanza; it's as if the narrator is rebuking himself for ever trusting the moon and stars and boughs with their midnight scents. Is this view of the natural world compatible with the various theories of Nature/nature that we have seen in the poems we've discussed over the past few months, or does this poem introduce a new reading of Nature/nature?   Bill Morgan

Sat Sep 2 0:25:26 US/Central 2000
ROSEMARIE MORGAN (rm82@pantheon.yale.edu)
Subject: Shutting Out

This is a palpably physical poem: each one of the five senses is addressed, from *seeing* (the moon which must be "shut out"), or reading (the names carved on the gravestones), or viewing (the celestial constellations), to *touching* ("brush not that bough"), to *smelling* (the "lingering" night "scents"), to *hearing* (the "lutes" now strewn with dust), to *tasting* ("too tart the fruit"). But it is most emphatically *"seeing"* which, of all the five senses, receives the most attention, and it is *"seeing"* primarily which must be "shut out." The reiteration of negatives attending the physical body, the life of the senses, renders this all the more emphatic. This is important and purposeful because at the heart of the poem lies the attempted ending of a life, an enforced forgetting of a life, a shutting out of all sense of that life: "when living seemed a laugh and love / All it was said to be."

Fittingly, given that memories of that blissful time bring nothing but heartache – an ache to the senses – the shape of the very word "love" is shut off (by line-ending) from "All it was said to be." I think at this point we are left in little doubt that this is not so much a poetic evocation of stars and moon, midnight scents and the world of nature, but of the unbearable burden of memory. And perhaps even, imagination (memory and imagination are, after all, indivisible).

Seeming to yearn for something akin to that Wordsworthian moment when slumber will the spirit seal, the speaker here urges on himself the numbness of forgetfulness, a release from memories that can only torment, even if this is at the expense of closing out all vision and with it the "seeing" which is also the seeing mind of the poet whose form of expression is physical: words. The orison? that the mind be stripped of all sensory sensitivity, including the pain of imagination, preferably to be reduced (safely?) to "mechanic speech."

Rosemarie Morgan

Fri Sep 8 11:36:50 US/Central 2000
PHILIP ALLINGHAM (philip.allingham@lakeheadu.ca)
Subject: Decreasing Possibilities in "Shut Out That Moon"

The note of insistence that Bill Morgan detects throughout the poem is rendered obvious by the number of imperative verbs (one each in stanzas one, three, and four) and the repetitions of "too" (lines 3, 23, and 24), the poem's title itself being a command. The rhyming pattern suggests a diminution, from the bounding, abundant energy and ceaseless variety of youth (stanza one: abcded) to the almost total lack of choice and freedom that advanced age brings with it (stanza four: ababab) as we plod toward the grave. The linguistic variety of the rhyming bank spirals downward almost immediately after stanza one, reflecting the reduced possibilities for new experiences as one ages. The sights, textures, odours and scents of Nature become almost unbearable to the persona because they act as objective correlatives for intense moments of sensual pleasure experienced in youth and never to be experienced so intensely and exquisitely again.

Nature somehow seems to represent freedom here, and "the common lamp-lit room" the unnatural environment in which the aged persona has imprisoned himself because the sight of freedom without the experience of that freedom is unbearable. Nature's apparent beauty and sweetness are a reflection of the general deceptiveness of human experience, for the "early bloom" (like the nocturnal assignation, the Greek mythological personages in the sky, the lutes, and "sweet sentiments") does not result in what was hoped for and expected: the "fruit" (the consequence of youthful romance) is "tart" rather than "sweet." The pessimistic images of the closing stanza are unrelieved as in the former stanzas by any trace of youthful optimism and sweetness, and the poet, player with the endless variety of language, is reduced to "mechanic speech" about "dingy details."

Philip Allingham

Sat Sep 9 10:24:52 US/Central 2000
BOB SCHWEIK (schweik@fredonia.edu)
Subject: Pronouns in "Shut Out That Moon"

In addition to the host of other linguistic details that enhance the contrasting grimness of the final stanza of "Shut Out That Moon" with those before it – "common," "prison," "dingy," "crudely loom," and "mechanic" – Hardy introduced one other small but telling contrast. The preceding three stanzas all include plural pronouns that refer to the couple – "we," "our," and "you and me" – at a time "When living seemed a laugh, and love / All it was said to be." In the final stanza, the only pronoun is "my," and the contrast further emphasizes the separation and sad solitariness of the speaker.   Bob

Sun Sep 10 10:46:54 US/Central 2000
ROSEMARIE MORGAN (rm82@pantheon.yale.edu)
Subject: Pronouns in "Shut Out That Moon"

I like this point of Bob's – to be reduced from the coupled-coupling "we" to the uncoupled state of the solitary "one"; from the bliss of the twosome to the loneliness of the "one," from the plural to the singular with not even a "me" to pick up something of the forerunning "we," but, instead, a "my" which (if the point I made earlier, about *seeing*, is apropos), finds its echo in that organ of sight: the eye. "Prison my eyes and thought," begs the speaker; shut out that luminous, encircling, celestial body – significantly not that other source of light, the sun, but the moon, that illuminator of darkness and night. With what deft subtlety does the humble pronoun work in this poem!

However, on a completely different tack, I don't feel – as does Philip – that the title issues a command; the poem isn't quite loud enough for that. My sense is, rather, that it signals a plea.

Rosemarie Morgan

Tue Sep 12 7:45:23 US/Central 2000
PHILIP ALLINGHAM (philip.allingham@lakehead.ca)
Subject: The singular pronoun in the last stanza

Since Bob and Rosemarie have drawn my attention to the sudden shift to the singular first person ("my") in the final stanza after Hardy's consistent use of the first person plural in preceding stanzas, I have been mulling over how that (apparently slight) change impacts on the rhetorical context. The plurals suggest at least a companionship as the speaker and the other descend into the gloomy pessimism of advanced age, so that the injunction (plea? command? exhortation?) "Shut out That Moon" is clearly directed towards the other (if one wishes to get biographical, Emma or even Florence). However, if the other is no longer present (that is, has predeceased the persona), we are confronted by a very different rhetorical context: is the "other" a caretaker, an illusion, or simply the speaker talking to himself? Or is the "other" in the final analysis the reader, whom Hardy is cautioning about uncritically accepting the superficial, transient beauty of nature as real and all-enduring rather than spurious and ephemeral?   Philip Allingham

Mon Sep 18 9:59:42 US/Central 2000
JAMES GIBSON (James.Gibson@ukgateway.net)
Subject: "Shut Out That Moon"

John Piper, the distinguished artist, said of Hardy that he taught us how to be nostalgic without being sentimental. "Shut Out That Moon" is a fine example of this. With its romantic vocabulary – the moon, the stars, the midnight scents, life's early bloom – it could easily slip into the sentimentality of the popular songs of the 30s. But Hardy sees the moon as a symbol of cold reality, indifferent to our joys and sorrows, and by its ever-changing, never changing presence, emphasising the passing of time. He looks back at it as he saw it in the days of youth and love, and is overtaken in those later years by the nostalgia that so often accompanies retrospection.

Dated 1904 and published for the first time in 1909 it comes from a particularly sad decade for Hardy. His beloved mother died in 1904 and his relationship with Emma was reaching an all-time low. The first part of *The Dynasts* was published and had lukewarm reviews. He was now 64 and more than ever a poet of retrospection.

In *Complete Poems* it will be found that "Shut Out That Moon" is placed by Hardy between "Autumn in King's Hintock Park" and "Reminiscences of a Dancing Man", both poems in similar mood about the past. The 18th century poet, William Cowper, has something of interest to say about this: "He who cannot look forward in comfort must find what comfort he can in looking backward." There is obviously a way in which Hardy draws comfort from the writing of these retrospective poems, and we read them because of their universality and beauty of utterance.

"Shut Out That Moon" is a brilliantly constructed and worded poem. Hardy loved the "rule of three" as in, "as it was in the beginning, is now, and ever shall be", or, "I came, I saw, I conquered", and we begin with the three imperatives, "Close up", "draw", and "Shut out". Three of the four stanzas also begin with imperatives, but the fourth is different and reminds us of Hardy's observation about "cunning irregularity", a practice he learnt from Gothic architecture.

There is so much to say about this poem, its use of alliteration (When living seemed a laugh, and love...) and assonance (room, crudely loom, too, bloom), and its clever use of neologisms made up of compounds, "years-deep dust", "dew-dashed lawn".

And then there is the contrast between the "dingy" vocabulary of the final stanza and the softer language of the earlier ones.

James Gibson

Mon Sep 18 17:17:09 US/Central 2000
ROY BUCKLE (erb@segr.demon.co.uk)
Subject: The Moon

Yes! The moon is a sinister influence in Hardy, not necessarily when viewed only through the windowpane. In the poem "I Rose and Went to Rou'tor Town" Emma's journey to see her father (from St Juliot to Kirland near Bodmin) was started early enough in the morning for her to see the moon looking down. Its baleful presence seems to suggest some relevance to the disastrous outcome of that journey, at least as far as her "cherished" plans for marriage to Hardy were concerned (I refer to the original text of the poem).

Roy Buckle

Tue Sep 19 14:43:39 US/Central 2000
BETTY CORTUS (hardycor@mailhost2.csusm.edu)
Subject: Hardy and the moon

I agree with Roy Buckle's statement that Hardy sees the moon as a sinister influence in this poem. Apparently there are other poets who view it in a similar way. I am reminded of Philip Larkin's poem "Sad Steps," a response to Sir Philip Sidney's Sonnet 31, which begins "With how sad steps, Oh Moon, thou climb'st the skies" and goes on to question the constancy of love when reminded of the moon's mutability. Larkin, like Hardy, sees the moon, that archetypal "[l]ozenge of love," as a cold, solitary observer of the human condition, and an unwanted reminder of the fact that love and youth are transient, and irretrievable once gone. It ends: "The hardness and the brightness and the plain / Far-reaching singleness of that wide stare / Is a reminder of the strength and pain / Of being young; that it can't come again, / But is for others undiminished somewhere."

Larkin freely admitted his debt to Hardy, but is this an example of influence? Or is it just an expression of a universal emotion evoked by the moon?

Betty Cortus

Sat Sep 23 10:10:27 US/Central 2000
BOB SEITZ (rseitz1009@aol.com)
Subject: Sun and Moon

The poem "Neutral Tones" concludes with a looking-back, a visual remembrance of the experience at the pond; her face, the smile that was "the deadest thing alive enough to have strength to die" (what a great line), and that damned, impotent sun. Might we not imagine that from time to time throughout his life Hardy would have been reminded of that occasion, when he observed that same cold winter sun hanging low on the horizon, apologetically providing light without warmth. Now, thirty-seven years later, we find a somber Hardy asking that the moon be removed from his sight. Why? Because it is the same moon that had shone on now-dead persons once known and loved, now lost; the same moon that had shone on the young couple ("When living seemed a laugh") that then were experiencing lively love, now lost.

In both cases we witness summer love lost, expressed in winter sun and ageless moon. In the first we find the twenty-seven year old man experiencing a relationship that had run its course. Devastating? No, but causing him to write movingly of the experience and its aftermath. In the latter we find the sixty-four year old man facing the realization that youth, with all its loves and hopes and sense of endlessness, has not only ended, but has ended on a bitter note. "Too fragrant was Life's early bloom / Too tart the fruit it brought!" Devastating? So it seems. In the first case there yet was time aplenty; in the second little hope but for more of the same. To me, while the early poem is a lament, tinged with misgivings and a sense of regret, the latter poem is fatefully tragic, with a sense of hopeless despair. The relationships lost this time, and the joys they brought, are lost forever, without hope of second chance. No youth, no time; no love, no moon.   Bob Seitz

Sun Sep 24 8:38:53 US/Central 2000
PHILIP ALLINGHAM (philip.allingham@lakeheadu.ca)
Subject: Hardy's Sinister Moon

Romeo.

>Lady, by yonder blessed moon I vow,
>That tips with silver all these fruit-tree tops—

Juliet:

>O, swear not by the moon, th' inconstant moon,
>That monthly changes in her circle orb,
>Lest that thy love prove likewise variable
>   *(Romeo and Juliet*, II. ii. 107-111).

Whether Hardy recalled this passage either consciously or unconsciously I cannot say, but the passage underscores the illusions that moonlight fosters and the transitory nature of sublunary experiences.

Often in Shakespeare, characters reckon time by the moon's cycles (one immediately thinks of the thirty dozen moons of the marriage of the Player King and Queen in "The Mousetrap" in *Hamlet*), so that shutting out the moon may stem from a desire not merely to disregard youthful passions and relationships but also to defy the passing of time and what its passage must inevitably bring in its wake.

Philip Allingham

Tue Sep 26 23:11:58 US/Central 2000
ROSEMARIE MORGAN (rosemarie.morgan@yale.edu)
Subject: Moon-ing

Ahh . . . and while we are moonstruck we might also remember that it was on the night of a lunar eclipse that Eustacia and Clym plighted their troth:

> This marked a preconcerted moment: for the remote celestial phenomenon had been pressed into sublunary service as a lover's signal. . . . [T]he shadow on the moon perceptibly widened. . . . In a moment the figure was in his arms and his lips upon hers . . . and the shadow on the moon's disc grew a little larger (*RN*, III. iv).   Rosemarie Morgan

Wed Sep 27 6:16:54 US/Central 2000
PHILIP ALLINGHAM (philip.allingham@lakeheadu.ca)
Subject: Shutting Out Moon, Romance, Time, Fancy

We have already associated the moon with lovers' vows and the passing of time. In the old Anglican hymn, the faithful look forward to the end of days, "when moons shall wax and wane no more." As I mentioned in an earlier posting, Juliet enjoins Romeo not to swear by the moon. The inconstancy of a lover who so swears is well illustrated by the Eustacia/Clym relationship, which is based on misperceptions and misunderstandings. The fabric of a love contract so sworn is a tissue woven by Queen Mab, a fabric which dissolves by the light of day, of reality, of reason. Ironically, then, shutting out the moon means, among other things, shutting out the world of fantasy, illusion, and imagination that nourishes the poet's visions of alternate realities and "faerie lands forlorn" (Keats).   Philip Allingham

Sat Sep 30 21:57:57 US/Central 2000
SULEIMAN M. AHMAD (smahmad@mail.sy)
Subject: The Moon's Sinister Influence

This defence of the moon should have been posted on Monday ('day of the moon'). The statement that the "moon is a sinister influence in Hardy," put forward by Roy Buckle and supported by Betty Cortus, Rosemarie Morgan, and Philip Allingham, seems an overgeneralization. The request to "Shut out that stealing moon" is because of her association with the music-making which the speaker and his companion enjoyed earlier in life. It has nothing to do with any "sinister influence" of hers. It is a part of a decision by the speaker to withdraw from a fresh natural outdoor world, lit by the moon and the bright constellations of the northern hemisphere, into a dingy "common lamp-lit" room. Having grown older and having experienced loss and disillusionment, he has apparently decided to give up, as some old people do.

Nor is the Earth's only natural satellite depicted as a harmful influence in Hardy's other moon poems. Surveying the world by her "chilly ray," she sees the whole picture ("The Moon Looks In"). Though "So aloof, so far away," she answers the poet's questions in a friendly way and seems to act as his mouthpiece ("To the Moon"). He knows well her "furtive feminine shape"; she is the "Lady of all [his] time" ("At Moonrise and Onwards"). Finally, in "Seeing the Moon Rise," (Aug, 1927), when Hardy was eighty-seven, the speaker regrets that he is no longer able to "go to Froom-hill barrow/ To see the round moon rise / Into the heath-rimmed skies," "... and gaze, and ponder, / Singing a song." One does not regret one's inability to expose oneself to an evil influence. Suleiman Ahmad

Fri Nov 17 5:58:13 US/Central 2000
JAMES WHITEHEAD (jsw@radley.org.uk)
Subject: Shut Out That Moon

This interpretation of "Shut Out That Moon" has been written by Kim Myers (aged 16), a pupil at Radley College, Oxfordshire, England.

Hardy wrote this poem at the age of 64. Its well constructed and worded format appears to depict a chapter in his life, or more specifically the turning of a page from one chapter to another. He writes bitterly of this period in his life ultimately with a regretful tone concealed within the verse. It appears that his relationship with his wife is the source of this regret as Hardy seeks a form in which to express his feelings on this subject.

Hardy endeavours, it seems, to send out a warning at the start of each verse in the poem. The imperatives he uses such as "close up" and "step not", appear to alert the reader of potential future perils that could shatter dreams. I would imagine that such caution has been triggered by individual experiences that Hardy himself underwent. These incidents aren't revealed in the poem, but snippets of information are scattered within individual verses that would imply such occurrences. These include the advice to annul the threat of the "stealing moon". The creeping of the moon goes to heighten an uninvited nature that Hardy looks to "shut out". The fact that the poem is introduced with three of these commanding expressions emphasises Hardy's intent, and it forcefully sets the tone for the remainder of the poem. However it is important to note that the final verse does not echo the same trend, but instead steers the reader towards the "common lamp-lit room."

Hardy uses a rhyming pattern throughout the majority of the poem. Its presence moves the verse along without sounding too contrived. I gain this impression by the mere fact that the rhyme occurs continuously but on alternate lines. This is the case for the whole poem bar the odd numbered lines in the first verse. For example the second verse's even-numbered lines end in "Chair", "Bear", and "fair" respectively, with the odd numbered lines in between preventing the poem from appearing too engineered but at the same time not choking the rhythmic effect of the rhyme.

By using other methods, such as alliteration, Hardy adds emphasis to his feelings. He manages to entwine a neologism and an alliterated phrase into the second verse. His description of the "dew-dashed lawn" is highlighted as a result and with the imperative at the start of the line, the phrase as a whole is given weight. The same can be said for line 15 with the phrase, "the same sweet sentiments". This line nicely sets up the last two lines of the verse, which appear to form the source of Hardy's discontent. He writes of "when living seemed a laugh, and love all it was said to be". This entices us to believe that the love he had for his wife never lived up to the stereotypical image that such a feeling upholds, but nevertheless he has seen better times.

Hardy finishes the poem on a despondent note that sums up his present response to thoughts of his early life. By starting both lines with "too" we expect an up-front statement, which is what we receive. Hardy writes "too fragrant was Life's early bloom, too tart the fruit it brought!" This bitter implication is reiterated as he suggests that life – especially the early part of it – fails to live up to its name when love is restricted to such a stage in your life. "Shut Out That Moon" relates to the reader Hardy's feelings of love, using his example with his wife. He implies that such a wonderful experience isn't always as breathtaking as it may seem.

By using such methods as the rhyming pattern carefully developed and also the music of alliteration this intention is successfully achieved, as Hardy's bitterness is emphatically depicted.

Kim Myers

Divertissement

Once again I'm switching channels and moving over to TTHA's Forum where, co-incidentally, a spontaneous "moon" discussion has arisen – in this instance over Hardy's poem "Once at Swanage." Ed

Once at Swanage

Wed, 11 Oct 2000 17:02:30 GMT remarkable wertyu3221
ROY BUCKLE <erb@segr.demon.co.uk>
Subject: The Moon at Swanage

May I pose a question or two regarding a musical project that I have in progress? It concerns the Hardy poem "Once at Swanage,"[25] especially the interpretation to be put on the meaning(s) underlying the use of the word *green*. The colour is associated with the appearance of the moon seen through sea-spray at Swanage by Hardy and Emma, "and all its light loomed green" and with the seemingly repetitious, "And (it) greened our gaze." Harking back to the discussions on the *POTM* it is notable that Bailey concludes that "Once at Swanage" has baleful undertones for the future of the two spectators holding hands. (Witches and all that!) I always thought the beautiful last line was evocative of an ecstatic experience but now I'm not so sure – quite a problem for someone who intends to express it all in music!

Roy

Moon and Sea-Storm at Swanage: courtesy, Roy Buckle (www.segr-music.net)

[25] *CP*, 783-784

Wed, 11 Oct 2000 11:32:58 -0700
BETTY CORTUS <hardycor@owl.csusm.edu>
Subject: The Moon at Swanage

Dear Roy, I've just been looking at the many connotations of "green" in the *OED*, and three of them attracted my attention in regard to this poem.
- "said of the sea (properly of the sea near the shore)."
- "of people, immature, of tender age."
- "of the complexion, having a pale, sickly, or bilious hue, indicative of fear, jealousy, ill-humour, or sickness."

I see other disturbing forebodings in the poem, as well as that of the green resembling "a witch-flame's weirdsome sheen." I am troubled by the roaring of the sea symbolizing "the slamming of doors" or the bellicose sound of "a regiment hurrying over hollow floors."

Perhaps the two holding hands are young innocents, whose love is fresh (green), but they are being warned by signs and tokens in nature, first by the splashing of the sea changing the color of the moon to green, which in turn greens their gaze, or alters their mood, that their relationship will eventually change for the worse, as suggested by the third connotation.   Betty Cortus

Wed, 11 Oct 2000 15:16:02 -0400
ROSEMARIE MORGAN <rosemarie.morgan@yale.edu>
Subject: The Moon at Swanage

The Hardys stayed near Peveril Point, in Swanage. So they may well have known that the underwater reefs at The Point wrecked a fleet of Viking Ships back in the days of the invasion (circa 10th C.) The story goes that the wrecked ships remain buried in the reefs to this day and, local legends notwithstanding (ghostly ship's bells echoing at night etc), there is certainly a disturbance of the waters in that area which gives the impression of unnatural turbulence.

Cheers, Rosemarie

Thu, 12 Oct 2000 13:03:41 +0100
PATRICK ROPER <patrick@prassociates.co.uk>
Subject: The Moon at Swanage

There was recently a long discussion of the significance of the colour green on the Arthurnet e-group (about King Arthur etc.). Very broadly green is renowned as the colour of fairies and pixies and is also the colour of fertility – in the Middle Ages women used to wear green, rather than white, wedding gowns. This association of green with sex has persisted until modern times. There is, for example, an 'urban myth' about selecting a green sweet (candy) as a come-on sign.

One thing that occurs to me about 'Once at Swanage' is that Hardy might not have meant sea-spray but spray as in foliage (like 'the rime was on the spray' in 'When I Set Out for Lyonnesse'), or he might have been deliberately or subconsciously ambiguous. George Meredith in his poem "Love in the Valley" refers to moonlight shining through foliage:

> .... you
> Lucid in the moon, raise lilies to the skyfields,
> Youngest green transfused in silver shining through

There also seems to me to be a strong reflection of part of Coleridge's "Ancient Mariner" in Hardy's poem. For example:

> About, about, in reel and rout
> The death-fires danced at night;
> The water, like a witch's oils,
> Burnt green, and blue, and white.[27]

And:

> Beyond the shadow of the ship,
> I watched the water-snakes:
> They moved in tracks of shining white,
> And when they reared, the elfish light
> Fell off in hoary flakes.
>
> Within the shadow of the ship
> I watched their rich attire:
> Blue, glossy green, and velvet black,
> They coiled and swam; and every track
> Was a flash of golden fire.[28]

Because of its mixed connotations, green is a very ambiguous colour and can, I think, be seen in both a positive sap-rising sense and as something sinister, if not baleful. This is perhaps why it came to be associated with fairies and pixies: they combine both good and bad, the delightful and the sinister. Patrick Roper

---

[27] Samuel Taylor Coleridge, "The Rime of the Ancient Mariner," Part II, stanza 11: reprinted in *The Penguin Book of English Romantic Verse*, edited by David Wright (Harmondsworth, Middx, 1968), 155-175.
[28] Ibid, part IV, stanzas 12 and 13.

Thu, 12 Oct 2000 17:18:20 GMT
ROY BUCKLE <erb@segr.demon.co.uk
Subject: The Moon at Swanage

Thanks for your responses.

Things are moving fast musically! I am very attracted to Betty's "third connotation". It would not have greened their faces but it would have greened their *outlook*. That is, in the sense of what they are viewing and how they are feeling. I use *View* here in place of *Gaze*.

There's a lot of alliteration in the poem, and this may have induced Hardy to use another g-word. Incidentally, Hardy was having trouble deciding on the phase of the moon too. "Cusps" replaced "Face" and "demilune" replaced "plenilune". I fancy he liked cusps for its sound. A cusped moon would not be so effective at greening their gaze. Anyone care to check the moon's phases in back numbers of the newspapers of the time? (Only joking!)   Roy Buckle

Thu, 12 Oct 2000 12:05:17 –0500
MARK BROWN <brown@jc.edu>
Subject: The Moon at Swanage

Patrick Roper wrote: "There also seems to me to be a strong reflection of part of Coleridge's 'Ancient Mariner' in Hardy's poem." I thought of Coleridge too, and what makes these lines from the *Rime* so appropriate to this discussion of the different connotations of green is not just the comparison to "witch's oils," but how the passages reflect two different attitudes towards the sea creatures, which the "Ancient Mariner" first views contemptuously as "slimy things" but later reveres as "happy living things."

But the Coleridge poem that I was reminded of first was "Dejection: An Ode," which begins with a reference to the ancient ballad, "Sir Patrick Spence" ("the new moone / Wi'th the auld moone in hir arme" foretelling foul weather), and describes the "Old Moon" seen at dusk in a sky that is said to be a "peculiar tint of yellow green." Cf. the green light of Hardy's "cusps of the moon" (though from "that night at demilune" I gather that Hardy is looking at the moon in its first quarter, i.e., the "half" moon). There is also in the *Rime* "The hornèd Moon, with one bright star / Within the nether tip," the "star-dogged Moon" which, Coleridge explained, sailors deemed a portent of evil.   Mark Brown

P.S: Re the green wedding gown, cf. Herrick, "Corinna's Going A-Maying": "Many a green-gown has been given. . . ." He doesn't mean a wedding gown.

The Last Chrysanthemum & The Year's Awakening

Sun Oct 1 22:54:17 US/Central 2000
BILL MORGAN (wwmorgan@ilstu.edu)
Subject: Introducing "The Last Chrysanthemum"[29] and "The Year's Awakening"[30]

In these two pieces, the narrator questions elements of the natural world (a chrysanthemum, a bird, and a crocus root) about the principles that govern their behavior – principles that, presumably, are a part of the fundamental order of the natural world which the narrator wishes to comprehend.

1. Does this different rhetorical premise produce noticeably different results – either poetically or philosophically? In other words, do these poems lead to intellectual or aesthetic conclusions that are different from those suggested by "Nature's Questioning"?
2. The two poems are themselves rhetorically different: the first one reserves its "point" for the last stanza (thus producing a moment of self-correction somewhat like the one that occurs at the end of "An August Midnight"), whereas the second one makes its point early and often: "How do you know?" it asks. Does this different rhetorical arrangement produce interesting or important aesthetic differences between the two reading experiences?
3. Finally, I note that neither of these is one of Hardy's great poems; how do we speak with respect and interest (or in other ways) about poems that may reveal something important about a great poet but are not in themselves great poems?   Bill Morgan

Tue Oct 3 8:49:45 US/Central 2000
PHILIP ALLINGHAM (philip.allingham@lakeheadu.ca)
Subject: "Some blessed Hope"

The speculative natural philosopher (naturalist/philosopher) who is the persona of both poems seems very close to the voice of Thomas Hardy himself, the countryman with an eye for environmental details who speaks directly to us in the eulogy "Afterwards." Whereas "Nature's Questioning" seems almost excessively dramatic in its personifying pool, field, flock, and lonely tree, and having them speak

---

[29] *CP*, 335
[30] *CP*, 149

like a synthesis of Hamlet and a Browning character, both flower poems seem less artificial and more natural owing to simpler syntax, diction, form, and style. "Nature's Questioning" leads us to the nihilistic conclusion that "Life and Death are neighbours nigh" (l, 28), filling us with despondency and a sense of Nature' misery; both "The Last Chrysanthemum" and "The Year's Awakening" lead us to unanswerable questions, and fill us with a sense of Nature's fathomless mystery. Certainly, there seems to be a metaphysical and even religious certainty behind "The Last Chrysanthemum" and "The Year's Awakening" that is wholly different from the ontological dubiety of "Nature's Questioning"... much closer to the yearning spirit of the persona in "The Darkling Thrush," which appears directly after "The Last Chrysanthemum" in the Wordsworth complete text of Hardy's poetry, presumably maintaining a sequence that Hardy instituted.

In "The Last Chrysanthemum," Hardy continually questions the flower's and nature's motivations, either directly (stanzas 1, 2, and 5) or indirectly (stanza 3). A nice touch is the poet's berating himself for fondly personifying the belated flower and ascribing to it both motive and consciousness: "I talk as if the thing were born / With sense to work its mind (lines 21-22). The real point, so long delayed, has maximum impact ... compelling the reader to re-think the whole poem as being not a description of a single flower but of "the Great Face" who may be the Christian God or Shelley's Preserver, Renewer, and Destroyer. The pattern of delay and punch line engages the reader philosophically.

In "The Year's Awakening" there is no such surprise; rather, the instinct that drives the "vespering bird" in the air is related to that which impels the crocus root, a Shavian Life Force that permeates all creation. "How do you know?" (oft repeated) enjoins the reader to answer on the bird's and flower's behalf. The reiteration and the implied connection between sentient bird and insentient root engage the reader philosophically, too, without the certainty of there being any "Great Face" behind either fauna or flora. New Critic-like, here I attempt not to worry about the writer's greatness and to confront each poem as a found document, no social or biographical context appertaining. Of course, such an approach is to deny the New Historicist respect for *Zeitgeist*, for the dominant body of thought and feeling from which the work sprang, and my own inclination to regard all of Hardy's work, but especially his verse, as a reflection of his beliefs, doubts, and values. Unable to escape these works' historical contexts, we recognize the philosophical/religious and Darwinian implications of both "The Last Chrysanthemum" and

"The Year's Awakening," but enjoy them irrespective of their late nineteenth-/early twentieth-century origins, recognizing their inherent longing, and responding to their questions with questions of our own. Inevitably, though, we conclude once again that Hardy was not a convinced atheist or determined agnostic, but a lapsed Christian still searching for some foundation for a religious faith that scientific evidence and life's wrongs have undermined. [31]   Philip Allingham

Wed Oct 11 13:07:37 US/Central 2000
PATRICK ROPER (patrick@prassociates.co.uk)
Subject: The robin's song

I thought people, especially those not familiar with English birds, might be interested in an explanation of Hardy's line "Now is the time of plaintive robin-song" in his poem "The Last Chrysanthemum." According to the "The Birds of the Western Palaearctic" the ro-bin's autumn song differs from that used in spring. It is softer and more wistful and tends to contain longer phrases. I would think very few people today, apart from those who have made a specific study of the bird, would be aware of this and it shows how remarkable and deep Hardy's knowledge of the English countryside was.   Patrick

"Robins": courtesy Terence Lambert, *Collins British Birds* (1982).

---

[31] See the earlier *Forum* discussion of Hardy's beliefs (above).

Mon Oct 16 14:06:25 US/Central 2000
BETTY CORTUS (hardycor@mailhost2.csusm.edu)
Subject: Hardy's Minor Poems

Concerning Bill's question 3: "How do we speak ... about poems that may reveal something important about a great poet but are not in themselves great poems?" First, any poet as prolific as Hardy could scarcely be expected to create work as consistently fine as his very finest poems, no matter what the subject or his particular frame of mind at the time of writing. But this does not mean that his minor poems lack intrinsic interest and value of their own. I find the two poems in question appealing in their revelation of the poet's mind pensively engaged in a close observance of nature, but feel that they are hardly likely to provoke a great deal of commentary or controversy. As William E. Buckler in *The Poetry of Thomas Hardy: A Study in Art and Ideas*[32] has expressed a defence of the minor poems far better than I can make, I hope you will forgive my quoting a longish passage from his book:

> Hardy ... did not prune from his canon the many minor pieces that, of no great merit and importance in and of themselves, have an authentic part to play in the mosaic panorama of representative human experience that was, from first to last, his distinctive imaginative ambition. . . . They are the interstices, connections, or traditional pathways among the more eye-catching displays of "mood and meter" in his poetic country. They, too, are legitimate marks of human passage, and the impact of the canon as a whole would be greatly altered and weakened without them (104).

Betty Cortus

The Night of the Dance

Sat Nov 4 20:37:03 US/Central 2000
BILL MORGAN (wwmorgan@ilstu.edu)
Subject: Introducing "The Night of the Dance"[33]

Philip Mallett, in an essay called "Noticing Things: Hardy and the Nature of 'Nature'"[34] describes two contrasting 19th century notions of Nature: a Ruskinian view and a Darwinian view – one that sees

---

[32] NYUP, 1983

[33] *CP*, 231-232

[34] *Human Shows: Essays in Honour of Michael Millgate*, edited by Rosemarie Morgan and Richard Nemesvari (The Hardy Association Press, 2000) 23-39.

Nature as infinite but unified, and bearing, as it were, God's signature on it, the other as a confusing mass of detail, subject to chance, the impersonal operation of natural laws, and inevitable .... Many of the Hardy poems that we have discussed here in the early part of this past year can be seen to support Mallett's general contention about Hardy's post-romantic reading of Nature; indeed, even though he is mostly interested in making a point about the novels, he cites "Nature's Questioning," "The Mother Mourns," and "The Lacking Sense" as part of his general characterization of Hardy's views.

But recently, we have been looking at poems that, rather than dirrectly theorizing about the nature of Nature, turn to the natural world for concrete detail and thematic resonance – and that sometimes present a more or less benign "reading" of Nature/nature. "The Night of the Dance," for instance, attributes to the moon and stars the ability to gaze at and be curious about things human; in fact, the natural world ("far and nigh things") seems even to be friendly in its role as observer of the human scene. So here is my general question for this last discussion of the Nature/nature poems: Is it useful to complicate the claim that Hardy is more nearly Darwinian than Ruskinian by reference to such poems as this one – and perhaps others, such as "Afterwards," "On a Midsummer Eve," and "Shut Out That Moon"? Is there in Hardy *another*, less firmly Darwinian view of Nature/nature that we can assemble from the bits and pieces provided by the poems we've been discussing (and others)? Or are the moments of benign natural influence just the wishful thinking of the various Hardy narrators? Bill Morgan

Sun Nov 5 8:06:18 US/Central 2000
PHILIP ALLINGHAM (apalling@tbaytel.net)
Subject: Nature in "The Night of the Dance"

Perhaps Hardy is too much the pragmatist, or too much the countryman, to let his experience of nature (that is, the natural habitat of the country people) be filtered by a philosophy such as Ruskin's (that nature is a system of mutual helpfulness, and therefore essentially benign) or by a thesis such as Darwin's (that nature, committed to the prin-ciple of Survival of the Fittest, is, as Tennyson saw matters, "red in tooth and claw"). Nature in "The Night of the Dance" is a world (al-beit, as the poet describes it, an animated and even sentient world) apart from man. For example,

>   The stars, like eyes in reverie,
>   Their westering as for a while forborne,
>   Quiz downward curiously (3-5)

... Capable of understanding, they cannot understand humanity. The persona, not a mature and cynical observer of the scene but a youthful participant, affirms that "...far and nigh things seem to know /Sweet scenes are impending here; / That all is prepared; that the hour is near" (11-13) because he has observed (and misinterpreted) the responses of his fellow creatures to the preparations for the dance: "The half-awakened sparrows flit / From the riddled thatch; and owls begin / To whoo from the gable-slit" (8-10.). Only to the young in love, who see the surrounding natural world as not merely benign but concerned and supportive, is the Wordsworthian (upon which Ruskin based his views) conception of nature entirely plausible. "That She will return in Love's low tongue/ My vows as we wheel around" (19-20) colours the youthful persona's way of seeing the moon, the stars, the sparrows, and the owls. The habitat, then, wears a friendly face and bears the signature, not necessarily of God, but of Love. It becomes, then, a reflection of the attitudes and aspirations of the human observer, who, Hardy implies, can never be objective and detached. This is the opposite side of the coin that has been currency in "Shut Out That Moon" and other apparently anti-Nature poems we have experienced over the past months. Hardy might say of humans as observers of the natural scene, "We are arrant knaves and fools – believe none of us."

How little of love the lover remembers when love is over.

Philip Allingham

Sun Nov 26 16:46:35 US/Central 2000
SULEIMAN M. AHMAD (smahmad@mail.sy)
Subject: Some Comments

I would like to comment on Hardy's "idiosyncratic mode of regard." The Darwinian or Ruskinian view of nature expressed in some of these poems seems to reflect the setting or the mood of the speaker. Thus, the Darwinian view appears in poems where the setting is gloomy or where the speaker is sad. "Nature's Questioning" is set "at dawning," when everything in a rural landscape is conducive to gloom; "The Mother Mourns" begins with "When mid-autumn's moan shook the night-time"; the "Scene" of "The Lacking Sense" is "A sad-coloured landscape"; in "In a Wood," the speaker is "Hearthalt and spirit lame/City-opprest"; and the setting of "The Last Chrysanthemum" is "the time of plaintive robin-song." On the other hand, when the speaker is in a happy mood, a Ruskinian view seems to inform the poem, as can be seen in "The Night of the Dance."

Suleiman Ahmad

Hardy: Drama and Movies

INTRODUCTION

At the moment, The Thomas Hardy Association's *DRAMA* site at www.yale.edu/hardysoc/Welcome/drama/drama.htm limits itself to information about productions, both amateur and professional, staged in Hardy's life-time – i.e. productions of which he was aware and with which in many cases he had some direct involvement. The site does not yet feature information on movie productions based on Hardy's work nor does it have a discussion group. However, if we step across the corridor (from Ottawa to California) and enter TTHA's Forum we find critical debates in plenty, including much ado about Hardy in film. So this is where we begin.

Rosemarie Morgan

Kingdom Come

Wed, 05 Jan 2000 17:05:46 -0500
ROBERT SCHWEIK <schweik@ait.fredonia.edu>
Subject: New Hardy Film: Kingdom Come

In the process of updating our Hardy Association Link A 48, "Filmography on Thomas Hardy" – which taps into the vast Internet Movie Database – I came upon a listing so odd it seems scarcely credible. Briefly, there is planned to begin production in February, 2000, a film "western" titled *Kingdom Come*, which is billed as a "female version" of Hardy's *Mayor of Casterbridge*, directed by Michael Winterbottom and with a cast including Natassja Kinsky and Wes Bentley. Does anybody on the list know any more about this?   Bob Schweik

Wed, 5 Jan 2000 15:18:57 -0800
BETTY CORTUS <hardycor@mailhost2.csusm.edu>
Subject: Re: New Hardy Film

In "The Editor's Notes and News" in the *Thomas Hardy Journal* (Oct 1999, p17), I was flabbergasted to see that *Madonna* was at one time being considered for the leading role in that film!   Betty Cortus

Thu, 6 Jan 2000 06:43:25 EST
W W. KERRIGAN <Kerrigan@aol.com>
Subject: Re: New Hardy Film

Why are we surprised? To get to *Kingdom Come* from *The Mayor of Casterbridge* one need only transpose the genders and change the time and place. Every theatre department in the English-speaking world seems to think of these two simple moves as the height of "creativity" and "originality" – the very hallmarks of "high concept" drama.

Wally

Thu, 6 Jan 2000 01:23:50 EST
LISA CACICIA <Lmpc219@aol.com>
Subject: Re: New Hardy Film

I fear the rumours are true. I read that a couple of weeks ago while surfing in England, and the same week at work (I work at a TV Station) "E-Wrap" that comes from E! Entertainment Network ran a story on that. If I get a chance this week I will try to find the script that went with the story. I wanted to run it under Ripley's "Believe it or Not." Regards, Lisa Cacicia

Fri, 7 Jan 2000 08:00:00 -0800
BETTY CORTUS <hardycor@mailhost2.csusm.edu>
Subject: Re: New Hardy Film

I wonder if *Kingdom Come* is going to have a husband-selling-scene in it. Betty Cortus

Fri, 07 Jan 2000 13:53:24 -0500
ROSEMARIE MORGAN <rosemarie.morgan@yale.edu>
Subject: Re: New Hardy Film

Or a Skimmington Ride that so shames him he'll die of shock!
Rosemarie Morgan

Fri, 7 Jan 2000 20:25:46 -0700
JOAN SHESKI < harrys@cnetco.com>
Subject: Re: New Hardy Film

Good idea, Lisa – Ripleys! You pulled a laugh out of me. How crazy some humans are, to try to commercialize, hype, and twist Hardy's work — and how nice that the integrity of his words resists! Joan

Sat, 08 Jan 2000 00:15:16 -0500
ROSEMARIE MORGAN <rosemarie.morgan@yale.edu>
Subject: Re: New Hardy Film

A small tweak: for sheer joy in – what would one call it? the dismantling of the autotelic text? – I have to emphasise that Hardy's work has a *long* way to go before it catches up with Shakespeare's upon which many a dramatic variation-on-a-theme has been based (presumably the ultimate sign of greatness). How about some playful parallels:
> *Where's Richard?* (-- *Waiting for Edred?*)
> *West Side Story* (-- *East of Egdon?*)
> *Prospero's Books* (-- *Mrs Edlin's Diaries*)

And while I'm in a frivolous frame of mind, was anybody around when – at one of those night-time poetry-readings on Weymouth beach (Hardy International Conference, 1970s) – a passing policeman, strolling by under the lamplight and stopping to listen to the learned recitations, observed, "Hm! I think I know this writer – hm... Yes! Yes! "Under The Milkwood Tree!"

Rosemarie Morgan

Sun, 9 Jan 2000 11:41:39 –0500
SETH LACHTERMAN <sl@banet.net>
Subject: Re: New Hardy Film

At the risk of offending other Hardy lovers, and playing my usual role as apostate, I'll keep an open mind about this upcoming film, *The Claim*. Firstly, Winterbottom (the director) is *not* a commercial guy. His *Butterfly's Kiss*, a phantasmagoric variation on the Thelma/Louise theme, was shocking to all sensibilities and has become something of a cult classic.

Secondly, his second film was *Jude*. Now, I know I'm in the minority here, but I found subtlety and vision in this film. Not faithful to nor nearly as powerful as Hardy, but still, a good flick. (Like the final Christminster scene – the procession played to the Bach St. Matthew Passion – the final chorus – an ironic foreshadowing).

Anyway, I know serious, thoughtful individuals who had never read Hardy and found the film of *Jude* remarkable. At least one that I know decided to read the original (and was so much more deeply affected). The premise of this new film sounds utterly crazy and deceitful to any Hardy lover, but maybe Winterbottom is talented enough to make this work – in spite of Madonna or Kinski! One thing – it will be a film I'll certainly want to see.

Seth Lachterman

The Claim

Tue, 01 May 2001 21:36:56 GMT
RICHARD NEMESVARI <rnemesva@stfx.ca>
Subject: *The Claim*

So has anybody on the list seen *The Claim* yet? I've read a number of online reviews, which I would summarize as "mixed." Many of the writers suggest that the cinematography is successful, the acting somewhat less so, and the plot/character development weakest of all. Does that match up with anybody else's impressions? I won't dwell on the poor benighted reviewer who declared that the film moves Hardy's novel off of "the Yorkshire moors." I guess Henchard must have wandered a long way north in his rambles. Wonder if he ran into Heathcliff and Catherine Earnshaw out there. Anyway, I haven't seen it yet, but would appreciate some feedback from those who have. Richard

Tue, 01 May 2001 21:36:56 GMT
BOB SCHWEIK <schweik@fredonia.edu>
Subject: *The Claim*[2]

I have not only not seen it, I haven't even seen signs of it—here in the Buffalo area. I have a hunch that when we do see it, it will be at one of the local "art" theatres here or in Buffalo. But, having read some of the reviews, I, too, would be much interested in hearing from people on the list who have seen it. Bob

Tue, 1 May 2001 19:51:27 -0600
GOLDIE MORGENTALER <goldie.morgentaler@uleth.ca>
Subject: The Claim

I have just come from seeing *The Claim* in Toronto after having taught *The Mayor of Casterbridge* in my 19th-century novel course at the University of Lethbridge this past semester. I think the film is beautiful! The photography is gorgeous and the recreation of a gold rush town in the Sierra Nevadas in the 1860s feels authentic. The film creates an atmosphere at once bleak, haunting and inspiring. But let me say right away that this movie is not Hardy's novel, nor does it claim to be more than "inspired" by the novel. The plot is a simplified version of what is in the book and all the main characters are like-

---

[2] Inspired by Hardy's *Mayor of Casterbridge*

wise simplified and lack the complicating attributes that make them so intriguing and infuriating in the novel. Also lacking is the early close relationship between Henchard and Farfrae and all the implications that go with that. Having said this, however, I think that if one is willing to accept the film on its own terms, then it is definitely worth seeing. I saw it with two people who had not read the book and who were very moved and impressed. As was I. I think it is an excellent film, but it is definitely *not* an adaptation of the novel. I'd be curious to read how others have reacted. Goldie Morgentaler

---

Background to ***The Claim*** *quoted from GENESIS online: at http://www.theclaimmovie.com/timeline.php3?section=1*

*Kingdom Come (now retitled The Claim – an epic story of love in the chilly Californian Gold Rush), started life over a cup of coffee at Euston Station, London in 1995. A chance encounter between director Michael Winterbottom and writer Frank Cottrell Boyce (who he had worked with on Butterfly Kiss and several short films) at the station led to Michael explaining that his producing partner, Andrew Eaton, had been discussing an idea for a Western. 'I just said because I was reading **The Mayor of Casterbridge** at the time, "yeah, it should be **The Mayor of Casterbridge**"', explains Frank, 'And we never discussed it again, it was just absolutely obvious, one of those ideas that takes two seconds to come up with but so obviously a good western plot'. Andrew, who had recently set up Revolution Films with Michael initially in order to produce **Jude**, adds: 'We kicked around a lot of ideas and I had an idea from a guy I used to work with at the BBC, who coined the phrase 'potato western', which we thought would be a new genre of Western where it would be holed up with Irish actors.'*

Thomas Hardy's 1886 novel tells the story of a man who swaps his wife and child for money at a country fair only to have their return twenty years later pre-empt a self-destructive journey. Hardy himself lifted these plot elements from a true story printed in local newspaper 'The Dorset County Chronicle'.

However the Hardy influence is played down, cited more as an inspiration than an adaptation. 'I think Michael would not want to identify Thomas Hardy with Kingdom Come because I think we feel we've just stolen the first part of the story and then moved the setting!' says Andrew. So is it fair to say it's less an adaptation and more an inspiration? 'Being asked now I would probably say it was adapted from the same newspaper story that Thomas Hardy used for the Mayor of Casterbridge' agrees Frank. 'They're both based on the same story but they've got nothing in common in terms of treatment.'

Tue, 01 May 2001 22:26:35 -0400
ROSEMARIE MORGAN <rosemarie.morgan@yale.edu>
Subject: The Claim

I'm eagerly waiting for this movie to come to New Haven, CT (forthcoming this week) with great expectations! The *New York Times* review was insightful but what was *unexpected* for me was the interview I had with the London *Sunday Times*' drama critic who asked me (teleconferencing), when the film was still in the making, whether I had any ideas to offer, viz the making of the movie and the transference of novel- to film-narrative. I was intrigued – how, for instance, would one treat the issue of death-by-reputation, upon which the destiny of many hang in the novel. We are accustomed these days to "killing" a reputation by media (many mirror issues in Hardy) but parallel transfers – if applicable – from Hardy's literary text to the cinematic narrative seem challenging.   I'll be back – and thank you! Rosemarie

Wed, 2 May 2001 11:34:58 -0600
GOLDIE MORGENTALER <goldie.morgentaler@uleth.ca>
Subject:: The Claim

Dear Rosemarie, apropos of your remarks about reputation and the way that issue is played out in the novel, I would like to elaborate on the comments I made yesterday about the film. I said in my message that the film simplifies Hardy's plot. It does more than that – at crucial moments it changes it. There is never a hint in the film, for instance, that the Elizabeth-Jane character is not the mayor's biological daughter. And the entire plot around Lucetta has been changed. She never marries the Farfrae character. Since prostitutes and saloon society figure so prominently in the film, and since murder and violence in this environment is common and unexceptional, the issue of losing one's reputation never really comes up. I won't say anything more about the changes from novel to film, because I don't want to spoil the movie for anyone. But as I said yesterday, the film takes the basics of Hardy's plot and builds a story of the American West around them. It is not quite Hardy, but it is a very good movie.   Goldie

Wed, 02 May 2001 15:54:51 -0400
ROSEMARIE MORGAN <rosemarie.morgan@yale.edu>
Subject: Re: *The Claim*

Thanks Goldie – what a pity to omit the full extent of Elizabeth-Jane's complicated relationship with Henchard. By the way there's a marvellous BBC audio production of *The Mayor of Casterbridge* in which Henchard's deep passion for and jealousy over his "daughter" is brought out so profoundly one feels compelled to go back to the book. I am keenly interested in the "changes from novel to film" –

Cheers, Rosemarie

Wed, 2 May 2001 16:48:29 +0100
PATRICIA MANN <patricia.mann@btinternet.com>
Subject: *The Claim*

I haven't yet seen *The Claim* but after looking at the official web site I must say I'm inspired. If anyone would like the web site address it is: <http://www.theclaimmovie.com> It has a synopsis, a cast list and some decent pictures and more. I was pleased to see that the actress who played 'Tess' is in it. (Natassja Kinski) Patricia

Wed, 2 Dec 2001 16:48:29 +0100
BETTY CORTUS hardycor@mailhost2.csusm.edu
Subject: *The Claim* Revisited

Earlier this year, when it was announced that a film production based on *The Mayor of Casterbridge* was underway, rumor had it that its setting would be the nineteenth-Century American West, and that the role of protagonist would be played by a woman. This drew a few skeptical comments from *Forum* members, myself included, premature though they turned out to be in some respects – the Henchard character would not be played by a female actor for one thing.

Then, in May of this year after the film in question, *The Claim*, was released in limited distribution, some members who had not yet had a chance to see it expressed interest in hearing the opinion of anyone who had. Goldie Morgentaler, the only one to report having seen it, praised it as a very good film *per se*, but cautioned that, although it uses many of the basic elements of Hardy's plot, it is definitely not an adaptation of *The Mayor of Casterbridge*.

I finally had an opportunity to see a video version of *The Claim* myself last week, and wholeheartedly concur with Goldie. Hardy's plot is considerably pared down, and some of its parts altered enough to make it almost entirely a separate work of art. However, once this distinction is made *The Claim* is indeed a beautiful film, touching, darkly opaline in its shifting moods, and sensitively acted and directed. There are, too, some oblique allusions to the fate likely to befall the Henchards of this world. To cite an example, in one rowdy bar-room scene a voice is heard in the background reciting Shelley's "Ozymandias," subtly reiterating the proverbial warning that pride comes before a fall. Ken Fox, reviewing the film for *The New York Times* states that director Michael Winterbottom "proves you *can* take

Hardy out of his country ... but why on earth would you want to?" It could very well be asked with equal cogency, if you must turn to a source from the past for a truly remarkable plot, why not go to the very best?   Best wishes, Betty Cortus

Far From the Madding Crowd

Sat, 10 Feb 2001 09:30:21 -0500 (EST)
KEITH WILSON <kgwilson@aix1.uottawa.ca>
Subject: Hardy night in Canada

For anyone in Ontario and the Northern U.S. who receives TV Ontario (Ontario's PBS station, with *no* advertisements), there's a double treat tonight. Actually the first one isn't much of a treat, and the Hardy connection somewhat tenuous: the film from Fowles's *The French Lieutenant's Woman* [1] is on at 8 p.m. I remember this as a very unsatisfactory adaptation, but with nice shots of Lyme Regis, particularly the Cobb. But the *big* event follows: the 1967 *Far From the Madding Crowd* with Alan Bates, Julie Christie, Terence Stamp and Peter Finch.

I have to say that, Polanski's *Tess* and the recent *Jude* notwithstanding, I still think of this as the best cinematic (as opposed to televisual) Hardy, and suspect that Hardy would have thought so too. Entirely unpretentious, gorgeously filmed (the Troy sword-exercise/ lock cutting scene is shot at Maiden Castle, down the flanks of which Terence Stamp rides an imaginary horse), well acted, and unusually faithful to the text it seems to me (yes I *know* Julie Christie's hair colour is wrong, but this was the 1960s and Jean Shrimpton ruled). There is also some good Hardy-known music. In short, probably as good as Hardy gets on the screen. It starts at 10.20 p.m., Ontario time.

One reason I thought it worth mentioning this movie is because a couple of years ago I referred to it in passing, to a class, as a film that obviously everyone would know. Not only had no-one in the class ever heard of it, but they had never heard of Alan Bates, Julie Christie or Peter Finch either, although Terence Stamp rang a bell with a couple of students, who identified him as a grey-haired British character actor who played seedy crooks. My TV guide gives a minimalist

---

[1] According to Fowles, this novel was written in an attempt to exorcise Hardy from haunting his imagination

and less than gripping plot summary: "Farmer, soldier and squire court Victorian beauty." Oh well, that's one way of putting it.

All the best, Keith

Sat, 10 Feb 2001 00:36:23 -0800
BETTY CORTUS <hardycor@owl.csusm.edu>
Subject: Re: Hardy night in Canada

Like Keith, I thought the 1967 film version of *FFMC* was an excellent production, well cast and acted, and beautifully filmed. Also, it is probably as true to the novel as film can come. When I taught *FFMC* a few years ago I invited the class to watch the video version ahead of time, and it was a great success. It was available in my local public library, a fact which those unable to catch the Canadian showing might like to check.

However, not everyone is as enthusiastic about the production as I. A. Mary Murphy, in her essay in the 2000 edition of *The Hardy Review* has some quibbles about deviations from the novel, and some of the casting. Betty

10 Feb 2001 11:25:07 MST
ELIZABETH HUGHES <taintedangel@usa.net>
Re: Hardy Night in Canada

My, but this is embarassing. Can't seem to hold my tongue any longer, however. I'm a humble undergraduate English major with no real right or reason for being in this discussion group except a voracious appetite for all things Hardy; he's why I became an English major. With that qualification made, I have to ask: Am I the only person who absolutely abhorred *FFMC*? Not because Hardy lacked in style or talent or the usual things that make his writing so enjoyable; technically, the book is delightful.

But the *characters* – it was an engrossing read, I will give it that, but I will unabashedly admit to wanting to throw the blasted thing across the room on more than one occasion. I could not bring myself to sympathize with a single character; Bathsheba was an egotist, Gabriel was a doormat, and don't even get me started on Troy and Boldwood. It took me aback, because at that point in my Hardy education, I had yet to read a work where I did not fall in love with at least one of the characters. To this day, *FFMC* remains the only work of his which has the particular distinction of garnering my annoyance and disgust with every fictional person involved.

I realize good literature elicits a strong response, whether positive or negative, and in that respect *FFMC* will always be, in my mind, one of the most powerful books Hardy wrote. My blood pressure goes up at the mere mention of it. I just wonder if anyone else found the same frustration with *FFMC*, and for those of you who love it, and love the characters, please help me to understand why. I don't like not liking one of my favorite author's most highly-acclaimed books.   Elizabeth Hughes

Sat, 10 Feb 2001 14:25:36 -0500
ROSEMARIE MORGAN <rosemarie.morgan@yale.edu>
Subject: Re: Hardy night in Canada

Dear Maddened Elizabeth, how refreshing! (your candour...) I too, on first reading of *FFMC* (in my teens), found the principals frustrating – Bathsheba, in particular, utterly infuriating! Stubborn, impulsive, self-willed, passionate to the point of rashness, undisciplined, arrogant – far, far too much like me!   Uncomfortably, Rosemarie

Sat, 10 Feb 2001 18:15:53 -0500
SUZANNE J. FLYNN <sflynn@gettysburg.edu>
Subject: Hardy night in Canada

Elizabeth – I too find your candour refreshing. I remember confessing to one of my graduate school professors that I found Henry James's novel *The Ambassadors* infuriatingly awful, only to learn later that it was this much-admired professor's favorite novel.

Although *FFMC* has never much bothered me (although I agree with your assessment of its characters), *Jude the Obscure* is the Hardy novel that I cannot abide reading more often than once every 5 years. It has all the tragedy and darkness of Hardy's best work, but that darkness is unrelieved by the beauty which pervades *Tess*, *The Woodlanders*, *Return of the Native*, etc. So, you're not alone. I'm sure that most of us who, like you, have loved Hardy's work since (or before) our undergraduate years would – if pressed – admit to finding some of his work lacking. Fortunately, he lived a long, long life, and left all of us much fiction and poetry from which to choose. Glad to hear your thoughts,   Suzanne Flynn

Sun, 11 Feb 2001 15:59:33 -0600
BILL MORGAN <wwmorgan@mail.ilstu.edu>
Subject: Hardy night in Canada

Hello, Elizabeth Hughes – I doubt if anyone can lead you to like or identify with a character by giving you "reasons," since our responses to the characters in a piece of fiction are so closely enmeshed in our response to the narrative moments in which they appear, but nonetheless I would suggest that while Gabriel is probably incompetent and even objectionable *as a lover*, he is competent and admirable (after his early disaster) in other zones of life: fire-fighting, rick-saving, nature-reading – farm-management in general, in fact. And he's responsible (perhaps to a fault) as well as kind and sympathetic to Fanny and to Boldwood. Might it be possible for you to admire him for such behaviors while still finding him exasperating as a lover? I always find myself sighing over his behavior vis à vis Bathsheba but admiring him as a resourceful and thoughtful citizen of the community otherwise – and I've come to think that the distinction between lover and citizen might even be part of Hardy's point in his characterization of the shepherd: perhaps love threatens to make even the most competent among us into "doormats." I certainly agree with Suzanne that we all have our intolerances about some of Hardy's characters, scenes, even whole novels – so if the professional critics among us are any model, you're in good company. In my own case, I think I'd say that I have to make allowances of one kind or another in *all* of Hardy's novels: to my mind, he never wrote a flawless piece of fiction (or poetry, come to that) – but then, he never wrote a dull one either. Thanks for a refreshing posting; you certainly got me thinking,   Bill

Sat, 10 Feb 2001 18:45:38 -0500
PHILIP ALLINGHAM <0>
Subject: Hardy (romantic hockey) night in Canada

Having seen (and played, and re played) videotapes of *The Mayor of Casterbridge* starring a rather hirsute Alan Bates, I think it an interesting and well detailed but less moving production than either *The Return of the Native* (with Catherine Zeta-Jones humanizing Eustacia into a sympathetic heroine), or *Far From the Madding Crowd* (Julie Christie infuriatingly infatuated with Troy and foolishly flirting with Boldwood). Since I saw the Christie film before reading *FFMC* my reading was doubtless coloured by the film, but I can remember thinking, "How can an intelligent, beautiful woman make such bad choices before coming to her senses and realizing the moral value of Gabriel Oak?" Her choices seemed preposterous at the time, but having taught secondary school for three decades and witnessed girls as clever and pretty as Bathsheba select Neantherthals far more brutish than Troy (whose redeeming feature is his love for Fanny), I can only sigh and repeat the Feminist adage, "Smart women – stupid choices." Don't even get me started on Tess and Alec D'Urberville!
  Philip

Sun, 11 Feb 2001 01:15:11 +0100
DAVID CLARK <dclark@udc.es>
Subject: Hardy night in Canada

I must admit that my opinon about *FFMC* has been much influenced by Rosemarie Morgan's chapter on the novel in her *Women and Sexuality in the Novels of Thomas Hardy* (1988). It changed my whole conception of the figure of Gabriel, which I'd held since I first read the novel in the late 1960s. Oak, a sympathetic figure for a sixteen-year old white male, became the spy, the censor who tries to re-write the "natural" world of the novel. Questioning the hitherto unquestionable Gabriel leads, at least in my case, to a whole re-reading of the novel. The loss of (the reader's) innocence conditions further readings. I still admit, however, that Bathsheba was the first woman I fell in love with.   Aye, Dave C.

In May of 1998 PBS did a production of FFMC on its Masterpiece Theater, which I for one, found far less satisfactory. It drew some interesting comments on this list which I have pulled out of the archives and repeat below for the benefit of anyone interested.
Betty Cortus

Masterpiece Theatre's
Far From the Madding Crowd
Dialogues from 1998

Mon, 18 May 1998 14:49:44 -0800
BETTY CORTUS <hardycor@mailhost2.csusm.edu>
Subject: Masterpiece Theater *FFMC*

I'm sorry to say I found it rather disappointing. First of all, I couldn't help comparing, unfavorably, Paloma Baeza's Bathsheba with Julie Christie's interpretation some years ago. Baeza seemed to lack the flexibility to capture the subtle nuances of Bathsheba's personality.

Several key scenes fell dismally flat to my mind. For example Bathsheba's first meeting with Troy in the fir plantation by night, and the sword play episode in "The Hollow Amid the Ferns." These conveyed none of the teasing eroticism tinged with more than a hint of danger the scenes demanded.

Secondly, Hardy's wry humor, a major contributor to the novel's charm, lost much of its edge in this slow-moving and rather earnest production. On the other hand, the film-makers did make a sincere attempt to adhere closely to Hardy's novel. A great deal of his dialogue was repeated verbatim. This in itself is commendable in an age when outrageous liberties are sometimes taken with a source. I am thinking, for example, of the recent movie which called itself *Great Expectations*.

I was sorry, however, that some minor, but compelling, elements were omitted such as the doings of the Gurgoyle, and Fanny's faithful canine helper. But I suppose that even a dramatic production of this length cannot include everything. By and large I found it a well-intentioned but lackluster piece of work. I am sure some of you will find plenty to defend, so don't hesitate to shoot me down in flames.

Betty Cortus

Tue, 19 May 1998 10:53:26 -0600 (MDT)
EARL. E. STEVENS <eestms@frii.com>
Subject: Re: Masterpiece Theater *FFMC*

I found the production to be quite rewarding because it did effectively capture so much of the Hardy world. The swordplay captured impressively the danger and the eroticism of the original. Baeza's performance was lacking, for it did not seem to present the power of Bathsheba. Earl

Tue, 19 May 1998 09:23:29 -0500 (CDT)
MARK SIMONS <mws@ripco.com (Monz)
Subject: Re: Masterpiece Theater *FFMC*

I agree completely with your assesment of the program. I still give the nod to the 1967 version, though not only for Julie Christie. The photography in the 1967 version was far superior and made up (in my mind) for whatever liberties were taken with the text. Nicolas Roeg was the director of photography and most of the credit should probbably go to him for this aspect of it. He had a rather interesting career as a director himself, doing adaptations of classic works like Wilde's Salome as well as his own work (I hope I'm remembering correctly!). But also the ending of the 1967 film with its shot of the toy soldier brought in the proper ironic twist and coloured it just right – I don't think there was any such twist in the Granada version. While not quite as bad a travesty as the ending of the *Jude* film, it still was a little off. But I can't complain too loudly about an attempt to bring Hardy to the screen, large or small: I hope more filmmakers do it! Mark Simons

Sun, 24 May 1998 21:35:37 -0400
DAVID HARRIS <dharris@bbc.edu>
Subject: Playing to the Vast Powers of the Mind

It's doubtful that film is capable of competing with the ability of literature to, as K.L. Billingsley states in his book *The Seductive Image,* "play to the vast powers of the mind."

The moving images were stunning in the recent film version of *Far From the Madding Crowd.* However, as Billingsley notes, "film, unfortunately does not portray thought very well. I did see Farmer Oak at the opening of the film. What I didn't see, and which transcends in importance the image of a shepherd, is only possible to understand from reading Hardy's thoughts about his protagonist":

> He was at the brightest period of masculine life, for his intellect and emotions were clearly separate: he had passed the time during which the influence of youth indiscriminately mingles them in the character of impulse, and he had not yet arrived at the state wherein they become united again, in the character of prejudice, by the influence of a wife and family. In short, he was twenty-eight, and a bachelor.[2]

In addition to the above mentioned concern, the film would have fared better without the harmful additions and subtractions imposed on Hardy's story.

At the end of chapter XIX, Gabriel, prompted by Bathsheba's valentine letter to Mr. Boldwood, says:

> "And even Miss Everdene if you seriously inclined towards him you might have let him discover it in some way of true loving-kindness, and not by sending him a valentine's letter."[3]

In the film, Gabriel says:

> "If you do care for him, you should let him know in a more dignified manner than sending him a silly girl's valentine."

It's quite difficult for me to conceive of Hardy's Gabriel, "one of the quietest and most gentle men on earth," resorting to placing Bathsheba on the level of a "silly girl." There is also a significant difference between "loving-kindness" and "dignified manner." Perhaps some might think this a minor indiscretion; however, for me it changes the personality of Hardy's character.   David Harris

---

[2] Thomas Hardy, *Far From the Madding Crowd,* edited by Rosemarie Morgan (Penguin World Classics, 2000), 4-5.

[3] Ibid, 118. Please note that the Penguin World Classics edition is based on the holograph MS version in which the chapter numbers differ from the (bowdlerised) Wessex. version.

Sat, 10 Feb 2001 08:19:02 -0800
BETTY CORTUS <hardycor@owl.csusm.edu>
Subject: Hardy night in Canada

Since we are talking about the filming of Hardy novels, whether for the movie theater or television, I thought you might be interested in another archive file discussion of a 1998 A&E production of *Tess*.

Betty Cortus

Arts and Entertainment's
Tess
Dialogues from 1998

Mon, 14 Sep 1998 08:57:59 -0800
BETTY CORTUS <hardycor@mailhost2.csusm.edu>
Subject: *Tess* on A&E

Dear All, I hope some of you were able to watch part one of A& E's production of *Tess* last night. I was quite impressed, a pleasant surpprise in contrast to PBS's disappointing version of *FFMC* last May. After looking at Part II tonight I would like to discuss it with you. Do check your local listing for the time. Regards, Betty Cortus

Tue, 15 Sep 1998 10:47:33 -0400
ROSEMARIE MORGAN <rosemarie.morgan@yale.edu>
Subject: *Tess* on A&E

Hi Betty – a quickie! We missed the first few minutes of *both Tess* episodes (will have to view again at another time) – thought it the most imaginative Hardy-on-film ever!. Astutely departed from the text at strategic points to enhance the emotional tone, mood etc. This worked, visually, very well indeed and preserved the spirit of the book in a way that keeping literally to the text would not have done (best: the baptism scene/dairymaids carried across the flooded lane).

The dynamics of the Tess/Alec and the Tess/Angel relationships were especially fine – sensitively *felt* rather than textually-dictated. Gripes? the musical score (ugh!) and the bathing of too many scenes in the proverbial golden-glow (overdone). Have to fly – but can't wait to hear what other viewers thought (and thanks Betty for giving out all the broadcasting times – very helpful!) Cheers, Rosemarie

Tue, 15 Sep 1998 09:36:01 -0800
BETTY CORTUS <hardycor@mailhost2.csusm.edu>
Subject: *Tess* on A & E

I agree with you Rosemarie. I just loved this production of *Tess*. Even the reedy music seemed to me to be appropriate to the pastoral setting. My only real gripe (apart from the insistent commercials) was the substitution of "mankind" for "the President of the Immortals" at the end. I thought this was a needless violation of the author's intent, placing the blame for her destiny totally on human failure rather than allowing for the mindless workings of the Immanent Will. I too am anxious to hear what others thought. Betty

Tue, 15 Sep 1998 1:29 pm EDT (17:29:02 UT)
ROBERT C. SCHWEIK <SCHWEIK@fredonia.edu>
Subject: Tess on A& E

At the beginning of the A& E *Tess* I felt a little disappointed; the version in which Natassa Kinski played Tess brought, it seemed to me, the opening of the novel more vividly to life. But as the drama progressed, and particularly in the second half, I found myself all but completely won over by the extraordinary acting of the characters of Tess, Angel, and Alec. By the end, I was caught up in what had become for me one of the most moving films I've seen in quite a while.

Both Polanski and whoever scripted the A&E version decided to leave out the final scene with Angel and Liza-Lu walking off hand-in-hand. Would the novel have been better for the same excision? Unike some, I had no problem with the music – in fact agree with Betty Cortus that it worked well. I *did* have a negative reaction to the voice-overs: they struck me as generally clumsy and intrusive. One exception, though, was the scene near the end where a figure looking remarkably like Hardy walks by Tess and Angel and remarks on what he sees by quoting from Hardy's poetry. Finally, I've often said to myself after viewing cinema adaptations of Hardy's novels that they suffer (and I think they do) from the lack of narrative voice that in so many ways adds such a rich dimension to Hardy's fiction. Would, I wondered, the films be improved by an artful use of voice-overs to compensate for that loss? The clumsy effect of the voice-overs in the A&E version persuades me that adaptors have been right to depend on the resources of the medium to compensate. But without that narrative voice, and those descriptions and comments in the last chapter of *Tess*, an introduction of a bare comment on the President of the Immortals would seem oddly out of place. Here, I wonder, would it have been better to have had no narrative comment at all? Bob

Tue, 15 Sep 1998 14:59:32 EDT
MICHELLE DENEVAN <mdenevan@bss2.umd.edu>
Subject: A&E *Tess*

Greetings Hardy Scholars! I enjoyed A&E's production of *Tess*. I was especially impressed with the actor (whose name escapes me at this time) who played Alec. He was quite convincing. The voice overs did bother me a bit. I agree with Prof. Schweik in regard to the lack of narrative voice. Indeed, that is one element of adapting novels for film and television that has always been a problem with me. I miss things such as Hardy's comments in the closing chapters and his general insights .... I'm curious to see what other viewers thought of the depiction of the farming life, i.e. how the industry became more mechanized as time passed. Did viewers believe that this theme was accurately rendered in the film or could more have been done?

Michelle

Thu, 17 Sep 1998 20:49:31 -0300
JAMES KENDALL <jamesk@tstt.net.tt>
Subject: *Tess* on A&E

Hello everyone. I must agree with Michelle that not enough was done to emphasize how the farming industry became more mechanised as time went by. However, I must also say that I was very impressed by the otherwise accurate portrayal of the events in the movie according to the novel. Yours Truly, Kim Kendall

Fri, 18 Sep 1998 00:04:29 -0800
DALE KRAMER <dalek@darkwing.uoregon.edu>
Subject: *Tess* on A&E

Judging from the responses so far posted to this site, I'm the only person who feels that the A&E production of *Tess* left a lot to be desired ... Granted, the novel, *Tess,* trips along the edge of sentimentality, so in one sense the TV production was faithful to the source; but Hardy also manages to maintain a tone that is acerbic and bleak and angular, whereas, to my mind at least, the TV production was smooth and even-handed and careful.

In particular, the TV production was timorous in its avoidance of any of Hardy's stories that adequately suggests the hardness of agricultural life. Also, I liked the casting of Tess. The woman who portrayed Tess conveyed well both innocence and weariness. Angel, on the other hand, was conveyed as maladroitly as Sue was by Kate Winslet in the movie *Jude* (1996).

The actor playing Angel looked more like a libertine on a rural weekend than someone as uptight as Hardy suggests Angel is. The actor playing Alec did a fine job: it's not his fault that the powers-that-be on the set decided that Alec should be so decent and well-realized. (One of the great appeals of the novel, *Tess,* is the incoherence of Alec that so well parallels the incoherence of the universe that wrecks Tess's chances for happiness.)

Finally, while I agree with Rosemarie Morgan about the golden-glow of the camera work being a bit self-conscious, this disturbed me less than the production's second-guessing Hardy about the best way to express his, or a, view of life. Powerful, if *outré*, symbols are preferable to the production's smoothing things to a rational of the sharp and the fantastical that are characterististic of Hardy.

Did anyone watching the TV production feel that the thresher was demonic and destructive – or just exhausting and picturesque? The murder of Alec was commonplace, not magical – no doubt the scriptwriters and director felt that to have blood soak through a ceiling was implausible thus unuseable. Who can take seriously one of the most famous images in English fiction? We mustn't risk risibility, particularly with teenagers who might rely on the TV production as a substitute for actually reading the novel.

I could accept that argument, but to portray in Tess and Alec's final argument an Alec who was both tolerant and declaring his love for Tess may fulfill a desideratum strongly desired by Hardy readers who object to the crude and melodramatic if subliminally admirable Alec, but it produces also an Alec who didn't really deserve to die. After all, he is correct to call Angel a "bastard." And, no doubt there wasn't time enough to present Tess pushed to the last extremity of wishing she could be inside the d'Urberville vault.

It was much easier, and a quicker move to the "tragedy" of the return to Alec, just to stress the unpleasantness of the Durbeyfields being forced to move from their cottage. While I (obviously) thought the decisions about the script must have been made by a committee of soap writers, in some respects the TV production would serve very well for students and general readers as a guide to agricultural processes in the 19th century. It was good to see the thresher in its realistic portrayal (despite its platitudinousness as a symbol).

All in all, this was the first ordinariness. Well, this is a long posting. I expect some flaming responses.

Dale Kramer

Fri, 18 Sep 1998 09:03:33 EDT
MICHELE DENEVAN <mdenevan@bss2.umd.edu>
Subject: *Tess* on A&E

Dale, I have to agree with you on the portrayal of Alec, particularly in the scene of his murder. While I did think that the actor who played Alec had his moments in which he was especially good at portraying his more, shall we say, sleazy side; I did think that in the final scenes the character was presented in a surprisingly sympathetic light. For me, one of the most powerful images in the novel is that of the thresher as menacing and destructive. From this production one picked up the idea that the work being done was hard and back-breaking, it didn't seem, though, to go into the deeper issues presented by Hardy regarding the mechanization of agriculture and what that meant for people like Tess and her family. Indeed, I at times felt that the production tended to stress the more soap opera elements of the novel and did not handle well the deeper issues contained within the work. Yet, I remind myself that there is only so much that can be done on a television production, and that there is no substitute for reading the actual text and being mesmerized by the words of Mr. Hardy himself.
Michelle

Sun, 20 Sep 1998 01:09:59 -0400
ROSEMARIE MORGAN <rosemarie.morgan@yale.edu>
Subject: A&E *Tess*

More marvellous A&E *Tess* tonight – but I am still 'out' on the musical score. Wish it really were '*reedy*'! Sadly, I think it could fit any old romantic movie any ole time any ole where. Tonight, though, I was very excited to see more of *Tess*, Part II, and thought the final scene with "Humanity" in place of the "gods" very Hardyan and very appropriate. Didn't Hardy, in any case, switch to "Aeschylus" to avoid the thunders? (I'm trying to recall the original—the ms) Was he not actually hitting, by parenthetic alignment here with pagan barbarism, at an inhumane judicial system which, until fairly recently (in Hardy's lifetime) had sent starving boys to the gallows for stealing bread and (in his own living memory) hanged young women for killing their abusive husbands? Surely "Aeschylus" – as one for whom human lives are as "flies to wanton boys" – stands in lieu here of humanity's system of justice, in a judicious position of proxy, given that Hardy's publishers wouldn't print many of the other iconoclastic or sacrelig-ious episodes in this book? (this is irrelevant probably, but "Aesculapian" connotes, in Greek, healing – a double irony given the "remedy" humanity provides for Tess?)   Besties, Rosemarie

Sun, 20 Sep 1998 13:25:28 -0800
BETTY CORTUS <hardycor@mailhost2.csusm.edu>
Subject: *Tess* on A&E

Like Rosemarie, I also watched quite a bit of *Tess* for the second time over the weekend, and found it just as enjoyable as I did at first. Unlike Dale I thought the actor playing Angel gave a fine and sensitive performance. I do agree, however, that the murder of Alec was less than effective, portraying him as just a little too sympathetic to justify his end. Perhaps it would have been better carried out off-stage and left to the imagination as it was in the Polanski version. I also think that the failure to show the blood soaking through the ceiling was to omit the single most graphic image in the novel – melodramatic no doubt, but awfully gripping nevertheless.   Betty Cortus

Sat, 10 Feb 2001 23:13:20 -0600
AYSHA D. BEY <kabey@bellsouth.net>
Subject: *Tess*

After all the positive responses to the A&E *Tess* film, I was so glad to see Dale Kramer's evaluation of the film. I have watched every Hardy film made and find few of the newer ones really in tune with the Hardy mood. I purchased the A&E *Tess* so that I could study it at home and try to figure out what I really didn't like about it. Basically, I believe that modern day cinema-makers find it difficult to make a film where so much of what really drives the characters is internally motivated and represented with Hardy's marvelous psycho-narration. When the film-makers meet up with this type of internal motivation, they then have to find a way to have the characters reveal these motivations; therefore, they create dialogue which doesn't always match Hardy's narrative mood or style of discourse either. In the scene as Tess finishes the conversation with Angel (after his return to her), Hardy writes that marvelous paragraph that

> Tess had spiritually ceased to recognize the body before him as hers – allowing it to drift like a corpse upon the current, in a direction dissociated from its living will.

In the film, Tess simply goes upstairs and confronts Alec about Angel's return. The powerful anger expressed doesn't fit with Hardy's previous words, nor does it fit well (in my opinion) with the broken syntax of Tess's "soliloquy" or "dirge." Hardy's famous mood words are too often ignored in filming. It seemed to me that the argument between Tess and Alec changes the viewer's understanding of Tess – to me she becomes a rather ordinary murderer, rather than a woman caught in the web of social and natural laws that are more powerful than she – and less forgiving. I would personally love to see a film that finds a way to depict the levels of plot as described by Gillian Beer. I find her analysis of Hardy's plot schemes in *Darwin's Plots*[4] absolutely superb, and I think that it is the problem of the optative plot that drives film-makers crazy (not that they know anything about that level of plot). Since the films do make use of a narrative voice in the film, perhaps they could also find a way to include more of Hardy's mood-setting narration. Tess was played beautifully; I did not care for Alec particularly. The scenery was gorgeous as it usually is in Hardy films. To the young lady who disliked *FFMC,* perhaps it is the rather unusually happy ending provided that disturbs. It was the first Hardy novel I read as a teenager years ago, and I was a Hardy fan ever-after. I adore *Tess*, but I really enjoy Hardy's earlier novels in their original published form (*Pair of Blue Eyes* and *Ethelberta*). His experimentation with genre and narrative form fascinates me.

Thanks to everyone for the terrific conversation.

Aysha

Sun, 11 Feb 2001 14:55:48 –0000
EDWARD HIRST <edwardkh@freenetname.co.uk>
Subject: A&E *Tess*

As a keen music composer myself, with an interest in film music I disagree with your comments on the music for A&E's *Tess*. Alan Fisk uses his music to underline Hardy's irony to great effect. Notice the tune when Tess sees Angel Clare (twice) is also used when she leaves him after the wedding. I found this very powerful indeed. The music suits the mood of Wessex too and the traditional music of the time.
Edward Hirst

Sun, 11 Feb 2001 18:33:29 EST
LISA CACICIA <Lmpc219@aol.com>
Subject: Hardy, media and movies

I wonder how many people have actually been introduced to Hardy through the television and film medium? Which brings up another question: as far as I can tell there were at least two film adaptations of Hardy works while he was alive – both *Tess of the d'Urbervilles*. The first one was in 1913 made by Famous Players Film Co. (US) and directed by J. Searle Dawley. I have never been able to find out who the screenwriter was. A lost film. The second *Tess* was made in 1924 by MGM. It was directed by Mickey Neilan, Mary Pickford's favorite director. The writing credit to that one goes to Dorothy Farnum.

---

[4] Gillian Beer, *Darwin's Plots* (London, Boston, Melbourne, New York, 1983)

She wrote a few of Garbo's silent films. You can still find the book edition that went with this film. On its cover is Blanche Sweet who played Tess along with Conrad Nagel who played Angel. Another lost film. Knowing how England had the block-booking system at that time, this film would have played all over England and Europe. Being a fan of silent films, which is an art form unto itself, I haven't given up hope that one day one of these prints will show up.   Lisa

Sun, 11 Feb 2001 21:36:11 -0500 (EST)
KEITH WILSON <kgwilson@aix1.uottawa.ca>
Subject: Hardy films in Hardy's life-time.

The 1913 silent film version of *Tess* had Minnie Maddern Fiske (the actress who had brought *Tess* to the American stage in 1897) in the title role.[5] In his lifetime, in addition to the two *Tess* films (the second one [Blanche Sweet] grotesquely Americanized, with Alec meeting Tess in a nightclub), there were the following films made:
➢ A 12-minute *Far From the Madding Crowd* made by Edison in 1911.
➢ Another *FFMC* produced by Larry Trimble in 1915.
➢ A 1921 *The Mayor of Casterbridge*, produced by Sidney Morgan.[6]

And the year after Hardy's death there was an *Under the Greenwood Tree* (Harry Lachman 1929).

Hardy's letters show recurrent negotiations for film rights. Vol. IV,[7] for example, has about a dozen letters between June and December 1913 that mention the first film *Tess*, which Hardy saw, and seems to have been somewhat bemused by.

Of film possibilities discussed but that came to nothing there are the following:
➢ Swedish film of *The Distracted Preacher* (see *Letters* VI, 6, 29/1 /1920).
➢ A patriotic film of *The Dynasts* for the war effort (see *Letters* V, 130 [1915], and the letter to TH from H.C. Macilwaine in Dorset County Museum).
➢ A film of *Jude* (see letter from S. Wimborne in DCM, received 12 February 1918, and TH's pencilled answer over FEH's name not in *Letters*]).

---

[5] Hardy attended the British premiere on 21 October 1913.
[6] In July 1921 Hardy witnessed the shooting of some scenes in Dorchester and Maiden Castle. For further information on Hardy in the Cinema, Radio and TV, see *The Oxford Reader's Companion to Hardy*, edited by Norman Page (Oxford University Press, 2000) 17-518.
[7] *The Collected Letters of Thomas Hardy*, ed., Richard Little Purdy and Michael Millgate, 7 Vols (Oxford: 1978-88).

- A film of the Hardy Players production of *The Famous Tragedy of the Queen of Cornwall*, permission for which was requested by S. H. Bathe of Pegasus films, 24 October 1923. Hardy pencilled a negative reply over his secretary May O'Rourke's name (not included in *Letters*).
- 1922-23 negotiations with Société des Films Albatross about filming *The Return of the Native* (*Letters*, Vol. VI, 192, 195, 198). Albatross paid 250 pounds for film rights, but no film was produced.
- Lucifer Films of France wanted rights to film *Tess* in 1920, and TH pencilled reply that rights were already disposed of (DCM).
- Société des Gens de Lettres of Paris wanted to negotiate general film rights (24th February 1922, DCM). Hardy pencilled reply on 10 March 1922 (not in *Letters*), asking to know what means the society had for film production.

There are others, but time presses. In a nutshell, there was ongoing interest in filming Hardy's work, and while this did not result in a very large number of actual films (seemingly five in all in Hardy's lifetime), Hardy always showed willingness in principle to considering possibilities, arranged for film rights to be sold, and maintained a rather puzzled interest in the oddities of the new medium.

All the best, Keith.

Mon, 12 Feb 2001 10:39:21 –0000
DAVID HERRICK <David.Herrick@bristol.ac.uk>
Subject: Hardy films in Hardy's life-time.

And the year after Hardy's death there was an *Under the Greenwood Tree* (Harry Lachman 1929). I recall this being mentioned on the BFI website a while back, as an example of the sort of films they were hoping to restore / preserve by some sort of sponsorship arrangement I think. I seem to recall them mentioning that it is one of the earliest surviving British 'Talkies'. This brings me onto the obvious question about how much of the film material Keith detailed still survives.

Dave

Mon, 12 Feb 2001 15:10:30 -0500 (EST)
KEITH WILSON <kgwilson@aix1.uottawa.ca>
Subject: Hardy films in Hardy's life-time.

I am not sure which of the completed films survive (I haven't seen any of them), although the British Film Institute index has information on them. My memory (I don't have the book readily available) is also that Peter Widdowson's book *Hardy in History: A Study in Literary*

Sociology (Routledge 1989) has a bit more information on them in its chapter on film and television adaptations.

One very interesting item in the Dorset County Museum collection is the souvenir booklet that Turner Films put out for the first showing (at the West End Cinema, 16 November 1915 at 11.30 a.m.) of Larry Trimble's 1915 *FFMC* (Trimble did the adaptation too). This booklet has eleven photographs from the film and a full cast list:

- Bathsheba/Florence Turner
- Troy/Campbell Gullan [from the Royalty Theatre]
- Boldwood/Malcolm Cherry [from the Royalty Theatre]
- Fanny Robin/Marion Grey
- Lyddie/Dorothy Rowan
- Gabriel Oak/Henry Edwards

Even Oak's dog gets a credit – it labours under the distinctly un-canine screen/stage name of "Jean."

But of still greater interest is the plot summary, prepared – or so the booklet claims – by Hardy himself. The booklet's prefatory comments include the following:

> This booklet is offered as a partial souvenir of the first exhibition of 'Far From the Madding Crowd,' though words, even when written by Thomas Hardy himself, and 'still' photographs, however effective, are no substitute for the reality of a picture play.

The summary is headed

> This synopsis of the story was written by Thomas Hardy especially for the private exhibition on the 16th of November, 1915.

There are some quite interesting turns of phrase (if it is indeed Hardy's work), particularly in relation to Bathsheba:

> He [Oak] has thus fallen into the tantalising position of being servitor to a woman with whom he is still desperately in love, and whose knowledge of his feelings causes her to throw mischievous little tyrannies into her commands to him. She, meanwhile, by a coquettish freak, draws upon herself the attentions of a reserved bachelor, the rich Farmer Boldwood, who gets to love her with a moody and taciturn passion that rather alarms her.

I won't give any more of Hardy's summary, but its existence is further evidence of the quite active interest he seems to have taken in the production. Also fascinating is the presentational rhetoric surrounding this early cinematic event: it is "a picture play" and the November 1915 performance a "private exhibition."

All the best, Keith

Hardy and the Cinema
Jude

Thu, 26 Apr 2001 12:46:04 +0200
RIMONDI <chirimo@libero.it>
Subject: Hardy and the Cinema: *Jude*

Hello everybody! My name is Chiara, I'm a student of the University of Foreign Languages and Literatures in Milan. I've always been fond of Thomas Hardy so I've decided to do my thesis on the film adaptation of *Jude the Obscure* (my favourite book). The movie is called *Jude* (1996) directed by Michael Winterbottom. I think the themes of the book are very direct and immediate, and that's what attracted me to it. It's a story that appeals to young people, because it's about outsiders challenging conventional ideas. Hardy is always modern, in the sense that his stories, his characters are eternal. That's why there are so many film adaptations of his books. I think that the adaptation of Winterbottom is very faithful to the spirit of the book. If any of you has seen the movie, I desperately need to know what you think of this film adaptation, because I've really run out of ideas. Thus I will appreciate any kind of information, opinion you may send on this subject.

This list is most enjoyable, informative and full of interesting points of view. Thank you very much for your help. Grazie mille!!

Chiara

Thu, 26 Apr 2001 13:12:52 GMT
BOB SCHWEIK <schweik@fredonia.edu>
Subject: Hardy and the Cinema: *Jude*

Dear Chiara, you can get some help with your request by going to TTHA's "Links to Other Sites" and selecting "Filmography for Thomas Hardy," which is A 28 in the "Hardy Related" list. You can also find that link in the Index under "Film." Follow the directions and you'll get access to a list of films based on Hardy's writings, including the Winterbottom film, and links to 27 "external reviews" of that film and 20 "user comments." Bob

Sat, 28 Apr 2001 11:59:07 EDT
DONNA <Donnalpha@aol.com>
Subject: Hardy and the Cinema: *Jude*

Hi Chiara, I recently watched *Jude*. I was also taken with the fact that

Hardy was way ahead of his time with the treatment of Jude's and his cousin's relationship (living together, scoffing at marriage!) education and perhaps the psychological reasoning behind the deaths of Sue's children. The acting was super and so were the authentic locations.

Sincerely, Donna

Sun, 29 Apr 2001 13:06:58 +0100 (GMT+01:00)
WAN-YU LIN <wanyu@another.com>
Subject: Hardy and the Cinema: *Jude*

I've seen *Jude* before and after I read the novel. I found the novel a lot richer, but I also have to say that Kate Winslet is a superb actress for the character of Sue Bridehead. I like those scenes where the main characters have to go to places by train. Don't you think these scenes also show Hardy's reasoning of the new technology and its influence to the character's lives? Wan-yu-Lin

Sun, 29 Apr 2001 11:24:25 -0400
SHANNON ROGERS <srogers@mailhost.sju.edu>
Subject: Hardy and the Cinema: *Jude*

Hello all, am I the only one who didn't like this film? I thought the ending was a Hollywood cop-out – having Jude live at the end, with Sue's kiss still warm on his lips, completely guts Hardy's message of hopelessness.

The casting also troubled me – the acting was fine, but since Hardy puts such an emphasis on the earthy physicality of the well-rounded Arabella, and the lack of it in Sue, having the sexy, earthy Kate Winslet as Sue just didn't make me ever think that she could live the life of the mind. Rachel (ooooh, her last name has now escaped me) as Arabella was physically better as a Sue – she doesn't ooze the sort of sexuality to lure the bookish Jude upstairs for a rousing good time between the sheets.

It was beautifully filmed and I'm always thrilled to see Hardy alive-and-well at the box office to keep the flame alive outside of academe – I love film adaptations for that reason alone.

But oh that ending!
Best,
Shannon Rogers

P. S Roused from end of term grading for a breather and a rant! Back to the pile of papers.

Mon, 30 Apr 2001 11:05:42 –0400
KEVIN R. SWAFFORD <swaffokr@jmu.edu>
Subject: Re: Late on the scene/*Jude* movie

Not only is the ending poor, but the near total displacement of the issues of class is almost embarrassing. The film's emphasis upon the sexual tensions is sensationalized. *Jude* the film is private – *Jud*e the novel is social. Class determination is still hands off, I suppose – even for supposed leftist film makers. Kevin Swafford

Wed, 02 May 2001 20:04:03 EDT
MAUREEN MARNEY < MMarney99@aol.com>
Subject: Hardy and the Cinema: *Jude*

Hello All, One thing you can't disagree with is the soundtrack – it's absolutely beautiful! Maureen

THE THOMAS HARDY ASSOCIATION "NOTES AND QUERIES" FORUM

> *The following queries have been culled from the Association's discussion group –* ***The Forum.***
> *Readers willing or able to provide informative responses are invited to subscribe to the group (no fee) at*
> *<HARDY-L@coyote.csusm.edu>*
> *where they can post their replies.*

Fri, 29 Sep 2000 19:25:51 GMT
BOB SCHWEIK <schweik@fredonia.edu>
Subject: Hardy a "Literary Criminal"

Hardy was familiar with some of the writings of "Lucas Malet" (Mary St. Leger Kingsley Harrison*). On March 18, 1892, he wrote to her thanking her for a copy of her *The Wages of Sin* published in London in 1891 (see the Purdy/Millgate *Collected Letters*, I, 120), and on April 14, 1892, in a letter to Millicent Fawcett, he commented on how a work of fiction could show "how the trifling with the physical element in love leads to corruption" by having "no mincing of matters." He then added:

> This I fear the British public would not stand just now .... The other day I read a story entitled "The Wages of Sin" by Lucas Malet, expecting to find something of the sort therein. But the wages are that the young man falls over a cliff, & the young woman dies of consumption – not very consequent, as I told the authoress.

But recently a claim has been published that Hardy flagrantly plagiarized from Harrison's *The Wages of Sin*. The claim is made in Talia Schaffer's *The Forgotten Female Aesthetes: Literary Culture in Late-Victorian England* published by the University Press of Virginia in 2000. I have not yet seen that book, but it is reviewed under the title "The First Dandy Dorian" by Sarah Churchwell in *TLS* of September 15, 2000, p. 25. According to Churchwell,

> Schaffer pulls no punches in accusing Hardy of plagiarizing Malet's *The Wages of Sin*: "the usual literary history [of *Jude the Obscure*] may not only be factually wrong but may perpetuate a monumental injustice, perhaps indeed a literary crime."

Churchwell goes on to say that Schaffer omits thorny questions of literary merit, but then seems to accept Schaffer's contention by saying,

> The misogyny of [Hardy's] revision is undoubtedly obnoxious, but Hardy was prompted to rewrite Malet's book at least partly because its sentimental ending irritated him.

I'm not familiar with *The Wages of Sin*, nor have I yet had the opportunity to read Schaffer's argument about Hardy's having plagiarized it. Would anyone on the list have an opinion about the strength and persuasiveness of Schaffer's argument? Bob Schweik

*Hardy had met Harrison in person (see*The Life and Work of Thomas Hardy by Thomas Hardy*, ed. Michael Millgate, 1984, p. 258).

Wed, 31 Jan 2001 10:39:01 –0000
PATRICK ROPER<patrick@prassociates.co.uk>
Subject: Greenwood Tree tune

Hardy's novel *Under the Greenwood Tree* presumably takes its title from Shakespeare's poem. But would Hardy have been familiar with the (in my opinion) delightful English country dance tune usually called simply "The Greenwood Tree"? Both the Shakespeare and the music can be enjoyed at: http://www.moongear.com/thebearypatch/skp14.htm The music in particular, though a bit 'canned', certainly took me back to 'former days' of mid-19th century Dorset. Patrick Roper

Mon, 5 Mar 2001 07:31:45 -0500
JOHN GOULD <jgould@andover.edu >
Subject: Convergences

Last week I assigned to a group of 10th-grade students a paper discussing the title of Flannery O'Connor's "Everything That Rises Must Converge." In that story, you'll recall, a well-meaning but condescending white woman offers a penny to a young black boy riding with his large and truculent mother on a bus in the South in 1961. The two women are wearing identical (ugly) hats. The proffered gift results in the black woman's bopping the white woman with a purse that seemed to be "filled with stones." The white woman sinks to the ground, apparently the victim of some sort of stroke.

To get the students going as they considered risings and convergings in the story, I referred them to "The Convergence of the Twain." Although initially amused at my own wit (for me a far too common failing), as I got going with the poem, I began to think more about the aptness of the comparison. O'Connor seems quite comfortable with the idea of an Immanent Will, for one thing. The hats make the two women "twin halves of one august event." The collision between the twain in her story is almost enough to "jar two hemispheres." (Indeed, when we consider the course of racial integration in the last 40 years, perhaps it has.) I think Hardy would have enjoyed O'Connor thoroughly. I wonder if anyone has ever seen any writing that puts them together. How familiar was O'Connor with Hardy, and did she know "The Convergence of the Twain"?   John

Mon, 23 Apr 2001 15:07:14 -0400
PHILIP ALLINGHAM <apalling@tbaytel.net>
Subject: Du Maurier's plates for Hardy's *A Laodicean*

Dear Hardy List Members: In 1881, *Punch* illustrator George du Maurier collaborated with Hardy on a programme of illustration for *A Laodicean* as serialised in *Harper's New Monthly Magazine*.
Two questions with respect to these illustrations have arisen.
1. Why were the European and North American editions out of *sync*, so that the serial run began in December, 1880, in one but January, 1881, in the other.
2. Why were Hardy and the *Harper's* management so displeased with du Maurier's work that he did not get another commission from them for quite some time (in fact, Du Maurier* never illustrated any of Hardy's works of fiction after *A Laodicean*)?   Philip

"Is the Resemblance Strong?" George du Maurier, *Harper's,* May 1881

Mon, 2 Jul 2001 17:25:09 +0100
MARTA RABIKOWSKA <M.Rabikowska@slavonic.arts.gla.ac.uk>
Subject: Venus and her arm

Dear Members, I'm working on *Jude* – considering the text from a semiotic perspective. I feel I have a problem with a sign of Venus mentioned in chapter III, part II. For me the following fragments refer to a figure of Venus who had both arms or at least one undamaged:
> They were in the main reduced copies of ancient marbles, and comprised divinities of a very different character from those the girl was accustomed to see portrayed, among them being a Venus of a standard pattern ....Occasionally peeping inside the leaves to see that the Venus arm was not broken (Penguin Classics. 1998: 93, 94)

I wonder now, whether the figure was treated as a copy that was "improved" and had two arms, or one whole arm? What does "standard pattern" of Venus mean, or rather why did Hardy call this figure "standard" if it was possible for Sue to check if the arm was not broken. This question is very important for my work; the idea of Venus improved (created, rearranged, rewritten) can become a significant argument for my research in which I deal with simulacra signs. Venus from the above fragments seems to be one of them. But maybe I read these passages too subjectively?   Marta

Tue, 17 Jul 2001 16:48:12 -0500
JOHN FARRELL <jackfar@mail.utexas.edu>
Subject: Edmund H. New

Can anyone furnish me with information – or a source of infomation —about Edmund H. New, who illustrated Bertram Windle's *The Wessex of Thomas Hardy* (London, 1902)? I've checked various resources on the net and in some standard Hardy books and have only found an account of New's visit to Kelmscott. Unfortunately I don't have a *DNB* lying around anywhere.   Many thanks. John P. Farrell

Sat, 15 Dec 2001 12:44:20 +0000 (GMT)
MARTIN RAY <enl090@abdn.ac.uk>
Subject: Re: Lorna the Second

Very sadly, I noticed in this morning's *London Times* (Saturday, 15 December 2001) the announcement of the death of Lorna Gore-Browne last Wednesday, in Highgate, London. These are the only details given in the newspaper.

This is another link with Hardy which we have lost. Lorna was the subject of Hardy's very late poem, 'Lorna the Second', written in 1927. She had married Stewart Gore-Browne (1883-1967) on 23 July 1927, when she was 19 and he was 44. Many years earlier (around 1904), Gore-Browne had proposed to Lorna's mother (also called Lorna), who was the daughter of Hardy's old friend, Reginald Bosworth Smith. Lorna-the-First refused him and married a German surgeon in 1906 (Hardy and Emma were at the wedding). Lorna-the-Second was born in 1908 and her mother died of consumption in 1919.

During a brief return from Africa, Gore-Browne met Lorna-the-Second at the funeral of her grandmother, Flora Bosworth Smith, at St Andrew's Church, Binghams Melcombe, Dorset, in March 1927. It does not appear that Hardy attended the funeral. After their marriage, Gore-Browne took Lorna to his great mansion in Northern Rhodesia (now Zambia). She bore him two daughters, the elder of whom was 'Lorna-the-Third', although her father always called her 'Mark' (longing for a male heir, no doubt). After that, she suffered from what sounds like postnatal depression. They separated in 1942 and divorced in 1950. Lorna-the-Third and her husband were murdered by burglars in 1992 in the great house which they had inherited.

By a coincidence, I've just finished reading an excellent biography of Gore-Browne by Christina Lamb called *The Africa House* (Viking, 1999; now available in Penguin).

There was a hopelessly mangled account of this book in the October 1999 issue of the *Thomas Hardy Journal.* I warmly recommend *The Africa House* to anyone wanting some holiday reading with a Hardy connection, or anyone wanting to know what becomes of the well-beloved. Martin Ray

The du Maurier print from the May instalment of Harper's is reproduced here by courtesy of TTHA's ***Novels*** *page – director: Birgit Plietzsch:*
http://www.zusas.uni-halle.de/~ttha/illustrations/al/harpers/6.htm

The Checklist
Celebrating the New TTHA Checklist and Other Web Resources for Research on Hardy

ROBERT SCHWEIK

A year ago, in *The Hardy Review*, III, I ended a report on The Thomas Hardy Association's **Links to Other Web Sites** with the following words:

> I want to conclude by drawing attention to a feature missing from the World Wide Web but one which a Web page would be eminently suited to provide: a continuously updated bibliography of newly published books and articles about Hardy . . . . My hope is that, when in the next *Hardy Review* I once again report on current developments related to Hardy on the Web, the emergence of such a site will be one of the events I will be able to celebrate.

And celebrate I can: for in January, 2001, The Association created a web page that provides a continuously updated **Checklist of Hardy Publications** that has already become an indispensable resource for anyone doing research on Hardy.[1]

Of course the **Checklist** is only one of a number of special research and reference resources the TTHA provides or is in the process of providing for its members. Those include an on-line edition of Hardy's *Collected Poems*, an extended bibliography of writings by and about Hardy, a concordance to Hardy's poetry, and a digitized version of the Gerber/Davis two-volume annotated bibliography. But it is particularly the **Checklist** that I want to celebrate here.

The **Checklist** is currently produced by a team of eighteen scholars around the world – aided by other special correspondents - who review, at least every other month, nearly one hundred sources, including more than 25 bibliographies, trade lists, catalogues, and electronic databases, as well as the current contents of over 70 scholarly journals, and the archives of major Internet discussion lists. The

---

[1] With grateful thanks to Seth Lachterman for providing software assistance on this project..

resulting ***Checklist*** cites recent Hardy scholarship published in English, Arabic, French, German, Italian, and Japanese. It provides a list of writings by and about Hardy that have appeared in the immediately preceding year and in the current year, with, in addition, listings of prepublications and announced publications for the following year. The current ***Checklist*** covers the years 2000, 2001, and 2002, and includes editions and reprints; readings, dramatizations, and musical settings; books and annuals on Hardy; books with significant Hardy content; articles and review articles; audio cassettes and CDs; reviews of works published earlier; announcements, notes, letters, and reports; dissertations and theses; miscellaneous earlier publications; and archives of internet discussions.

Many of those Checklist citations are annotated, and the contents of book-length publications are often analyzed. Even the relevant contents of three major Internet archives are provided in detail. Related entries are hyperlinked to make finding connections between them easier, and the entire ***Checklist*** may be searched for keywords; moreover, its table of contents is hyperlinked to allow for easy access to its various divisions. But the primary advantage of the ***Checklist*** is its currency. Listings are usually a year – often two years or more – in advance of standard bibliographies. In short, for anyone who wishes to keep up with the latest publications related to Hardy, the TTHA ***Checklist*** is the one indispensable resource to consult. [2]

But although TTHA provides some of the most sophisticated and current information about Hardy available on the World Wide Web, there is that wide range of other resources to which it is connected via its ***Links*** (To Other Sites) pages, and I want to expand my celebration to include some of the very best of them here. There are, of course, institutional web sites to be celebrated, such as the fine catalogue of the Richard Little Purdy collection at Yale,[3] but I want here to single out for praise sites that are the products of individuals whose efforts deserve special commendation.

First, kudos go to Norman Page, who, as editor of the encyclopedic *Oxford Reader's Companion to Hardy*, is particularly suited to impersonate Hardy and provide answers to all kinds of questions on a *Times Educational Supplement* web site titled "Talking to Thomas Hardy."[4] It's a delightfully informal site, which invites questions from persons of all ages – questions that are authoritatively answered by

---

[2] For information about how to access the ***Checklist***, go to
<http://www.yale.edu/hardysoc/Members/MRRHome.htm>.
[3] See TTHA Links A33 <http://www.fredonia.edu /hardysoc/linksone/yale.htm)>
[4] TTHA Links A 201 < http://www.fredonia.edu/hardysoc/ linksone/tes.htm>

"Hardy" himself. And, though the format is playful, and the tone and detail of the answers adjusted to the maturity of the questioners, the information available from this site is encyclopedic in scope, highly reliable in matters of fact, and, in matters of judgment, critically solid. And there's a "search" function that enables anyone to locate answers already given on a wide variety of subjects.

There are other sites whose focus is anything but encyclopedic, but which provide, for the narrower topic they address, well-documented information and/or solid critical insights about Hardy. Of these, perhaps the narrowest is Daniel Patrick Quinn's "The Dorset Ooser" site[5] which not only provides two pictures of the grotesque horned mask of the folklore figure mentioned by Hardy both in *The Return of the Native* and in "The First Countess of Wessex," but also supplies a fully detailed account of Quinn's researches into the obscure history of that folk figure. Here is everything you might ever have wanted to know about Hardy's "Ooser" but were afraid to ask.

On the other hand, there are sites that provide thoughtful and solidly documented studies of Hardy novels in relation to their intellectual background. For example, Peter Morton, Senior Lecturer in English at Flinders University of South Australia, provides a valuable study of the impact of Victorian theories of heredity on Hardy's *Tess of the d'Urbervilles*,[6] and David Garlock reproduces his extensive scholarly essay titled "Endangered Genders: Sexuality and the Individual in Darwin, Hardy and Beauvoir" whose thesis is that in *Jude the Obscure* Hardy rejects traditional gender roles in several of his major characters, and, like Darwin, writes in a way that suggests that such classificatory gender categories are illusory.[7]

Finally, although this has been a celebration of some of the many Hardy-related web sites with scholarly emphasis, I must include some whose delights are more popular in character but nevertheless are careful about facts and cautious in judgment. Anyone who has visited W. Robert Seitz's "Thomas Hardy Country" site[9] will be grateful for his excellent pictures of scenes related to Hardy's life and work, with their accurate identifications and supplementary commentaries, including relevant quotations from Hardy's texts. But my final words of celebration must be devoted to the site of Dave Sands, owner of The Paper Shop in Dorchester, who has taken upon himself a project to

---

[5] TTHA Links A 194 < http://www.dorsetooser.fsnet.co.uk/>

[6] TTHA Links A 72 < http://www.fredonia.edu/hardysoc/linksone/heredity.htm>

[7] TTHA Links A 160 < http://www.fredonia.edu/hardysoc/linksone/garlock.htm>
[9] TTHA Links A 123
<http://www.fredonia.edu/hardysoc/linksone/photographic.htm>

provide information for those interested in Hardy and Dorchester. His site[10] is in part a guide for first-time foreign visitors to Dorchester, with emphasis on the basics of getting to and around the town, its environs, and Hardy-related sites; in part it is a bulletin board for information about events in Dorset for those interested in Hardy; and in part it is a miscellany of other Hardy-related materials, including information about various services, a Hardy chat page, photographs (including many related to the Hardy Conferences), books and guides, local news – even weather reports. For anyone interested in news about current matters related to Hardy and Dorset – or in need of basic information about travel to Dorchester and getting around there – here is God's plenty.

Of course there is so much more to celebrate! One can only be grateful, for example, to Emily Ezust, a computer scientist, who has gone to the trouble of creating a web site that is an archive of texts which have been arranged to music, with indexes of poet, title, and first line – a site that identifies over 120 Hardy texts set to music by Sir Arthur Bliss, Benjamin Britten, Andrew Downes, Gerald Finzi, Ivor Gurney, John Ireland, and Robin Humphrey Milford.

But limits of space require that this celebration must come to an end. I hope that readers will be tempted to visit some of the sites I've described above, and that all those interested in keeping up with what has most recently been written on Hardy will find TTHA's **Checklist** of recent Hardy publications an indispensable resource to consult.

SAMPLE OF MUSICAL SETTINGS TO HARDY'S POEMS ON THE EZUST SITE
http://www.recmusic.org/lieder/h/hardy/

A Wagtail and Baby: Britten (Wagtail and Baby)
A Night in November: Downes
A Wife Waits: Downes
At the Piano: Wallach (At the Piano)
A Young Man's Exhortation: Finzi
After the Club Dance: Downes
After the Fair: Downes
Amabel: Finzi
At Castle Boterel: Downes (At Castle Boterel)
At a lunar eclipse: Finzi
At day-close in November: Britten

A Collation of the Gibson and Hynes Editions of Hardy's Poems

MARTIN RAY[*]

This article lists the numerous differences between James Gibson's New Wessex Edition of *The Complete Poems of Thomas Hardy* (Macmillan, 1976) and Samuel Hynes's *The Complete Poetical Works of Thomas Hardy* (Clarendon Press: vols. I–III, 1982–85). Variants in Gibson's edition have been checked against his 1979 *Variorum* edition, and one further variant between the two Gibson editions is noted (see 'She Hears the Storm'). In total, some 350 poems have different readings in the Gibson and Hynes texts.

The following points should be noted about this collation:

➤ I omit minor differences of punctuation or house-styling in headnotes and footnotes
➤ I ignore Hynes's titles in quotation marks when they are not present in Gibson
➤ I ignore Gibson's capitalization of the opening word or phrase of a poem
➤ I have not noted the changed order of Uncollected Poems in Hynes

In the following list, Gibson's reading is given first; the parentheses (gray numbers) after titles indicate his numbering of the poems, and the additional numbers (in black) indicate line numbers.

Domicilium (1) Placed by Hynes at the opening of 'Uncollected Poems'.
The Temporary the All (2) 1 youthtime,] youthtime 14 in:] in; 20 I....] I...
Hap (4) Hynes adds '16 Westbourne Park Villas.'
In Vision I Roamed (5) 14 taciturn and] trackless, distant,

---

[*] Martin Ray has compiled an electronic Concordance to Hardy's Poems; this can be ordered (free to TTHA members) by going to the order form at the following link: http://www.yale.edu/hardysoc/Welcome/orderf.htm Martin is also a TTHA Vice President and **SHORT STORY** Page Director.

At a Bridal (6) Hynes adds '8 Adelphi Terrace.'
A Confession to a Friend in Trouble (8) Hynes adds '16 Westbourne Park Villas.'
Her Dilemma (12) Headnote: Church] church
Revulsion (13) 8 superfluously] superfluous when Footnote: Hynes adds '16 Westbourne Park Villas.'
She, to Him I (14) 5 When, in your being,] When in your being
She, to Him III (16) 10 came:] came;
She, to Him IV (17) Footnote: Hynes adds '16 Westbourne Park Villas.'
The Sergeant's Song (19) Footnote: Hynes omits *Published in 'The Trumpet-Major' 1880*
Valenciennes (20) Headnote: Hynes adds '(Wessex Dialect)'
San Sebastian (21) 29 Passed] Past [*Collected Poems*, 1930, has 'Past']
The Stranger's Song (22) Footnote: Hynes omits *Printed in 'The Three Strangers', 1883*
The Burghers (23) 63 on] from
Leipzig (24) 15 quartered] camped 67 heard;] heard: 95 deathbed] deathbed 116 bridgeway track:] bridge-way track; 128 Marshal's] Marshals'
The Peasant's Confession (25) Headnote: c'est] C'est 5 cross'd] crossed 33 Grouchy?] Grouchy! 50 clash] crash 57 view] view, 73 nighed] struck 118 round. . . .] round . . . . .
The Alarm (26) 24 char-wench] chore-wench 39 clatters; –] clatters; 40 My] ... My 53 were cars and chariots, faring] cars and chariots fared them 62 come,] come 74 arms] arms, 81 me! ...] me! .... 94 Till nearing coast and harbour] Till, nearing coast and harbour, 98 Fencibles] Fencibles, 106 tarried:] tarried;
Her Death and After (27) 23 there,] there; 67 dear –] dear, 82 once] had
The Dance at the Phœnix (28) 36 on] to 40 swords,] swords 55 selfsame] self-same 77 by] towards 79 sergeant tall] sergeant's call 86 for] for, 89 mid] 'mid 107 chime went] chimed to 131–2 When forthward yestereve she crept, And as unwitting,] When with lax longings she had crept Therefrom at midnight,
A Sign-Seeker (30) 23 well] well,
My Cicely (31) 6 aforehand] aforetime 61 dwells] is 62 aforetime?'] aforetime?' – 63 to disguise] and disguised 76 life's] Life's 77 For, on my ride down I had] For riding down hither I'd 97 wayfared] wayfared,
Her Immortality (32) 19 bride:] bride;
A Meeting with Despair (34) 15 perverse,] perverse –
To Outer Nature (37) 16 re-adorning] readorning
In a Wood (40) Headnote: *See*] From 31 black] blank
Nature's Questioning (43) 6 ways] way 7 days] day

128

The Impercipient (44) 11 they've] they have 29 deprived] beshorn

The Bride-Night Fire (48) Headnote: (*A Wessex Tradition*)] Or, The Fire at Tranter Sweatley's / (Wessex Dialect) 10 clinking off] vanishing 11 near,] near 18 pair] twain 19 leer] lear 27 tidetimes] tidetimes 30 laitered] loitered 33 main] main, 34 Around] And round 41 cwold] cold 60 husbird,] husbird 64 'ithin en] within him 68 horsed her by jerks, till] bending his back, there 73 ere long where a halter-path] erelong where a bridle-path 74 Sighted Tim's house by dawn, on'y] Lit on Tim's house at dawn, only 75 day,] day; 108 o' wold] of old Footnotes: omitted by Hynes

Heiress and Architect (49) 13 me,'] me', 25 frame,'] frame',

The Two Men (50) 25 down] out 40 long-lingering] long lingering 48 poverty. . . .] poverty. . . 49 Meantime] Meanwhile Footnote: Hynes adds '16 Westbourne Park Villas.'

Lines (51) 7 good-will] good-will, 24–5 No stanza break in Hynes 34 ill] ills

V.R. 1819–1901 (53) 10 Her] – Her

The Colonel's Soliloquy (56) 33 her;] her!

The Going of the Battery (57) Headnote: (2 *November 1899*)] (*Casterbridge: November* 2, 1899) 21 Some one] Someone

The Souls of the Slain (62) 64 new] dew Footnote: omitted by Hynes

Shelley's Skylark (66) 8 immortality:] immortality.

Rome: On the Palatine (68) 7 gleams, its] gleams in

Zermatt: To the Matterhorn (73) 13 end;] end:

The Bridge of Lodi (74) 1 body,] body 31 But,] But Footnote: omitted by Hynes

The Mother Mourns (76) 5 aëry] aërie 16 dirge-like] dirgelike 37 mindsight] mind-sight 51 lure] lure,

A Commonplace Day (78) 17 slides,] slides

The Problem (85) 5 hearken intently and carry an eagerly upstrained sense] listen intently with strained and eager and reaching sense 7 reign:] reign; 10 pain.] pain!

The Bullfinches (86) 29 the day's] to-day's 30 those be] they sleep

God-Forgotten (87) 26 severance,] severance 47 – Oh,] – O often] still

The Bedridden Peasant (88)] The Bedridden Peasant to an Unknowing God 9 giv'st us men our] givest men their 14 us] it 19 meant'st that] meantest 29–30 Then, since Thou mak'st not these things be, But these things] Since, making not these things to be, These things Thou

Mute Opinion (90) 5 I scarce had means] I almost failed 9 When, grown] When as

To an Unborn Pauper Child (91) 35 thou'lt] thou wilt

On a Fine Morning (93) 11 iris-hued] iriséd

To Lizbie Browne (94) 23 disappeared] disappeared,
Song of Hope (95) 15 Larks,] Larks 22 broken:] broken;
The Well-Beloved (96) 2 the dear one's home] my Dear's abode 3 Kingsbere] Jordon 4 sun upclomb] noon-tide glowed 7 Nigh] Near 18 by] to 21 erstwhile] the while 22 Out from] Adown 26 be] be, 38 Kingsbere] Jordon 56 sayest] say'st 59 I have] I've 62 Kingsbere] Budmouth
Her Reproach (97) 14 moment;] moment, Footnote: *Westbourne*] 16 Westbourne
The Inconsistent (98) 3 sweetness,'] sweetness', 7 recent] later
How Great My Grief (101) 6 loving-kindness] lovingkindness
The Coquette, and After (103) 2 me] me, 4 For] For,
A Spot (104) 8 be. . . .] be.
Long Plighted (105) 3 descried] decried
The Widow Betrothed (106) 7 thereby] thereby, 40 before.] before. . . .
Birds at Winter Nightfall (115) 3 cotonea-aster] cotoneaster Footnote: *Max Gate*] Max Gate. 1900.
The Comet at Yell'ham (120) 8 that sweet form of] face of mine or
A Wasted Illness (122) Headnote: Hynes has '(Overheard)'
A Man (123) 26 sickened;] sickened,
The Dame of Athelhall (124) 13 uprose to] appeared in 29 Home, home to Athelhall] Home – home to Athel 49 quick] due
The Seasons of Her Year (125) 10 song-birds] songbirds
The Milkmaid (126) 6 Upheaves] Uplifts 13 bends] throws
The Levelled Churchyard (127) 23 plane] plane,
The Ruined Maid (128) 12 Some] A 13 bleak] bleak,
The Respectable Burgher (129)] The Respectable Burgher On 'the Higher Criticism' 14 whate'er,] whate'er;
The King's Experiment (132) 34 Ere her too] Before her
The Tree (133) 19–21 'Years back, within this pocket-hole / I found, my Love, a hurried scrawl / Meant not for me,' at length said I;] I said to her: 'I found a scrawl, / My Love, within this pocket hole / Years back, not meant to meet my eye; 37 aye, wife] aye, wife!
Her Late Husband (134) 13 obeyed:] obeyed;
The Church-Builder (139) 1 flings forth] projects 2 moon-blanched] moon-lit 4 hoard;] hoard: 8 in] in, 9 Of] Set 78 morn] dawn
The Lost Pyx (140) 1 banned:] banned; 33 uphung] hung 53 'mid] mid Footnote: omitted by Hynes
Tess's Lament (141) 8 Of] O' 11 staunch] stanch 19 perhaps] p'rhaps 35 they all] all o'm 36 A-standing] A standing 37 o'us] o's 48 gone all] leave no

The Supplanter (142) 3 day-dawn until eve] dawn till eventide 5 day-dawn until eve] dawn till eventide 25 He drops his wreath, and enters] He downs his wreath when entered 45 all drawn with heavy] drawn down as by a 54 forgot.'] forgot.'…61 She cowers; and, rising, roves he then] Out from her arms he takes his track 66 awhile.] awhile. . . .67 year beholds him wend again] year: and he is travelling back 68 her] one 69 day-dawn until eve] dawn till eventide 71 day-dawn until eve repairs] dawn till eventide he bears 72 Towards her mound to pray] A wreath of blooms and bay 80 me.] me! 91 passion-tossed;] passion-tossed:

Sapphic Fragment (143) 6 thy shade shall] shall keep thee

I Have Lived with Shades (149) 37 pain] pain,

Memory and I (150) 1 youth] Youth 7 joy] Joy 9 in gaunt gardens lone] on a lonely lawn 13 hope] Hope 19 faith] Faith 25 love] Love

The Revisitation (152) 11 stronger] stronger, 71 come,'] come', 84 dread. . . .] dread . . . .96 unconsciousness. . . .] unconsciousness . . . . 128 more. . . .] more . . . .

A Trampwoman's Tragedy (153) 29 cosy] cozy 80 flung.)] flung). Footnote: not in Hynes

The Two Rosalinds (154) 23 self-same] selfsame 28 indeed. . . .] indeed . . . . 37 play. . . .] play . . . . 51 here. . . .] here . . . .

A Sunday Morning Tragedy (155) 23 shame,'] shame', 37 herb. . .?] herb. . . .? 39 is,'] is', 69 chimes] chimes, 70 In Pydel Vale] Next Sunday came 95 this. . . .] this . . . . 122 Stone dead] Stone-dead

Bereft (157) [Hynes places this poem after 'The Farm-Woman's Winter]

The Curate's Kindness (159) 17 one] our 35 anyhow,'] anyhow',

The Rejected Member's Wife (161) [Hynes places this poem after 'Geographical Knowledge']

Autumn in King's Hintock Park (163) 8 leaves,] leaves

Shut Out That Moon (164) 3 wears] bears

Reminiscences of a Dancing Man (165) 22 Argyle] Argyll

I Say, 'I'll Seek Her (172) 2 interposes;'] interposes';

Four Footprints (175) 15 scores,"] scores",

In the Mind's Eye (177) 3 there,] there

Misconception (185) 24 I find most pleasure] My nature revels

The Market-Girl (197) 6 said] said,

The Inquiry (198) 3 Hermitage] Hermitage,

A Wife Waits (199) 7 Willy,] Willy Footnote: omitted by Hynes

After the Fair (200) Footnote: omitted by Hynes

The Dark-Eyed Gentleman (201) Footnote: omitted by Hynes

The Spring Call (204) 7 dear',] dear,'

Julie-Jane (205) 16 name . . . .] name . . . . 18 too. . . .] too . . . . 21 suppose,'] suppose', Footnote: omitted by Hynes

News for her Mother (206) 2 is,] is 7 made] wrung 16 now,] now 26 Yes,'] Yes',

The Husband's View (208) 2 my hid] hidden 24 Hidden] Concealed 26 then!...] then!....

Rose-Ann (209) 13 son;'] son';

The Homecoming (210) 10 there-right] thereright

The Rash Bride (212) 47 what....] what ... 51 beside] besides [Misprint in Hynes] 53 naught....] naught ... 60 Saint Stephen's] 'Saint Stephen's'

A Dream Question (215) 7 When] 'When   20 still....] still ....

A Wife and Another (217) 43 him....] him ....   65 so....] so ....

The Vampirine Fair (219) 38 cheer,'] cheer', 73 Lord] lord

The Rambler (221) 15 far back] removed 16 me!] me.

She Hears the Storm (228) [Hynes places this poem before 'Autumn in King's Hintock Park'] 4 this!] this. 13 sooty-wick'd] sooty wick'd [Gibson's Variorum edition, however, has 'sooty wick'd']

Before Life and After (230) 6 heart-burnings] heartburnings

New Year's Eve (231) 1 year,'] year', 6 said,] said. 11 "who in] who "in

God's Education (232) 19 be,] be

Panthera (234) 24–5 No stanza break in Hynes 43–4 [between] Centred line in Hynes only 44 unlike,'] unlike', 46 day,] day 47 Judæa....] Judæa ... 54 Governor] governor 88–9 No stanza break in Hynes 89 'Among] Among 112 terebinth] terebinth [Misprint in Hynes] 112–3 No stanza break in Hynes 122–3 No stanza break in Hynes 131–2 No stanza break in Hynes 141–2 No stanza break in Hynes 169–70 No stanza break in Hynes 176 again....] again .... 218 that] the 219 memory....] memory ....

The Unborn (235) 23 desired,] desired

One Ralph Blossom Soliloquizes (238) 10 dryly] drily

The Noble Lady's Tale (239) 37 won:] won; 133 he,] he. 178 entered] entered – 179 Sanctified,] Sanctified – 200 unfold).] unfold.)

Unrealized (240) 21 died!] died,

Aberdeen (242) Headnote: And] 'And [Misprint in Gibson: *Collected Poems*, 1930, has quotation mark]

In Front of the Landscape (246) 49 scenes,] scenes

Channel Firing (247) 26 be,'] be',

To Meet, or Otherwise (251) 17 Demon] Daemon

The Sun on the Bookcase (253) 13 done,] done

The Torn Letter (256) 30 on:] on;

Beyond the Last Lamp (257) 12 glance,] glance

The Face at the Casement (258) 27 to:] to; 28 day:] day.

Wessex Heights (261) 22 thin-lipped] thin lipped 23 railway train] railway-train

The Place on the Map (263) 18 our] out [Misprint in Hynes]
A Plaint to Man (266) 13 device,'] device', 16 Somewhere] 'Somewhere
Ah, Are You Digging on My Grave? (269) 1 grave,] grave 5 now,"] now",
    9 no:] no; 25 grave....] grave ...
Self-Unconscious (270) Headnote: Hynes has '(Near Bossiney)'. Gibson
    puts this as a footnote. 19 sea-line] sea-line,
Tolerance (272) 1 thing,'] thing',
Before and after Summer (273) 4 street] street,
The Year's Awakening (275) 5 Ram,] Ram. [Misprint in Hynes]
Your Last Drive (278) 23 heed,] heed
The Walk (279) 10 way;] way:
Rain on a Grave (280) 9 rain:] rain.
I Found Her Out There (281) Footnote: Hynes adds '*December* 1912'.
Lament (283) 35 things,] things
His Visitor (286) 9 cosy] cozy
A Dream or No (288) 8 brown-tressed.] brown-tressed,
After a Journey (289) 26 lazily;] lazily,
A Death-Day Recalled (290) 3 Vallency's] Valency's 17 Vallency] Valency
    23 Breath] breath
The Phantom Horsewoman (294) 5 haze] haze,
The Spell of the Rose (295) 7 apple-trees] apple trees 26 This,'] This',
Where the Picnic Was (297) 30 evermore] evermore. [Misprint in Gibson]
The Cheval-Glass (300) 3 plume] plume,
The Re-Enactment (301) 33 years'-long-binned] years-long-binned
The Newcomer's Wife (304) 8 forget:] forget.
A Conversation at Dawn (305) 92 could;] could. 96 claim;] claim. 153 So,]
    So 160 sentiment:] sentiment. 172 dear!] dear.
The Coronation (307) 27 like,'] like',
Aquae Sulis (308) 21 'Repress]' – Repress 24 song] song that 28 Come,]
    Come –
The Elopement (310) 4 You] you 6 fair,] fair.
In the British Museum (315) 16 Paul;] Paul,
The Obliterate Tomb (317) 93 went,] went 123 well,'] well', church-ward-
    en] churchwarden 129 read;] read,
The Telegram (323) 13 herself] her self
The Moth-Signal (324) 6 candle flame] candle-flame 13 think,'] think',
Seen by the Waits (325) 14 dead:] dead;
The Two Soldiers (326) 19 known;] known,
In the Days of Crinoline (328) 26 To-day,'] To-day',
The Roman Gravemounds (329) 5 Rome,'] Rome', 17 Cæsar's] Caesar's
    20 Cæsar] Caesar
The Sacrilege (331) 36 dallyings,] dallyings. [Misprint in Hynes] 77 night.
    ...] night ...

133

The Abbey Mason (332) 95 knew,'] knew', 103 to-day;] to-day: 177 so,] so 194 fascinations] fascination [Misprint in Hynes] 196 halls,] halls. 199 part] part,

The Satin Shoes (334) 39 her,'] her',

A Poet (336) 14 him;'] him';

At Tea (337) 1 cosy] cozy

By Her Aunt's Grave (339) 1 week,'] week', 10 know] know.

At a Watering-Place (341) 7 pair,'] pair',

In the Nuptial Chamber (346) 5 townsfolk's] townsfolks'

In the Restaurant (347) 9 here] here, [Gibson's note in the Variorum edition says that he re-introduced the comma, but he omitted to do so] 12 Let us] Let's

At the Draper's (348) 10 *fashion;"*] *fashion"*; 14 *mourning,"*] *mourning"*,

In the Moonlight (351) 5 moon] moon,

The Voice of Things (353) 3 below] below,

She, I, and They (365) 14 meaning,'] meaning',

Copying Architecture in an Old Minster (369) 16 quatre-foiled] quatrefoiled

Quid Hic Agis? (371) Footnote: Hynes omits 'During the War'

The Faded Face (377) 19 sorrow-wrung] over-wrung 21 Sorrow-wrung] Over-wrung

The Duel (379) 16 you your] your [Misprint in Hynes] 39 't would] 'twould

To My Father's Violin (381) 28 cannot] can not

Lines (388) 19 such rashness,] such richness,] richness, rashness,

His Heart (391) 7 if,'] if',

The Photograph (405) 6 eyes;] eyes, 9 furtivewise] furtive-wise

The Pink Frock (409) 2 sha'n't] shan't 4 hardly can] can hardly 9 frock?] frock,

Transformations (410) 11 often] vainly

The House of Silence (413) 24 aion] aeon

Great Things (414) 4 Ridgway] Ridgeway 28 thee:'] thee':

The Figure in the Scene (416) 4 scene;] scene. Footnote: *an*] and [Misprint in Hynes]

The Blow (419) 6 unbiassed] unbiased

At Middle-Field Gate in February (421) 9 rolls,] rolls

On Sturminster Foot-Bridge (426) 8 flows:] flows;

The Five Students (439) 11 I,] I 28 course] course,

The Wind's Prophecy (440) 17 coastlands] coastlines

During Wind and Rain (441) 14 across!] across.

At a Seaside Town in 1869 (447) 37 said;] said:

The Memorial Brass: 186– (452) 11 remarried] re-married

The Upper Birch-Leaves (455) 23 you] *you*

It Never Looks Like Summer (456) 3 looks] look

134

Everything Comes (457) 6 around,] around
He Fears His Good Fortune (459) 16 claim,'] claim',
He Wonders About Himself (460) 10 sources] forces 11 the poise of forces,] creature-courses,
Jubilate (461) 13 hearkening] harkening
Fragment (464) 11 Cause);] Cause;)
Honeymoon Time at an Inn] (466) Honeymoon-Time at an Inn 39 good,'] good', 40 aftergrinds] after-grinds
The Clock-Winder (471) 11 clock] clock,
In a Whispering Gallery (474) 12 this gaunt gray] from this gaunt
The Enemy's Portrait (476) 40 I thought they were the] Strange, I thought they were
The Clock of the Years (481) 7 Peace;'] Peace'; 15 me –] me. 25 Better,'] Better',
At the Piano (482) 12 sigh;] sigh,
In the Garden (484) 9 Throwing a shade to] Shading its finger
Looking at a Picture on an Anniversary (488) 22 rebirth?] rebirth!
The Choirmaster's Burial (489) 21 think,'] think',
His Country (494) 9 parts] parts,
England to Germany in 1914 (495) 11 rancorously] rancorously,
An Appeal to America on Behalf of the Belgian Destitute (497) 3 dead] dead, 14 wooingwise] wooing-wise
In Time of 'The Breaking of Nations' (500) Footnote: omitted by Hynes
Before Marching and After (502) 19 overseas] over-seas
Often When Warring (503) 8 not] not.
The Dead and the Living One (506) 20 curl] curl, 31 you!] you,
Afterwards (511) 8 sight.'] sight'. 12 gone.'] gone'. 19 rise] swell
Epeisodia (515) 15 drearisome] drearisome, 23 quiver] quiver,
Barthélémon at Vauxhall (519) 11 morn,'] morn',
The Curtains Now Are Drawn (523) 15 vain;'] vain';
Welcome Home (527) 16 you. . . .] you . . .
Her Song (532) 21 face,] face
The Strange House (537) 10 some one] someone 20 Any one] Anyone
The Contretemps (539) 20 Plainly] 'Twas clear
A Gentleman's Epitaph on Himself and a Lady, Who Were Buried Together (540) 25 vernal] vernal, Footnote: omitted by Hynes.
A Duettist to Her Pianoforte (543) 32 hushed, you] hushed you
Where Three Roads Joined (544) 14 near] near,
'And There Was a Great Calm' (545) 39 to-day;'] to-day';
Haunting Fingers (546) 16 endures?'] endures? 59 grayer] grayer,
The Woman I Met (547) 76 Forms] Flesh
The Two Houses (549) 49 come,'] come',

On Stinsford Hill at Midnight (550) 25 are,'] are', Footnote: omitted by Hynes.
A Wife Comes Back (554) 23 clothed] drest
At Lulworth Cove a Century Back (556) Footnote: omitted by Hynes.
I Worked No Wile to Meet You (562) 12 stumbling-blocks] stumblingblocks
An Autumn Rain-Scene (569) 1 merry-making] merrymaking 16 No care if he] Careless to
An Experience (571) 10 round] round,
The Beauty (572) Footnote: omitted by Hynes.
The Collector Cleans His Picture (573) 14 artfeat] art-feat 18 grimefilms] grime-films 36 lifetime . . .] lifetime. . . .
Voices from Things Growing in a Churchyard (580) Footnote: omitted by Hynes.
At the Royal Academy (585) 12 summer's] summer's,
By Henstridge Cross at the Year's End (588) 26 now'] now,'
I Look in Her Face (590) 3 blossoming;'] blossoming'; 7 no;'] no';
The Chapel-Organist (593) 15 upstaring] upstaring, 73 bosom'] bosom',
He Follows Himself (604) 16 man,'] man', 31 beards] beards,
Last Words to a Dumb Friend (619) 23 nor] not [Misprint in Hynes?]
The Old Workman (624) 7 blocks,'] blocks', 13 up,'] up',
A Sound in the Night (629) 7 half an hour] half-an-hour 47 heard,] heard 49 on't,] on't.
The Inscription (642) 14 Soules,'] Soules', 58 that, since earth's joys most drew her, past doubt,] that the joys of the earth had so wound her about, 59 Friends'] That 65 no;'] no';
Intra Sepulchrum (648) 3 dead,] dead 20 unconscious;] unconscious.
The Seven Times (652) 37 how,'] how',
Rake-Hell Muses (656) 15 communion] communion –
After Reading Psalms XXXIX, XL, etc. (661) 14 Shall,'] Shall',
Waiting Both (663) 3 our] his
A Cathedral Façade at Midnight (667)   Footnote: Hynes adds 'Salisbury'.
The Turnip-Hoer (668) 7 out-wore] outwore 64 far.] far,
The Monument-Maker (671) 17 emotion] emotion,
An East-End Curate (679) 4 Mr] Mr.
In St Paul's a While Ago (683) 19 coquetting] conquetting [Misprint in Hynes]
The Month's Calendar (687) 3 weeks,] weeks
Sine Prole (690) Headnote: *Mediaeval Latin*] Latin 4 one –] one
A Night of Questionings (696) 25 time, shrined] time (shrined 29 earth,] earth) 73 fret,] fret 80 Through] In
Night-Time in Mid-Fall (699) 10 home-coming] homecoming

136

Winter Night in Woodland (703) 19 twelve] twelve,

At Wynyard's Gap (718) 22 Gap'.] Gap.' [65] *The carrier comes up. Her companion reluctantly hails him.*] Hynes places this after line 73.

At Shag's Heath (719) 35 showed:] showed 69 me. . . .] me . . .

The Faithful Swallow (725) 4 evermore,'] evermore',

In Sherborne Abbey (726) 26 do] do it Footnote: *Family*] *family*

The Pair He Saw Pass (727) 25 morning,'] morning',

The Mock Wife (728) 4 seventeen-hundred and five] seventeen-hunddred five

The Caricature (731) 40 And,'] And',

The Aërolite (734) 21 we,'] we',

Genitrix Laesa (736) Headnote: Measure of a Sarum Sequence] Sarum Sequence Measure 24 dissolubility?] dissolubility.

The Fading Rose (737) 11 come,"] come",

Vagrant's Song (743) Footnote: omitted by Hynes

The Sexton at Longpuddle (745) 7 well,] well.

The Harvest-Supper (746) 37 merry-making] merrymaking

At a Pause in a Country Dance (747) 13 mind,] mind. [15] Hynes includes additional line: ''Tis "The Dashing White Serjeant" we love so.' 15 And] Let's 17 your husband full trusts you] my husband full trusts me

Not Only I (751) 12 newcomers] new-comers

She Saw Him, She Said (752) 5 heart-sore] and sore

Under High-Stoy Hill (760) 1 Ivelwards] Ivel-wards

Retty's Phases (765) Footnote: omitted by Hynes.

A Poor Man and a Lady (766) 34 to).] to.)

To a Sea-Cliff (768) 5 solid] stolid

Donaghadee (772) 3 In Donaghadee I shall never be:] And I am sure there never to be: 19 tuned] turned [Misprint in Hynes] 23 tender-toned] tender toned

A Refusal (778) 20 master,] master 37 Poets'] Poet's

The Protean Maiden (780) 3 noon] eve

Bags of Meat (787) 17 beer;'] beer'; 21 stand,'] stand',

The Forbidden Banns (795) 11 folk,] folk 35 found;] found:

The Paphian Ball (796) 12 say] sat [Misprint in Hynes] 15 They] We [also ll. 21, 23, 26, 31, 38, 40, 42, 54, 56 and 58] 25 they found them] we found us 35 slow hours wore them] hours onbore us 36 their guineas heaped before them] our guineas heaped before us   43 their] our 47 supine] sleeping 60 they'd] we'd 63 *Rejoice,*] *Rejoice*   69 earth!] earth.

Nothing Matters Much (801) 5 the letter] each letter

The Bird-Catcher's Boy (809) 47 sit,] sit

Discouragement (811) Subtitle: '(Natura Naturans)': not in Gibson.

The New Dawn's Business (815) 19 bed):] bed:)
Proud Songsters (816) 7 brand-new birds of twelve-months'] brand new birds of twelvemonths'
The Bad Example (821) 5 you,] you
Expectation and Experience (831) 9 face] face,
Aristodemus the Messenian (832) 54 nought] naught
The Three Tall Men (834) 34 'Many] Many 35 sea.'] sea.
The Lodging-House Fuchsias (835) 1 Mrs] Mrs.
The Whaler's Wife (836) 11 on,] on 45 grim:] grim 46 before;] before: 52 wife.] wife. 54 stain,] stain
Throwing a Tree (837) 16 years'] years
The War-Wife of Catknoll (838) 10 seem] seems 23 gallantry,] gallantry 32 known!"] known!' [Misprint in Hynes] 47 Knight. . . .] Knight . . . Footnote: omitted by Hynes
Yuletide in a Younger World (841) 22 far-time] fartime
The Son's Portrait (843) 17 wooer:] wooer;
Childhood Among the Ferns (846) 12 death;'] death';
A Countenance (847) 10 lower] bottom
To a Tree in London (852) 3 Never,] Never 19–21 Not in Hynes
He Did Not Know Me (854) 6 'But] – 'But 15 'But,'] – 'But', 17 'True] – 'True 18 'But] – 'But 19 'Yea] – 'Yea
So Various (855) 25 saw] say [Misprint in Hynes] 32 gladness:] gladness. 60 please. . . .] please . . . 61 Now. . . .] Now . . .
A Self-Glamourer (856) 5 far,'] far', 6 than] Than
The Clasped Skeletons (858) 6 dear] Dear 14 loves] Loves 30 Héloïse'] Héloïse'
We Field-Women (866) 16 three-score] threescore
Squire Hooper (868) 31 To] 'To 35 anon;'] anon';
We Say We Shall Not Meet (870) 3 leaden] heavy
Song to Aurore (872) 15 Sweet] sweet
Burning the Holly (878) 7 Yes;] Yes:
A Philosophical Fantasy (884) 1 you] thou 35 me?)'] me?') 55 greatly).] greatly.) 70 whatever),] whatever,) 83 Thy] They [Misprint in Hynes] 89 not).] not.) 107–8 No stanza break in Hynes 111 them] then [Misprint in Hynes] 126 "unfulfilled intention",] 'unfulfilled intention,'
The Letter's Triumph (886) 11 whether] whether, [Misprint in Hynes]
Whispered at the Church-Opening (888) 5 man,'] man',
The New Boots (891) 7 husband,'] husband', 11 to wear whenever] for the wet weather, [Misprint in Hynes] 13 "Yes,"] "Yes,' [Misprint in Hynes] 20 them. . . .] them . . . .
Lorna the Second (893) 16 Lorna!] Hynes puts this at end of previous line [Misprint in Hynes]

Drinking Song (896) 70 bending-ocean] ether-ocean
A Musical Incident (899) [Wrong line numbering in Gibson's *Variorum* edition]
June Leaves and Autumn (900) 16 June] June.
No Bell-Ringing (901) 17 Day.] Day, Footnote: omitted by Hynes
I Looked Back (902) 14 three-score] threescore
The Gap in the White (911) 4 glass.] glass,
The Catching Ballet of the Wedding Clothes (913) 39 O,] O. [Misprint in Hynes] 92 clerk).] clerk.) 120 again.] again [Misprint in Hynes]
The Ballad of Love's Skeleton (915) 52 One] one
A Private Man on Public Men (916) 8 rumour's] rumour's quiet [Misprint in Hynes]
A Victorian Rehearsal (923) 18 the other way;'] th'other way'; 19 haggarded] haggard
Thoughts from Sophocles (924) 2 Has] Feels
Eunice (925) Footnote: omitted by Hynes.
She Would Welcome Old Tribulations (927) 19 decree;] decree:
The Night of Trafalgár] The Night of Trafalgar (929) Footnote: omitted by Hynes.
[*Albuera*: not included by Gibson]
Budmouth Dears] Hussar's Song (930) Subtitle: (*Hussar's Song*)] Budmouth Dears Footnote: omitted by Hynes.
My Love's Gone a-Fighting (931) Footnote: omitted by Hynes.
The Eve of Waterloo (932) 23 rheum] rheum, 32 The] – The 35 bed,] bed; 37 shivers as sinks] sighs as he shifts 39 tomorrow's] tomorrow's Footnote: omitted by Hynes.
Chorus of the Pities (933) Hynes adds SEMICHORUS I and II. Footnote: omitted by Hynes.
Last Chorus (934) *The Years*] SEMICHORUS I OF THE YEARS (and II) 9 dream] a dream *The Pities*] SEMICHORUS I OF THE PITIES (and II) 15 loving-kindness'] lovingkindness' Footnote: omitted by Hynes.
[*Motto for the Wessex Society of Manchester*: not included by Gibson]
The Yellow-Hammer (938) 8 road.] road,
A Jingle on the Times (939) 32 Today] To-day
Prologue] Prologue to *The Dynasts* (940) 19 ago. . . . . .] ago. . . .
Epilogue] Epilogue to *The Dynasts* (940) 2 three hours'] three-hours' 4 such!] such. 10 eyes!] eyes – Footnote: omitted by Hynes.
A Hundred Years Since (941) 39 be] have
[*The Sound of Her*: not included by Gibson]
They are Great Trees (943) Footnote: omitted by Hynes.
[*'Could he but live for me'*: not included by Gibson]
[*'Let's meet again to-night, my Fair'*: not included by Gibson]

At a Rehearsal of One of J.M.B.'s Plays] On J. M. B. {944} Footnote: omitted by Hynes.
The Hatband {945} 19 came;] came: Footnote: omitted by Hynes.
Epitaph for G. K. Chesterton] Epitaph [for G. K. Chesterton] {946}
Epitaph for George Moore] {947} On One who Thought No Other Could Write Such English as Himself Headnote: *On one who thought no other could write such English as himself*] Epitaph [for George Moore] 4 beauty (perfection)] beauty 5–6 Printed by Hynes as one line.

THOMAS HARDY: 1880

INDEPENDENT ESSAYS

I

The Excavating Consciousness in Hardy's Two on a Tower.

ANDREW RADFORD

Under any other circumstances Lady Constantine might have felt a nameless fear in thus sitting aloft on a lonely column, with a forest groaning under her feet, and palaeolithic dead men feeding its roots; but the recent passionate decision stirred her pulses to an intensity beside which the ordinary tremors of feminine existence asserted themselves in vain.

(*Tower*, 108-109)[1]

Lady Viviette Constantine "sitting aloft on a lonely column" evokes images of the Nelson monuments that were spontaneously created close upon the news of the famous Lord's naval victory (1805) in the Battle of Trafalgar. Monuments like that in Trafalgar Square (under construction between the 1820s and 1840s) commemorated the heroic virtues of men; rarely were they built in honour of a woman. Rings-Hill Speer "had been erected in the eighteenth century as a substantial memorial of [Sir Blount's] great-grandfather, a respectable officer who had fallen in the American War" (*Tower*, 6).

Viviette's position at the top of the Speer also suggests the Christian ascetics who demonstrated their devotion to God by living on similar towers, such as Saint Simeon Stylites (390-459), the first and most renowned of the Pillar-Hermits, who occupied a pillar for thirty years. Hardy's pairing of images not ordinarily joined and which on a cursory reading make little sense together – the male Christian ascetic and the married patrician lady – reveals a grim aptness after all: Viviette has been compelled to adopt an enervating existence of severe

---

[1] Thomas Hardy, *Two on a Tower*. Ed. with Introd. Suleiman M. Ahmad (Oxford: The World's Classics, 1988). Referred to throughout as *Tower*.

self-repression as a demonstration of devotion to her dissipated husband. She has taken a "solemn oath" (*Tower*, 20) not to mingle in genteel society until his return from Africa; so her clandestine visits to the Speer have much more serious implications than they will for the young astronomer with whom she is in love.

In the sharply unsettling image of "palaeolithic dead men" Hardy ponders to what extent the psychological past is a dead event in modern society. Tylor's *Primitive Culture* (1871), which Hardy read before or during the writing of *The Return of the Native*, convincingly demonstrated that "through remoter periods, as we recede more nearly towards the primitive conditions of our race, the threads which connect new thought with old do not always vanish from our sight" (Tylor, I, 274). To what extent then did the individual inherit from preceding generations not only his physiological but also his psychological structures? That the remains of "palaeolithic dead men" actively fertilize the roots of the trees which groan beneath Viviette's feet is suggestive. Hardy implies that mental survivals are still operant, governing human behaviour from below the threshold of rational consciousness. He exploits Rings-Hill Speer to introduce a vertical timescheme: palaeolithic dead men buried beneath a Romano-British earthwork on which is built an eighteenth-century tower surmounted by Swithin's equatorial telescope. The archaeological term "palaeolithic" was coined by Sir John Lubbock, author of the seminal *Prehistoric Times* (1865),[2] to designate a first Stone Age greatly antedating all written records:

> From the careful study of the remains which have come down to us, it would appear that Pre-historic Archaeology may be divided into four great epochs.
>
> I. That of the Drift; when man shared the possession of Europe with the Mammoth, the Cave Bear, the Woolly-haired rhinoceros, and other extinct animals. This we may call the "Palaeolithic" period. (Lubbock, 2)

Hardy glimpses through the "palaeolithic dead men" passional imperatives which do not submit to the rigid proprieties governing polite Victorian society. He asks whether the social milieu of *Two on a Tower* complicates these imperatives, or are the timeless energies simply malicious: inexorably cruel natural laws under whose sway we see Viviette Constantine? Although Hardy retains an honest ambivalence about this issue, he shifts towards the latter conclusion when Louis Granville discovers Viviette is carrying an illegitimate child by

---

[2] Lubbock also coined the term "Neolithic" to refer to the later or polished Stone Age. The book became a best-seller for half a century; the seventh edition was published in 1913.

Swithin. As a result, he embarks on a journey to marry her off to the Bishop of Melchester:

> Louis entered the train at Warborne, and was speedily crossing a country of ragged woodland which, though intruded on by the plough at places, remained largely intact from prehistoric times; and still abounded with yews of gigantic growth and oaks tufted with mistletoe. It was the route to Melchester. (*Tower*, 254)

Louis's route to a stronghold of Christianity on the modern train ironically takes him through some of the most ancient pagan landscape in Wessex. The "oaks tufted with mistletoe" foreshadows Hardy's description of The Chase in Chapter 5 of *Tess* ("a truly venerable tract of forest land, one of the few remaining woodlands in England of undoubted primaeval date, wherein Druidical mistletoe was still found on aged oaks"), and is a potent image given the antiquarian Charles Hardwick's comments in his *Traditions, Superstitions and Folklore* (1872):

> The mistletoe and the oak were both of sacred...origin amongst the Aryans...It is a parasite...everywhere believed to spring from seed deposited by birds on trees. When it was found on the oak, the Druids ascribed its growth directly to the gods. (Hardwick, 67)

Hardwick comments later:

> The peculiar and regular equiangular form of the branches of the mistletoe, doubtless, had much influence in its selection as a mystical plant endowed with supernatural properties. (255)

It is possible that Hardy knew of ancient boundary and bridal oaks in Dorset, like the ones Hardwick mentions,

> around which newly-married couples danced three times and afterwards cut a cross...unquestionably one form of the many phallic symbols. (75)

The Greenwood Tree under whose branches the celebration of Dick and Fancy's wedding takes place is an oak.

Eight years after the publication of *Two on a Tower* in 1890, James Frazer's *The Golden Bough* would thoroughly investigate the mythical significance of the mistletoe and the oak trees on which it was commonly found. The plant was "from time immemorial", the "object of superstitious veneration in Europe." (750) Women believed that carrying mistletoe about with them would enable them to conceive. (*The Golden Bough*, 751).[3]

---

[3] See also (Frazer, *Golden Bough*, 796-800): "The inference is almost inevitable that *The Golden Bough* was nothing but the mistletoe seen through the haze of poetry or of popular superstition."

It seems highly probable then, considering the nature of Louis's mission to Melchester, that Hardy slyly exploits the link between "oaks tufted with mistletoe" and pagan fertility rites, a link which first reviewers of the novel such as the *Saturday Review* (18 November 1882) no doubt found "extremely repulsive" (Cox, 675). Convinced in *Two on a Tower* of the impossibility of realizing one's individuality in a society dominated by ridiculously strict conventions, Hardy incorporates more bitterly grotesque effects into his comic repertoire. There is a cruel, even venomous relish in Hardy's portrayal of the *ruined* Lady Constantine becoming the "spiritual queen of Melchester" (*Tower*, 184) after passing off Swithin's child as the middle-aged bishop's. The prehistoric features of the Wessex countryside suggest the volatile passional imperatives (the begetting of an illegitimate child) traditionally and naturally associated with the primitive world, as late Victorian folk-lore attests and which Frazer confirms in *The Golden Bough*.

The same tension behind an incongruous situation imbues the depiction of Swithin's marriage preparations in the tower cabin. Hardy's roving archaeological imagination again charges the Speer with arresting associations, but the disenchanted tone of the writing – its refusal to honour the false pieties of a moribund late Victorian culture – remains the dominant feature. Hardy considers the issue that was a source of such ugly controversy in the final novels: the features of a genuine marriage and its relationship to the religious rite and the legal contract which guarantees its social acceptance. In earlier novels, Hardy might have countered the oppressive fact of an unbridgeable gulf between primitive and modern conceptions of marriage by adopting a fresh way of looking at it; here the "find" remains painfully stark, the narrative voice sombre, almost despairing.

> It was a strange place for a bridegroom to perform his toilet in, but considering the unconventional nature of the marriage a not inappropriate one. What events had been enacted in that earthen camp since it was first thrown up nobody could say; but the primitive simplicity of the young man's preparations accorded well with the prehistoric spot on which they were made. Embedded under his feet were possibly even now rude trinkets that had been worn at bridal ceremonies of the early inhabitants. Little signified those ceremonies today, or the happiness or otherwise of the contracting parties. (*Tower*, 118)

This bitter representation of incongruity strikes a note of irrecoverable loss. Hardy focuses on young rabbits watching Swithin's

> preparations through the open door from the grey dawn with-

> out, as he bustled half-dressed in and out under the boughs, and among the blackberries and brambles that grew around. (*Tower*, 117-118)

It is as if Hardy wants to believe the young astronomer has the "primitive simplicity" to establish an instinctual rapport with his prehistoric surroundings; to be subsumed in the natural world like the partially blind, furze-cutting Clym Yeobright on Egdon Heath. But to establish this kind of primal link is impossible for a dispassionate agent of modernism.

In *A Laodicean* (1881), Hardy's previous published novel, there was a spirited insouciance in the "New Light" Paula Power taking possession of Stancy Castle, a medieval "survival". However, there can be no such harmony between Swithin and his even older surroundings; for as Seymour-Smith observes, the young man is a "hard-faced Darwinian" (*Hardy*, 292), a rationalist scholar whose education renders him incapable of fully immersing himself in the eerie ambience of the site, beneath which "[m]any ancient Britons lie buried" (*Tower*, 60). Nor can the agnostic astronomer be viewed as a vigorous modern equivalent of the ancient seers and sun-worshippers who stood on more basic temple-towers and mediated between the heavenly and sublunary realm, blessed with the magical gift of decoding the riddles of the stellar universe. Although Rings-Hill Speer is "the temple of that sublime mystery on whose threshold he stood as priest" (*Tower*, 61), Swithin is a clear replacement of that ancient type utterly divorced from him in attitude, function and sympathy. Hardy recognises that his own imaginative "excavations" are making the general scene bleaker not better, and looks *beyond* the human for fecundating energies, but exposes only "horror" at the intractable "vacancy" of the night sky.

> There were gloomy deserts in those southern skies such as the north shows scarcely an example of...The inspection of these chasms brought [Swithin] a second pulsation of that old horror which he had used to describe to Viviette as produced in him by bottomlessness in the north heaven. The ghostly finger of limitless vacancy touched him now on the other side...Space here, being less the historic haunt of human thought than overhead at home, seemed to be pervaded with a more lonely loneliness. (*Tower*, 268)

The "lonely loneliness" reflects Hardy's anxious sense that language does not possess the expressive resources to capture in consolingly human terms the frightening vastness of astronomical distance. In 1885 Hardy noted the following from a review of Henry Amiel:

> To look on our own time from the point (of view) of universal history, on history from the point of view of geological periods, on geology from the point of view of astronomy - this is to enfranchise thought. (*Literary Notebooks*, I, 1340)

But Hardy offers Swithin a view of the heavens that can do little to "enfranchise thought." For Tennyson in his poem "Parnassus" (1889), astronomy was one of the "terrible muses" (geology being the other). These two sciences were frequently connected in that they both opened up dizzying perspectives which seemed to dwarf man and his history. Sir Charles Lyell throughout his *Principles of Geology* (1830-33), compares the "immensity of past time" revealed by Victorian geology to the austere "sublimity" of the astronomer's view:

> Worlds are seen beyond worlds immeasurably distant from each other, and beyond them all, innumerable other systems are faintly traced on the confines of the visible universe (Lyell, I, 63).

But Hardy could not respond buoyantly to the existential emptiness of this vision, for he is fast losing faith in his own special techniques, in his ability to offer hopeful or enabling ways of perceiving the "unacceptable". In this disquieting incident *Two on a Tower* foreshadows that crisis point when all the resources of Hardy's mature art conspire to produce a feeling of unmitigated desolation.

Although alert to how they could be corrupted, Hardy in *A Laodicean* is generally thrilled by the new inventions set amid a crumbling castle (such as a telegraph machine) which could make the farthest reaches of the earth less isolated. But in the description of the galaxies overhead in *Two on a Tower* there is an overpowering feeling of blankness which characterizes Hardy's thought-adventures in the novel as a whole, because the varieties of tone which his humour can accommodate are not allowed anything like as free an expression. *Two on a Tower*, written at a mid-point in Hardy's literary career (twelve years after *Desperate Remedies* and twelve years before *Jude*), is an uneasy work, at times even tragic, in which the menacing threat of time is felt more than its promise of progress and amelioration. The impish Hardy of *A Laodicean* who relishes the anomalous position survivals occupy in contemporary culture is increasingly troubled in *Two on a Tower* by his own witty address; feeling its inadequacy to alleviate the flagrant hypocrisy and selfish corruptions besetting his cultural moment.

At this stage, Hardy's attitude towards the English bourgeoisie becomes more truculent and combative, illustrating how "instincts did not square well with the formalities of...existence" (*Tower*, 48); and his richest vein of satirical vivacity turns in on itself. Yet the anthropological material contained in *Two on a Tower* anticipates *Tess*'s elaborate use of anthropological themes to portray irrational forces that are unleashed for destructive human ends. Hardy implies that ancient myth, and the often nonrational, violent and disturbing elements it includes, may help readers to reconcile themselves to the unavoidable constraints inflicted, by nature and by civilised society, upon the human condition at the modern moment and through all history. It is this sense of a possible mental connection with his remotest forebears that Hardy becomes increasingly preoccupied by in the final novels. The role he plays therefore in the rediscovery of anthropological materials, examining "the times of the Classical Dictionary" (*Tower*, 9) in late-nineteenth century fiction should not be underestimated.

WORKS CITED

Cox, R. G. (ed.). *Thomas Hardy: The Critical Heritage*. London: Routledge & Kegan Paul, 1970.

Frazer, James George. *The Golden Bough. A Study in Magic and Religion*. A New Abridgement from the Second and Third Editions, ed., with Introd, Robert Fraser. London and New York: The World's Classics, 1994

Hardwick, Charles. *Traditions, Superstitions and Folklore (chiefly Lancashire and the North of England:) Their affinity to others in widely-distributed localities: their Eastern Origin and Mythical Significance*. London: Simpkin, Marshall & Co, 1872; repr. Manchester, England: E. J. Morten, 1973.

Hardy, Thomas. *The Literary Notebooks of Thomas Hardy*, 2 vols. Ed. Lennart A. Bjork. London: Macmillan, 1986.

―――― *Two on a Tower*. Ed. with Introd. Sulieman M. Ahmad. Oxford: The World's Classics, 1988.

Lubbock, John. *Pre-historic Times as illustrated by Ancient Remains and the Manners and Customs of Modern Savages*, 4th edn. London: Frederic Norgate, 1878

Lyell, Charles. *The Principles of Geology, Being an Attempt to Explain the Former Changes of the Earth's Surface, by Reference to Causes now in Operation* 3 vols. London: John Murray, 1830-33.

Seymour-Smith, Martin. *Hardy*. London: Bloomsbury, 1995.

Tylor, E. B. *Primitive Culture: Researches into the Development of Mythology, Philosophy, Religion, Language and Art*, 2 vols. 4th edn. London: John Murray, 1903.

INDEPENDENT ESSAYS

II

"A Complete Diorama": The Art of Restoration in Hardy's The Return of the Native

CHARLES LOWE

The aspect of the opponent was now singular. Apart from motions, *a complete diorama* [italics my own] of the fluctuations of the game went on in their eyes. A diminutive candle-flame was mirrored in each pupil, and it would have been possible to distinguish therein between the moods of hope and the moods of abandonment, even as regards the reddleman, though his facial muscles betrayed nothing at all. Wildeve played on with the recklessness of despair[1]

In 1822, Louis Daguerre and Charles Bouton opened a diorama in Paris and introduced this theater a year later in Regent's Park in England. Daguerre was expert in lighting and scenic effects, and using a vast array of life-sized devices produced the naturalistic illusion that gave the diorama its immediate appeal. Immense pictures, varying from 69 x 45 to 70 x 50 to 72 x 42 feet in size, were painted on a transparent surface with a canvas on each side. The opaque portions

---

[1] Hardy, Thomas. *The Return of the Native*. (Oxford: Oxford University Press, 1998) Bk. III, ch. 8, p. 232. Further citations will be from this edition.

were lit by directly reflected light from the skylight over the corridors. As Richard Altick (1978) describes it

> in the wall of the building wing behind each picture – that is, at the end of the corridors – were tall ground-glass windows, the light from which shone through the translucent portions of the picture (165).

Alison and Helmut Gernsheim (1968) add perceptively that its architecture played an important role in bringing about the naturalistic illusion of the theater (22). Indeed, its capacity to insulate its spectators almost entirely from the outer world made the theater, in the eyes of an anonymous reviewer in the *Times* (October 4, 1823), superior in the force of its artifice to that of the panorama. Thus, it is insisted of the diorama, "the whole thing is nature itself" (17). However, the claim by the *Times* journalist that the diorama could reproduce a natural scene indistinguishable from its real-life counterpart invites a provocative suggestion that a spectator, no matter his sophistication, cannot be trusted to tell apart imaginative and natural phenomena.

The trope of a diorama in *The Return of the Native* (1878), Hardy's sixth-published novel, picks up on the tension by focusing on how the spectator's reading of "the handwriting" on the dice is informed by his individual "mood" (233). The scene is an intimate part of a narrative in which a character's vision is exposed not so much to be a picture of what is but more accurately to be subject to her or his highly individual bent (1, 2, 12). The significance of the whole phrase, "a complete diorama," is that it takes the narrow perspectives of two actors in a contest which is apparently captioned off by the "darkness" of the heath and locates the implied concern over subjectivity in an urban architecture that could have been visited by any of Hardy's contemporary readers (3, 8, 233).

I propose here to give a thick reading of the passage above from *The Return of the Native*. I consider how Hardy's interest in the diorama could have originated during the course of his architectural training and how the dioramic play of light might have held a special significance to him as a Gothic architect who was deeply engaged with problems of historical perspective – a professional concern of which he wrote stirringly in his essay entitled "Memories of Church Restoration" (June, 1906). As I see it, an understanding of the connection between his interest in the theater and his background in architecture can deepen one's appreciation of the interplay between lighting and structure in *The Return of the Native*.

Hardy, a professional trained in the art of restoration, sought to uncover in his fiction how light, the explicit instrument of the dioramic illusion, did not fall freely (or naturally) on its subjects. The diorama has been the subject of one inquiry in Hardy scholarship: *Hardy's Poetic Vision in **The Dynasts:** The Diorama of a Dream*. Here Susan Dean (1977) undertakes an approach to *The Dynasts* that interprets the poem as "vision in action" (7). A speech by the Semi-chorus II of the Pities is cited: "And their great Confederacy dissolves like the diorama of a dream" (I, vii, 168; qtd. in Dean 36). Briefly, it is recognized that the allusion to the diorama in *The Dynasts* is a relatively minor entry in Hardy's dramatic poem. While noting that the diorama itself may not have played a significant role in giving "form to the vision of his poem," Dean shows that the figure does offer a useful scheme for envisioning the theatrical workings of *The Dynasts*. Like *The Return of the Native*, *The Dynasts* is told from many points of view – from the perspective of a demigod, Napoleon, as well as from that of its choral spirits. The value of Dean's research can be seen as supporting what has become central to Hardy scholarship: namely, that his literary and dramatic allusions, such as the one to the diorama, exhibits his well thought-out and worked-over design and not an exhibition of flaws in an otherwise inspired vision.

My contribution is firstly that the diorama appears as a literary trope not once but at least twice over the duration of Hardy's career. This invites the question of what drove him to employ the diorama in a work from an early-to-middle-portion of his career and then, later in his vast dramatic poem. Dean's study finds a number of promising sources for Hardy's allusion to the dioramic theater in *The Dynasts*. In George Eliot's *Middlemarch* (1872), memory is said to have "as many moods as the temper, and shifts its scenery like a diorama" (Ch. 13; qtd. in Dean 37). In a January of 1876 article by L. Tollemarche in the *Fortnightly Review*, the diorama is suggested as a metaphor for literature's potential for realistic representation: "Literature is able...to give a diorama of what it depicts, while art can give only a panorama" (38).

Additionally, Richard Altick (1978) in *The Shows of London* identifies the diorama as having a currency, which is exhibited prominently in the well-known inventor's, Charles Babbage's, description (1851) of the Crystal Palace as "this Diorama of the Peaceful Arts" (Altick 457).[3] But unlike perhaps these other speculations, an investigation of Hardy's architecturally informed interests does enter directly into an examination of what Altick sees as Hardy's "subtle" use of the trope in *The Return of the Native* (174n).

---

[3] An almost full listing of allusions to the diorama in nineteenth-century literature including the reference to the diorama in *The Return of the Native* can be found in Richard Altick's *The Shows of London*, p. 174n.

In *The Life of Thomas Hardy*, Hardy (1928) records that he carried with him on his first arrival to London as an apprenticing architect a letter of introduction to

> an architect who had been a pupil of the elder Pugin's [and] was connected with the West of England, and had designed a Dorset mansion of which Hardy's father had been one of the builders, carrying out the work to that gentleman's complete satisfaction (35-6).

Pugin-the-elder, one of the foremost architectural draftsmen of the Gothic Revival during the 1820s and early 30s, planned the architecture which housed an especially well-known diorama in Regent's Park in London, opening in 1823 (22). Hardy would have likely been familiar with Pugin's lead role as architect in the theater's construction; the depth of Hardy's research and interest in the field is reflected in a scholarly essay of his entitled, "On the Application of Colored Bricks and Terra Cotta to Modern Architecture" (Millgate 79).

In a 1906 essay on architecture entitled "Memories of Church Restoration," Hardy argued the implausibility of restoring a medieval building to its original condition. The essay was most likely inspired by his experience as a member of the firm, Hicks & Company, when he was obliged to participate in the attempted restoration of St. Juliot's church, or as he described the endeavor in his autobiography, when he was "instrumental" in the "obliteration" of a "building as he had first set eyes on it having been so associated with what was romantic in his life" (F. E. Hardy 79).[4] As Hardy saw it, this was an undertaking that was fraught with economic and epistemological issues. The architect was not an independent economic actor who was privileged to render a likeness of a medieval building as he saw it. He was contractually obliged to draft designs in accordance with the wishes of a patron who might have his own peculiar vision of history – who might have viewed the restoration of a building as having value for "decorative" purposes alone ("Memories of Church Restoration" 204). However, if he could evade the preconditions imposed by the marketplace, the informed architect could perceive dilemmas that, as Hardy saw it, were intrinsic to the task of restoring a building to its earlier circumstance:

> The first is uniqueness; such a duplicate as we have been considering can never be executed. No man can make two pieces of matter exactly alike.

---

[4] In his biography of Hardy, Michael Millgate (1982) gives a rich discussion of the association that Hardy drew between the church and his courtship with Emma Hardy and additionally, its possible influences on his later poetry (124-5; 515-6).

The architect cannot "truly" reproduce "even such an easily copied shape as, say, a traceried window....The old form inherits or has acquired an indefinable quality" (Orel 214). Most significantly, the architect is faced with his own intellectual and historical distance from the object of his endeavor:

> The influence that a building like Lincoln or Winchester exercises on a person of average impressionableness and culture is a compound influence, and though it would be a fanciful attempt to define how many fractions of that compound are aesthetic, and how many associative, there can be no doubt that the latter is more valuable than the former (Orel, 215).

The architect's designs will not only be an outcome of his research on Gothic architecture. He will be influenced by his adherence to "aesthetic" principles and by the "human associations" that the structure sparks. Given a task that permits a greater license, the architect's "sentiment of association" can render an architecture that is humane in its vision and original in its design; however, in terms of the endeavor of historical restoration,

> the damage done by replacement, by the rupture of continuity, is mainly what makes the enormous loss this country has sustained from its seventy years of church restoration so tragic and deplorable (Orel, 215).

It is advised when presented with the project of reviving the ruins of a church such as St. Juliot's, that the architect should keep to a "policy of masterly inaction" (Orel, 216-7).

The particular attention paid to the problem of the architect's historical perspective suggests an origin of Hardy's considerable sophistication about issues of subjectivity in his participation as an architect in a restoration, which he noted in his autobiography, remained a cause of considerable regret (F.E. Hardy 79).

Hardy's allusion to the dioramic theater in *The Return of the Native* is representative of a similar preoccupation. His special use of the trope puts in the foreground how an aspiring tradesperson's and trained engineer's views of a contest are bent by their individual "moods" and by their susceptibility to the diorama's "diminutive candle-flame" (3, 8, 232). Although he might have come across a reference to the diorama in his studied reading of Eliot's *Middlemarch*, his chance perusal of a newspaper column and his early encounter with the Crystal Palace, Hardy's treatment of the theater in *The Return of the Native* appears to be colored primarily by his architectural training.

In *The Return of the Native* the lighting of scenes is informed by the observer's perspective on a historical "structure" (1, 2, 12). One prominent example can be found in the reddleman's and the narrator's first sighting of Eustacia Vye, the tragic heroine of *The Return of the Native*. The scene is endowed with attributes that indicate the restricted nature of the narrator's vision and identify the genesis of his perceptual framework in architectural principles:

> There the form stood, motionless as the hill beneath. Above the plain rose the hill, above the hill rose the barrow, and above the barrow rose the figure. Above the figure there was nothing that could be mapped elsewhere than on a celestial globe.
>
> Such a perfect, delicate, and necessary finish did the figure give the dark pile of hills that it seemed to be the only obvious justification of their outline. Without it there was the dome without the lantern: with it the architectural demands of the mass were satisfied. The scene was strangely homogeneous. The vale, the upland, the barrow, and the figure above it, all of these amounted only to unity. Looking at this or that member of the group was not observing a complete thing, but a fraction of a thing.
>
> The form was so much like an organic part of the entire motionless structure that to see it move would have impressed the mind as a strange phenomenon. Immobility being the chief characteristic of that whole which the person formed portion of, the discontinuance of immobility in any quarter suggested confusion.
>
> Yet that is what happened. The figure perceptively gave up its fixity, shifted a step or two, and turned round. As if alarmed it descended on the right side of the barrow, with the glide of a water-drop down a bud, and then vanished. The movement had been sufficient to show more clearly the characteristics of the figure: it was a woman's (1, 2, 11-2).

The ephemeral "form" in the opening paragraph recalls the *Times* reviewer's account "of passing through a gloomy anteroom" of the diorama's "circular chamber" (Gernsheims 15-6). The other-worldliness of the "scene" is underscored by the description of the heath: "Above the figure there was nothing that could be mapped elsewhere than on a celestial globe."

As the "lantern" in contrast with the heath's "exhaling darkness" is consistent with the marked distinction in a diorama between its scenic lighting and darkened viewing chamber, so the scene presents a theater of mutability. This illusion of "movement" is integral to the diorama's claim as superior to a panorama in its potential to reproduce a natural scene. However, the question suggested by the heroine's being figured as a "lantern," unlike the *Times* reviewer's statement, is not centered on the dilemma of "the whole thing[s]" identity to "nature itself" (Gernsheims 17). The focus is on whether the fluid "figure" is "native" to an "immobile" heath or whether her appearance as an aspect of a naturalistic "scene" represents an elaborate misperception. This inquiry into the difference between a "native" and an artifice, introduced in this opening passage, becomes a visible theme of *The Return of the Native*.

A number of phrases in the passage are indicative of the narrator's training as an architect. "Structural" terms, such as "form" and "figure," are applied to delineate the appearance of the heroine. Her "figure" is considered requisite to appeasing "the architectural demands of the mass." The barrow exhibits the "perfect, delicate, and necessary finish" of a finished construct and, as a man-made addition to the heath, is appropriately the site on which the well-informed narrator trains his attention. Significantly, this observer of Egdon Heath bears a resemblance to an architect who has been conditioned to draft a design of a "structure," which is fixed to the ground: "The discontinuance of immobility in any quarter" suggests for the trained eye "confusion," the fluidity of a "woman's" "glide" falling outside its field of reference.

The idiosyncratic use of the possessive case to close the passage reinforces the emphasis on the limited reliability of the reddleman's and narrator's visions, restricted as they are by the narrowness of their individual trainings; and subtly, the special syntax turns attention to the interpretive processes by which these professionals fill in the gaps in their individual readings of the "queen of the night" (17). The subjectivity of their shared impression is affirmed in the next paragraph when these spectators understand the heroine's "movements" in the background of a "pantomime" – another nineteenth-century entertainment. The reddleman and narrator are drawn (like the reader and author) to what is pleasurable to the eye about her theatrical process across an "organic" and "motionless structure" (17, 16). And the specialist is recognized to be no more or less an authoritative guide than is any other of the theater's audience – a cautionary about storytelling, which is reiterated throughout Hardy's fictive chronicle.

A broad-based consideration of the use of the dioramic lighting and framing in *The Return of the Native* might start with an examination of the painterly references to Dürer and the architecturally-grounded rendering of the bonfire in the next chapter of the first book. It would almost certainly center on the use of lighting to color Eustacia Vye's "great Dream" and the reference in that dream to a landscape architecture, the "parterre" (2, 3, 115-120). Equally important is the use of light from a lantern in the tragic denouement of the novel where the reddleman attempts to recover the heroine's body from the weir – a man-made construct, "the sides" of which, it is emphasized, are constructed "of masonry, to prevent water from washing away the bank" (5, 9, 374). However, the reddleman, a notably calculating observer, is only partially successful in his work. He can recover an "unconscious man" who has been given the illusion of thickness by the embrace "of another man, who had hitherto been entirely beneath the surface" (376), but cannot master the art of restoration.

Hardy's allusion to the diorama and to other popular theaters and architectures in his novel suggests that his contemporary readers were, likewise, susceptible to a play of lights. The "compound influence" of the "aesthetic principle" behind the popular theater and the "human associations" that are evoked by the woman's fluid "movements" undercut the implied claim of the spectator – regardless of whether he is an architect, a scientist, or a reviewer – to render a detached account of "nature itself" or of the "native" herself. The raising of an obligatory skepticism is, as is recollected in Hardy's "Memories of Church Restoration," one cornerstone of his "social duty" as an architect and author (Orel 215).

WORKS CITED

Altick, Richard, *The Shows of London* (Cambridge: Harvard University Press, 1978)

Crary, Jonathan, *Suspensions of Perception: Attention, Spectacle, and Modern Culture* (Cambridge: The MIT Press, 1999)

Dean, Susan, *Hardy's Poetic Vision in **The Dynasts:** The Diorama of a Dream* (Princeton: Princeton University Press, 1977)

Gernsheim, Alison and Helmut, *L. J. M. Daguerre: the History of the Diorama and the Daguerreotype* (New York: Dover Publications, Inc, 1968)

Hardy, Florence Emily, *The Life of Thomas Hardy, 1840-1928* (Hamden: Archon Books 1970)

Hardy, Thomas, *The Return of the Native*, edited by Simon Gatrell (Oxford: Oxford University Press, 1998)

Millgate, Michael, *Thomas Hardy: A Biography* (New York: Random House, 1982)

Orel, Harold, editor, *Thomas Hardy's Personal Writings* (London: Macmillan, 1967), 203-217

THE THOMAS HARDY ASSOCIATION

FOUNDED IN 1997

BY
LOVERS OF HARDY FOR LOVERS OF HARDY

BOCKHAMPTON COTTAGE: COURTESY TERRY LINNEE

NOTES ON CONTRIBUTORS

The Thomas Hardy Association is deeply indebted to all contributors, whether named here or not, especially those who have been participating in our debating groups – the *Poem of the Month* series and the *Forum* discussion group. Whereas each and every contribution is valued and *all* are archived (see the relevant TTHA Director), we regret that due tothe limitations of space only a selected sample of our debates can be published in *The Hardy Review*.

> **BETTY CORTUS** received her Ph.D. from the City University of New York. In retirement she continues to research and write as an independent scholar. She volunteers her time to teach literature in a Learning-in-Retirement Program at Mira Costa College in Oceanside, California. She is a Vice President of the Thomas Hardy Association and moderates its on-line Discussion Group, the ***Forum***

> **CHARLES LOWE** has recently completed his doctorate in English at the University of Massachusetts at Amherst. His dissertation is entitled, *The Geography of Silence: Women in Landscape in Thomas Hardy's Fiction.* He has also published articles on landscape architecture and on the crisis in perception in late nineteenth-century sciences and aesthetics.

> **ROSEMARIE MORGAN**, editor and publisher of *The Hardy Review*, has taught at Yale University since 1984. She is President of TTHA and Vice President/Symposium Chair of the Hardy Society (UK). Her publications include *Women and Sexuality in the Novels of Thomas Hardy* (Routledge, 1988), *Cancelled Words* (Routledge, 1992), also essays on Charlotte Brontë, Mary Chesnut, Thomas Hardy, Toni Morrison and women writers of the American "Frontier." Her edition of the holograph manuscript version of *Far From the Madding Crowd* (Penguin World Classics) came out in 2000.

> **WILLIAM W. MORGAN** is a TTHA Vice President and director of The Thomas Hardy Poetry Page *(POTM)* for the Association. He is Professor of English at Illinois State University, where he

teaches courses in Victorian Literature, Poetry as a Genre, English as a Field of Study and, occasionally, Women's Studies. He has published essays on Hardy in *PMLA*, *JEGP*, *Victorian Poetry*, *The Hardy Review*, and other journals. In 1998 he published his first chapbook of poems, *Trackings: The Body's Memory, The Heart's Fiction* (Boulder: Dead Metaphor Press).

➤ **ANDREW RADFORD** is currently lecturing in nineteenth and twentieth century literature at the University of Durham, UK. He is completing a book-length study on Hardy's abiding interest in Victorian sciences of humankind, especially geology, archaeology and anthropology.

➤ **MARTIN RAY** teaches at Aberdeen University. He is the editor of the *Thomas Hardy Journal* and is a TTHA Vice President. His works include *Thomas Hardy: A Textual Study of the Short Stories* (1997), *Thomas Hardy: A Variorum Concordance to the 'Complete Poems'* (1998), *Joseph Conrad: Interviews and Recollections* (1990) and *Joseph Conrad* (1993). He also wrote *Thomas Hardy: An Annotated Critical Bibliography* with R. P. Draper, and his revised edition of Conrad's *Chance* is about to appear in the OUP World's Classics series. He has also published over fifty chapters and articles on such authors as Ford Madox Ford, Nathaniel Hawthorne, H.G. Wells and Arnold Bennett. He is currently working on a fully annotated edition of Hardy's *Complete Poems*.

➤ **ROBERT SCHWEIK** is Distinguished Teaching Professor and Faculty Exchange Scholar, Emeritus, of the State University of New York, College at Fredonia. He is Vice President of the Thomas Hardy Society (UK) and of TTHA. He is director of TTHA's ***Links*** which provides over 200 evaluations and hyperlinked connections to Hardy-related websites worldwide. He is also TTHA director of the *Members' Research Resources* Page which features a regularly updated *Checklist* of Hardy works – critical, literary and evaluative. His publications include a Critical Edition of *Far from the Madding Crowd* (Norton), *Reference Sources in English and American Literature* (Norton), *Hart Crane: A Descriptive Bibliography* (U of Pittsburgh Press), as well as over fifty book chapters and articles on Hardy, Robert Browning, J. S. Mill, Oscar Wilde, and various topics in Western intellectual and cultural history.

ADVERTISEMENTS
As featured on **TTHA PROMOTIONS** www.yale.edu/hardysoc

TO RENT: BEAUTIFUL BARTON BARN, West Stafford (Talbothays Country): contact Robert and Ruth Eshelby, 01305-269949 email : <RandR@barnarts.com>

TUPPENY COTTAGE, near Shaftesbury, in the heart of picturesque "Wessex"– spacious, comfortable, fully-equipped kitchen; sleeps 5; charming enclosed garden; close to extensive holiday facilities: Call Hugo: 0171 223 5461/email; hugo@gn.apc.org/Fax: 0207 223 5461

B & B at THE OLD RECTORY, Cornwall, where Hardy stayed and met Emma: Contact Sally Searle: 01840 250225/<sally@stjuliot.com>

STAY AT THE OLD MANOR, Kingston Maurward, Dorchester: Tel: (0)1305 261110/Fax: (0)1305 263734/<thomson@kingston-maurward.co.uk>

STAY AT THE CHANCEL, in the heart of Hardy country, Dorchester. Contact Chris or Heather: 0208-777-073/<ChrisRick@compuserve.com>

ADVERTISING RATES
for
The Hardy Review
Up to 3 lines: $25 (£16)
Half Page: $50 (£35)
Full page: $85 (£60), if predesigned
For advertising copy designed by TTHA there is an added charge of $30 (£20).
Copy and payment to be sent to the editor on floppy disk or e-attachment
Rosemarie Morgan
124 Bishop St
New Haven
CT 06511

"The Retreat"
BEAUTIFUL DORSET LONG HOUSE FOR RENT

Available for Summer Rental 2002
(April through September)
16th Century Dorset Long House
IN THE HEART OF HARDY COUNTRY

3 Bedrooms (1 queen w/en suite, 1 double, 1 twin), 2 Shower Rooms /wc, Parlour, Sitting Room, Great Room (w/snooker table & piano), Study, Dining Room w/Aga, Modern Kitchen w/all appliances , Solarium, Summer House w/table tennis & darts/ beautiful gardens.

In the Quiet, Exclusive Village of Frome St. Quintin, County of Dorset, U.K.
Equidistance (10 miles) to Dorchester, Yeovil & Sherborne. 16 miles to coast.

IDEAL for THREE COUPLES

$725 (500 LS) total per week – June/July/August
$600 (415 LS) per week – April/May/September
Photos on request – or view online at:
http://www.yale.edu/hardysoc/Promotions/annebob.htm

Contact Bob or Anne Hammond: E-mail address bh5705@btinternet.com
Phone: 44 (0) 1 193 583 086

Membership Form

THE THOMAS HARDY ASSOCIATION

Please photocopy this form, fill it in, and mail it with your check *made out to:*
Rosemarie Morgan 124, Bishop St, New Haven, CT 06511

Payment can be made using UK sterling checks and International money orders. Amount may vary according to the current rate of exchange.

NAME: ....
ADDRESS: ....
....

E-MAIL ....
PHONE NUMBER: ....
FAX NUMBER: ....
OCCUPATION:...
EDUCATION ....
INTERESTS: ....

....
IDEAS FOR SOCIETY ACTIVITIES: ....
....

MEMBERSHIP PRIVILEGES INCLUDE

- ➢ Receipt of the Hardy Society *Journal* : issued Feb/May/Oct: (dual membership only)
- ➢ Receipt of TTHA annual *Hardy Review*
- ➢ Receipt of TTHA Poetry Concordance, CDRom: *Please apply direct to Martin Ray: Order form on* www.yale.edu/hardysoc
- ➢ Access to Members Research Resources
- ➢ Advertising on TTHA PROMOTIONS page: *PROMOTIONS advertising is now $40 per annum to* TTHA *members: please add this fee to your renewal check*

FOR OFFICE USE ONLY

MEMBERSHIP NUMBER ASSIGNED: Expiration DATE: DIM:

THE THOMAS HARDY ASSOCIATION

MEMBERSHIP INFORMATION

Please go to http://www.yale.edu/hardysoc & read membership ordinances pertaining to TTHA, the Thomas Hardy Society & dual membership

A. **INDIVIDUALS APPLYING FOR DUAL MEMBERSHIP** with **TTHA** & The Thomas Hardy Society . . . . . $55.00/£45.00
B. **COUPLES APPLYING FOR DUAL MEMBERSHIP** with **TTHA** & The Thomas Hardy Society . . . . $60.00/£48.50
C. **STUDENT** (please state affiliation) **FOR DUAL MEMBERSHIP** with **TTHA** & The Thomas Hardy Society. . . . . . $36.00 /£28.00
D. **INDIVIDUALS APPLYING FOR MEMBERSHIP OF TTHA** (separately from the THSoc) . . . .$30. 00/£20.00
E. **COUPLES APPLYING FOR MEMBERSHIP OF TTHA** (separately from the THSoc) . . . .$40.00/£30.00
F. **STUDENT** (please state affiliation) **FOR MEMBERSHIP OF TTHA** (separately from the THSoc). . . . .$20.50/£18.00

TTHA MEMBERSHIP OFFERS THE FOLLOWING TO ALL

- Free copy of annual publication: *The Hardy Review*
- Membership option to purchase earlier editions of *The Review*: at half price (plus postage) & *Occasional Series*: $7.50/£5.00
- Free CD-Rom of the *Thomas Hardy Poetry Concordance* Please apply direct to Martin Ray giving your membership #
- <www.yale.edu/hardysoc/Order Form >
- Free UK snailmail service: see Martin Ray:
  < http://www.yale.edu/hardysoc>- VP BOX
- Reduced advertising fees on TTHA Promotions See PROMOTIONS page on www.yale.edu/hardysoc
- Access to TTHA Members Research Resources

DUAL MEMBERSHIP OFFERS THE FOLLOWING TO ALL

- All of the above plus three annual copies of:
  The Thomas Hardy Society *Journal*

THE THOMAS HARDY ASSOCIATION PUBLICATIONS

TTHA publications can be ordered by copying & returning this form with payment cheque *made out to:*
**Rosemarie Morgan,
124 Bishop Street, New Haven, CT 06511, USA**

Title . . . .
Qty . . . .

The Hardy Review, Vol I, (1998) ISBN: 0-9669176-0-X	£18/$25
The Hardy Review Vol II, (1999) ISBN: 0-9669176-3-4	£18/$25
The Hardy Review Vol III,(2000) ISBN: 0-9669176-5-0	£18/$25
The Hardy Review Vol IV,(2001) ISBN: 0-9669176-7-7	£18/$25

Days to Recollect: Essays in Honour of Robert Schweik
ISBN:0-9669176-4-2   £25/ $36

Human Shows: Essays in Honour of Michael Millgate
ISBN: 0-9669176-2-6   £25/$36

Occasional Series, Vol I: Editing Hardy (1999)
ISBN: 0-9669176-1-8   £10/$15
Occasional Series, Vol II: Emma Poems (2001)
ISBN: 0-9669176-6-9   £10/$15

Postage & Packing per volume: £4.50/$5.50

Grand Total . . . . ._____
. . . . . .

Title: ....
First Name: ....
LastName: ....
Department: ....
Position: ....
Establishment: Address:...
....
Town................................. Zip/Postcode: ....
Country: ....Telephone: ....
Date: ....   Signature: ....
DISCOUNT to TTHA Members: 50% off all TTHA publications

THE THOMAS HARDY ASSOCIATION
TTHA Vice Presidents and Board of Directors

Gillian Beer: VP

Elena Carp: VP: *News From Romania*

Betty Cortus: VP: *Forum Moderator*
<Hardycor@owl.csusm.edu>

Shanta Dutta: VP: *News From India*
< shanta_dutta16@yahoo.com>

Ralph Elliott: VP
<Ralph.elliott@anu.edu.au>

James Gibson: VP: *Poetry Consultant*
<JamesGibson@ukgateway.net>

Sumiko Inoue: VP: *News from Japan*
<ks-inoue@mx2.nisiq.net>

Yasushi Kamiyama: VP

Suzanne Keen: VP: *Student Journal* General Editor/*Elections* Director
<Skeen@wlu.edu>

Seth Lachterman: VP: *Network Consultant* < <slach@bcn.net>

Rosemarie Morgan: *President/The Hardy Review* Editor/*Resources* Page Director/*Maps* Page Director/*News Updates* Director/*Bibliography* Page Director/*Promotions* Page Director/
<Rm82@pantheon.yale.edu>

William Morgan: VP/*Executive* Vice President/*Poetry* Page Director
<wwmorgan@mail.ilstu.edu>

Richard Nemesvari: VP
Life Page Director
<rnemesva@stfx.ca>

Linda Peterson: VP
<Linda.peterson@yale.edu>

Birgit Plietzsch: VP: *Novels* Page Director/*Internet Asst/*
<bp10@st-andrews.ac.uk>

Martin Ray: VP:*Short Stories* Page Director
<Enl090@abdn.ac.uk>

Shannon Rogers: VP: *Book Reviews* Page Director
<srogers@sju.edu >

Robert Schweik: VP: *Links* Page Director /*Syllabi* Page Director/ MRR – *Checklist* Page Director
<schweik@fredonia.edu>

Rosemary Sumner: VP:
Student Journal European Editor

Dennis Taylor: VP: *Poetry Consultant*<Taylor@bc.edu>

Keith Wilson: VP: *Drama* Page Director
<Kgwilson@uottawa.ca>

Ling Zhang: VP

The Hardy Review

Volume V Winter 2002

THE HARDY REVIEW

EDITED BY

ROSEMARIE MORGAN

THE HARDY ASSOCIATION PRESS
ISBN 0-9669176-8-5

First published in the United States in 2002
by The Hardy Association Press
124 Bishop Street, New Haven, CT 06511

© Copyright for the collection is retained by the Hardy Association
Press. Copyright for individual essays is retained by the author.

All rights reserved. No part of this publication
may be reproduced, stored in a retrieval system,
or transmitted in any form or by any means,
electronic, mechanical, photocopying,
recording or otherwise without the
prior permission of the Copyright holders.

ISBN 0-9669176-8-5

Typesetting & cover design by Rosemarie Morgan.
Designed and originated in-house.
Printed by Goodcopy Inc, NewHaven

THE THOMAS HARDY ASSOCIATION

PRESIDENT:
ROSEMARIE MORGAN
www.yale.edu/hardysoc

EDITORIAL BOARD

James Gibson	Christchurch Coll. Canterbury
Rosemarie Morgan	Yale University
William W. Morgan	Illinois State University
Richard Nemesvari	St Francis Xavier University
Linda Peterson	Yale University
Martin Ray	Aberdeen University
Robert Schweik	SUNY at Fredonia
Keith Wilson	University of Ottawa

THE HARDY REVIEW
Editor: Rosemarie Morgan

Volume V   Winter 2002

Copyright is retained by TTHA. Individual items will not be reproduced without the author's permission. Contributors may reclaim their work for inclusion in book publication

CONTENTS

List of Illustrations.	ii
Editor's Column.	iii

TTHA POETRY DISCUSSION GROUP : -   1

❖ "The Dark-Eyed Gentleman."	2
❖ "She At His Funeral," and "Her Confession."	8
❖ "Tess's Lament," and "The Pine Planters."	13
❖ "The Pink Frock," and "The Beauty."	19
❖ "The Chapel Organist."	26
❖ "A Sunday Morning Tragedy."	32
❖ "A Trampwoman's Tragedy."	35

TTHA FORUM DISCUSSION GROUP : -   40

❖ Hardy's Tragic Heroes.	41
❖ Biblical Allusions in *Tess*.	51
❖ Possible New Hardy Poems.	62

Poems by Isobel Robin: "The Haunting," "The Little Bottle Shop"   90

PAPERS FROM THE "HARDY AND DANCE" SYMPOSIUM : -   93

❖ Jan Lloyd-Jones, "In the Whirl and Wildness of the Dance."	96
❖ Roy Buckle, "Mop Ollamoor's Reel."	105
❖ Eugene Davis, "Dance Songs: A Meaningful Hybrid in . . ."	113
❖ Philip Allingham, "An Illustrated Discussion . . . "	122
❖ David Havird, "'The Commonwealth of Hearts & Hands . . .'"	135

RESEARCH PAPERS AND ESSAYS :-

Martin Ray, "*The Life and Work of Thomas Hardy:* Allusions . . . ."	145
Andrew Radford, "The Marriage of Ancient & Modern in . . . "	184
Betty Cortus, "The Cycle of Regeneration."	193

Poem by William W. Morgan: "Contract Holdout."	201
Poem by Joanne Schweik: "Those Autumns."	202
Notes on Contributors	205
TTHA Information and Membership Form	209

ILLUSTRATIONS

Vignette by Hardy: "She At His Funeral," *Wessex Poems*.	12
Vignette by Hardy: "She To Him," *Wessex Poems*.	39
E. J. Detmold: Illustration to "About Lizards."	71
E. J. Detmold: Illustration to "Yellow-Hammer."	73
Illustration by Hardy, "Soldier's Joy."	95
Gordon Smith, "Cremorne Gardens."	106
"Country Dancing," Anon.	112
"The Girl I Left Behind Me," arranged by W. E. Davis.	120
"The Sergeant's Song, " arranged by W. E. Davis.	121
Charles S. Reinhart, "Margery and the Baron."	123
Robert Barnes, "Farfrae Footing a Quaint Little Dance..."	124
William Hatherell, "She Chanced to Pause on the Bridge..."	125
Dunster Church Tomb.	193
Vignette by Hardy: "Her Immortality," *Wessex Poems*.	201
Agnes Miller Parker, Illustration to *The Return of the Native*.	202
Hardy's Drawing of the West Gallery at Stinsford Church.	203
West Gallery of Puddletown Church.	204

EDITOR'S COLUMN

ROSEMARIE MORGAN

WELCOME to the fifth volume in the Hardy Association's annual series: *The Hardy Review*. Over the past year, since the publication of Volume IV in 2001, TTHA's activities have, as ever, burgeoned in all directions and at such an increasing pace that recruiting new directors has, yet again, become a necessity.

While Professor Shannon Rogers' appointment to the directorship of TTHA's innovative "Book Reviews" page[1] added a vital new dimension to the ever-expanding "Members' Research Resource" (MRR), and while she was diligently learning HTML and FLASH in order to web-design her own page, so yet another new initiative – Bob Schweik's "Checklist" – was growing, cuckoo-wise, far too mighty for the Schweikian nest which still nurtures the famed "Links" page.[2] The "Checklist," an ever-evolving bibliography, updated twice-monthly, fuelled by an international team of sixteen Hardy scholars, is now the prodigy of bibliographies: no other in existence can match it for its currency, immediacy and comprehensiveness.

On the other hand, by 2002 "Links" was sporting over 300 hyperlinked Hardy-related subpages – each one evaluated succinctly (no easy task), in a single paragraph in order to save researchers wasting their time in tracking down "Hardy" sites that might not always prove useful to their researches. Clearly the time has come to relieve Bob (at his request) of the more established of his pedigree stock – time for "Links" to move on to a new directorship. This, after careful planning at TTHA, will be implemented at the earliest opportunity.

Alongside these developments, and moving into a completely new field altogether, TTHA has also, recently, entered the world of book

---

[1] http://www.yale.edu/hardysoc/Welcome/welcomet.htm – also for the "Checklist." Grateful thanks for prompt technical support from Birgit Plietzsch.
[2] http://www.yale.edu/hardysoc/Links/linksone/Links.htm

collections. Actually, this hit me right out of the blue. I'd received an e-mail from David Cosgrove a few months ago asking if he could donate to TTHA his copy of an early work on Hardy – *Life and Art* by Hardy's (temporary) friend, Ernest Brennecke. I have to admit that I was not in the least "surprised by joy" – rather by panic. I had no idea what I should do with such a gift nor did I want to take responsibility for it. I tried persuading David to donate it to Yale's Beinecke Library or, possibly, the Dorset County Museum, but he was adamant. TTHA had to have it. Accordingly, I took the matter to my colleagues and Bill Morgan came to the rescue. TTHA, he said, would start a book collection: a collection of early Hardy criticism.

And so we did. We made several investigations and finally Bill approached curator, Professor Steven Meckstroth at Milner Library (ILSU) who responded to the proposal with prompt and spirited enthusiasm. Within a matter of weeks The Thomas Hardy Association Collection of Early Hardy Criticism was born: it would be housed at Milner Library under the dedicated care of Steve Meckstroth – and the official inauguration would take place at the end of April in Illinois. As of now, as we go to press, I'm planning to drive to Illinois from New Haven, arriving on the scene with my car absolutely stacked (I hope) with recent donations of books![3]

While all this activity has been buzzing in the e-corridors of TTHA so too has the organisation of the joint hosting of a mini-conference: "Hardy in Cambridge" at Magdalene College in July. This convention is a significant "First." For many years TTHA has been supporting the Hardy Society (UK) behind the scenes – providing dual memberships, aiding and advising at conferences, promoting and advertising the Society – its St Juliot Appeal, Essay Contests, London Lectures, its Max Gate tours: in sum, generating interest via its world-wide membership and internet presence. Now, for the first time in the history of both organisations, we come together, in collaboration, thanks to the Society's newly elected Council (2002) and its "Way Forward" planning committee. It is a privilege and a compliment to the Hardy Association that every one of the conference lecturers is a director of TTHA.

Each speaker will touch on topics related to the manuscript holdings at Cambridge – notably the *Jude* MS, *Time's Laughingstocks* and *Moments of Vision*.[4] For the more romantic of conferees there are the candle-lit dinners, the summer nights punting on the River Cam,

---

[3] So far about two dozen books have been donated: see
http://www.yale.edu/hardysoc/Welcome/COLLECTION.htm

[4] See the Cambridge Agenda at:: http://www.yale.edu/hardysoc/agendaca.htm

the glories of King's College choir and the sylvan glades Hardy also meandered through on his visits to his beloved, poet-philosopher friend, Horace Moule.[5]

As if this were not quite enough activity for the irrepressible TTHA there was now the proposal, from one of TTHA's most loyal and hardworking members, Sarah Bird Wright,[6] that the Association should present a Session at the next MLA conference in San Diego, in December 2003. Sarah (Committee Woman *extraordinaire*) had discovered that not a *single Hardy session* had taken place at MLA meetings over the past decade. Accordingly, she promptly took charge of the entire operation and what was initially a rather scattered group of TTHA Laodiceans is now a gathered team of devotees. As I write we are all still grappling with protocols, paper outlines and who does what where and when, but, undoubtedly, we will all come through with flying colours when the day comes. Professor Linda Peterson[7] has agreed to be our Session Leader – a great boon to the erstwhile Laodicean.

Aside from these "matters of consequence," TTHA's intellectually stimulating discussion groups, namely the "Forum"[8] and "The Poem of the Month" (POTM[9]), continue to thrive under the expert directorship of Betty Cortus and Bill Morgan respectively. A small selection of these lively exchanges comprise the first half of this issue (1-62); they range from discussions on Hardy's use of female personae in his verse (1-35), to the role of the tragic heroes in his fiction (41), to biblical allusions in *Tess* (51), and to putative Hardy poems – that is, the renowned "Baby" poems composed for the Detmold books (62).

In keeping with my previous editorial practice with *The Hardy Review* I have tried to preserve the spontaneity and vigour of the original online conversations while at the same time ensuring the linear clarity expected of edited scholarly writing. In my efforts to reconcile these somewhat conflicting ends I have corrected commonplace errors of spelling and punctuation, clarified the documentation if and where necessary and, occasionally, restructured the online dialogues in the interests of coherency and linearity (frequently, several online topics will be running at once; similarly, several voices might cross one another). I have retained, as far as possible, the "voice" and style

---

[5] See: http://www.yale.edu/hardysoc/magdalen.htm

[6] Sarah Bird Wright is author of *Thomas Hardy – A to Z: The Essential Reference to His Life and Work* (Facts on File, Inc. 2002)

[7] See: http://www.yale.edu/hardysoc/VPBOX/linda.htm

[8] http://www.yale.edu/hardysoc/Welcome/Forum/forum.htm

[9] Poem Of The Month: http://www3.ftss.ilstu.edu/hardysoc/poemonth.htm

of individual speakers, including their abbreviations, contractions, and symbols; it is not my wish or intention to render uniform the style and content of free self-expression. On the contrary, it is precisely the preservation of that quality of spontaneity, informality, open confrontation and impromptu response, characteristic of online debates, that distinguishes *The Hardy Review* as an organ promoting a unique form of seminar rarely to be found in the classroom or in reportage. To enhance these qualities longwinded or repetitious material has been pruned: this is marked in the text by means of ellipses.

The poets featured here are already well established. Isobel Robin (90), whose work first appeared in *The Hardy Review, Vol I*, 1998, and in subsequent editions, has recently celebrated her first major publication, *Freud's Back-Yard* (Five Island's Press, 2002). We are proud to present her two poems, "The Haunting" (*FBY*) and "The Bottle Shop": the latter has not yet been collected and Robin fears it may be rather too frivolous for a scholarly publication, but she is in good company here: Hardy felt much the same about several of *his* poems. Bill Morgan's new poem, "Contract Holdout," may also form part of a future collection (201), and Joanne Schweik's "Those Autumns" (202) was chosen from a selection of her verse because it aptly complements Hardy's own preoccupations with time and change.

The section entitled "Symposium Papers" (93) comprises short papers presented at the "Hardy and Dance" Symposium, Dorchester, August, 2002. These pieces represent student research and work-in-progress except in the case of Professor W. Eugene Davis whose customised presentation is researched and written specifically for the Symposium "sing-song" which concludes this popular event (113).

Succeeding these papers Martin Ray offers one of his exceptionally fine pieces of scholarly research – in this instance, a detailed, annotated compilation of Hardy's allusions in the *Life* (145). Andrew Radford's essay follows on the *Laodicean* in which any illusions about Hardy's resistance to new technology are convincingly rebutted (184). Concluding this section on scholarly research papers, "The Cycle of Regeneration," by Betty Cortus (193) returns to one of her favourite themes, Hardy's treatment of metamorphosis and transcendence

In bringing this annual number together I have kept in mind, at all times, that first and foremost ours is a celebration of Thomas Hardy and of those of his followers who so treasure his literary endowment that they are prepared to give freely of their time, and generously of their scholarly expertise – in trust and appreciation, to TTHA.[10]

---

[10] I am deeply indebted to Martin Ray for giving of his precious time and energy to scrupulous proofreading; if errors there be, they are mine alone.

THE THOMAS HARDY ASSOCIATION POETRY DISCUSSION GROUP

AN OVERVIEW OF TTHA POETRY PAGE
William W. Morgan
wwmorgan@ilstu.edu

THE THOMAS HARDY ASSOCIATION'S Poetry Page (POTM) has undergone two changes since my last report here: We are now using WebBoard for the Poem of the Month discussions (instead of NetForum), and the main page now has a different look and better functionality (http://www3.ftss.ilstu.edu/hardysoc/). The transition to WebBoard is almost complete. I still need to reconstruct some of the older NetForum discussions and post them at the site, but as of this writing there are thirteen discussions available at:
  http://webboard.ilstu.edu/~TTHA_POTM_DISCUSSIONS/
I encourage visitors to the site to be curious and patient about learning the new software, since it has some substantial advantages over NetForum. And I want to thank Illinois State University for allowing TTHA to use its licensed copy of WebBoard for our monthly conversations. The POTM discussions themselves remain lively, insightful, disciplined, and vigorous exchanges that are a pleasure to read and participate in – as readers will see when they read the nine discussions about Hardy's poems with female narrators that are reprinted below.

The new, more efficient Poetry Page now has links to *Authoritative Texts* (Dennis Taylor's essay comparing the Hynes and Gibson editions of Hardy's poems); to *Collecting Hardy's Poetry* (Mark Simons's well-illustrated and thoughtful guide to first, collected, and significant other editions of Hardy's poetry); to *Teaching Hardy's Poetry* (offering a questionnaire for teachers of Hardy's poetry at all grade levels and another WebBoard for discussion of teaching issues). The *Teaching* division still seems to me to be under-used, so I would particularly invite readers' attention to it. And, as before, I would be pleased to hear from scholars who might want to direct a division of the Poetry Page devoted to *Translations, Musical Settings, and Performances* of Hardy's poems.

SUMMARIES AND SAMPLES OF THE POEM OF THE MONTH (POTM)
DISCUSSIONS
December 2000-August 2001

IN preparing these discussions for print publication, I have tried, as I usually do, to preserve the character of the original conversations while bringing them closer to the standard of edited scholarly writing. In pursuing these two goals, I have sometimes silently corrected obvious errors and have omitted extraneous matter such as personal greetings and the like. But I have tried to preserve the "voice" of each posting as it appeared at the site: hence, if the writer used contractions, abbreviations, and the like, I have retained them in my edited version of the posting. If one writer used single quotes and another double ones, I have left their choices as they made them rather than trying to impose uniformity. Likewise with styling and spelling (UK vs. US): I have preserved the original writers' choices. I hope that readers of the *Review* will find that these discussions have the vigor of informal intellectual conversations and the linear clarity of professional writing.

Welcome to the TTHA Poem of the Month discussions for

December 2000 through August 2001.

—Bill Morgan

THE DARK-EYED GENTLEMAN

Fri Dec 1 9:20:11 US/Central 2000
BILL MORGAN <wwmorgan@ilstu.edu>
Introducing "The Dark-Eyed Gentleman"[1]

This poem is the first in a series of female-narrated Hardy poems that I plan to offer for our discussion here over the next few months. Although Hardy's interest in actual women and in femaleness as a dimension of human experience has been a major preoccupation of his biographers and of the critics of his fiction, his female-centered poetry has received surprisingly little attention; perhaps the POTM discussions for the next months can go some way towards remedying that deficiency.

There are many female-narrated Hardy poems: setting aside all the pieces in which women are central characters and all the others in which they have major dramatic or narrative roles to play, there are still more than 60 titles in Hardy's body of work that belong entirely

---

[1] *The Complete Poems of Thomas Hardy*, edited by James Gibson (Macmillan London, Ltd, 1976) 243. Hereafter *CP*

to female voices. And they range in date from his earliest pieces (e.g., the four "She, to Him" sonnets of 1866) to poems probably of a very late date (e.g., "We Field-Women" from *Winter Words*). They also vary widely in kind: there are ballads (such as "A Trampwoman's Tragedy," "A Sunday Morning Tragedy," and possibly this month's poem?); there are memorial poems in which the dead woman speaks (such as "The Haunter," "His Visitor," and "The Spell of the Rose" in which the spirit of his dead wife Emma is the speaker); there are laments over various kinds of losses (e.g., "Autumn in King's Hintock Park" and "A Wife Waits"); and there are monologues in verse by characters from his fiction (e.g., "Tess's Lament" and "The Pine Planters"). Clearly, Hardy believed he purchased some kind of emotional or artistic advantage by writing poems in a female voice. What can we as readers and commentators say to articulate the motives for and effects of his choices? Here are some issues to consider that, while they relate mainly to this month's poem, may also lead us to some insights into the more general topic:

1. Is the narrator's class as significant as her gender in determining her attitude towards her experience?
2. What does it mean that most if not all of Hardy's female narrators are concerned with the place of love and sexual experience in their lives?
3. What does it mean that these female narrators so often have remarkable powers of endurance?
4. What does it mean that Hardy's female narrators are almost all presented as sympathetic characters?

Mon Dec 4 14:59:20 US/Central 2000
BETTY CORTUS <hardycor@mailhost2.csusm.edu>
subject: Female Narrators

The subject of Hardy's female narrators in the poems is a fascinating one, and one that, as Bill has pointed out, is overdue for serious study. One of the effects that Hardy achieves through this and several other related poems is to project his own non-judgmental, even sympathetic approach to what the rest of society might deem "the fallen woman." Although the speaker in "The Dark-Eyed Gentleman" bewails her plight at first, years later, in retrospect, she sees her lapse as nothing more than an almost forgotten "slip" (line 16), and for her the wages of sin are ultimately far more rewarding than punitive. Similarly unrepentant is the irrepressible Julie-Jane in the poem named for her. Dying in childbirth she chooses her bearers from her "fancy-men." Although she is not the principal speaker of the poem her own words are quoted in stanza six:

> 'I suppose,' with a laugh, she said,
> 'I should blush that I'm not a wife;
> But how can it matter, so soon to be dead,
> What one does in life!'[2]

Even more insouciant in spite of her lost reputation is 'Melia in "The Ruined Maid." Then, in another example, Eve Greensleeves in "Voices from Things Growing in a Churchyard," who in real life "was the handsome mother of two or three illegitimate children" according to Hardy's note, seems to actually regain her virtue in her after-life transformation to "innocent withwind." The yielding nature and fecundity of this woman, who in life had been "[k]issed by men from many a clime," has undergone a purifying metamorphosis to the pliancy of a vine, whose fruitfulness, in the manner of the plant world, is now dependent on her passive, and freshly innocent submission to the kisses and caresses of pollinating insects. Through the voices of these four women, at least, Hardy reveals his belief that the loss of womanly virtue is a very human condition, that it may even bring its own rewards, and that it need not exclude ultimate redemption if only after death.

Surely Hardy was ahead of most of his contemporaries in his tolerance of, and perhaps even admiration for, the resilient female narrators in these particular poems. Betty Cortus

Sat Dec 30 13:36:18 US/Central 2000
SULEIMAN H. AHMAD <smahmad@mail.sy>
subject: Motherhood in Women's Lives

The ballad-like poem "The Dark-Eyed Gentleman," one of "A Set of Country Songs" in *Time's Laughingstocks*, underscores the importance of motherhood in women's lives. For the speaker, mothering compensates for the pain and social stigma of becoming a fallen woman and for the difficulties of being a poor single parent. Her son is all what an ideal son should be: "My own dearest joy is he, comrade, and friend, / He it is who safe-guards me, on him I depend."

Unlike Tess's son, "No sorrow brings he." Apparently she has brought him up very well, treating him as "comrade, friend." Well done! one finds oneself saying in response. Still, one wonders at the

---

[2] *CP*, 245-246

ease and speed of her falling into temptation. The few details she gives may suggest why: coming home "'Twixt sunset and moonrise" after a long day of gleaning in the fields, she, a maiden, encounters a handsome gentleman who has "a winning tongue" (to quote M.G. Lewis's ballad: "The Banks of Allan Water") and is ready to use his hands in a way that shows that he is no novice in love-making. The intimate contact of tying up her garter leads to the yielding of her virginity to the complete stranger. The fact that she becomes pregnant immediately indicates that she had been ready for impregnation and consequently easily aroused. As the narrator of *The Well-Beloved* puts it, "Nature was working her plans for the next generation"[3]; and what matters for Nature in this case is the fertilization of the girl's egg to ensure the survival of the human species. From the natural, as opposed to the social, point of view and judged by results, the girl may be looked at as lucky: the cross-fertilization[4] is perhaps responsible for the production of the "fine lissom lad," a combination of peasant and middle-class stocks and the fruit of what seems to have been a satisfying sexual experience. It is significant that the speaker is not resentful but thankful and affectionate: notice her use of the word "dear" each time she refers to her anonymous lover. His disappearance soon after the sexual encounter is an action which is not uncommon among the males of the species. He leaves her to fend for herself. As in all seductions that lead to pregnancy, it is the woman who pays.[5] A brave girl, she weathers the storm of social opprobrium and raises her child single-handedly. She endures, no doubt helped by motherhood. As a mother who cares for her offspring, she is bound to win sympathy and respect. Many, if not the majority, would take the tolerant position expressed in "The Husband's View"[6]:

> Misfortunes are no crime:
>
> 'And what with our serious need
> Of sons for soldiering,
> That accident, indeed,
> To maids, is a useful thing!'

Suleiman M. Ahmad

---

[3] Thomas Hardy, *The Well–Beloved*. New Wessex Edition, p. 102

[4] "Cross-fertilisation" is the fertilisation of one species by a different species, say a human male with a bovine species, hence the mythic Minotaur. The inference here is not clear. – ed.

[5] See also *Jude* for a contrasting perspective; the male also pays -- ed.

[6] *CP*, 248-249

Sun Dec 3 12:37:50 US/Central 2000
DAVID M. CLARK <dclark@udc.es>
subject: Class, Gender and the Corn King

It seems to me that both class and gender are inextricably linked in this poem, and the narrator's response to her situation reflects a stoicism which is implicitly a-temporal. The reference to the "leazings" in the first line, and the phonological relationship of this word with the adjective "lissom", which the narrator uses to describe her child, bring to mind the concept of fertility through the Corn King. The poem seems to imply a mythical quality in the relationship, whilst at the same time projecting an idea of the independence of the female character who is able, it is implied, to raise her child without the financial or emotional aid of her lover. Both class and gender are foregrounded in this poem, which seems to transcend its form in order to create an enduring vision. David Clark

Tue Dec 5 13:00:40 US/Central 2000
PHILIP ALLINGHAM <philip.allingham@lakehead.ca>
subject:"The Dark-Eyed Gentleman": Comus, not Satan

In the "Preface" to *Time's Laughingstocks* (1909), Thomas Hardy identifies the form of many of these poems collected from periodicals "as dramatic monologues by different characters." He adds that these monologues tend "to take the reader forward, even if not far, rather than backward." In that "The Dark-Eyed Gentleman" follows the objectively narrated "After the Fair" (1902) and first-person-voiced "To Carrey Clavel," this poem begins ominously but ends optimistically, contributing a lighter tone and mood to the sequence about country girls. The opening line establishes our speaker as an agricultural labourer by her "day's leazings" (bundle of gleaned corn), but certainly "lithe" (flexible, supple) enters the mind of the average reader unaccustomed to Dorset dialect. Perhaps, by implication, she is adaptable, able to adjust to circumstances, even able to adjust her morality and her outlook. The "dear" man (expensive, costly, well-dressed, but one whose flatteries and attentions will cost the speaker dearly in society's eyes) is specifically a "gentleman," a member—at least, in appearance and utterance—of the master class, and attractive to the speaker, "dark-eyed," a not unwelcome partner sent by chance, and, at least initially, malignant fate. She implies she was a willing participant at the moment; she later reveals herself disinclined to dwell on the past; indeed, the present and the moment are comfortable to her. He is a creature of the twilight, of deceptive appearances and seductive eyes, accosting the speaker "Twixt sunset and moonrise." He is barely quoted; he is not an individual, but a type, a darkling who catches the maiden between waking and dreaming, a Comus rather than a Satan whose single remark reveals his opportunistic and sensual nature. Indeed, the "dear gentleman" could be construed as the archetypal stranger who takes from the maiden consecrated to Astarte-Diana, goddess of the moon and the menstrual cycle, what nevermore she will find; she is impregnated by the anonymous traveller, an agent of fructifying nature.

By the end of the second stanza, the persona is a plaintiff "Tess," sobbing at her fate, cast off, alienated, self-pitying — bitter and sobbing, by her own description. She is "Tess," violated and abandoned, potentially an object of derision and scorn —"the ruined maid." But she is a working girl who has been equipped with both the skills and morality to make her own way in the world — "I can mind" reveals that the second stanza is her version of herself recollected, as she was when she first realized all that the encounter had "brought."

Time draws the curtain; the years slip by in the white space between stanzas two and three. She makes no direct comment about her experiences as an unwed mother-to-be; if of a pessimistic turn of mind, the reader may imagine that she faced what Tess faces after Alec D'Urberville has had his way with her in The Chase. But such a reflex of thought is probably not what Hardy intended; we are to move "forward, not backward." The adaptive former-maiden does not dwell on the intervening events; her boy is specifically "lissom" (lithe, agile, and supple) like his mother. Both he and she are amazingly free of society's taint; "No sorrow brings he." He is not, like Tess's child, a "Sorrow" but a blessing unmixed: comrade, friend, protector, and supporter.

The potential for tragedy has been unrealized, even though the persona is a member of the underclass whose body like her labour (her "leazings" imply low-paid agricultural work) has been exploited by the master-class. Her resiliency is her defining characteristic; she mourns momentarily, but is not excessively reflective or maudlin. Life goes on, and she goes with it.

That surely is the value that Hardy sees in her and wants us, his middle-class, educated readership (much of it, presumably, male at the time he wrote and for the periodical text in which he published) to see: an essentially optimistic outlook that refuses to allow life to be blighted by what cannot be mended if broken, or found if lost.

Philip Allingham

SHE AT HIS FUNERAL & HER CONFESSION

Sun Dec 31 20:27:23 US/Central 2000
BILL MORGAN <email:wwmorgan@ilstu.edu>
subject: Introducing "She At His Funeral" and "Her Confession"[7]

WHAT can we say about not only the two lyrics here cited for discussion but also about the larger group they represent — a group which, Hardy says in the *Life and Work*, was once a good deal larger, before much of the longer "She, To Him" sequence, in Hardy's word, "perished"[8]). Here are some more specific questions:

1. What does it tell us about his self-concept as a poet in the 1860s to early 1870s that he gave over a good deal of his energy to the creation of female speakers discoursing on a variety of themes? "She At His Funeral" seems to be an early treatment of the idea that moral respectability is not reliably linked to sexual conventionality — a theme that surfaced more than once in last month's discussion of "The Dark-Eyed Gentleman." "Her Confession," on the other hand, seems to be an effort to explore the psychology of love from a female perspective. And the other poems of the period take up some additional themes. In hindsight, it looks as if Hardy is "practicing" for the creation of the female characters and gendered issues in his novels, but that can't have been his intention before he ever thought of writing a novel. What is the best explanation for his choice?

2. Even though we are talking about female voices in these poems, their titles might be seen to register a male, female, or ungendered authorial presence that stands outside the text and names the experience as gendered female: "*Her* Confession," "*She* At His Funeral," and so forth. Who speaks those titles and takes responsibility for their gender specificity? If we read that presence as Hardy's, are we being too literally biographical? If the titles don't belong to Hardy, to whom or what do we assign them?

3. And finally, with the exception of "From Her in the Country," all these female narrators are concerned exclusively with love. Is this fact a mark of Hardy's own gender? Perhaps like most men he knows women only as they figure most prominently in his life and imagination – that is, as lovers. If so, do we call this limited

---

[7] *CP*, 12-13 & 234 respectively

[8] Thomas Hardy, *The Life and Work of Thomas Hardy*, ed. Michael Millgate (London: Macmillan, 1984), 55. Hereafter *Life and Work*.

vision a kind of egotism on his part, or do we congratulate him for writing about only what he can know? Bill

Fri Jan 5 15:14:21 US/Central 2001
WILEY CLEMENTS <susque@jdweb.com>
subject: She at His Funeral and Her Confession

Bill, you have set up three very good questions, to none of which I am a qualified respondent. So I confine myself to admiring these further examples of Hardy's genius with rhyme: the perfect symmetry of the scheme in "She at His Funeral" and the surprising (to me) success of his rhyming *a debtor says* with *forgetfulness* in "Her Confession." I do not recall reading either of these pieces before. Thanks for bringing them to my attention. Wiley

Wed Jan 10 12:15:24 US/Central 2001
PHILIP ALLINGHAM <philip.allingham@lakeheadu.ca>
subject: Glimpses of Greatness.

We may call these "She" poems collectively "A Glimpse of Greatness or Enlightenment Yet to Come." Enlightenment or enlarged understanding does not always equal greatness, but these early sketches of the female psyche offer us a glimpse of that greatness of artistic achievement that is the company of Hardy's female protagonists, a line that stretches from Fancy Day through Eustacia Vye to Tess Durbeyfield and Sue Bridehead .... In "She at His Funeral," the third person pronouns in the title immediately suggest a determination to sketch in a type and a fascinating situation that might arise .... in any culture.

The "She" and "His" suggest a portrait painter or photographer capturing the young woman's image ... what thoughts lie beneath that anguished surface? The persona, in each case, clearly a young woman, speaks directly to us in an interior monologue without any male consciousness mediating ..... In the first case, our sympathies are directed towards the poor girl who suffers so because, although treated like a "stranger" by the dead man's family (who without genuine feeling are going through the appropriate, middle-class, socially-sanctioned funeral routines), her grief is more than superficial and her "regret consumes like fire!" The climactic line conveys the success of the sketch: what-ever the gender of the reader, s/he feels exactly what the poet feels his subject feels.

The second poem, "Her Confession," directs our sympathies away from the feigning, supercilious beauty who waived her would-be lover's "proffered kiss / With quick divergent talk ... to enhance [her]

bliss." We are put off by her egocentricity: the relationship is "all about her"... from the male perspective she "owes" him affection in return for his investment of "long thought," and his looks are full of "consternation" when she makes no attempt to "pay." But appearance and reality once again diverge, as in "She at His Funeral," for her "uneagerness" to respond affectionately is as specifically "false" as the sorrow of the other mourners, their true feelings revealed by their dry ("griefless") eyes. If all these "shes" are alienated lovers (cut off, or cast off, or denying), isn't the young poet psychologically arrested, seeing women in only one role, the role that at that stage in his life he deems most important? Male ego does seem to lie at the heart of each situation. In a reversal of the poor man and the lady, in "She at His Funeral" the poor woman remains to offer up her love on the altar of the dead rich man. In "Her Confession," the rejected male lover struggles to understand the mentality of a beautiful woman who, although attracted to him, refuses to commit herself to him.

In the first poem of the "She to Him" sequence the poet picks up the theme of the injustice between lovers: if what principally attracts a young man to a young woman is her outward beauty how will each of the lovers feel when that physical attractiveness has faded and "heart concedes to mind"? In the second poem, the female, imagining herself dead and her lover in another relationship, upbraids him for forgetting her ... so easily dismissing her when something about the second woman reminds him of her. [Life is] a "fitful masquerade"... reducing the one dead to "A Thought." The injustice of the lover here does not anger us so much as make us feel the poignancy of the situation. Different kinds of alienation afflict the "shes" of the last two "She to Him" poems .... they are in very different circumstances and states of thought and feeling, so that the poems constitute variations on a psychological exercise that stems from a young man's simply asking himself, "How does a woman feel?"   Philip

Mon Jan 8 16:55:31 US/Central 2001
JOHN GOULD jgould@andover.edu
Subject: "She At His Funeral" (and "The Ruined Maid"?)[9]

I've thought a good deal about "She At His Funeral," because I've taught it and I've done a presentation about it some years ago. I find it extremely compelling as a lyric – compressed, tightly-wrought, built out of carefully balanced phrases moving back and forth.

There's a different poem I'd like to set it against, though: "The

---

[9] *CP*, 158-9

Ruined Maid." There, a country girl ... bumps into an old friend, a young woman that has left the "barton" and come to the city, where she is now "ruined." For her, this depiction means she is well dressed, eats fine food, and lives the good life – presumably all paid for by the man that keeps her. Her counrty sister is suitably impressed, and wants very much to be ruined herself. "The Ruined Maid" was written in 1863, a decade or more earlier than "She At His Funeral," and the later poem certainly suggests Hardy has had a sea change in his thinking about ruined women. Ruination is no longer a laughing matter. Lying still further ahead, of course, is Tess, whose ruin leads not merely to exclusion from a funeral party, but to death.

These remarks are sketchy, but they do suggest that Hardy's decision to take a woman's voice in "She At His Funeral" is a step in a progression of thought that began earlier and will go further, becoming more empathetic and more complex as it does so.   John Gould

Wed Jan 24 16:49:12 US/Central 2001
SULEIMAN AHMAD <smahmad@mail.sy>
subject: Hardy's Choice of Female Narrators

Hardy's choice of looking at experience from a female perspective in "She At His Funeral" and "Her Confession" seems to have come naturally to him. It was his "idiosyncratic mode of regard" — to use his own words in another context.[10] To account for this mode is a matter of conjecture, of course. According to the *Life and Work*, "a clue to much of his character and action throughout his life is afforded by his lateness of development in virility."[11] In the light of his biography, one is tempted to substitute "lack" for "lateness."

Women attracted him, and he loved them: Elizabeth Bishop ("Lizbie Browne"), Louisa Harding, Tryphena Sparks, Emma Gifford, Florence Henniker, etc. That love, however, seems to have been mainly in his imagination. Apparently he believed that "Love lives on propinquity, but dies of contact.[12] By loving women imaginatively rather than physically he developed an understanding of the female psyche which one would have attributed to a woman poet. Perhaps it was this understanding that made some early reviewers of the anonymously published *Far from the Madding Crowd* in the *Cornhill Magazine* uncertain of the gender of the writer.[13]   Suleiman

---

[10] *Life and Work*, 235
[11] Ibid, 37
[12] Ibid, 230
[13] Ibid, 100-101

Thu Feb 1 12:15:08 US/Central 2001
ELIZABETH HUGHES <hughese@rocky.edu>
subject: Stepping stones to greatness

I feel a bit timid posting here, as I'm only an undergrad English major, but if it weren't for Hardy, I wouldn't have gone in this particular direction with my schooling. I agree with what has previously been posted. Hardy does seem to be "practicing" in preparation for his ensuing psychological sculptures of the female mind —if anything, showing a sort of contrast between the Tess-Eustacia dichotomy – the lover almost pathetic in her steadfast qualities, vs. inconstant passion based from a love of power. Indeed, the second stanza of "Her Confession" brings to mind almost immediately the scene of Wildeve and Eustacia's first meeting on the Heath, when Wildeve departs:

"May I kiss your hand"
"Oh, no."
"May I shake your hand?"
"No."
"Then I wish you goodnight without caring for either."

Conversely, the vignette painted in "She at his funeral" seems to bring to mind Tess watching Angel's brothers, too frightened to introduce herself merely because she was selfconscious of her own appearance.

Watching these sketches, and then looking at his novels later in his life, seems to show a picture of the natural progression of any artist, starting small, practicing, and eventually creating amazing things of elaborate color and intricate design. Though perhaps the artist, when first experimenting with the pen, does not realize their exquisite doodles are a shadow of things to come.   Elizabeth

VIGNETTE BY HARDY ACCOMPANYING "SHE AT HIS FUNERAL," IN
WESSEX POEMS AND OTHER VERSES
(NEW YORK & LONDON: HARPER AND BROTHERS, 1898), 19. HEREAFTER *WESSEX POEMS*.

TESS'S LAMENT & THE PINE PLANTERS

Thu Feb 1 20:59:06 US/Central 2001
BILL MORGAN <wwmorgan@ilstu.edu>
subject: Introducing "Tess's Lament" and "The Pine Planters"[14]

FOR this month's conversation, I offer two poems that Hardy has invited us to read with characters from his novels in mind. But immediately I must qualify my statement by noting that "Tess's Lament" in the holograph is called simply "Lament," and "The Pine Planters" (part II only) appeared in the *Cornhill Magazine* (June 1903) with no reference to Marty South; at some point in its history, in other words, Hardy imagined each of the poems being read without reference to its respective novel.

1. Do the poems gain from their association with the novels, or are they better read on their own terms? With or without their connection to *Tess of the d'Urbervilles* and *The Woodlanders*, these poems obviously feature narrators who suffer considerable pain in their relations with men.
2. What value are we expected to attach to their suffering: are we expected to see it as heroic —or as perhaps masochistic? Both of these poems employ fairly intricate verse forms ("Tess's Lament" especially so) that feature a number of short lines. Are the short lines emotionally effective – perhaps more effective in one poem than in another?
3. There are six differences (in lines 8, 19, 35, 36, 37, and 48) between the Hynes and Gibson texts of "Tess's Lament."[15] These are interesting for what they reveal about Hardy's way of imagining his narrator in his holograph and first edition (as reprinted in Hynes) and later (as reprinted in Gibson). Two of the variants seem to be attempts to clarify rhythm and diction, but four of them turn on the question of the intensity of the speaker's dialect – whether Tess should say "O' my day's work," (Hynes) or "Of my day's work," (Gibson), "p'rhaps," or "perhaps," "all o'um," or "they all," "what they say o's now," or "what they say o'us now." I have followed Hynes in each case. As a reader of the poem, which narrative language do you prefer —one strongly

---

[14] *CP*, 175-177 & 271-273 respectively

[15] Note on the text: "Tess's Lament" is transcribed from *The Complete Poetical Works of Thomas Hardy*, I, ed. Samuel Hynes (Oxford: Clarendon, 1982) (hereafter *Hynes*) , cross-checked against the poem as it appears in *The Variorum Edition of the Complete Poems of Thomas Hardy*, ed. James Gibson (London: Macmillan, 1976).

flavored by dialect or one that is (mostly) standard English?

Bill Morgan

Fri Feb 2 18:07:33 US/Central 2001
BIRGIT PLIETZSCH <bp10@st-andrews.ac.uk>
subject: inter-textual relationship

I would like to offer some thoughts on the intertextual relationship between "Tess's Lament," "The Pine Planters," *The Woodlanders* and *Tess*. Reading these poems within the context of the respective novel offers background information on Hardy's female narrators but at the same time limits possibilities for their interpretation. It automatically draws the attention to particular characters and their history. Being told, for example, that "The Pine Planters" is narrated from the perspective of Marty South restricts the interpretation of the poem to the episode in *The Woodlanders* in which Giles and Marty are planting fir trees.

To reverse Bill's question of whether the poems gain from their association with the novels, I feel that "Tess's Lament" and "The Pine Planters" open up a wider context for the reading of each novel. They retrospectively add an emotional dimension to the fiction that is not expressed as clearly in the episodes to which they refer.   Birgit

Sat Feb 3 11:57:51 US/Central 2001
PATRICK ROPER <patrick@prassociates.co.uk>
subject: Pine Planter observations

I would like to make some comments on "The Pine Planters," especially in the light of Birgit Plietzsch's remarks. First, not having read *The Woodlanders* in its entirety for many years, on my first quick reading of "The Pine Planters" I assumed that Marty was a male – two men out planting trees. A more careful reading does show that Marty is a woman (or possibly a homosexual man), but much of the poem would be obscure to someone not familiar with *The Woodlanders*. This often seems to be the case with Hardy – it is necessary to know quite a bit about his life or work before a poem can be fully appreciated. And I think it is not only necessary to have read *The Woodlanders*. Many general readers would be likely to forget the pine planting section of the novel (as I had done) after a passage of time. In *The Woodlanders* the pine planting episode seems to me to be explicitly erotic whereas this aspect is scarcely in the poem and I wondered why Hardy had chosen to do this. The novel is earthy and sensuous using the pines and their foliage plainly as sexual analogies, but the feeling is far more wistful and dreamy in the poem.

I also have a rather more matter of fact observation on the trees themselves. In *The Woodlanders* Hardy refers to the saplings as pines or firs, then, in his moving final paragraph in *The Woodlanders*, as larches. Maritime pines and other exotic species were planted in Dorset in the 19th century, but I suspect that not many larches were. The real pine-planting rage did not get going until the two World Wars when there was considerable concern about the country running out of wood and being blockaded. This was especially so in regard to the supply of pit-props. Since Hardy wrote thousands of acres have been afforested with conifers and many of the woods and heaths with which he was familiar have disappeared under these alien species and the former associated wildlife has gone. I am sure Hardy would have been sensitive to this alteration of the traditional landscape for economic reasons, but I am not sure quite how it relates to the poem and the novel, especially as he seems slightly confused as to which sort of tree he means. Larches are deciduous and would not, therefore, have any needles through which the wind could sigh in winter. This creates a problem in both the poem and the novel. Perhaps TH really did mean pines, but if so why did he change their designation to larches at the end of *The Woodlanders*?   Patrick Roper

Sun Feb 4 12:35:22 US/Central 2001
PHILIP ALLINGHAM <philip.allingham@lakeheadu.ca>
Positioning "Tess's Lament" and "Marty South's Reverie"

Hardy's entitling the first poem "Tess's Lament" (which appeared in *Poems of the Past and the Present*, 1901) rather than merely "The Forsaken Maid's Lament" prompts the reader familiar with Hardy's prose works to compare the voice of the poem to that of Tess in the novel, and to search for clues in the verse as to where to "position" this complaint in the text of the novel. Clearly Hardy wants us to make such connections. He is thinking of Tess after she has been abandoned by Angel Clare ("How gay we looked that day we wed") and before she has agreed to live with Alec as his wife. In other words, the "lament" is possibly situated in Chapter XLI of *Tess of the D'Urbervilles* when "Mentally she remained in utter stagnation." This is not the passionate, indignant, desperate voice of Ch. LVI.

In the poem, she takes up her "Cross" but with more than a touch of self-pity blames herself for Angel's abandoning her: "'Twas I who made the blow to fall / On him who thought no guile." (Significantly, the persona never names the man who has left her: this moment is one that all human beings at one time or another experience, and not naming the man adds to the experience's universality.) Ever since the novel's serial publication readers have been apportioning considerable blame to Angel since he initially expresses contempt for conventional morality but easily succumbs to it, failing to see Tess as she is and making the age-old male error of blaming the victim instead of the malefactor.

Do we need to "position" the poem in order to enjoy or understand it? Probably not. The poem informs us adequately of the maid's situation, and compels us to consider not so much the cause as the result of the rupture between the speaker and the man who has left her. The interest is primarily lyric as we are to focus on the speaker's feelings of rejection and not on the incidents that led to that rejection.

.... The textual placement of the second poem, "The Pine Planters," is not so problematic since it is an interior monologue to accompany the third-person narrative of Ch. VIII in *The Woodlanders*. The speaker, Marty South, is again maudlin and self-pitying, but more stoical in the face of her two sorts of suffering: cold and anguish.

Patrick Roper wonders why Hardy changed "pines" to "larches" at the end of *The Woodlanders*, but chapter VIII specifically mentions "a thousand young fir tress to be planted in a neighbouring spot which had been cleared by the wood-cutters"[16].... Unlike Tess, Marty has never expressed her love and never been rejected; her love for Giles will "for ever / Remain a seed." Her "lament" then is of a very different nature from Tess's, though both young women of the soil lack hope and see death as a release from their intolerable situations.

.... In "Tess's Lament," the short lines, ballad-like dimeter refrains (in contrast to the iambic tetrameter of five of eight lines of each stanza), show the speaker dwelling morbidly on her situation, her hope and energy ebbing away at the close of each stanza, whereas the short lines (the second and fourth lines of each stanza are dimeter, the first and third lines generally trimeter) are typical of the backward-forward motion of the traditional folk-ballad, which "Marty South's Reverie" emulates with its quatrains and a-b-c-b rhymes.

Because of the sheer volume of these short lines in "Marty South's Lament" they offer less of a contrast than do the short lines of "Tess's Lament." With only three short lines per stanza, "Tess's Lament" has the quality of interrupted narrative: the long lines carry the tale, the short lines being interjections of regret, despondency, and despair. With respect to the appropriate language of the ballad

---

[16] Thomas Hardy, *The Woodlanders* (Macmillan London Ltd, 1974), 93.

form, the dialect of Tess seems more truthful than the standard English of Marty, and thereby renders "Tess's Lament" more 'oral', effective, and individualised than "Marty South's Reverie." Philip

Mon Feb 5 12:53:15 US/Central 2001
PATRICK ROPER <patrick@prassociates.co.uk>
subject: Trees in "The Pine Planters" & *The Woodlanders*

Just a bit more on trees. Firs and pines, so far as TH was concerned, seem to be the same thing. In *A Pair of Blue Eyes* he refers to "Scotch Fir" which is what people today would call "Scot's Pine." Strictly speaking firs have single needles arranged along the branches while pines have clusters of needles, though the definitions are fairly fluid. Larches, like yews and junipers, seem to be in a category of their own, though obviously all are conifers.

I suspect "larch" would have been a rather unusual word when TH was writing, though "pine" and to a lesser extent "fir" would have been well-known. People in forestry in Dorset in the 19th century were clearly planting all three species but not as a time-honoured tradition. Giles and Marty were doing something relatively novel like sowing GM crops today. This seems to me to hint at a changing countryside with changing people and customs and thus rather subtly reinforcing a sense of loss that pervades the poem.

Also, is the idea that it might have been better to have remained a seed TH's way of suggesting it would be better if people did not replace indigenous broad-leaved woodland with conifers?

Wed Feb 21 17:14:51 US/Central 2001
WILEY CLEMENTS <susque@jdweb.com>
subject: Tess's Lament/Pine Planters

I'll comment only on the short lines. We have been taught, at least in more recent times, that long lines are best for serious subjects, short lines for lighter. If that was the thinking at the juncture of the 19th/20th centuries, why would Hardy have chosen short lines for these poems? It would seem that for Tess's "Lament" he also wished to invoke the cadence of a three or four-part hymn. I have earlier remarked that the repeated second line in each stanza reminds me of the bass line in "When the Roll is Called up Yonder." However, it may be that the association of short lines with lighter verse is a newer thing. One thinks again of Thomas Hood (1798-1845) and his *Bridge of Sighs*, certainly a serious theme, but most effectively rendered in very short dactylic dimeter. Perhaps someone knows how and when this association came to be accepted? Wiley Clements

Fri Mar 2 16:04:49 US/Central 2001
SULEIMAN AHMAD <email:smahmad@mail.sy>
subject: Hardy's Provision of "Internal Links"

The textual history of "Tess's Lament" and "The Pine Planters: (Marty South's Reverie)" shows Hardy providing "internal links" between his poetry and fiction, thereby enriching both and indirectly revealing an interesting point about himself as a creator. (I borrow the term "internal links" from the realm of web site design. Had Hardy lived at the present time, he would in all probability have had a web site that one would describe as "user-friendly")

Making the link with the respective novel was easy in the first poem: Hardy changed the title from "A Lament" to "Tess's Lament." But the link of the second poem involved more work. Hardy deleted the hyphenation in the title, substituted a subtitle for the headnote in the *Cornhill* version, added Part I, and revised the first stanza of what became Part II.[17] In both cases, the result enriches the reading experience. While the two poems and their respective novels can be enjoyed separately without activating the links, a fuller enjoyment is available to the reader who reads them in conjunction. The emotional impact of each, originally strong, seems much stronger now through the reverberations and echoes that each provides for the other. As Birgit Plietzsch has pointed out in her posting of 2 February, the poems "open up a wider context for the reading of each novel. They retrospectively add an emotional dimension to the fiction." In addition to that, the reader, hearing Tess's and Marty's voices unmediated by an omniscient narrator, gets much closer to these characters and knows them better. Still, after reading "Tess's Lament" and *Tess of the d'Urbervilles*, for example, some readers would wonder why Tess's creator presents a weak self-accusing Tess instead of the Tess of the letter in Chapter XLVIII. This presentation seems unfair to her. In the last paragraph of the novel, one reads that "'Justice' was done, and the President of the Immortals (in Aeschylean phrase) had ended his sport with Tess." Her creator, however, seems to have continued his "sporting" with her, high-lighting her weakness rather than her strength.

The stoical and loyal Marty receives a similar treatment in her "Reverie," and the same "idiosyncratic mode of regard" appears to inform the other female-narrated poems. This makes one suspect

---

[17] Richard Little Purdy. *Thomas Hardy: A Bibliographical Study* (Oxford: Clarendon, 1954. [Repr. 1968]), 145-146

that, though Hardy shows deep understanding of women, his attitude towards them seems basically that of a male chauvinist.   Suleiman

THE PINK FROCK & THE BEAUTY

Fri Mar 2 19:50:20 US/Central 2001
BILL MORGAN <email:wwmorgan@ilstu.edu>
subject: Introducing "The Pink Frock" and "The Beauty"[18]

FOR this month's discussion, I have chosen two poems that address themes of female beauty and female vanity –- but from very different perspectives. The first piece seems to be a rather ungallant gesture meant to expose the speaker's heartless preoccupations with clothing and personal charm, but the second one presents beauty as an unwelcome burden – perhaps even a fatal one. Interestingly, both poems seem to have originated in something close to fact. In the *Life and Work* Hardy identifies the model for the narrator of "The Pink Frock" as Marcia, Lady Yarborough:

> At the Countess of Y—'s, a woman very rich and very pretty, she informed him mournfully in tête-à-tête that people snubbed her, which so surprised him that he could hardly believe it, and frankly told her it was her own imagination. She was the lady of the "Pretty pink frock" poem, though it should be stated that the deceased was not her husband but an uncle.[19]

The note that accompanies "The Beauty" is as follows:

> The Regent Street beauty, Miss Verrey, the Swiss confectioner's daughter, whose personal attractions have been so mischievously exaggerated, died of fever on Monday evening, brought on by the annoyance she had been for some time subject to.[20]

1. Is it possible or desirable to infer a consistent Hardyan view of women's beauty and vanity from these two contrasting poems –- or from other Hardy texts, for that matter?
2. Note that "The Pink Frock," like "Under the Waterfall," appears within quotation marks, thus indicating the silent presence of someone who hears the speaker's words and passes them on to

---

[18] *CP*, 472 & 616-617 respectively

[19] *Life and Work*, 281

[20] *Hynes* (514) says that the sentence appears in Hardy's notebook as a quote not from a London paper but from the *Dorset County Chronicle*.

us, whereas "The Beauty" is direct, unmediated first-person narration. How does this subtle difference in presentation affect our response to the two poems?
3. And finally, are the poems persuasive as speaking voices: that is, does Hardy successfully bring meter and rhyme and other technical features of the poems under the control of a credible narrative voice?

Bill Morgan

Sun Mar 4 11:17:47 US/Central 2001
PHILIP V. ALLINGHAM <philip.allingham@lakeheadu.ca>
subject: The Contrasting Rhetorical Stances of "The Pink Frock" and "The Beauty."

The note of despair or anguish in "The Pink Frock" at the persona's being unable to wear an attractive and fashionable dress (instead of the conventional, pietistic and drab mourning garb dictated by society) reminds one of the superficial and frivolous heroines of Alexander Pope's mock-epic *The Rape of the Lock* and John Gay's mock-elegy "On the Death of a Lap Dog." Surprisingly, Hardy has not chosen the traditional verse form for such satire, the Heroic Couplet of "The Ruined Maid" (1866) or at least a couplet form, as in "The Respectable Burgher." Rather, he has adapted the folk ballad, with its a-b-c-b rhyme and its three-four beat metre, to social satire.

....When the female persona of "The Pink Frock" confuses inconveience with grief, the reader may be tempted to categorize all young, fashion-conscious beauties as egocentric and insensitive. And yet the reader here, as in the eighteenth-century satires alluded to, finds the persona almost charming in her naïveté; certainly, the reader finds it difficult to condemn one who is so artlessly and unconsciously amusing. All these satires place the reader in the Olympian seat of moral judgment, rendering the mere mortals observed – by virtue of their follies, vices, and foibles –– inferior but rather entertaining creatures. The reader reprovingly laughs at the vacuous young woman because she is a negative exemplum, a lesson in how not to approach the sufferings of others.

In contrast, the iambic tetrameter lines and alternating rhyme of "The Beauty" compose the vehicle for a more serious and subtle consideration of female beauty, although once again Hardy gets into the skin of his subject, adopting the persona of a beautiful woman – a beauty of a different moral and intellectual complexion. In spite of her much praised outward attractiveness, the persona of "The Beauty" is quite the reverse of the persona of "The Pink Frock." In contrast to the bubble-headed fashion-plate of the satire, the pensive beauty of the second poem strikes an elegiac note, reinforced by her contemplation of the inevitable "gray hour" in the final stanza. Her anguish at her condition stems from the inability of others (especially, one suspects, members of the opposite gender) to appreciate what she is rather than what she appears to be. In "The Pink Frock," we are merely hearing the belle's words second-hand; they are hearsay, perhaps exaggerated for satiric effect. In "The Beauty," the persona seems to be speaking to us directly, engaging rather than distancing us, and by implication blaming us for our superficiality (according to the poem's rhetorical stance, the interlocutor has just praised her in order to win her love when all she wants – and presumably cannot find – is a relationship not charged with passion, friendship). Thus, the moral stance in which Hardy places his reader is the opposite in the second poem: we are not more but less wise than this beauty, from whom we have a life-lesson to learn.

Victorian (patriarchal) society is to blame for the plight of thoughtless and thoughtful beauty alike. In "The Pink Frock," the root of the persona's difficulty is not so much the untimely demise of a close male relative (we note that Hardy does not even bother to specify whether the one dead is a brother, father, or uncle) so much as the mores surrounding the appropriate attire for one in mourning. Similarly, society's insistence on defining women by their appearances rather than their characters is responsible for the anguish of the second beauty...To Hardy's persona, feminine beauty is a burden in that it prevents others from seeing what lies beneath the surface.

Philip

Fri Mar 23 8:50:27 US/Central 2001
SULEIMAN AHMAD <smahmad@mail.sy>
subject:Hardy's Negative View of Women

Hardy's "The Pink Frock," "The Beauty," and other female-narrated poems seem to be informed, in the main, by a negative view of women. Women are presented as vain, men-centered, and afraid of what "the toils of Time" bring. The callousness of the lady, in "The Pink Frock," towards a dying male relative originates apparently in a desire to please other men while she "may." For the woman in "The Beauty," being beautiful is a liability rather than an asset. What seems to make it so is her belief that men are attracted to external appearances and not to "inner" reality. This is an aspect of weakness since it shows that she does not trust that her man's love will survive into old age. Hence her plea for friendship, a less passionate but more enduring relationship than love. This plea, similar to that of the speaker in

"She to Him, I," indicates that Hardy the creator seems to look at women as incapable of imagining Eros developing, through the years, into Agape. Judged by real life experience, such a view is both untrue and unfair.
Suleiman

Fri Mar 23 9:00:16 US/Central 2001
PETER COXON <coxon@btinternet.com>
subject: Poem(s) of the Month

I'd hardly noticed "The Pink Frock" before other than to puzzle over its curious duple-triple rising rhythm (a3b3c3b2) — noted by the incomparable Elizabeth Hickson (*The Versification of Thomas Hardy*, p.98) but not, I think, picked up by Dennis Taylor in his metrical studies. The satirical presentation of the would-be wearer of pink instead of Victorian fustian compares well with the widow-to-be in "At the Draper's" who views the latest fashion in mourning all the while observed unseen by her dying husband.

A different note is struck in one of Hardy's earliest poems, "She at His Funeral," where the "gown of garish dye" worn by the deceased's sweetheart, in contrast to the conventional mourners' attire ("sable-sad") is no expression of superficial emotion. On the contrary, a pretty frock is worn by one whose regret "consumes like a fire." Similarly, in "The Chapel-Organist," the deacons engage a stunningly beautiful woman ("A bosom too full for her age; in her lips too voluptuous a dye") to play the chapel organ but fail to appreciate that they they are dealing with a serious musician who finds greater fulfilment in church music than "lovers, or beauty, or gold." The first of the "She to Him" poems looks for "friendship down Life's sunless hill" when "lauded beauties" have disappeared and seems to echo the theme of "The Beauty" tho' the latter is set in the tawdry environment of Victorian Regent Street (the haunt of "The Promenade of Prostitutes" according to TH in *The Life and Work*.[21])

There is a TH poem (the title eludes me) of the attractions of a Covent Garden (Eliza Doolittle?) flower girl whose natural beauty contrasts with the finely dressed upper-class women who throng to the theatre but whose worth is recognised by the poet. In the opening chapter of *Far From the Madding Crowd* Gabriel Oak faulted Bathsheba's admiration of her reflected image, crimson jacket and all, and the narrator recognised "woman's prescriptive infirmity" stalking into the sunlight. The poems cited take a more multi-faceted viewpoint.
Peter Coxon

---

[21] *Life and Work*, 217

Mon Mar 26 20:37:39 US/Central 2001
DON ULIN <ulin@pitt.edu>
Subject: Hardy on women and vanity

I would point out that even the ostensibly anti-vain speaker in the second is still fixated on her "beauty in the glass." So both of these poems could be used to support the critical commonplace regarding Hardy's own scopophilia (that women typically appear first in the gaze of a man or an apparently male reader, and that their downfall is associated with a recognition of their own image.) But I find Hardy too ironic to read quite so directly, which is what I came to love (after too many literal readings) of the ending to "The Ruined Maid," which allows the "ruined maid" something better than the sympathy, cond-escension, or condemnation that one might have expected there.

On a different note, I think the seemingly advanced thinking of "The Beauty," with its plea for a more holistic view of women, is attenuated by the fact that she has just died. If his marriage can be taken as any indication, it seems that Hardy's fullest appreciation of a woman's humanity may have required her death. So, having started off in this message trying to redeem Hardy's attitude toward women, I find myself leaning back in the other direction – as it seems I so often do in working through these marvellously, deceptively simple bits of verse. (Even "The Pink Frock" might be read with a kind of double-irony, a reminder, not of woman's vanity, but of the truly stifling observances expected of a woman in the event of the death of even so distant a family member as her uncle.)   Don Ulin

Thu Mar 29 20:56:41 US/Central 2001
ROSEMARIE MORGAN <rosemarie.morgan@yale.edu>
subject: "Pink Frock"

"The Pink Frock" stirs thoughts along the lines of Phillip Allingham's ideas on satire. Yes. But satirical of whom or of what? Of those who think – like Ahmad – that woman's vanity speaks here as opposed to being mimicked (yes! the speech marks are a clue – thanks Bill!). It is the mannered clichés and "flash" empty rhetoric which bespeaks a mockery of what might have been a fleeting regret here aggrandised to fit the cultural stereotype of female vanity.

Hardy's speaker alone helps us towards this perception. Here, we are invited to eavesdrop, morbidly curious, vicariously enjoying a "dressing" moment and thieving it for self-gratification, to fuel our sexual prejudices and to parody the entire event in "feminine"tones of petty vanity. Why else, if not in mockery, would the speaker utter words in what I would call the "colour of frivolity" which is predictably "pink" (not light vermilion or pale red, but *pink*)? Why else, if not in scorn, would s/he iterate "sounds" of childish petulance (not frustation, irritation or annoyance, but pouting discontent): "I can hardly bear it!" Why also the "Puff" sleeves and more, the running of "pleated" into "cheated" as if to degrade the very stuff of the garment itself?

There is no fleeting regret of this kind which would normally course along into so many clichés and stereotypical images. We might mutter "Pity – can't wear my feathered hat" but it would be left to an unsympathetic interlocutor to take the momentary thought to such extremes of cultural stereotyping as occur in this poem. Note too how amorphous the owner of the pink dress is, in terms of identity. She has not a single feature or attribute by which we might know her. Yet another characteristic of stereotyping. It is only the narrator we are permitted to see clearly, rather as we "see" the Duke in "My Last Duchess" who reveals himself through his rhetorical flourishes and nothing more. It is identification with this eavesdropper which determines our reading of this poem. Just as the spying Gabriel Oak perceives "vanity" in Bathsheba's actions in the mirror-scene (but the narrator does not) so readers are invited to take the espial position here. Hardy is past master at this kind of contra-self-identification. His novels abound with it: we either share his (her?) point of view and join his (her) world of sexual prejudice or we stand aside and thoughtfully regard the (narrative) company we are in.

Rosemarie Morgan

Sat Mar 31 13:06:03 US/Central 2001
ROBERT SCHWEIK
subject: Quotation Marks in "The Pink Frock"

In his introductory commentary, Bill Morgan remarked:
> Note that 'The Pink Frock,' like 'Under the Waterfall'... appears within quotation marks – thus indicating the silent presence of someone who hears the speaker's words and passes them on to us, whereas "The Beauty" is direct, unmediated first-person narration.

I want here to consider in some greater detail Hardy's use of quotation marks in such poems. First, Hardy uses quotation marks as a convention to indicate that the words of the poem are intended to represent the speech patterns, diction, and other inflections of a character or characters. Such quotation marks are, of course, conventions marking the poet's pretense of catching speech inflections even while using such devices as rhyme, alliteration, stanza breaks, and the like. Hardy uses this device to signify dialogue (as in "The Bird-catcher's Boy," "The Ruined Maid," "Under the Waterfall," and "The Sacrilege"); he also uses it for representing interspersed snatches of speech (as in "An Unkindly May"), or for poetic monologue (as in "The Pink Frock"). He even uses it to signify a verbal form of unspoken thought (as in "The Obliterate Tomb").

As his use of it to represent a verbal form of thought might suggest, Hardy does not, so far as I can tell, use quotations in his poems to signify that they are "mediated" by "the silent presence of someone who hears the speaker's words and passes them on to us." When he wants to, Hardy does use quotation marks to signify speech in dramatic contexts where one character's speech is overheard by another (as in "The Dame of Athelhall," Stanzas VII-X, for example). It seems mistaken, then, to assume that by using quotation marks alone in a poem Hardy means anything more than to indicate that what is intended to be represented is the inflections of some character's spoken words or unuttered thoughts. When he wants to indicate that a character's speech is being overheard, as in "The Dame of Athelhall," he provides a character to overhear and report it.

It seems unwarranted, then, to assume that Hardy uses quotation marks in a poem to "indicate the silent presence of someone who hears the speaker's words and passes them on to us." And such unwarranted assumptions can lead to eccentric interpretations. Someone may mistakenly think that Hardy used quotation marks in "The Ruined Maid" to indicate to us the silent presence of someone who overhears the speaker's words and passes them on to us. "Well, then," the reader wonders, "what kind of person would do that? Certainly not the author, whom I know to be a superb human being and close observer of humanity. Why, then, the words quoted in the poem must be the words of some morbidly curious eaves-dropper with stereotyped preconceptions about the ignorance of country girls and, even worse, stereotyped misconceptions about the supposed financial advantages prostitutes gain for themselves. By his rhetoric, the eavesdropper-narrator of "The Ruined Maid" clearly reveals what a shallow, superficial, facile observer he is. I for one, want no part of him, and I don't think those nice girls really said that at all!"

In short, I think Bill Morgan's assumption that quotation marks alone in a poem "indicate" that the words within them are "mediated" through "the silent presence of someone who hears the speaker's words and passes them on to us" is not an accurate description of what uses Hardy makes of quotation marks in his poetry. The use of such marks to signal the pretense of representing speech patterns of fictional characters – with no implication that they are to be understood to be "reported" or "passed on" by anyone but are, rather, the immediate creations of the author — is so common that to insist otherwise seems mistaken. When there are unreliable narrators depicted in poetry – e.g., Browning's Duke in "My Last Duchess" – his unreliability is *not* indicated with quotation marks at all. And when Hardy wants to indicate that one speaker is overheard by another – as in "The Dame of Athelhall"— he dramatizes the listener. I'd be wary, then, of interpretations of Hardy's poetry that depend on the assumption about Hardy's use of quotation marks that Bill Morgan voiced in his opening statement. Bob Schweik

THE CHAPEL-ORGANIST

Tue May 1 16:30:15 US/Central 2001
BILL MORGAN wwmorgan@ilstu.edu
subject: Introducing "The Chapel-Organist"[22]

HERE are the ideas that occur to me:

1. "The Chapel-Organist" has many features that could remind one of the work of Robert Browning, especially the use of a dramatic narrator in a crisis situation (complete with music and poison, both of which appear regularly in Browning); are there fruitful parallels or contrasts to be drawn between this poem and, say, "The Laboratory," or one of the music poems such as "Abt Vogler," "Master Hughes of Saxe-Gotha," or "A Tocatta of Galuppi's"?
2. most of the paid work done by the female narrators of Hardy's poems is agricultural labor; here work is differently inflected; can this poem serve as a means of entry into the idea of women and "work" in Hardy's poetry?
3. there are relatively few female artists in Hardy's work; are there important points to be made about Hardy's women and artistic endeavor that can begin with observations on this poem?
4. note that the poem is in rough hexameters and that each verse paragraph ends with a "couplet" rhyme; are there useful observations to be made about the poem's form and meter?
5. the narrator is strikingly aware of herself as a sexual being but rather detached from sexual feelings of any kind (usually attributing comments about her body, for instance, to others); what are

[22] *CP*, 633-636

we to make of her attitude towards sexuality (and, for that matter, her attitude towards her art)?

Sat May 5 15:23:46 US/Central 2001
PHILIP ALLINGHAM <philip.allingham@lakeheadu.ca>
subject: Browning's Organists Revisited in a Coherent Plot, or, Play It Again, Tom –

Although poison, passion, and playing the organ occur variously or in conjunction with one another in a number of Browning's "dramatic lyrics" or "dramatic monologues" (since only one voice is heard), Hardy's "The Chapel-Organist"(sub-dated "A.D.185-"), although very much an interior monologue, seems have affinities with a number of Browning's poems, especially the highly reflective "A Tocatta of Galuppi's." "Abt Vogler" (1864) is more soliloquy than monologue (although a variation of ballad stanza rather than blank verse), since the musician's "extemporizing" is more to himself than to others present, and suggests little dramatic action. Its 12-line stanzas of alternating rhyme are equally disciplined as but quite different in form from the rough pentameter couplets of "The Laboratory" (1844), which suggests both an auditor and a dramatic action involving poison.

In "Master Hughes of Saxe-Gotha" (1855), Browning uses a more experimental stanza of five lines (alternating rhyme, the first two and last lines being tetrameter and lines three and four pentameter of trochees and iambs), the speaker being the Bach-imitator's organist and not the composer himself. The triplets and long lines of "A Tocatta of Galuppi's" (1855) – perhaps intended to simulate the effect of the organ music – are as close as we can come to the equally long lines and the couplets of Hardy's organist-cum-poison offering.

However, the rhetorical stance of the speakers is somewhat different in that, while Browning has a present-day (largely gender-neutral but middle-aged) organist mentally addressing the Venetian composer of the touch-piece as he plays it on the organ, Hardy has his overtly female musician narrate her story in stream-of-consciousness as she plays, awaiting the moment when the poison will take effect and she will take her vengeance on a patriarchal, puritanical Deacon for terminating her position. Browning's point seems to be that in hearing the Renaissance composer's music we can mentally reconstruct the society for which he wrote, that we can experience that magical, decadent world gone-by. Hardy's point, in contrast, is that we identify ourselves, regardless of our gender, with the musician to whom playing is more important than living, and against the patently male voices of respectability who have, in imposing their morality upon her, attempted to silence her.

.... Through the persona of "The Chapel-Organist" (unlike Fancy in *Under The Greenwood Tree*) Hardy explores the consciousness of a woman who is very much both a sexual being and a dedicated artist. However, Hardy's interest seems to lie in the dilemma of such talent struggling to express itself in a female body – one senses the Dissenter elders would have had fewer scruples about employing a male organist, although a sexually-permissive male musician would have been discharged if he failed to alter his public behaviour. Like Tess, she carries sexuality as a burden because of the male perspective that sees her body rather than her character or abilities; Tess, too, had "A bosom too full for her age" (line 17) – Hardy seems aware that early-bloomers tend to become sexually active, whether they really wish to or not, and that beauty (especially feminine beauty) cannot hold commerce with chastity.

The organist resents the captain's exploiting her sexually in return for her passage, but feels compensated by being able to exploit the Dissenter-chapel's need for her services: "But get such another to play here we cannot for double the price!" (line 30).   Philip

Tue May 8 16:26:34 US/Central 2001
BETTY CORTUS <hardycor@mailhost2.csusm.edu>
subject: Body versus Soul

The chapel organist's dilemma reminds me a little of the arguments set forth in those medieval dialogue poems in which body and soul contend with each other for supremacy. She is very much a sexual being, and her voluptuous appearance arouses suspicions of lascivious behavior, at least in the rather prurient mind of the "inquirer" (line 13), even before rumors of her equivocal conduct in her home town become widespread throughout the chapel congregation

At war with her frankly sexual nature is her powerful spiritual craving for creative fulfillment in sacred music. It is to this need she gives priority over "lovers, or beauty, or gold." She first dismisses responsibility for her beauty with the statement: "But who put it there? Assuredly it was not I." Her apathy toward money is evidenced by the fact that her commuting expenses are not even compensated for by the meager stipend she receives, and which she is even willing to forfeit altogether for the supreme joy she derives from her music alone. Lovers, however, are a different kind of temptation. They are captivated by her ripe beauty, and these she seems far less able to resist. She does not deny having led a less than chaste life, even allowing that she has libelled her soul to the sensuality of men. As compelling as is her need to express her spiritual element in music, she ultimately shows no evidence of having been able to suppress the carnal side of her nature to give it the ascendancy.

Finally, she resolves the conflict with the melodramatic act of public suicide. This is the kind of dichotomy that I believe Hardy, himself, would have found insupportable. I envision him being much more inclined to the view that body and spirit require equal nourishment in the making of a fully realized individual. Yet this concept is so subtly interfused throughout the poem that even the most rigidly pious chapel-goer could scarcely take exception to the values expressed therein, while to the more open-minded reader the organist appears a sympathetic, if not tragic figure. How wonderfully duplicittous our poet can be!   Betty

Thu May 24 9:33:59 US/Central 2001
ROBERT SCHWEIK <schweik@fredonia.edu>
subject: "The Chapel-Organist"

I've got two questions about "The Chapel-Organist" I want to raise here. First, is the poem ambiguous about what role sex plays in the woman's life? Or are there indicators in it that are sufficiently determinate to say that her sexual activity is *not* the consequence of her sexual desire but, rather, of her need to support herself so that she can play the music that is her life's great passion? Two things seem to make the second interpretation more plausible.

One is that Hardy went to the trouble of changing line 51, which had earlier read, "High love had been beaten by lust; and the senses had conquered the soul" to read, "My bent, finding victual in lust, men's senses had libelled my soul" – and, in doing so, seemed to stress that, although the woman had to prostitute herself for "victual," that physical act was a "libel" on her soul which (as the poem makes abundantly clear) was devoted to the music that was truly her love. In short, her sexual activity was simply an undesired necessity. But, on the other hand, line 47, "Above all embraces of body by wooers who sought me and won" suggests that her sexual activity was more than that – that she was "wooed" and "won." So, too, may her words "But past all the heavings of passion" (l. 83). My own preference is for the first of those interpretations because it fits so well with the other ironies of the poem. One of those ironies is the way that, as the deacons and other members of the congregation use their doubts about her morality to reduce her stipend – already not enough to support her – she, in turn, is driven by them to prostitute herself even more. The crass financial considerations that prompt them to underpay her (ll. 30-31) and then accept her work for no pay (ll. 37-41) are precisely the things that drive her to increased and more open activity as a prostitute.

Second, her motive in killing herself is also possibly ambiguous. It would be consistent with the kinds of ironies I've mentioned that her death was one final ironic consequence of the deacon's termination of her opportunity to do the one thing that was truly her life's passion. That being lost, her "soul" dies (ll. 50-53) and she simply puts an end to the physical self that was really for her no more than the means for the spiritual passion she had for her music. Or, does the "far-reaching plan" she has (l. 60) imply some kind of punitive act as well?   Bob Schweik

Tue May 29 15:17:00 US/Central 2001
DON ULIN <ulin@pitt.edu>
subject: Hexameters

Given the observations and questions already posted this month regarding the poem's attitude toward its subject, I wonder what we can gather from Hardy's use of the epic hexameter for this poem. Surely this poem could not have been written as early as the 1850s, but the date would situate it in the midst of Clough's experiments with hexameter in *The Bothie* (1848) and *Amours de Voyage* (1858). Clough's are mock-epics (the undergraduate reading party in the highlands and the blasé upper-middle-class tourist in Europe), but they are also much more self-consciously Homeric than Hardy's poem is, which seems to bring a much more prosaic feel to meter. Other poems are written in lines of six feet (most famously "Wessex Heights"), but the others that I know of are mostly iambic, whereas this one is mostly anapests –- closer to Clough's more traditional hexameters with the series of dactyls concluding with a spondee.

This is all very technical, though, and irrelevant (to my thinking) unless it says something about what the poem is saying or how it is saying it. Perhaps it is significant that a woman artist (of which there are very few in Hardy's work, as Bill Morgan points out) should express her stream of consciousness in a meter associated with Homer even as she alters it to fit her own needs. One might say that the anapests join the grandeur of Homer with lower perspective of popular verse. But I don't know. I've spent more time puzzling over this already today than I can really afford!

So I'll leave an open question for others who may know Hardy's poetic oeuvre far better than I.   Don Ulin

Wed May 30 12:24:51 US/Central 2001
SULEIMAN AHMAD <smahmad@mail.sy>
subject: The Chapel-Organist: A Pure Woman

"The Chapel-Organist" presents a young woman, physically and artistically gifted, hounded to an early death by poverty in a male-dominted society. Naturally endowed with physical qualities that any woman would desire, she wonders why these natural gifts are viewed nega-tively. Overhearing a chapel-goer murmuring, "'A handsome girl,'... / 'But – too much sex in her build; fine eyes, but eyelids too heavy; /A bosom too full for her age; in her lips too voluptuous a dye'" (ll. 15-17), she mildly comments: "(It may be. But who put it there? Assure-dly it was not I.)" (l. 18).

The words of the chapel-goer tell much about male mentality. It seems that many men cannot see in a woman more than a sex object. Though a superb artist, a player of sacred music and a contralto singer of psalms and hymns, only her sexual traits are emphasized. If these are the thoughts of a worshipper at a chapel, where one assumes that things spiritual should dominate the mind, what can one expect from a sexually starving sea-captain in Havenpool? Such a girl has little chance in a world of "coaxers" and "catchers" (if I may adapt the narrator's words in "To Lizbie Browne," l. 40). How can an exploited poor girl like her remain physically chaste, particularly if she has neither family nor friends to support her, as the last line of the poem suggests? The chemist-deacon, whom she calls (ironically, I should think) "a worthy man" (l. 25), states that her "stipend can hardly cover her fare hither twice in the week" (l. 8). Yet it never occurs to him that her starvation wages would lower her resistance to temptation. As she herself makes clear, it was necessity that drove her into prostituting her body: "(O yes; I was thereto constrained, lacking means for the fare to and fro)" (l. 44). Wooers "sought" and "won" her by the power of their money and their "blandishments."

As Tess says, "Once victim, always victim: that's the law"[23] Even the pastor, the shepherd of the flock, seems more interested in his own "peace" of mind (l. 42) than in following the example of Jesus and preventing the congregation from casting stones at his chapel-organist. Still, though, conventionally, a "prostitute," this young woman is purer than the dirty-minded chapel-goers who condemn her. She is not a hypocrite: "I have never once minced it. Lived chaste I have not. Heaven knows it above!" (l. 83). It seems that she enjoys

---

[23] Thomas Hardy, *Tess of the d'Urbervilles*, ed. Gatrell and Grindle, (World's Classics, 1988), 321

Eros. But she considers "all the heavings of passion" (l. 83) as "lower delight" (l. 23), far below her "life-love" for sacred music (l. 83).

Apparently, she has come to some kind of terms with her situation, cleansing her men-"libelled" (l.51) soul twice a week by playing and singing at the Chapel. When she is denied this cleansing process, life becomes impossible for her. Hence her decision to commit suicide on "the last [day] of [her] functioning" (l. 62) as a chapel-organist. She dies in triumph, a pure woman at the end of a spiritually cleansing performance. Suleiman Ahmad

A SUNDAY MORNING TRAGEDY

Fri Jun 1 14:19:08 US/Central 2001
BILL MORGAN <wwmorgan@ilstu.edu>
subject: Introducing "A Sunday Morning Tragedy"[24]

ALTHOUGH I would welcome comment on any dimension of the poem, I call your attention especially to three features:
1. its use of ballad-like repetition: each stanza creates its own internal tension by confining the forward motion of narrative to the first and third lines (the a rhymes), and reining back that motion with almost static commentary in the second and fourth (the b rhymes); is this structure too rigid and predictable, or is it appropriately relentless, like the movement of tragedy?
2. its insistently tragic female thematics: the mother-narrator blames not only herself but something like "women's lot" (see line 118, for example) for the tragedy; what is the nature of this tragic burden that women bear in the poem; is the burden childbearing/mothering itself or something else?:
3. its critical history as a poem that challenges conventional morality: Hardy first intended to use the story as the plot of a tragic play, but he gave up on that idea when he realized that the subject matter would not be acceptable on the London stage; his sketches for two different dramatic treatments are in the Dorset County Museum. And even when he had reworked the material as a ballad, he had trouble getting the poem published: *The Fortnightly* and *The Cornhill* both rejected it. Ford Madox Hueffer (Ford) later claimed that he and Arthur Marwood started *The English Review* specifically to publish the poem – and thus to challenge the prevailing conventions that had led other editors to reject it.

---

[24] *CP*, 201-205

Hardy himself seemed to see two separate themes that might be controversial – the "false shame" of unwed pregnancy and "the crime" of attempting to induce an abortion.[25] How controversial is the poem for today's audiences, and can we still respond to it as a brave challenge to stifling convention; if not, has it lost some of its appeal? - Bill

Sat Jun 2 8:04:22 US/Central 2001
PHILIP ALLINGHAM <philip.allingham@lakeheadu.ca>
subject: "Sunday Morning Tragedy": controversial or Merely Improbable?

Tragedy sometimes forces its audience to accept the grossly improbable, and "A Sunday Morning Tragedy" is no exception to the age-old problem of what Coleridge termed "the willing suspension of disbelief." No wonder that the *Fortnightly* and the *Cornhill* both rejected it – this was strong stuff for Edwardian England. In musing over this ballad, I did something I rarely do – I discussed the poem of the month with my wife, a former corrections-facility teacher and high school guidance counsellor. She responded that young women today would not be inclined to take the chance that the protagonist's daughter does, swallowing a herbal remedy used on sheep to induce abortion. (Of course, some young women today are prepared to consume other natural products to lose weight or alter their consciousnesses or simply narcotize themselves, but I suppose those natural products constitute less of an unknown). And as for mothers today, continued my wife, this poem would be a particularly "tough sell." "Why didn't she simply send her daughter to relatives and well away from the prying eyes and wagging tongues of the parish?"

However, consider the situation of this rural, poor, unsophisticated mother – without money, she cannot send the girl away, and the local doctor would hardly be inclined to induce an abortion, although I'm sure Casterbridge's Mixen Lane harboured more than one back-alley abortionist. In the end, we can either go on quibbling about details of the tragic circumstance, denying their likelihood, or accept the tragedian's terrible proposition and respond to it emotionally rather than logically. Tragedy from the time of Aeschylus has usually been set on a stage generations before our own to distance us a little from its protagonist, and certainly Hardy's adaptation of the ballad form (its iambic tetrameter lines, oral delivery, simple language, strong sense of character, clearly delineated moral conflict, terse dialogue, recursive refrains are all appropriate to the folk form, even

---

[25] Hardy to Hueffer, September 9, 1908, *Collected Letters*, III, 331

though it has a-b-a-b rather than a-b-c-b rhyme) helps us place the action much earlier than 1904, although the poem is clearly commenting upon the values and attitudes of contemporary society.

.... The lines "Of how she found her in the plight / That is so scorned in Christendie" (35-36) swiftly establish the moral context in which mother and daughter operate .... Unfortunately, most younger readers would be terribly practical in their responses to the poem ("Why didn't she take her daughter to an abortion clinic? Even young women in Ireland, where abortion is unavailable, take the ferry to Liverpool"), and would not regard the mother as heroic or defiant, but merely gullible. The issue of abortion is certainly still charged with emotion and controversy: to some Canadians, Dr. Morgentaler is a saint, to others a devil, for setting up abortion clinics across the country so that young women can exercise their right to choose whether to give birth and take on the responsibility of child-rearing.

Philip Allingham

Mon Jun 4 1:32:53 US/Central 2001
ANGELA RICHARDSON <angela@oaktown.demon.co.uk>
subject: mother and daughter

Although the brave subject of abortion makes us think about the young woman and the choices before her, we do not hear her voice in the poem. It is the voice of the doomed mother we hear, who acted instead of the chief protagonists — the daughter and her lover. Her actions are extreme in the context and are more to do with the loss to her of the image of the perfect daughter rather than the living child. She'd rather she was dead than matured. Angela

Tue Jun 26 15:23:15 US/Central 2001
BETTY CORTUS <:hardycor@mailhost2.csusm.edu>
subject: Poem as Tragedy

If one were to adopt Aristotle's principle that the effect of tragedy should be to elicit pity and fear in the audience I doubt that this poem would entirely meet that philosopher's criterion. Perhaps it would have been more successful in evoking these emotions in dramatic form as Hardy first intended it. However, as a ballad I find the numbing repetitions, and the mother's histrionics at times to be more in keeping with melodrama than pure tragedy, and the ironic twist at the end leaves me less sympathetic to the plight of the young woman than frustrated and impatient at the pointless blunders leading to her death. As for fear, the poem would be unlikely to evoke it in a reader today, although it might have frightened young women of an earlier generation into caution regarding pre-marital sex. Nevertheless, the poem does tell a rather compelling story, which certainly would have constituted a real tragedy to the inhabitants of rural Wessex "circa 186-" So although its ability to shock may have faded since the time of its composition, and the ballad is not seen much as a contemporary poetic genre, it is not entirely without relevance, as well as a degree of historic interest, both in form and content today.   Betty

A TRAMPWOMAN'S TRAGEDY

Sun Jul 1 15:20:04 US/Central 2001
BILL MORGAN <wwmorgan@ilstu.edu>
subject: Introducing "A Trampwoman's Tragedy"[26]

FOR this, the last in our series of discussions of Hardy poems with female narrators, I have chosen the piece that Hardy purportedly considered "upon the whole, his most successful poem."[27] I suggest three broad areas of inquiry (plus a fourth question of a different kind – see Note on the Text below):
1. the poem's narrative structure: what can we say about it as a tale well- or ill-told?
2. meter and form: is its reputation as an example of Hardy's formal mastery well deserved?
3. its participation in the enterprise that is represented by the larger group of Hardy poems with female narrators: does the poem offer any distinctive insights into Hardy's handling of such female-specific issues as we have been talking about for the past eight months (women and love, female sexuality, women and class, women and beauty, etc.)?

Note on the text: I have transcribed "A Trampwoman's Tragedy" from *The Variorum Edition of the Complete Poems of Thomas Hardy*,[28] and cross-checked my transcription against the text of the poem as it appears in *The Complete Poetical Works of Thomas Hardy*.[29] Although the two editions record quite a number of interesting variant readings in the

---

[26] *CP*, 195-199
[27] Florence apparently added this to Hardy's holograph version of *The Life and Work of Thomas Hardy* (see p335). See also *The Life*, 312.
[28] *The Variorum Edition of the Complete Poems of Thomas Hardy*, edited by James Gibson (London: Macmillan, 1979)
[29] *The Complete Poetical Works of Thomas Hardy*, I, edited by Samuel Hynes (Oxford: Clarendon, 1982).

poem's many states (from holograph to Hardy's last *Collected Poems*, there is only one inconsequential disagreement between the two editors' reading texts: in line 30 Gibson (following *Collected Poems* 1919 and later) has "cosy" whereas Hynes (following the first edition) has "cozy." I have accepted Gibson's reading. Another interesting difference between the two editions lies in the fact that Gibson chooses to print Hardy's notes on the same page with the poem itself, whereas Hynes moves the notes to the end of his volume, where they appear within his own explanatory and biographical notes. With this difference in mind, I offer a fourth question:

4. do we prefer to read Hardy's notes in the same textual zone as the poem itself, as part of the experience of reading the poem, or in another location, as part of the commentary or editorial apparatus? Bill Morgan

Mon Jul 2 7:56:32 US/Central 2001
BOB SCHWEIK <schweik@fredonia.edu>
subject: Some Questions About Wording and Punctuation in "A Trampwoman's Tragedy."

Although lacking the moral delicacy of the editor of the *Cornhill Magazine*, who rejected Hardy's "A Trampwoman's Tragedy" as something impossible to print in a family periodical, I share the view of the editor of the *North American Review* who regretted that Hardy changed the word "traipsed" (which he had originally used in line 81) to "walked." The editor gave his reason this way:

> The latter [word 'traipsed'] seemed so natural on this trampwoman's lips, and her use of it in her hopeless sorrow surely emptied it of the slightest trace of the idea of jauntiness or light-heartedness and left only that aimless wandering through a friendless world."[30]

There's one rare case where I think Hardy might profitably have listtened to an editor's advice.But even more, I regret Hardy's removal of four periods after the words "Alone, alone" in line 82 and his replacement of them with an exclamation mark. One of the features of "A Trampwoman's Tragedy" that unfortunately weakens it for me are its melodramatic exclamation marks not only in line 82 but in lines like 34 ("O deadly day! –") and 63 ("God knows it was not! But, O despair!"). That "O despair!" in particular makes me wince, as much for the wording as the exclamation mark. Bob Schweik

---

[30] Hynes, ibid, 381

Mon Jul 2 15:01:49 US/Central 2001
PHILIP ALLINGHAM <apalling@tbaytel.net>
subject: Hamartia in "The Trampwoman's Tragedy"

Having to dismiss the Aristotelian requirement of nobility and high social status for a tragic hero to discover whether Hardy's protagonist is a tragic heroine, the reader of "The Trampwoman's Tragedy" must focus on the nature of her tragic flaw or *hamartia*. Only through an examination of the trampwoman's tragic flaw can the reader determine whether the ballad meets Aristotle's condition of "causality of character"or whether its catastrophe is imposed purely by circumstance. In attempting to formulate a theory of character-generated suffering, in *The Poetics* (330 B. C.) Aristotle by the term *hamartia* implies two kinds of "tragic flaw": the inherent personality or character flaw that inevitably leads an otherwise noble person into disaster (Oedipus's impetuosity, temper, and curiosity; Macbeth's ambition; Michael Henchard's "introspective inflexibility"), or a fatal error in judgment resulting from that character flaw.

....Where is the justification for the Trampwoman's teasing her fancy man in "wanton idleness" (V), intimating that the child she carries is not his but Jeering John's? She acknowledges her "lover's dark distress," but like Anne Garland[31] enjoys inflicting the pain his anguished look betokens. Suddenly, of course, the Trampwoman achieves an Aristotelian *anagnorisis*. She perceives her error, but her epiphany comes too late, for her beloved lies dead.

However, instead of merely seeing herself as partly to blame, as "an accessory before the fact," so to speak, she takes upon herself the entire burden of guilt, although she is not the one charged with the crime ... By coincidence, which seems a piece of the pattern of poetic justice, Mother Lee dies, leaving the surviving alpha female of the pack to fend for herself. The Trampwoman's complete acceptance of a guilt not entirely hers is characteristic still of her egotism. Her fancy man made a moral choice and was compelled to face the consequences of that choice, but as far as she is concerned Jeering Johnny's murder is simply her fault. Her *anagnorisis*, then, is not the suprarational revelation or self-insight achieved by Shakespeare's Lear, although her error in judgment, like Lear's, is at least partially responsible for the poem's catastrophe, which is not merely personal suffering but social disintegration.

On the other hand, since the Aristotelian tragic hero's fate (self-sacrifice) makes possible a restoration of the social order, we must

---

[31] Central character in Thomas Hardy's *The Trumpet-Major* (1880)

conclude that Hardy's Trampwoman falls short as a tragic protag-ist. She provides causality of character, but fails to achieve fully tragic self-awareness and her suffering does not have positive social ramifications. Despite these difficulties, the poem justly deserves its reputation as a well-told ballad tale, swiftly establishing the setting, the characters, the conflict, and the narrative voice.

The repetition of part of the first line of each stanza in a second, short line creates the impression of both a chorus and a lament, leading the first-time reader to believe that a tragic event must be the inevitable conclusion since the repeated line implies a sense of fatality and an overwhelming sense of guilt. The problem with Hardy's handling of the persona, as I have suggested above, is that he has her act capriciously and without logical motivation when she teases her fancy man regarding the child's paternity and her feelings for Jeering Johnny. Hardy knows the ballad requires she act thus, but fails somewhat in his characterisation of the Trampwoman.

A final point to be addressed is the placement of explanatory notes: if the annotations are Hardy's and reflect authorial intent, they deserve to be placed as close to the passages glossed as is possible. On the other hand, an editor's notes are more accessible if placed as endnotes rather than buried at the back of a volume. Philip

Thu Aug 2 9:27:14 US/Central 2001
ROSEMARIE MORGAN <rosemarie.morgan@yale.edu>
subject: Extremity in "A Trampwoman's Tragedy"

After reading Bob's comments on "A Trampwoman's Tragedy" and the hyperbolical stresses conveyed by the use of exclamation marks – exclamation marks which Bob feels to be "melodramatic" – I wanted to say that I feel these emphases to be entirely appropriate. Why? because from Stanza I onwards in the journey "northward" as "we beat afoot" one extremely tense melodrama is being played out. And if Spielberg were to make a movie of this we would have settings of unbearable intensity: Stanza 1: Heat: "sun-blaze burning on our backs." Stanza II: Beat: "twenty miles" more of endless tramping. Stanza III: Stress: Gale force winds, river-crossings, stinging insects. Surely then the language of these people would be thick with the curses of exhaustion not to mention the ill-begotten sayings and doings of the over-burdened and inebriated (even if later regretted).

This is what we do – this is how it is when we are pushed to the limit of physical and emotional endurance. Hence, to cry "O deadly day!" aghast and with expressive feeling (exclamation mark) seems to me tonally apt.

Nowadays I suppose four-letter words or street vernacular would (in modern parlance) express it just as emphatically and in terms we would recognise as expressive of the condition of the indigent poor, not to say the heavily pregnant and homeless tramp. This is a homicidal situation after all! (exclamation mark). Feelings are running very high.

By stanza IX the knife is drawn and Johnny is dead. Surely an exclamation mark or two is the least a poet-linguist might do under the (leading) circumstances?   Rosemarie

VIGNETTE SKETCHED BY HARDY PLACED AT THE OPENING OF THE 'SHE TO HIM' SEQUENCE OF POEMS IN THE FIRST EDITION OF *WESSEX POEMS*, 28.

THE THOMAS HARDY ASSOCIATION: FORUM DISCUSSION GROUP[1]
Director: Betty Cortus
hardycor@owl.csusm.edu

INTRODUCTION

THE discussions that follow speak for themselves. In any given year TTHA's Forum conversations cover a wide variety of topics and the small samples collected here have been chosen primarily for the way they stirred the interest of other Forum listeners and became, of their own volition, a "thread." The Forum is not moderated in any way. It exists as a free speech arena and is wholly self-governing. Credit is due solely to those Hardy lovers worldwide – those who avail themselves of Forum privileges – for the quality of the debates and for the sustained courtesy and freedom from abuse that distinguishes this particular List-serve at all times.

One of the most remarkable features of TTHA's Forum is the speed and quality of the responses triggered by the questions and observations posted online. The Hardy Association's own Board of Directors and Vice-Presidents is largely responsible for supplying these responses but by no means exclusively. To everyone's interest and delight new names, new contributors crop up every week with answers to queries, solutions to problems, ideas for research, suggestions for students and, of course, insights and observations on the current "threads"– there's a veritable goldmine of Hardy enthusiasts out there!

At the end of the day, though, our grateful thanks must go to Betty Cortus for her patience in handling the technical side of things, her forbearance with the many subscribers who call upon her for priate assistance and her dedication to Hardyans everywhere who only ever meet with her gentle understanding and unerring goodwill. Our deep appreciation also goes to John Cortus who labours behind the scenes filing and archiving the dozens of different discussion threads so that they can be made available to researchers on any day at any time. Long may the Forum thrive!   Rosemarie Morgan

---

[1] http://www.yale.edu/hardysoc/Welcome/Forum/forum.htm

HARDY'S TRAGIC HEROES
February 27th - March 2nd 2002

Wed, 27 Feb 2002 18:23:07 -0600
GLEN & SARA van ALKEMADE <gvanalkemade@jpusa.org>
Subject: Hardy's tragic heroes?

I've been thinking about Michael Henchard lately, though it's been a while since I've read *The Mayor of Casterbridge*. I just completed a book club study of *Tess* – part of one's reaction to Tess as a character is indignation or outrage as you watch this decent, innocent girl's life destroyed by lousy men and cruel fate, even while she consistently tries to make good, responsible decisions. Michael Henchard also demonstrates his capacity for consistently good, responsible, decision-making, but he reaches a point where his finer traits succumb to the baser traits, after which his decisions are informed by jealousy, revenge, pride, violence, etc. As a result, I read his ultimate fate as inevitable, or of his own doing, or his just deserts, or the natural consequences of rotten decisions. What is the word for how we feel about such characters? In the former camp I would group Tess, Clym Yeobright, Giles Winterborne, Hamlet, Cordelia, Antigone – persons of noble character driven down by their circumstances and fate, but who retain their dignity and elicit our admiration and compassion. In the latter, Henchard, Troy, Eustacia Vye (?), Macbeth, King Saul, Javert, Oedipus – persons of seriously flawed character, with a warped moral sense that is in significant discord with their universe, and which is largely the cause of their own undoing.

In high school they taught us "Oh, that's called a Tragic Hero." But how do we *feel* about Hardy's tragic heroes? The best I can come up with is pity, pity at a misspent life, heedlessly wasted on rotten choices when the individual either *did* or *could* have known better. I can't find admiration, and I won't stoop to contempt. What do you think? Which other Hardy characters would you put into which group?   Glen

Wed, 27 Feb 2002 17:11:27 -0800
BETTY CORTUS <hardycor@owl.csusm.edu>
Subject: Re: Hardy's tragic heroes?

I think pity is a good term for the emotion Henchard's character evokes in my case too Glen, although I think that pride being one of his characteristics, flaws if you will, he would have hated being pitied. Interesting too that pity is one of the two emotions Aristotle believed true Tragedy should elicit.   Betty

Wed, 27 Feb 2002 18:10:14 -0800 (PST)
BRETT HARTLINE <brettbat@yahoo.com>
Subject: Re: Hardy's tragic heroes?

Yes indeed, all of the characters Glen mentions could to some extent be classified as "tragic heroes"; however, in the classical definition of the term, a tragic hero is undone primarily by his/her tragic flaw. Hardy's characters (particularly Jude, Tess, Henchard, and Eustacia) *do* have flaws, but it seems to me that they are primarily victims of fate (or Fate). That is the dominant theme of Hardy's work —that we are not necessarily in control of our destinies, that we are ultimately powerless. The aforementioned characters do indeed elicit feelings of pity, but I believe the pity comes from witnessing how helpless and tossed about these people are by circumstances beyond their control.

Brett

Wed, 27 Feb 2002 22:08:08 -0500
ROSEMARIE MORGAN <rosemarie.morgan@yale.edu>
Subject: Re: Hardy's tragic heroes?

The Aristotelian definition of tragedy — a dramatic action of some magnitude which evokes deep pity and fear in the audience and thereby allows for catharsis (via psychological integration of intensely powerful emotions) – typically involves an individual of *considerable social standing whose character is balanced*; neither unusually good nor exceptionally bad. The audience (if we assume each is the center of her or his own universe), then sees its own deceit, say, or jealousy, or brash boasting, as the potential source of its own downfall, but far less readily identifies with the stereotypical villain or the stainlessly-virtuous character in the same way, with the same empathy, to the same end.

In order to arouse pity and fear in the audience the hero's fall must be significant – that is, a "fall" from a tremendous height (socially, morally etc). Hamartia, and the "tragic flaw" mentioned by Brett, of which the most heinous fault was pride (hubris), may concur with a character's error of judgment, lack of courage etc., but can also result from a misstep, mistake, or even accident of fate that leads protagonists – errors and all – to their downfall.

For these reasons of form there are schools of thought that claim that there is no true tragedy in modern literary terms; modern works tend to feature ordinary folk: Arthur Miller's Willy Loman, Tennesse Williams' Blanche and – of course – our Hardy people aforementioned (customarily dubbed anti-heroes to distinguish them from the noble, high-class protagonists of the past).

However, if many Aristotelian tenets no longer apply to our modern "tragedies" there is one which does – certainly in Hardy's case. This tenet holds that where cataclysmic events befall the protagonist the ensuing tragedy ultimately celebrates the dignity of the human spirit in confronting them: that overwhelming misfortune meets with human acceptance of the tragic consequences is heroic. In this respect, Tess reigns supreme. Cheers, Rosemarie.

Wed, 27 Feb 2002 22:00:22 -0800
DALE KRAMER <dalek@darkwing.uoregon.edu>
Subject: Re: Hardy's tragic heroes?

Yes, pity is an appropriate rational and emotional response to Hardy's destroyed heroes; and of course their flaws lead to, sometimes in the sense of creating, their fates. But I think that attributing their destruction to powerlessness may be accepting Hardy's rhetoric, and his strong sympathy with his characters, too uncritically. Giles Winterborne, for example, is the most effective person in his world. He's silent, but hardly powerless. His death would seem to be a paradigm of a decent person dying because he's just too nice; but he has alternatives to lying in the wet so as not to bring into question Grace's virtue. If he's a victim he's a victim of his own excessive conventionality.

Is Tess powerless? To my mind, only in the sense that women are taken stereotypically to be powerless in a patriarchal world. True, she is sent by her mother into a perilous situation without adequate preparation, but she participates, however innocently and perhaps even blindly, in creating a situation where she can plausibly surrender her virtue in confusion. After recovering from her grief at the death of Sorrow, she pursues happiness at Talbothays, and puts herself in way of achieving it, failing primarily because Angel is an idiot to convention. She saves her family from penury by accepting that only Alec is in a position to support them all. When she kills Alec, she is scarcely "powerless." Impractical and impetuous and bitter and rash, perhaps. But not powerless. She is exacting revenge, not necessarily in terms of such universals as malehood, but for quite specific mistreatment by specific individuals. (Modern readers might speculate she kills Alec because it's too far a stretch for her to kill Angel. I wouldn't go this far. Instead, I'd say that her devotion to Angel is one of the features that limits her as a tragic figure). Pity is one of the feelings a tragic writer is traditionally expected to evoke; the other is "terror". Why terror? It's probably because tragedy depends on admiration more than on softer grounds such as cordiality. Pity, itself, is not a soft empathy, so much as it's the "there but for the grace of god goes I" sense that dreadful things can happen to people just like me. It's cheek-by-jowl with terror, in fact, because the basic result of admiring the central figure (who is destroyed by the action within a narrative) is an awareness of the likely terrible consequences of being true to one's character (i.e., our own, assuming we feel positive toward ourselves). If a character is *not* true to him/herself, that's a disqualification to thinking she or he is tragic. Tragedy is significant: nothing significant can be made out of inconsistency. Hardy's characters, and not just his tragic figures, do tend to be true to themselves.

Sergeant Troy and Wildeve, and Alec d'Urberville, are all true to their inner natures. Because of their roles in their narratives, we tend not to admire them, however much we may understand them. But in different plots they could have been tragic: it's not necessary to feel chummy with a tragic hero.

These assumptions go toward explaining why Henchard is a satisfactory tragic figure. Henchard tests out, as it were, the various aspects of his character — ambition, sexual love, envy and resentment, pride, parental love — and takes them to their (rational) limits. When none of them results in a condition he can find acceptable, he takes himself away (twice). Like Macbeth, like Oedipus, he accepts the consequences of what he does, however socially intolerable are the traits that cause him to act as he does. (And he is, like Oedipus, his own most severe judge.) Clym (for example) doesn't accept consequences: he sloughs them aside, imposing a glossing idealism on his worldly decisions, especially so at the very end of the novel. Clym and Jude are sentimentalized sufferers (in different ways), and thus can be admired (well, by me, anyway) only with provisos. With Henchard, it's easy to denigrate his clumsiness and brute selfishness; but he is always himself, aware of his own needs, ready to act and willing to suffer. His stubbornness makes him more a real human being like most of us, just as Macbeth's succumbing to political temptation is a more empathetic failing than Hamlet's waffling combined with an impulsive lunging toward contingent opportunities.

Sorry about going on at such length; but once started on a subject I'm hard to stop. Dale

Thu, 28 Feb 2002 07:49:54 -0500
PHILIP ALLINGHAM <apalling@tbaytel.net>
Subject: Re: playwrites vs. playwrights

Of course, Aristotle would have objected to Hardy's being a writer of prose rather than a dramatist or playwright. The origin of that very English conception of the dramatic writer alerts us to the fact that an acting company's resident writer revised and revamped existing texts as well as wrote new ones. The story of Tess, in particular, smacks of an oral tradition, the seduction of a maid in a great house...or, the rape victim bringing her attacker to justice. Can we experience Aristotelian catharsis in our armchairs as opposed to seats in a theatre?

Philip

Thu, 28 Feb 2002 10:05:03 -0500
NATHAN ELLIOTT <nelliott@nd.edu>
Subject: Henchard's character, tragedy, and other stuff

My apologies if other people have brought this up, but it might be interesting to think about Henchard's rise and fall not only in terms of tragedy, but as Norman Page points out, also in terms of the Medieval Wheel of Fortune, (or Fortune's Wheel, for those of us who want to avoid gameshow implications). Page writes that:

> Before the end of the novel, Henchard has reached, socially and economically, the precise point at which he started: his dramatic rise has been exactly matched by a catastrophic fall. Fortune's wheel has come full circle.

Tragedy, according to Aristotle, should make us feel pity and terror (and Henchard does make me feel this). But what should fortune's wheel make us feel? Is there supposed to be a particular emotive response to that genre? What was the purpose? Any thoughts from Hardy fans who happen to be medievalists would be most welcome.

Thanks, Nathan

Thu, 28 Feb 2002 10:23:51 -0500
ROSEMARIE MORGAN <rosemarie.morgan@yale.edu>
Subject: Re: Hardy's tragic heroes?

Dale writes:

> Clym and Jude are sentimentalized sufferers (in different ways), and thus can be admired (well, by me, anyway) only with provisos. With Henchard, it's easy to denigrate his clumsiness and brute selfishness; but he is always himself, aware of his own needs, ready to act and willing to suffer.

This, like so much else pointed out by Dale, is the essence of it. I would add that our fear for Henchard is complicated by both admiration and frustration: "admiration" because he does have the courage to take action under stressful circumstances and his courage is so often born of a deep, self-unthinking generosity of spirit (as in the raging bull sequence), that our loyal affections can only be aroused for him commingled with a strong urge to protect him from himself; "frustration," too, because his courage has rash edges to it and that's when we fear, dreadfully, for him — that is, when heroic risk-taking breaks its own boundaries and becomes recklessness.

I feel Eustacia has these qualities too, but latently, because hers is the dilemma of the prisoner (trapped: no money to facilitate escape, no opportunities to grasp — unlike Henchard) and her hero status is more that of the Prometheus (Bound) kind: she'll seize all and any chance that comes her way but none has the size of salvation. Her attempts to fight her condition, mirrored by her efforts to play the warrior, the Turkish Knight, are pitiful. Her faith in Possibility, mirrored by her dreams of Paris with the man who has been living and working there, is also pitiful. A different kind of heroism maybe?

Best, Rosemarie.

PS I've just caught Nathan's message and cannot agree with Norman Page's "Wheel of Fortune" analogy. Henchard *doesn't* end "socially" where he began; he now has a reputation and a history of some significance. He also has, in Elizabeth-Jane, a compassionate disciple who will bear witness to his struggle. He had none of this at the outset.

Thu, 28 Feb 2002 18:10:21 –0000
MARCUS BARRETT <MMB@barrett.supanet.com>
Subject: Hardy's tragic heroes?

As one of the List's normally silent majority I offer my gratitude for the current, fascinating discussion on the nature of "Tragedy" in Hardy and offer a modest contribution gleaned from, I think, Millgate (ed), *The Life* (London: Macmillan, 1984):

> 1878 "April - Note. A Plot, or Tragedy, should arise from the gradual closing in of a situation that comes of ordinary human passions, prejudices, and ambitions, by reason of the characters taking no trouble to ward off the disastrous events produced by the said passions, prejudices and ambitions."

Also: "May [1889] 'That which, socially, is a great tragedy, may be in Nature no alarming circumstance."

Apologies if these words have been used before, recently, but — opinions on "Classical Tragedy" apart — don't these comments from Hardy exemplify that great man's ability to make a remarkable tale from the stuff of everyday feelings and fears? He really was one who used to notice such things.

Best wishes from Dorset — Marcus Barrett

Thu, 28 Feb 2002 18:55:23 –0000
MICHAEL BARRY <michaelj.barry@talk21.com>
Subject: Re: Hardy's tragic heroes?

What a truly wonderful summary of Tragedy – thanks Rosemarie, from a humble practitioner who never seems to have time to read the books he should!

My acquired "wisdom" has always been that the Greeks provide us with tragic heroes, whose tragedy is entirely inflicted upon them by the Gods or Fate ("as flies to wanton boys are we to the Gods" – actually a Shakespearian quote), and that in theatrical terms this is (almost by definition) less interesting than the Shakespearian version of Tragedy (or should I say "Elizabethan" as it almost certainly is a response to the times and to current thought). This posits a hero who comes to a sticky end because of his own flaws and faults, in other words is the cause of his own undoing – and this is really interesting to watch, because like us, this type of guy *does* have choices to make and decisions to take and it is this process which is so fascinating for us, because we do all this likewise.

The Deus ex Machina weakens what is, at its best, the study of human beings struggling with their own humanity. Having said that, watching the Greeks on stage is always fascinating, so my argument doesn't perhaps have much drive behind it! When it comes to anti-heroes, I must say I've never seen them as somehow more downmarket or lower class than Heroes. I may be wrong, but an anti-hero in my book is a central character, who is morally more negative than positive, but with whom I am being invited to identify.

The supreme example to me is that wonderful Scottish classic (the subject of my very first, and still unmade, film script) "The Confessions of a Justified Sinner" by that truly splendid writer (and personal hero) James Hogg (perhaps best known to non-Scots as author of the song "Charlie is my darling").

Michael

Thu, 28 Feb 2002 17:06:41 -0400
RICHARD NEMESVARI <rnemesva@stfx.ca>
Subject: Hardy's tragic heroes/heroines

I don't have much to add to this topic, since the previous posters have provided eloquent and comprehensive comments on Hardy and tragedy.

Here are just a few random observations. It seems to me that often Hardy's tragic effect is centred on our awareness of wasted potential. Whatever combination of fate/coincidence, material circumstance, and character brings about the downfall of the protagonist, it is the sense of "what might have been" that creates the poignancy.

The Aristotelian pity generated, therefore, is free of the possible condescension which is the risk whenever we think of someone as "pitiful." I think this remains true of even the most "flawed" characters, since each of them has a kind of potentiality for better things which the text reveals even as it remorselessly arranges their catastrophe. As well, and without delving into the morass of Hardy's so-called philosophy ("Let me repeat that a novel is an impression, not an argument"), the tragedy is often generated by the "curse of consciousness."

It is humanity's self-awareness which creates tragedy because, unlike physical pain or even death itself, for something to be tragic it must be constructed as such within a psychological context. This is something Hardy comes back to over and over again – the idea that "it would have been better not to be" is simply unavailable to any other species, for good or ill. My dog can be hurt or afraid (although I do my best to prevent such things), but he can never perceive his situation as tragic. It is Hardy's powerful ability to communicate this additional and uniquely human level of suffering which gives his fictions such an impact. Richard

Fri, 1 Mar 2002 12:39:12 EST
EDDIE ARNAVOUDIAN: <EArnavoud@aol.com>
Subject: Re: Henchard's character, tragedy, and other stuff

As an aside to the substance of this discussion I feel that Henchard's fall as depicted by Hardy lacks authenticity and thus fails to communicate the essence of a tragic experience however that may be conceived. Henchard's collapse is all too sudden and apparently inexplicable. Here is a man who stubbornly keeps to an oath to refrain from drink, who reconstructs his life, establishes himself, is held in high regard by most and who manages a successful business almost by instinct. Is it quite possible for such a person to succumb so easily, and without real resistance, before a young upstart, albeit talented and charismatic? Is it consistent with his character to so suddenly become a passive victim to his past misdemeanours? Perhaps some Achilles Heel within his character I have missed. Perhaps I have not grasped something. The tragedy would be evident in the process of his collapse. Did I miss the unfolding psychological and social process?

Eddie

Fri, 1 Mar 2002 20:11:51 –0000
GARY ALDERSON <Gary.Alderson@btinternet.com>
Subject: Re: Henchard's character, tragedy, and other stuff

Yes, but Henchard was already not on top of his game. At the time that Farfrae turns up, he's already suffering from the bad grain. He's losing his reputation with the people of Casterbridge. And he's not just a passive victim. In some respects he's the author of his own downfall; it's his previous affair that brings Lucetta to Casterbridge, he makes Elizabeth-Jane take his surname and afterwards looks into his parentage. He goes into competion against a more up-to-date opponent. And it's Farfrae's modern-ness, at the end of the day, that sets him apart from the backward Casterbridge locals. Henchard's been a big fish in a small pool, but the pool's getting bigger. And once Farfrae starts to win, it's Henchard's pride that really does him in. That said, of course Hardy's got to be a bit melodramatic. After all, it is a novel. Gary

Sat, 02 Mar 2002 08:59:25 -0500
PHILIP ALLINGHAM: apalling@tbaytel.net
Subject: Re: Hardy's tragic heroes/heroines

According to Sidney Lamb in *Tragedy* (CBC: Toronto, 1964), although the form of tragedy written in Elizabethan England differs somewhat from that written in ancient Greece, in both eras tragedy was a reflection of a hierarchical society, even as Hardy's Novels of Character and Circumstance are. Even late in the twentieth century with the tragedy of the average man well-established critically, we still tend to think of a tragedy as "the story of the fall from greatness of an exalted personage" – a king (Sophocles' Oedipus or Shakespeare's Lear), a general (Aeschylus' Eteocles or Shakespeare's Macbeth), or a man of great wealth, rank, and social prestige (The Old Testament's Job or Shakespeare's Romeo). Consequently, the fall of Michael Henchard from prosperity and power to obscurity and alienation is certainly the stuff of Aristotelian tragedy. Even though the French tragedian Beaumarchais argued that "The nearer the suffering man is to my station in life, the greater is his claim upon my sympathy" (*Essay on the Serious Drama*, 1767), whether there can be a truly tragic middle-class hero is highly debatable, and therein may lie the problem with Henchard: he is simply not exalted enough, whereas Tess's suffering (rather than her D'Urberville lineage) is sufficient to exalt her.

Aristotle in *The Poetics* (330 B. C.) required two things of the tragic protagonist: he or she must be noble (whether in spirit or social status), and must be responsible for causing his own suffering (not necessarily death). Making references to his favourite tragedy, *Oedipus Rex* by Sophocles, the Greek philosopher proposed

1. A leader in his society, exemplifying both the good and bad elements of that society ('a person neither wholly good nor bad').
2. Disclosed to the audience at the height of his prosperity, power, and influence in that social group so that his fall from its favour will seem that much greater (and, therefore, more tragic).
3. Driven to his fall (social alienation, suffering, death, or exile) by some innate flaw (Greek: hamartia) in his nature or some fatal error ("misstep"), yet appear to have the ability to alter his course. (In other words, a tragic hero should appear to possess free will, and yet be a victim.).
4. Made a scapegoat for the sins or errors of his people – and accordingly be exiled or punished by them in such a way that his suffering is irreversible (since Oedipus is blinded, his suffering cannot be reversed).
5. The cause of his own punishment through his own folly and pride (hubris).
6. Ready to take upon himself the burden of his society's (and hence the audience's) sense of guilt, shame, inadequacy, or shortcoming.
7. Grander and more noble as the result of his futile struggle with fate.
8. Through his suffering instrumental in the resolution of a problem that plagued his society at the outset, and in the restoration of a harmony that was not present at the opening of the story.

Despite the fact that *The Mayor of Casterbridge* is not a drama in which we vicariously participate by watching an action and identifying ourselves with certain characters on stage, we may argue that Michael Henchard satisfies many of the Aristotelian requirements for the tragic hero. His physical power and strong-willed determination to succeed, to expiate his sin, and to do what he feels is best for Elizabeth-Jane are consistent with the usages of his society – as are his impulsiveness, quick temper, and manly pride.

Hardy reveals Henchard first as itinerant hay-trusser burdened by a wife and child as a sort of prologue; this antecedent circumstance renders his corporate and municipal rise all the more impressive, but also reveals how tentative this outward success is. As the suffering outcast whose daughter cannot reciprocate his affection, Henchard is far grander – and far more sympathetic – than the leader of the town council at the King's Arms' dinner. As he falls socially, we tend to acc-ept his sullenness and temper as part of the emotional makeup of this complex character. I am never sure as I re-read the novel's conclus-ion, however, as to whether Henchard satisfies the eighth point, except that his fate enriches Elizabeth-Jane's understanding of the human condition. Philip Allingham

BIBLICAL ALLUSIONS IN *TESS*
March 8th - 25th 2002

Fri, 8 Mar 2002 04:03:57 EST
SCOTTY <Scotty2705@aol.com>
Subject: *Tess of the D'Urbervilles*

I am doing a study of *Tess* at college and in particular I am investigating Hardy's use of Old Testament text in the narrative and what effect if any it has on the story. Would you or any of the members have any views on this. Thanks for your help.

Iain Walker.

Fri, 8 Mar 2002 08:21:53 -0800
BETTY CORTUS <hardycor@owl.csusm.edu>
Subject: Re: *Tess of the D'Urbervilles*

Dear Iain, You are right about Hardy's extensive use of biblical allus-ion in his works. He had a thorough knowledge of the Bible and ref-erences to biblical passages are to be found all through his writings. I do not know of a single book or essay that deals with this topic excl-usively, although if such a work exists I'm sure one of our members will bring it to our attention. Robert Schweik's essay "The Influence of Religion, Science, and Philosophy" in *The Cambridge Companion to Thomas Hardy* (ed. Dale Kramer, 1999), deals with this subject in part. And the article under the word "Bible" in the *Oxford Reader's Compan-ion to Hardy* (ed. Norman Page, 2000), notes that 87 biblical allusions have been detected in *Tess*, but unfortunately it does not list them. These may be good articles for getting you started nevertheless. There was an extensive discussion of a particular biblical allusion in *Far From the Madding Crowd* on the Forum back in 1998, but I couldn't find anything in the archives of a similar nature on *Tess*. Good luck with your research. Betty

Sun, 10 Mar 2002 15:07:30 -0600
GLEN ALKEMADE <gvanalkemade@jpusa.org>
Subject: Re: *Tess* and *Old Testament*

Iain, since the biblical references in *Tess* have been numbered at 87 but not identified, maybe this is an opportunity for you to do original research. You know what happens to essays like that, don't you? They get published. If you are not already pretty familiar with the *Old Testament*, though, you would have a hard time spotting the allusions. Hardy's literary allusions often take the form "as Shelley says..." or "in the Aeschylean phrase," but his biblical ones are much more discreet. Perhaps if several Forum members all share their favorite biblical *Tess* allusions with you, it would give you a fair start towards your study. Ch. 16 mentions Tess' affinity for the **Psalms (**Ps 148). In Ch. 39, the Clares read **Proverbs** 31 (In Praise of an Excellent Wife) in respect of the absent Tess. But my favorite is Hardy's reference to the "ironical Tishbite" in Ch.11, an allusion to 1 **Kings** 18:27, Elijah's taunt of the prophets of Baal.

A really compelling use of the *New Testament* occurs when Tess, returning to Marlott, encounters the disciple tagging scriptures on all available surfaces. His use of "Thy, Damnation, Slumbereth, Not" is provocative, because it is a misuse of the referenced scripture, 2 **Peter** 2:3 which actually reads "their damnation slumbereth not," and Peter is referring to false prophets, those who misquote and misuse the Word of God for their own purposes. The layers of irony here are endless. But my favorite NT ref is in the Stonehenge scene, "Like a greater than himself, to the critical question at the critical time he did not answer," an allusion to Christ before Pilate. I always weep. G.

Mon, 11 Mar 2002 16:53:29 -0500
ROSEMARIE MORGAN <rosemarie.morgan@yale.edu>
Subject: Re: *Tess* and *Old Testament*

Alec's self-modelling, in his conversion, upon the "chief of sinners," the "bachelor-apostle, whose deputy I thought I was" (St Paul), may be superficial (XLVII) but his deep knowledge of the scriptures is not. It is profound. I wonder what you make of this? Rosemarie

Mon, 11 Mar 2002 19:31:36 -0600
BILL MORGAN <wwmorgan@mail.ilstu.edu>
Subject: Re: *Tess* and *Old Testament*

I don't think anyone has mentioned the following studies that address – some more directly than others – the questions posed in the original posting: Deborah L. Collins, *Thomas Hardy and His God: A Liturgy of Unbelief* (NY: St. Martin's, 1990). Timothy Hands, *Thomas Hardy: Distracted Preacher,* (NY: St. Martin's, 1989). Marlene Springer, *Hardy's Use of Allusion* (London: Macmillan, 1983). And there's another book-length study by, I think, Jan Jedrewski (sp?), but I can't summon it at the moment; perhaps some other listmember will know.[2] Best, Bill Morgan

Mon, 11 Mar 2002 17:39:57 -0800
BETTY CORTUS <hardycor@owl.csusm.edu>
Subject: Re: *Tess* and *Old Testament*

Glen wrote in part:
> But my favorite is Hardy's reference to the "ironical Tishbite" in Ch 11, an allusion to 1 **Kings** 18:27, Elijah's taunt of the prophets of Baal.

Glen, although this has nothing to do with *Tess,* your posting reminded me of "Jezreel," a wonderful poem conjuring up Elijah by Hardy, which was inspired by the capture of the Plain of Esdraelon in Palestine by English troops in 1918. Hardy, curious about whether the entering soldiers were aware that Esdraelon and the biblical Jezreel were one and the same, jotted down these lines rapidly, calling them "just a poem for the moment" in a letter to Mrs. Henniker. In it he evokes the confrontation between Elijah and King Ahab and wond-ers if the soldiers remembered the events of long ago:

Did they catch as it were in a Vision at shut of the day –
When their cavalry smote through the ancient Esdraelon Plain,
And they crossed where the Tishbite stood forth in his enemy's way–
His gaunt mournful Shade as he bade the King haste off amain?[3]

He evokes further images in the poem from that biblical story, picturing Jehu "he who drove furiously" and Jezebel "that proud Tyrian woman who painted her face." This is just one of numerous instances where Hardy reveals just how vividly these biblical stories linger in his imagination. Betty

---

[2] From: Jeanie Smith <jean_e_smith@hotmail.com>: Bill Morgan's reference is to Jedrzejewski, Jan., *Thomas Hardy and the Church* (Basingstoke: Macmillan, 1996).
[3] *Thomas Hardy: The Complete Poems* (hereafter *CP*), edited by James Gibson (Macmillan London, 1976), 569

Tue, 19 Mar 2002 08:54:48 –0000
ALAN SHELSTON <alan@shelston.freeserve.co.uk>
Subject: Re: *Tess of the D'Urbervilles*:

Betty, Trevor Johnson's Manchester PhD thesis ('Churchy Hardy', plus subtitle) which I supervised, deals very much with all this and he has a chapter on *Tess*. The date is 1998 or 1999 – sorry not to be more specific but I'm sending this from home, and all my records are at the university. I can check it out if you need.   Alan Shelston

Mon, 11 Mar 2002 21:03:08 -0600
GLEN ALKEMADE <gvanalkemade@jpusa.org>
Subject: Re: *Tess* and *Old Testament*

> Alec's self-modelling, in his conversion, upon the "chief of sinners," the "bachelor-apostle, whose deputy I thought I was" (St Paul), may be superficial (XLVII) but his deep knowledge of the scriptures is not. It is profound. I wonder what you make of this?

The paragraph from which your quote is excerpted is the only one I see in which Alec demonstrates any specific Bible knowledge. I have two theories to account for Alec's seemingly obscure reference to Hymanaeus and Alexander.

1. Alec was converted by the preaching of Rev Clare, whom Hardy explicitly describes as thoroughly Pauline in his theology. Whatever discipleship he received was either from Clare or from the likes of the fence painter ("the brethren"). The complete context for the Hymanaeus remark is 1 **Timothy** 1:18-20, wherein Paul exhorts the young preacher Timothy to "fight the good fight, keeping faith and a good conscience," and then warns of the apostates Hymanaeus & Alexander. Taken together, I can readily see this passage as among the first Alec was taught.

2. The tone and structure of this particular line of dialogue sound more like Hardy's voice to me than Alec's, a criticism applied somewhat more often to his earlier novels. I think Hardy may have wanted to use this allusion somewhere because it fits Alec so well; maybe in an earlier draft it started in the narration but ended up in the dialogue. Hardy's own thorough bible knowledge may have sometimes obscured his judgement of what his readership would accept as coming from a shallow cad like Alec.

Glen

Tue, 12 Mar 2002 00:08:05 -0500
ROSEMARIE MORGAN <rosemarie.morgan@yale.edu>
Subject: Re: *Tess* and *Old Testament*

Glen, I'm intrigued by this question for several reasons, the main one being TH's curious inclination to have his "baddies" exceptionally well versed. Sgt Troy is a good example: he is by far the most well-read person in *FFMC*; Oak's reading isn't even close although he *is* one of "nature's aristocrats'" as Hardy would put it — well-versed in the natural world. Back to Alec: the intriguing aspect in his case is that if Parson Clare is an influence on his reading how and where does this occur? There is an unpleasant scene between the pair when, according to Angel, his Parson father is humiliated in his messianic zeal to preach at Alec. Later, Alec expands on this encounter in an attempt to convince Tess of his own true Pauline calling, his radical nonconformism, as one who has suffered derision at the hands of the Church (ie., Clare). In holding forth to Tess about the "extreme wing of Christian believers to which I belong" he makes a clear different-iation between his set of beliefs and Parson Clare's.

The truth is that Alec almost certainly knows his stuff (not simply the book of **Timothy**), and in contrast to Angel's intellectual suffoc-ation of Tess he draws out of her some serious philosophical ex-changes – (e.g., the Sermon on the Mount conversation). To add grist to the mill, according to Angel his Parson father is an Evangelical yet the Clare sons, at the outset of the book, are said to be reading *A Counterblast to Agnosticism* (altered from the original in the MS where their reading is topically Broad Church). This indicates their interest in the current schools of biblical revisionism. This interest was not characteristic of the Evangelical persuasion.

I'd like to add just one more grain to the grist: Angel assumes Tess (who is a churchgoer but not necessarily a believer – in common with her author) to be a "Tractarian and Pantheistic in essence." A "Tractarian"? This is an extraordinary perception under the circum-stances, especially given her Pagan appropriation of church litanies (is this intended to be one of his many misperceptions maybe?). No doubt Hardy is deliberately appealing to his Victorian readers' fervent interest in these current sectarian movements, the conflict they generated and the fury they aroused. Alec, in expatiating to Tess on the "extreme wing of Christian believers to which I belong" is impli-cated in this conflict (he has already been to the North of England to proselytise) albeit, like Arabella after him, a convert with a good deal of "con" and less of the "vert" (sorry to end with such an – ugh! – feeble pun). Cheers, Rosemarie

Wed, 20 Mar 2002 01:26:43 –0000
GARY ALDERSON <Gary.Alderson@btinternet.com>
Subject: *Tess* and the *OT*

Well I thought I'd see how many allusions I could spot in *Tess*. After a week's reading, I've come out with about 50 references and a burning desire to kick Angel Clare in the seat of the pants. Of course, what doesn't help is sorting the *New Testament* from the *Old Testament* references, particularly where there are actually passages in the *NT* referring to the *OT* (eg "Babylon").

Ch I: "how are the mighty fallen" 2 **Sam** 1:19 [David's lament on the deaths of Saul and Jonathon]
Ch IV: "Better to drink with Rolliver in a corner of the housetop than with the other landlord in a wide house" **Prov** 15:17 ["Better a dinner of herbs where love is, than a stalled ox and hatred therewith."]
Ch XI: "the ironical Tishbite" 1 **Kings** 18 [Elijah, asking what the god Baal is up to when he doesn't answer his prophets]
Ch XI: "sins of the fathers" **Ex** 34:7 ["Keeping mercy for thousands, forgiving iniquity and transgression and sin, and that will by no means clear [the guilty]; visiting the iniquity of the fathers upon the children, and upon the children's children, unto the third and to the fourth [generation]."]
Ch XII: "the serpent hisses" **Gen** 3
Ch XII: "thou shalt not commit –" **Ex** 20:14 [adultery]
Ch XII: "dust and ashes" **Gen** 18:27 ["And Abraham answered and said, Behold now, I have taken upon me to speak unto the Lord, which [am but] dust and ashes"
Ch XIV: "Aholah and Aholibah" **Ezek** 23:4 [Unfaithful Israel and Judah, portrayed as women]
Ch XIV: "Sorrow, I baptize thee" **Gen** 3:16 ["Unto the woman he said, I will greatly multiply thy sorrow and thy conception; in sorrow thou shalt bring forth children; and thy desire [shall be] to thy husband, and he shall rule over thee."
Ch XV: "D'Urberville, like Babylon, had fallen" **Rev** 14:8 (**Dan** 4:30) [A New Testament quote, but the **Revelation** passage is looking back to passages such as in **Daniel**, where Babylon is the embodiment of godless evil].
Ch XVI: "O ye Sun and Moon" **Psalm** 148:3 ["Praise ye him, sun and moon: praise him, all ye stars of light."]

Ch XVIII: "Angel" Various; ["Angel" in Greek means "messenger." But in the *Old Testament*, an "Angel" can be God's messenger, or God himself. Which, in a way, is what Angel becomes to Tess?]

Ch XVIII: "strumming upon an old harp" 1 **Sam** 16 [King David played upon a harp. There are references to Angel being like David (or rather, of Tess being like Bathsheba) later in the novel.]

Ch XVIII: "the road to dusty death" **Psalm** 22:15 ["My strength is dried up like a potsherd; and my tongue cleaveth to my jaws; and thou hast brought me into the dust of death."]

Ch XIX: "the man of Uz" – "my soul chooseth strangling" **Job** 1:1, 7:15 [Job suffered and let God know about it.]

Ch XIX: "Abraham" Various; [in **Genesis** Abraham ended up with a lot of sheep.]

Ch XIX: "his spotted and his ring-straked" **Gen** 30:32 ["I will pass through all thy flock to day, removing from thence all the" speckled and spotted cattle, and all the brown cattle among the sheep, and the spotted and speckled among the goats: and [of such] shall be my hire." Jacob (Abraham's son) when looking after Laban's sheep.]

Ch XIX: "the Queen of Sheba" 1 **Kings** 10 [Not renowned for being poor – just not as wise as Solomon.]

Ch XX: "Adam and Eve" **Genesis** 3

Ch XXIII: "a time for everything" **Ecclesiastes** 3 ["A time to cast away stones, and a time to gather stones together; a time to embrace, and a time to refrain from embracing."]

Ch XXIII: "Three Leahs to get one Rachel" **Gen** 29 [Jacob served 7 years to marry Rachel; but Laban gave him Leah to marry instead. So he had to serve another 7 years for Rachel.]

Ch XXVII: Eve and Adam **Gen** 3

Ch XXXI: "She walked in brightness, but she knew that in the background those shapes of darkness were always spread" **Isa** 59:9 ["Therefore is judgment far from us, neither doth justice overtake us: we wait for light, but behold obscurity; for brightness, [but] we walk in darkness."

Ch XXXVI: "The intuitive heart of woman knoweth not only its own bitterness" **Prov** 14:10 ["The heart knoweth his own bitterness; and a stranger doth not intermeddle with his joy."

Ch XXXIX: "Words of King Lemuel" "Who can find a virtuous woman?" **Prov** 31

Ch XXXIX: "Like the prophet on the top of Peor" **Num** 23:28 [Balaam, who was paid to curse Israel but could only bless them.]

Ch XXXIX: "No prophet had told him, King Lemuel" **Prov** 31

Ch XLI: "All is vanity" **Ecc** 1:2 ["Vanity of vanities, saith the Preacher, vanity of vanities; all [is] vanity."]

Ch XLV: "the old Adam" **Romans**, looking back at **Gen** 3 [Yet another *New Testament* reference, referencing the *Old.*]

Ch XLV: "fleshly tabernacle" 2 Peter, **Exodus** [The *NT* writers take up the *OT* concept of "tabernacle" (a non-permanent temple) to apply to their bodies.]

Ch XLVI: "the gins and nets that the wicket may set for them" **Ps** 140:5 ["The proud have hid a snare for me, and cords; they have spread a net by the wayside; they have set gins for me."]

Ch XLVI: "Angels of Heaven" *NT*, looking back at **Genesis** "And he dreamed, and behold a ladder set up on the earth, and the top of it reached to heaven: and behold the angels of God ascending and descending on it."]

Ch XLVI: "I thought I worshipped on the mountains, but I find I still serve in the groves!" Various; eg 2 **Chron** 33:3 [Groves were the site of pagan worship; the "high places" weren't normally so bad, as the children of Israel normally worshipped God there (albeit in an individualistic way). Best of all was "Mount Zion," the temple in Jerusalem.]

Ch XLVI: "Maddening mouth since Eve's" **Gen** 3

Ch XLVII: "creature from Tophet" **Jer** 7 [Within the valley of Hinnon (later "Gehenna"), where the Israelites sacrificed their children to the god Molech by burning them. So, by analogy, the dark place.]

Ch XLVII: "chaos" **Gen** 1 [Chaos = the Void, = the sea-monster Rahab]

Ch XLVII: "stern prophet Hosea" **Hos** 2:7

Ch XLVIII: "Jacob's ladder" **Gen** 28:12

Ch XLVIII: "the punishment you have measured out" Various; eg **Jer** 30:11 ["For I [am] with thee, saith the LORD, to save thee: though I make a full end of all nations whither I have scattered thee, yet will I not make a full end of thee: but I will correct thee in measure, and will not leave thee altogether unpunished."]

Ch XLIX: "Abraham might have mourned over the doomed Isaac" **Gen** 22:2 [When God tested Abraham by telling him to sacrifice his son.]

Ch XLIX: "the gleaming of the grapes of Ephraim better than the vintage of Abi-ezer" **Judges** 8:2

Ch L : "paradise" **Gen** 3 (**Rev** 2) [The concept of heaven as a garden; *NT* looking back at **Gen** 2-3

Ch L: "everything under the sky" **Ecc** 3 ["To every [thing there is] a season, and a time to every purpose under the heaven."]

Ch LI: "Egypt – land of promise" **Genesis/Exodus/Judges** [Jacob and his family went to Egypt; under Moses they left and went

to the Promised Land. But the Israelites wanted to go back, suddenly claiming life in Egypt (where they were slaves, and their sons were murdered at birth) was much better than life in the desert.]
Ch LII: "the little finger of the sham d'Urberville" 1 **Ki** 12:10 ["My little [finger] shall be thicker than my father's loins." – Rehoboam taking over when his father Solomon dies.]
Ch LII: "Canaan – Egypt" [See above]
Ch LIII: "children of the soil" **Gen** 2 [A reference to Adam, who is made from the dust of the earth?]
Ch LIII: "wife of Uriah" 2 **Sam** 11:3 [Bathsheba, with whom David slept – he then made sure Uriah got bumped off.]
Ch LIV: "how are the mighty fallen" 2 **Sam** 1:19 [The theme of the book, really.]
Ch LV: "prophet's gourd" **Jonah** 4 [The gourd grew up and gave Jonah shade, then suddenly died.]
Ch LVII: "it came to me like a shining light" **Prov** 4:18 [Ironic allusion? — "But the path of the just [is] as the shining light, that shineth more and more unto the perfect day."]
Ch LVIII: "did they sacrifice to God here?"**Exodus** [and others.]

Gary

Wed, 20 Mar 2002 08:08:11 -0500
ROSEMARIE MORGAN <rosemarie.morgan@yale.edu>
Subject: Re: *Tess* and the *OT*

Gary's comment:
> Of course, what doesn't help is sorting the *New Testament* from the *Old Testament* references, particularly where there are actually passages in the *NT* referring to the *OT* (eg "Babylon")

set me a'thinking. I'm reminded of the concept of "kernel sentences" – a component part of Chomsky's discourses on generative linguistics. It occurred to me that, for example, "dust and ashes," originating in Psalm 22: 15, produces a plethora of variations of which Shakespeare's "way to dusty death" (*Macbeth*) is but one. Likewise with "Angel of Heaven" (*NT/***Genesis**) and "O ye Sun and Moon" (**Psalm** 148:3) both of which, as primary or elementary structures of language, surface in Hamlet's speech formations. This is rather a long way around to Gary's "sorting" but an intriguing route to travel by if there is a thesis in the making? Good luck, Gary!

Cheers, Rosemarie

Wed, 20 Mar 2002 18:28:26 –0000
GARY ALDERSON <Gary.Alderson@btinternet.com>
Subject: Re: *Tess* and the *OT*

Fascinating stuff ... because of course as Rosemarie points out, the specific phrase "angels of heaven" occurs in the *NT* (eg **Matt** 24) rather than the *Old*; I picked the **Genesis** reading because it's the first specific link of angels with heaven that I could find. So Hardy is alluding to Shakespeare, who is taking an expression from **Matthew** who is using the concept of **Genesis**... Gary

Sun, 24 Mar 2002 13:27:44 -0600
GLEN ALKEMADE <gvanalkemade@jpusa.org>
Subject: Re: *Tess* and *Old Testament*

This goes back a few days to some terrific remarks Rosemarie made. TH's curious inclination to have his "baddies" exceptionally well versed. I missed last year's discussion on Hardy's religious beliefs.

Perhaps it's been beaten into the ground, but suffice to say Hardy had some sort of grudge against religious types that forms one of the dominant themes in his life work. Did he have a particularly devastating experience with hypocrisy in the Church, some time as a young man? He was so private, and destroyed so many of his own records, can we ever be sure, or only infer from his treatment of "baddies"?

Next, "*if Parson Clare is an influence on his [Alec's] reading how and where does this occur*?" You're right; I re-read Ch XLV and clearly Alec came to faith some time after his encounter with Clare, who writes his encouraging letter to Alec some time later yet. So Alec has only been hanging out with the fence-painting crowd.

Later, Alec expands on this encounter in an attempt to convince Tess of his own true Pauline calling, or his radical nonconformism....he makes a clear differentiation between his set of beliefs and Parson Clare's. I do not see this. I think Alec is proud and pleased to be aligned with Clare...as evidenced by his regard for his letter from Clare.

The truth is that Alec most certainly knows his stuff (not simply the book of Timothy) ...some serious philosophical exchanges –- (ie., the Sermon on the Mount conversation). Tess lived in reverential adoration of Angel and did not discuss faith matters with him as a token of respect to his lofty thoughts. She explains as much to Alec. I don't think Alec draws anything out of Tess. She speaks frankly (or carelessly) to him because she doesn't care a whit what he thinks.

To add grist to the mill, according to Angel his Parson father is an Evangelical ....revisionism – not, I think, an Evangelical persuasion! As the novel unfolds, Angel's brothers are portrayed as profoundly conventtional, of narrow views, and perhaps of cardboard personality. They seem to lack any passion or zeal, and although there is no evidence from the text, I wonder if in later life Parson Clare was not as disappointed with his two ordained sons as with his heterodox son.

Angel assumes Tess ...to be a Tractarian and Pantheistic in essence .... apppealing to his Victorian readers' fervent interest in these current sectarian movements. I don't know anything about the current sectarian movements but for Angel to perceive Tess as a Tractarian even after she remarks that it had long troubled her that she can't quite hang on to what she hears in Church is surely a great misperception.

I've idealized girls I was fond of, and made them over in my own image. That's why (I'm afraid) I identify most with Angel in this novel. When I confessed this in a recent book study I was leading, my students (all women) nearly threw me out. Glen.

Wed, 20 Mar 2002 18:28:26 –0000
CHARLES ANESI <Charles.Anesi@wellsfargo.com>
Subject: RE: *Tess* and *Old Testament*

On this subject, does anyone know if Hardy spent any time studying the Talmud? In translation, obviously. I ask because the Yahwistic god image – irascible, and afflicting righteous and sinful alike for reasons known only to himself -- is so obviously pronounced in Hardy's works. Chuck Anesi

Mon, 25 Mar 2002 04:23:56 –0000
GARY ALDERSON <Gary.Alderson@btinternet.com>
Subject: Re: *Tess* and *Old Testament*

To add grist to the mill, according to Angel his Parson father is an Evangelical yet the Clare sons, at the outset of the book, are said to be reading ***A Counterblast to Agnosticism.***

Mr Clare's evangelicalism is always very much commented on -- but Hardy makes it clear that it's not fashionable any more. To quote Michael Saward in "Evangelicals on the Move" –- "Numbers, then, they had. What they had lost was respect."

The high-water mark of nineteenth century evangelicalism was about 1860; thereafter, intellectually they were overtaken by the

Tractarians (which we would call Anglo-Catholics today), and more dangerously the liberals. We can see the rise of the Tractarians even as early as c. 1840 in *UGT*.

Hardy makes it pretty clear that the younger Clares don't share their father's evangelical beliefs:

> They were both dutiful and attentive sons, and were regular in their visits to their parents. Felix, though an offshoot from a far more recent point in the devolution of theology than his father, was less self-sacrificing and disinterested. More tolerant than his father of a contradictory opinion, in its aspect as a danger to its holder, he was less ready than his father to pardon it as a slight to his own teaching. Cuthbert was, upon the whole, the more liberal-minded, though, with greater subtlety, he had not so much heart.

So while their beliefs are actually going in the direction of Hardy's, he respects them less than the Old School. Some kind of tribute to the Moules? But then Hardy never seems to be that impressed with liberal Christianity — eg "The Respectable Burgher."   Gary

POSSIBLE NEW HARDY POEMS
April 8th - June 20th 2002

Mon, 08 Apr 2002 20:06:03 -0400
ROBERT SCHWEIK <rschweik@fiam.net>
Subject: Likely New Hardy Poems

Those who are members of the TTHA may have noticed a new entry in the "Editions" section of the TTHA Checklist for the year 2002 that reads as follows:

> Hardy, Thomas (?).*Fifty-seven Poems by Thomas Hardy*. Ed.with introduction by Bernard Jones.Gillingham, Dorset: Meldon House, 2002.
>
> [Fifty-seven poems for children previously published in three volumes respectively in 1911, 1912, and 1915, with pictures by E.J. Detmold and descriptions by Florence E. Dugdale. The introduction provides substantial evidence, both external and internal, that these poems may be attributed to Hardy. Three, on the basis of R.L. Purdy's evidences and authority, have already been included in scholarly editions of Hardy's verse. The issue of the authenticity

of the remaining poems will no doubt be the subject of scholarly discussion in this and future years.]

The question mark is, of course, unusual.[4] But so is the possibility that more than fifty new poems written by Hardy have been uncovered in this limited edition.

I thought that many on this list might want to read the poems and introduction for themselves and perhaps to take part in the discussion of the authenticity of their attribution to Hardy that will surely follow. For those, I'm giving here information about how to order a copy of the pamphlet:

> Address: Bernard Jones, Meldon House, The Red House, East Stour, Gillingham, Dorset SP8 5JY. Price is £10.50 plus £2.50 for overseas postage (one pound only for UK postage).

And because of the exorbitant cost of converting foreign currency checks via British banks Mr. Jones regretfully has to specify that all payments need to be in sterling checks or money orders. Copies may be available at the DCM, but whether any of the 250 they have will be left by the time of this summer's Hardy conference is at this time uncertain.

And, having stuck my neck out this far, I'd invite comments from Forum members on the question of whether these poems should be added to the canon of Hardy publications. Bob Schweik

---

Mon, 08 Apr 2002 22:57:04 -0400
ROSEMARIE MORGAN <rosemarie.morgan@yale.edu>
Subject: Re: Likely New Hardy Poems

Thanks Bob. I have suggested to Bill that we might look at some of these poems on TTHA's POTM, to gain a consensus (or not so to gain) on their provenance.

Alternatively, some of the poems could be transcribed and placed on TTHA's Members' Page for readers to enjoy. But, for now, let's start off, here on the Forum, with the first of the poems printed in the Jones edition (transcribed below).

Any other suggestions?

Besties, Rosemarie

---

[4] The editor of *Fifty-Seven Poems by Thomas Hardy*, Bernard Jones, does not include the question mark in his title.

THE POLAR BEAR

Where the lone Arctic snow-flake flies,
              I daily roam;
The dark night creeps, the tempest cries
                    About my home.

I have, in foreign lands afar,
                  A brother-bear;
He is held by iron bolt and bar
                  A captive there.

So, while I range here uncontrolled
                  In wildest mood,
He has to do what he is told,
                  And wait for food.[5]

Tue, 9 Apr 2002 13:32:21 +0100
JAMES GIBSON <James.Gibson@ukgateway.net>
Subject: The 'Baby' poems

Whilst working on TH's *Complete Poems* in the Seventies I came across R. L. Purdy's statement that one poem in each of the three 'Baby Books' with 'Illustrations by E. J. Detmold' and 'Descriptions by Florence E. Dugdale' had been written by Hardy, and on Purdy's authority included them at the end of *Complete Poems*. Each bird, pet and beast has a piece of verse after Detmold's illustration of it and this is followed by Florence's prose contribution. Looking at the verses which had not been described as being by Hardy I could not see very much difference in the quality, and it seemed to me possible that Hardy had written them all, but for some reason or other did not want it known, and, of course, he has a history of this kind of behaviour. At the time I discussed this with Desmond Hawkins and he thought that it was probable. Since the beginning of the year Michael Irwin and I have been carefully studying the vocabulary and construction of these 'Baby' poems and with the aid of Martin Ray's invaluable Concordance[6] we have made some progress, which we

---

[5] Thomas Hardy, *Fifty-Seven Poems by Thomas Hardy*, edited by Bernard Jones (Meldon House: Dorset, 2002), 3 Hereafter *Fifty-Seven Poems*.

[6] To order the Poetry Concordance, go to The Thomas Hardy Association's Concordance Order Form at: http://www.yale.edu/hardysoc/Welcome/orderf.htm
The Poetry Concordance comes free to TTHA members.

hope will lead to a scholarly paper on it being published later in the year. In the meantime, the question-mark remains!

All good wishes, Jim Gibson

Thu, 25 Apr 2002 15:45:06 -0700
BETTY CORTUS <hardycor@owl.csusm.edu>
Subject: Re: Likely New Hardy Poems

Dear Members, Rosemarie Morgan recently printed on the Forum the first poem in a series of 57 new poems attributed to Hardy. I was very happy to hear that James Gibson and Michael Irwin are working on a scholarly study to attempt to determine if these are indeed Hardy's work. Rosemarie hoped that Forum members might not feel constrained to comment on the likelihood of Hardy's authorship of these poems – perhaps because experts are working on the subject many, myself included, may have felt a little intimidated about expressing an opinion.

Nevertheless, I will stick my vulnerable neck out with two simplistic, decidedly unscientific comments:
- ❖ First, the content of the poem is in perfect harmony with Hardy's well-known compassion for animals, particularly for animals caged, or suffering in any way at the hands of humankind.
- ❖ Secondly, while the language in these poems written for children is simple, the author does not "write down" to his readership. This is also true of the poems attributed to Hardy in the three 'Baby Books' with 'Illustrations by E. J. Detmold' and 'Descriptions by Florence E. Dugdale.'

Particularly, in regard to Hardy's concern "that innocent creatures should come to no harm," I would be most interested to hear further comments from admirers of the "man who used to notice such things." Best Wishes to All, Betty Cortus

Thu, 25 Apr 2002 19:46:17 –0400
ANDY BELYEA <andybelyea@rogers.com>
Subject: RE: Likely New Hardy Poems

Okay Betty, me too – I'll take the leap. I entirely agree with your observations and would add:
1. Hardy, the master of perspective, often uses animals in his "animal"or "nature" poems (I hate to pigeon-hole them, as they are all philosophical poems of "seeming" or "impression," like most of his others) to comment on how animals might imagine

the human condition. Frequently, he relies on birds, who (and I'll say "who" and not "which," since he personifies so many of them) have the ultimate spatial perspective and no fixed address. Here, similarly, we are invited to imagine ourselves looking down on the earth between two semi-fixed locations – the "Arctic" and "some foreign land" –- and to tap into the irony such a doubling or comparison enables. Here, Hardy toys with natural vs domestic freedom, the inappropriateness and arrogance of humans controlling nature, and human interference – maybe that's too strong, maybe "presence" is better –- in long-term natural and evolutionary processes).

2. Even though some of the terms and phrases here seem familiar – "lone," "roam," "captive," "uncontrolled," "wildest mood" – they all have Hardy's often ghoulish flavour (ie. him as spectre floating around watching, à la his comment in *The Life*). Note, too, how other inanimate objects of Nature merit personification: the dark night creeps and the tempest cries.

3. I wonder if his animals may be intended to form part of his unconscious Will and that they are pondering consciousness. Our sympathy might determine whether they do. In many of his animal poems, like this one, we get the impression that they are watching us as we read about them, in a somnambulistic, semi-conscious way and with a subtle ability to "wonder" whether they ought to model the only form of consciousness available: ours. Maybe it's all part of Hardy's desire to wake humans up to the possibility that how we treat animals and each other may have long-term evolutionary impact (ie. Unconscious Will). Wary of the risk of fitting this poem into my idea, I think the idea tangentially suits the poem.

How does the polar bear know about his brother? Because, the poet suggests, he (like us), has the power of imaginative observation. If he can see his fellow creature, then maybe he can see us, too. Maybe they both can, and that's the whole point of the personification. The polar bear can sympathize: can we? Sounds like Hardy to me.

Andy Belyea

Sat, 27 Apr 2002 18:10:23 +0100
MICHAEL BARRY <michaelj.barry@talk21.com>
Subject: Re: Likely New Hardy Poems

I hadn't really tuned into this debate until right now – and this sounds intriguing and amazing! A range of poems newly discovered, possibly by Hardy, written for children? The Wessex Actors Company has the Community Chest, a portfolio of (currently) 10 small-scale productions for community venues like village halls, schools, libraries, museums etc. ("The Indiscretion of an Heiress" is one of these, as performed at the Hardy Conference 2 years ago). Is there any chance we might get a chance to perform them – even before validation (ie while an "air of mystery" still surrounds them!) to libraries and primary schools in our 5 county constituency? We are a deserving and unfunded charity, if that sways anyone, with a fondness for Hardy (5 productions to date).   Michael Barry

Mon, 29 Apr 2002 07:34:23 -0400
ROSEMARIE MORGAN <rosemarie.morgan@yale.edu>
Subject: Re: Likely New Hardy Poems: 2 & 3

Here are two more "Baby" poems:

- II -

THE DONKEY
Alas for the humble goal
That looms in the life anon
Of a thoughtful Ass's foal
Like me, when I muse thereon!

Perhaps I shall pull a cart —
Perhaps I shall carry a pack —
Perhaps at a sea-resort
I shall bear little boys on my back.[6]

- III -

THE CHIMPANZEE
Being one of the Monkey tribe
I have to suffer many a gibe.
And it is true I lack the grace
That marks the human form and face.
But yet, perhaps, I may say this,
We do not always act amiss.
For instance, I can climb a tree
With quite immense rapidity;
And some can see-saw by the tail

---

[6] *Fifty-Seven Poems*, 5

> From branches the most thin and frail;
> And every one among us chatters
> Until we sound as mad as hatters.
> But I should seem to brag to you
> If I told more that we can do.[7]

Using Martin Ray's wonderful Poetry Concordance I found that "Mad as Hatters" also features in Hardy's poem, "Channel Firing," also 55 instances of things that suffer. Cheers, Rosemarie

Tue, 30 Apr 2002 22:02:06 +0100
JAMES GIBSON <James.Gibson@ukgateway.net>
Subject: Re: Likely New Hardy Poems

Dear Michael, You will have to be careful about the copyright situation until the writer of the 'Baby' poems is known with more certainty. If Hardy wrote them, they are out of copyright because they were published before his death in 1928, and such items came out of copyright in 1999, seventy years after his death. If they were written by Florence they are still in copyright. As she died in 1937, her writings will remain in copyright until 1 January 2008.

Best wishes, James

Wed, 08 May 2002 11:15:10 -0400
ROSEMARIE MORGAN <rosemarie.morgan@yale.edu>
Subject: Re: Likely New Hardy Poems/New poems 4 & 5

Greetings all: Although some of us have had, by private email, some intriguing responses to the "Baby" poems folks are apparently feeling shy about voicing their thoughts publicly on the Forum. This is such a shame! However small the "thought" it is still of immense value to the rest of us as we all try to assess the authorship of these poems. Every single point adds up. Remember the precepts of wise Brother William to Adso in *The Name of the Rose* – that the world doesn't yield up its truths in the single instance or momentary perspective but in the endless array of symbols it presents to the mind of the truth-seeker? So, how about a Forum "array"?

Here goes with poems 4 & 5.

Cheers, Rosemarie

---

[7] *Fifty-Seven Poems*, 7

- IV -

THE HIPPOPOTAMUS
Yes, I am a Hippopotamus;
You would not like to be born thus,
Though, as for me and all my kind,
We are used to it and do not mind.
My baby mouth is rather large
Even when I am in my mother's charge.
My skin is loose and wrinkled too,
But it suits me, as yours suits you;
For, living mostly in a river,
The soaking wet would make me shiver
If I had not a thick great-coat
About my body, neck and throat.
My very name means "River Horse,"
In reference to my haunts, of course.[8]

- V -

THE GIRAFFE
I am no camel, cow, or calf,
But a queer thing they call "Giraffe,"
At whose long neck some people laugh.

And I am really soft and mild,
And would not hurt the smallest child,
Or frailest life that roams the wild.[9]

Thu, 09 May 2002 10:30:21 -0400
MICHAEL MILLGATE <michael.millgate@utoronto.ca>
Subject: Re: Likely New Hardy Poems

Bob Schweik's suggestion was a good one: The three canonised "baby" poems do help, especially since one comes from each of the three original Detmold volumes. The problem, I suspect, with the "new" poems shown on the List – the reason why people are hesitant

---

[8] *Fifty-Seven Poems*, 9.
[9] *Fifty-Seven Poems*, 13.

to jump in with comments – is precisely that they are being seen in isolation rather than within the context of Bernard Jones's booklet as a whole, including Jones's brief but, to me, persuasive introduction.

Reading the poems together one gets the sense, I believe, of hearing Hardy everywhere (as a notable Hardyan put it to me), of encountering characteristic turns of phrase, variations in metres and rhyme-schemes, touches of humour, and gestures of imaginative sympathy towards the animals themselves.

And while no one, I think, is likely to argue that these are to be numbered among Hardy's greatest works, they are surely charming and engaging poems written specifically for children – to be judged within that special generic context and recognised, in any case, as perfectly comfortable in the company of "The Calf," "The Yellow-hammer," and "About Lizards."

Again, those who haven't read the Jones introduction may not have realized the strength of the circumstantial evidence for Hardy's authorship of the poems. The title-pages of the three "baby" books acknowledge Detmold as the illustrator and Florence Dugdale as the author of the prose "descriptions" of the illustrated animals but say nothing about the poems that appear, effectively, as epigraphs to those descriptions.

And in light of the three already accepted "baby" poems, Purdy's expressed suspicions about others (based on his conversations with Florence and her sisters, see especially p. 316), TH's known penchant for "secret sharer" relationships, and the absence of any evidence of verse-writing (or capacity for such) on Florence's part, one is virtually forced to the conclusion that Hardy must have written not just "The Calf" and "The Yellow-hammer" and "About Lizards" but all of them – some, maybe, with his left hand! And Hardy's clearly established engagement with the three volumes provides in any case welcome evidence of his having retained his sense of humour and empathy with children long beyond the time by which he is popularly assumed to have sunk into hopeless gloom!

Bernard Jones is evidently publishing the booklet at his own cost and it would be grossly unfair to him – and tricky in copyright terms – to display all 57 poems on the TTHA list. But copies of the booklet itself are still, I believe, available, and the price being asked strikes me as very reasonable for an item that is in itself charming and well-produced and that promises to be of long-term value as a limited-edition first collective printing of what I personally am happy to accept as Hardy's poems for children.   Michael Millgate

"ABOUT LIZARDS" *THE BOOK OF BABY PETS: PICTURES IN COLOUR* BY
EDWARD JULIUS DETMOLD PUBLISHED BY HENRY FROWDE AND
HODDER AND STOUGHTON, LONDON, (1915), 75.
HEREAFTER *DETMOLD*.

Thu, 09 May 2002 02:04:03 -0400
ROSEMARIE MORGAN <rosemarie.morgan@yale.edu>
Subject: Re: Likely New Hardy Poems

Bob Schweik tells me he posted this message yesterday but it didn't appear on the Forum, as he intended, so here it is:

In response to Rosemarie Morgan's recent postings, it seems to me it might be very helpful to have before the Forum a posting with the text(s) of one or more of the three "Baby" poems now generally accepted to be Hardy's on the basis of various kinds of compelling evidences. I don't have any of those on hand as I write this, but perhaps someone else does. Those accepted poems could form a useful basis in comparing the others attributed to Hardy.

RM: So here are the three "Baby" poems Bob requested; they are already in print publication and attributed by R. L. Purdy to Hardy.[10]

- VI -

THE CALF

You may have seen, in road or street
    At times, when passing by,
A creature with bewildered bleat
Behind a milcher's tail, whose feet
    Went pit-pat. That was I.

Whether we are of Devon kind,
    Shorthorns, or Herefords,
We are in general of one mind
That in the human race we find
    Our masters and our lords.

When grown up (if they let me live)
    And in a dairy-home,
I may less wonder and misgive
Than now, and get contemplative,
    And never wish to roam.

And in some fair stream, taking sips,
    May stand through summer noons,
With water dribbling from my lips
And rising halfway to my hips,
    And babbling pleasant tunes.[11]

- VII -

THE LIZARD

If on any warm day when you ramble around
Among moss and dead leaves, you should happen to see
A quick trembling thing dart and hide on the ground,
And you search in the leaves, you would uncover me.[12]

---

[10] Richard Little Purdy, *Thomas Hardy: A Bibliographical Study*, 1954

[11] *Thomas Hardy, The Complete Poems*, edited by James Gibson (Macmillan London, Ltd, 1976), 945. Hereafter *CP*. See also, *Fifty-Seven Poems*, 19.

[12] *CP*, 952.

- VIII -

THE YELLOW-HAMMER[13]

When, towards the summer's close,
    Lanes are dry,
And unclipt the hedgethorn rows,
    There we fly!

While the harvest waggons pass
    With their load,
Shedding corn upon the grass
    By the road.

In a flock we follow them,
    On and on,
Seize a wheat-ear by the stem,
    And are gone....

With our funny little song,
    Thus you may
Often see us flit along,
    Day by day.[14]

What a crisply-perfect little poem: it sprints and darts with such palpable flurries that you can almost *hear* the heavy waggons lumbering on, by contrast, "with their load." – RM

DETMOLD "THE YELLOW-HAMMER," *BOOK OF BABY BIRDS* (1912), 75

---

[13] Gibson indents lines 2 & 4 by only one space as opposed to 4 spaces in Jones.
[14] *CP*, 946.

Thu, 09 May 2002 11:49:33 -0400
ROSEMARIE MORGAN <rosemarie.morgan@yale.edu>
Subject: Re: List of Likely New Hardy Poems

By way of an addendum to Michael's message my thinking is that 12 "baby" poems in total might be a reasonable limit to set. We have had, so far, "The Polar Bear," "The Donkey," "The Chimpanzee," "The Hippopotamus," "The Giraffe," and (from the Gibson Collection), "The Yellow-Hammer," "The Calf," and "The Lizard." This leaves four to go. I'll print below the poem titles and if you'd like to pick one (or all four) from the list I'll transcribe accordingly.

The Squirrel	The Rat	The Elephant
The Rhinoceros	The Tiger	The Camel
The Kangaroo	The Dog	The Kitten
The Colt	The Lamb	The Llama
The Fawn	The Magpie	The Long-Tailed Tit
The Willow Warbler	The Cygnet	The Oyster-Catcher
The Duckling	The Rhea	The Capercailzie
The Blue Tit	The Skua	Chickens
The Jay	The Gannet	The Redshank
The Green Tree-Frog	The Tropic Bird	The Whitethroat
The Long-Eared Owl	The Chaffinch	About Lambs
About Guinea-Pigs	About Rabbits	About White Mice
About Goldfish	About Kittens	About Hedgehogs
About Elephants	About Canaries	About Puppies
About the Kid	About Doves	About Squirrels
About the 'Cordon Bleu'	About Chicks	About Tortoises
About the Love-Bird		

Thu, 9 May 2002 10:38:27 -0700
BETTY CORTUS <hardycor@owl.csusm.edu>
Subject: Re: List of Likely New Hardy Poems

Even from the first few samplings of these poems appearing on the list so far, they seemed to me to have a decidedly Hardyesque quality. Now that I have seen the complete list of titles I am even more impressed by the fact that so many of them are about birds. I count eighteen, and possibly more if such critters unknown to me as "the Skua," "the Redshank," and "the Capercalzie" are identified as birds – are they in fact? I have often been impressed by the number of poems about birds and the pervasiveness of bird imagery in the canonized poems. An unnamed source quoted by William H. Pritchard writes that "the lot of a bird, for Hardy, is human life writ small."[15]

Hardy's pattern of drawing parallels between the fate of birds and that of humans is reiterated by F.B.Pinion, who writes at length about this subject. He argues: "The most persistent symbol in Hardy is connected with birds. Its significance varies, but its main theme is human happiness and suffering."[16] Of all living things, birds, because of their frailty, defencelessness against the elements and larger and stronger predators, do seem to represent, in miniature, the way Hardy frequently depicts human helplessness at the hands of fate.   Betty

Thu, 09 May 2002 15:22:36 -0400
ROSEMARIE MORGAN <rosemarie.morgan@yale.edu>
Subject: Re: List of Likely New Hardy Poems

Yes Betty, "such critters" are all birds: The Skua – (I looked this one up) is a large predatory sea-bird which pursues other birds and forces them to disgorge their catch. The poem craftily draws sympathy down on their heads by invoking the "baby's," the nestling's, innocent point of view! (very Hardyan) The Redshank is, I think, the equivalent of the American sandpiper. According to the poem they have red legs and seem to migrate north (!) The Capercalzie (or Capercallie) is a wood-grouse. I thought this had to be Scottish (given the Gaelic name) but maybe not. The poem doesn't indicate any specific locale, aside from the deep woods where (in the poem) they live contentedly on green buds but also, as harsh reality would have it, in fear of the gun.   Cheers, Rosemarie

Thu, 9 May 2002 19:47:31 –0400
JULIAN WHIPPLE <JWWHIPPLE1@attbi.com>
Subject: Re: List of Likely New Hardy Poems

Though I am unfamiliar with the Capercalzie, the Skua is a sort of gull and the Redshank a hawk. I wonder if Hardy's admiration of avian species might be at all connected to Gilbert White's "The Natural History of Selborne," a delightful book which Hardy might well have read. A friend told me it is the fourth most-published book in England! Just a thought. I must add my thanks for the brightening of Hardy's poetic reputation, which I have always thought unnecessarily dour.   Julian

---

[15] Hardy's Anonymous Sincerity," *Agenda*, Spring-Summer 1972, 100-116
[16] F.B.Pinion, *A Hardy Companion* (Macmillan, 1974).

Thu, 9 May 2002 19:49:22 –0400
JULIAN WHIPPLE <JWWHIPPLE1@attbi.com>
Subject: Re: List of Likely New Hardy Poems

Perhaps my memory is faulty – there is a kind of hawk here known as a "red-leg" or "red-shank." I bow to Rosemarie!   Julian

Tue, 14 May 2002 17:32:12 +0100
JAMES GIBSON <James.Gibson@ukgateway.net>
Subject: Likely new Hardy poems

The copyright position of the "Baby" poems is intriguing and will need to be taken into account when they are published today. As I said in a previous e-mail on the subject, *if* they are written by TH there is no copyright...but *if* they were written by Florence the executors of Florence's will will want payment. This could provide the Dugdale Estate with a good deal of money in the remaining years of the copyright. Now, as there is no mention of TH in any of the three books whereas all announce that the 'Descriptions are by Florence E. Dugdale,' it will have to be proved *beyond doubt* that TH wrote all of them, and that is going to be difficult to do.

The very fact that Florence said that he wrote three of the pieces of verse could be taken as evidence that he did write only three. I think that we shall need more evidence than has been presented so far that Hardy was the 'onlie begetter' of them all. Have we any lawyers in TTHA to advise us?   Best wishes, James Gibson

Tue, 14 May 2002 15:20:42 -0400 (EDT)
STEVE PASTORE <rarebks@aiconnect.com>
Subject: Re: Likely new Hardy poems

I'm a lawyer in the USA. Florence owns the copyright on the Baby Poems without any doubt. Even if TH did write all of them, he assigned his rights to her when he turned them over for publication under her name.   Steve

Tue, 14 May 2002 16:21:51 -0400
ROSEMARIE MORGAN <rosemarie.morgan@yale.edu>
Subject: New Hardy poems?

(oops –- just spotted a lawyer on the Forum – will post this anyway..)
A significant ambiguity lies in the fact that Purdy added to his three

attributions to Hardy – "The Lizard," ("About Lizards" in Jones) "The Yellow-Hammer" and "The Calf" – a note saying, "It is probable that [Hardy] had a hand in the revision of other poems in the book, " and that "Hardy's unacknowledged 'assistance' to Florence had gone beyond the contribution of just the three identified poems."[17] What does this mean? That Hardy's hand is omnipresent but that he wishes to keep a low profile? That Hardy merely advised on the occasional word, or phrase, or line? If the former – the omnipresent but anonymous hand – to whom might authorship be assigned (as in "anon" poems which are later identified) where none in the Detmold book is claimed for the poems? Apparently the book is mainly, or was mainly, intended to be a celebration of Detmold's illustrations?

There is an additional ambiguity here with regard to "The Yellow-Hammer." In Purdy's entry for this poem he takes note of the fact that it was unsigned but pencilled in Hardy's hand on the verso of a Macmillan presentation slip and accompanied by the following question addressed "presumably to Florence while the Baby Birds book was in preparation."[15] "Have seen them flitting thus, but do they eat corn? They may not have been there for that purpose – If so, will write a different verse."[18] What we now need is for someone to find a bunch of Macmillan presentation slips.   Cheers, Rosemarie.

PS. Although I cannot name them here, TTHA does have a sizeable bunch of lawyers among its members. But copyright lawyers? I believe USA copyright law differs from that of the UK & Europe – is this correct?

Tue, 14 May 2002 16:39:59 -0400 (EDT)
STEVE PASTORE < rarebks@aiconnect.com>
Subject: Re: New Hardy poems?

Copyright law is essentially uniform between the UK, Europe and the US. Any later admission by TH that he wrote the poems in question still does not cure the publication of them under FEH's name – a tacit admission that he transferred rights to her. I do not believe that anyone, except here perhaps, could argue with the logic of this. This is not to be confused with the far more puzzling logic of letters sent.

---

[17] *Fifty-Seven Poems*, iv
[18] Purdy, ibid, 316

Here, the writer retains the copyright although title to the actual words and paper passes to the recipient; note, however, that the name of the author appears by way of signature. Only recently have courts and legislators recognized that artworks (paintings) do not transfer copyright to the purchaser unless the artist specifically states in writing that there is such a transfer. Prior law, for centuries, differed with this modern change. In short, Cyrano did not retain the copyright to the utterances he attributed to his mouthpiece.   Steve

Tue, 14 May 2002 19:24:25 -0400
ROSEMARIE MORGAN <rosemarie.morgan@yale.edu>
Subject: Re: New Hardy poems?

I will try to clarify: I too am a little uncertain of what I'm trying to get at. So: three of the poems in question have already been attributed to TH (on Purdy's evidence, primarily) and are published under Hardy's name in James Gibson's edition of *The Complete Poems* and other editions. The Gibson Notes to the 3 poems say, in each case,
> First printed in *The Book of Baby Beasts/[Birds]/[Pets]*, illustrated by E. J Detmold, descriptions by Florence E. Dugdale (Oct 1911).

However, these same poems originally appeared in the Detmold Books as not attributed. The only names appearing on the title page are that of Detmold (for the "illustrations," in large print) and Florence Hardy (for the "descriptions," – not the verses – in small print).

If I understand you correctly, Steve, the verses appear, originally and legitimately, under Florence Hardy's copyright because they are not attributed to any one else? But then why not (for the sake of argument) attribute them to Detmold? Why would they necessarily be attributed to the "description" writer and not the "illustrator"? Incidentally (sorry to be complicated about this) what happens in the case of "anon" poems? Should the original author be discovered and proven to be the author of the poems do the poems become the copyright of the newly attributed "anon." Or is "anon" discounted altogether in terms of copyright law? Is "anon" considered a pseudonym for a legal entity or simply a legal nonentity? So – back to TH – how does this affect any future attributions if, for example, some of the other "Baby" poems can be shown (by some evidence or other) to be the work of Hardy? (as are the three already mentioned above).

I apologise for these convolutions. All best wishes, and many thanks for your kind help and good advice.   Rosemarie

Wed, 15 May 2002 05:58:59 -0400 (EDT)
STEVE PASTORE <rarebks@aiconnect.com>
Subject: Re: New Hardy poems?

Now I understand your original question. I presumed the poems were published under Florence's name. If they are under Detmold's name, they are either Detmold's copyright or the publishers' copyright. Anon poems remain the property of either the poet or the publisher depending on their deal. You may notice that sometimes an author retains the copyright to his published work – all that legal jargon on the back of the title page. It is interesting to figure out what happens with a book where no author or no publisher is stated – I suppose some limited edition pamphlets etc might fill this bill. Here as in all cases the issue becomes "who is asserting rights?" Let's say you decide to re-publish this book under your own name. The true author or publisher can assert a claim of copyright infringement – we all know you neither wrote nor published the original. As between Hardy and Florence (or Detmold), Hardy has the superior claim. As between a re-publisher (like Gibson), Florence or Detmold has the superior claim. An "attribution" is worthless legally speaking. Gibson could attibute "Convergence of the Twain" to his grandmother. Hardy still retains the copyright unless Gibson can show that Hardy provably obtained the poem from Grandmother Gibson who specifically retained the copyright but licensed it to Hardy for a one-time publication. Copyright does not vanish simply because we do not know who owns it. If you re-publish, one thing is certain, *you* are not the creator. As to the estate of anon work they have a difficult battle – they have to prove their antecedent created/published the work and that you didn't.   Steve Pastore

Wed, 15 May 2002 07:54:15 -0400
ROSEMARIE MORGAN <rosemarie.morgan@yale.edu>
Subject: Re: New Hardy poems?

Thank you so much, Steve, for giving this your valuable time and attention. Greatly appreciated.   Cheers, Rosemarie

Wed, 15 May 2002 09:24:23 -0400 (EDT)
STEVE PASTORE <rarebks@aiconnect.com>
Subject: Re: New Hardy poems?

The issues raised here are interesting but the actual controversy is *de minimis* (trivial as they say in the law). Lack of bad intent, peripheral fair use issues, a lack of real damage to Florence render the cause of action minor in the extreme. Had a multimillion pound/dollar deal been struck for the revelation of the Baby Poems, things would be different. I have copies of all of Florence's books, but not where I am now. My recollection is that her name prominently figures on all her books and the inference is most certainly that Detmold, a renowned illustrator, is not the poet/writer. *Lucy's Garden, Cousin Christine*, e.g., have her as the author. Given Detmold's fame, I cannot imagine what Florence's role would be in a collaboration if not to write the text. And, again as I recall, the Baby books all say "Illustrated by Detmold" which would imply that the text is by F.   SRP

Fri, 17 May 2002 09:31:38 -0400
ROSEMARIE MORGAN <rosemarie.morgan@yale.edu>
Subject: Re: Posting of numbers 9 & 10 of the Baby poems

Here are two more "Baby" poems, chosen by Michael Millgate.

- IX -

THE KITTEN
I like warm milk, and fires aglow
On hearths; for I am, as you know,
                A Kitten.

I like to jump at your two feet,
Or clutch the inky letter sheet
                Just written.

Or something hanging from above,
A bobbin, say; or claw your glove,
                Or mitten;

Or handkerchief, or anything
That can without much damaging
                Be bitten.

While, if you enter at the door,
And stroke me, I shall like you more,
For I am, as I said before,
                A Kitten.[19]

---

[19] *Fifty-Seven Poems*, 16

THE LLAMA

Mere beast of burden though I be,
I am proud of my utility;
And therefore should not feel depressed
But for one fact to be confessed:
It is that, being a simple Llama —
An understudy in Nature's drama
Of him that heads our family,
The Camel — large, compared with me,
(I only carry a hundredweight
And he a thousand as his freight) —
I feel myself looked down upon
In pitying comparison,
As if, whatever my application,
I only were an imitation.

However, now, as I have heard
Without much grief, Mules are preferred.[20]

Fri, 17 May 2002 06:43:25 -0700
BETTY CORTUS <hardycor@owl.csusm.edu>
Subject: Re: Posting of numbers 9 & 10 of Hardy's "Baby" poems

Dear Rosemarie, Thanks for posting Baby Poems 9 and 10. All I can say is how delightful they are. And if Hardy didn't write them I, for one, will eat my hat! Betty Cortus

Fri, 17 May 2002 10:50:28 -0400
ROSEMARIE MORGAN <rosemarie.morgan@yale.edu>
Subject: Re: Posting of numbers 9 & 10 of Hardy's "Baby" poems

I share your feeling, Betty! Tone, sentiment, point of view and even structure – particularly the extended line (tail?) for the kitten's "last flourish"– all seem peculiarly Hardyan. Unlike Steve at <rarebks@aiconnect.com> I don't have Florence's writings but if

---

[20] *Fifty-Seven Poems*, 20.

she's the author here I'd like to see some textual evidence, wouldn't you? Cheers Rosemarie

Fri, 17 May 2002 19:37:28 -0500
BILL MORGAN <wwmorgan@mail.ilstu.edu>
Subject: Authorship of the "Baby" poems

I've read all 57 of the "Baby" poems several times now, as well as Bernard Jones's "Introduction" and the correspondence here on the matter, and I'm convinced that the poems are indeed Hardy's work. The circumstantial case is very strong, the stylistic evidence is mostly persuasive, and the themes and rhetorical strategies of the pieces (e.g., the arguments in favor of ethical treatment of animals) are very characteristic of Hardy. So, I'm signing on: I'm convinced. I'm still interested to see what Jim Gibson and Michael Irwin's attribution study will turn up, of course, but I expect it to reach a similarly positive conclusion. If it does not, I will reconsider my endorsement.

Here is one circumstantial point that I don't think has yet been made. There are four plausible authors for the poems – Detmold, Florence, some staff writer for the publisher, and Hardy. Of those four, Hardy is by far the most likely author. If you think the poems are not by Hardy, then you will need to posit some other possible writer as yet undiscovered, I think.

One caution: since one of the three books is called *The Book of Baby Birds* and contains 19 poems, we probably shouldn't treat the high incidence of birds in the poems as evidence of Hardy's authorship: by definition, at least one third of the 57 poems have to be about birds – and it seems unlikely that Hardy would have had a hand in the choice of overall subject for the books (Baby Birds, Baby Pets, and Baby Beasts).

So, for now, I say welcome to these new items in Hardy's poetic canon – and thanks to Bernard Jones for calling them to our attention. Who'd have thought that at this late date we'd have new Hardy poems to consider? Cheers, Bill Morgan

Fri, 17 May 2002 21:32:41 -0400
ROSEMARIE MORGAN <rosemarie.morgan@yalc.edu>
Subject: Re: Authorship of the "Baby" poems

Bill — one question: is there any way of telling which came first – the Detmold or the Hardy? I suppose the illustrations came first since it was "Detmold's book" but is there any way of knowing? Is there any correspondence on the matter? any textual indications?

Cheers, Rosemarie

Fri, 17 May 2002 21:10:44 -0500
BILL MORGAN <wwmorgan@mail.ilstu.edu>
Subject: Re: Authorship of the "Baby" poems

Hi, Rosemarie, I would assume that the idea of the books came from Detmold or his publishers and that Florence was signed on (perhaps with Hardy's help) after the main outlines of the book had been agreed upon by other parties. Hardy then would have been the silent collaborator with Florence, and probably Detmold and the publishers were none the wiser. My inference about the sequence of events comes from a single sentence in one of Florence's letters in April of 1914 (to Rebekah Owen): "To my great grief I am just obliged to refuse to write, for my publisher, a book about dogs – to be illustrated by that splendid artist – Detmold."[21] I understand this to mean that she had been asked to prepare the text for another book of Detmold illustrations (this would be after the other three, *Beasts* in 1911, *Birds* in 1912, and *Pets* in 1913). We might guess that Hardy had a part in this refusal, since by the time of the letter he and Florence were married, and it would have been easier for someone to associate him with the text of any new Florence book. There may be textual indications in the poems to suggest that the illustrations came first; I haven't read them with that question in mind. There are, I think, no references to Detmold in *Collected Letters* or in *The Life and Work*. Bill.

Wed, 22 May 2002 12:25:54 -0400
ROBERT SCHWEIK <schweikr@localnet.com>
Subject: The "Baby Poems"

I've been fortunate to have a copy of Bernard Jones' edition of the fifty-seven poems he attributes to Hardy. What I (and I suspect many others) have not seen are examples of the Detmold illustrations and the "descriptions" provided by Florence Dugdale (not included in the Jones edition). Would anyone on the list be able to provide such examples for members of the Forum? Bob

---

[21] *Letters of Emma and Florence Hardy*, edited by Michael Millgate (Oxford: Clarendon, 1996) 95.

Thu, 23 May 2002 15:24:01 +0100
HELEN GIBSON <helen.gibson@ukgateway.net>
Subject: Re: The "Baby Poems"

We have a copy of the Baby Birds book, and I could scan a page or two and post them, if that would help.　　　　　　Helen Gibson.

Thu, 23 May 2002 11:44:39 -0400
ROSEMARIE MORGAN <rosemarie.morgan@yale.edu>
Subject: Re: The "Baby Poems"

That would be wonderful, Helen. The only problem is that I think Betty wants no attachments on the **Forum** (viruses). If this is correct then, with her permission, you could send them to me and I'll post them on TTHA's **News Updates** instead.　　　Cheers, Rosemarie

Thu, 23 May 2002 08:58:47 -0700
BETTY CORTUS <hardycor@owl.csusm.edu>
Subject: Re: The "Baby Poems"

This is true Helen, I would strongly discourage sending attachments of any kind to the List, but having them at the TTHA web-site would be wonderful. I for one would love to see them.　　　　　　Betty

Sat, 01 Jun 2002 18:37:35 -0400
ROSEMARIE MORGAN <rosemarie.morgan@yale.edu>
Subject: Re: "Baby" Poems

Greetings all: I'm half way through the new page of "Baby" poems, the Detmold illustrations and Florence's descriptions, but I'm afraid my progress has been painfully slow. You can take a peek at:
http://www.yale.edu/hardysoc/updates.htm.
I hope to complete this page next week.　Apologies for the delay,
　　　　　　　　　　　　　　　　　　　　　　Cheers, Rosemarie

Sat, 1 Jun 2002 18:38:40 –0400
JULIAN WHIPPLE <JWWHIPPLE1@attbi.com>
Subject: Re: "Baby" Poems

Dear Rosemarie, You are doing an admirable job, both artistically and technically. Thanks so very much. Looking forward to seeing and listening to you in Dorchester.　　　　　　　　　　　　Julian

Mon, 03 Jun 2002 15:38:31 -0400
ROSEMARIE MORGAN <rosemarie.morgan@yale.edu>
Subject: Re: "Baby" Poems

Thanks Julian. I too, am looking forward to meeting everyone, new and old, at Dorchester very soon. As for the "Baby" page – it struggles along. I now have 17 "Baby" poems online, 8 Detmold illustrations and 11 pages from Florence.   Rosemarie

Wed, 05 Jun 2002 19:32:39 -0400
ROBERT SCHWEIK <schweikr@localnet.com>
Subject: "Baby Poems"

First, thanks to Rosemarie Morgan, Helen Gibson, and Birgit Plietzsch for the service they've performed for TTHA. They've given us all a resource that exists absolutely nowhere else except for the individuals who have access to the Detmold volume. And what a revealing resource they have provided! Faced with it, I've tried — really tried – to conceive that the person who wrote those mind-numbingly pedestrian "descriptions" could be the same person who wrote those charming, playful, and often wittily composed poems that accompany the Detmold illustrations of the "baby" volumes. I can't. At best I can conceive that Florence might have made some suggestions about the poems and that the author (lovesick as he may have been) *might* have adopted some to please her. There is no doubt more objective evidence about the authorship of those poems will be adduced. I look forward to seeing it. But what I've seen has left me with a powerful prejudice in favor of Hardy's authorship.   Bob

Fri, 7 Jun 2002 13:07:04 +0100
HELEN GIBSON<helen.gibson@ukgateway.net>
Subject: re: "Baby" poems

It was a pleasure to be able to scan some of the Detmold pictures so that people can see how the books were originally presented. The books are large – nearly 12in. high by 9in. and the font used for the prose is very large – clearly meant for adult and small child joint reading. I think the choice of animals and birds is interesting, some of them being quite exotic for the British market (but maybe they were also sold abroad). Detmold was the illustrator of other books for children – notably Kipling's *Jungle Book*, *The Arabian Nights*, *Aesop's Fables*, and also Fabre's *Book of Insects*. His interest in tiny creatures and detail is evident in the "Baby" books, I think. In fact, I feel there is an interesting correlation between this close observation in his work and Hardy's acute perceptions of the creatures. I do agree that Florence's prose is a tad pedestrian, and the tone a trifle 'twee'![22]

All best wishes, Helen

Wed, 12 Jun 2002 22:43:51 +0100
JAMES GIBSON <James.Gibson@ukgateway.net>
Subjecct: "Baby Poems": "A kitten, just written"

Those members of the Forum who have been following the discussion on the Detmold/Florence Hardy "Baby" books may like to know that the T.L.S. of 7 June has a review of Bernard Jones's *Fifty Seven Poems*. The reviewer is Christopher Reid, and he entitles his review "A kitten, just written." He concedes that Hardy may have had some hand in some of the poems, but finds that the sheer badness of much of the writing makes it difficult to accept Hardy's authorship of all without protest. Bernard Jones's argument that Florence is not recorded as having written any other poetry, (she did, in fact, write several other short poems in her other books), far from discounting her as the author in this case, might "rather explain the inane doggerel note that sounds so often in these pages"!

These 'babies' are certainly giving us some trouble!
Best wishes to all, James Gibson

Wed, 12 Jun 2002 19:04:48 -0400
ROSEMARIE MORGAN <rosemarie.morgan@yale.edu>
Subject: Re: "Baby Poems": "A kitten, just written"

Thanks Jim. If one is to take Reid at his word, I'm not sure (are you?) why he or any other critic should hold the view that a great poet might not write doggerel at some point. There is always room for some rhyming sillies – in fact there's a venerable tradition of it: Chaucer had a go in his "rym dogerel" in "The Tale of Sir Thopas" (*Canterbury Tales*) and Swift has his rainy day, dining alone:

> Upon a chick, and pint of wine,
> On rainy days, I dine alone,
> And pick my chicken to the bone;
> But this my servants much enrages,
> No scraps remain to save board wages.

And TH certainly had something of a "doggie" moment in "A Young Man's Epigram on Existence":

---

[22] Affectedly childish.

> A senseless school, where we must give
> Our lives that we may learn to live!
> A dolt is he who memorizes
> Lessons that leave no time for prizes.[23]

Yup! — you're right, Jim! These "Babies" are certainly going to be a bunch of trouble!   Cheers, Rosemarie Morgan

Mon, 17 Jun 2002 13:33:42 -0400
ROBERT SCHWEIK <schweikr@localnet.com>
Subject: The "Baby Poems"

Reid's contention is that Hardy could not be the independent author of these poems because of what he calls "the sheer badness of the writings," and he adduces lines like these as evidence that Hardy could not have written them:

> I hardly like to own to you
> That my odd name is – Kangaroo!

or

> We are named Magpies; bird-folk that are
> By some considered singular.

or

> A puppy is, I should suppose,
> A pet that everybody knows.

Reid's argument seems to me to be singularly wrong-headed. Apart from the fact that Florence Dugdale is not known to have written any poetry, what Reid does not seem to have noticed is that these poems are for *children*. Their quaintly odd rhymes and metres seem calculated to appeal to the young in the same way the Dr. Seuss rhymes do to children today. To judge them as if they were written as serious poetry is to consider them for what they are obviously *not* intended to be. So, his conclusion that they were a joint project of Hardy and Florence seems unconvincing. Rather, their rhymes and metres seem to me to be all of a kind – just the sort of thing a talented poet might write when having the fun of writing about animals for amusement. Just the kind of thing T. S. Eliot did with his book on cats. Of course, there may be more definitive evidence for or against Hardy's authorship coming, but what Reid adduces is, it seems to me, not at all convincing.   Bob Schweik

---

[23] *CP*, 299

Thu, 20 Jun 2002 07:48:10 +0100
PHILIP IRWIN <philip.irwin@btinternet.com>
Subject: Re: The "Baby Poems"

I have not read Christopher Reid's article, but I do understand his reported views. There does seem to be a contradiction in the "Baby Poems." I think I hear the voice of Hardy in their language and style, and yet for my part I find it difficult to believe that a poet of Hardy's power and stature could write some of these lines, or having written them, permit their publication.

I have a couple of questions that for me would provide indications of authorship or otherwise.

1. Did the work of other poets writing for children at the beginning of the twentieth century have echoes of the style and language of Hardy's adult poems (in other words, do we hear the voice of Hardy in the "Baby Poems" because we are focused on him)?

2. Did other notable poets writing for children at the beginning of the twentieth century allow themselves to slip into bad verse?

Philip Irwin

Thu, 20 Jun 2002 04:26:37 -0700 (PDT)
ANDREW HEWITT <aghewitt@yahoo.com>
Subject: Re: The "Baby Poems"

Philip, I have been looking at Christina Rossetti's poems for children for comparison, many of which are about small birds, animals, flowers etc and were also published in illustrated editions. Here are a few from *Sing-Song*[24]:

- **1** -

> Hear what the mournful linnets say, –
> "We built our nest compact and warm, –
> But cruel boys came round our way
> And took our summerhouse by storm.
>
> "They crushed the eggs so neatly laid;
> So now we sit with drooping wing,
> And watch the ruin they have made,
> Too late to build, too sad to sing."

---

[24] I am grateful to Martin Ray for searching out the Rossetti lines and advising that they come, in fact, from three separate poems (untitled) in *Sing-Song*..

- 2 -

Dead in the cold, a song-singing thrush,
Dead at the foot of a snowberry bush
Weave him a coffin of rush,
Dig him a grave where the soft mosses grow,
Raise him a tombstone of snow.

- 3 -

A linnet in a gilded cage, –
A linnet on a bough, –
In frosty winter one might doubt
Which bird is luckier now.

But let the trees burst out in leaf,
And nests be on the bough,
Which linnet is the luckier bird,
Oh who could doubt it now?

It is interesting to read these side by side with the "Baby Poems" under discussion. I am utterly unqualified to comment on the authorship of the "Baby Poems." But by comparison with Rossetti I would say that they are actually a bit too grown-up in their use of language, a bit too stylised, to be really successful as poems for "babies." I can imagine a small child becoming quite still and absorbed as its parent reads, or better still sings, of the plight of the "mournful linnets." The so-called "Baby Poems" arouse a different response, they are rather more knowing and ironic.   Andrew Hewitt

This is where the "Baby Poems" discussion thread ended – as exploratively and as indeterminately as it began six weeks ago. If readers have any new light to shed on the question of Hardy's authorship please write to us at:
http://www.yale.edu/hardysoc/Welcome/Forum/forum.htm

THE HAUNTING
For Rob

Be quiet! I can no longer understand
yet can not sweep my way through shadows
of your voice— the way they infiltrate
music we both loved, stopping my breath.

Would it free you if I let you go,
if I consumed your memory, and would not
answer the interrogations of your photograph?
Should I hold back my outstretched hand?

You are impatient at my tardiness.
You grumble in my blood. I make you wait,
not stepping from my frame to come to you.
But oh, I am not ready. Let me be late.

Isobel Robin, Monash University,
Melbourne, 2002[1]

THE LITTLE BOTTLE SONG
(*With apologies to Pete Seeger*)

Little bottles, little bottles
On the top shelf of the linen-press,
In the bathroom, the bedroom
And the old kitchen drawer;
With unfinished boxes
Of capsules in bubble-packs,
But I'm darned if I remember
What they're all of them for.

---

[1] Robin, Isobel, *Freud's Back Yard: Poems by Isobel Robin* (Wollongong University: Five Islands Press, 2002), 44. Reproduced here with kind permission of the author. "The Little Bottle Song" is published here for the first time: 2002 © Isobel Robin.

Oh mystery! Social history
In ointment and anodyne;
A family saga
Of ailments and germs.
Homeopathic and herbals –
Oil for Pussy's fur-balls
That was twice as effective
When the poodle had worms.

❖

Look! Oceans of potions
And rather smelly lotions,
A gaggle of gargles
And a poultice or three;
Starters and stoppers
Both mini-sized and whoppers,
Sticking plasters for disasters,
And camomile tea.

❖

Here's a physic for colic
Or upsets alcoholic.
But I don't remember this one,
Like stale, congealed wax.
Can't imagine why we got it,
But I've made a discovery –
If you drop it on the carpet
It pulls out the tacks.

❖

Runny unguents, oozy ointments
(Used once – disappointments);
A salve for Mum's twinges,
And some blood pressure pills.
Feeling groggy? Here's a soggy
Packet of pick-me-ups,
Or a pretty, pink linctus
For bronchitis and chills.

❖

There's a tonic for a chronic
But I can't tell a chronic what
Because half its label
Is no longer there.
Wheezy breathing? Baby teething?
Ah! Now I remember it.
Dad used it for dandruff
Then lost all his hair.

❖

Disinfectants for scabies;
Pills to stop having babies
And others to make you
More fertile by far.
Heaven help me! What's this thing?
It's Grandfather's gallstone
Preserved in its majesty
Here in a jar.

❖

Soothing syrups for neurotics;
Aunty's antibiotics,
(Now Aunty has passed over
Are they any use to you?
They didn't help Uncle
With his boils and carbuncle,
But it's wicked to waste
Any good they might do.)

❖

What leather-skinned patient
Required this rubefacient
So furiously fiery
It could barbie a chook?
Well, we've done what you suggested;
We've inhaled, rubbed, ingested.
Can you tell me, dear doctor,
Why we're still feeling crook? [2]

Isobel Robin

---

[2] "Crook" is an Australianism in this context for feeling unwell.

THE THOMAS HARDY INTERNATIONAL CONFERENCE 2002
SYMPOSIUM PAPERS

THOMAS HARDY AND DANCE

INTRODUCTION
ROSEMARIE MORGAN
Symposium Chair

Toward the end of the week at the 2002 Hardy International Conference in the Corn Exchange, Dorchester, Dorset, I hosted a "Hardy and Dance" Symposium at which graduate students and independent scholars could present short research papers.[1] Time was allocated after each presentation for a session of questions and observations from the audience: these have been incorporated by individual speakers into their papers (below) as each has seen fit. The Symposium traditionally ends with a "sing-song" led by Professor Eugene Davies – choral director. Earlier in conference week Gene convenes a choir, fondly known as The Mellstock Quire. In true Hardyan style of occasional mischief the Quire performs short pieces, based on Hardy's poems, set to familiar tunes prepared by Gene and sung in parts. The audience, invited to sing along, invariably comes up with a remarkable number of singers ready and able to read from notation – thus, lustily, the event provides a fitting end to conference week. By way of introducing the Hardy and Dance programme I gathered a few snippets from Hardy's personal recollections of the delights and joys of the dance – from the *Life*, as follows:

- I -

As a young man of 20 years or so he would rush off with his fiddle under his arm, sometimes in the company of his father as first violin and uncle as 'cellist, to play country-dances, reels, and hornpipes ... not ret-urning sometimes till nearly dawn, the Hardys still being traditionally string-bandsmen available on such occasions, and having the added recommendation of charging nothing for their services.[2]

---

[1] See snapshots at: <http://www.yale.edu/hardysoc/confsnap.htm>
[2] Florence Emily Hardy, *The Life of Thomas Hardy, 1840-1928* (London: Macmillam, 1975), 32. Hereafter, *Life..*,

- II -

A year later, in 1862,

> Balls were constant at Willis's Rooms, earlier Almack's, and in 1862 Hardy danced at these rooms, or at Almack's as he preferred to call the place, realizing its historic character. He used to recount that in those old days, the pretty Lancers and Caledonians were still footed there to the original charming tunes, which brought out the beauty of the figures as no later tunes did, and every movement was a correct quadrille step and gesture. For those dances had not at that date degenerated to a waltzing step, to be followed by galloping romps to uproarious pieces.
>
> Cremorne and the Argyle he also sought, remembering the jaunty senior-pupil at Hicks who had used to haunt those gallant resorts. But he did not dance there much himself, if at all, and the fascinating quadrille-tune has vanished like a ghost, though he went one day to second-hand music shops, and also to the British Museum, and hunted over a lot of such music in search for it. Allusions to these experiences occur in more than one of his poems, "Reminiscences of a Dancing Man" in particular; and they were largely drawn upon, so he once remarked, in the destroyed novel *The Poor Man and the Lady*.[3]

- III -

And in 1895, at 55yrs old,

> It may be worth mentioning that, passionately fond of dancing as Hardy had been from earliest childhood, this was the last occasion on which he ever trod a measure ... on the greensward, which is by no means so springy to the foot as it looks, and left him stiff in the knees for some succeeding days. It was he who started the country dances, his partner being the above-mentioned Mrs (afterwards Lady) Grove.[4]

- IV -

And as recorded in a local paper (not named by Hardy):

> After nightfall the scene was one of extraordinary picturesqueness and poetry, its great features being the illumination

---

[3] Ibid, 42-43.
[4] Ibid, 269

of the grounds by thousands of Vauxhall lamps, and the dancing of hundreds of couples under these lights and the mellow radiance of the full moon. For the dancing a space was especially enclosed, the figures chosen being mostly the polka-mazurka and schottische, though some country dances were started by the house-party and led off by the beautiful Mrs Grove .... Probably at no other spot in England could such a spectacle have been witnessed at any time.[5]

- **V** -

And on a warm summer's night in 1896, at the Imperial Institute in the city of London,

> they met, with other of their friends, the beautiful Mrs. Grove, afterwards Lady, Grove; and the 'Blue Danube' Waltz being started, Hardy and the latter lady danced two or three turns to it among the promenaders, who eyed them with a mild surmise as to whether they had been drinking or not.[6]

"SOLDIER'S JOY" – VIGNETTE BY HARDY TO ACCOMPANY HIS CHRISTMAS POEM "THE DANCE AT THE PHOENIX," *WESSEX POEMS*, 108.

---

[5] Ibid, 269
[6] Ibid, 281.

- I -

IN THE WHIRL AND WILDNESS OF THE DANCE
JAN LLOYD JONES

"SHALL I sing," asks Hardy in "Song to an Old Burden",[1] "dance around around around/When phantoms call the tune"? This is a frequent theme of his: can one in good faith make merry when death is all around — absent friends, vanished lovers, ageing beauties are all evidence of the approaching night, and Hardy reminds us of this again and again — with evident relish. In his poetry the dance is often used as a compact metaphor for all that is sweet in life — for youth and gaiety and love: in "Music in a Snowy Street"[2] some street musicians are playing an old dance tune:

> The tripletime beat
> Bounds forth on the snow,
> But the spry springing feet
> Of a century ago,
> And the arms that enlaced
> As the couples embraced,
> Are silent old bones
> Under graying gravestones.

Displaying a similar obsession with bones, in "Reminiscences of a Dancing Man,"[3] Hardy asks:

> Who now recalls those crowded rooms
> Of old yclept 'The Argyle',
> Where to the deep Drum-polka's booms
> We hopped in standard style?

---

[1] *The Complete Poems of Thomas Hardy*, edited by James Gibson (Macmillan, 1976), 830. Hereafter *CP*

[2] *CP*, 735-6.

[3] *CP*, 216-17

> Whither have danced those damsels now!
> Is Death the partner who doth moue
> > Their wormy chaps and bare?
> Do their spectres spin like sparks within
> The smoky halls of the Prince of Sin
> > To a thunderous Jullien air?

And "The Fiddler"[4] has witnessed too much dancing not to recognize that it frequently results in tragedy:

> The fiddler knows what's brewing
> > To the lilt of his lyric wiles:
> The fiddler knows what rueing
> > Will come of this night's smiles!
>
> He sees couples join them for dancing,
> > And afterwards joining for life,
> He sees them pay high for their prancing
> > By a welter of wedded strife.
>
> He twangs: 'Music hails from the devil,
> > Though vaunted to come from heaven,
> For it makes people do at a revel
> > What multiplies sins by seven.
>
> 'There's many a heart now mangled,
> > And waiting its time to go,
> Whose tendrils were first entangled
> > By my sweet viol and bow!'

One can only speculate upon what sort of things it is "people do at a revel / [That] multiplies sins by seven"; but it is possible that Jenny, in that wonderful poem "The Dance at the Phoenix"[5] (who, in her younger days, "knew the regiment all!"), would have understood. She enjoys a final fling, in her sixtieth year, when the King's-Own Cavalry comes to town. Leaving the side of her trustful, sleeping husband, she makes her way to the ball and dances all night:

> Hour chased each hour, and night advanced;
> > She sped as shod with wings;

---

[4] *CP*, 248
[5] *CP*, 43-48

> Each time and every time she danced -
> Reels, jigs, poussettes, and flings:
> They cheered her as she soared and swooped,
> (She had learnt ere art in dancing drooped
> From hops to slothful swings).
>
> The favourite Quick-step 'Speed the Plough' -
> (Cross hands, cast off, and wheel) -
> 'The Triumph', 'Sylph', 'The Row-dow-dow',
> Famed 'Major Malley's Reel',
> 'The Duke of York's', 'The Fairy Dance',
> The Bridge of Lodi' (brought from France),
> She beat out, toe and heel.

Nevertheless, the sudden return to dancing has been too much for Jenny. She just manages to make her way back to her husband's bed, and in the morning he finds her dead beside him. However, he is the very best sort of husband, and remains utterly unsuspecting:

> When told that some too mighty strain
> For one so many-yeared
> Had burst her bosom's master-vein,
> His doubts remained unstirred.
> His Jenny had not left his side
> Betwixt the eve and morning-tide:
> — The King's said not a word.

And Hardy concludes in a tone of lament that is half-wistful, half-humorous:

> Well! times are not as times were then,
> Nor fair ones half so free;
> And truly they were martial men,
> The King's-Own Cavalry.
> And when they went from Casterbridge
> And vanished over Mellstock Ridge,
> 'Twas saddest morn to see.

These poems on the dance are all prime examples of Hardy's love of the lachrymose. But one needn't feel that he was too tortured by his subject matter. Hardy's second wife, Florence, revealed the evident satisfaction he experienced when writing in a minor key, recording her opinion that her husband's good spirits on a certain day were probably to be accounted for by his being in the midst of writing a particularly miserable poem.

And Hardy did, in fact, "dance around around around", despite the phantoms – or because of them. In his autobiography, written cagily in the third person, he described one of his earliest memories:

> He was of ecstatic temperament, extraordinarily sensitive to music, and among the endless jigs, hornpipes, reels, waltzes, and country-dances that his father played of an evening in his early married years, and to which the boy danced a *pas seul* in the middle of the room, there were three or four that always moved the child to tears, though he strenuously tried to hide them....He used to say in later life that....he danced on at these times to conceal his weeping.[6]

At other points in the autobiography, Hardy described himself as being "wildly" even "passionately" fond of dancing. This is a claim he made for no other art or occupation. What was it about the dance that could have caused him to express himself so immoderately and enthusiastically in its favour?

Life is characterized before all else by movement; and the ecstasy of life is no better expressed than in the free and flowing movement of the body in space. The dance distils into stylized form the very essence of the primal experience of life as motive power, as animation, vibrancy, flexibility (a favourite word of Hardy's for his heroines) and throbbing (another favourite: one thinks of — and conjectures upon — his well-known "throbbings of noon-tide"[7]). The exhilaration of the dance comes from the immediacy of participation, of defying gravity, floating, soaring, and — almost — flying. The rhythmic movement of the body through space reflects the rhythm of the inward beat – the heart-beat – which never stops while life continues and which relentlessly impels the involuntary movement through time. Dancing can be seen as a curiously gratuitous act that both expresses and gives delight purely for its own sake. Like playing, or loving, or worshipping, dancing is an entirely unnecessary thing to do: it is an adornment to life, an expression of freedom and a transcendence of words; in a dance, the spirit and body are not separate but one: as Yeats asks, without expectation of reply, "How can we know the dancer from the dance?"[8]

The dance was of immense symbolic importance in ancient philosophical speculation. Lucian wrote,

---

[6] Florence Emily Hardy *The Life of Thomas Hardy, 1840-1928* (London: Macmillan, 1962; repr.1973), p. 15. Hereafter, *Life*.

[7] This line is from Hardy's poem "I Look Into My Glass" *CP*, 81

[8] From W. B.Yeats' poem "Among School Children."

> Dancing is coeval with the birth of the Universe, and sprang forth at the same time with Love, the eldest of the gods . . . and is at length the most muse-like, all comprehending, all harmonious, first of things.[9]

The dance has long been seen as epitomizing the nature of the ongoing creation. Pythagoras speaks of the creation of life as when "dancing . . . began to be." Dancing symbolizes the order and design of creation, and, as Alan Brissenden writes, the idea of

> the cosmic dance, the rhythmic movement of all things in relation to one another, lasted until the eighteenth century beside the great chain of being and music itself as a commonly accepted metaphor of order, a concept closely allied to the Pythagorean belief in the primacy of number.[10]

Thus one reads of "the dance of the atoms", "the dance of the planets", and "the dance of the angels", all going on of course to the celestial harmony of the music of the spheres.

Dance, of course, has more than one aspect. Dance as a social activity is a celebration, a confirmation of the shared life and values of the community, and a means of its perpetuation through the courtship rituals involved. If one were to use Nietzsche's division of art into the Apollonian and the Dionysian, this sort of dancing would be Apollonian: it symbolizes and embodies balance and harmony.

No mere spectator at a country dance could hope to capture the vital essence of the experience in the way Hardy did, and the dance scenes in Hardy's novels are justly celebrated for their immediacy and vibrancy – they convey the mood, the life, the rush, the gaiety, the sound and the movement of the dance with unparalleled attention to detail and feeling for the warmth and spirit of the occasion. There is the Christmas dance at the tranter's house in *Under the Greenwood Tree*, which starts only after midnight, as Mrs Penny says, "If you do have party on Christmas-night, 'tis only fair and honourable to the sky-folk to have it a sit-still party. Jigging parties", she says, "be all very well on the Devil's holidays." And Mr Spinks, the schoolmaster, pronounces "Dancing . . . is a most strengthening, livening, and courting movement, 'specially with a little beverage added."[11]

And so the dance begins, with "Triumph, or Follow my Lover" and Dick Dewey succeeds in making the delectable Fancy Day his partner. But then, Mr Shiner (the villain of the piece)

---

[9] Lucian, "On Dancing" trans. Thomas Francklin, 1781

[10] Alan Brissenden, *Shakespeare and the Dance* (London: Macmillan, 1981), 3

[11] *UGT*, 70. All citations from Hardy's novels are from the New Wessex Edition

according to the interesting rule laid down, deserted his own
partner and made off down the middle with this fair one of
Dick's — the pair appearing from the top of the room like
two persons tripping down a lane to be married. Dick
trotted behind with what was intended to be a look of
composure, but which was, in fact, a rather silly expression
of feature – implying, with too much earnestness, that such
an elopement could not be tolerated.[12]

But sometimes the dance has a more Dionysian aspect. In various places Hardy used phrases such as "the enchantment of the dance", "the fascination of the dance", "in the mazes of an infinite dance", indicating that sometimes in his work the dance represents possession of the body against the will: irrational, puppet-like behaviour is the result, impelled as if by an evil magician. In *The Dynasts*, it is the Creator of all who is credited with animating the hapless Buonaparte: "You'll mark the twitchings of this Buonaparte / As he with other figures foots his reel, / Until he twitch him into his lonely grave."[13] In "The Fiddler of the Reels", the magician is Mop Ollamoor, whose virtuoso playing makes Car'line Aspent a slave of his will on account of what is described as "the excruciating sweetness of his bow": "Presently the aching of the heart seized her simultaneously with a wild desire to glide airily in the mazes of an infinite dance;" "she convulsively danced on;" she "continued to dance alone, defiantly as she thought, but in truth slavishly and abjectly."[14]

Similarly, "A Necessitarian's Epitaph"[15] expresses the trance-like behaviour of one who is "danced" by another:

> A world I did not wish to enter
> Took me and poised me on my centre,
> Made me grimace, and foot, and prance,
> As cats on hot bricks have to dance
> Strange jigs to keep them from the floor,
> Till they sink down and feel no more.

And the dancers at Chaseborough (in *Tess of the d'Urbervilles*), once they are satisfied with their partners, stop changing, and

> It was then that the ecstasy and the dream began, in which
> emotion was the matter of the universe, and matter but an

---

[12] *UGT*, 71-72

[13] Thomas Hardy, *The Dynasts*, (London: Macmillan, 1924), I, Fore Scene.

[14] See Thomas Hardy, *The Complete Stories*, edited by Norman Page (London: Dent).

[15] *CP*, 889

> adventitious intrusion likely to hinder you from spinning where you wanted to spin.[16]

In *Return of the Native* there are several dances. At Mrs Yeobright's on Christmas Eve, Eustacia hears "Nancy's Fancy" and thinks of Clym:

> He was there, of course. Who was she that he danced with? Perhaps some unknown woman, far beneath herself in culture, was by that most subtle of lures sealing his fate this very instant. To dance with a man is to concentrate a twelvemonth's regulation fire upon him in the fragment of an hour.[17]

And later there is a village dance where everyone joins in:

> A whole village-full of sensuous emotion, scattered abroad all the year long, surged here in a focus for an hour. The forty hearts of those waving couples were beating as they had not done since, twelve months before, they had come together in similar jollity. For the time Paganism was revived in their hearts, the pride of life was all in all, and they adored none other than themselves.[18]

Eustacia dances illicitly with Wildeve:

> Eustacia floated round and round on Wildeve's arm, her face rapt and statuesque; her soul had passed away from and forgotten her features, which were left empty and quiescent, as they always are when feeling goes beyond their register.
>
> How near she was to Wildeve! it was terrible to think of. She could feel his breathing, and he, of course, could feel hers. How badly she had treated him! yet, here they were treading one measure. The enchantment of the dance surprised her....Her beginning to dance had been like a change of atmosphere; outside, she had been in arctic frigidity by comparison with the tropical sensations here. She had entered the dance from the troubled hours of her late life as one might enter a brilliant chamber after a night walk in a wood. Wildeve by himself would have been merely an agitation; Wildeve added to the dance, and the moonlight, and the secrecy, began to be a delight. [19]

But the dance becomes anarchical impulsion that they cannot refuse:

> for different reasons, what was to the rest an exhilarating movement was to these two a riding upon the whirlwind.

---

[16] *TD*, 97.

[17] *RN*, 156

[18] Ibid, 281

[19] Ibid, 283

> The dance had come like an irresistible attack upon whatever sense of social order there was in their minds, to drive them back into old paths which were now doubly irregular.[20]

In "The History of the Hardcomes", the placid wife Jane sums up rather prosaically the mystery of what the whimsical narrator of that tale calls "the whirl and wildness of the dance." She muses on why she suddenly changed her equally-placid betrothed for his cousin, who was "of a more bustling nature, fond of racketing about and seeing what was going on in the world", just in the course of a single evening, and says "'Twas the dancing," said she. "People get quite crazy sometimes in a dance."[21]

Hardy defined poetry as "emotion put into measure"; and, significantly, measure was a word he commonly used as a synonym for dance. The second Mrs Hardy said she found, after her husband's death, many skeletons of poems — no words, just the metre and the scheme of rhyme and accentuation, as yet unfilled by any meaningful symbols. This is an illuminating fragment of information. It indicates that Hardy's poetry was not so much inspired by the need to convey a message (and it is well known that he repeatedly denied having any coherent "philosophy" or designs upon his readers) as by his aesthetic appreciation of tone and timbre, of the agreeable lilt of the words, their resonances in sound as well as in meaning – their rhyme, their alliteration, their very dancing together in the sublime, Dionysian sense.

It has been well said that "at the heart of Hardy's novels there is always a kind of dance;"[22] and this applies to his poetry as much as to his prose. Sometimes it is an allemande, with a stately, slow, and serious tread; but it should not be forgotten that sometimes it is a dance of exultation and delight. Just as Hardy reports of himself that, when aged only three, he danced ecstatically to his father's fiddle-playing – dancing even while weeping – so does his poetry move, now with joy, now with sorrow, but always in a dance: You will recall that one of the most damnable characteristics about Angel and his brothers (in *Tess*) is that they do not dance. At least, Angel does dance at the beginning of the story, but most lamentably and unforgivably with the wrong girl. His brothers prefer not to join in the dancing at all, on the grounds that, as one remarks: "We must get through another chapter

---

[20] Ibid, 284

[21] *The Complete Stories*, 486-94

[22] Joan Grundy, *Hardy and the Sister Arts* (London: Macmillan, 1979), p. 171.

of *A Counterblast to Agnosticism* before we turn in."[23] How very far this anti-dancing attitude was from Hardy's own frame of mind. The poem "Great Things"[24] extols just three things: cyder and love – and dance:

> The dance it is a great thing,
>   A great thing to me,
> With candles lit and partners fit
>   For night-long revelry;
> And going home when day-dawning
>   Peeps pale upon the lea:
> O dancing is a great thing,
>   A great thing to me!

WORKS CONSULTED

Brissenden, Alan. *Shakespeare and the Dance.* London: Macmillan, 1981.

Ellis, H. *The Dance of Life.* London: Constable, 1923.

Fraleigh, Sondra Horton. *Dance and the Lived Body: A Descriptive Aesthetics.* Pittsburgh, Pa.: University of Pittsburgh Press, 1987.

Grundy, Joan. *Hardy and the Sister Arts.* London: Macmillan; New York: Barnes-Noble, 1979.

Hardy, Florence Emily. *The Life of Thomas Hardy.* London: Macmillan, 1962; repr. 1973.

Miller, J. Miller. *Thomas Hardy, Distance and Desire.* Cambridge, Mass.: Belknap Press of Harvard University Press, 1970.

Miller, James, L. *Measures of Wisdom: The Cosmic Dance in Classical and Christian Antiquity.* Toronto; Buffalo: University of Toronto Press, 1986.

Sheets-Johnstone, Maxine, ed. *Illuminating Dance: Philosophical Explorations.* Lewisburg: Bucknell University Press; London: Associated University Presses, 1984.

Sparshott, F. E. *Off the Ground: First Steps to a Philosophical Consideration of the Dance.* Princeton, N. J.: Princeton University Press, 1988.

Turner, Paul. *The Life of Thomas Hardy: A Critical Biography.* Oxford: Blackwell, 1998.

---

[23] *TD*, 44.
[24] *CP*, 474-5.

THE THOMAS HARDY CONFERENCE 2002: SYMPOSIUM PAPERS

- II -

MOP OLLAMOOR'S REEL
ROY BUCKLE

OF central interest in the Hardy tale "The Fiddler of the Reels" (from the collection in 'Life's Little Ironies') is the notion that there is hypnotic power in music for dancing. The idea features in various Hardy poems as well as in several of his stories touching on rural life in "Wessex".[1] It seems to have grown out of his own early experiences when dancing to his father's fiddle-playing and later when as a fiddler himself he helped to provide the music at social gatherings of a convivial type. In this article I will consider the feasibility of reconstructing and performing the dances of the story from Hardy's descriptions.

The sensation of reverie one experiences when dancing peacefully to a regular beat at moderate tempo is comparable perhaps to that of being *gently* rocked in the cradle or perambulator. What Hardy describes in this particular story though is different, for it suggests that in certain circumstances dancers might find themselves in the control of the musician, who enforces obedience to vigorous dance figures of *his* choosing, prolonged during *his* pleasure and varied at *his* command. This last point is important because it suggests to Hardy that it is an example of the will of the listener being taken over by the need to conform to the will of the dominant performer. What exactly is the nature of this need?

The sound of a regular beat in strict tempo will provide support for a pattern of rhythmic movement, as in primitive tribal dancing or ceremonial military marching, where the beating of drums or other instruments of percussion communicates messages of instruction or command. The movements typical of children's dancing games (including skipping) appear to have a forceful influence on the mind of the child especially when the action is accompanied by the chanting of a monotonous jingle. Other instances of coordination between singing and physical exertion are found in the shanties, or chanteys, of the seamen of old.

---

[1] See, e.g., "The Fiddler"(*CP*, 248); "A Necessitarian's Epitaph" (*CP*, 889); "The Ballad Of Love's Skeleton" (*CP*, 925-927). See also Hardy, Evelyn. *The Countryman's Ear* (Tabb House: Padstow, Cornwall 1982) 69-77.

In all these cases the thoughts of the performer are concentrated by the need to remain alert and attentive to the rhythm and to respond appropriately in their physical movements. Further influences may be at work when a dance is accompanied by instrumental music or song, which in addition to the pulse of the rhythm supplies *melody* "tune") and perhaps also *harmony*, both of which can affect the mood of the listener.

GORDON SMITH POSTCARDS: INTERIOR OF CREMORNE GARDENS
www.victorianlondon.org/entertainment/cremone.htm

As in all folk dancing, the tunes in Hardy's story are appropriate to the form the dance is to take, and a particular choice of tune therefore is connected with the pattern of physical movement expected of the dancers. The dancers themselves therefore, through what they expect to hear, are in the grip of the tune, and it follows that once the dance has begun the musician may find it in his power to exert his will on the dancers to a certain extent not only by *what* he plays but even by the *way* he plays. This is, broadly speaking, the principal theme of the story, which describes how a roving fiddle player persists in using the hypnotic power he discovers in his subtle style of playing to force his will on a village girl and bring her to ruin.

The fiddler, Wat, or 'Mop', Ollamoor, a person of uncertain background, appears from nowhere to practise his malevolent arts on the simple village girl, Car'line Aspent. So marked is his natural ability with the violin it is even suggested that but for a certain idleness of character he might have achieved in musical performance the greatness of a second Paganini. Here Hardy may be hinting at the fanciful myth of the *satanic* power said by contemporary listeners to have been at the call of that musician of genius.

While in the story Hardy describes the hypnotic effect of music and movement on the dancers he also mentions the stance and demeanour of the fiddler as one of utter concentration, his eyes apparently being closed for much of the time as he plays. It might be supposed then that what is occurring is self-hypnosis and that the fiddler's influence over the dancers, with whatever disastrous events follow, is ultimately traceable to the effect of his playing on the fiddler himself! (This is not, however, a point made by Hardy.) What is also interesting is Ollamoor's choice of tunes for the dancing. His main purpose from the outset would seem to have been to indulge a wanton urge to dominate and humiliate poor Car'line. Having already brought her to shame on a previous encounter by seduction he now seems set upon bringing further disaster now she is a married woman. Like Hardy himself there were certain tunes to which she was susceptible. For example, the one used to entice her into joining the dancing at the Quiet Woman Inn was 'My Fancy-Lad', struck up by Ollamoor *'in the key of D major'*.

There is much confusion to be faced in searching for the music Hardy specifies in this story. Although described by one modern writer as "a charming tune used for five-handed reels" and "a favorite with Hardy from boyhood,"[2] a song or dance tune called 'My Fancy Lad' has not so far been discovered. It is briefly mentioned in the *Life*

---

[2] Firor, Ruth A. *Folkways in Thomas Hardy* (Barnes: New York 1962) 195.

(chapter: "Birth and Boyhood") with 'Johnny's Gone to Sea' as an alternative title. One of the dances named in Hardy's poem 'The Dance At The Phoenix' is called "Fancy Lad", and there exists among the collections of Hardiana in the Dorset County Museum a page of manuscript with two lines of music written in two sharps (key of D major or B minor, i.e.) and with the title 'Tenor of Fancy Lad'. Now 'Fancy Lad' is the title of a broadsheet song published in the early 1800s but without music.[3] The wording of the first verse resembles closely that of the song 'Katy Cruel', for which we have the tune. Our record for this, including the melody, relies on North-American sources.[4] Like many old tunes (one authority thinks it may be of Northumbrian origin dating back to 1610) it is in the common minor mode although cadences shift the *mood* between major and minor modes with haunting effect. A Scottish song called '(The) Leaboy's Lassie' has words similar to those of 'Katy Cruel' but there is little or no resemblance in its sad tune. The wording of a Hexhamshire song of the 1790's entitled 'Jess Macpharlane' also shows similarities to 'Katy Cruel', throwing further doubt on its true origin and that of 'Fancy Lad'.

Regarding alternative titles, songs or melodies entitled
1. 'Johnny's Gone to Sea'
2. 'Johnny's Gone for a Soldier'
3. 'Johnny's Gone to France'

are also on record. In no case, however, is the music that of 'Katy Cruel' nor are the words those of 'Fancy Lad'. Apart from its different phrasing, the melody of II closely resembles that of 'Leaboy's Lassie'! However apt it may or may not be to our story, we may note that the outstanding tune of III, in the key of E minor with brief visits to *D major* (like so many dances of Irish tradition), is ideal for a fast reel. We are clearly faced with problems if we wish to learn what it is about the *music* of '(My) Fancy Lad' that was supposed to enslave Car'line Aspent (and perhaps at some time Hardy also). It should at least be possible to provide music for the fiddling of a reel by adapting the memorable tunes of 'Katy Cruel' and 'Johnny's Gone to France' in a medley of dances including also the well-known 'Fairy Dance' with which Ollamoor's murderous bowing ends.

The dance movements have still to be considered, and here the brevity of Hardy's descriptions involves us in some further difficulty. Car'line watches from under her veil as the first dance begins with a

---

[3] Bodleian Ballads Catalogue: 2806 c. 17(123).

[4] Linscott, E.H. *Folk Songs of Old New England* (2nd. Edit. Dover 1993) 225.

'longways' set (ladies opposite the men; two parallel lines). The number of couples is not specified but after it has got under way she is urged to join in by a man at the bottom of the line whose dance partner has dropped out. She does so, 'plunging in' together with small daughter Carry.

Hardy does not say just how the odd dancer coped as they all 'whirled about'. Such technicalities as are given are reserved for later in the tale, when the detail becomes especially interesting but it appears that at the outset Car'line, not wishing to be recognised by her seducer, did not really *want* to dance and actually longed for it all to *stop*. When eventually there was a break, the tired and emotional woman was revived with a quantity of beer and gin before a five-handed reel was proposed as the next dance. Still reluctant she was induced to join in again especially when Mop began 'aggressively tweedling' the tune of 'My Fancy Lad'. One feels this is where Hardy is really beginning to enjoy his tale as the action presses on to a climax with its woeful outcome.

It is interesting that a modern expert has described the five-handed reel as a 'confusing' dance[5] since Hardy with tongue in cheek wryly suggests to the reader that not everyone may know how it is danced. It begins with four of the dancers taking up positions at the points of a cross while the fifth starts in the centre.[6] There is no pairing of the dancers and, according to Hardy, by the ruse of shortening the tune it is within the power of the fiddler to oblige the dancer (such as Car'line) in the middle to continue dancing from that position, with its energetic role of constant movement, with no chance of relief.

As the story continues, other dancers drop out, the dance becoming a four- and then a three-handed reel. Hardy does not dwell on the four-handed figure beyond saying the reel "instantly resolved itself into a four-handed one". Later, for the three-handed one, the tune changes to 'Fairy Dance' and poor Car'line is forced into the middle of a hectic reel of three! Finally left to dance somehow on her own she collapses with exhaustion, whereupon Ollamoor ends his fiddling performance with an 'elfin shriek of finality' and disappears for ever taking with him little Carry, who everyone including husband Ned knows is really the fiddler's daughter and not his own! So the story ends.

To be able to emulate the somewhat frantic dancing programme in Hardy's story we will have to specify *the steps* for ourselves. It

---

[5] Torfason, T. *The Ghillies Gazette*, **20** (2), March-April 2001, i-iv.

[6] Wilson, T. *An Analysis of Country Dancing* (London: J S. Dickson 1811) 194pp.

seems preferable to keep to a dance plan of simple basic figures[6] and to see how far we can get while following those details he has provided. Simple but vigorous traditional rustic dances often include as one of their figures the 'hey' of the morris dancer, where each person weaves in and out of their partners-in-line by skipping or hop-stepping (no plain walking in England!) energetically through a serpentine figure (Hardy's 'figure of 8'), turning at the end to follow a similar twisting path back to their starting places. In a reel-of five, for example, one line of three first dances a hey leaving the two remaining dancers on the other line to face inwards and "foot it" (skipping or side-stepping to and fro on the spot) while waiting their turn to join the middle dancer in a similar sequence, beginning with a hey in directions at right-angles to the previous one.

On the other hand, there is nothing stationary about the three-handed reel with just the one line of dancers skipping or stepping to every beat. This also begins with a hey (the so-called 'reel of three'). Since this is the simplest of the dances to be considered I will continue to describe it first.

The tune of 'Fairy Dance' is a reel of 16 bars in 2/4 time divided into two parts, each part a phrase (or strain) of **four** bars played twice over. As Hardy says, it is eminently suited to the fast three-handed dance. After the hey (the eight-bar figure of part one) the centre dancer skips outwards to 'set' to the first outside dancer who is at the same time advancing inwards. This involves each of them in two skips forwards and two more on the spot during two bars. They then move similarly but in reverse to return to place (another two bars).

The middle dancer will have turned round as if to 'set' to the other outsider while the tune goes through the four bars of part two for the second time. Now, however, instead of setting to one another and stepping back again the new pair *continue forward to pass and change places*. This completes the dance figure, after which the tune and the dance return to the first part again (heys) with a new dancer in the middle position.

Normally, therefore, when the end of the tune is reached the original centre person will have 'escaped' from that position to take up an outsider's place. Escape from the middle could of course be prevented *if instead of changing places in the last four bars the incoming outsider chooses to step back to the outside position*. In Hardy's tale, however, it was *the fiddler* who made Car'line stay in the middle by missing out part of the tune (in our case the last four bars) and switching to the beginning again. 'Fancy Lad' could easily be played in this way (if the tune were

---

[6] See Radford, A. *The Thomas Hardy Journal* **15** (2), 72 (1999).

known as well as the tenor part) but although the point is not mentioned *it would still seem to require the tacit agreement of the other dancers* for the whole figure to be repeated satisfactorily by switching prematurely to a new hey. This would be a simple matter if they were dancing to familiar tunes in the time-honoured fashion.

As we have seen, the three-handed dance involves only two directions; to-and-fro in the fixed line of three. In a cruciform five-reel the complete figure is twice the length with dancing to and fro in two lines at right angles. Therefore 32 bars in 2/4 time are necessary for the five-handed reel (four directions) if the movements are not to be completed by a stampede in half the time. What we have in the Hardy music manuscript for the structure of *'Fancy Lad'* is the tenor part of a tune in two parts, each a strain of **eight** bars and each played twice in succession; a total length of 32 bars. It is clear why Hardy's fiddler saw fit to "modulate" into the shorter tune of 'Fairy Dance' as the company, having first shrunk from five dancers to four, eventually declined to a row of three.

A satisfactory interpretation of the five- and three-handed dances is therefore possible but the way in which any one of *four* dancers could be persuaded to take up a 'middle' position leaves an interesting question. Hardy describes neither the tune nor the dance pattern to which the five-handed reel was "instantly" converted when another dancer left the floor. Traditionally the 'reel of four' commences with a single line or a square set. That the 16-bar 'Fairy Dance' is said to be "better suited to the contracted movement" of the three-handed figure implies perhaps that a *longer* tune ('Fancy Lad'?) was still appropriate in the four-handed dance.

As a last point to be considered in reconstructing the action of the story it should be noted that Hardy takes the trouble while describing the final stages of Car'line's dancing to emphasise her effort to react to every subtlety the fiddler injected into his playing and her seemingly *defiant will* to respond in this way to the very end. It might be expected that the way the accompanist plays his instrument for a group of dancers, including any exhibitionist improvisations he skilfully works into familiar tunes, will tend to influence the way they dance (their mannerisms, for example) *if they are so inclined.* Except when things are proceeding at a stately pace the responsive attitude of the dancers might give the impression to an onlooker of *automatism* whereas it would normally signify intense *concentration*. It is part of the mystery of Hardy's tale that Car'line is not so inclined. If dance steps and music alone fail to provide the vital clue to Car'line's seemingly dogged persistence, wherein lies the source of Ollamoor's uncanny ability to will her on? It could be that through his playing he somehow exerts a mysterious *sexual* power to which she is fated to remain slave.[7] If so we are left to puzzle over the likely nature of Car'line's terpsichoric inventions during her desperate final dance. Bearing in mind that they end in collapse on the floor and a convulsive fit Hardy seems to have provided his readers, and would-be interpreters, with yet another challenging opportunity for the exercise of the imagination.

COUNTRY DANCING (Anon)

---

[7] Sumner, R., *ibid.*, 15 (3), 103 (1999).

DANCE-SONGS: A MEANINGFUL HYBRID IN
Far From the Madding Crowd [1]

W. EUGENE DAVIS

IN response to Ian Gregor's contention that "Hardy's novels are above all concerned with *process*," that is with the "ongoing" involved in story and the "web of human doings" Joan Grundy adds the qualification that

> the weaving of the web is in some respects a musical process. Music is the most "ongoing" of the arts: it moves through time as well as in time. Hence its close association with dance. At the heart of Hardy's novels there is always a kind of dance.[2]

In the earlier novels like *Far from the Madding Crowd,* she observes, the sense of a small group of people in their relationships with each other moving through the intricacies of a dance is strong.

The rightness of her interpretation is underscored by the frank use of dances in this novel, either in dance scenes or in references to traditional dance tunes. The most fully developed scene is the one in the Great Barn to celebrate a successful harvest and the wedding of Bathsheba and Frank Troy, whom the band honors by playing "The Soldier's Joy." The tune closely associated with Gabriel Oak, "Jockey to the Fair,"[3] is also a dance tune, as is one associated with Troy and his earlier occupation as member of Her Majesty's 11th Dragoon Guards, who march away from Casterbridge to the strains of "The Girl I left Behind me." All three tunes, by the way, were widely known and performed in late Victorian England.

---

[1] Hardy, Thomas, *Far from the Madding Crowd.* World's Classics Edition, edited by Suzanne B. Falck-Yi. London and New York: Oxford University Press, 1993. This edition is used throughout this essay.

[2] Joan Grundy. *Hardy and the Sister Arts* (London: Macmillan, 1979), 171.

[3] See Appendix

The interrelationship between musical form, then, with its "ongoing" or evolving pattern of melodic contour marked, especially in dances, with clear rhythmical patterns, and the evolving narrative, which takes shape as characters form shifting patterns of relationships, is therefore an important aspect of the art of *Madding Crowd*. It is further enriched and complicated by an aspect of the role of dance which Grundy did not investigate. In novels like this one it is inappropriate to consider dances purely as rhythmical songs-without-words, because the meaning of dance tunes is sometimes glossed by their lyrics, texts that were commonly sung to them.

Most dance scenes in the novels include a band or at least one instrumentalist to set bodies swaying to music. But there are those other musical scenes which are devoid of dancing. Familiar examples include carol singing around the parish at Christmas, the collaboration of quire and congregation to produce music for religious services, and of course the many scenes in which individuals or groups sing songs to accompany their work, or to heighten their enjoyment of feasting or other communal activities. When his characters are met to dance, as at the Christmas celebration in *Under the Greenwood Tree* or the dance at Trantridge on the night of Tess's seduction, they do not spend time singing, they *dance*. Similarly, when songs are called for (as they literally are during the latter stages of the harvest feast in *Madding Crowd*) no one offers to dance; instead, the focus is clearly on song. Thus Hardy seems to separate his musical concerns and scenes into two distinct categories: song and dance.

Given this separation, it piqued my interest that in his pastoral tale of the faithful shepherd, the flute-player Gabriel Oak, and his undying love for the sweet singer Bathsheba Everdene, Hardy sometimes blurs the boundaries between song and dance. For example, after the "pastoral tragedy," Gabriel's loss of his sheep and his subsequent ruin, Hardy creates an intriguing theme song of a dance-like nature for his impoverished hero. Since Gabriel fails to find an employer at the Casterbridge hiring fair, he temporarily becomes a busker to raise necessary funds. Hearing some

> merry men . . . whistling and singing by the corn exchange [Gabriel] drew out his flute and began to play "Jockey to the Fair" in the style of a man who had never known a moment's sorrow. Oak could play with Arcadian sweetness, and the sound of the well-known notes cheered his own heart as well as those of the loungers.[4]

---

[4] *FFMC*, 45.

Two chapters later when Oak, having gained employment on Bathsheba's farm as a shepherd, goes off to Warren's Malthouse to celebrate, the tune recurs. Henery Fray, who remembers seeing Oak playing his flute at Casterbridge (and evidently liking what he heard) makes a request: "But we could thank ye for a tune, if ye baint too tired."[5]

Oak obliges. He
> then struck up "Jockey to the Fair" and played that sparkling melody three times through accenting the notes in the third round in a most artistic manner by bending his body in small jerks and tapping with his foot to beat time.[6]

His listeners are moved by his performance: Susan Tall's husband almost wishes that he could play a flute as well as Gabriel does, and Joseph Poorgrass goes so far as to say that "'tis a true comfort for us to have such a shepherd." His explanation for saying that is clear, but it raises questions about the nature and purpose of Gabriel's theme song. Hardy's description and Gabriel's playing might lead one to assume that "Jockey to the Fair" was simply a dance tune. We must, however, reconsider that in light of Joseph's words.

> We ought to feel full o' thanksgiving that he's not a player of ba'dy songs instead of these merry tunes; for 'twould have been just as easy for God to have made the shepherd a loose low man – a man of iniquity, so to speak it – as what he is.

Joseph says this just because "Jockey to the Fair" is a lively, merry tune or rather because *he knows the words commonly sung to it*. In other words, Joseph helps identify "Jockey to the Fair" as one of those fascinating musical hybrids, dance-songs, which play a role in this novel. It is certain that "Jockey to the Fair" existed in both wordless instrumental versions for dancing and as part of a song of the same name. *The Fiddler's Companion* website observes that

> The melody, dating at least from the mid-18th century, was a popular tune throughout England and served several functions, including dancing and marching. Morris dance versions are wide-spread and numerous and have been collected from [among others] the Sherborne areas of England's Cotswolds.[7]

---

[5] Ibid, 69

[6] Ibid

[7] Edward Kurtz, Compiler and Editor. *The Fiddler's Companion: A Descriptive Index of North American and British Isles Music for the Folk Violin.* Version V2.00 (11/2000). WWW.

The word "Jockey" in the song is devoid of equestrian denotation. One theory traces the word to Scotland, from "joculator," which by the 17th century meant an itinerant minstrel. Another theory stresses the purely English origin and views "jockey" as deriving from "jogging." In any case, "Jockey to the Fair" must have had lyrics for over a hundred years by the time Hardy recalled it during the writing of this novel. Probably best known in Wessex was that ballad of innocent young love which John Hullah included in his *The Song Book: Words and Tunes from the Best Poets and Musicians*, published in London in 1866, a work Hardy might have purchased during his years in London.

This wedding of lyric and tune is suitable to the amorous but virtuous Gabriel. While his proposal of marriage to Bathsheba did not lead her to join her minstrel in abandoning the security of family life to encounter the more dangerous delights of "the fair," the tale of Jockey and Jenny ends as does that of the novel's couple:

> Soon did they meet a joyful throng,
> Their gay companions blythe and young;
> Each joins the dance, each joins the song,
> To hail the happy pair.[8]

The second instance, the choice of "The Soldier's Joy" by the lead fiddler of the band playing for the harvest dance in the Great Barn is also an example of a theme song, another one probably chosen for its clear-cut associations with a major male character.

But before turning to it we should consider one mentioned earlier in the novel which also has obvious associations with Francis Troy. William Smallbury tells Bathsheba that Fanny Robin has "run away with the soldiers." In Casterbridge at the Barracks, Smallbury learned that Troy's unit, The Eleventh Dragoon Guards, had left the previous week for Melchester: "they pranced down the street playing 'The Girl I left Behind me,' so 'tis said, in glorious notes of triumph." There might not be much to be said about this casual reference to an old song often chosen by military bands for marching away from home or familiar billets, except that it had wide currency in Hardy's Wessex, and indeed long before, as a dance tune and that it was often sung.

The Fiddler's Companion has 15 pages of information on this tune, known in the US as "The Arkansas Traveler," and in England, as

---

[8] John Hullah. *The Song Book: Words and Tunes from the Best Poets and Musicians* (London, 1866), 81.

Hardy himself observed in notes to a scene in *The Dynasts*, usually as either "Brighton Camp" or "The Girl I Left Behind Me." Of course for the reader, as well as for Smallbury and Oak, the ironic parallel between the soldiers' figurative abandonment of the girls they have wooed when they march away and Sgt. Troy's actual abandonment of Fanny is hidden at this point, but becomes clear before long.

Grundy's notion about the dance of life, mirrored in rhythmical, passionate dancing, is an important feature of the scene in the Great Barn. The scene also reveals Bathsheba's epiphany regarding the bed she had chosen to lie in by wedding Troy. Hardy's artistry is evident here not in his invitation to a dance to celebrate that wedding but in its dramatic cancellation. Dancing, this personal and social activity so vital to young and old, married and single as Hardy often depicts it, is of course a communal activity, a gathering of individuals into an intricately dancing group, a social unit. It is therefore possible, to belabor the obvious, only when a sociable environment is preserved.

At first, the communal enjoyment of the dance seems unbounded. Gabriel, busy about the farm, had not come to the dance earlier. But now, "As Oak approached the building the sound of violins and a tambourine, and the regular jigging of many feet, grew more distinct"[9] The description of the improvised ballroom, bandstand and chandeliers, is rich in suggestive details about the fullness of the harvest – "the remaining end [of the room] was piled to the ceiling with oats" – and the gay, frenzied nature of the dance:

> Here sat three fiddlers, and beside them stood a frantic man with his hair on end, perspiration streaming down his cheeks, and a tambourine in his hand.[10]

But the sociable atmosphere will be short lived. When Bathsheba does not exercise her option to name the next dance, the leader makes a fateful choice, one full of ironies.

> "Then," said the fiddler, "I'll venture to name that the right and proper thing is "The Soldier's Joy" – there being a gallant soldier married into the farm – hey, my sonnies, and gentlemen all?"[11]

Troy accepts the compliment, but notes that there are certain ironies in the choice:

> though I have purchased my discharge from Her Most Gracious Majesty's 11th Dragoon Guards, to attend to the duties awaiting me here, I shall continue to be a soldier in

---

[9] *FFMC*, 251
[10] Ibid
[11] Ibid

spirit and feeling as long as I live.[12]

The irony deepens before long. The erstwhile soldier, Sgt. Troy, has not abandoned his former loose living, and the dance-gathering soon becomes a travesty of a harvest celebration. Instead of acting to preserve the harvest's rich garnering he deliberately risks it. When Gabriel asks to talk to him to warn him of the danger to the ricks, Troy sends back the message that "Mr. Troy says it will not rain... and he cannot stop to talk to you about such fidgets."

Then he further shows his unwillingness to attend to his new responsibilities at the farm by radically changing the nature of the celebration by ordering strong brandy and hot water to be served to the guests. When Bathsheba objects, he orders the women to go home so "we cock-birds will have a jolly carouse" by themselves. Frank doesn't want to dance, he wants to drink himself into insensibility, an abdication of his responsibility as farm owner and husband. The band, furthermore, that essential driving force of the gaiety and festivity of the dance, takes Troy's order as tantamount to a dismissal: "The musicians, not looking upon themselves as 'company,' slipped quietly away to their spring waggon and put in the horse."[13]

Before this unfortunate metamorphosis, however, there is the triumphant scene in which the notes of "The Soldier's Joy," accentuated by the "frantic man's" tambourine, lead the guests in what must have been an animated, bacchanalian dance, as the narrator suggests.

> As to the merits of "The Soldier's Joy" there cannot be, and never were, two opinions. It has been observed in the musical circles of Weatherbury . . . that this melody, at the end of three quarters of an hour of thunderous footing, still possesses more stimulative properties for the heel and toe then the majority of other dances at their first opening. "The Soldier's Joy" has too an additional charm in being so admirably adapted to the tambourine aforesaid – no mean instrument in the hands of a performer who understands the proper convulsion, spasms, St Vitus's dances and fearful frenzies necessary when exhibiting its tones in their highest perfection. [14]

Another old, pre-Napoleonic tune, like "The Girl I Left Behind Me," "The Soldier's Joy" was also a favorite of Morris dancers. *The Fiddler's Companion* observes that "the melody was used in North-West

---

[12] Ibid
[13] Ibid, 252-3
[14] Ibid, 251

England morris dance tradition for a polka step, and also is to be found in the Cotswold morris tradition, where it appears as 'The Morris Reel.' The *Companion* further cites an authority which believes the tune was "one of the earliest dances recorded in England, but no date of origin has been established."

It is fair to ask, however, about the claim that "The Soldier's Joy" belongs in a list of dance-songs. Indeed, though no words are given for it in the novel, it must have been widely sung. The *Companion* lists fragments of several lyrics for the tune, though no provenance is given for them. These include

> Chicken in the bread tray scratchin' out dough
> Granny will your dog bite? No, child no.
> Ladies to the center and gents to the bar,
> Hold on you don't go too far.

And

> Twenty-five cents for the malteen,
> Fifteen cents for the beer,
> Twenty-five cents for the malteen,
> I'm gonna take me away from here.

The Companion also quotes a set of lyrics that nicely fit, and suit, the tune – complete with a reference to "Brighton Camp." Certainly "The Soldier's Joy" must have been a dance-song, one probably well known to Hardy's first readers.

Is it coincidence, moreover, that Hardy's "The Sergeant's Song" suits the tune nicely, both regarding its metre and its blend of satire and jocularity? Further support for the claims of "The Soldier's Joy" as a dance-song is supplied by none other than Robert Burns, who chose this tune to undergird his feisty ballad "I am a Son of Mars" in his Cantata *The Jolly Beggars*.

So the realms of song and dance certainly do overlap in *Madding Crowd*. Rather than the tunes Hardy's narrator mentions merely bearing witness to the country folk's love of dance, they often had lyrics, that is *texts* whose characters, little dramas and concerns relate in meaningful ways to the principal characters' own dramas and concerns.

To what degree our interpretations of Gabriel as shepherd and lover or Frank Troy as soldier, farmer and husband are affected by our awareness of the tunes and texts Hardy associates with them is an intriguing question, but one I shall leave for later consideration.

APPENDIX

The Sergeant's Song

The Soldier's Joy—traditional. Arr. W. E. Davis

When ___ law- yers ___ strive ___ to ___ heal a breach, And ___
When ___ Jus- ti- ces ___ hold ___ e - qual scales, And ___
When ___ Rich ___ Men ___ find ___ their ___ wealth a curse, And ___
When ___ hus- bands ___ with ___ their ___ Wives a - gree, And ___

par - sons ___ prac- tice ___ what they preach; Then ___ Bo- ney ___ he'll ___ come.
Rogues. are ___ on- ly ___ found in jails;
fill ___ there- with ___ the ___ Poor Man's purse;
Maids ___ won't ___ wed ___ from ___ mo - des - ty;

poun - cing down And march ___ his ___ men ___ on ___ Lon - don town! Ro -

___ li- cum- ___ ro - ___ rum, ___ lol - ___ lol - ___

lo - ___ rum, Ro - ___ li- cum- ___ ro - ___ rum,

tol- ___ lol- ___ tol - la - lay!

Lyric by Thomas Hardy, from The Trumpet Major (1878)

The Girl I Left Behind Me

The Girl I Left Behind Me--trad.(from Fiddler's Companion)

marcato

I'm lone-some since I crossed the hill, And o'er the moor land sed - gy, such heavy thoughts my heart do fill since parting with my Peg-gy. I seek for one as fair and gay but find none to re-mind me How sweet the hours I passed a-way with the Girl I Left Be-hind Me. I seek for one as fair and gay but find none to re-mind me How sweet the hours I passed a-way with the Girl I Left Be-hind Me.

O ne'er shall I for-get the night, the stars were bright a-bove me And gently lent their sil-v'ry light, when first she vowed to love me. But now I'm bound to Brigh-ton Camp kind hea-ven then pray guide me, And send me safe-ly back a-gain to the Girl I Left Be-hind me. But now I'm bound to Brigh-ton Camp kind hea-ven then pray guide me, And send me safe-ly back a-gain to the Girl I Left Be-hind me.

THE THOMAS HARDY CONFERENCE 2002: SYMPOSIUM PAPERS

- IV -

AN ILLUSTRATED DISCUSSION OF THREE ARTISTS' INTERPRETATIONS OF HARDY'S CHARACTERS AND DANCE:

C. S. REINHART'S ILLUSTRATION OF MARGERY AND THE
BARON PREPARING FOR THE BALL IN
"The Romantic Adventures of a Milkmaid" (*Graphic*, 1883),
ROBERT BARNES'S DONALD FARFRAE AND ELIZABETH JANE
IN *The Mayor of Casterbridge* (*Graphic*, 1886),
AND WILLIAM HATHERELL'S REPRESENTATION OF
"The Fiddler of the Reels" (*Scribners*, 1893)

PHILIP ALLINGHAM

AS CHARLES DICKENS in 1836 examined Sunday "under three heads," I propose to examine the topic of Hardy and the dance under three headings that are illustrated by three plates involving three Victorian artists' realizations of moments associated with the dance in Hardy's prose fiction. Further, I propose to speak to this Cerberan[1] topic in two modes, personas, or voices – the former effusive, the latter analytical.

Interpretation One: As Pater or Carlyle

PLATE ONE
"Margery and the Baron Dressed for the County Ball": from "The Romantic Adventures of a Milkmaid by Charles S. Reinhart (1844-1896) from the Extra Summer Number of the London *Graphic*, 1883: p. 22 (19 cm high x 23.5 cm wide).

---

[1] Three-headed

Dance as Theatre, Costume Ritual, Class-Marker, and Portal to Romance.

The first of the three representations of dance reveals how, through going gorgeous in formal, 'aristocratic' costume, the would-be dancer seeks release from the humdrum diurnal round of working, feeding, and resting, like Cinderella yearning to go to the ball. Her changing to ballroom from workaday apparel enables acolyte Margery momentarily to join the superior orders, to become a brighter, purer being who steps away from the tawdriness of the Green Room for the artificial light and passion of the stage, a world of make-up, chandeliers, and choreographed motion. This is where archetypes are enacted, where the girl from the lower orders moves in equality for the evening with the patriarchal landowners at the yeomanry ball, passed off like Eliza Doolittle as a duchess rather than seen in her true 'class' colours, as a milkmaid.

However, as artist C. S. Reinhart emphasizes in his illustration, the solid, natural world holds back its devotee from the glittering, illusory world of surfaces.

PLATE TWO

"Farfrae was footing a quaint little dance with Elizabeth Jane" by Robert Barnes (1840-1895) in the London *Graphic* (p. 189, Vol. 33), Plate 7, 16.5 cm wide by 21.5 cm high (13 February, 1886), for Chapter Fifteen of *The Mayor of Casterbridge*.

Dance as Courtship Ritual, as Social Order, as *Entrée* to Marriage
Before the community in a time-honoured social ritual associated with the rhythms of sowing and harvest, the bachelor and spinster come together as partners under the watchful eyes of matronhood, seen for four beats as a joint entity before separating. The dancers in Barnes's plate are specifically fashionable burghers, products of urban society and mercantile class, well-dressed city-dwellers whose costumes are London imports, rendering them exemplars of middle-class respectability, manager wooing employer's daughter in the bourgeois capitalistic idyll. The next time we as novel-readers will encounter the pair dancing will be on their wedding day.

PLATE THREE
"'She Chanced to Pause on the Bridge near His House to Rest Herself,'" by William Hatherell for "The Fiddler of the Reels" in *Scribner's Magazine* (New York) 13 (May, 1893): page 601 (15.5 cm high x 11 cm wide).

Dance as Erotic Metaphor, Fetishistic Coupling, & Precursor of Sex.
The pattern is maintained with a village girl, native of Wessex, partnered with an outlander, for Margery's partner for the evening is a melancholy German baron, Elizabeth Jane's a sensitive Scot, and Car'line's an olive-complexioned, long-haired Gypsy. However, in a sense, Car'line's partner is not a person at all (and certainly not a dancer) but an erotic strain of music, an atavistic impulse that must be satisfied or placated before Car'line Aspent, green and giddy maiden, can be transformed into Mrs. Edward Hipcroft, homemaker and mother.

In Hatherell's plate, her partner, unseen, tickles and excites her fancy; perforce, she must yield to instinct (as in a D. H. Lawrence story) and abandon conscious control, the inhibiting intellect, to dance until she exhausts herself, and unconsciously engages in the procreative act. At her second rape, she pays the Rumpelstiltskin price for this social and personal transformation as Mop Ollamoor[2] harvests his crop, her first-born. As in the case of the rape of unsophisticated village girl Tess by urban master Alec D'Urberville, we have no narrative description of their coupling; rather, as a phallic principle, Mop takes her between a waking and a sleep (to quote Edmund in *King Lear*), impregnating her and later returning to exact sacrifice.

Interpretation Two: As a Post-Modern Paratextualist
PLATE ONE

Whereas the country-dance is an extension of those traditions rooted in the soil and the seasons, the polka like the Baron's steam yacht is an outlandish invention that will inevitably participate in modernity's eclipsing the traditional ways of the Wessex folk. Margery's enchantment by the Baron here looks forward to Car'line Aspent's more explicitly sexual submission to Mop Ollamoor in "The Fiddler of the Reels."

Well past the story's exposition, mid-way through Chapter III, the Baron has intimated that he will arrange to take this bucolic Cinderella to the Yeomanry Ball at the Assembly Rooms (possibly at Bath), even though her dance steps are old-fashioned, and we are left in suspense as to whether or not he will carry out his intention after he has made enquiries about the forthcoming ball: "The Baron mentioned an evening and an hour when he would be passing that

---

[2] Not merely "Of the Moor," an agent of nature, but "*à l'amour*," an agent of the eternal life-force.

way again; then mounted his horse and rode away."[3] We are concerned that her antiquated notion of dancing will prevent her going – the
> Reels, and jigs, and country-dances like the New-Rigged-Ship, and Follow-my-Lover, and Haste-to-the-wedding, and the College Hornpipe, and the Favourite quickstep, and Captain White's dance."[4]

Or perhaps it will prevent her from enjoying herself, should she go, for the Baron has already (ironically) evaluated her dancing as too enthusiastic, too all-encompassing:

> But you dance too well – you dance all over your person – and that's too thorough a way for the present day. I should say it was exactly how they danced in the time of your poet Chaucer.[5]

Plate I immediately answers the question implicit in the earlier part of Chapter III as to whether the Baron intends to take the green and giddy girl to the urban ball: Margery (stage-right) and the Baron (stage-left) are both formally dressed. Consequently, in Plate 1 we "read" Margery in a fuller, womanly light. C. S. Reinhart captures a moment of suspense and dilemma as Margery (as at the beginning of the story) is again blocked or thwarted, not merely by the hollow tree which prevents her leaving her native environment (as represented by woods that serve as the backdrop), but also because the low *décolletage* of the ball gown exposes more of her body than she is accustomed to show. The illustration simultaneously raises another question: will outward and inward hindrances, the hollow tree and her self-consciousness prevail over her desire to accompany the Baron to the ball?

Margery is depicted in a moment of crisis, for, having changed into a voluminous ball gown, she cannot exit as she entered, the rustic dressing room being inconsistent with the identity that the fashionable dress has conferred upon her. The pictured dress of high 'urban' fashion symbolizes those imaginative and materialistic yearnings which subsequently seduce Margery into aspirations beyond her social class and regional background.

A minor problem in the chronological match of text and plates is that, while the costuming of Dairyman Tucker in another of the Reinhart plates suggests an early nineteenth-century setting, such details as the Baron's and Margery's formal dress (Plate I) and the

---

[3] Chapter III, *Graphic*, 5.

[4] Ibid.. "Antiquated" in the sense of traditional; the steps to which the young Thomas Hardy, as a boy, would play his fiddle.

[5] Ibid.

Baron's extolling the polka as formerly "an ancient Scythian dance" now "adopted by Society," suggest a mid-century setting, the polka having been introduced from Bohemia via Vienna in 1844. According to Benazon, Hardy had no clear chronological setting in mind for the serial; however, the Baron specifically identifies the polka as the fashionable dance that has recently replaced Terpsichorean "movements which are even yet far from uncommon in the dances of the villages of merry England."[6]

The time period seems appropriate, however, for although the full impact of the industrial revolution had not yet reached Dorset when Hardy was a boy, it is at just this point in history that innovators from beyond Wessex, such as Farfrae in *The Mayor of Casterbridge*, were introducing concepts and machines that would "disrupt the peace and order of the agricultural communities Hardy describes."[7] In temporal setting, then, as in the theme of the disastrous effects of giving way to sexual passion, there is much that connects "The Romantic Adventures of a Milkmaid" to *The Mayor of Casterbridge* and other Novels of Character and Environment.

PLATE TWO

Noted for his skill with figures and genre subjects periodical illustrator and artist Robert Barnes possessed the ability to produce characters who have apparently sprung "straight from English soil."[8] All the Barnes figures that people the pages of his *Graphic* illustrations for Hardy's novel exemplify the robust solidity typical of his work elsewhere. Note the careful detailing, for example – Farfrae's elegant white trousers with "inset straps" – very much in vogue in the early 1840s.

Barnes excelled at juvenile figures, as is evident in his rendering of Elizabeth-Jane: scarce eighteen, she is very fetching in both face and figure, as one might expect from reading Hardy's novel, although her head seems to suggest little of the intellectual striving with which Hardy invests her. Even if Barnes' illustrations for *The Mayor of Casterbridge* do reveal a certain absence of imagination, his women here do not run to the "bovine type of beauty" for which Reid criticizes Barnes. The illustrations reveal that Barnes was very much at home in the rural, working-class idiom, as in this scene Donald

---

[6] Ibid. See also Benazon, Michael. "'The Romantic Adventures of a Milkmaid'": Hardy's Modern Romance." *English Studies in Canada*, 5.1 (1979).

[7] Benazon, 58.

[8] See Forrest Reid, *Illustrators of The Eighteen Sixties* (New York: Dover. 1975) 269.

Farfrae and Elizabeth-Jane are surrounded by those local characters that appear in the background elsewhere in his illustrated programme for the novel, as in Hardy's text.

Let us now examine the plate in relation to Hardy's letter-press. The moment illustrated is significant in that Farfrae's popularity as the active and inventive young foreigner who has purified Henchard's grain and provided an ingeniously hung pavilion tent for a dance to celebrate "a national event"[9] prompts Henchard to give him notice just afterward. In the romantic aspect of the novel's plot, the scene connects the young Scot and the mayor's daughter in the public mind. Henchard's entertainments – involving agricultural feats of skill, a free public tea and dance[10]– have failed because of six hours of unexpected rain. The Henchards and their daughter wander over to the West Walk to investigate Farfrae's alternative, 'under-cover' entertainment.

First, in Hardy's text we see the young Scot in the character of a nimble-footed, kilted dancer of the Highland Fling, a performance suggestive of mating rituals in the animal kingdom. Since Donald Farfrae has developed the persona of a "usually sedate," sober businessman we, like the crowd and Henchard (whose perspective the plate gives us), are surprised to witness him "flinging himself about and spinning to the tune." While Henchard is prompted to laugh at the transformation that the music has effected in his manager, the female spectators are lost in "immense admiration." Now a new dance, presumably a figure in which the crowd can join, is proposed; "Donald ... disappear[s] for a time to return in his natural garments..." Although he has his choice of partners, by the time we spot Farfrae again he is

> footing a quaint little dance with Elizabeth-Jane – an old country thing, the only one she knew, and though he considerably toned down his movements to suit her demurer gait, the pattern of the shining nails in the soles of his boots became familiar to the eyes of every bystander. The tune had enticed her into it; being a tune of a busy, vaulting, leaping sort – some low notes on the silver string of each fiddle, then a skipping on the small, like running up and down ladders –'Miss M'Leod of Ayr' was its name, so Mr. Farfrae had said, and that it was very popular in his own country.[11]

---

[9] Perhaps Queen Victoria's wedding in February, 1840.

[10] *Le thé dansant* was introduced in 1845.

[11] *Graphic*, 13 February 1886, Ch. XVI (bottom of centre column, p. 190)

This is a virtuoso performance indeed, for Farfrae's feet must more often be airborne rather than earth-bound if he is pouring such energy into his steps that his shining boot-nails are dazzling the eyes of his spectators.

Shortly after the dance, Henchard discharges Farfrae in a fit of pique occasioned by by-standers' remarks about how the manager has bested the master, then feels remorse, and finally concern that Farfrae has taken this notice seriously – the same emotional pattern we witnessed years before in the furmity vendor's tent at Weydon-Priors. At the suggestion of "a nodding acquaintance" Elizabeth-Jane misinterprets Henchard's anger as originating in her public dancing:

> As the Mayor's step-daughter, she learnt, she had not been quite in her place in treading a measure amid such a mixed throng as filled the dancing pavilion.[12]

Although the illumination provided by the gas-jet seems a little fanciful, the pavement beneath the dancers' feet and the canvas tarpaulins draped a few feet above their heads (the boughs in the Walks having been used by the ingenious Farfrae to construct "a gigantic tent") indicate that the artist has scrupulously attempted to realize the text's word-picture Since a row of bonneted women, many of them eyeing Farfrae enviously, flanks Elizabeth Jane and since the woman at the top (right) is holding her skirt in preparation for taking her turn, we can assume that Barnes has stationed us on the male side of the country dance known as "Miss McLeod's Reel," which was usually footed to the tune of the same name. Hardy designates the tune "Miss M'Leod of Ayr," perhaps to imply that the tune and dance originated in Ayrshire, the home of Scotland's national poet, Robbie Burns. *The Life*[13] records that this old dance tune was one of Hardy's favourites when he was a child: "an old Scotch tune to which Burns may have danced." Thus, since this choice of music (like the plaintive lyric about his "ain countree" sung at The Three Mariners earlier) is presumably Farfrae's, it further establishes his Romantic nature.

Top hats and workmen's caps behind Farfrae imply that going off the frame there is a line of male dancers representing all levels of Casterbridge society. Presumably, Farfrae and Elizabeth-Jane have

---

[12] Ibid, (bottom of right-hand column, p. 190) "Miss McLeod's Reel."
http//www.111.hawaii_edu/contra/dances/mcleod.html

[13] Hardy, Florence Emily, *The Early Life of Thomas Hardy, 1840-1891* (London: Macmillan, 1933), 18.

already come down centre, and are now in the process of turning as a couple on four beats before dividing and yielding the top to another set of partners. The dark dresses, buxom figures, and full faces of the female chorus are in sharp contrast to Elizabeth-Jane's white, diaphanous dress (connecting her visually to Farfrae in his immaculate white trousers); Barnes heightens the contrast by making her thin-necked and long-faced, and by giving her no bonnet. The details of Farfrae's formal dress – swallow-tail, cut-away coat, vest, top hat, and stirrup – are all perfectly consistent with the period evoked by the novel. While Farfrae seems careful and controlled in the precision of his movements, Elizabeth-Jane seems abstracted or withdrawn, almost dancing within herself. Thus, while the caption focuses on her partner, the artist is focusing on the novel's heroine, who possesses a pensive visage in contrast to her elegant dress and complementary Indian shawl, an imported commodity indicative of the wearer's social standing. Although, like Margery, Elizabeth-Jane is a newcomer to such fashion, she carries herself easily and without embarrassment, but lets Farfrae take the initiative.

PLATE THREE

We begin, as it were, in the present and *in medias res*, since "Talking of Exhibitions" seems to refer to the 1889 Exhibition in Paris, memorialized by La Tour Eiffel. Hardy's narrator, an "old gentleman," reverts to a time four decades previous, taking us back, like the narrators of *The Mayor of Casterbridge* and *The Romantic Adventures of a Milkmaid*, to the 1840s and the Wessex of Hardy's youth.

The narrator (quite properly, since the tale's title is "The Fiddler of the Reels") begins with the dubious character of the markedly "un-English" gypsyish Mop Ollamoor and a description of

> his power over unsophisticated maidenhood, a power which seemed sometimes to have a touch of the weird and wizardly in it,[14]

to which the illustrator has added a mesmerizing influence of children. Although Hardy invokes the textual authority of *Under the Greenwood Tree* when he has his narrator quote Theophilus ('Lover of God') Dewey, one of the Mellstock church musicians, to deride Mop's repertoire as "devil's tunes,"[15] Hardy arranges matters so that Mop exercises his peculiar, other-worldly fascination "by simply fiddling one of the old dance-tunes"[16] that are heretical departures

---

[14] *Scribner*, 597.
[15] Ibid, 598
[16] Ibid

from the musical traditions of old Wessex. Once again, Hardy's bias against modernism asserts itself in his discussion of the dance and its music, which in their original possessed an almost atavistic force now much diluted in derivative modes and works. Like Margery, Car'line viscerally falls under the spell of the old dance music, but her "infatuation" with it is so great that it induces in her an "attack" which Hardy's narrator describes as "a species of epileptic fit"[17] in which the victim temporarily loses all control of mind and body. Thus, Mop's dance music seems to be a palpable link with the pre-Christian and pagan fertility traditions of Wessex: He "represents paganism and effects conversion to his own creed of sensuality through his violin-playing."[18] The music appeals to some deep, sexual instinct in Car'line which compels her to abandon momentarily her social roles as wife and mother; and, as in so many Hardy stories, the heroine's succumbing to instinct results in catastrophe.

One assumes that Hatherell quite deliberately selected as the subject for his illustration the first time that Car'line Aspent hears the beguiling fiddle music of Mop Ollamoor. Hatherell has correctly read the story as not being about the fiddler himself, but about the influence of the fiddler on the heroine. The word "chanced"[19] in the caption is one of great significance in most Hardy stories, and no less so here, for chance determines that Car'line falls prey to Mop's fascinating playing in her initial meeting, which occurs not in her own village of Stickleford, but when she is on her way home through Lower Mellstock. He is initially the wolf to her Little Red Riding Hood (we note his beguiling three children in the background). Her second, ill-fated meeting with Mop occurs much later in the story, when she and her husband have returned to their native Wessex. On the first occasion, she loses her maidenhead to the diabolic musician; on the second, she loses her child. Thus, from this brief overview of the role of chance in Car'line Aspent's history, we see that the artist has chosen to illustrate one of the two key 'fated' moments, and yet has avoided telegraphing the story's pathetic outcome.

Unfortunately for the purposes of this discussion, the artist has chosen to show the first moments of Mop's spell rather than Car'line engaged in one of the many old dances that the fiddler is accustomed to accompany. His music blights the spring of Car'line's life, signified by the cherry blossoms above her head, and leads to her yielding to the indiscriminate mating instinct signified by the ducks (right).

---

[17] Ibid
[18] Ibid, 80.
[19] Ibid, 598

Dancing and music in this story seem to combine to compel an out-of-body experience in the female protagonist, a member of that "unsophisticated maidenhood"[20] whose weak wills are completely subservient to "the weird and wizardly" power of the outlandish itinerant musician who deploys his dance-music as if it were the date-rape drug rohipnol.

The conclusion of Hardy's "The Fiddler of the Reels," a celebration of the pagan life-force that folk-music enables even the "unsophisticated" to access, envisions a geriatric Mop still fiddling and his now middle-aged daughter dancing to his strains as her mother once did, but this scene occurs (in the narrator's imagination) in The New World, a land of second chances and fresh starts: "There. . . they may be performing in some capacity now, though he must be an old scamp verging on three-score-and-ten, and she a woman of four-and-forty." However, by "may" Hardy seems to be inviting each reader to enter into this creative process, producing whatever ending he or she wishes to bring closure to Ned's anguish and loss. Although conscientious stepfather Ned Hipcroft is alarmed that Mop may be "torturing [the child] to maintain him" his wife is curiously unconcered. Mop remains the incarnation of paganism, a figure representative of the Dionysian revels of pre-Christian Greece and Italy, and not a real child-exploiter.

WORKS CONSULTED

Bénézit, E. *Dictionnaire Critique et Documentaire des Peintres, Sculpteurs, Dessinateurs et Graveurs*. (Paris: Librairie Gründ, 1976). Vol. I: 451.

Brady, Kristin. "Miscellaneous Stories: Reflections on a Career." *The Short Stories of Thomas Hardy: Tales of Past and Present*. (London and Basingstoke: Macmillan, 1982).

Cassis, A. F. "A Note on the Structure of Thomas Hardy's Short Stories." *Colby Library Quarterly* 10 (1974): 287-296.

Champlin, John Denison, Jr. *Cyclopedia of Painters and Paintings*. (New York: Empire State, 1927). Vol. IV.

Foster, Vanda. *A Visual History of Costume*. (London: B. J. Batsford Drama Book Publishers, 1984).

---

[20] Ibid, 597.

Graves, Algernon. *A Dictionary of Artists Who Have Exhibited Works in the Principal London Exhibitions from 1760 to 1893*. (London: Henry Graves, 1895).

Hardy, Thomas, *Collected Short Stories*, ed. F. B. Pinion. (London: Macmillan, 1988)

---. "The Fiddler of the Reels," il. William Hatherell. *Scribner's Magazine* (New York) 13 (May, 1893): 597-609.

---. *The Mayor of Casterbridge*, *The Graphic* (London) Vol. 33. 2 Jan.-15 May, 1886.

---. *The Romantic Adventures of a Milkmaid*. *The Graphic* , Summer Number (pub. 25 June) 1883, pp. 4-25; *Harper's Weekly*, 23 June-4 August, 1883.

---. "Serial Rights in Stories." *Athenæum* 16 May 1903: 626.

Harris, Wendell V. *British Short Fiction in the Nineteenth Century: A Literary and Bibliographic Guide*. (Detroit: Wayne State University Press, 1979).

---. "English Short Fiction in the Nineteenth Century. III. The Rise of the Short Story in England. . . ." *Studies in Short Fiction* 6, 1 (Fall, 1968): 45-57.

Houfe, Simon. *The Dictionary of Nineteenth-Century British Book Illustrators and Caricaturists*. (Woodbridge, Suffolk: Antique Collectors' Club, 1978, rev. 1996).

Jackson, Arlene M. *Illustration and the Novels of Thomas Hardy*. (Totowa, NJ: Rowman and Littlefield, 1981).

Mallalieu, H. L. *The Dictionary of British Watercolour Artists up to 1920*. 2nd ed. (Woodbridge, Suffolk: Antique Collectors' Club, 1986.

McManus, Diane. "Dance and Ballet." *Victorian Britain: An Encyclopedia*, ed. Sally Mitchell. (New York: Garland, 1988). 207.

Page, Norman. "Hardy's Short Stories: A Reconsideration." *Studies in Short Fiction* 11, 1 (Winter, 1974): 75-84.

Pennell, Joseph. *The Adventures of An Illustrator Mostly in Following His Authors in America and Europe*. (Boston: Little, Brown, & Co., 1925).

Purdy, Richard Little, and Michael Millgate, eds. *The Collected Letters of Thomas Hardy*. Volume One. (1840-1892). (Oxford: Clarendon, 1978-88).

Quinn, Maire A. "Thomas Hardy and the Short Story." *Budmouth Essays on Thomas Hardy: Papers Presented at the 1975 Summer School* (Dorchester: Thomas Hardy Society, 1976). Pp. 74-85.

Ray, Martin. *Thomas Hardy: A Textual Study of the Short Stories*. (London: Ashgate, 1997).

Seymour-Smith, Martin. *Hardy*. (London: Bloomsbury, 1994).

Temperley, Nicholas. "Dance Music." *Victorian Britain: An Encyclo-pedia*, ed. Sally Mitchell. (New York: Garland, 1988). 208.

"THE COMMONWEALTH OF HEARTS AND HANDS": DANCING IN
The Return of the Native.

DAVID HAVIRD

THE *Return of the Native* opens with dancing around a bonfire on the night of November 5th, Guy Fawkes Day, and ends two-and-a-half years later with a wedding-day dance, which comes on the heels of a Maypole-day dance. In between these customs, Eustacia has a dream of dancing with a knightly Clym. Then there is dancing at the Yeobrights' at Christmastime. Outside the house, Eustacia listens, assumes that Clym is taking a turn. It's doubtful that he is. At no other time in the novel does he dance. There is no dancing to celebrate their wedding. But some two or three months afterward, there is the "gipsying," where the rebellious, reckless wife trips the light fantastic with her former lover. What does this dancing signify?

For T. S. Eliot, for the 16th-century ancestor whom he quotes in "East Coker," dancing signifies marriage, and marriage "concord":

> The association of man and woman
> In daunsinge, signifying matrimonie –
> A dignified and commodiois sacrament.
> Two and two, necessarye coniunction,
> Holding eche other by the hand or the arm
> Whiche betokeneth concorde. . . .

The corresponding phrase in *The Return of the Native* is "the commonwealth of hearts and hands." According to Hardy, Eustacia's "grandeur of temper," a cast of mind that reveals itself in unrealistic, romantic notions about marriage, threatens "the commonwealth of hearts and hands."[1]

---

[1] Thomas Hardy, *The Return of the Native*, ed. Simon Gatrell (Oxford: Oxford UP,

Eustacia is "desperately" fond of dancing." She understands that to "dance with a man is to concentrate a twelvemonth's regulation fire upon him in the fragment of an hour."[2] Now, in the novels of Jane Austen it is no less than imperative that a woman in want of a husband —as is Eustacia —should dance with the man. But nothing could be more alien to dancing in Austen's novels than is Eustacia's frank eroticism. Perhaps that dance in "East Coker," with the agreeable meaning that Eliot ascribes to it, corresponds to occasions in Austen's novels and if at all to a dance in *The Return of the Native*, then to the festivity that winds up the evening of Thomasin's wedding to Venn. Perhaps this marriage at the end of the novel is the paradigm for Hardy's "commonwealth of hearts and hands." Or maybe concord, if vital, is unstable. Eliot's interpretation of dancing introduces oddly a scene that rather depicts Dionysian frenzy than Apollonian concord. The scene is of rural folk "dancing around [a] bonfire" –

> Round and round the fire
> Leaping through the flames, or joined in circles,
> Rustically solemn or in rustic laughter . . .

Though this scene in Somerset (scarcely 20 miles from Egdon Heath) takes place on a "summer midnight," it calls to mind the chaotic dance of the rustics around the bonfire on Guy Fawkes Day, the "custom of the country" that opens *The Return of the Native* – "a whirling of dark shapes amid a boiling confusion of sparks, which leapt around the dancers as high as their waists." Plunge into the vortex of a dance like this and you may find yourself, with Eliot's bacchants, "under the hill." That's where Eustacia finds herself. At the beginning of the novel she is the figure against the sky that gives "Such a perfect, delicate, and necessary finish . . . to the dark pile of hills that it seemed to be the only obvious justification of their outline."[3] Again atop Blackbarrow near the end of her story, she appears to be "drawn into the barrow by a hand from beneath."[4] Eliot condemns his dancers to "dung and death," a phrase that captures his "rejection of the earthly life and its oblivious pleasures...It is from the joining of

---

1990), Book V.. Chapter 4. Hereafter *RN* and numerals only will be cited. The phrase, "the commonwealth of hearts and hands," appears in 6.4.

[2] *RN*, IV, 3 & II, 5.

[3] Ibid, 1, 2-3

[4] Ibid, VII, 7. Hardy changed "Blackbarrow" to Rainbarrow for the 1895 edition of the novel. The actual Barrows number 3 and flank different parts of the heath.

men and women that Eliot recoils most strongly."[5] Clym Yeobright has that same fastidious attitude toward erotic expression -- an attitude that Hardy rejects, despite the doom that awaits Eustacia -- despite the "primarily sexual" nature of her "tragedy." For however "intellectual" Clym's tragedy may be in contrast, his sexual pathology poses at least as great a threat to the precarious, vital "commonwealth of hearts and hands" as does Eustacia's potentially "disruptive[,] unfocused sexuality."[6]

I have referred to the dance of the rustics at the beginning of the novel. Actually, the dance that opens *The Return of the Native* – apart from the Dionysian dance of the flames: "Maenades, with winy faces and blown hair" – is Grandfer Cantle's "private minuet." Perhaps this scene recalls an early memory of the author's – as if in his portrait of Grandfer Cantle, Hardy, in early middle age, were already anticipating and affectionately burlesquing his own second childhood. In the *Life* he recalls how "extraordinarily sensitive" he was to music, remembering

> the endless jigs, hornpipes, reels, waltzes, and country-dances that his father played of an evening in his early married years, and to which the boy danced *pas seul* in the middle of the room.[7]

This memory finds its way into verse in "The Self-Unseeing." In this nostalgic poem, the speaker surveys a room where his father played the violin. His mother meanwhile enjoyed the fire that danced to her husband's music, and he, a child then, danced with only the fire as partner:

> She sat here in her chair,
> Smiling into the fire;
> He who played stood there,
> Bowing it higher and higher.
> Childlike, I danced in a dream

Whether or not that child becomes Grandfer Cantle, the merriment of a child – foolishness in the eyes of a censorious adult and the venerability of an ancient combine in him. As Mrs. Yeobright laments, "O that what's shaped so venerable should talk like a fool!"[8] As

---

[5] Lyndall Gordon, *Eliot's New Life* (New York: Noonday, 1989), 104

[6] See Boumelha, Penny. *Thomas Hardy and Women: Sexual Ideology and Narrative Form.* (Madison: U of Wisconsin P, 1982), 48-53

[7] Thomas Hardy, *The Life and Work of Thomas Hardy*, ed. Michael Millgate (Athens: U. of Georgia Press, 1985), 19

[8] Ibid, I, 3.

with Hardy himself in later years, "Time ... shakes this fragile frame at eve / With throbbings of noontide."[9] For some of the foolishness that Grandfer Cantle talks (outside of Mrs. Yeobright's earshot) concerns Eustacia. Lusty as well as cheerful, only he among the superstitious rustics boasts such bravery as to openly desire the Queen of Night as "partner": "I'd be very glad to ask her in wedlock, if she'd hae me, and take the risk of her wild dark eyes ill-wishing me."[10]

Even more scornful of superstition, Clym, though he does not dance, shares for a while that healthy, erotic interest in Eustacia. An intellectually liberated man and, seemingly, a socially ambitious one, Clym is the man of her dreams:

> [a] young and clever man ... coming into that lonely heath from, of all contrasting places in the world, Paris. It was like a man coming from heaven.[11]

If only the Yeobrights had invited her to their Christmas party: "what an opportunity would have been afforded her of seeing the man whose influence was penetrating her like summer sun." Before she sees his face, she dreams of him, a "man in silver armour" with whom she dances. "Suddenly," as Hardy describes the dream, the pair escape the "ecstatic mazes of the dance" and dive into a pool, the pool to which Eustacia had summoned Wildeve with her bonfire on Guy Fawkes Day and the same pool beside which she and Clym will seal their betrothal with a kiss. The rainbow-arched utopia into which they then emerge prefigures the "Eden" of their first three or four weeks of marriage, when the couple "[are] like those double stars which revolve round and round each other and from a distance appear to be one." Except in Eustacia's dream of Clym as a knight in shining armor, it is only as "those double stars" early in their marriage that the two of them "dance" together.[12]

Meanwhile, music and dancing greet the mummers at Blooms End. Unable to dance with Clym, Eustacia is unable to set him aflame with her erotic heat. Instead, her "emotions" project, without her knowledge, a "mysterious," venereal "emanation" as when (in Hardy's words), "the disguised Queen of Love appeared before Aeneas, [and] a preternatural perfume accompanied her presence and betrayed her quality" – and this arouses Clym. That classical allusion, the analogy in which Eustacia plays Venus to Clym's Aeneas (whose *mother* Venus is), both acknowledges the repressed eroticism that

---

[9] Thomas Hardy, *The Complete Poems*, ed. James Gibson (London: Macmillan, 1976), 81
[10] Ibid, I, 5.
[11] Ibid, II, 1
[12] Ibid, II, 3-4 & IV, 5.

infuses Clym's undemonstrative and "absolutely indestructible" love for his mother and implies that this is the moment when Eustacia becomes, if for a while, "his mother's supplanter."[13] The mumming, then, stands in place of Eustacia's dreamed-of dance.

Eustacia, who perceives that her power depends on her sexual allure, fears that her "change of sex," her masculine disguise, has disempowered her by denying the beauty of her face and "the charm of her motions"– has left her with "nothing but a voice."[14] Perhaps the disguise has the opposite effect from what Eustacia fears. Perhaps, in other words, Eustacia's "phallic" presence is no less alluring than her erotic feminine aura; for these two characteristics combine to fit her as an ally in his struggle for freedom from his mother's domination. As Clym's only living parent, Mrs. Yeobright "wears the pants." While she means for him to accomplish through his profession the social aims that his ineffectual father failed to do – and so positions Clym within an Oedipal contest with his dead father – she denies him his manhood by pressuring him to keep a job that he disdains as "effeminate." Clym intends, by challenging his mother's masculine authority, to become a man: "Mother, I hate the flashy business" – jewelry, that is.

> Talk about men who deserve the name, can any man deserving the name waste his time in that effeminate way, when he sees half the world going to ruin for want of somebody to buckle-to and teach 'em how to breast the misery they are born to.

Clym, then, regards Eustacia as a knight, however "inadequate" in her "thrust" during the mummers' performance, who can successfully challenge his domineering mother's phallic authority and ventture with him on his quest. At the same time, he regards her as a *woman* with whom he can be a man, with whom, in other words, he can express the repressed eroticism that fuels his undemonstrative love for his mother. But Clym also seeks maternal nurture. He means not only to marry her himself, but also to marry her to his project: he sees her as "a good matron in a boarding school."[15] When Clym identifies himself to his dying mother – "I am your Clym," he insists – and then lifts her in his arms as Aeneas did his *father*, he signals not only a shift in emotional allegiance from Eustacia back to his mother, but also his psychological regression. He has become again his mother's boy – and his socially feckless father's son. His atonement

---

[13] Ibid, II, 5-6 & V, 6.

[14] Ibid, II, 4 & 6.

[15] Ibid, III, 2-3

with his father is manifest in his persistent indifference to "social failure" even as he returns to his mother's house and makes a home there with her spirit.[16]

Loss of social standing and her own mental depression prompt in Eustacia a Promethean rebellion. By this time, when Eustacia resolves to attend the gipsying, Clym has ceased to be a deity; he has exchanged his brilliant armor for brown leather. Clym patronizes his discontented wife: "Now don't you suppose, my inexperienced girl, that I cannot rebel in high Promethean fashion."[17] But nowhere does he adduce any evidence for the assertion. When the heath-dwellers, even those whose occupation is cutting furze, rebel, they set fire to furze faggots; and "to light a fire," as Hardy maintains, "indicates a spontaneous Promethean rebelliousness against the fiat that this recurrent season shall bring foul times, cold darkness, misery, and death." Then they dance around the tufts of flame. Until then, "so involved in furze" has each one of them been "by his method of carrying the faggots that he appeared like a bush on legs."[18]

That drama at the beginning of the novel presents an allegory of the evolution of an organic culture that gives the heath a human look. Civilization is Egdon's enemy, but Clym derives a "barbarous satisfaction" from the furze-tufted heath's resistance to cultivation. The "oppressive horizontality" of the heath arouses in Clym a similar response when, right after his betrothal to Eustacia, it imparts "a sense of bare equality with and no superiority to a single living thing under the sun" and so enervates his passion for her. Now, after the marriage, it is to that horizontality that Clym now descends: "He was a brown spot in the midst of an expanse of olive-green gorse, and nothing more." And Eustacia resolves to "shake off" this drab monotony: "I'll begin by going to this dance on the green." Thus she enacts her Promethean rebellion by dancing, which creates – thanks to the emotional heat of the 20-odd couples – an atmosphere of "tropical sensations" that keeps at bay the "arctic frigidity" that otherwise infuses her (though it is August).

Hardy characterizes Eustacia's "scheme" as "an afternoon of reckless gaiety."[19] The "gipsying," where Eustacia encounters Wildeve, represents for the participants a Dionysian revolt against the order imposed by the monotony of habit and a puritanical denigration of life itself, which derives from Christian idealism. As Hardy insists,

---

[16] Ibid, IV, 2.
[17] Ibid, IV, 2-3
[18] Ibid, I, 2-3
[19] Ibid, III, 2 & V, 3 & IV, 2-3

"The forty hearts of those waving couples were beating as they had not done since, twelve months before, they had come together in similar jollity. For the time," he concludes (paraphrasing 1 John 2.16), "Paganism was revived in their hearts, the pride of life was all in all, and they adored none other than themselves" – a paraphrase that celebrates the world that's "not of the father," the world of flesh that the Evangelist deplores. Eustacia's sense of propriety prompts her to hesitate before accepting Wildeve's invitation to dance; and even after they've entered the circle, she experiences pangs of conscience. But "fairly launched into the ceaseless glides and whirls...Eustacia's pulses [begin] to move too quickly for longer rumination of any kind." The heart overwhelms the mind, and "a new vitality enter[s] her form." This Dionysian experience challenges at least an unwritten code of respectability: "The dance had come like an irresistible attack upon whatever sense of social order there was in their minds, to drive them back into old paths which were now no longer regular." Out of harmony with the established order and evincing that precarious vitality which her chilly marriage lacks, the dance transports Eustacia at least into the Timeless: amid the pale ray of evening" and then the moonlight, she

> floated round and round ... her face rapt and statuesque; her soul had passed away from and forgotten her features, which were left empty and quiescent.[20]

If this transcendence recalls the early weeks of her marriage, when she and Clym "were enclosed in a sort of luminous mist which hid from them surroundings of any inharmonious colour, and gave to all things the character of light," it also anticipates Eustacia's death. In death she almost appears to be a body of sculpted light. "White" cannot describe the "pallor" of her complexion: "it [is] almost light." Hardy observes the "pleasant" expression of her finely carved mouth and concludes, "Eternal rigidity had seized upon it in a momentary transition between fervour and resignation." In short, the gipsying's "maze of motion" prefigures the "vortex" into which she and Wildeve plunge near the end of the novel.[21]

While that reckless dance on the green in August anticipates the fateful "Night of the Sixth of November," Eustacia's earlier participation in the mumming and the attention that Clym pays to his dying mother together prefigure the nocturnal journey undertaken by the characters. Clym's rescue of his snake-bitten mother, when Hardy compares him with Aeneas and her with Anchises, has elements of

---

[20] Ibid, IV, 3.
[21] Ibid, IV, 1 & V, 9 & IV, 3 & V, 9.

the archetypal journey of the hero into the folds of the dragon and his subsequent "marriage" to Woman and atonement with the father. Now, late in the novel, Eustacia herself embarks on this journey, "occasionally stumbling," as she does, over twisted furze-roots, tufts of rushes, or "oozing lumps of fleshy fungi, which ... lay scattered about the heath like the rotting liver and lungs of some colossal animal," beset all the while by psychological stings and arrows, which Hardy externalizes as the pins that Susan Nunsuch thrusts into a wax effigy of Eustacia and as the lashes of scorpion-like rain.[22] In her earlier role as Turkish knight, she had a voice. Now her lack of money costs her her "masculine" authority. And as ignorant of the revival of her husband's affections as she is now penniless, Eustacia finds herself atop Blackbarrow estranged "from all of humanity except the mouldered remains inside the barrow," a virtual mirror image of her isolated ego. This is the second time that she has had to consider her lack of money: in an earlier altercation between Eustacia and Mrs. Yeobright beside the pool at Mistover the subject was the money meant for Thomasin and Clym. Afterward, after the "excited mother ... withdrew ... Eustacia, panting, stood looking into the pool." It is worth remembering that it was to this same pool that Eustacia summoned Wildeve with her bonfire, and then she boasted that she had called him up and

> triumph[ed] over [him] as the Witch of Endor called up Samuel. I determined you should come; and you have come. I have shown my power.[23]

Earlier, at the threshold of their relationship, Clym presented to Eustacia a prehistoric, bone-filled urn unearthed from a barrow, an urn that his mother then coveted. Having experienced a symbolic emasculation thanks to an "effeminate" occupation that had his mother's approval, he was, in effect, resurrecting his dismembered self and offering it to Eustacia, a gesture that said, "I am your Clym." That it now appears "as if [Eustacia] [is] drawn into the barrow by a hand from beneath," the hand of those "remains," implies her own dismemberment.[24] Hardy juxtaposes Clym's presentation of the burial urn to Eustacia with the scene in March of their betrothal. Beside the pool at Mistover, they pledge themselves to one another with a kiss amid the "stir of resurrection." Symbolically, Clym's crossing of his mother's threshold and his union with Eustacia promise reanimation, transfiguration. But the blindness that comes with the transfer of

---

[22] Ibid, V, 7-8.
[23] Ibid, V, 7 & IV, 2 & I, 6.
[24] Ibid, III, 3 & V, 7.

libidinal energy from mate to books – to a project that he is pursuing in defiance of his mother's wishes – that blindness reveals how impotent is his rebellion against his mother. Clym is her eunuch. His loss of sight, of virility, prepares then for his shift of allegiance from his wife to his mother, who becomes in death "the sublime saint whose radiance even his tenderness for Eustacia could not obscure."[25]

Now, late in the novel, Clym's attempt to rescue Eustacia from the pool at the base of Shadwater Weir represents psychologically an attempt to return to the pool at Mistover. It is as if he can remember his role as the silver knight that danced with Eustacia in her dream, then dove with her into the pool and reached thereby that "iridescent" utopia prefiguring the "Eden" of the early weeks of their marriage. There has awoken in Clym "some of his old solicitude for his mother's supplanter." Unaware of that revival of tender emotions, Eustacia foresees her existence at Egdon only as that of "a painful object, isolated, and out of place." Her death by drowning – a (perhaps suicidal) plunge into the libidinous "vortex" of ego – signifies her rejection of her would-be savior, whether that hero is Clym or Wildeve. Clym also dies – he is not breathing when Venn drags him from the pool – and though he does revive, he finds that every "pulse of lover-like feeling which had not been stilled during Eustacia's lifetime [has] gone into the grave with her."[26]

Clym's reanimation comes at the hands of the now-widowed Thomasin, who applies a bottle of "hartshorn" to his nostrils. While Eustacia has impulsively rejected him as Artemis does Acteon (whose discovery of her in a pool costs him life and limb), the maternal Thomasin, his mother's choice of bride for Clym, embraces him. His subsequent "distress" at what he perceives to be a new erotic complexity in their relationship, when he mistakenly perceives that she has made herself pretty for him on the day of the Maypole dance, reveals that those "lover-like feelings" have a pulse after all. Hardy has depicted Clym's relationship with his widowed cousin as one of "boy and girl under his mother's eye." Now it appears that the period of sexual latency is ending for that boy. Clym flees Blooms End right as the festival of spring is beginning just beyond its palings: "He could not bear to remain in the presence of enjoyment to-day, though he had tried hard." Thus, a conscious effort yields to a more powerful unconscious taboo. Clym similarly shuns the feasting and dancing that follow Thomasin's wedding to Venn, which Grandfer Cantle celebrates by twirling himself about. The consequence is the repression

---

[25] Ibid, III, 3 & VI, 4.
[26] Ibid, II, 3 & IV, 1 & V, 6-7 & VI, 1

of whatever erotic feelings Thomasin's loveliness may have aroused and the sublimation of that energy toward the mother, who becomes "almost a presence," and toward a new occupation. [27]

Though his eyes remain weak, Clym does find his voice, and "to speak," according to Freudian thought, means to be potent; inability to speak means castration: Speaking "not only in simple language on Blackbarrow and in the upland hamlets round, but in a more cultivated strain elsewhere" as "an itinerant open-air preacher," the erstwhile hero has become an archetypal bearer of the word. But however stirring may be the "tones of his voice," his discourses on "morally unimpeachable subjects" appear unlikely to faze "the commonwealth of hearts and hands," which draws sustenance from the occasional revival of Bacchic frenzy. Anyhow, he will not be enacting its customs.[28]

WORKS CONSULTED

Boumelha, Penny. *Thomas Hardy and Women: Sexual Ideology and Narrative Form*. Madison: U of Wisconsin P, 1982.

Campbell, Joseph. *The Hero with a Thousand Faces*. Bollingen Ser. 17. Princeton: Princeton UP, 1972.

Eliot, T. S. *Four Quartets*. San Diego: Harvest/HBJ, 1971.

Freud, Sigmund. "On Narcissism: An Introduction." *The Freud Reader*. Ed. Peter Gay. New York: Norton, 1989. 545-562.

Gordon, Lyndall. Eliot's New Life. New York: Farrar-Noonday, 1989

Hardy, Thomas. *The Complete Poems of Thomas Hardy*. Ed. James Gibson. London: Macmillan, 1976.

— *The Life and Works of Thomas Hardy*. Ed. Michael Millgate. Athens: Uni. Georgia Press, 1985.

— *The Return of the Native*. Ed. Simon Gatrell. Oxford: Oxford UP, 1990.

Holland, Norman N. "Fantasy and Defense in Faulkner's 'A Rose for Emily.'" *Literary Theories in Praxis*. Ed.Shirley F. Staton. Philadelphia: Uni. Pennsylvania Press, 1987. 294- 307.

---

[27] Ibid, V, 8 & Vi, 1, 4.
[28] Ibid, VI, 4.

THE LIFE AND WORK OF THOMAS HARDY:
ALLUSIONS AND ANNOTATIONS

MARTIN RAY

INTRODUCTION

THIS ARTICLE is primarily concerned with attempting to identify the many allusions to the work of other writers which Hardy includes in his autobiography. For instance, there are some eight or nine allusions to Robert Browning's poetry which the modern reader is unrealistically expected to recognize: few readers now would readily identify the source of "mountainous fugues" or "wronged great soul of an ancient master", yet Hardy obviously assumed that in his own day readers would accept without suspicion that even Florence Hardy, the book's nominal author, would have a thorough familiarity with the Victorian poet and a facile ability to quote an apposite phrase. Other writers to whom Hardy alludes include favourites such as Shelley, Wordsworth, Milton, Tennyson, Swinburne, Byron and Keats (the last name surprisingly appears only once in this article as the source of an allusion). Shakespeare, of course, features prominently, as do Latin and Greek literature (especially Horace), along with a dozen references to the Bible.

It seems highly unlikely that any publisher will produce a fully annotated edition of the *Life* in the foreseeable future, and therefore I have also taken this opportunity to add some notes and glosses to numerous references in Hardy's text which seem to me to need explication. I would stress that this aspect of the article is not at all intended to be comprehensive but should be regarded simply as a preliminary step towards the kind of annotated edition which the *Life* will one day enjoy and which it certainly merits. Some of these notes give the kind of historical or contextual information which Hardy did not feel any need to add: what did Queen Adelaide die of? what did Lady Florence Paget do in Marshall and Snelgrove's? what was the Crawford-Dilke case? Other annotations collate information from standard biographical sources, such as the works of Michael Millgate and Robert Gittings, and present them in a form convenient to a reader of the *Life*.

A third kind of annotations give some observations of my own, again in no systematic way, of points which I thought might be of some interest to fellow Hardyans: for instance, it is not immediately apparent that Hardy, in recording the Whitechapel murder of 1888, is in fact describing the death of the second of Jack the Ripper's five victims. Similarly, I mention a recent photograph of Arlington Manor, the Jeunes' splendid country home in Berkshire which Hardy visited, and which can now be viewed online, a source of information which has not been available to earlier commentators.

I have not annotated quotations from Hardy's letters, which have already been thoroughly annotated in the *Collected Letters*, and I have not duplicated information which is already given in the excellent Index to the *Life*. However, one particular feature of my use of the Index should be mentioned: I have produced what internet search engines call by the ungainly term of a Reverse Lookup Directory. That is, the Index gives the name of Elizabeth Swire, say, and directs the reader to the "Irish ancestress" whom Hardy mentions, but a reader coming across "Irish ancestress" in the text would not be able to identify her as Elizabeth Swire in the Index. This article seeks to remedy such an inevitable shortcoming of the Index.

All page references in this article are keyed to Michael Millgate's edition of *The Life and Work of Thomas Hardy* (London: Macmillan, 1984). The following works are frequently referred to in the notes:

Lennart A. Björk, ed., *The Literary Notebooks of Thomas Hardy*, 2 vols. (London: Macmillan, 1985).

Robert Gittings, *Young Thomas Hardy* (Harmondsworth: Penguin, 1978).

Robert Gittings, *The Older Hardy* (Harmondsworth: Penguin, 1980).

Michael Millgate, *Thomas Hardy: A Biography* (Oxford: Clarendon Press, 1982). This is 'Millgate' unless otherwise stated.

Michael Millgate, *Thomas Hardy: His Career as a Novelist* (London: Bodley Head, 1971).

R. L. Purdy, *Thomas Hardy: A Bibliographical Study* (London: Oxford University Press, 1954).

R. L. Purdy and Michael Millgate, eds., *The Collected Letters of Thomas Hardy*, 7 vols. (Oxford: Clarendon Press, 1978–88).

Allusions and Annotations

7 *retired military officers*: one of whom was Captain Meggs. Millgate notes that "The hamlet's earlier nickname of 'Veterans' Alley' derived from the military men who had retired to live along its single street, and although Hardy himself would have known only one of these, a Lieutenant Thomas Drane who had fought at Trafalgar, his father told him anecdotes of an army officer, Captain Meggs, who had lived in the 'house by the well' – presumably the one subsequently inhabited by John Cox, the relieving officer and registrar" (p. 24).

old navy lieutenant: Thomas Drane.

small farmer and tranter: William Keats.

relieving officer and registrar: John Cox.

old militiaman: George Downton.

nurse: Elizabeth Downton.

11 *one of those Swetmans*: John Swetman.

West Briton: a Whig (Liberal) newspaper founded in 1810. Based in Truro and giving coverage of Cornwall. It was the county's second newspaper, and it is still being published.

Herbal and *Dispensary*: Nicholas Culpeper's *Complete Herbal* (1653) is an alphabetical listing of herbs offering remedies to all known ills. His *London Dispensatory* of 1653 was the first translation into English of the second London pharmacopoeia (1650) and proved immensely popular: it was pirated in 1654 and reprinted fourteen times before 1718. Culpeper was a well-known herbalist and astrologer, and not a medical doctor; he had an enormous influence on folk medicine.

daughter: Jemima Hardy.

12 *young man*: George Hand.

tambouring: embroidering material which has been stretched within a tambour, or circular frame.

mantua-making: dress-making.

13 *Croft*: in 1724 he published his most famous work, a two-volume collection of church music entitled *Musica Sacra*, containing 30 anthems and a setting of the Church of England burial service that is still in use. It was the first collection of anthems to be printed in score format.

sons: James and Thomas Hardy.

wrote Walpole: in a letter to Lord Hertford of 12 April 1764, Walpole wrote that "Poor Lord Ilchester is almost distracted; indeed, it is the completion of disgrace – even a footman were preferable; the publicity of the hero's profession perpetuates the mortification. [...] I could not have believed that Lady Susan would have stooped so low". See the *Yale Edition of Horace Walpole's Correspondence*, 48 vols. (1937–81), XXXVIII, 367.

14 *The Double Dealer*: by William Congreve.

The Constant Couple ... The Beaux' Stratagem: plays by George Farquhar.

16   *Pope's Ode*: "Ode on St. Cecilia's Day". Hardy is probably referring to Maurice Greene's 1730 setting of the Ode. St. Cecilia is the patroness of church music.

    "*mountainous fugues*": Robert Browning, "Master Hugues Of Saxe-Gotha": "Answer the question I've put you so oft: // What do you mean by your mountainous fugues?" (ll. 3–4)

    description by Fairway: see *The Return of the Native*, Book First, Chapter 5.

18   *Vandyke-brown*: a deep brown colour, characteristic of Vandyke's paintings. Cf. the description of Grace Melbury in *The Woodlanders*: "She had well-formed eyebrows which, had her portrait been painted, would probably have been done in Prouts's or Vandyke brown" (Chapter 5).

19   *Broken Heart*: during a feast, Calantha hears, in close succession, of the deaths of her father and lover. She dances on, apparently unmoved, in a show of Spartan self-control. When the feast is done, she dies broken-hearted.

20   "*And now another day is gone*": Isaac Watts's hymn of 1715. The full text is as follows: "And now another day is gone, I'll sing my Maker's praise, my comforts every hour make known, his providence and grace. // I lay my body down to sleep; may angels guard my head, and through the hours of darkness keep their watch around my bed. // With cheerful heart I close my eyes, since thou wilt not remove; and in the morning let me rise rejoicing in thy love".

    cousin: Augustus Hardy.

    vicar: Arthur Shirley.

    same composer: George Frederick Handel. Gittings accounts for Hardy's confusion by noting that military funerals in Dorchester "were accompanied by solemn music on the way to church, and brisk marches on the way back" (*Young Thomas Hardy*, p. 42).

21   *schoolmaster and mistress*: Thomas Fuller and Mrs C. Fuller.

    Walkingame's Arithmetic: Francis Walkingame's *Tutor Assistant* (1751) passed through numerous editions and was the most popular "Arithmetic" in England and America until the mid-nineteenth century. See *Far from the Madding Crowd*, Chapter 8, and the poem, "He Revisits His First School".

    Paul and Virginia: romance by Jacques Henri Bernardin de Saint-Pierre, published 1787.

    her sister: Martha Sharpe, who lived in Hatfield, Hertfordshire.

    Squeers: Wackford Squeers, the malevolent headmaster of Dotheboys Hall in Dickens's *Nicholas Nickleby*.

22   *Great Northern Railway to London*: opened 1850.

    Pantheon: a large building in Oxford Street, opened as a place of public entertainment in 1772.

    Marble Arch: built in 1828 as the chief entrance to Buckingham Palace, but when the Palace was extended in 1851, the Arch was moved to its current site as an entrance to Hyde Park.

    Pantechnicon: a word "invented as the name of a bazaar of all kinds of artistic work" (OED).

headmaster: Isaac Last.

23 *lady of the manor*: Julia Augusta Martin.

master and mistress: Thomas Fuller and Mrs C. Fuller.

24 *harvest-supper*: held in the early autumn of 1850, in an old barn on the Kingston Maurward estate. See Hardy's poem, "The Harvest-Supper".

small farmer's daughter: Charlotte Keats (?).

little niece: Miss Campbell (?); see Index.

25 *the railway*: it reached Dorchester in 1847.

"*The Outlandish Knight*": in this ballad, a knight woos a lady and says he will marry her if she runs away with him. He leads her to the seashore and threatens to drown her as he has drowned others before. She makes him turn his back and kills him instead. She returns home and bribes her parrot to keep her secret.

26 *landlord*: James Fellowes.

corn-law agitations: the repeal of the Corn Laws in 1846 was opposed by the gentry, and therefore support for the Anti-Corn-Law movement was usually secret.

Wiseman: the No-Popery agitation of 1850–51 was sparked by Wiseman's arrival in London as the first cardinal Archbishop of Westminster in November 1850. The incident which Hardy recalls occurred during the Guy Fawkes celebrations of 5 November 1850.

27 *vicar*: Arthur Shirley.

schoolmaster: Isaac Last.

old Eton grammar: Hardy's second-hand Eton grammar (1846), in which he wrote his name in 1852, had its origins in the early 16th century. The lines on the genders of nouns begin "Propria quae maribus".

Eutropius: "Eutropius' compact survey of Roman history down to AD 364 has the merit of simplicity, but it is dull and now largely forgotten. Hardy's signature in his 1846 text, again second-hand, is dated 1854" (Jeremy Steele's entry on "Classics" in Norman Page, ed., *Oxford Reader's Companion to Hardy* (2000), p. 53).

Caesar: Hardy's "copy of Caesar's *De Bello Gallico* (1854) was new, and its condition indicates that he studied part of Book 1 and all of Book 4, doubtless chosen because it included Caesar's first expedition to Britain" (Jeremy Steele's entry on "Classics" in Norman Page, ed., *Oxford Reader's Companion to Hardy* (2000), p. 53).

colouring the nouns: Hardy's second-hand King Edward VI Latin Grammar (c.1844) contains five pages in which he coloured the genders in watercolour, using red for masculine, blue for neuter and leaving feminine white. See Jeremy Steele's entry on "Classics" in Norman Page, ed., *Oxford Reader's Companion to Hardy* (2000), p. 53.

Fellow: Charles Walter Moule (?).

    new Latin primer: Kennedy's *Revised Latin Primer*, which appeared in 1888.

28   *Dumas*: best known for historical romances such as *The Three Musketeers* and *The Count of Monte Cristo* (both 1844–5).

29   *His son*: William Isaac Last.

    his namesake: Thomas Hardye of Frampton endowed the Dorchester Grammar School in 1579.

    Beza's Latin Testament: inscribed "T. Hardy. A reward for diligence in studies from Mr. Last. Mids[ummer] 1855".

    Tate's Mechanics: Thomas Tate's *Mechanics and the Steam Engine, for the Use of Beginners* was published in 1855 as part of Gleig's School Series.

    Nesbitt's Mensuration: Anthony Nesbit's *A Treatise on Practical Mensuration* was first published in 1816 and went through many later editions. Hardy's spelling of the author's surname is mistaken.

    fell madly in love: the incident is reproduced in *The Well-Beloved*, I.vii.

30   *vicar's sons*: Sewallis and Robert Shirley.

    dairy-maid: Jane Gilliam (?).

    Windsor Castle: published 1843.

    another young girl: Elizabeth Sarah Bishop.

    well-to-do farmer: Stephen Coghill Harding.

    Louisa: Louisa Harding.

31   *Woodsford Castle*: a fourteenth-century house on the south side of the Frome valley, to the east of Lower Bockhampton. It is the setting of Hardy's poem, 'A Sound in the Night', and he may have heard the poem's tradition when working there with his father.

32   *pupil of twenty-one*: Herbert F. Fippard.

32–3   *a man was to be hanged*: James Seale was executed on 19 August 1858.

33   *that of a woman*: Martha Browne was executed at Dorchester prison on 9 August 1856, for the murder of her husband.

    vicar: Arthur Shirley.

    Hooker: Richard Hooker's *Of the Laws of Ecclesiastical Polity* was the primary source of Anglican/Episcopal "doctrine" on all subjects such as church governance, worship, interpretation of Scripture and Christian ethics. It was written in the 1580s and 90s.

    architect's wife: Amelia Hicks.

34   *hard-headed Scotch youths*: Frederick and William Henry Perkins.

    Griesbach's: in the 1859 Bohn edition, which Hardy signed in February 1860. Jude acquired the same edition.

35   *great friend of Hardy's*: Alfred More Perkins.

"*plain living and high thinking*": Wordsworth, "Written in London, September, 1802", l. 11.

Baptist minister in A Laodicean: Mr Woodwell. See especially Book the First, Chapter Seven.

37 *one of the partners*: John Hussey.

Essays and Reviews: published in 1860, it is a collection of seven essays on religion, covering such topics as religious thought in England, the Biblical researches of the Higher critics, the evidences of Christianity, and the cosmology of Genesis. The book was highly controversial and the essayists, seven liberal Anglican churchmen, were known as "The Seven Against Christ." The book was a key part of the challenge to Biblical history by the Higher Critics and by scientists working in the new disciplines of biology and geology. The most important piece is Benjamin Jowett's essay entitled "On the Interpretation of Scripture".

Bagehot: Walter Bagehot's *Estimates of Some Englishmen and Scotchmen* was published in 1858. It was Bagehot's first book, and included nine long review essays, on "the first Edinburgh Reviewers" (including Sydney Smith), William Cowper, Edward Gibbon, Bishop Butler, Shakespeare, Shelley, Hartley Coleridge, Sir Robert Peel, and Macaulay.

anonymous skit: see Purdy, pp. 291–3. Purdy believes that Hardy's memory "played him false after sixty years" in his description of this article.

38 *one or two of the dramatists*: Aeschylus and Sophocles.

He settled ... based Oun: Browning's "A Grammarian's Funeral", ll. 129–30. *Hoti* and *Oun* are Greek particles meaning "that" and "therefore". The grammarian thus settled difficult points in Greek grammar.

danseuse: Gittings notes that this is a euphemism, since the girls were all prostitutes (*Young Thomas Hardy*, p. 91).

41 *Dorset mansion*: Gittings suggests that this building was near Stinsford, "either Clyffe House to the north-east, or, more likely, Stafford House to the south-east" (*Young Thomas Hardy*, p. 41).

42 *inquirer*: C. K. Shorter.

Embankment: the Victoria Embankment was built in 1864–70.

Charing-Cross Bridge: this railway bridge across the Thames was built in 1863–4.

Garrick: the actor had lived next door at No. 6 Adelphi Terace from 1772 until his death at the house in 1779.

Johnson: Samuel Johnson had moved to London, accompanied by Garrick, in 1737. They were both members of the Literary Club (formed 1764). In 1748, Johnson had moved into a large house in Fleet Street and began work upon his dictionary.

43 *the lady*: Julia Augusta Martin.

butler: William Henry Adams.

Cider Cellars: in Leicester Square. Gittings notes that "the notorious 'Lord Chief Baron' Renton Nicholson, having settled himself with a cigar and brandy-and-water, would 'try' a case of prostitution, with girls and bawds represented by male actors; when the last ounce of indecent humour had been extracted, this was succeeded by more-or-less nude *poses plastiques* with real girls" (*Young Thomas Hardy*, p. 92).

Dr Donovan: of 111 The Strand. See Gittings, *Young Thomas Hardy*, p. 115.

Pearl ... "Skittles" ... Willoughby ... Menken: Gittings describes them as "notable courtesans": Menken was "the powerful equestrienne of Astley's, who fascinated Swinburne, and performed her sensational ride as Mazeppa in a vest and shorts that made her appear naked. [Hardy's] memory as an old man, however, somewhat telescoped the years. In 1862, the first two ladies had deserted London for more profitable conquests in Paris, while Menken, beloved by the literati as much for her quite professional poetry as for her apparent nudity, had not yet left her native America. Another lady he mentions, Agnes Willoughby, had in fact just hooked a rich husband and retired in triumph" (*Young Thomas Hardy*, pp. 91–2).

44   *Lady Florence Paget*: on 16 July 1864 she announced that she needed to do some shopping for her trousseau. She went to the fashionable departmental store of Marshall and Snelgrove in Oxford Street, but left the store secretly and met her lover, the Marquis of Hastings, outside. They were married later that day.

Charing-Cross Station: opened on 11 January 1864.

Thames Embankment: built 1864–70.

Temple Bar: one of the eight gates that surrounded the old City of London. It stood at the junction of Fleet Street and The Strand in London until dismantled in 1878 because it caused major traffic congestion.

Law Courts: G. E. Street's Law Courts were built 1868–82.

Skinner Street: the Godwin family lived at 4 Skinner Street, Holborn. The street still exists but the Godwin residence has disappeared.

bridge across Ludgate Hill: the western approach to St. Paul's was completely marred by the obtrusive iron railway bridge of the London, Chatham, and Dover Railway, which crossed Ludgate Hill at its lower end, and destroyed the view from Farringdon-circus at its foot. The bridge was built in 1874 and demolished in the late 1980s. A contemporary image can be viewed at http://www.storyoflondon.com/article1003.html.

South Kensington Museum: opened in 1857 on the north side of Brompton Road, east of Exhibition Road.

underground railway: the first was opened in 1863.

Kilburn: a newly-built district at the far end of the Edgware road.

45   *Our American Cousin*: a comedy by Tom Taylor, in which a character called Lord Dundreary appears.

Cremorne: in Chelsea.

Argyle: in Great Windmill Street.

senior-pupil: Herbert F. Fippard.

46   *Maritana*: by William Vincent Wallace.

The Bohemian Girl: by Michael William Balfe.

47   *the bodies of her parents*: Mary Shelley died on 1 February 1851. A few days later, the remains of Mary Wollstonecraft and William Godwin were moved from St. Pancras to the churchyard at St. Peter's, Bournemouth, and on 8 February Mary Shelley was buried between her parents.

50   *Princess Royal*: Princess Victoria was the eldest daughter of Queen Victoria and in 1858 was married to Crown Prince Friedrich of Prussia, later Kaiser Friedrich III. The laying of the foundation stone for All Saints' Church in New Windsor occurred on 21 November 1863, two years earlier than Hardy remembers here. Blomfield had been commissioned to build the church, a photograph of which can be seen in Ellen Dollery's "New Windsor All Saints' Church and Thomas Hardy", *Thomas Hardy Journal*, 3:1 (January 1987), 37–9. The incident with the trowel "seems almost certainly to have been preserved in a scene between the architect hero and the heroine" in *The Poor Man and the Lady* (Gittings, *Young Thomas Hardy*, p. 150).

51   *Lalla Rookh*: by Thomas Moore.

"*Nescit vox missa reverti*": Horace, *Ars Poetica*, ll. 389–90 ("A word once uttered cannot be recalled").

52   *a friend*: Horace Moule.

53   *Westminster Abbey*: Millgate comments that "a note in his prayerbook, however, shows that the Westminster Abbey communion [...] was actually taken not in July 1865 but in July 1863" (p. 91).

54   *companion*: W. O. Milne.

Phelps: Millgate notes that "Hardy particularly admired Samuel Phelps's Falstaff, and he could have seen him in that role as early as March 1864. He saw Phelps in *Othello* in 1865 and recalled fifty years later the 'knocking scene' in Phelps's *Macbeth*" (p. 99).

58   "*save his own soul he hath no star*": Swinburne, *Prelude to Songs before Sunrise*; also quoted as epigraph to Part Second of *Jude the Obscure*.

socialistic: the first British citation in the OED is dated 1858.

59   *Battle of the Nile*: Nelson's crushing naval defeat of the French in 1798.

61   *editor of the Saturday Review*: Alexander James Beresford Hope.

65   "*Morgenblätter*": "Morning Paper Waltz" (1864).

new assistant: Millgate, noting that the portrayal of Springrove seems autobiographical, comments that "it is by no means impossible that the 'new assistant' was Hardy himself" (p. 118).

71   *the Patron*: Richard Rawle.

73   *the Patron*: Richard Rawle.

74   *cousins*: Edith Ching and Kate Gifford.

75 *old friend*: Anne d'Arville.

76 *a pupil*: William Searle Hicks.

78 *Bishop of Exeter*: Frederick Temple.

firm to which he was a stranger: Hardy had in fact submitted *The Poor Man and the Lady* to Tinsley in 1869.

81 *Battle of Wörth*: Prussian victory during the Franco-Prussian War.

"*quicquid delirant reges, plectuntur Achivi*": "Whatever folly the kings commit, the people suffer" (Horace, *Epistles*, I.ii.14).

battle of Gravelotte: the largest battle of the Franco-Prussian war took place on 18 August 1870 and resulted in some 33,000 casualties. It led to a French retreat.

82 "*In Time of 'the Breaking of Nations'* ": this poem was written in 1915 and first printed in the *Saturday Review*, 29 January 1916.

scarfings: joining two pieces of wood together so as to appear as one piece.

85 "*Thou wouldst ... no matter*": *Hamlet*, V. ii. 194–6.

87 *the reviewer*: John Hutton.

"*a desperate remedy for an emaciated purse*": Millgate notes that Hardy's account "incorporates a small yet significant misquotation: the reviewer had written of his hope of stirring the author 'to better things in the future than these "desperate remedies" which he has adopted for ennui or an emaciated purse'". The omission of " 'ennui' stresses the insinuation of poverty; it also suggests Hardy's sensitivity to this implication at a moment of extreme financial vulnerability" (*Thomas Hardy: His Career as a Novelist*, p. 36).

88 "*Things at their worst ... what they were before*": *Macbeth*, IV. ii. 24–5.

another publishing house. Tinsley Brothers.

"*accomplished critic*": John Morley.

89 *his letter to you*: see letter of 17 August 1871 to Malcolm Macmillan, in *Collected Letters*, I, 12.

91 *about the last week in May*: Purdy writes that "though the novel was advertised as early as 18 May, it was not announced as ready until 15 June" (p. 8n).

92 *Copinger on Copyright*: Copinger's *Law of Copyright* was first published in 1870. It was known as *Copinger on Copyright* and became the standard work on Copyright Law in England. Gittings, however, notes that Hardy's copy of Copinger in the Dorset County Museum is inscribed 1873 (*Young Thomas Hardy*, p. 227).

the artist: J. A. Pasquier.

94 *On this day*: 28 September 1872.

"*The Tranter*": William Keats (see Index for mistaken dating of death).

95 *the Tranter and the Tranter's wife*: William and Mary Keats.

Brasseur: this was the French comic actor's first appearance in England. The evening of "French Plays" (thus advertised) took place at the Princess's

Theatre. Brasseur performed nine different characters to illustrate his repertoire.

98 *Saturday Review*: the review declared that *A Pair of Blue Eyes* was "one of the most artistically constructed among recent novels" (vol. XXXVI, 2 August 1873, pp. 158–59).

buried at Fordington: see the poem, "Before My Friend Arrived".

99 *publishers*: Smith, Elder.

rick-'staddles': "stones with tapering tops and round flat under-surfaces, a number of which are placed on posts beneath ricks and granaries to raise them from the earth and keep rats out" (OED). See *Far from the Madding Crowd*: "The corn stood on stone staddles" (Chapter 6).

101 *The Times*: the passage in *Far from the Madding Crowd* (Chapter 8) which the review praised was the description of Levi Everdene making his wife take off her wedding ring: "And as soon as he could thoroughly fancy he was doing wrong and committing the seventh, 'a got to like her as well as ever, and they lived on, a perfect example of mutual love" ([Frederick Napier Broome] "Recent Novels", *Times*, 25 January 1875, p. 4). The review commended "this surface talk of an intensely realistic and amusing kind".

103 *married at St. Peter's*: on 17 September 1874.

his second wife: Margaret Symons Gifford.

odd coincidence: the subject of Hardy's late poem, "The Opportunity". On 22 August 1874 Helen Paterson married William Allingham (1824–89), the Irish poet and member of the Rossetti circle, who was virtually twice her age.

104 *the lady he had so admired*: Julia Augusta Martin.

105 *as she entered church*: the memory of the noise of Mrs Martin's gown is reproduced in "The Withered Arm", when Gertrude Lodge's "gownd […] whewed and whistled so loud when it rubbed against the pews".

"*to keep base life afoot*": *King Lear*, II. iv. 214.

author of Lorna Doone: Richard Doddridge Blackmore wrote *Lorna Doone* in 1869. Blackmore did not consider himself a writer. He lived for most of his life in the then rural London suburb of Teddington as a market gardener.

108 "*Ars est celare artem*": the true art is to conceal art.

"*A sweet disorder … every part*": Robert Herrick, "The Poetry of Dress".

act of 1870: the Clerical Disabilities Act, enabling clergy to renounce their orders.

109 *vortex*: "in modern scientific use: a rapid movement of particles of matter round an axis; a whirl of atoms, fluid, or vapour" (OED). This indicates the influence of Comte's Positivism on Leslie Stephen.

Stylites: saints who took up their abode on top of pillars.

delegation: representing the Copyright Association, which met Disraeli on 10 May 1875.

Waterloo Day: 18 June.

110 *The Hundred Days*: the period of Napoleon's escape from Elba, return to power, and defeat at Waterloo in 1815.

"*captain*": Joseph Masters.

111 *article appeared*: Léon Boucher, "Le Roman Pastoral en Angleterre", *Revue des Deux Mondes*, 15 December 1875, pp. 838–66.

112 *Bernard Shaw*: Hardy seems to be referring to the "impossible situation" in *Pygmalion* (1914), in which the cockney Eliza is accepted by polite society as a lady.

"*Artemus Ward*": Charles Farrar Browne.

113 "*between the banks that bear the vine*": Byron's *Childe Harold's Pilgrimage*, Canto the Third, LV: "the wide and winding Rhine, // Whose breast of waters broadly swells // Between the banks that bear the vine".

Königsstuhl: the Koenigstuhl ("King's Chair") is the mountain overlooking Heidelberg.

114 *Duchess of Richmond's ball*: held on 15 June 1815, two nights before Waterloo, the ball was attended by Wellington and numerous other distinguished guests. It took place at the Duchess's home in the rue de la Blanchisserie, Brussels.

115 *wizard*: "Dr" John Buckland.

116 "*All is vanity*", *saith the Preacher*: see Ecclesiastes 1:2.

Revue des Deux Mondes: there does not appear to be a review of *A Pair of Blue Eyes* in this periodical in the first half of 1877.

117 *fife*: a small high-pitched kind of flute. Cf. Hardy's "Summer Schemes", which also associates birds with fifes: "When friendly summer calls again, // Calls again // Her little fifers to these hills" (ll. 1–3).

"*She is not fair to outward view*": the title of Hartley Coleridge's only poem to be included in Palgrave's *Golden Treasury* (1875).

118 "*the light that never was*": Wordsworth's "Elegiac Stanzas Suggested by a Picture of Peele Castle, in a Storm, Painted by Sir George Beaumont": "Ah! then, if mine had been the Painter's hand // To express what then I saw; and add the gleam, // The light that never was, on sea or land, // The consecration, and the Poet's dream" (ll. 13–16).

Our servant: Jane Phillips (?).

Her father: Edwin Phillips (?).

windrows: rows in which mown grass or hay is laid before being made up into heaps (OED).

119 *Mrs* ——: Georgina Long.

Jamie: James Godolfin Long.

churched: "said of a woman after child-birth, when thanks are publicly offered for her safe delivery" (OED).

Her husband: Robert Godolfin Long.

real names: Christoph Bless and Matthäus Tina.

Hambledon Hill: the largest battle in Dorset during the Civil War was not fought between Cavaliers and Roundheads. It occurred in August 1645 when a force from Cromwell's army, outnumbered by some 4 to 1, engaged in battle with the Dorset Clubmen, a body which owed no allegiance to either side and which was driven by anger at the damage to crops and land which the war had caused. The Clubmen were countryfolk armed with clubs and pitchforks, and they were quickly put to flight.

120   *G. W.*: Great Western.

"*Eustacia*": Eustacia Belvale.

121   *battue*: the driving of game from cover (by beating the bushes, etc. in which they lodge) to a point where a number of sportsmen wait to shoot them (OED).

Superintendent of Police: William Grant.

124   *Heidelberg ... Scheveningen*: "to the commonest tourist, spots like Iceland may become what the vineyards and myrtle-gardens of South Europe are to him now; and Heidelberg and Baden be passed unheeded as he hastens from the Alps to the sand-dunes of Scheveningen' (*The Return of the Native*, Book First, Chapter 1). Heidelberg is a pleasant town in south-west Germany with an ancient university, and Scheveningen is a windy seaside resort on the Dutch coast near the Hague.

125   "*Jingle*": James Albery's 1878 adaptation of *The Pickwick Papers*, in which Irving took the principal role.

Eugene Aram's 'Dream': Thomas Hood's "The Dream of Eugene Aram". Irving had starred in a dramatic version of "Eugene Aram" in 1873 and he had performed *Richard III* in 1877.

Kingston Lacy: the seat of the Bankes family, near Wimborne, Dorset. There are paintings by Raphael, Rubens, Sebastiano del Piombo, Titian, seventeenth-century Spanish pictures and portraits by Lely.

West-Stafford Rectory: Reginald Southwell Smith was the rector.

Ford Abbey: in north-west Dorset. This mansion, a mediaeval building with seventeenth-century additions, occupies the site of a Cistercian Abbey. Hardy recalls the visit to Ford Abbey with Moule in *Collected Letters*, VI, 87.

126   *Treasure Island*: published 1883.

jaunty young man: Herbert F. Fippard.

127   *Chelsea Hospital and Ranelagh Gardens*: The Royal Hospital, Chelsea, was founded by Charles II as a retreat for old or disabled soldiers and opened in 1692 by William and Mary. It is still fulfilling its original purpose, as a home for the "Chelsea Pensioners". Access to Ranelagh Gardens is from a gate in the Royal Hospital grounds.

The Times: their review began by noting that "In his 'Return of the Native,' Mr. Hardy keeps us as 'Far from the Madding Crowd' as ever, or further" ("Recent Novels", *Times*, 5 December 1878, p. 3).

128 "*there had past away a glory from the earth*": a reference to Wordsworth, *Ode: Intimations of Immortality from Recollections of Early Childhood*, l. 18.

Arabic arch: an architectural term for a style of arch found in Arabia.

129 *G. R.——*: George Rackstrow Crickmay.

130 *shoemaker*: Robert Read.

his mother: Ruth Read.

Harrow: Reginald Bosworth Smith had been House Master of The Knoll, a large house at Harrow School, since its opening in 1870.

baby: Mervyn Henry Bosworth Smith, nephew of the dying man.

Mrs H. S.: Alice Bertha Smith.

131 *Knapdale*: the name of Macmillan's house in Upper Tooting perhaps suggested "Ringdale", earlier "Kingdale", the name of Barnet's new home in "Fellow-Townsmen".

A Laodicean: see Chapter 15.

132 "*Plon Plon*": the sobriquet of Prince Joseph Charles Paul Napoleon. He was nicknamed *Craint-plon* (Fear-bullet) in the Crimean war (1854–1856), later corrupted into "Plon-Plon".

134 *Good Words*: an illustrated monthly magazine founded in 1860 with which Hardy had recently agreed to serialize *The Trumpet-Major* the following year. The Lord Mayor's Show this year took place on Saturday, 8 November.

137 *The Gamekeeper at Home*: published in 1878 by Smith, Elder & Co, when Jefferies was 30 years old.

139 *Edmonton*: Charles Lamb's home, near Enfield, Middlesex. The Procters were married in 1824.

140 *the Tombstone*: in "Fellow-Townsmen" (*Wessex Tales*), Downe initially has plans for a "vast altar-tomb and canopy" for his late wife, but he eventually decides upon "a coped tomb of good solid construction, with no useless elaboration at all".

airy does: see Tennyson's *The Princess*, VI.

Freshwater: Tennyson's home at Farringford House, Freshwater Bay, Isle of Wight.

The Battle of Dorking: George Chesney's hugely successful novel was published in 1871; it popularized fiction about preparations for a German invasion.

143 *mother's grandfather*: William Hand.

145 *architect*: Reginald Ely (died 1471), Henry VI's master mason. The foundation stone of the Chapel was laid on 25 July 1446, by the king. Three other master masons worked on the Chapel after Ely's death.

"*glorious work of fine intelligence*": Wordsworth, "Inside of King's College Chapel, Cambridge", l. 5.

"*dim religious light*": Milton, *Il Penseroso*, l. 160.

"*white-robed scholars*": Wordsworth, "Inside of King's College Chapel, Cambridge", l. 4.

149 *Fryston*: Fryston Hall, Castleford, Yorkshire; Lord Houghton's family home (now demolished).

surgeon: Henry Edward Beck.

150 *George Eliot died*: 22 December 1880.

151 *Arnold is wrong*: see his essay, "The Literary Influence of Academies", and Björk, 1166.

152 *Carlyle died last Saturday*: on 5 February 1881, in London.

Aerostation: "the art of raising and guiding balloons or other machines in the air" (OED).

plan adopted by Sue: see *Jude the Obscure*, IV. vi.

The Hundred Days: the period of Napoleon's escape from Elba, return to power, and defeat at Waterloo

153 "*See the wretch ... Paradise*": Thomas Gray, *Ode on the Pleasure Arising from Vicissitude*, ll. 45–52.

Lady Day: March 25.

154 *new comet*: Tebbutt's Comet, visible to the naked eye from late May 1881 until the end of July. First visible to observers in the Northern Hemisphere in the second half of June. It was recorded as being of the first magnitude with a 20 degree tail on 25 June, when Hardy saw it.

Roslin: six miles south of Edinburgh.

155 *Roslin Castle and Chapel*: Roslin Castle is romantically situated on the wooded steep banks of the Esk. It dates from the 12th century and is a plain, massive ruin. Rosslyn Chapel is a beautiful, ornate medieval chapel built in 1446. It is renowned for its famous stone carvings, many of which relate to the symbolism of the Old Testament, Freemasonry, the Knights Templar, etc. See the official website at http://www.rosslynchapel.org.uk/.

Hawthornden: the Castle is located about a mile east of Roslin and was the home of the poet, William Drummond (1585–1649).

serjeants-at-law: members of "a superior order of barristers (abolished in 1880), from which, until 1873, the Common Law judges were always chosen" (OED).

157 *Coleridge says*: Hardy summarizes part of Coleridge's essay on *The Tempest*: see T. M. Raysor, ed., *Coleridge's Shakespearean Criticism* (London: Constable, 1930), I, 128–9.

158 *The Origin of Species*: published 1859.

yarn-barton: rope-yard.

rollick: frolic.

159   *The Cobb*: the harbour wall at Lyme Regis.

160   *family of Darius at the feet of Alexander*: the mother of the Persian King Darius, defeated by Alexander the Great in 330 BC, threw herself at his feet in terror, having just prostrated herself before the wrong man. Alexander graciously forgave her.

end of the autumn: Caddell Holder died on 27 November 1882, aged 79 years.

161   *cholera visitation*: probably the Bristol epidemic of 1832, when Holder was about 29 years of age.

to be churched: churching was a religious service for women after childbirth.

163   *more than one case in his fiction and verse*: e.g., *Tess*, "For Conscience' Sake" and poems such as "The Dark-Eyed Gentleman" and "Julie-Jane".

164   *M.*: Mary Hardy.

John: John Lawrence.

165   *Mrs ——*: Miriam Florence Folline Leslie.

Lady Duff-Gordon: *Burke's Peerage* (see entry under "Gordon") records her only issue as being Caroline Lucy, born 21 August 1874.

167   *God-ist*: Ralph W. V. Elliott suggests that the word is "perhaps modelled on the seventeenth-century word *religionist*, still current in the nineteenth century, or an anglicization of deist" (*Thomas Hardy's English* [Oxford: Blackwell, 1984], p. 207).

168   *The Dynasts*: Part First, Act II, Scene v.

169   "*The glass-stainer ... stripes, and bars*": a largely accurate quotation from a review of Victor Hugo's *L'Archipel de la Manche*, in *Athenæum*, 3 November 1883, pp. 561–2.

170   *Billy C——*: William Coward.

"*Ye shall weep and mourn, and the world shall rejoice*": a misquotation of John, 16:20: "ye shall weep and lament, but the world shall rejoice".

James S——: James Selby.

ragged robins: the popular name of *Lychnis Floscuculi*, a bright crimson colour.

171   *Miriam*: she held a tambourine and led the Israelites in song as they crossed the Red Sea during the Exodus from Egypt (see Exodus 15:20–1).

173   *Niniche*: Hardy is perhaps referring to the operetta *Mam'zelle Nitouche* by the French composer, Hervé.

their daughters: Lady Eveline Camilla Gurdon, Lady Rosamond Alicia Christie, Lady Dorothea Hester Bluett Wallop, Lady Gwendolen Margaret Wallop and Lady Henrietta Anna Wallop.

174   *warm*: rich, affluent.

Lord Mayor: Sir Robert Nicholas Fowler.

ex-Lord Mayor: Sir Henry Edmund Knight.

176   *St. Peter's belfry*: described in the poem, "The Chimes".

Eggesford: Eggesford House, near Chudleigh, North Devonshire.

her daughters: see note to p. 173 above.

179   *Mrs Hardy's relations*: Edwin and Margaret Gifford.

political excitement ... small-and-early: this event is recalled in *The Well-Beloved*, II. i.

General Gordon: killed in Khartoum on 26 January 1885. News of his death reached London on 5 February. Gladstone was blamed for not relieving the siege.

C——: 4th Earl of Carnarvon.

181   *wife's son*: Lloyd Osbourne.

cousin: Katharine de Mattos (?).

his father: Sir Aubrey de Vere.

183   *"This is the chief thing: Be not perturbed; for all things are according to the nature of the universal"*: this is George Long's 1862 translation of Marcus Aurelius's *The Meditations*, Book Eight. The saying is referred to in *A Laodicean*, IV.i, and *Tess*, Chapter 39. Millgate notes that on New Year's Day 1865 Horace Moule presented Hardy with a copy of *The Thoughts of the Emperor M. Aurelius Antoninus*, trans. Lang, which he was to keep at his bedside until he died, inscribed with this quotation (p. 87).

sympathetic ink: a name for various colourless liquid compositions used as ink, the writing with which remains invisible until the colour is developed by the application of heat or some chemical reagent (OED).

184   *T. B.*: William Biles (?).

185   *dictum of Hegel*: "What is rational is real; And what is real is rational" (from the Preface to *Philosophy of Right*, 1821).

Hindu Buddhist: Mohini Mohun Chatterji.

"The Pilgrim and the Shrine": published 1868.

collaboration: *The Perfect Way; or, The Finding of Christ* (London, 1882).

187   *great naval engagement*: Lady Camperdown was the widow of the grandson of Admiral Adam Duncan (1731–1804), who lifted the threat of Napoleonic invasion when he defeated the Dutch fleet at Camperdown, off the Dutch coast, in 1797.

188   *Hardy met Grieg*: in 1906. See *Life*, p. 355.

Edinburgh Review: Reeve edited the *Review* from 1855 until his death in 1895.

Greville Memoirs: the three series of *The Greville Memoirs* (1874–87) comment on the course of English politics and society from the accession of George IV to the year 1860. They are the memoirs of Charles Cavendish Fulke Greville.

189   *Crawford-Dilke case*: William A. Davis describes the "famous Crawford-Dilke case of 1886, or, as it was known officially, *Crawford v. Crawford and Dilke*, a suit brought by Donald Crawford, M.P., against his wife and Sir Charles Wentworth Dilke, M.P." Crawford filed the case on the ground of his wife's alleged adultery with Dilke. The case was heard in the London Divorce Court and the judge eventually pronounced a decree nisi. Hardy appears to have attended the court in July 1886, and he was probably gathering divorce material for use in *The Woodlanders* which he was then writing. See Davis, "Happy Days in *Jude the Obscure*: Hardy and the Crawford-Dilke Divorce Case", *Thomas Hardy Journal*, 13:1 (February 1997), 64–74.

191   "*He*": Alfred John George Byng.

        Highclere: Highclere Castle, Hampshire, six miles south of Newbury. Built for the 3rd Earl of Carnarvon, 1839–42.

        filled several bookshelves: the magnificent library can be seen online at <http://www.highclerecastle.co.uk/>.

        friendly Winifred Herbert: Millgate believes she is featured as the "kindly young lady of the house, his hostess's relation" in *The Well-Beloved*, II.i (Millgate, *Thomas Hardy: His Career as a Novelist*, p. 301).

195   *another English resident*: Julia Dunn.

196   "*altae moenia Romae*": the walls of lofty Rome (from the seventh line of the *Aeneid*).

        "*ochreous gauntness*": Hardy seems to be thinking of the description of the "housebacks pink, green, ochreous" in "Genoa and the Mediterranean", l. 8. "Gaunt" appears in "Rome: Building a New Street in the Ancient Quarter", l. 4.

        "*umbered walls*": Hardy slightly misquotes the phrase "umbered cliffs" in the opening line of "Rome: Building a New Street in the Ancient Quarter".

        more verses: "Rome: At the Pyramid of Cestius near the Graves of Shelley and Keats".

        another poem: "Rome: The Vatican: Sala delle Muse".

        that of another: "Rome: On the Palatine".

        Faustinas: Faustina was the wife of Emperor Antoninus and was notorious for debauchery: she died in 141 AD. Hardy had no doubt visited the Temple of Antoninus and Faustina.

197   "*wronged great soul of an ancient master*": Robert Browning, "Old Pictures in Florence", VI.

198   *The Ring and the Book*: see the opening lines of Chapter 7.

        inquisitive bore's conversation: Horace's *Satire*, I, 9, which begins "Ibam forte via sacra" and in which the bore ignores all of Horace's ploys to shake him off.

        Wendell Holmes: he wrote that "the octogenarian Londoness has been in society – let us say the highest society – all her days. She is as tough as an old macaw, or she would not have lasted so long": "Our Hundred Days in Europe", *Atlantic Monthly*, LIX (March 1887), 343–56.

Thackeray's letters: "A Collection of Unpublished Letters of Thackeray", *Scribner's Magazine*, 1:4 (April 1887), 387–409.

200   *Mrs Browning's tomb*: in the Protestant Cemetery.

Euganean Hills: see Shelley's "Lines Written Among the Euganean Hills".

ferri: the ornamental ironwork on both ends of the gondola (sing. "ferro", p. 202).

201   *Ruskin*: in *Stones of Venice*, Ruskin writes that St Mark's is, for instance, "to be regarded less as a temple wherein to pray, than as itself a Book of Common Prayer, a vast illuminated missal, bound with alabaster instead of parchment, studded with porphyry pillars instead of jewels, and written within and without in letters of enamel and gold".

"*sun-girt*": see Shelley's "Lines Written Among the Euganean Hills", l. 115.

202   "*silent ... gondolier*", "*Tasso's ... no more*": Byron, *Childe Harold's Pilgrimage*, Canto the Fourth: "In Venice Tasso's echoes are no more, // And silent rows the songless gondolier".

203   *took their pleasure ... for the morrow*: an adaptation of Browning's "A Toccata of Galuppi's", ll. 10–12.

Italian Contessa: see "Lady Mottisfont".

Milan Cathedral scene: *The Dynasts*, Part First, Act I, Scene vi.

famous Napoleonic struggle: French victory over Austria at Lodi in May 1796, after which Napoleon entered Milan.

204   *Crown jewels*: the French Crown Jewels were sold at auction by the government.

207   "*the empty shrine*": "The Statue and the Bust", l. 189.

208   *Lady Marge W—— ... going to a ball*: Millgate notes the correspondence to "Lady Mabella Buttermead, who appeared in a cloud of muslin and was going on to a ball" in *The Well-Beloved*, II. i (Millgate, *Thomas Hardy: His Career as a Novelist*, p. 301).

Thrice happy ... at noon: James Thomson, "Summer", *The Seasons*, ll. 458–64. "At noon" should read "in noon".

"*Natural Law in the Spiritual World*": published 1883.

Calderon's Plays: *Six Dramas of Calderon*, "freely translated" by Edward Fitzgerald (London: Pickering, 1853). The plays were *His Own Dishonour*; *Keep Your Own Secret*; *Gil Perez, The Gallician*; *At a Blow*; *The Mayor of Zalamea*; *Beware of Smooth Water*.

209   *Junius*: unidentified writer of letters (1769–1772) to the London Public Advertiser, criticizing the government of George III. "Junius" is now believed to have been Sir Philip Francis. Marcus Junius Brutus was one of the assassins of Julius Caesar.

Round luminous enquiring eyes: Millgate notes that Nichola Pine-Avon has "round, inquiring, luminous" eyes in *The Well-Beloved*, II. ii (Millgate, *Thomas Hardy: His Career as a Novelist*, p. 302).

210 *Anniwalia*: properly Harnam Singh, Ahluwalia of Kapurthala (1852–1930), second son of the Raja of Kapurthala.

Ajalon: the valley over which Joshua commanded the moon to stand still. See Joshua 10:12: "Sun, stand thou still upon Gibeon; and thou, Moon, in the valley of Ajalon".

211 *say unto a flea, 'Thou art my sister'*: an ironic inversion of Proverbs 7:4: "Say unto wisdom, Thou art my sister; and call understanding thy kinswoman".

212 *he quotes from Addison*: this particular comment by Addison on *Paradise Lost* originally appeared in the *Spectator*, No. 321, 8 March 1712; rpt. in *Milton: The Critical Heritage*, ed. John T. Shawcross (London: Routledge & Kegan Paul, 1970), p. 183. Addison writes "unactive", not "inactive".

Coleridge: in Biographia Literaria, Coleridge writes that "a poem of any length neither can be, nor ought to be, all poetry" (Chapter 14).

Vic. of W.: Goldsmith's *Vicar of Wakefield*.

Worsley: his translation of the Odyssey in Spenserian stanzas was published in 1861.

213 *Two were dying*: one of these friends was presumably Mrs Procter, who was ill at New Year and who died in March 1888 (see *Collected Letters, I, 172*).

214 *Life of Darwin*: *The Life and Letters of Charles Darwin* (1887), ed. Francis Darwin, includes an autobiographical chapter.

215 *Crucifixion*: Gérôme's *Consummatum est Jerusalem* (1867), now in the Musée d'Orsay, Paris.

216 *Matthew Arnold's death*: the quotation from the *Times* does not appear in its obituary notice of 17 April, and there appears to be no reference to Arnold's death on 16 April. Perhaps Hardy was quoting from a late edition of the newspaper of that date.

so many doctors as the German Emperor: Friedrich III had been diagnosed as suffering from throat cancer in February 1888. He became Emperor on 9 March.

Queen Adelaide: she suffered for many years from what would now be diagnosed as tuberculosis. Dr Chambers had been one of her physicians for the last dozen years of her life.

Alma Tadema's ... house: in Grove End Road, St John's Wood, London. Alma-Tadema turned the house into a virtual palace, designing every feature himself, such as the doorway modelled on one from Pompeii and the marble-floored studio crowned with a polished aluminium dome.

217 *Grand Prix de Paris*: the Grand Prix was a 3000-metre race for three-year-old horses from any country, held at the Longchamp track in the recently re-landscaped Bois de Boulogne. The final race in the spring season, the Grand Prix signalled the close of the society season before the summer vacations. Gittings notes that Hardy "had not realized that the starter on this occasion was, in fact, an Englishman, Dick Fijus, and that the French jockeys' swearing was meant to intimidate the foreigner in his own terms" (*The Older Hardy*, p. 89).

Bon Marché: renowned department store in Paris, opened in 1876 and designed by Eiffel and Boileau.

normous arch: the Arc de Triomphe has the names of 128 battles of the Republic and Napoleon's Empire inscribed on the inner walls under the vault.

St. Denis: the Abbey of Saint Denis, which is located about 10 miles north of Paris, is the last resting place of most of the French kings and queens.

218 *Emperor of Germany:* Friedrich III died of throat cancer on 15 June 1888 in Potsdam, after a reign of only 99 days.

arouses sad feelings: because Mrs Ritchie's sister, Harriet Marion, had been Leslie Stephen's first wife until her death in 1875.

"Peace be unto you": after the Resurrection, "Jesus himself stood in the midst of them, and saith unto them, Peace be unto you" (Luke 24:36).

219 *July 7:* this note records a germ *for the short story "The Son's Veto". The Hardys' bedroom faced on to Kensington High Street.*

St Mary Abbots: designed by Sir George Gilbert Scott and built in 1872, it is one of the finest examples of Victorian Gothic. It has the tallest spire in London as well as fine stained glass windows. An image of the interior can be viewed online at http://www.stmaryabbots.freeserve.co.uk/index.htm.

Paradise Lost: Book I, ll.767–9: "Thick swarmed, both on the ground and in the air, // Brushed with the hiss of rustling wings. As bees // In spring-time […]".

"The Taming of the Shrew": at the Gaiety Theatre.

220 *sun-and-moon argument: The Taming of the Shrew,* IV. v.

direct ancestor: Sir Henry Wallop.

221 *Egyptian Exhibition:* it opened on 18 June 1888 in the Egyptian Hall in Piccadilly and was a great popular success.

Amazon: a woman of manly strength (from the Amazons of Asia Minor, a warlike tribe).

Atalanta: in Greek mythology, a beautiful virgin who agreed to marry any man who could defeat her in a running race. Those whom she defeated were slain by her dart. She lost to Hippomenes when she paused to pick up three golden apples which he had deliberately dropped.

Faustine: a reference to Swinburne's poem of that name, whose heroine embodies what Swinburne described as "the transmigration of a single soul, doomed as though by accident from the first to all evil and no good, through many ages and forms, but clad always in the same type of fleshly beauty".

222 *Dick Facey:* Richard Feacey.

223 *Whitechapel murder:* Hardy records (more or less verbatim) part of the lengthy report in the Times of the murder of Annie Chapman, who is now known as the second of Jack the Ripper's five victims. Her body was discovered four hours after leaving the lodging-house on 8 September 1888.

224 *[paternal] grandmother:* Mary Head (Hardy) was about 21 years of age when Marie-Antoinette was executed in 1793.

225 *great Titian: Bacchus and Ariadne*, acquired 1827 and measuring 172 × 188cm.

227 *Village story*: the anecdote which follows would seem to be the origin of the poem, 'The Catching Ballet of the Wedding Clothes'. 'Mary L.' was Mary Lovell of Askerswell, Dorset, who married William Keats of Higher Bockhampton on 23 April 1821 at Stinsford Church. She died in 1869 and is buried in Stinsford, where her headstone records that she was eighty years of age, which would have made her about 32 years old at the time of her marriage and some ten years older than her husband. For many years, and throughout Hardy's childhood, the Keats family lived in the end cottage on the north side of Cherry Lane, opposite the Hardy cottage. William Keats is the model for the tranter Reuben Dewy in *Under the Greenwood Tree*.

Hardy's source for his anecdote was almost certainly one of his parents. In this respect it is perhaps significant that Hardy recorded the story of the wedding shoes on 4 March 1889, which was a Monday: he could thus have heard the story 'yesterday' on his weekly Sunday visit to his parents, when he would walk over from Max Gate.

228 *skeletons in the church*: the bones of 4000 Capuchin friars decorate the four chapels of the Capuchin Crypt in Rome.

in love with a Louisa: Louisa Harding. See the poem, "To Louisa in the Lane".

230 *her age*: Lady Coleridge was born in 1853, so she was about 36 years of age.

"*Her lips are roses full of snow*": Mrs Thornycroft was the physical model for Tess, and, as Millgate notes (p. 298), her mouth here is praised precisely in terms echoing those used of Tess's mouth: "He had never before seen a woman's lips and teeth which forced upon his mind, with such persistent iteration, the old Elizabethan simile of roses filled with snow" (Chapter 24). This is a reference to Thomas Campion's "The Garden" (1617): "Those cherries fairly do enclose // Of orient pearl a double row, // Which when her lovely laughter shows, // They look like rosebuds filled with snow".

"*a deeper deep*": *In Memoriam*, LXIII: "So mayst thou watch me where I weep, // As, unto vaster motions bound, // The circuits of thine orbit round // A higher height, a deeper deep".

Grein: Millgate notes that Hardy mentions only Grein, but the request to which Hardy was responding came jointly from Grein and C. W. Jarvis (*Thomas Hardy: His Career as a Novelist*, p. 408).

231 *Iphigenia*: Agamemnon had sacrificed Clytemnestra's daughter, Iphigenia.

Oak-apple day: 29 May, the anniversary of the Restoration in 1660. It was formerly commemorated by the wearing of oak apples or oak leaves, recalling the oak in which Charles II hid after the battle of Worcester in 1651.

232 *the editor of Murray's Magazine*: Edward Arnold. Hardy omits any reference to the earlier contract for the novel with Tillotson's, subsequently cancelled.

the editor of Macmillan's Magazine: Mowbray Walter Morris.

third editor: Arthur Locker.

233 "*Incidents in the development … worth study*": quoted in "Mr. Robert Browning", *Athenæum*, 21 December 1889, pp. 858–60 (p. 858). The quotation is originally from Browning's preface to *Sordello*.

Athenæum: "intellectual subtlety is the disturbing element in his art. He is both too intellectual and too subtle. These are qualities the reverse of poetical"; from "Mr.Robert Browning", *Athenæum*, 21 December 1889, pp. 858–60 (p. 859).

234 *cousin*: Tryphena Sparks.

235 *article on Ibsen*: "it may be said of the drama as it may be said of fiction, that it is not for edification. A play with a purpose is considered by the best critics to be as great a mistake as a novel with a purpose; and if this is a mistake it is one which Ibsen never fails to commit"; from Oswald Crawfurd, "The London Stage", *Fortnightly Review*, 47 (1 April 1890), 499–516 (p. 516).

236 "*The Bells*": play (1871) by Leopold David Lewis. Henry Irving achieved fame in 1871 with his portrayal of Mathias in "The Bells", a role he often repeated. The performance which Hardy attended was presumably at the Lyceum Theatre, London, which Irving managed. Hardy's reference to "kiln-dried" in this paragraph is prompted by a scene in the play in which the body of the murder victim who haunts his killer is disposed of in a lime-kiln: Hardy is suggesting that the millions of inhabitants are like the ghosts of dead men who return to haunt London.

237 *publishers of his travels*: the publishers of Stanley's *In Darkest Africa* (London, 1890) were Sampson, Low.

238 *dwarfs*: the Central African explorer verified previous reports of Pygmy people in his book, *A Journey to Ashango-Land* (1867).

Bishop of Ripon: William Boyd Carpenter.

Lord Carnarvon: died 29 June 1890.

Athenæum: Hardy was elected a member in late April 1891, Carnarvon having proposed him in 1888.

239 *illness and death of her father*: John Attersoll Gifford died of senile decay and a long-established prostate condition.

Epilogue: the poem "Lines".

240 *Goschen*: at the time of his dramatic resignation as Chancellor of the Exchequer, Randolph Churchill (see note below) said of Goschen, who succeeded him: "All great men make mistakes. Napoleon forgot Blücher, I forgot Goschen".

Randolph Churchill: he had resigned as Conservative Chancellor of the Exchequer in 1886. His deteriorating health prevented any comeback.

241 *Parnell*: in December 1890, Parnell was deposed as leader of the Irish Party after being cited in a divorce case the previous month.

various: see the poem, "So Various".

"*the viewless wings of poesy*": Keats, *Ode to a Nightingale*, l. 33.

243 *George Peabody*: a bronze statue of the American banker and philanthropist was unveiled on 23 July 1869 behind the Royal Exchange in the City of London.

244 *first night at a play*: *All the Comforts of Home*, by William Gillette and H.C. Duckworth, Globe Theatre, 24 January 1891: see *Collected Letters*, I, 227.

house where Hardy was staying: Mary Jeune's, at 37 Wimpole Street.

Ellen Terry ... all the works fly open: Michael Millgate notes the use of this passage in the description of a leading actress in *The Well-Beloved*: "a creature in airy clothing, translucent, like a balsam or sea-anemone, without shadows, and in movement as responsive as some highly lubricated, many-wired machine, which, if one presses a particular spring, flies open and reveals its works" (II.ii; see Millgate, *Thomas Hardy: His Career as a Novelist*, p. 300).

E. Ashley's laugh: cf. *The Well-Beloved*, II. ii: "a representative of Family, who talked positively and hollowly, as if shouting down a vista of five hundred years from the Feudal past" (noted by Millgate, *Thomas Hardy: His Career as a Novelist*, p. 300).

death's-heads: a large species of moths, perhaps.

Judge of the Supreme Court: Millgate notes the correspondence to the mention of the "wife of a Lord Justice of Appeal" in *The Well-Beloved*, II. ii (Millgate, *Thomas Hardy: His Career as a Novelist*, p. 300).

Judge-and-Jury: Renton Nicholson's music hall act. See note on "Cider Cellars", p. 43, above.

rode on horse-back for ... the last time: Millgate notes however that "Emma continued to ride on horseback – making some of her more distant social calls by that means – at least until the autumn of 1893" (p. 318).

245   *poor young fellow*: William Hardy.

Lady Byron's secret: i.e., why she left the poet after a year of marriage. She told only her solicitors.

Spurgeon: Charles Haddon Spurgeon (1834–1892) was the most popular preacher of the Victorian age. A Baptist, he moved to the specially built Metropolitan Tabernacle in 1861: this was situated on the main Elephant and Castle roundabout in London. The vast auditorium could hold six thousand people, and Spurgeon spoke without amplification and at a rate of 140 words per minute. Spurgeon died on 31 January 1892, aged 57, but he gave his last sermon at the Tabernacle on 7 June 1891, so Hardy only just managed to hear him preach at the very end of his 38 years as a pastor. The original Tabernacle of Spurgeon's time was burnt down in 1898.

Hedda Gabler: opened in London on 20 April 1891 and ran for six weeks. The leading role was played by Elizabeth Robins.

248   *flétries*: wilted (Fr.).

249   ——*s of Newstead*: the Webb family owned Byron's former estate at Newstead Abbey in Nottinghamshire.

tragic Damers: John Damer, who married Horace Walpole's cousin, Anne Seymour Conway, shot himself in 1776 after contracting heavy debts. Hardy learned about the Damer family from Walpole's correspondence. Some of the Damer family history provides a basis for the short story, "The Doctor's Legend".

venust: beautiful (the latest recorded usage in the OED is 1698). For Hardy's use of the word in the manuscript of *Tess*, see Michael Millgate, *Thomas Hardy: His Career as a Novelist*, pp. 285–6.

250 *how long ...rot*: *Hamlet*, V. i. 148.

Tess should put on the jewels: on their wedding night, Angel gives Tess the jewels which had been bequeathed to him by his godmother (Chapter XXXIV).

Springwood Park: near Kelso in the Scottish Borders. At this time it was the site of the mansion of the Douglas family, but it is now a caravan park and showground. The only vestiges remaining are the grand gates next to Bridgend Park.

Northumbrian: Swinburne was born in London and was raised partly on the Isle of Wight and partly at Capheaton Hall, near Wallington, Northumberland. He always regarded Northumberland as his native county.

Edie Ochiltree's grave: the grave of Andrew Gemmels, a blue-coat "gaberlunzie", who died at the age of 106, and upon whom Sir Walter Scott based Edie Ochiltree in *The Antiquary*, is in Roxburgh, near Kelso.

Smaylho'me Tower: Smailholm Tower, near Kelso, belonged to the Scott family, and had become derelict by the end of the 18th century. Sir Walter Scott used to stay at the nearby Sandyknowe Farm, owned by his uncle, as a child. His poem, *The Eve of St John*, has Smailholm as its location, and is a ghostly tale in the Gothic tradition.

252 *Mrs Hardy's mother*: Emma Gifford.

256 *Philosophy of Rhetoric*: first published 1776. The sentence from which Hardy quotes reads in full as follows: "A fourth way in which tropes may promote vivacity, is when things sensitive are presented to the fancy instead of things lifeless; or, which is nearly the same, when life, perception, activity, design, passion, or any property of sentient beings, is by means of the trope attributed to things inanimate" (London 1850 edition: Book III, Chapter 1).

258 "*Weatherbury*": Hardy's name for Puddletown, five miles north-east of Dorchester.

door-trig: door-stop.

259 *review of 'Tess'*: [Mowbray Morris], "Culture and Anarchy", *Quarterly Review*, 174 (April 1892), 317–44. "Bludyer" (Morris) described *Tess* as "a coarse and disagreeable story", yet proceeded to say that "Coarse it is not, in the sense of employing coarse words". Millgate remarks that Hardy "does not seem to have discovered that the review itself was the work of Mowbray Morris, who had so officiously declined to accept the novel for *Macmillan's* and thus set Hardy upon the path to its dismemberment" (p. 320).

260 *Letters of Henry James*: James wrote to Stevenson about *Tess* on 17 February 1893. See *Letters of Henry James*, ed. Percy Lubbock (London: Macmillan, 1920), I, 204–5.

261 "*men, not measures*": Edmund Burke remarked that "Of this stamp is the cant of, Not men, but measures" (*Thoughts on the Cause of the Present Discontent*).

262 *house in which he was born*: see the poem, "On One who Lived and Died where he was Born".

"*Thou hast been ... equal thanks*": *Hamlet*, III. ii. 61–4.

263 *Irish ancestress*: Elizabeth Swire. Hardy described her as "pure Irish" in a letter to Lady Gregory (*Collected Letters*, IV, 37).

265 *Daily News*: see "Literature of the Future", *Daily News* (London), 11 October 1892, p. 4.

I look in the glass: see the poem, "I Look into My Glass".

Hawkins ... Tichborne: a spectacular but ultimately unsuccessful attempt by an impostor to obtain the Tichborne family estates occurred in the early 1870s. The cross-examination by Henry Hawkins of the leading witnesses for the false claimant completely exposed the fraudulent nature of the claim.

267 *stonemason*: Thomas Hounsell.

271 *Phoenix Park*: site in Dublin of the assassination on 6 May 1882 of Lord Frederick Cavendish, British secretary for Ireland, and Thomas Henry Burke, his under-secretary. They were stabbed to death by members of the "Invincibles", a terrorist splinter group of the Fenian movement.

Lady de Ros: Georgiana, Lady de Ros (1811–1891). Her brother, Lord March, had been A.D.C. to the Duke of Wellington. Her grandson was perhaps Victor Alexander Augustus Henry Cowley: see Index.

Chief Secretary's Lodge: situated within Phoenix park.

succeeding Secretary: Sir George Otto Trevelyan.

Gap of Dunloe: a scenic path between mountains, some four miles long, in Co. Kerry, south west of Killarney. The path comes out into the Black Valley.

Kate Kearney: fictional subject of a song by Dublin writer Lady Sydney Morgan (1783–1859).

272 "*Little-ease*": a Tower dungeon cell in which one could not stand or lie in comfort (a cube of about 4 feet per side).

273 *Bishop of Oxford*: William Stubbs (see Index).

Duke of York: later George V.

the Club: the Athenæum.

274 *editors*: one of whom was Henri Mazel.

Wenlock Abbey: at Much Wenlock, Shropshire, about 13 miles south-east of Shrewsbury. The Hardys signed the visitors' book on 13 August 1893.

the ruins: of St. Milburga's Priory, adjoining Wenlock Abbey.

275 *In Memoriam*: a reference to XCIV, where "tapers" illuminate bats (not moths).

Comus: Milton wrote the masque *Comus* (1634) in honour of the Earl of Bridgewater and it was performed for the first time in the Council Chamber of Ludlow Castle.

Hudibras: Samuel Butler was working on his great religious satire while acting as steward at Ludlow Castle in 1661.

276 *Arlington Manor*: the Jeunes' country home in Berkshire, three miles north of Newbury. The house is now a residential school for deaf children: a photograph of the building can be viewed at
<http://www.bme.jhu.edu/~tratnana/mhgs.html>.

"*An Imaginative Woman*": Hardy mistakenly gives the date of composition as December 1893. It was actually written in August and September of that year.

278 *angelic quire*: Wordsworth's "Stanzas Suggested in a Steamboat Off Saint Bees' Heads, On The Coast Of Cumberland": "When her sweet Voice, that instrument of love, // Was glorified, and took its place, above // The silent stars, among the angelic quire" (ll. 55–7).

put into verse: "On Stinsford Hill at Midnight".

hostess: Lady Londonderry.

279 *the Doctor*: George Henry Kingsley.

280 *son and daughter-in-law*: William and Margaret Meredith.

Matterhorn: see the poem "Zermatt: To the Matterhorn".

281 *"Pretty pink frock" poem*: i.e., "The Pink Frock".

282 *prominent actor*: Johnston Forbes-Robertson (?).

284 *her park and house*: identified as Charborough Park, the original of Welland House, in *Life*, p. 513. Charborough Park is situated between Wimborne and Bere Regis.

285 *Burford Bridge*: the hotel, dating back to the sixteenth century, is in Dorking, Surrey, at the foot of Box Hill. Keats lodged at the hotel in November and December 1817.

286 *Rushmore*: the Pitt-Rivers estate was at Tollard Royal, near Salisbury in Wiltshire, high up on the Cranborne Chase. The Larmer Tree Gardens were ornamental grounds created by General Pitt-Rivers in 1880 for the enjoyment and education of his estate workers and local people; the name derives from the ancient Wych Elm, known as "The Larmer Tree", which stood on the Wiltshire/Dorset border. The dancing is recorded in the poem, "Concerning Agnes".

287 *double profit*: Mrs Oliphant in "The Anti-Marriage League" had said that Hardy had "taken elaborate precautions to secure the double profit of the serial writer, by subduing his colours and diminishing his effects, in the presence of the less corrupt, so as to keep the perfection of filthiness for those who love it" [*Blackwood's Magazine*, CLIX (January 1896), 135–49; rpt. in R. G. Cox, ed., *Thomas Hardy: The Critical Heritage* (London: Routledge & Kegan Paul, 1970), p. 259].

288 "*nice minds with nasty ideas*": cf. Swift: "A nice man is a man of nasty ideas", *Thoughts on Various Subjects* (1711).

essay on Byron: Macaulay's "On Moore's Life of Lord Byron" (1830).

"*Pierrette*" and "*L'Enfant Maudit*": by Balzac.

289 *he wrote to an enquirer*: see *Life*, p. 425.

292   *Poet-Laureate*: Alfred Austin.

294   *letter to the papers*: Bishop Walsham How announced in a letter to the *Yorkshire Post* on 9 June 1896 that "I bought a copy of one of Mr Hardy's novels, but was so disgusted with its insolence and indecency that I threw it on the fire" (see F. D. How, *Bishop Walsham How* [London: Isbister, 1898], pp. 343–5).

295   *Eighty Club*: a grouping of Liberal MPs first elected in the 1880 General Election.

301   *same hotel*: the Hôtel de la Poste.

        note in The Dynasts: Part Third, Act VI, Scene ii.

302   *the Digue*: the parade, constructed of solid granite, which extends for over a mile along the shore.

        Crabbe: see the opening of Letter II of Crabbe's *The Borough*, where he describes "The living stains which Nature's hand alone, // Profuse of life, pours forth upon the stone: // For ever growing; where the common eye // Can but the bare and rocky bed descry".

        mother's grandfather: John Swetman.

303   *the Trachiniae*: by Sophocles. Hyllus's closing speech reads thus in the Jebb translation: "Lift him, followers! And grant me full forgiveness for this; but mark the great cruelty of the gods in the deeds that are being done. They beget children, they are hailed as fathers, and yet they can look upon such sufferings. [...] No man foresees the future; but the present is fraught with mourning for us, and with shame for the powers above, and verily with anguish beyond compare for him who endures this doom. Maidens, come ye also, nor linger at the house; ye who have lately seen a dread death, with sorrows manifold and strange: and in all this there is nought but Zeus".

        certain papers: notably the *World* on 24 March 1897 (see *Collected Letters*, II, 155).

        periodical: the *Academy*, 3 April 1897, printed Hardy's letter.

304   *an editor*: Lewis Hind of the *Academy*. See *Collected Letters*, II, 155.

311   *Wengern Alp*: offering the best view of the Jungfrau.

        Manfred: Byron's poem of 1816.

        Ruskin recommended: in the *Pall Mall Gazette* in 1886, Ruskin had said that "Gibbon's is the worst English that was ever written by an educated Englishman".

312   *Chillon*: a mediaeval castle built on the shore of Lake Geneva. It is the setting for Byron's sonnet, "On the Castle of Chillon" (Hardy's copy of *Baedecker's Switzerland*, now in the British Library, quotes six lines from the poem).

313   *disappearance of an Englishman*: Hardy's letter to the *Times* is headed "The Disappearance of an Englishman at Zermatt" (8 July 1897, p. 10) and it was written from the Hôtel de la Paix in Geneva on 3 July. The missing man was James Robert Cooper (see Index).

        Austrian Empress: Elizabeth (see Index).

        anarchist: Louis Luccheni stabbed the Empress (see Index).

ancestor: Sir Humphry Davy. Emma noted in her diary, "July 3. I went to Plain Palais Cemetery & found my ancestor's grave. Sir H. Davy – grandmama's cousin I think" (*Emma Hardy Diaries*, ed. Richard H. Taylor [Mid Northumberland Arts Group and Carcanet New Press, 1985]. He died in Geneva in 1829, at the age of 50, following a stroke. Davy was the inventor of the miner's safety lamp, and a friend of Wordsworth, Coleridge and Walter Scott. A photograph of the grave can be seen online at http://home.t-online.de/home/mkstu/Davy.htm.

Diodati: the Villa Diodati on the shores of Lake Geneva, where Byron, Shelley, Mary Godwin (later Shelley), Mary's step-sister Claire Clairmont and Polidori spent a scandalous summer in 1816.

Montalègre: the Shelleys rented a house here in 1816.

Ferney: Voltaire purchased the Château Ferney in 1758.

314   *the Editor*: James Thomas Harris (Frank Harris).

315   *Duke of Buckingham*: he was beheaded in the Market Square after his failed insurrection against Richard III in 1483.

316–7   *Madeleine Rolland*: she had recently translated *Tess* (1897) and wished to consult Hardy about the possibility of translating *Jude* (a project which did not materialize). She was in fact staying in Oxford at this time, and she stopped at Salisbury on her way to the Isle of Wight. She visited Max Gate on 15 August 1907.

317   *well-known periodical: Aus Fremden Zungen*.

Some Dogmas of Religion: published 1906.

Russell: the War Correspondent for the *Times* in the Crimean War, the American Civil War, the Austro-Prussian War and the Franco-Prussian War.

Gladstone had just died: on 19 May 1898.

320–1   *Verdi*: he wrote *Il Trovatore* in 1853, at the age of 39. His later works are *Otello* (1887, age 73) and *Falstaff* (1893, age 79). Mozart died at the age of 35 years.

321   *Undistributed Middle*: it was a rule of traditional logic that the middle term of a valid syllogism (the term common to the premisses) must be distributed in at least one of its occurrences: not meeting this requirement was the fallacy of undistributed middle.

324   "*Gradus*": "Short for *Gradus ad Parnassum* 'a step to Parnassus', the Latin title of a dictionary of prosody until recently used in English public schools, intended as an aid in Latin versification, both by giving the 'quantities' of words and by suggesting poetical epithets and phraseology" (OED).

Frederic Harrison: The comment by Harrison occurs in his review of *Collected Poems* (1919): "One heading might serve as title for nearly every poem in this collection. It is *Memento Mori*. […] There are bridals – but Nature cares not if they turn out well or ill. One wedding ends in a fire and leaves the bridegroom 'a charred bone'" ("Novissima Verba", *Fortnightly Review*, 107 [February 1920], 181).

326   *country-house*: Dorothy Allhusen's, in Stoke Pogis, Bucks.

Gray's mother: Gray is buried in the church at Stoke Pogis, beside his mother. This was "well known" because of the famous epitaph which Gray put on her tomb, as Hardy described in a letter to his sister: "Erected by her son, who had the misfortune to survive her" (*Collected Letters*, II, 222).

dairymaid: Jane Gilliam (?).

327   *sudden death*: Blomfield died on 30 October 1899.

329   "*best sellers*": the first recorded usage in the OED is 1905.

330   *her sister*: Helen Catherine Holder died on 6 December 1900. She was living in the Hampshire seaside town of Lee-on-Solent.

331   "*octaves*": Sir Henry's Octaves were a meal of eight courses for eight men at eight o'clock.

332   *rose-bush*: rosehips from Omar's tomb were germinated at Kew and planted on Fitzgerald's tomb in 1893. The original plant has died, but its descendants still bloom.

an inquirer: Frederic Chapman. See *Collected Letters*, II, 290.

the Lass: The tune to "The Lass of Richmond Hill" was written by James Hook (1746–1827), an English composer, and was published circa 1790. The words are by Leonard McNally (1752–1820).

334   *with his wife*: Emma did not in fact attend the wedding: see *Letters*, III, 3.

Victor Hugo's birth: Hugo was born on 26 February 1802. Hardy's tribute was published in Italian in *Il Piccolo della Sera* (Trieste) on the day of the centenary.

339   *Coriolanus*: in a letter of 27 April 1924, Harley Granville Barker correctly informed Hardy that Kean had actually taken the part of Octavian in *The Mountaineers* by George Colman the younger (see *Collected Letters*, VI, 248n).

340   *lately commemorated*: the 250th anniversary of Charles the Second's period of three weeks spent as a fugitive in Dorset following the Battle of Worcester in 1651.

"*All his faults … by rote*": *Julius Caesar*, IV. iii. 96–7.

china shop: the building was in High West Street, Dorchester.

341   *correspondent*: Howard Maynard Shipley.

Cornhill Magazine: edited by Reginald John Smith.

editor of L'Européen: Louis Dumur.

346   *Mrs Malcolm Nicolson*: Violet Nicolson died in Madras on 4 October 1904, aged 39 years. She poisoned herself following the death of her husband in the previous August.

348   *associated with Byron*: it is impossible to identify the specific places which Hardy might have visited. A detailed account of Aberdeen in Byron's time is given by

J. D. Symon in "Byron: The Aberdonian Epoch", *Aberdeen University Review*, 11 (1923–24), 1–36.

Lord St. Helier: died on 9 April 1905.

Mrs Hardy's aunt: Margaret Jeune was married to Emma's uncle, Edwin Gifford.

349   *Lord Mayor*: Sir John Pound.

nearly drowned: in September 1868, Swinburne was swept two miles out to sea while bathing off the coast of Normandy, before being rescued by French fishermen. The previous year, he had begun writing *Bothwell*, his play about the life of Mary Stuart, which was eventually published in 1874.

Augusta: Augusta Leigh, Byron's half sister.

350   *her father*: Basil Montagu (actually Anne Procter's step-father).

Exhibition of Wessex Pictures: the exhibition of "Thomas Hardy's Country" seems to have opened at the Leicester Galleries on Saturday, 24 June 1905: see Clive Holland, *Wessex*, illustrated by Walter Tyndale (London: Adam & Charles Black, 1906). Many of Tyndale's seventy-five colour illustrations show settings and buildings from Hardy's novels.

351   *Crabbe*: born 24 December 1754.

New York Tribune: in an article entitled "Genius Misapplied", the *Tribune* had noted that publication of later volumes of *The Dynasts* was "'not guaranteed'" and added that "it is sincerely to be hoped that Mr. Hardy will put no further instalments of this work into book form" (23 January 1904: pasted into Hardy's scrapbook of reviews).

352   *great-uncle*: John Hardy.

"*like unto them that dream*": Psalm 126:1: "When the Lord turned again the captivity of Zion, we were like them that dream".

357   *death of Mrs Craigie*: Pearl Craigie, the novelist "John Oliver Hobbes", died of heart failure during the night of 12–13 August 1906.

362   *a connection of Hardy's*: the Revd. Caddell Holder, Emma's brother-in-law, was the son of a Judge of Barbadoes, where he was born.

collateral ancestor: one of the Swetmans: see *Life*, p. 10.

368   *Duchess of St. Albans*: Hardy met her at a dinner at Lady St. Helier's, in Portland Place, on 20 May 1908. Nell Gwynne's illegitimate son by Charles II was created 1st Duke of St. Albans in 1684.

Hackwood Park: near Basingstoke, where Hardy went on 9 June 1908.

369   *Milton Celebration*: the celebration of the tercentenary of Milton's birth, held at Christ's College, Cambridge, on 10 July 1908.

Japanese Ambassador: Count Jutaro Komura.

died three months after: on 17 October 1908.

relations: one of whom was Edwin Gifford, Emma's uncle, who died in 1905: see *Life*, p. 349.

370   *"unmerciful disaster"*: from Poe's "The Raven": "some unhappy master whom unmerciful Disaster / Followed fast and followed faster" (ll. 63–4).

371   *representation*: three scenes from *The Dynasts* were presented at the Town Hall, Dorchester, 6–7 May 1908.

       10th April: the day on which Swinburne died at Putney.

       Dear —— : perhaps Florence Dugdale. See *Collected Letters*, IV, 15–16.

       critic: Robert Aris Willmott.

372   *Swinburne's funeral*: he was buried at Bonchurch in the Isle of Wight.

       "*O sole … songs were*": "Cor Cordium", l. 10.

       "*With all … ye hate*": "Two Leaders", l. 15.

       "*Save his … no star*": Prelude to *Songs before Sunrise*.

       odd verdict of the Spectator: the quotation which Hardy cites is from R. H. Hutton's review of *Modern Love* in the *Spectator*, XXXV, 24 May 1862; rpt. in Ioan Williams, ed., *Meredith: The Critical Heritage* (London: Routledge & Kegan Paul, 1971), pp. 92–6.

373   *lady of New York*: Sue M. Farrell.

375   *the dramatist*: Alfred Herbert Evans.

376   *Secretary*: Henry Stephens Salt.

377   *letter written earlier*: see pp. 373–4.

       King Edward: Edward VII died during the night of Friday, 6 May 1910. Hardy had initially thought of leaving London on the day of the funeral, "to avoid the frightful crush" (*Letters*, IV, 89), but he did eventually decide to witness the funeral, on 20 May. Henry Rider Haggard describes how Hardy witnessed the funeral: "On my return to London I saw King Edward's body lying in state in Westminster Hall, and afterwards watched the noble panorama of his funeral from the upper balcony of the Athenaeum. Thomas Hardy and I sat together; there were, I remember, but few in the club" (*The Days of My Life: An Autobiography*, ed. C. J. Longman, 2 vols. (London: Longmans, Green, 1926), II, 214).

378   *Mayor*: Charles Francis Symes.

379   *woman hanged*: Martha Browne was executed at Dorchester prison on 9 August 1856, for the murder of her husband.

380   *architect*: Benjamin Ferrey (?).

       "*Nothing is permanent but change*": the German author is Ludwig Börne (1786–1837), who commented in an 1825 memorial tribute to Jean Paul Richter that "Nichts ist dauernd als der Wechsel". Börne's saying is alluded to in *The Well-Beloved*, I, ix. It was originally said by Heraclitus, circa 500 B.C.

       "*a slope of green access*": Shelley's *Adonais*: "the spirit of the spot shall lead // Thy footsteps to a slope of green access // Where, like an infant's smile, over the dead // A light of laughing flowers along the grass is spread" (XLIX).

381   *comedy*: *The Mellstock Quire*.

captain: William Rees Rush.

commander: Seaton Schroeder.

end of this year: Hardy confuses the date of publication (1912) with the date of completing the poem (1910). "God's Funeral" was first printed in the *Fortnightly Review*, March 1912, pp. [397]–399.

King-of-Dahomey: the kings of Dahomey were associated, in life and at the time of their deaths, with extensive human sacrifice.

the editor: W. L. Courtney.

"phrasemongering literary contortionist": G. K. Chesterton. "Blasphemy" was used in Chesterton's first reference to Hardy in *The Victorian Age in Literature* (1913): "no one outside Colney Hatch ever took Nature so unnaturally as it was taken in what Mr Hardy has had the blasphemy to call Wessex Tales". (Colney Hatch was a mental hospital.) In his poem, "Epitaph for G. K. Chesterton", Hardy refers to him as a "literary contortionist", a favourite phrase of Hardy's, long before he had heard of Chesterton, and used to describe critics of his alleged "atheism": see *Life*, p. 302.

382 *Mayor*: Charles Francis Symes.

Winter's Tale: see IV, iv, 190–8.

accomplished editor: the parodies were written by G. H. Powell. Owen Seaman was the editor of *Punch*.

383 *Earl Marshal*: Henry Fitzalan-Howard, 15th Duke of Norfolk.

dungeons: Hardy would no doubt have remembered that Carlisle Castle is where Fergus Mac-Ivor was imprisoned before his execution at the end of Walter Scott's *Waverley*. He was also perhaps thinking of the legendary "licking stones", where parched Jacobite prisoners found enough moisture to stay alive, only to be brutally executed on Gallows Hill.

"evil men ... evil things": an adaptation of Luke 6:45.

384 *Saxelby ... a name which resembled his own*: in "The Duchess of Hamptonshire" (rpt. in *A Group of Noble Dames*), the Duke of Hamptonshire "came of the ancient and loyal family of Saxelbye, which, before its ennoblement, had numbered many knightly and ecclesiastical celebrities in its male line".

385 *General Henniker*: died 6 February 1912.

Bunty Pulls the Strings: the male lead in the London production at the Haymarket Theatre was James Finlayson (1887–1953). He achieved fame when the play transferred to Broadway in 1912, and he later became one of the original Keystone Cops. He is best remembered now as the comic foil with the bushy moustache in numerous Laurel and Hardy films.

three-crow: a reference to the popular Victorian nursery song about three crows who sat on a stone: two flew away so the third one just went home.

386 *under the guise of a novel*: Morley Roberts's *The Private Life of Henry Maitland: A Record Dictated by J. H.* (1912) was held to be a fictionalized account of the life of George Gissing (see *Collected Letters*, IV, 234–5).

387 *two ladies*: Rebekah and Catharine Owen.

doctor: Benjamin William Nettlefold Gowring.

390 *poem on Swinburne's death*: "A Singer Asleep".

Newnes Librarian: the Newnes Public Library, Putney, was close to Swinburne's last home, No. 2 The Pines.

392 "*Porte-Latin Feast*": properly "Port Latin" Feast. The college archivist at St John's, Cambridge, Mr. M. G. Underwood, has kindly informed me that there are no specific memorabilia of Hardy's visit to the college (the Feast took place on Wednesday, 6 May 1914), but, by chance, a copy of the printed menu for the nine-course dinner has survived (see my Editor's Notes in the October 2002 issue of the *Thomas Hardy Journal*). Mr. Underwood explains the origin and history of the feast as follows: "The name Port Latin derives from the story that St. John the Evangelist was miraculously preserved from harm after being cast into a vat of boiling oil by the Emperor Domitian (81–96 AD) outside the Latin Gate (Porta Latina) of Rome. The College celebrated it as a complement to the major St. John's Day feast on 27 December. It became the feast in celebration of the commemoration of College benefactors, particularly after the reduction in the number of commemoration days in the nineteenth century. It has been the custom to invite a range of official guests from the University and City, and other distinguished guests, some at the nomination of the Master. Guest lists have been traced back only to 1936, so it is not possible to say in what list, or according to which principles, Thomas Hardy was invited".

394 "*quicquid delirant reges, plectuntur Achivi*": see note to p. 81, above.

An Englishman's Home: this play by Major Guy du Maurier was first staged at Wyndham's Theatre, London, on 27 January 1909 (Hardy was in London during this week). The jingoistic story involves a Territorial soldier who seeks the hand of a girl, but her father opposes the marriage. It is only when the Germans invade and shoot his son in front of him that the father is pleased to have the aid of the Territorials.

397 "*breaking of nations*": an allusion to Jeremiah 51:20: "Thou art my battle axe and weapons of war: for with thee will I break in pieces the nations, and with thee will I destroy kingdoms". Cf. Hardy's poem, "In Time of 'The Breaking of Nations'".

398 *ended The Dynasts*: "But – a stirring thrills the air // Like to sounds of joyance there // That the rages // Of the ages // Shall be cancelled, and deliverance offered from the darts that were, // Consciousness the Will informing, till It fashion all things fair!"

"*Desine fata Deûm flecti sperare precando*": "Cease to hope that the decrees of the gods can be changed by prayer" (*Aeneid*, vi. 376).

400 *cousin*: Frank William George.

401 *Phillpotts*: he and his wife lived in Torquay.

Militavi non sine gloria: I have fought not without glory: Horace, *Odes*, Book III, 26.

Wilfred: Sheridan was lost in action on 15 September 1915.

402 "*Dixi Custodiam*": "I said, I will take heed to my ways": the opening of Psalm

39 in the Order for the Burial of the Dead.

"*The strange fatality ... to face them*": *The Dynasts*, Part First, Act I, Scene iii.

"*Unprecedented ... men will learn*": *The Dynasts*, Part First, Act I, Scene iii.

403   *poems about Sturminster*: this comment may apply to the quartet of poems: "The Head above the Fog"; "Overlooking the River Stour"; "The Musical Box"; "On Sturminster Foot-Bridge".

her sister: Edith Ching.

404   *Hymns Ancient and Modern*: Psalm 34 is rendered as Hymn 153, "Through all the changing scenes of life", and was usually sung to the tune "Bedford". The hymn covers only the first nine verses of the Psalm, and therefore it is impossible to identify which verse Hardy regrets was omitted: perhaps he is thinking of verse 10 or 20, both of which were included in the Tate and Brady version. *Hymns Ancient and Modern* was published in 1861.

405   *Junkers*: reactionary Prussian aristocrats.

406   *God of Mercy*: the concluding sentence of W. L. Courtney's article reads, "Perhaps, after the convulsion of an appalling war, the wounded heart of man may turn for healing and guidance – in all humility and faith – to 'a Divinity who shapes our ends, rough-hew them how we will' – a God of Goodness and Justice and Mercy" ("Mr Thomas Hardy and Æschylus – II", *Fortnightly Review*, 101 [April 1917], 629–40).

One writer: G. K. Chesterton.

Dashwood: see Horace Walpole's letter to Sir Horace Mann of 16 October 1742; rpt. in the *Yale Edition of Horace Walpole's Correspondence*, 48 vols. (1937–81), XVIII, 79. Dashwood is mocking Lord Shrewsbury's Catholicism.

"*invariable antecedent*": see *Life*, p. 235.

407   *cousin*: Theresa Hardy.

other writers: William Lyon Phelps records in his autobiography that "[Barrie] told me that in this very flat on one evening during the war, there were gathered together sitting on the floor around one lighted candle, for on account of Zeppelin raids they were not allowed to show much light, Thomas Hardy, Bernard Shaw, Joseph Conrad, John Galsworthy, Arnold Bennett, and himself; when suddenly a tremendous bomb fell from the sky and exploded on the pavement very close to their apartment. Anyone may now verify this for himself. The bomb fell at the foot of the obelisk on the embankment, and while the pavement has since been repaired, the holes made in the base of the obelisk are as they were. It would have been a sad and sensational loss to English literature if the bomb had struck a few yards north" (*Autobiography with Letters* [London: Oxford University Press, 1939], p. 570). See also *Life*, p. 521.

408   *Absit omen*: may the omen be absent.

409   *Sordello*: a poem by Robert Browning, published 1840.

414   "*Never dreamed ... would triumph*": Browning's "Epilogue", l. 13.

the reviewer: Robert Lynd, in his review of *Moments of Vision*, had said that "Many of Mr Hardy's poems are dramatic lyrics on the pattern invented by Robert Browning – short stories in verse" ("Mr Hardy in Winter", *Nation* (London), vol. XXII, 22 December 1917, pp. 412–4). On 30 July 1919, Hardy wrote to Lynd: "I will not dwell upon other statements in the review: e.g. that Browning invented short stories in verse. He invented the name 'Dramatic Lyrics', but not the thing, which has existed for centuries" (*Collected Letters*, V, 319). See also the note to p. 422 below.

Victorian skirt: the *Westminster Gazette*'s review of *Moments of Vision* discussed "The Pink Frock": "It is possible that Mr Hardy's language is old-fashioned in the style of the remarkable piece of dressmaking which he describes – not with the antique pomp of the Augustans, but with the heavy stiffness of the later nineteenth century" ("Mr Hardy's Poetry", *Westminster Gazette*, 8 December 1917, p. 3). In a letter to Florence Henniker on 7 February 1918, Hardy remarked, "Did you see the super-precious review of the verses in the Westminster Gazette? It amused me much (having no weight or value as criticism) as it was obviously written by a woman. It condemned the poem entitled 'The pink frock' because the frock described was old-fashioned & Victorian!" (*Collected Letters*, V, 250).

415   *United States periodical for March*: no such review as Hardy describes here is listed in the standard bibliographies, nor does there seem to be one in his scrapbook of reviews.

419   *a lady*: Winifred Fortescue, wife of John William Fortescue.

420   Hardy omits any mention of the Armistice in November 1918.

her friend: Ada Russell.

422   *great-grandfather*: Thomas Browning.

recent English review: "Mr Hardy in Winter", *Nation* (London), vol. XXII, 22 December 1917, 412–4. Hardy added "[Written by Robert Lynd]" to his scrapbook copy. This is the same review which Hardy mentions on p. 414 of the *Life*.

like milk in a cart: Lynd had quoted the poem's first verse and criticised Hardy's "intolerably prosaic utterance", adding that "One could make as good music as that out of a milk-cart".

took the trouble to explain: see Hardy's letter to Lynd of 30 July 1919 in *Collected Letters*, V, 318–9. Hardy's comment in the letter that he had read the review in the *Nation* contradicts his description in the *Life* of reading a quotation from it in an Australian newspaper.

423   *Bishop of Durham*: Handley Carr Glyn Moule.

"*All the days ... my change come*": Job 14:14. The verse gave Hardy the title for his short story, "A Changed Man".

Vicar of Fordington: Moule's father, Henry, vicar of Fordington, 1829–1880.

cholera-years: there were epidemics in Fordington in 1849 and 1854. Hardy's portrayal of Maumbry in "A Changed Man" reflects Henry Moule's heroic efforts during the later of the two outbreaks.

424 *picturesque account*: "A Tradition of Eighteen Hundred and Four", first published in 1882.

a friend: Sydney Carlyle Cockerell.

425 *Mr ——*: Archie Stanton Whitfield, who wrote to Hardy on 30 October 1919 to enquire if *Jude* was Hardy's "personal history" (see *Collected Letters*, VI 16).

Bishop's death: Frederick Edward Ridgeway died on 4 May 1921.

426 *written before or after*: Tate and Brady's *A New Version of the Psalms of David* was published in 1696, and Isaac Watts's version of Psalm 90 is dated 1719.

427 *President*: Cecil Hanbury.

428 *Jacob's Join*: see "Jacob family" in Index.

430 "*some new thing*": Acts 17:21.

432 *representatives*: including Charles Langbridge Morgan.

sister Daisy: Margaret Jeune Gifford.

Poet-Laureate: Robert Bridges.

433 *Gallio*: a reference to Acts 18:17: "And Gallio cared for none of these things".

Conder: properly Josiah Condor (1852–1920). He had practised as an architect in Japan since 1876 and became Minister of Works. He also taught at Tokyo University and is regarded as the father of western architecture in Japan. He published *The Flowers of Japan and the Art of Floral Arrangement* in 1891, the first English-language book on Ikebana, which popularized the form in the west.

Scott: Hardy received the R.I.B.A. prize from Thomas Leverton Donaldson, not Sir Gilbert Scott.

Wentworth Place: Keats's home in Hampstead was saved from demolition by public subscription and was opened as a museum in 1925.

434 "*Bidding … sound*": Browning's "Abt Vogler", ll. 2–3.

Bishop of Durham: Handley Carr Glyn Moule had died on 8 May 1920.

passed away: Charles Walter Moule died on 11 May 1921.

"*the half is more than the whole*": spoken by Hesiod to his brother Perseus, here implying that a few sincere words of comfort are preferable to a gush of sympathy.

435 *Lord Mayor*: Sir Edward Ernest Cooper.

Cambridge Vice-Chancellor: Peter Giles.

Prime Minister: David Lloyd George.

"*I call mine own ways to remembrance*": Psalm 119.

436 *Cornish friend*: Christopher Childs (?).

17–: the *West Briton* had actually been founded in 1810; see note to p. 11 above.

437 *roi-fainéant*: a do-nothing king.

438 *Society*: Royal Society of St. George.

446 *Canterbury Tales*: Prologue to "The Clerk's Tale", ll. 16–18.

448 *The Triumph*: John Masefield described the ship in a letter to Audrey Napier-Smith in 1955: "About the Thomas Hardy model. It is a dreadful thing: but in talk once TH said that as a little boy he had longed for a model & had never had one; so I asked if I might try to make him one; so I tried to make 'The Triumph, the new-rigged ship', of the old song he quotes somewhere (in a poem) [see "One We Knew"]. It looked quite gay when new, but I was a wretched hand at tools at the best. I blush to see it now, but I think TH was pleased: & that is much to remember" (*Letters to Reyna*, ed. William Buchan (London: Buchan & Enright, 1983), p. 114). The model is now in the Dorset County Museum.

new Prayer Book: a new *Book of Common Prayer* was published in February 1927. This revision of the Prayer Book was basically the 1662 Book with additional newer versions of services.

449 *battle of Hohenlinden*: French defeat of Austria, 3 December 1800, during the Napoleonic wars.

451 *Dorset man*: George Tilley Gollop.

452 *died soon after*: Elizabeth Allhusen died in the spring of 1926 after a long illness.

Pro-Provost of Queen's College: Edward Mewburn Walker (not p. 432, as given in Index).

454 *Provost*: John Richard Magrath.

Shelley Memorial: a statue of the poet in University College, on the High Street opposite Queen's College.

455 *seven brethren*: Matthew 22:25. This was the name which the brothers used to call themselves humorously: see *Collected Letters*, VI, 87.

458 *The Immortal Hour*: Boughton's opera, whose text was adapted from the writings of "Fiona Macleod" (William Sharp), was first performed in 1914 and enjoyed an enormously popular revival in London in 1922–23.

"*The Blue Danube*": a waltz composed by Johann Strauss Jr. in 1876.

"*The Morgenblätter Waltz*": "Morning Paper Waltz" (1864) by Strauss (see also *Life*, p. 65).

"*Overture to William Tell*": Rossini's last opera, composed in 1829.

political views: Boughton was a Communist.

459 *Emerson*: the quotation is adapted from the closing lines of Emerson's essay, "New England Reformers" (1844).

460 *Pearsall Smith*: the quotations are from Logan Pearsall Smith's *Four Words: Romance, Originality, Creative, Genius*, Society for Pure English Tract No. XVII (Oxford: Clarendon Press, 1924), pp. 38, 41.

461 *Iphigenia at Aulis*: by Euripides.

462 *one of the company*: Margaret Carter.

correspondent: Richard Little Purdy.

463 *friend of the Hardys*: Thomas Henry Tilley.

465 "*the man with the watching eye*": as Millgate observes, "the phrase may simply represent Florence's imperfect memory of the line 'Friend with the musing eye' from '"Men Who March Away"' " (p. 562).

Oxford correspondent: Roy McKay.

467 *a friend*: St. John Greer Ervine.

469 *the Rector*: George Cecil Niven.

473 *headmaster*: Ralph William Hill.

475 *new edition*: *Chosen Poems*, not published until August 1929.

476 *two men sitting on chairs*: Gittings suggests that the two men "were probably merely smugglers, sitting on their contraband tubs to try and conceal them" (*Young Thomas Hardy*, p. 38).

description of Apollyon: "So he went on, and Apollyon met him. Now the monster was hideous to behold: he was clothed with scales like a fish, and they are his pride; he had wings like a dragon, and feet like a bear, and out of his belly came fire and smoke; and his mouth was as the mouth of a lion" (Part 1, Stage 4). Cf. Jude's fear of "Apollyon lying in wait for Christian" (I. iii).

480 *local practitioner*: Edward Weller Mann.

a friend: Newman Flower.

486 *Mayor*: Wilfred Francis Hodges.

492 "*Artemus Ward*": Charles Farrar Browne.

THE MARRIAGE OF ANCIENT AND MODERN IN
A Laodicean

ANDREW RADFORD

> [T]he singing of the wire, which for the last few minutes he had quite forgotten, again struck upon his ear, and retreating to a convenient place he observed its final course: from the poles amid the trees it leaped across the moat, over the girdling wall, and thence by a tremendous stretch towards the keep where, to judge by sound, it vanished through an arrow-slit into the interior. This fossil of feudalism, then, was the journey's end of the wire, and not the village of Sleeping-Green.[1]

HARDY'S *A Laodicean* is perhaps more deeply concerned than any of his previous Wessex novels with the subtle processes of his own artful composition. He allows himself unprecedented freedom to manoeuvre and to refine the controlled historical promiscuity or 'eclecticism' of which Stancy Castle is the central symbolic setting. *A Laodicean* is a bracing expression of Hardy's erratic time-voyaging, mischievously gathering in an often capricious arrangement the scattered fragments of the past. The protagonist George Somerset – a Gothic architect and avid amateur antiquarian like his creator – is thrilled by the sight of the six-hundred year old Stancy Castle, a 'fossil of feudalism', bizarrely equipped with up-to-date paraphernalia such as the buzzing telegraph wire and neo-Greek gymnasium. Somerset's interest in this medieval 'survival' reflects Hardy's own retrospective curiosity: an imaginative possession of history by 'the class of *dilettanti*', the 'people that know all about styles and dates – travelled men, sketchers, ecclesiologists, and the like.'[2] Somerset's 'unlimited appreciativeness'[3] resisting a single-minded devotion to any one style and temperamentally wary of the closed-off

---

[1] Hardy, Thomas. *A Laodicean*, ed. with introd. Jane Gatewood. (Oxford: The World's Classics, 1991), 22. Hereafter *AL*.
[2] Anon., 'The State of English Architecture', *Quarterly Review* 132 (Jan-Apr, 1872), 298.
[3] *AL*, 12.

nature of philosophical systems, is portrayed as a force for good in this underrated novel. That modern contrivances and antique remnants might coexist is a concept Hardy can revel in and utilize:

> There was a certain unexpectedness in the fact that the hoary memorial of a stolid antagonism to the inter-change of ideas, the monument of hard distinctions in blood and race, of deadly mistrust of one's neighbour in spite of the Church's teaching, and of a sublime unconsciousness of any other force than a brute one, should be the goal of a machine which beyond everything may be said to symbolise cosmopolitan views and the intellectual and moral kinship of all mankind.[4]

Where we might have expected a provocative clash Hardy impishly provides a romantic harmony. That *A Laodicean* displays a superabundance of this creative zest which both dazzles and amuses is apparent when Paula's telegraph message to Somerset

> sped through the loophole of Stancy Castle keep, over the trees, along the railway, under bridges, across three counties – from extreme antiquity of environment to sheer modernism – and finally landed itself on a table in Somerset's chambers in the midst of a cloud of fog.[5]

'When railways and telegraphs extend from London to the remotest cities and villages', observed a contributor to the 1842 *Quarterly Review*, 'the sensation of time may be transmitted along with the elements of language.'[6] Another writer remarked in 1877 that the

> telegraph has taken such a large place in the practical business of life, that the world in general is apt rather to look upon electricity only in light of an agent of rapid communication.[7]

This dynamic energy is conveyed by Hardy's descriptive prose: the wit resides not merely in Paula's using a telegraph machine inside the mouldering remains of feudal glory, then transmitting her note across a landscape dotted with dolmens and tumuli; we also see how the sense of breathless velocity evoked by modern communication contrasts with the rustic lethargy of 'Sleeping-Green', whose inhabitants are far removed from the tide of progress. For Paula, time is precious; she belongs to that 'rising generation' who 'would think themselves ill-treated if they did not read in the *Times* each morning the report of any important event which had occurred in India the

---

[4] *AL*, 22-23.

[5] *AL*, 210.

[6] Anon., 'The Encyclopaedia Britannica', *Quarterly Review* 70 (June 1842), 57.

[7] Anon., 'The Science of Electricity as applied in Peace and War', *Quarterly Review* 144 (July 1877), 139.

day before.'[8]

Whereas *Far from the Madding Crowd* and *The Return of the Native* hark back to the mid 1870s and early 1840s respectively, portraying communities relatively untouched by recent technology, *A Laodicean* is self-consciously a 'story of today', striking a note of deliberate contemporaneity. Instead of offering a jaded, escapist complaint against the profligacy of the present, *A Laodicean* comprises a brisk, outgoing endorsement of modernity. Hardy honours the apostles of scientific experimentation, and how they accommodate (and reanimate) the unlikeliest vestiges of the past. He does not depict Paula, the modern flower in her medieval flowerpot, as an 'upstart interloper'[9] or a shallow *parvenue* whose newfangled toys represent the polluted forces of a decadent bourgeoisie.

Pugin in his 1836 manifesto for the Gothic Revival angrily denounces 'the lukewarm feelings with which religion is regarded by the majority in this country.'[10] However, it is one of the novel's greatest triumphs that Paula, the 'lukewarm' woman, who aims to manufacture Hellenic pottery in her imposing Norman castle becomes the embodiment of modern exuberance and entrepreneurial flair. Paula has few qualms about taking contradictory views of life. Hardy also enjoys the image of her polished second-measuring castle clock – 'bearing the name of a recent maker'[11] – incongruously set amid Stancy Castle's decaying mortar.

William Dare's use of his 'patent photographic process' on the eerie de Stancy portraits is another instance of Hardy presenting with beguiling verve the 'hymns ancient and modern' in the Victorian age. An artistically minded photographer, writing in 1852, lamented that perhaps no science or art that has been revealed to mankind has had to encounter a 'greater amount of opposition and prejudice than the science of photography'.[12] However, Hardy shows that photography can fit smoothly into the established hierarchy of pictorial media then in place in European culture.

This jars with John Ruskin, who in 1872 declared of photographs that 'for geographical and geological purposes they are worth ... a

---

[8] Ibid, 144.

[9] Page, Norman. *Thomas Hardy*.(London: Routledge & Kegan Paul, 1977), 107.

[10] Pugin, Augustus Welby Northmore. *Contrasts: or A Parallel between the Noble Edifices of the Middle Ages, and Corresponding Buildings of the Present Day; shewing the Present Decay of Taste*, introd. H. R. Hitchcock. (New York: Humanities Press, 1969), 48. Hereafter, *Pugin*.

[11] *AL*, 25.

[12] Vines, H. *A Brief Sketch of the Rise and Progress of Photography, with Particular Reference to the Practice of Daguerreotype*. (Bristol, 1852), 32.

good deal less than zero'.[13] Though not unqualified in his embrace of the latest inventions, Hardy employs them with originality to demonstrate how a new medium – Dare's photography for instance – entertains an archaic medium (the mildewed ancestral portraits), and so opens up demanding new perspectives for his art.

When George Somerset visits Sir William de Stancy, he finds the impecunious aristocrat settled snugly amid the 'mushroom modernism' of 'Myrtle Villa' whose '[g]enuine roadside respectability sat smiling on every brick of the eligible dwelling.' This mordant irony is elaborated when the baronet, a retired roué whose conversation Somerset expects to be 'the essence of historical romance,' expatiates instead on contemporary money-markets and the overriding need for frugality.[14]

Perhaps the most memorable escapade in this teasing wit occurs when the 'New Light' Paula briefly experiences the sights, sounds and smells of the 'Dark Ages':

> [Paula] was transported to the Middle Ages. It contained the shops of tinkers, braziers, bellows-menders, hollow-turners, and other quaintest trades ... It was a street for a medievalist to revel in, toss up his hat and shout hurrah in, send for his luggage, come and live in, die and be buried in. She had never supposed such a street to exist outside the imaginations of antiquarians. Smells direct from the sixteenth century hung in the air in all their original integrity and without a modern taint. The faces of the people in the doorways seemed those of individuals who habitually gazed on the great Francis, and spoke of Henry the Eighth as the king across the sea.[15]

In his *Life of Carlyle*, published in the 1880s, J. A. Froude declared that Carlyle's unparalleled greatness as a historian resided in his ability

> to bring dead things and dead people actually back to life; to make the past once more the present, and to show us men and women playing their parts on the mortal stage as real flesh-and-blood human creatures.[16]

Paula Power's medieval experience is an acerbic comment on Froude's assessment. Hardy relishes the artistic challenge of reviving

---

[13] Ruskin, *Works*, IV, 142 : see Nickel, Doug. 'The Camera and other Drawing Machines.' In *British Photography in the Nineteenth Century*, ed. Mike Weaver (Cambridge: Cambridge University Press, 1982).

[14] *AL*, 44-45.

[15] *AL*, 399.

[16] Froude, James Anthony. *Thomas Carlyle: A History of his Life in London, 1834-1881*, 2 vols. (London: Longmans, Green, 1884), II, 342.

the sights and sounds of former days, making 'the past once more the present'. Indeed, his time-voyage reveals an improvisatory virtuosity rarely found in his earlier fiction. He illustrates how an amateur antiquarian, always eager to separate the genuine 'survival' from a false copy, would rejoice at inhaling a sixteenth century odour in all its original pungency. The passage is not throwaway or frivolous, but reveals in Hardy (who then confers it on Paula) a keen imagination empowered by incongruity and ready to use it so that we might perceive the complex workings of a brave new world from surprising angles. Hardy does not recoil in shock from an environment dominated by a Norman castle whose owner invites Somerset to construct a neo-Greek courtyard within its weather-stained walls, or a railway track weaving around prehistoric barrows.

The dilettante's commonsense 'eclecticism' that Hardy indulges to such disarming effect extends to the assorted decorations and modish reading matter on display in Paula's living quarters. As well as 'books from a London circulating library, paper-covered light literature in French and choice Italian, and the latest monthly reviews,' we see a Bible, the *Baptist Magazine*, Wardlaw on Infant Baptism, Walford's County Families, and the *Court Journal*. 'These things,' Hardy writes,

> ensconced amid so much of the old and hoary, were as if a stray hour from the nineteenth century had wandered like a butterfly into the thirteenth, and lost itself there. [17]

His tone implies an amused and slightly baffled fascination with this heterogeneous clutter; he is stirred and stimulated by the 'cosmopolitan, fashionable modernity.'[18] He himself moves promiscuously between those archaic and contemporary styles which best appeal to his own idiosyncratic temperament. 'To regard all things and principles of things as inconstant modes or fashions', Pater remarks in *The Renaissance*, 'has more and more become the tendency of modern thought'.[19] The book on county families and the *Court Journal* reflect Paula's concern for social standing; the Bible and *Baptism Magazine* indicate religious denomination and establish her as a dabbler in eclectic religious philosophy. Hardy later described *A Laodicean* as a 'mechanical and ordinary production',[20] but its treatment of archaic features grafted onto a disconnected present is *extra*ordinary, continually

---

[17] *Al*, 38.

[18] Fisher, Joe. *Hidden Hardy* (London: Macmillan, 1992), 104.

[19] Pater, Walter. *The Renaissance: Studies in Art and Poetry*, ed. with introd. Adam Phillips (Oxford: The World's Classics, 1986), 186.

[20] Florence Emily Hardy, *The Life and Work of Thomas Hardy*, ed. Michael Millgate (London: Macmillan, 1984), 154.

courting oddness and whimsicality.

A Laodicean possesses a new optimism about the way modernity takes account of medieval and prehistoric 'survivals'. It is slavish respect for, or unthinking absorption in the artefacts, styles and institutions of medieval times that is shown as sham; Captain de Stancy's 'close study of the castle history' and 'notes which referred to the pedigree of his own family',[21] appear to be merely an attempt to wheedle his way into Paula's affections. We might expect the architectural purist in Hardy, who calls for 'the protection of an ancient edifice against renewal in fresh materials' in his 1906 essay 'Memories of Church Restoration', to deride Paula's wish to build a Greek colonnade in the precincts of her Norman castle. She wants a fountain in the middle, and 'statues like those in the British Museum' – perhaps a plan to transport the Elgin Marbles into this isolated portion of Wessex! Ironically, Hardy's purist impulse is voiced by the unscrupulous architect Havill, whose letter to a newspaper disparages the neo-Hellenic spirit and Paula's criminal lack of veneration for the battered magnificence of Stancy Castle, which has outlasted English Civil Wars only 'to be made a complete ruin by the freaks of an irresponsible owner'.[22]

Havill's tirade is couched in terms reminiscent of 'The State of English Architecture', a fierce polemic published in the 1872 *Quarterly Review* condemning 'this Gothic reign of terror' which sacrifices 'simplicity of outline and rhythm of parts' for 'meretricious vanity' and 'agonizing superfluity of contrivance'.[23] With his relish for exploiting uncoordinated impressions, Hardy uses throughout *A Laodicean* the outlandish fusion of obsolete and chic that is Gothic renovation, yet he disavows it in his essays and poems. Hardy comes across as simultaneously a child of his era (reflecting its perverse mixture of bright confidences and enervating angst), and within that a writer giving a response to it that is uniquely his own. Externalizing his own individ-ual impulse when confronting the paradoxes of the period, he seems fretful when the spirit of the age was marked by hubristic eloquence (for example, about the perfectibility of man). But as Havill's letter reveals on a subject close to Hardy's heart, he could be dryly amused in the light of vitriolic resistance to 'dainty', 'softhanded' gentleman architects whose 'amateur dilettante diversions' were supposedly desecrating an august English heritage. An 1831

---

[21] *AL*, 185

[22] *AL*, 109.

[23] Anon, ' The State of English Architecture', 309, 310, 319. See also, Anon., 'Hamilton &c. on Architecture', *Quarterly Review* 58 (February 1837), 61-82.

reviewer asserted that 'incongruity is, in our estimation, a strong, perhaps a conclusive argument, against the adaptation' of 'the Gothic style'.[24] On this matter of sharp controversy, Hardy offers not a jeremiad on the 'pue-rile' pseudo-Gothic[25] but a jubilee; he divorces himself from the cen-sorious Havills of late Victorian England, and acclaims Paula's crusa-ding desire to quarry multifarious techniques of construction and design. He sees in it the impatient, visionary eclecticism to which he was instinctively drawn: his natural imaginative habit of randomly collecting motifs from diverse past cultures and placing them in in-creasingly eccentric arrangements. Hardy's inquiries are not merely into continuity with the past; he shows a concern with prudent adap-tation to the present, and astute awareness of the future.

Paula Power's fanciful improvements to her castle home are not associated with that which is undesirable or life-denying; rather Hardy warns against uncomprehending immersion in the patrician past. The de Stancys are a lost yet partially preservable thirteenth century order; like Rings-Hill Speer, which dominates the landscape of *Two on a Tower* (1882), defunct sites should be put to an entirely new use. No dirge for a vanishing past, *A Laodicean* reinforces Paula's nobility of talent and ambition, and scoffs at the enervated de Stancys, whose medievalism cannot meet the dislocating complexities of the modern moment. If Hardy espoused the shrill rhetoric of Havill's letter, the novel would be a cautionary tale of orderly feudalism displaced by tasteless and turbulent democracy. But like Paula, Hardy enjoys cas-ually raiding the storehouse of history, given the Victorians' deepen-ing knowledge of unfamiliar epochs and cultures.

Although conscious of the unreliable technology of the train – one nearly runs Somerset over – Hardy's upbeat attitude towards the railway and the tunnel built by Paula's pioneering father underpins his strategy of furnishing a dilapidated Norman castle with the leading inventions of the day. Dickens's attitude to the ongoing expansion of the British rail network could be apocalyptic: 'beyond the Station, an ugly dark monster of a tunnel kept its jaws open, as if it had swallow-ed them and were ravenous for more destruction.'[26] But Hardy repudiates the rhetoric of severe trauma and ideas of social collapse

---

[24] Anon., 'Old English Domestic Architecture', *Quarterly Review* 45 (July 1831), 471-504 : 472. See also, Anon., 'Principles of Gothic Architecture', *Quarterly Review* 69 (December 1841), 111-149.

[25] Anon., 'Hope's *History of Architecture*', *Quarterly Review* 53 (April 1835), 338-371.

[26] Dickens, Charles. 'Associations of Childhood', *All the Year Round* (June 30 1860), 274-278: 274.

which were strenuously promulgated by the opponents of railway travel; he offers instead a more temperate, reassuring assessment:

> Somerset looked down on the mouth of the tunnel. The absurdity of the popular commonplace that science, steam, and travel must always be unromantic and hideous, was proved on the spot. On either slope of the deep cutting, green with long grass, grew drooping young trees of ash, beech, and other flexible varieties...The vertical front of the tunnel, faced with brick that had once been red, was now weather-stained, lichened, and mossed over in harmonious hues of rusty browns, pearly greys, and neutral greens.[27]

Rather than brutally cutting down antiquities and defacing on all sides, the tunnel has been happily absorbed into its surroundings and naturalized by time. Hardy is not repelled by this glaring incongruity but evinces a feeling of quiet wonder at the tunnel's deceptively organic appearance; this clashes with the sombreness of *Desperate Remedies*, in which the emergence of rail-travel has left Old Springrove's Three Tranters Inn a cheerless roadside relic.

In 1862 James Fergusson paid fulsome tribute to the design of tunnels: "Some of the entrances to the tunnels which are found on most railways in England are as grand as any city gates, and grander than many triumphal arches that are to be found in Europe."[28]

Hardy would have supported this sentiment rather than take a Ruskinian view of the railway's utilitarian meanness. We are invited to regard the railway not simply in terms of mechanical function but as an object worthy of aesthetic appreciation: the moss and the effects of weather, bringing the massive stonework into the organic cycle of nature, thus making technology seem picturesque and romantic.

Hardy's representation of the ancient Wessex countryside, overspread with telegraph poles and John Power's railway, is not the searing vision of a bleak dystopian fiction. Rather he hails

> 'those *new arts* which are on the eve of altering the forms and habits of social life. The wonders of railway intercourse, of locomotive engines, tunnels ... steam-boats' and the almost magical 'powers of the electro-magnetic telegraph'.[29]

A Laodicean shuns the didactic simplicity of Augustus Welby Pugin's juxtapositions of old and new in *Contrasts* (1836). The etched title-

---

[27] *AL*, 95.

[28] Fergusson, James. *History of the Modern Styles of Architecture: being a sequel to the Handbook of Architecture* (London: John Murray, 1862), 477

[29] Anon., The *Encyclopaedia Britannica*, 54-55.

[30] *Pugin*, 55.

page in the first and second editions refers to 'a parallel between the noble edifices of the fourteenth and fifteenth centuries and similar buildings of the present day; shewing the present decay of taste'. Hardy's tunnel episode, instead of illustrating the unrelieved sterility of Victorian life with its 'tide of innovations and paltry novelties,'[30] upholds the manifold opportunities created by Paula's venturesome and reformist generation.

Stancy Castle, rich in romantic historical associations, becomes a symbol not just of temporal conjunction but also of the ways in which Hardy can revivify the seemingly moribund relics of forgotten periods. He is excited by the artistic possibilities offered by 'survivals' because they cast their shadows across many different eras. The vivid image of a medieval castle, crusted with myriad bygone experiences, stimulates him to fresh insights when he might have been uneasy over an apparent collision of past and future. In *A Laodicean*, he persuasively contends that energy resides in modernity's accommodating our heritage (e.g. Paula's maverick plans for her castle home) rather than the past's undignified striving to ingratiate itself with the

15th CENTURY CANOPIED TABLE TOMB, DUNSTER CHURCH[31]

modern spirit (Captain de Stancy). This even extends to the machinery of Gothic supernaturalism, situating the conventional orphan of the castle in the bewildering milieu of Victorian scientific, social and political ferment. Although commentators would have us believe that Hardy was magisterially dismissive of Gothic stock-in-trade, it appears in this novel to exert an irresistible hold over his imagination.

---

[31] This tomb at Dunster Church, Somerset, commemorates a member of the Luttrell family of Dunster Castle – one of the models for Stancy Castle. See F. P. Pitfield, *Hardy's Wessex Locations* (Dorset:: Dorset publishing Co, 1992) 39.

THE CYCLE OF REGENERATION:
METAMORPHOSIS IN HARDY'S POEMS

BETTY CORTUS

BIRDS and bird song held a strong fascination for Hardy judging by the numerous poems in which these images appear. More than one commentator has surmised that the life of a bird, in Hardy's symbology, represents human life in miniature. Birds caged, blinded, or starving in winter, evoke visions of human misery. Birds free to go wherever they will, or throbbing in full-throated song, on the other hand, represent human life at its happiest. There are other times, however, when Hardy uses bird imagery to illustrate his conviction that death is not necessarily the ultimate termination of life. Although he could not share with orthodox Christians a belief in a celestial afterlife, he retained a conviction that some essence of a living entity persisted on an earth-bound level. Take for example the long-dead bird in "Shelley's Skylark"[1] which the earlier poet "made immortal through times to be" by enshrining it in a poem. Hardy multiplies the possibility of its earthly continuance in an even more material way when he envisages the bird passing through a process of metamorphosis to reappear in a series of other physical forms:

> Maybe it rests in the loam I view,
> Maybe it throbs in a myrtle's green,
> Maybe it sleeps in the coming hue
> Of a grape on the slopes of yon inland scene. (iv)

After living as a bird accustomed to soaring aloft in ecstatic song, an afterlife in the form of a grain of earth or part of a plant, stationary and mute, may seem a humble kind of existence. But the creature's essence is still throbbing, or at worst merely dormant for a time, in these lowly states of being. Through a cycle of disintegration and re-

---

[1] Hardy, Thomas, *The Complete Poems of Thomas Hardy* edited by James Gibson (London: Macmillan London Ltd, 1976), 101. Hereafter *CP*.

generation the possibilities of ascending the evolutionary ladder are as great as are those of descending it. For example, plants draw their sustenance from the soil, herbage becomes part of the domestic animals which consume it, and their elements, in turn, nourish, and become portion of the humans who ingest their flesh.

This concept, central as it is to Hardy's poetry, actually has a scientific basis as well as an imaginative one. Its influence can be traced back to the ancient Greek materialist philosophers Democritus and Epicurus, and their most articulate exponent, the Roman poet Lucretius. Frank M. Turner has investigated a heightening of interest in Lucretius which occurred around the middle of the nineteenth century; although he had long been admired for his poetry, at that time scientists began to discover unexpected parallels between his philosophy and contemporary atomic theory. A number of controversial articles which began appearing on this subject drew a great deal of public attention. In 1860 further interest was sparked when H. A. J. Munro published one of the first modern critical editions of *De Rerum Natura*, which he followed four years later with a new English translation of the poem.

The publication of Tennyson's poem "Lucretius" in 1868 marked a peak in the new surge of appreciation for the ancient poet and his philosophy.[2] Hardy, who made his first acquaintance with Lucretius as a young architectural apprentice in London, soon became an ardent admirer of his works, marking and annotating passages which held a particular appeal for him.[3] Writing to his friend Edward Clodd in 1897, Hardy referred to Lucretius as "that glorious Double-man" deserving of "due honour" as both a poet and a scientist.[4]

Considering his own philosophical bias Hardy would have found Lucretius's assertion that we have nothing to fear in death a particularly attractive one. Contrary to the superstitious belief in eternal punishment after death in Acheron, which made life a hell on earth for his contemporaries, Lucretius proclaimed that all sensation is lost after our bodies decay, and that we return to a state of oblivion such as existed before we were born. If life has been miserable we should rejoice at being released from pain. And if life has been happy we should depart graciously, sated with the good things it has given us. He believed, moreover, that while we are mortal, the atoms from

---

[2] Frank M. Turner, "Lucretius among the Victorians," *Victorian Studies* 16.3 (1973), 329-48. Hereafter *Turner*.

[3] *The Literary Notebooks of Thomas Hardy*. 2 vols. Ed. Lennart A. Björk. (London: Macmillan, 1985), I, 361, n 1146.

[4] *Thomas Hardy: Selected Letters*. Ed. Michael Millgate (Oxford: Clarendon, 1990), 111.

which we are formed are indestructible. His contention that nothing comes from nothing is seen by some as foreshadowing the second law of thermodynamics which states that matter can be neither created nor destroyed.[5] As death must come to all we should be content in the knowledge that the release of our atoms will provide substance for the growth of future generations who will have their fill of life and then pass away as we did.

T. H. Huxley, whom Hardy personally knew and greatly admired, describing the relationship between organic and inorganic matter, put this same principle into modern scientific terms in an essay which Hardy almost certainly read:

> The plant gathers ... inorganic materials together and makes them up into its own substance. The animal eats the plant and appropriates the nutritious portions to its own sustenance, rejects and gets rid of the useless matters; and, finally, the animal itself dies, and its whole body is decomposed and returned into the inorganic world. There is thus a constant circulation from one to the other, a continual formation of organic life from inorganic matters, and as constant a return of the matter of living bodies to the inorganic world; so that the materials of which our bodies are composed are largely, in all probability, the substances which constituted the matter of long extinct creations.[6]

Aside from these scientific considerations the whole poetic tradition of the metamorphosis of people and animals into plant life is, of course, also an ancient one. Ovid, after all, for all his genius, merely recorded myths dating back to the beginning of time. Poets have made use of the conceit over and over as a means of finding consolation after the death of a loved one. To name just a few examples, the speaker of the medieval alliterative poem *Pearl* is soothed by the fragrance of the gillyflowers, ginger blossoms, and peonies, springing from seeds germinating in the pearl maiden's burial mound. Laertes, at Ophelia's graveside, exclaims: "Lay her i' th' earth, / And from her fair and unpolluted flesh / May violets spring!"[7] And Thomas Gray, in his famous elegy, describes the "rugged elms"and shady yew trees of the country churchyard under which are the moldering heaps where "[t]he rude forefathers of the hamlet sleep."

---

[5] *Turner*, 341

[6] Huxley, Thomas Henry. *Man's Place in Nature and Other Essays* (London: Everyman, 1906), 158-9.

[7] *Hamlet* V.i, 240-2.

This long tradition achieves its ultimate expression in English poetry in Hardy's remarkable poem: "Voices from Things Growing in a Churchyard"[8] in which the dead, now flourishing in the plant forms springing from their graves, commune not only amongst themselves, but appeal as well to the ears of the living graveyard visitors who are attuned imaginatively to their mysterious frequency. A close reading of this poem reveals it to be a study in contrasts on two separate levels. First, it portrays the differences between the characters and personalities of its subjects. Second, it contrasts the quality and tempo of life before and after metamorphosis. On the first count, the six subjects of the poem can be grouped for comparison and contrast into three pairs, the little girl and the old man whose monologues begin and end the series, the two men, and the two women, whose utterances occur in between. Unlike the framing couple, little Fanny Hurd and old Squire Grey, the middle two pairs have at least gender, and possibly age in common. Beyond that they sharply diverge. Bachelor Bowring and Thomas Voss, for example, are unlikely neighbors in the graveyard. One has been a man of wealth and prominence during life, the other a poor man of obscure origins. Yet, ironically, Bachelor Bowring's costly coffin of shingled oak becomes a rigid prison balking his liberating transformation into "a dancer in green leaves on a wall" for over a century. Meanwhile, his thin-urned fellow has successfully burrowed free from his flimsy cerements and has burgeoned far more expeditiously into new life as the ruddy fruit clusters of the yew tree.

Equally disparate are the two women, the cool, formal Lady Gertrude, proud of her noble birth, and her sensual, yielding sister under the skin, Eve Greensleeves, "the handsome mother of two or three illegitimate children" according to Hardy's note. Appropriately enough Lady Gertrude's superfine satins become the stiff, lustrous leaves of the laurel tree after her transformation. The compliant Eve is changed, just as felicitously, to a supple vine whose fruitfulness, in the manner of the plant world, is now dependent upon her passive, and freshly innocent, submission to the kisses and caresses of pollinating insects. But if the two framing speakers are juxtaposed in this way they appear the most oddly assorted pair of all. Fanny Hurd is a simple, unformed girl-child who during her brief time on earth "Flit-fluttered" happily like a bird as she played. Squire Grey is a world-weary old man embittered by life's pains. During life they represented the extremes of innocence and experience. Yet after their absorption into the vegetable kingdom they are strangely at one. The little girl

---

[8] *CP*, 623-5.

flutters ebulliently in the daisy shapes on her grave, and the old man, his ache stayed at last, is free to cavort gaily in the attire of ivy-green.

By selecting such diverse characters and opposing them to bring out these contrasts Hardy depicts, in miniature, the color and heterogeneity of the human race as a whole. At the same time he contrasts the quality of life before and after transformation, showing the chief attractions of the latter state to be its dancing insouciance and its egalitarianism. Although each of these leafy avatars retain vestiges of the personality traits which distinguished them during life, the societal barriers which once would have segregated them one from the other seem strangely irrelevant after their metamorphosis. In fact they now seem to be enjoying a whole new level of carefree, companionable interaction:

> And so these maskers breathe to each
> Sir or Madam. (vii)

The word "maskers" brings a note of playful impersonation to the life of this graveyard community. And the mock ceremoniousness with which they address their audience "Sir or Madam" seems to indicate that they are having fun in their foliar disguise at the expense of those visitors to the churchyard who fail to perceive their original identity. Yet underlying these comic elements a mysterious thrumming vitality energizes the plants. They are vibrantly alive, and the "radiant hum" they emit is audible to those willing to linger and apprehend its human origins, now transmuted into the general life of growing things. Incidentally, although Hardy may not have been aware of it himself, his reference to the plants' breathing, coupled with his refrain: "All day cheerily, / All night eerily," curiously parallels the actual respiratory functions of the vegetable kingdom. By day plants purify the air by taking in waste gases and "cheerily" giving out healthy, life-supporting oxygen. By night, however, the process is "eerily" reversed as they inhale wholesome oxygen and exhale insalubrious carbon dioxide.[9]

Although the characters in the poem are drawn from people Hardy actually knew, he furnishes a more deeply personal instance of this metamorphic phenomenon when he depicts his late wife Emma, like little Fanny Hurd, living anew in the "daisy shapes" waving above her resting place in the poem "Rain on a Grave":[10]

---

[9] Strictly speaking plants also give off carbon dioxide during the day; proportional increase by night is more apparent than real due to the absence of photosynthesis and oxygen production which occurs only in the presence of light.
[10] *CP*, 341-2.

> Soon will be growing
> > Green blades from her mound,
> And daisies be showing
> > Like stars on the ground,
> Till she form part of them –
> Ay – the sweet heart of them,
> Loved beyond measure
> With a child's pleasure
> > All her life round.   (iv)

"Transformations"[11] is another arresting treatment of the theme. Although the rather graphic corporeality of the first two stanzas may be a little disconcerting, the calm transcendence of the final stanza works to temper the poem's mood.

> Portion of this yew
> Is a man my grandsire knew,
> Bosomed here at its foot:
> This branch may be his wife,
> A ruddy human life
> Now turned to a green shoot.
>
> These grasses must be made
> Of her who often prayed,
> Last century, for repose;
> And the fair girl long ago
> Whom I often tried to know
> May be entering this rose.
>
> So, they are not underground,
> But as nerves and veins abound
> In the growths of upper air,
> And they feel the sun and rain,
> And the energy again
> That made them what they were!

The metamorphosis of these individuals is nothing like the process whereby Ovid converts Daphne to a laurel tree and Adonis to a flower with the swiftness of time-lapse photography. Hardy's characters are transformed by minute degrees over a long period of time, reflecting far more accurately the biological facts. The man and wife

---

[11] *CP*, 472.

of stanza one have taken three generations to become part of the yew tree. The woman whose murmured prayers are now the whispering of the wind in the grass has been dead since the previous century. Even the fair girl who was the speaker's contemporary lived "long ago." And it is far less certain that her transformation is as complete as that of those who died earlier. He speculates that she may, only now, be in the process of entering the rose.

Hardy's belief in the interconnection between all living things may account for at least one of the ambiguities at the core of this poem. This is the fact that the distinctions between animal life and vegetable life tend to blur at times. These people have become plants, but they are also still uncannily human. They possess nerves which enable them to feel, and veins through which energy pulses. Furthermore, the poem wavers back and forth between certainty and conjecture about the process of metamorphosis itself as a possibility. The fact that the man "is" and the praying woman "must be" transformed, but the wife and the fair girl only "may be" so, creates tensions which lead to uncertainty about whether or not this is actually happening.

Similarly problematical is the poem "Drummer Hodge."[12] While it is primarily about the senselessness of war it is probably the most poignant poem in which metamorphosis is also an element. The young soldier of the title, an unsophisticated native of rural Wessex, dies far from home in a foreign land for a cause he probably does not understand. Denied the consolation of burial at home among his forefathers, he is thrown uncoffined into a crude grave in the South African veldt:

> Yet portion of that unknown plain
>   Will Hodge for ever be;
> His homely Northern breast and brain
>   Grow to some Southern tree,
> And strange-eyed constellations reign
>   His stars eternally.   (iii)

Here the equivocality of this kind of transmigratory afterlife is markedly present. The words "forever" and "eternally" indicate that Drummer Hodge has indeed gained immortality of a kind, but the fact that he becomes part of a foreign tree and not one of the familiar elms or yews of his homeland means that his transformation is less than a happy one. The cycle of metamorphosis, however, will continue to repeat itself endlessly, cresting at intervals in its evolutionary ascent as brand new living creatures draw their being from the

---

[12] *CP*, 90-1.

elemental pool. Hardy returns to bird imagery to record one of these climactic episodes in the charming small poem, "Proud Songsters"[13]:

> The thrushes sing as the sun is going,
> And the finches whistle in ones and pairs,
> And as it gets dark loud nightingales
> In bushes
> Pipe, as they can when April wears,
> As if all Time were theirs.
>
> These are brand-new birds of twelve-months' growing,
> Which a year ago, or less than twain,
> No finches were, nor nightingales,
> Nor thrushes,
> But only particles of grain,
> And earth, and air, and rain.

Hardy was never one to make dogmatic pronouncements on philosophical matters, yet one can envisage him, unable to believe in a heavenly afterlife, nevertheless deriving comfort from the thought that something of one's essence lives on beyond the grave, albeit in a humble earth-bound way. He may even have imagined that some of those deathless atomic particles now embodied in these proud young songbirds once throbbed with life, eons ago, in the selfsame skylark immortalized by Shelley.

WORKS CONSULTED

Cawley, A C., Ed. *Pearl, Sir Gawain and the Green Knight*. New York: Dutton, 1962.

Lucretius (Titus Lucretius Carus). *De Rerum Natura*. Trans. H. D. Rouse. Cambridge: Harvard UP, 1975.

Ovid (Publius Ovidius Naso). *The Metamorphoses*. Trans. Horace Gregory, New York: Viking, 1958.

Shakespeare, William. *Hamlet*. Ed. Edward Hubler. New York: Signet, 1963.

Shelley, Percy Bysshe. *Shelley: Poetical Works*. Ed. Thomas Hutchinson. London: Oxford UP, 1905.

---

[13] *CP*, 835-76.

CONTRACT HOLDOUT
Love calls us to the things of this world.
– Richard Wilbur

In March, the first timid woodchuck –
a sleek, attractive offer;
then the killdeer drawing arcs
across the April gray,
the catbirds, brown thrashers,
rushing, crowding back in:
like the barely-leafed-out trees,
they promise things green and golden.

But a cool, clear, breezy morning
among white-blossoming locusts
of early May – with goldfinches,
indigo buntings, yellowthroats,
and a sun-brightened scarlet tanager –
is enough to make me sign:
I'l take love's lease again –
same terms for another year.

Bill Morgan, Normal,
Illinois. 2002

VIGNETTE BY HARDY TO ACCOMPANY "HER IMMORTALITY,"
WESSEX POEMS, 133.

THOSE AUTUMNS

Those autumns we bought apples by the bushel
For school lunchboxes, for canning applesauce,
Picking them ourselves, in fact, those apples,
All of us happy in trees or reaching from the
        ground to loaded branches
To carry home the taste of summer's end.

Those autumns the house rang with noise,
Children coming and going,
Simon and Garfunkle on the stereo,
Sons playing loudly as they do,
Daughters secret in their rooms.

Those autumns were not soundless, as now,
Though apples still load the trees
And leaves still shout their rainbow.
Those autumns were not like these,
Silent and sad.

Joanne Schweik
Fredonia, New York. 2003

WOOD ENGRAVING BY AGNES MILLER PARKER FOR THOMAS
HARDY'S *THE RETURN OF THE NATIVE*, BOOK IV.
(NEW YORK: THE HERITAGE PRESS, 1942), 243

THE THOMAS HARDY ASSOCIATION

FOUNDED IN 1997

BY

LOVERS OF HARDY FOR LOVERS OF HARDY

THE WEST GALLERY OF STINSFORD CHURCH.[*]
DRAWN FROM MEMORY BY HARDY

---

[*] **Picture courtesy of Dorset County Museum.** The gallery was reconstructed and consecrated in the 1990s

THE WEST GALLERY OF PUDDLETOWN CHURCH, 1635[*]
[WHERE HARDY'S GRANDFATHER PLAYED]

---

[*] Hardy, Evelyn, *Thomas Hardy: A Critical Biography* (London: The Hogarth Press, 1954), Frontispiece.

NOTES ON CONTRIBUTORS

The Thomas Hardy Association is deeply indebted to all contributors, whether named here or not, especially those participate in our debating groups – the *Poem of the Month*, and the *Forum* discussion group. Whereas each and every contribution is valued and *all* are archived we regret that due the limitations of space only a selected sample of our debates can be published in *The Hardy Review*.

➢ **PHILIP ALLINGHAM** is an assistant professor in the Faculty of Education at Lakehead University, Ontario. His doctoral thesis is entitled "Dramatic Adaptations of The Christmas Books of Charles Dickens, 1844-1848: Texts and Contexts" (1988) and, his recent work on Hardy's illustrators includes "Six Original Illustrations for Hardy's *Tess of the D'Urbervilles* Drawn by Sir Hubert Von Herkomer, R. A., for *The Graphic* (1891)" (*Thomas Hardy Journal* 10, 1. Feb. 1994), 52-70.

➢ **ROY BUCKLE** – a Reader at the University of Sheffield until 1990 – now composes musical pieces which can be seen and heard on www.segr-music.net. He is keen to receive responses to his work.

➢ **BETTY CORTUS** received her Ph.D. from the City University of New York: her major area of concentration was on Hardy's poetry. In retirement she continues to research and write as an independent scholar. She volunteers her time to teach literature in a Learning-in-Retirement Program at Mira Costa College in Oceanside, California. She is a Vice President of the Thomas Hardy Association and Directs its online Discussion Group, the ***Forum.***

➢ **W. EUGENE DAVIS** is Professsor Emeritus of English Literature and has taught at Purdue University from 1963-1999 having gained his Ph.D in 1962 from Western Reserve University. Gene co-edited the two-volume Gerber-Davis annotated secondary bibliography of works on Hardy (Northern Illinois University Press), and has recently concentratad on the role of music in Hardy's novels. W. Eugene Davis acts as Choral Director of the "Psalming" events at the Thomas Hardy International Conferences in Dorchester.

➢ **DAVID HAVIRD** is a member of the English Faculty at Cent-eneray College of Louisiana where he also serves as Associate Dean of the college. His interest in Hardy stems from his studies in regionalism – he has also published on Flannery O'Connor, Elizabeth Spencer, Allen Tate and Robert Penn Warren. His poems have appeared in *The New Yorker*, *Poetry*, *Seneca Review*, *Shenadoah* and *Southwest Review*.

- **JAN LLOYD JONES** works with Professor Ralph Elliott at the Australian National University on the comic elements in Hardy's works. Her other research interests include the novels of Milan Kundera, theory of comedy and tragedy, and the figure of the hero in literature from Beowulf to James Bond.

- **ROSEMARIE MORGAN**, editor and publisher of *The Hardy Review*, has taught at Yale University since 1984. She is President of TTHA and Vice President/Symposium Chair of the Thomas Hardy Society (UK). Her publications include, *Women and Sexuality in the Novels of Thomas Hardy* (Routledge, 1988), *Cancelled Words* (Routledge, 1992), also essays on Charlotte Brontë, Mary Chesnut, Thomas Hardy, Toni Morrison and women writers of the American Frontier. Her edition of the holograph manuscript version of *Far From the Madding Crowd* (Penguin World Classics) came out in 2000; she is "Year's Work" essayist for *Victorian Poetry* and author of "Women" and "Marriage" in *The Oxford Reader's Companion to Hardy*. Work in progress includes a book on *Editing Hardy*.

- **WILLIAM W. MORGAN** is a TTHA Vice President and Director of The Thomas Hardy Poetry Page (*POTM*) for the Association. He is Professor of English at Illinois State University, where he teaches courses in Victorian Literature, Poetry as a Genre, English as a Field of Study and, occasionally, Women's Studies. He has published essays on Hardy in *PMLA*, *JEGP*, *Victorian Poetry*, *The Hardy Review*, and other journals. In 1998 he published his first chapbook of poems, *Trackings: The Body's Memory, The Heart's Fiction* (Boulder: Dead Metaphor Press). He is co-editor with Rosemarie Morgan of TTHA's *Occasional Series, Volume* II: *The Emma Poems* (2000) and is the driving force behind the Hardy Associations's Collection of Early Hardy Criticism held at Milner Library.

- **ANDREW RADFORD** is currently lecturing in nineteenth and twentieth century literature at the University of Durham, UK. He is completing a book-length study on Hardy's abiding interest in Victorian sciences of humankind, especially geology, archaeology and anthropology.

- **MARTIN RAY** teaches at the University of Aberdeen, Scotland. He is a Vice President of TTHA, Director of the Association's *Short Stories* page and editor of *The Hardy Journal*. His publications include, *Thomas Hardy: A Textual Study of the Short Stories* (1997), *Thomas Hardy: an Annotated Critical Biography* (co-author, Ronald Draper, 1989), *Joseph Conrad* (1993), and has edited several works on Conrad. Martin Ray has recently com-piled and produced a Thomas Hardy Poetry Concordance on CD Rom (free to TTHA members), a *Dynasts* Concordance and has also produced concordances on the novels.

➤ **ISOBEL ROBIN** embarked, late in retirement, on her M. A. thesis on Hardy, entitled "Devolutions of Power in *The Dynasts* and Other Works of Thomas Hardy." She was first published in *The Hardy Review*, Vol. I, in 1998; she has since produced her first book of poetry, *Freud's Back-Yard* (Five Islands Press, 2002), and has subsequently been commissioned by her publishers to produce new works.

➤ **JOANNE SCHWEIK** has worked as grammarian for a nation-al magazine, as a researcher for a court case, as a library publicist, and has published many nonfiction articles and features and a long-running column on foods and cooking, entitled "The Artful Kitchen." She has also freelanced as writer and editor. She has recently published a cookbook, *Chautauqua Cooks: A Century of Recipes* from *Chautauqua Kitchens*, and a history of a seminal decade in the growth of the State University of New York College at Fredonia: *The Lanford Years*. She is currently at work on the next college presidential history, 1970-1984.

ADVERTISEMENTS
As featured on **TTHA PROMOTIONS** www.yale.edu/hardysoc

Advertising rates for *The Hardy Review*
Up to 3 lines: $45 (£25)   Half Page: $60 (£45)   Full page: $90 (£70), if predesigned
For advertising copy designed by TTHA there is an added charge of $50 (£30).
Copy and payment to be sent to the editor on floppy disk or e-attachment
Rosemarie Morgan, 124 Bishop St, New Haven, CT 06511

HARDY AND HIS READERS

This study examines the fraught relationship Hardy had with his readers. He resented their bourgeois values and beliefs, in particular their hypocritical form of Christianity, with its repression of the body. Initially content to compromise, to provide them with congenial entertainment, Hardy resorted at first to "back-door" strategies of subversion, smuggling obscene and blasphemous material past his editors, and finally to outspoken attack. What emerges from this study is a new insight into the dynamics of Hardy's writing and into the wider literary field within which he operated.

palgrave/macmillan   ISBN 0333-96260-5   June 2003

THE THOMAS HARDY ASSOCIATION

Please photocopy this form, fill it in, and mail it with your check *made out to:*
Rosemarie Morgan 124, Bishop St, New Haven, CT 06511

Payment can be made using UK sterling checks and International money orders.
Amount may vary according to the current rate of exchange.

NAME: ....
ADDRESS: ....
....

E-MAIL ....
PHONE NUMBER: ....
FAX NUMBER: ....
OCCUPATION:..
EDUCATION ....
INTERESTS: ....
....
IDEAS FOR SOCIETY ACTIVITIES: ....
....

MEMBERSHIP PRIVILEGES INCLUDE

- ➢ Receipt of TTHA annual *Hardy Review*
- ➢ Receipt of TTHA Poetry Concordance, CDRom: *Please apply direct to Martin Ray: Order form on* www.yale.edu/hardysoc
- ➢ Access to Members Research Resources: http://www.yale.edu/hardysoc/Welcome/welcomet.htm
- ➢ Advertising on TTHA PROMOTIONS page: *PROMOTIONS advertising is now $40 per annum to* TTHA *members: please add this fee to your renewal check*

FOR OFFICE USE ONLY

MEMBERSHIP NUMBER ASSIGNED: Expiration DATE: DIM:

THE THOMAS HARDY ASSOCIATION

MEMBERSHIP INFORMATION

Please go to http://www.yale.edu/hardysoc & read membership ordinances pertaining to TTHA..

A. **INDIVIDUALS APPLYING FOR MEMBERSHIP OF TTHA** ....$35.00/£25.00
B. **COUPLES APPLYING FOR MEMBERSHIP OF TTHA**.............$45.00/£35.00
C. **STUDENT** (please state affiliation) **FOR MEMBERSHIP OF TTHA**. .... $25.50/£20.00

TTHA MEMBERSHIP OFFERS THE FOLLOWING TO ALL

- Free copy of annual publication: ***The Hardy Review***

- Membership option to purchase earlier editions of *The Review*: at half price (plus postage) & *Occasional Series*: $7.50/£5.00

- **Free CD-Rom** of the *Thomas Hardy Poetry Concordance* Please apply direct to Martin Ray giving your membership # www.yale.edu/hardysoc/Order Form

- Free UK snailmail service: see Martin Ray:
  < http://www.yale.edu/hardysoc>- VP BOX

- Reduced advertising fees on TTHA Promotions See PROMOTIONS page on www.yale.edu/hardysoc

- **Access to TTHA Members Research Resources**, featuring:
  1. **Bob's Checklist**: the most comprehensive and up-to-date literary Checklist in existence online: updated twice monthly by a team of 20 scholars and professors world-wide.
  2. **Reviews Page**: book reviews of recent works on Hardy.
  3. ***The Complete Poems*** (under construction—currently holds *Time's Laughingstocks*)
  4. **Ottakars Booklist**.
  5. **Jeanie's Bibliography:** a complete checklist of works on Hardy published through the 1990s – the perfect complement to **Bob's Checklist.**

THE THOMAS HARDY ASSOCIATION PUBLICATIONS

TTHA publications can be ordered by copying & returning this form with payment cheque *made out to:*
Rosemarie Morgan,
124 Bishop Street, New Haven, CT 06511, USA

Title ....
Qty ....

The Hardy Review, Vol I, (1998) ISBN: 0-9669176-0-X	£18/$25
The Hardy Review Vol II, (1999) ISBN: 0-9669176-3-4	£18/$25
The Hardy Review Vol III, (2000) ISBN: 0-9669176-5-0	£18/$25
The Hardy Review Vol IV, (2001) ISBN: 0-9669176-7-7	£18/$25
The Hardy Review, Vol V, (2002) ISBN: 0-9669176-8-5	£18/$25

Days to Recollect: Essays in Honour of Robert Schweik
ISBN:0-9669176-4-2   £25/ $36

Human Shows: Essays in Honour of Michael Millgate
ISBN: 0-9669176-2-6   £25/$36

Occasional Series, Vol I: Editing Hardy (1999)
ISBN: 0-9669176-1-8   £10/$15
Occasional Series, Vol II: Emma Poems (2001)
ISBN: 0-9669176-6-9   £10/$15

Postage & Packing per volume: £4.50/$5.50

Grand Total . . . . ._____

Title: ....
First Name: ....
LastName: ....
Department: ....
Position: ....
Establishment: Address:...
....
Town................................ Zip/Postcode: ....
Country: ....Telephone: ....
Date: ....   Signature: ....

DISCOUNT to TTHA Members: 50% off all TTHA publications

THE THOMAS HARDY ASSOCIATION
TTHA Vice Presidents and Board of Directors

Gillian Beer: VP

Elena Carp: VP: *News From Romania*

Betty Cortus: VP: *Forum* Director
<Hardycor@owl.csusm.edu>

Shanta Dutta: VP: *News From India*
< shanta_dutta16@yahoo.com>

Ralph Elliott: VP
<Ralph.elliott@anu.edu.au>

James Gibson: VP: *Poetry Consultant*
<JamesGibson@ukgateway.net>

Sumiko Inoue: VP: *News from Japan* <ks-inoue@mx2.nisiq.net>

Yasushi Kamiyama: VP

Suzanne Keen:VP: *Elections* Director <Skeen@wlu.edu>

Seth Lachterman: VP: *Network Consultant*
<slach@bcn.net>

Rosemarie Morgan: *President/The Hardy Review* Ed/*Resources* Page Dir./*Maps* Page Dir./*News Updates* Dir./*Bibliography* Page Dir/ *Promotions* Page Dir.
<Rm82@pantheon.yale.edu>

William Morgan: VP: *Executive Vice President/ Poetry* Page Director
<wwmorgan@mail.ilstu.edu>

Richard Nemesvari: VP
Life Page Director
<rnemesva@stfx.ca>

Linda Peterson: VP
<Linda.peterson@yale.edu>

Birgit Plietzsch: VP: *Novels* Page Director/*Network Consultant*
<bp10@st-andrews.ac.uk>

Martin Ray: VP:*Short Stories* Page Director
<Enl090@abdn.ac.uk>

Shannon Rogers: VP: *Book Reviews* Page Director
<srogers@sju.edu >

Robert Schweik: VP: *Syllabi* Page Director/ MRR – *Checklist* Page Director
<schweik@fredonia.edu>

Rosemary Sumner: VP:

Dennis Taylor: VP: *Poetry Consultant*<Taylor@bc.edu>

Keith Wilson: VP: *Drama* Page Director
<Kgwilson@uottawa.ca>

Ling Zhang: VP
China Consultant

Thomas Hardy
A Bibliographical Study

by Richard L. Purdy
edited by
Charles P. C. Pettit

This work brings the 1954 first edition **up-to-date** with over **five decades of new bibliographical reference additions** all contained in a new two-part supplement.

The first part guides the reader through the mass of material published on Hardy in recent decades by providing an annotated bibliography of key works that expand or update the information supplied by Purdy. The second part draws upon the contributions of a number of Hardy scholars in identifying errors in the book as originally published and significant bibliographical information that has become available since that time.

Co-published with The British Library.

2002, hardcover, 6" x 9", 432 pages, illustrated
ISBN 1-58456-070-3 **Order No. 69934-TH2**
~~Price $65.00~~ **Discount to members Price $57.50**
Sales Rights: Worldwide except UK. Available in UK
from The British Library.

To Order:
Oak Knoll Press 310 Delaware St, New Castle, DE 19720
800-996-2556 or 302-328-7232 Fax: 302-328-7274
email: oakknoll@oakknoll.com web: www.oakknoll.com

The Hardy Review

Volume VI   Winter 2003

THE HARDY REVIEW

EDITED BY

ROSEMARIE MORGAN

THE HARDY ASSOCIATION PRESS
ISBN 0-9669176-9-3

First published in the United States in 2003
by The Hardy Association Press
124 Bishop Street, New Haven, CT 06511

© Copyright for the collection is retained by the Hardy Association Press. Copyright for individual essays is retained by the author.

All rights reserved. No part of this publication
may be reproduced, stored in a retrieval system,
or transmitted in any form or by any means,
electronic, mechanical, photocopying,
recording or otherwise without the
prior permission of the Copyright holders.

ISBN 0-9669176-9-3

Typesetting & cover design by Rosemarie Morgan.
Designed and originated in-house.
Printed by Goodcopy Inc, New Haven

THE THOMAS HARDY ASSOCIATION

PRESIDENT:
ROSEMARIE MORGAN
www.yale.edu/hardysoc

EDITORIAL BOARD

James Gibson — Ex-Christchurch, Canterbury
William W. Morgan — Illinois State University
Richard Nemesvari — St Francis Xavier University
Rosemarie Morgan — Yale University
Robert Schweik — SUNY at Fredonia
Linda Peterson — Yale University
Keith Wilson — University of Ottawa
Martin Ray — Aberdeen University

THE THOMAS HARDY ASSOCIATION
IS SUPPORTED BY:

Yale University, Connecticut.
University of Ottawa, Ontario.
Illinois State University, Illinois.
State University of New York, at Fredonia.
California State University, at San Marcos.
St. Francis Xavier University, Nova Scotia.
Saint Joseph's University, Philadelphia.
University of Aberdeen, Scotland.
St Andrews University, Scotland.

GRATEFUL THANKS TO
EACH AND EVERY
SUPPORTING
INSTITUTION

THE THOMAS HARDY ASSSOCIATION
WAS FOUNDED IN:

1997 to promote the study and appreciation of Hardy's work in every corner of the world. Both its organising principle and its membership reflect this global character. TTHA is governed by an international team of world-class scholars (voluntary) — all are members of its Council of Honorary Vice Presidents and Board of Directors. Together they maintain a website with over a dozen different departments focusing on Hardy's life and work while also providing over 300 site evaluations, each of interest to Hardy lovers everywhere.

THE HARDY REVIEW
Editor: Rosemarie Morgan

Volume VI   Winter 2003

Copyright is retained by TTHA. Individual items will not be reproduced without the author's permission. Contributors may reclaim their work for inclusion in book publication

CONTENTS

List of Illustrations. ... ii

Editor's Column. ... iii

TTHA FORUM DISCUSSION GROUP : -   1

- *The Well-Beloved* – A Tragedy?   2
- Defining Genre.   8
- Arabella's Satiric Role.   19

An Overview of TTHA *Life* page.   24

TTHA MEMBERS' RESEARCH RESOURCES : -

- An Overview of TTHA's *Checklist.*.   27
- An Overview of TTHA's *Reviews* page.   35

TTHA POEM OF THE MONTH DISCUSSION GROUP : -

- "Winter Night in Woodland."   50
- "Ice on the Highway."   52
- "A Light Snow-Fall after Frost."   55
- "The Sheep-Boy."   58
- "A Sheep-Fair" and "Last Look round St. Martin's Fair."   61
- "A Backward Spring."   64
- "Shortening Days at the Homestead" and "Last Week in October."   65
- "No Buyers" and "An East-End Curate."   72
- "Life and Death at Sunrise."   77

TTHA NOTES AND QUERIES : -

- Canford Manor Frieze   83
- St Juliot   86
- The Wordworth Edition   91

A Hardy Hymn, Rosemarie Morgan.   93

Poems by Betty Cortus, "Sea Creatures," "Aeschynomene."   97

Poem by Isobel Robin, "Been There, Donne That."   98

Poem by Bill Morgan, "Winter Journal."   98

The Bodleian Manuscript of *Poems of the Past and the Present*, Martin Ray.   99

Chess and Social Game Playing in *A Pair of Blue Eyes*, Glen Downey.   105

Notes on Contributors.   147

TTHA Membership Information.   150

TTHA Publications.   151

TTHA Directors and Vice Presidents   152

ILLUSTRATIONS

Thomas Hardy, by Max Beerbohm.	10
"St George and the Dragon": Melodrama in the Pub.	17
Jude the Obscure: "See How He's Served Me!"	23
Thomas Hardy, by G. Grenville Manton	33
The Dynasts – Programme Cover.	49
Assyrian Frieze.	85
St. Juliot Memorial Window, by Simon Whistler.	86
"To Thee Whose Eye All Nature Owns."	96
A Pair of Blue Eyes: On the Cliffs.	146

EDITOR'S COLUMN

ROSEMARIE MORGAN

WELCOME to the sixth volume in The Thomas Hardy Association's annual series: *The Hardy Review*. Since we are confined, in this publication, to offering but a tiny sample of TTHA's continually developing online resources[1] I'll try to match selectivity with brevity in conveying something of the past year's *offline* activities.

As we approach the first anniversary, in April, of the inauguration at Milner Library (ILSTU), of TTHA's Collection of Early Hardy Criticism, Bill Morgan and I are proud to announce that, thanks to the generosity of donors, worldwide, we now have 80 books in the Collection – a Collection initiated this time last year with two dozen contributions. This is a noteworthy achievement and is characteristic, I think, of the pride and joy Hardyans take in supporting a philanthropic enterprise of this kind.[2]

Likewise, the enthusiasm for the joint enterprise – hosted by TTHA and the Hardy Society – of a mini-conference entitled "Hardy in Cambridge" at Magdalene College in July, 2003. "Cambridge" was not only a significant and highly successful first for our two Hardy organisations but was also, for the bard himself, a major event in his personal history. The "Jude" of frustrated ambitions and torn dreams whose self-castigating last words swore that there would be no "light given to him that is in misery," no "life unto the bitter in soul," revived and reversed in his creator later when he was awarded an

---

[1] The "Overviews" presented in this *Review* are self-explanatory and need no introduction. For further details and membership information see TTHA's online resources at: http://www.yale.edu/hardysoc/Welcome/welcomet.htm.

[2] For full details see http://www.yale.edu/hardysoc/Welcome/COLLECTION.htm

honorary degree by Cambridge University in 1913. Hardy had found *his* Christminster! Indeed, once gained it was so deeply cherished by Hardy that he couldn't spend enough time there: "How I wish I could be often at dear old Magdalene," he lamented to his devoted Cambridge friend, Arthur Christopher Benson.[5]

Magdalene was indeed an enchanting venue and the only complaints we had from conferees were that it was over far too soon. TTHA is currently planning its next conference to take place at Yale University in 2007. Progress reports for this event will be regularly posted on TTHA's ***News*** page and also on the ***Forum***. See ***News Updates*** at: http://www.yale.edu/hardysoc/updates.htm; also the ***Forum,*** at: http://www.yale.edu/hardysoc/Welcome/Forum/forum.htm.

Among other future projects: a series of CDRoms is being planned which will expand upon those already published by TTHA – compiled and edited by Martin Ray. Currently, a *Complete Poems* concordance[3] on CDRom is issued free to members and a *Life* "Allusions" concordance on CDRom is available at half-price to members.[4] *The Dynasts*, The Short Stories and *Jude the Obscure* have been added to the list and an online ***Concordance*** page, for taking orders on TTHA's website, is being designed as we go to press. TTHA is deeply indebted to Martin Ray for producing the concordances and to Shannon Rogers for burning and distributing them.

I suppose ultimately the Association's success is measured by the number of graduate students who have found the online research resources and discussion groups indispensable to their studies. For every paid-up student-member of the Association – those who most generously support the cause by digging into scant pockets – there are hundreds who lurk, and often contribute to, TTHA's discussion groups, the ***Forum*** (see pp 1-23), and ***POTM*** (see pp 50-82). According to the Yale Log several thousand visitors regularly haunt TTHA's electronic ivory towers; especially popular are ***Wessex Maps***, the ***Links*** pages, the ***Novels*** page, the ***Drama*** page, the ***Short Stories*** page, and the ***Life*** page. These visitors remain, unfortunately, faceless and anonymous. So it was with great pleasure that, this month, we received several letters out of the blue from graduate students who not only told of their success in gaining their higher degrees but also their gratitude to TTHA in so doing. This was an unexpected delight: the real world and the virtual are in fact one, after all!

---

[5] See also: http://www.yale.edu/hardysoc/magdalen.htm

[3] Order forms at: http://www.yale.edu/hardysoc/Welcome/orderf.htm

[4] Order forms at: http://www.yale.edu/hardysoc/Welcome/Allusions.html

This is of course the purpose, also, of *The Hardy Review* – bringing the "virtual" (a tiny portion of it) into physical form. A sample of **Forum** threads begins the volume (1-23), followed by an Overview of the **Life** page (24-26), a selection of items from **Members' Research Resources** (27-49), and **The Poem of the Month** debates (50-82). **Notes and Queries** concludes the converse section (83-96). The second half of the volume presents poems by Betty Cortus, Isobel Robin (which, despite my reassurances that Hardy is nothing if not eclectic, she fears may be too light-hearted for a scholarly journal), and Bill Morgan (97-98). Martin Ray contributes a research article on Samuel Hynes' transcriptions in *The Complete Poetical Works of Thomas Hardy* (99-104), and in place of the customary essay section Glen Downey presents a double-decker essay on the chess motif in *A Pair of Blue Eyes* (105-146).

A NOTE ON THE TEXT

In keeping with my previous editorial practice with *The Hardy Review* I have tried to preserve the spontaneity and vigour of the original online conversations while at the same time ensuring the linear clarity expected of edited scholarly writing. In my efforts to reconcile these somewhat conflicting ends I have corrected commonplace errors of spelling and punctuation, clarified the documentation if and where necessary and, occasionally, restructured the online dialogues in the interests of coherency and linearity (frequently, several online topics will be running at once; similarly, several voices might cross one another). I have retained, as far as possible, the "voice" and style of individual speakers, including their abbreviations, contractions, and symbols; it is not my wish or intention to render uniform the style and content of free self-expression. On the contrary, it is precisely the preservation of that quality of spontaneity, informality, open confrontation and impromptu response, characteristic of online debates, that distinguishes *The Hardy Review* as an organ promoting a unique form of seminar rarely to be found elsewhere. To enhance these qualities longwinded or repetitious material has been pruned: this is marked in the text by means of ellipses.

In bringing this annual number together I have kept in mind, at all times, that first and foremost ours is a celebration of Thomas Hardy and of those of his followers who so treasure his literary endowment that they are prepared to give freely of their time, and generously of their scholarly expertise – in trust and appreciation, to TTHA.[10]

---

[10] I am deeply indebted to Martin Ray for giving of his time and energy to proofreading; if errors there be, they are mine alone.

THE THOMAS HARDY ASSOCIATION: FORUM DISCUSSION GROUP[1]

OVERVIEW OF TTHA FORUM

AS THE OVERARCHING theme of the following Forum discussion is genre and its application to literature and other art forms, it might make for a diverting exercise to try to categorize a new writing form – a descendent of traditional literary criticism – the "electronic discussion" itself. On a spectrum of genres it could be viewed as occupying a space somewhere between the kind of formal criticism published in books and essays and the more casual kinds of discussions taking place in a classroom. Forum discussions do have much of the spontaneity, the tendency to digress, and general shapelessness of the latter, but, in common with more formal criticism, they allow participants at least a little time to make a considered response, to check references, and to take a quick glance over their comments before posting them. The three discussions which follow fit comfortably into this "in-between" niche – their sometimes off-the-cuff informal tone is always counterbalanced by content that is both thought-provoking and scholarly.

Beginning with comments on Hardy's skilful, tradition-breaking manipulation of genre, the discussion moves on to compare genre's impact on forms other than literature – film, stage, and the plastic arts. A discussion of melodrama, and its influence on nineteenth-century sensation fiction ensues.

The most challenging and lively Forum discussions almost invariably begin, as do these three, with a question. It is the generous way in which members respond, drawing on their insights, imagination, and above all their scholarly knowledge, that makes these discussions well worth plucking out of the ephemeral world of "cyber-talk" and preserving in print.

Betty Cortus
Forum Director
hardycor@owl.csusm.edu

---

[1] http://www.yale.edu/hardysoc/Welcome/Forum/forum.htm

THE WELL-BELOVED – **A TRAGEDY?**
May 12th – 15th 2003

Monday, 12 May 2003 16:53:29 -0400
ROBERT SCHWEIK <schweikr@localnet.com>
Subject: *The Well-Beloved* as Tragedy

A recent – in fact as yet not formally published – book on Hardy has this in its blurb: "an original and groundbreaking re-reading of Hardy's four major tragic novels." The novels treated are *The Mayor of Casterbridge*, *Tess*, *Jude*, and *The Well-Beloved*. The publisher is Palgrave. That someone would consider *The Well-Beloved* one of Hardy's "major tragic novels" seemed to me so odd I thought I'd call it to the attention of the Forum. Is there some case to be made for regarding this work as one of Hardy's "major tragic novels"? – Bob.

Monday, 12 May 2003 22:45:05 +0100
ROB ABBOTT <hobacus@clara.co.uk>
Subject: *The Well-Beloved*

I wouldn't want to argue that *The Well-Beloved* was by any means a major novel but I think that that nonetheless it is an interesting one. It does in many ways prefigure many of the changes in literary form that occurred a few years later in the works of writers such as Joyce and Woolf. It is a difficult novel to enjoy as it is neither possible to read it as a realist novel nor as a modernist text. While it does subscribe on one level to the conventions of mimetic realism it also contains elements that are recognisably modernist. Hillis Miller's essay on *Fiction and Repetition* is particularly interesting in what it says on this score. To take just a small example from the opening of the novel:

> A person who differed from the local wayfarers was climbing the steep road which leads through the sea-skirted townlet definable as the Street of Wells, and forms a pass into that Gibraltar of Wessex, the singular peninsula once an island, and still called such, that stretches out like the head of a bird into the English Channel. It is connected with the mainland by a long thin neck of pebbles 'cast up by rages of the sea,' and unparalleled in its kind in Europe (9).

This seems to be on the surface at least the language of mimetic realism. A man climbs a road, enters a town that leads onto an island peninsula. The details of the island's physical construction are laid out for us in linear form (road, townlet, pass, peninsula, island, channel, mainland, pebbles). This is a "wandering viewpoint" that picks out, on the surface at least, a succession of signifiers each relating to a recognisable "familiar" signified. It seems to be the language of mimetic realism in which the cumulative effect of selection and combination of details provides a simplistic reckoning of the novel's setting. Yet the first paragraph also contains five explicit metaphors: the townlet is "sea-skirted"; the island is "that Gibraltar of Wessex"; the singular peninsula "stretches out like the head of a bird into the English Channel"; the raised pebble beach that leads to it has "a long thin neck of pebbles"; these have been "cast up by rages of the sea." This last metaphor is yet further removed from the language of mimemetic realism by being an extract from a sixteenth century journal.

There is also the synecdochal use of terms such as "wayfarers," "Street of Wells," and the metonymical connection between the real Portland and the fictional Isle of Slingers. The more carefully you read the text the more confusing it all becomes. We seem to leap from one metaphor to the next and in the midst of this we lose sight of the figure whose progress we are ostensibly following. This evasiveness of language continues into the second paragraph:

> The pedestrian was what he looked like – a young man from London and the cities of the Continent. Nobody could see at present that his urbanism sat upon him only as a garment.

Looked at closely it is obvious that the two sentences plainly contradict one another. How can he be "what he looked like" when no one (other, that is, than the narrative voice) can see that his urban appearance is only artifice. In a story that is all about appearance, reality, and perspective and these three never quite aligning, I think the opening few pages set the scene both linguistically and thematically for events later in the novel. – Rob

Monday, 12 May 2003 20:41:20 -0500
CHARLES ANESI <Charles.Anesi@wellsfargo.com>
Subject: *The Well-Beloved*

Rob Abbott wrote:
> How can he be 'what he looked like' when no one (other, that is, than the narrative voice) can see that his urban appearance is only artifice.

I don't follow your argument. Are you saying that if no one could perceive that his urban appearance was only a "garment", then he could not be a young man from London and the cities of the continent? I read the two sentences to say that the young man came recently from London and the cities of the continent, and looked like it, but was still an Islander at heart. I don't see any contradiction or evasion. For me, *The Well-Beloved* was another treatment of The Eternal Feminine and the power She has over men of artistic temperament, Thomas Hardy included. Because an abstraction is incapable of returning love, the man who is in love with an abstraction will never find his love requited. This may be unfortunate and painful, but the consequences are not dire enough (in my opinion) to make it tragic. – Chuck

Tuesday, 13 May 2003 12:27:25 -0300
RICHARD NEMESVARI <rnemesva@stfx.ca>
Subject: *The Well-Beloved* as Tragedy

I have to agree with Bob that the characterization of *The Well-Beloved* as one of Hardy's "four major tragic novels" is decidedly odd. That oddness starts with the apparent exclusion of *The Woodlanders* from the group, since in my opinion it is decidedly both *more* major and considerably *more* tragic. I agree with Rob Abbot that *The Well-Beloved* is an interesting novel worthy of study, and there is undoubtedly something problematic about the assignment of "major" and "minor" labels to texts, tempting as that kind of rating system sometimes is. Nonetheless, to suggest that it is as successful an artistic realization as *Mayor*, *Tess*, or *Jude* strikes me as verging on indefensible.

The question of tragedy becomes more difficult, since it enters the notoriously tricky area of genre definition, although I think it is telling that Hardy classifies *The Well-Beloved* as one of his "Romances and Fantasies" in the 1912 General Preface. None of Hardy's tragedies are purely Aristotelian, but they obviously partake of some of the ideas in the *Poetics*, which I don't see happening in *The Well-Beloved* at all. Most obviously, there doesn't seem to be any kind of catharsis. Where is "pity and fear" provoked in the reader through Pierston's experience? His designation through the novel's various parts as "A Young Man of Twenty," "A Young Man of Forty," and "A Young Man of Sixty" suggests a failure of maturation and development which precludes the tragic stature achieved by Henchard, Tess, Jude, or, for that matter, Giles Winterborne.

If I was going to assign a generic category to *The Well-Beloved* I would describe it as a satire, the exploration of a temperament which is exposed as flawed in ways which create an ironic distance between character and audience, and that prevents the intense identification required by tragedy. That Hardy perhaps saw certain elements of

Pierston in himself doesn't prevent such a reading, since self-satire is hardly beyond his range.

The Well-Beloved is no more and no less "autobiographical" than, say *Jude the Obscure*; that is, it is an artistic transformation of authorial experience, and biographical information (or disinformation) can't be used in any significant way to "explain" the text. I don't think *The Well-Beloved* meets the characteristics of generic tragedy, however broadly defined, although I suppose I reserve the right to be convinced otherwise should the book Bob refers to produce a strong argument. In the meantime, the cover blurb seems more than a little questionable –. Richard

Tuesday, 13 May 2003 14:36:44 -0400
ROBERT SCHWEIK <schweikr@localnet.com>
Subject: *The Well-Beloved* as Major Tragedy

I've been asked to identify the book to which I referred. Here's the TTHA Member's Research Resources "Checklist" entry:
> Musselwhite, David E. *Social Transformation in Hardy's Tragic Novels: Megamachines and Phantasms.* New York: Palgrave Macmillan, 2003. [Listed in the Palgrave catalogue on 12 May 2003 as scheduled for publication in October 2003.]

Palgrave blurb reads:
> Drawing on the theoretical work of Deleuze and Guattari and that of Jean Laplanche – particularly his major and as yet still relatively unfamiliar notion of the phantasme – *Social Transformation in Hardy's Tragic Novels* is an original and groundbreaking rereading of Hardy's four major tragic novels …The theoretical work is complemented by the use of new and hitherto unregarded major empirical findings that reveal the very heart of Hardy's creative universe.

Table of contents:
> "Preface"
> "Introduction"
> "The Interrupted Return"
> "The Exploding Body in *The Mayor of Casterbridge*"
> "*Tess of the D'Urbervilles* [sic]: 'a becoming woman'"
> "Tess: The phantasmatic capture"
> "Retranslating *Jude the Obscure* I"
> "Traversing *The Well-Beloved*"
> "Retranslating *Jude the Obscure* II"
> "Notes"
> "Bibliography"

I hope this might put the author's claims about *The Well-Beloved* in some usefully revealing context. I confess to being entirely ignorant of the writings of Jean Laplanche. Perhaps someone on Hardy-L might be able to provide some information about that theorist. But I wait in anticipation for those "new and hitherto unregarded major empirical findings that reveal the very heart of Hardy's creative universe." – Bob

Tuesday, 13 May 2003 16:23:06 -0300
RICHARD NEMESVARI <rnemesva@stfx.ca>
Subject: *The Well-Beloved* as Major Tragedy

Thanks to Bob for providing the Palgrave description of *Social Transformation in Hardy's Tragic Novels: Megamachines and Phantasms.* The concept of "megamachines" is linked to Deleuze and Guattari, while, as stated, "phantasme" is apparently an idea of Laplanche's (although I'm not familiar with it). If anybody is interested in brief outlines of these theorists, see:

> Deleuze and Guattari:
> http://130.179.92.25/Arnason_DE/Deleuze.html
>
> Laplanche:
> http://www.l-w-bks.co.uk/journals/newformation/
> updatepages/currentnewform.html#sum

Delueze and Guattari are post-Marxist, post-Freudians, while Laplanche is a Lacanian psychoanalytic critic. How these three are going to be reconciled should prove interesting. And as far as my previous posting is concerned, I doubt anything as mundane as considerations of Hardy and genre is going to receive much space in the text. – Richard

Wednesday, 14 May 2003 09:18:09 -0400
ROSEMARIE MORGAN <rosemarie.morgan@yale.edu>
Subject: *The Well-Beloved* as Major Tragedy

Thank you Richard for the useful contacts. The ascriptions of "post-Marxist" and "post-Freudian" are curious to say the least, as applied in the profile at <http://130.179.92.25/Arnason_DE/Deleuze.html>.

It may well be a truism that "The life of any culture is always both collapsing and being restructured" – if one adheres to the Heraclitan school of thought. But that Deleuze and Guattari allow for a "post-Marxist" analysis "without accepting the historical inevitability of the dialectic" is – I would say – not so much "post" Marxist as "anti-" or even "pre-." The historical dialectic provides, after all, the crucible of Marxist thought. It predicates not the "collapse" (as agency) but the antithetical (as agency). Moreover the synthetic (in Marxist thought) indicates not so much a restructuring (of the culture) but, more precisely, a production of (social) compounds from their constituent parts. I searched for evidence, in the above synopsis on:

http://130.179.92.25/Arnason_DE/Deleuze.htm

(which may itself be antithetical), for "post" Marxist thought – "post" as in "later," or "occurring or existing after the fact" – but only found a return to the age-old anti-Parmenidean theory of social and cultural change. All of which suggests, as Bob and Richard have both maintained, that there may be almost nothing of Hardy in this discourse! – Cheers, Rosemarie.

Wednesday, 14 May 2003 15:57:33 -0300
RICHARD NEMESVARI <rnemesva@stfx.ca>
Subject: Re: *The Well-Beloved* as Major Tragedy

I agree with the entirety of what Rosemarie says. Unfortunately, it becomes difficult to describe the kind of theorizing done by Deleuze and Guattari, since they are clearly "cherry-picking" certain aspects of Marxist theory, while at the same time denying central aspects of that same theory. And they're doing something similar with Freud. Thus they are "post" in the sense of "coming after," but I'm not sure they can be called completely "anti," because they have accepted what they see as those elements which haven't been "disproven" by history (i.e., in their opinion, the existence of dialectical materialism). This is what I often find irritating about so-called "post-feminist" readings, which often employ feminist concepts to produce what look awfully like patriarchal readings.

Laplanche, on the other hand, because of his Lacanian focus, is still in the direct line of Freud, despite Lacan's elaborations / modifications on the Freudian model.

And just to bring this back to Hardy. I feel these approaches may have something useful to say about TH (although I'll wait to read the book to say that for sure), but the problem may be that the text will ignore foundational issues such as genre, and Hardy's approach to it, and go straight for the theoretical jugular. On the other hand, it may be that the "blurb" is typical of its kind, and is evoking what it thinks will sell the book (Hardy's "major tragic novels") while the author has completely different fish to fry. We'll see. Definitely a candidate for the Review Page! – Richard

Wedneday, 14 May 2003 22:26:08 -0400
ROSEMARIE MORGAN <rosemarie.morgan@yale.edu>
Subject: *The Well-Beloved* as Major Tragedy

Richard Nemesvari wrote:
> This is what I often find irritating about so-called 'post-feminist' readings, which often employ feminist concepts to produce what look awfully like patriarchal readings.

Bravo Richard! I'm with you 100% on this (some of the essays in Higonnet's *Sense of Sex* veer irritatingly in this direction) – Cheers, R.

Thursday, 15 May 2003 13:30:40 -0700
PHILIP GOLDSTEIN <lesl@uclink.berkeley.edu>
Subject: *The Well-Beloved* as Major Tragedy

Here is my first or second comment in the four or five years that I have been on the list: Isn't Peter Widdowson a kind of post-Marxist whose "Hardy in History" and other essays on Hardy recuperate a "genuine" Hardy – anti-realist, anti-humanist – from the conventional humanist realism. Widdowson says critics restate humanist realist views of Hardy as a flawed artist who still manages to be great. Either Widdowson or Eagleton shows that what critics call his minor flawed works, including *The Woodlanders* and *The Well-Beloved*, I think, experiment with a modernist sort of absurdist fiction. – Philip

DEFINING GENRE
IN HARDY'S IMAGINATIVE LITERATURE
May 16th – 20th 2003

Friday, 16 May 2003 03:49:42 +0100
MICHAEL BARRY <michaelj.barry@talk21.com>
Subject: Genre

Richard mentioned genre and that it was "foundational". I'd love to hear more. I am, however, non-academic and unskilled in literary criticism, not least in genre study. But my (partial) reading of Hardy's works has thrown up in my mind the fact that he does make occasional forays into genres different from his "main one." I don't know what to call them but how about: Tragedy, Informed by Naturalism and Lyricism and Driven by Social Criticism as his "main" or preferred genre (I suspect already this may be limiting the "major" works and that a more all-encompassing genre description is available?).

However then we have (in my reading experience) the lovely *Under the Greenwood Tree*, which might be: Romantic Comedy, Spiced with a Strong Thread of Irony and Visual Comic Timing (unique in his work?). Then there is one short story (from memory), "The Honourable Laura", which seemed to stand out from the rest as unadulterated Victorian melodrama. *The Hand of Ethelberta* maintains, I suspect, the social criticism, especially of the class structure, but doesn't qualify as either tragedy or romantic comedy. Maybe it's a Romance?

I'm running out of steam here! The questions are I guess: is Hardy known as a Master of Genre? Does he have a "main" preferred genre? Are the others one-off writing exercises for him? Are they considered successful? And what are these genres "officially" called? Can anyone enlighten me? – With thanks, Michael B

Friday, 16 May 2003 13:13:00 -0400
ROSEMARIE MORGAN <rosemarie.morgan@yale.edu>
Subject: Genre

Given that Hardy is a literary genre-crosser (the mixing of genres was discouraged – forbidden, even, before the eighteenth century), his prose works are particularly difficult to categorise. Genre classifications are, traditionally, prose /poem /fiction /drama /lyric /pastoral /satire within which there are sub-genres in the novel such as Picaresque, Gothic, the Sentimental novel etc.

Contemporary critics took Hardy's early novels such as *Under the Greenwood tree* and *Far From the Madding Crowd* to be pastoral novels and given the extensions (as provided by William Empson) which allow for inclusions of works that cloak complexity in simple guises this may be good for standardizing purposes. But it is far too general for analytical studies. Indeed, the recent (historically speaking) development of the novel has complicated the whole notion of genre and the conventions traditionally accorded to genre categories.

Ludwig Wittgenstein thought of genre in terms of "family resemblances." This offers, I think, a useful starting point in approaching what is arguably a set of loose and arbitrary categorisations.

Hope this helps – Cheers, Rosemarie.

THOMAS HARDY by MAX BEERBOHM, *Fifty Caricatures*, 1913.

Friday, 16 May 2003 10:02:00 +0100
MICHAEL BARRY <michaelj.barry@talk21.com>
Subject: Genre

Mmmm! Thanks Rosemarie, helpful I think, but some serious digestion is called for, I guess ("Picaresque" – where's my dictionary) ! Judicious "crossing of genres" is nowadays supposedly the name of the game for getting a film-script done, but modern film genres are obviously in a different league with the likes of Hardy being consigned to "arthouse"! I doubt that Hardy would recognize Slasher as a sub-genre of Horror – on the other hand Shelley & Co might include it under Gothic.

Then there's Polonius with genre-crossing and "historical-pastoral-comical"-whatever. Your reference to "recent development of the novel": is this later than Fielding? I suspect *Tom Jones* either includes a number of genres or is bundled up in "epic" perhaps – if only by length?

It's not high enough on my priority list to be able to track down and read a serious work, but has anyone done a simple Dictionary or Bluffer's Guide to genre? It would be a useful handbook to have around, and help a layperson such as me to be more aware of essential ingredients (or as you say "family resemblances"). In modern film scripting theory, genre is there to feed audience expectations and therefore to be acceptable, ie "publishable." Shakespeare too is usually categorized into his own genres – so too, I guess, were the Greeks and Romans with their drama.

Thanks again and best wishes – Michael B

Friday, 16 May 2003 16:12:06 -0300
RICHARD NEMESVARI <rnemesva@stfx.ca>
Subject: Genre

Since I'm the one who described genre as "foundational" for Hardy, I'll take the opportunity to respond to Michael Barry's posting.

I would say that Michael's list of Hardy's potential genres is certainly valid, but for me the bigger issue is his manipulation of form. That is, his fiction provides a heterogeneous mixing of genre which in itself destabilizes reader response, and therefore acts to subvert status quo assumptions and reactions. If Hardy is a "master" of genre it is because he knows how to effectively break the "rules" which supposedly delineate tragedy, comedy, romance, pastoral, realism, melodrama, sensationalism, satire, history, and didacticism (to name a few) in ways which disrupt his audience's comfortable belief in the established literary/social order.

For Henry James such a lack of unity demonstrated Hardy's flawed association with the "loose baggy monsters" of Victorian fiction. Of course I would argue that James mischaracterizes as a weakness what was in fact an effective rhetorical device that foreshadows modernist fragmentations and disjunctions, especially in later novels such as *Tess* and *Jude*. I would also say, however, that this approach can be seen in earlier texts as well, and also in the so-called minor novels, which is why it is important to acknowledge them. So when the blurb Bob quoted describes a critical work as dealing with Hardy's "four major tragic novels," I start to worry that issues which are themselves profoundly complex are about to get ignored out of existence. To describe *The Mayor of Casterbridge* and *The Well-Beloved* as inhabiting the same generic category without recognizing that such a position needs to be demonstrated, not just asserted (because everybody knows Hardy writes tragedies), and without recognizing that that demonstration will necessarily become involved with Hardy's refusal to provide "pure" fictional forms in any instance, is a recipe for trouble. But as I said in an earlier posting, this may just be blurb writer's enthusiasm.

Hardy is "playful" with genre (makes it a game, puts it into the play of meaning), a quality which got him into no end of trouble with Victorian reviewers who tried throughout his entire career to pigeonhole him and thus contain him. And the whole issue became further exacerbated when he began publishing his poetry. If anybody can provide a clear-cut genre definition of *The Dynasts*, well, you're a better man than I am Gunga Din (to quote an almost-equally-famous contemporary).

For Hardy questions of genre are crucial to his relationship with his readers and to his creative method, which is why I call them foundational. Hope this has been of some help.— Richard.

Friday, 16 May 2003 16:01:40 -0400
ROSEMARIE MORGAN <rosemarie.morgan@yale.edu>
Subject: Genre

Michael, I am very interested in film and have followed with keen curiosity the way in which cinematographic artists can successfully straddle genre-crossing (in the visual narrative) when dealing with such subversive writers as Dickens and Hardy both of whom make untoward switches from melodrama to psychological realism almost in the same breath.

Some of our generation (in contrast to our *Commedia dell'arte* great-great grandparents), are embarrassed by melodrama and it is this generational difference that interests me from a psychoanalytical point of view. So elegantly did the movie *Barry Lyndon* employ purist-style Constable settings – "Constable" in chiaroscuro and landscape-form – that there was small chance an anti-melodrama critic could have griped; equally your own cited *Tom Jones* – surely Fielding would have smiled at such subtle toning-down of his melodramatic art!

For good, balanced, traditional, critical theory on such issues as genre Northrop Frye's *Anatomy of Criticism* is matchless, followed by Wellek and Warren's *Theory of Literature* which provides some very useful distinctions between "outer" and "inner" forms of genre – R.

Friday, 16 May 2003 13:32:26 -0700
BETTY CORTUS <hardycor@owl.csusm.edu>
Subject: Genre

I agree entirely with Richard about Hardy's mastery of art of manipulating genre "in ways which disrupt his audience's comfortable belief in the established literary/social order." I am thinking particularly of the lighter novels which, after a conventional network of archetypal elements, lead the reader to expect the conventional happy ending of comedy and romance, usually involving a marriage, but invariably spring an ironic twist at the end which utterly shakes up and controverts the reader's expectations. The heroine may wind up marrying the wrong man (*The Trumpet-Major*), or she may marry for the wrong reasons (*The Hand of Ethelberta*), or marry the right man then have regrets about it (*A Laodicean*), or even drop dead because of too sudden joy after despair (*Two on a Tower*). Richard's characterization of this kind of generic manipulation as "an effective rhetorical device that fore-shadows modernist fragmentations and disjunctions," sounds convincing to me . – Betty

Monday, 19 May 2003 01:42:43 +0100
MICHAEL BARRY <michaelj.barry@talk21.com>
Subject: Genre

Thank-you Rosemarie and Richard – as always the picture is deeper and denser than one would like for instant appreciation, but then that's the fundamental attraction of the more worthwhile acts of man-made creation – whether genre theory or the works of TH!

Rosemarie's concern over the gap between realism and melodrama is a fascinating one and I guess one that is much open to differences in definition – perhaps even generational differences? My theatre perspective has long ago led me to consider melodrama as an "empty over-playing" in which form surpasses (not "transcends" I think!) content – and is in practical terms largely a concern of acting (and an on-going concern for me as director) – as it always seems important to me to ensure that the expression of a work's emotional life is at the fullest flood that the content of it will believably carry, but no further. If the expression increases without the motive power of the content, then an empty, formal, "hammy", overdone result can become laughable at worst, but at the least will destroy belief in the reality of a scene, or event, or relationship exchange. Now I guess there is an approximate literary equivalent of this – you mention Dickens – there is in *Pickwick Papers*, out of the blue, "A Madman's Manuscript", which shouted "melodrama" to me in terms of my definition – likewise (for slightly different reasons – viz cast of characters and sequence of actions and weather and setting) TH's "The Honourable Laura". Is it that modern generations are less aware of the Victorian tradition of acting and writing? I was there when 1956 gave birth to *Look Back in Anger* – though clearly there were increasing attempts to provide realism in acting from the first WW onwards. But apropos Hardy – apart from the one short story I mentioned, I've not registered melodrama as I understand it – quite possibly a lack of perception or a difference of definition on my part?

There must always be a danger of limiting your audience if you don't identify with genre – as people (by and large!) like to have life pre-digested for them – and to know in advance what they are getting for their money rather than supporting an "experiment". My theatre company can get excellent audiences for *Tess* which it can never get for modern writers – audiences know *Tess* and *Tom Jones* – they are "safe" to invest ticket money in!

Thanks for the book tips – I'll see if Somerset's library system can come up with them! – Cheers, Michael

Monday, 19 May 2003 14:51:28 -0300
RICHARD NEMESVARI <rnemesva@stfx.ca>
Subject: Genre

Just a quick response to Michael's message, since it touches on a few things I'm dealing with in my research. Within the theatrical community melodrama is mostly, as Michael notes, associated with a certain style of acting which, in its emphasis on "non-realistic" overstatement of emotion, is largely out of fashion. It is well to remember, however, that as a form it was *the* dominant mode of drama for much of the Victorian period, including presentations of Shakespeare, and that it therefore quickly developed a series of generic "characteristics" which became available for incorporation into novels. It is no coincidence that Dickens plays a major role in this, or that his melodrama *The Frozen Deep* (1857 – co-written with Wilkie Collins) has its central relationship transported pretty much wholesale into *A Tale of Two Cities* (1859). The most significant example of this was the rise of sensation fiction in the 1860s, which overtly utilized melodramatic situations and characters, and created a decade-long furor as reviewers did their best to repel what they saw as the "corruption" of fiction. It is worth remembering that Hardy was in London during the height of this debate, and had plenty of opportunity to follow the controversy and attend the theatre.

Keith Wilson is obviously much more qualified than I am to comment on Hardy and the theatre, but I think there can be no doubt that Hardy was influenced by what might be called the "melodramatic" qualities which existed both in Dorset folklore (see "The Withered Arm" and "The Fiddler of the Reels") and in contemporary theatrical productions. For a somewhat dated but still useful analysis of this aesthetic, see Peter Brooks' *The Melodramatic Imagination: Balzac, Henry James, Melodrama, and the Mode of Excess* (1975).

And just to provide two fairly obvious examples, both *Desperate Remedies* and *Tess of the d'Urbervilles* employ melodramatic villains. The "organ scene" in *Desperate Remedies*, with its bolts of lightning crashing down as Aeneas Manston pounds out his stirring music is almost a parody, while several reviewers of *Tess* called attention to Alec d'Urberville's obvious connection to any number of mustache-twirling seducers of the stage. That these characters appear at the beginning and the end of Hardy's career as a novelist suggests his resistance to "pure" realism was a consistent one. – Richard

Monday, 19 May 2003 01:39:10 +0100
MICHAEL BARRY <michaelj.barry@talk21.com>
Subject: Genre

Thanks for the connection Richard (Victorian theatre melodrama and Hardy) – not a connection I'd registered. And although melodrama is "out of fashion" in acting terms, it's an ongoing basic concern (for me at least) with any production to match acting style or level with the content, whatever that may be. By and large modern actors want to underplay, even to the point of not being clearly heard (too much focus on TV!) – I always try and push them into greater energy and a more full-blooded delivery, acting, myself, as arbiter of when they reach the acceptable limit (if ever – very few of ours do!).

Whilst I haven't personally registered melodrama (in my terms, I guess) in "The Withered Arm" and "The Fiddler of the Reels", I do acknowledge the difficulties of playing Alec in *Tess*. We were criticized in one review for drawing boos and hisses from the audience (only once I think), but did succeed in the main in making him realistic, by having him be (unfairly?) genuinely emotionally dependant on Tess (viz Lolita) and really suffering when he discovers she's married Angel. It may not have lasted, but it certainly goes a long way to eradicating melodramatic qualities in the character. – Cheers, M.B.

Monday, 19 May 2003 23:45:55 -0400
ROSEMARIE MORGAN <rosemarie.morgan@yale.edu>
Subject: Genre

It strikes me, reading your message, Richard, that the 19th century cultural imagination was already so deeply imbued, by the time Hardy arrived at "letters," with notions of an aesthetic elaboration at the most fundamental level of everyday life that it must have made theatrical and literary melodrama appear, at times, quite artless by contrast.

For example, the great elaborator of fashion, Beau Brummel, may have died at around the time Hardy was born but his influence lived on – and not just in the world of *haute couture*. I recall, in my work on *Punch,* that the military came under (was going to say "fire–"– but the pun is too dreadful), a good deal of criticism for sporting overly-ornate uniforms designed (critics said) to please the ladies. And, at a more intimate level, the newly-invented water closet (midcentury) would feature artwork, on the inside of the bowl, of an exotic nature – a cornucopia of succulent fruits here, bowers of tropical flowers there – at which the dandy of the day might unbutton before proceeding to the looking glass where he would wax and tweak his curling moustachios and adjust his delicate fripperies.

Hardy's Alec (to continue Richard's point) and Troy come close to this type of Victorian male and may have differed little, in this respect, from many members of the audience or, rather, readership. Even the stalwart Oak comes in for a little dandyism toward the peak of his career – in his taking over of Boldwood's holdings – at which juncture locals lightly mock him for becoming "quite the dand."

Perhaps it's worth remembering that melodrama had its origin in mime – mime with music. Hence an element of extravagance or over-elaboration, as in the art of miming, is the name of the game. – R.M.

Photograph, courtesy The Beinecke Rare Book and Manuscript Library, Yale University

MELODRAMA IN THE PUB
ST GEORGE AND THE DRAGON - MUMMERS PLAY

Tuesday, 20 May 2003 13:25:38 -0400
KEITH WILSON <kgwilson@uottawa.ca>
Subject: Genre

I shouldn't really be contributing to this discussion (despite Richard Nemesvari's kind tacit invitation to do so), having only just arrived home after an extended period away, during which the e-mail survival tactics I employed ruthlessly at occasional visits to cybercafes caused me to delete large numbers of listserve messages unread, including most of the antecedent postings to this thread. But for what it's worth (and apologies if this goes over ground already covered), it is my sense that the kind of drama in which Hardy had most genuine interest (notwithstanding his readiness to attend many other kinds during his London visits) – namely classical Greek, English blank-verse, and folk – shared certain characteristics with what I gather people have been identifying as the melodramatic proclivities of some aspects of his own work. His comments in the 1903 Preface to *The Dynasts* are particularly suggestive: ruminating on how "plays of poesy and dream" might be rendered on stage, he writes:

> a practicable compromise may conceivably result, taking the shape of a monotonic delivery of speeches, with dreamy conventional gestures, something in the manner traditionally maintained by the old Christmas mummers, the curiously hypnotizing impressiveness of whose automatic style – that of persons who spoke by no will of their own – may be remembered by all who ever experienced it.

The kind of stylization that he is describing here, emphasizing generic convention in gesture and speech-delivery, shares characteristics with melodrama, and is antipathetic to what Hardy saw as the spurious "realism" of the late-Victorian stage, with what he described in "Why I Don't Write Plays" as its

> real and sham-real appurtenances, to the neglect of the principle that the material stage should be a conventional or figurative arena, in which accessories are kept down to the plane of mere suggestions of place and time, so as not to interfere with the required high-relief of the action and emotions.

Melodrama, particularly to a modern audience, may seem to place the action and emotions in such "high-relief" as to become indistinguishable from the parodic or comic. But then modern audiences in every age tend to have unpredictable responses to the popular presentational conventions of the past. I once went to a screening of *Brief Encounter* in which a 1980s student audience were laughing like drains as an earnest Trevor Howard laboriously explained to a starry-eyed Celia Johnson what preventative medicine was, although fortunately by the time the audience had twigged to the fact that this, to them, far-from-moving non-event of an affair was not going to be consummated, they had at least been stunned into incredulous silence. Seemingly (although perhaps it was just a bad night down at the film society), the only aspects of what is arguably regardable as one of the best British films ever made that came through untainted to a young 1980s audience were the comic bits involving Stanley Holloway's chirpy cockney railwayman.

Sorry if all this is entirely irrelevant to the burden of the missed postings. – Keith

ARABELLA'S SATIRIC ROLE?
June 29th – 30th 2003

Sunday 29 Jun 2003 14:17:25 -0400
ROBERT SCHWEIK <schweikr@localnet.com>
Subject: Arabella as "satiric"

Some time ago there was a discussion on the Forum about genres into which Hardy's novels might fit. I have another question which relates to a claim made by Peter Widdowson about Arabella in *Jude*. Arabella, he argues, has a "satiric" role in the novel and cites ways that her critical comments on Sue's and Jude's ideals (and on Phillotson's releasing Sue to return to Jude after his recognition of her repulsion with his sexual advances) provide a "satire" on their ideals.[2]

That, it seems to me, is a misleading way of characterizing Hardy's treatment of the relationship between Jude, Sue, and Arabella. My own sense is, rather, that the stance Hardy takes through his narrator (who does indeed sometimes comment with amused condescension on Jude's ambitions and Sue's aspirations) is a more nuanced one – posing different ways of coping with the human condition against one another, none of which he portrays as satisfactory, though some – particularly those which include sympathy and loving kindness – he tends to depict with greater respect. But there have been other dissenters from my view of Arabella. For example, Chizuko Watari in "'Who Casts a Stone at Her?' – In Defense of Arabella."[3] And, I recall a paper on the same topic, given at a Thomas Hardy Society Conference by John Doheney, argued much to the same effect.

Of course, that Arabella stands as a foil for the aspirations of Jude and Sue I concede. So, indeed, does Vilbert. But that she or he is a "satire" on them I reject because I take the term "satire" to involve a moral judgment – that one way of behaving is morally better than another. Unless one can be persuaded that Hardy portrays Arabella's urging Phillotson to adopt "bondage" in order to break Sue's spirit as something the equivalent of the way Swift portrays the rationality of the Houyhnhnms as a model against which the brutality of the Yahoos is to be judged – "satire" it is not. But "satire" is a complex topic, and I hope to learn more of what I don't know from others on the Forum. – Bob.

---

[2] Peter Widdowson, *On Thomas Hardy: Late Essays and Earlier* (Basingstoke: Macmillan Press LTD, 1998), 188-195.

[3] See *Jude the Obscure Reconsidered: Eleven Ways of Twenty-first Century Interpretation*, edited by Nasu Masago, Tadao Fukuoka, Yukio Kaneko, Makiko Kazama, and Tokuko Kitawaki (Tokyo: Eihosha Co., Ltd., 2003.), 79-96.

Monday, 30 Jun 2003 17:43:48 -0300
RICHARD NEMESVARI <rnemesva@stfx.ca>
Subject: Arabella as "satiric."

I thought I would respond to Bob's question about Arabella's "satiric" role in *Jude*, since I also piled onto the last discussion we had about genre. It strikes me that Widdowson's use of the word "satire" in this way (although I haven't read the work Bob cites) is imprecise, and I would instead advance the idea that Arabella and her comments are ironic rather than satiric. This can operate on multiple levels, which I'll come back to, but the first thing I would suggest is that irony is a "larger" term and may or may not involve satire specifically, depending upon its employment by an author.

I don't think Hardy is using satire, but he is using irony. If irony is generated when (very broadly) there occurs a disjunction between appearance and reality, intention and accomplishment, then Arabella's deflating comments on Jude and Sue's idealism are ironic in that they serve to illustrate the severe dislocation between their aspirations and the often brutal social context which thwarts them. That her comments are sometimes overtly sarcastic, the lowest form of irony, only serves to emphasize her role as the voice of conventional "common sense." In this way she is not "satirizing" them because, as Bob pointed out, the text does not suggest that her "morality" is superior to theirs and should be followed, only that it allows you to get by much more easily. She isn't wrong, but she isn't right either. Indeed, I would argue that the irony rebounds back on Arabella, in that her pragmatic vision of the world (in which husbands and children are essentially disposable, sexual desire is a weapon to be wielded whenever there is gain to be had, and social conventions are a game to be played, not a system to be reformed) is itself ironically exposed as insufficient and destructive. In other words, she is a character in a novel whose author gets to unload the final irony by revealing her apparently successful method of coping as part of "the letter [that] killeth."

Arabella can be "defended" (I suppose) in that she plays the cards she has been dealt with superlative skill, and her refusal to be victimized by a system that so effectively neutralizes Jude and Sue demonstrates a Darwinian survival instinct which has a crude kind of biological worth. But she is hardly the character the text asks us to emulate. She is Hardy's ironic comment on the fact that survival of the fittest doesn't always mean survival of the best, which may be a satire on society, but not on the text's two main characters. Of course Hardy often explores "life's little ironies," and for him the word may be more accurately invoked by focussing on the disjunction between what should be and what is. Jude and Sue have flaws, and Arabella helps reveal them. The irony created isn't a judgment on them, however, but on a culture which takes those weaknesses and produces needless and tragic suffering. – Richard

Monday, 30 Jun 2003 16:44:56 -0400
SHANNON ROGERS <srogers@sju.edu>
Subject: Arabella as "satiric"

Dear Bob et al: while I would love – for the sake of a real debate – to make the argument that Arabella is intended to satirize Jude and Sue, I just can't do it. If she is a satire then would that make Phillotson equally a satire (but the other side of the coin)? Both stand at odds to Jude and Sue's ideals and I think that both represent trends of modern thoughts in diametrically opposed positions. Arabella just wants to get by and succeed in the world, and she doesn't care what she does to get there. I never get the feeling from Hardy that she is intended as a sympathetic character – rather she is a sad commentary on one element of modernity – those who have no compunctions or cares for others, and only think of themselves. Phillotson, on the other hand, while pathetic, isn't terribly sympathetic (to me) either. He stands initially as a representation of the older world of moral uprightness, and yet he is able to bend and give way – to tolerate modern thinking and allow his love and respect for Sue as a human being to outweigh his old-fashioned moral code. He is the positive side of what modernity brings. In the middle are those who cannot bend, but are only brittle and break under pressure – Jude and Sue.

I would argue that, rather than a satire on their ideals – for certainly Hardy feels a great pull toward them – he sets Arabella up as a foil to them. The world is not ready for their kind – they are too sensitive, like Hardy himself, and so in a new modern world, those like Arabella survive. Phillotson survives as well, and unlike Arabella, he has dignity and a certain level of compassion. I look forward, though, to a lively debate to prove us both wrong! – Cheers, Shannon.

Monday, 30 Jun 2003 19:36:47 -0400
ROSEMARIE MORGAN <rosemarie.morgan@yale.edu>
Subject: Arabella as "satiric."

I can see that satire could be applied in a loose way to describe Arabella's stance in relation to Jude and Sue, insofar as her use of sarcasm and ridicule exposes their smallest foibles and largest aspirations to higher things. But "loose" it is and unsatisfactory for that reason. Irony, as Richard points out, is more to the point.

First and foremost, the satirist (whether in Hardy's narrator or in Arabella herself) customarily employs wit in order to reduce the vaunted worth of someone or something to its lowest value. And we can certainly attribute wit to Hardy's narrator, as in the marriage scene where

> The two swore that at every other time of their lives they would assuredly believe, feel and desire precisely as they had believed, felt, and desired during the few preceding weeks. What was as remarkable as the undertaking itself was the fact that nobody seemed at all surprised at what they swore.[4]

But there is no instance that I can recollect where Arabella demonstrates comparable wit in making her (often insightful) observations.

Next, and equally important, the satirist seeks to provoke a response (as does the narrator in the marriage-contract comment above) designed to spur change or reform. Arabella's observations on Sue, in particular, and on Jude, occasionally, are often psychologically astute and nearly always perceptive (I'm now thinking of her "frowsty" bedroom scene where she delivers a startlingly accurate hit at Sue's sexuality), but as targets, neither Sue nor Jude exhibit the kind of folly, vice or immorality the satirist seeks to root out.

I suspect Hardy had trouble with Arabella – in keeping her sufficiently distanced from his own interests in order to sustain her antipathetical role, just as he had trouble with distancing Troy. There are many moments in *Jude* where her perceptions place her dangerously close to her narrator in attitude and sympathy, and Hardy *does* give her (with good reason) the last word on Sue. But satire, unlike sarcasm, simply doesn't hold up under scrutiny; it is too sophisticated (in all senses of the word), too intellectual for Arabella. From her intuitive perceptions, which are indeed sharp and (unlike Sue's) unfettered by self-regard, by self-analysis, to her nod-and-wink mode of expression Arabella shares a very special, knowing relationship with the reader (we are "in" on her secrets). This simply serves to accentuate the complexities, the incongruities in this novel in which both the "letter" and the "word" "killeth." – Cheers, Rosemarie.

---

[4] Thomas Hardy, *Jude the Obscure*, ed., Dennis Taylor (Penguin Classics: 1998), Part First, IX.

W. Hatherell's illustration for *Harper's New Monthly Magazine*: courtesy, Dorset County Library.

'See how he's served me!' she cried. 'Making me work Sunday mornings when I ought to be going to my church, and tearing my hair off my head, and my gown off my back!'[5]

---

[5] *Jude the Obscure*, Part First, XI. "And my gown off my back!" was added in 1895 proofs. The heavily bowdlerized serial version of *Jude* was published in *Harper's New Monthly Magazine* (December 1894-November 1895) in London and New York:. The first instalment was entitled *The Simpletons* but thereafter *Hearts Insurgent* (volume edn., 1895/6). For further copies of Hatherell's illustrations to *Harper's New Monthly Magazine's* serialization of *Jude, the Obscure* see The Thomas Hardy Associations's **Novels** page, Director Birgit Plietzsch: < http://www.st-andrews.ac.uk/~ttha/>

AN OVERVIEW OF TTHA LIFE PAGE

THE Thomas Hardy *Life* page continues to develop by adding links and references to works dealing with Hardy's biography. The site is divided into five sections:
- ❖ Chronology
- ❖ Biographies
- ❖ Reviews
- ❖ Resources
- ❖ Image Gallery.

The **Chronology** section provides not only a listing of the major events in Hardy's life, but various links which elaborate on them. Thus, for example, when Emma Lavinia Gifford is first mentioned the user may click on her name and pull up comments on her and her relationship with Hardy from the major biographers.

HERE IS A SAMPLE:

ROBERT GITTINGS	MICHAEL MILLGATE	MARTIN SEYMOUR-SMITH
She herself described her childhood home as 'a most intellectual one and not only so but one of exquisite home-training and refinement'. In her recollections in old age, there are idyllic pictures of family music and singing, of readings and discussions of books.	Emma Gifford's nervousness sprang from much anticipatory speculation 'as to what the Architect would be like'. Tiny and remote, St. Juliot offered little in the way of society beyond the occasional visiting clergyman or school inspector, and any visitor was welcome.	Although she attended nothing better than a dame school in Plymouth (run by 'dear refined single ladies of perfect manners'), Emma had tender memories of a genteel life, even if it was rather impoverished, and her father was given to alcoholic outbursts.

Similarly, the publication dates of "The Profitable Reading of Fiction," "Candour in English Fiction," and "The Science of Fiction" contain links which allow the user to pull up and read these works in their entirety. In some cases links are provided to Hardy's poetry. Thus the date of Horace Moule's death is followed by a link which provides the text of "Standing by the Mantelpiece (H.M.M., 1873)":

> This candle-wax is shaping to a shroud
> To-night. (They call it that, as you may know) –
> By touching it the claimant is avowed,
> And hence I press it with my finger – so.
>
> To-night. To me twice night, that should have been
> The radiance of the midmost tick of noon
> And close around me wintertime is seen
> That might have shone the veriest day of June!
>
> But since all's lost, and nothing really lies
> Above but shade, and shadier shade below,
> Let me make clear, before one of us dies,
> My mind to yours, just now embittered so.
>
> Since you agreed, unurged and full-advised,
> And let warmth grow without discouragement,
> Why do you bear you now as if surprised,
> When what has come was clearly consequent?
>
> Since you have spoken, and finality
> Closes around, and my last movements loom,
> I say no more: the rest must wait till we
> Are face to face again, yonside the tomb.
>
> And let the candle-wax thus mould a shape
> Whose meaning now, if hid before, you know,
> And how by touch one present claims its drape,
> And that it's I who press my finger – so.[1]

And the reference to Hardy's Boer War poetry is matched by a link to the text of "Drummer Hodge." The **Chronology** part of the site thus provides useful elaborations on the events of Hardy's life.

The **Biographies** section is a straightforward listing of the major biographical works on Hardy. Beginning with F. A. Hedgcock's *Thomas Hardy: penseur et artiste* (1911) it concludes with Paul Turner's

---

[1] Thomas Hardy, *The Complete Poems of Thomas Hardy*, edited by James Gibson (New York: Macmillan, 1976), 887.

The Life of Thomas Hardy: A Critical Biography (1998). Additional suggestions of other texts to be included are always welcome, and the goal of the list is to indicate the wide range of writers and approaches which have been drawn to exploring the relationship between the author and his work. Further, given that that relationship has sometimes been controversial, the **Reviews** section reproduces (as its title suggests) reviews of recent Hardy biographies. Thus, for example, reviews of Seymour Smith's *Hardy* (1994) are provided from the *Sunday Times Book Review*, the *Times Literary Supplement*, the *Ottawa Citizen*, and the *Toronto Star*. This allows the user to evaluate the critical response to the biographies and judge their strengths and weaknesses.

HERE IS A SAMPLE:

Sunday Times Book Review	Times Literary Supplement	Ottawa Citizen
This is a huge, exasperating, unforgettable book. Verbose, repetitive, jeering at previous biographers, grousing about modern life ... For all that, it is exceptionally well informed, and far more often right than wrong.	Perhaps it is his populism that makes Seymour-Smith indifferent to the professional custom of identifying sources; perhaps he believes that his book doesn't need footnotes because the common reader probably doesn't care about critical analysis or critical history ...	Even more remarkable is the extent of Seymour-Smith's indebtedness to the work of those benighted scholars he keeps trying to savage with his rubber teeth. Without the Hardy *Collected Letters* ... and without the Millgate and Gittings biographies, Seymour-Smith would have virtually no subject.

The **Resources** section is itself divided into four sections: "Letters," "Notebooks," "Essays and Prefaces," and "Memoirs and Interviews." It is thus a listing of additional sources of biographical information which expand on Hardy's research and on his own comments on his work. And finally, the **Image Gallery** provides a few pictures of Hardy and his life. This section of the site will be undergoing a major expansion soon.

TTHA's *Life* page thus aims to give the user ample information to pursue whatever facet of Hardy's biography he or she finds most interesting, in a way that is both accessible and accurate.

Richard Nemesvari
Life page Director
nemesva@stfx.ca

AN OVERVIEW OF TTHA CHECKLIST

An Unexpected Treasure
The "Checklist of Recent Hardy Publications"
Four Years After Its Inception

ANYONE in need of information on publications by or about Hardy will find retrospective bibliographies relatively full and readily available. The authoritative primary bibliography by Richard Little Purdy has recently been republished with supplements by Charles P.C. Pettit, and the massive two-volume annotated secondary bibliography published by Helmut Gerber and W. Eugene Davis is remarkably thorough for the years it covers. Other more selective bibliographies have appeared from time to time, and all those retrospective bibliographies can to a limited extent be brought up to date by reference to the current bibliographies appearing under the auspices of the MHRA and the MLA.

One problem with those current bibliographies, however, is that they are far from up-to-date: anyone consulting them will not find information about most publications that appeared in the previous or the current year; in reporting very many publications they lag even further behind. Nor, of course, do they provide information about forthcoming publications that could be important to a particular inquiry.

To help remedy this information gap, an international group of scholars, all members of The Thomas Hardy Association, organized to create a "Current Checklist of Recent Hardy Publications." Those compilers agreed to contribute information bi-monthly on current publications cited in a wide range of sources:

- ➢ Seven trade lists, including the major compilations of books in print and the electronic catalogues of publishers who in the past have frequently published books on Hardy.
- ➢ Over twenty electronic bibliographies, catalogues, and other databases, ranging from such vast resources as WorldCat

and Ingenta to the more specialized Digital Dissertations and Project Muse.

➢ Eighty-seven scholarly journals.

These sources were to be reviewed at least bi-monthly by the compilers, and citations of new items noted by them are regularly added to a Checklist that is now available to its members.

From its inception, the primary purpose of the Checklist has been to provide scholars and other interested persons who were members of TTHA with whatever reliable information *might be available* about new Hardy publications – a checklist fully searchable by author, title, or keyword that would be far in advance of such current bibliographies as the MLA and the MHRA. Implementation of that limited goal ("limited" because always subject to availability) has recently been improved. In the past, Checklist updates were posted every 15 days; now every Checklist update received is posted immediately to the Members' Page[2] so that the Checklist is updated from one day to the next. For the convenience of its users, the *current* Checklist is limited to three years: the previous year, the current year, and the following year – e.g., in 2003 the years covered would be 2002, 2003, and 2004. Checklists for previous years are archived but available to TTHA members wishing to consult them, and they, too, are fully searchable by author, title, or keyword.

The inclusion in the Checklist of citations to publications scheduled to appear in the following year is but one index of its aim to provide bibliographic information as up-to-date as possible. At the time this report was written (December, 2003), the Checklist already contained seven entries for the year 2004

Here is a small sample from Category "**A**."

A. EDITIONS, REPRINTS, AND TRANSLATIONS

- **Hardy, Thomas.** *The Mayor of Casterbridge.* **Edited by Dale Kramer with Introduction by Pamela Dalziel. Oxford: Oxford University Press, 2004.**

    ➢ **[On 22 October 2003 Books in Print listed this edition as scheduled for publication in July of 2004.]**

- **Hardy, Thomas.** *The Return of the Native.* **Mineola, NY: Dover Publications Incorporated, 2004.**

---

[2] At the Hardy Association Website:
http://www.yale.edu/hardysoc/Welcome/welcomet.htm

> [On 22 October 2003 Books in Print listed this edition as scheduled for publication in October of 2004.]

In the future, about August of 2004, advance announcements of forthcoming Hardy publications will again begin to appear, and by the end of 2004 there will already be again a substantial number of entries for 2005.

Currency, above all, then, was and is the primary goal of TTHA Checklist. But extended coverage has been an unexpected – though very important – development. Included in its coverage, for example, are books and articles which, although not devoted to Hardy, include substantial comment on him. Included, too, are electronic archives not presently covered by other current bibliographies. Included, too, is an extensive recording of review citations, letters, reports, and other more ephemeral materials relating to Hardy.

Here is a small sample from Category "**E**":

E. REVIEWS OF WORKS PUBLISHED BEFORE 2003

- **Page, Norman.** *Thomas Hardy: The Novels.* **New York: Palgrave, 2001.**

  > [See the 2001 Checklist for original entry with table of contents and other information.]

  > Reviewed by Heather Marcovitch. *English Literature in Transition* 46.2 (2003): 199-203.

  > Reviewed by Betty Cortus. TTHA Book Review (2003). Text available in TTHA Members' Research Resources pages: http://www.yale.edu/hardysoc/mrr/reviews/page.bc.html

  > Reviewed by Roger Ebbatson. *English* 52.203 (2003): 198.

- **Pite, Ralph.** *Hardy's Geography: Wessex and the Regional Novel.* **Houndmills, Basingstoke, Hampshire and New York: Palgrave, 2002.**

  > [See the 2002 Checklist for original entry with table of contents and other information.]

  > Reviewed by T. Loe. *Choice* 40.8 (2003): 305.

  > Reviewed by Bharat Tandon. *TLS* No. 5253 (5 December 2003): 3-4.

- **Purdy, Richard Little.** *Thomas Hardy: A Bibliographical Study.* Introduction and Supplement by Charles P.C. Pettit. London and New Castle, DE: Oak Knoll Press/St. Paul's Bibliographies and the British Library, 2002.

  - [For further information, see the Purdy entry for 2002.]

  - Reviewed by Phillip Mallett. *The Thomas Hardy Journal* 19.1 (February, 2003): 67-69.

  - Reviewed by Paul W. Nash. *The Library* 4.3 (2003): 320-2.

  - Reviewed by Stuart James. *Reference Reviews* 17.4 (2003): 33-4.

  - Reviewed by Rosemarie Morgan. TTHA Book Review (2003). Text available in TTHA Members' Research Resources pages:
    http://www.yale.edu/hardysoc/mrr/reviews/purdypettit.rm.html

- **Wickens, Glen.** *Thomas Hardy, Monism and the Carnival Tradition: The One and the Many in The Dynasts.* Toronto: University of Toronto Press, 2002.

  - [See the 2002 Checklist for table of contents and description.]

  - Reviewed by Robert Schweik. *English Literature in Transition* 46.3 (2003): 303-8

  - Reviewed by Robert Schweik. TTHA Book Review (2003). Text available in TTHA Members' Research Resources pages:
    http://www.yale.edu/hardysoc/mrr/reviews/Wickens_Monism_by_Schweik.html

  - Reviewed by C. M. Jackson-Houlston. TTHA Book Review (2003). Text available in TTHA Members' Research Resources pages:
    http://www.yale.edu/hardysoc/mrr/reviews/wickens.cjh.html

Just a few statistics may suggest something of the remarkable if unexpected scope and fullness of the TTHA Checklist. As of December 2003, the current Checklist for the years 2002-2004 consisted of 422 main entries and 115 review citations. There is no way of comparing the MLA and MHRA bibliographies with this up-to-date TTHA coverage because they lag so very far behind: as of December, 2003, their most recent citations were primarily for the year 2002. But it may help make clear the relative thoroughness of the Checklist coverage by comparing the TTHA Checklist with the MHRA and MLA bibliographies for 2002

DECEMBER 2002
MHRA's ABELL	MLA database	TTHA Checklist
61 Citations	47 Citations	257 Citations + 80 review citations

Roughly this same ratio holds true for the 2000, and 2001 Checklists, and there is no reason to think that subsequent Checklists will not exhibit the same relative thoroughness.

Furthermore, TTHA Checklist provides descriptive comment on the contents of its citations, ranging from the full tables of contents of books cited to briefer descriptive annotations of the contents of chapters, articles, and reviews. Although it.does not have the full-text capabilities now becoming in part available in the ABELL, it does provide access to the full texts of some reviews, as well as to full texts of major electronic publications of scholarly materials. In this respect, too, its inclusiveness when compared with the MLA and MHRA bibliographies is a welcome surprise.

With respect to purely electronic publications, now becoming a significant part of the information on Hardy available to scholars, MHRA's ABELL does make an attempt to include some, but it lists as part of its total citations on Hardy only ten sites, none particularly new; and – altogether characteristic of standard reference works which undertake to cite electronic sources – it can be remarkably naïve: for example, one it lists, *The Thomas Hardy Online Society*, is a site utterly worthless for any scholarly purpose.

But equally striking is what the TTHA Checklist does currently cover that the ABELL does not:

- The current archives for TTHA's own Forum
- TTHA's Poem of the Month discussions[3]
- Relevant material on *The Victorian Web*[4]
- Discussions in the archives of *Victoria*[5]

Moreover, apart from recording such ongoing electronic resources, the Checklist also captures one-time electronic publications that can be of exceptional importance for anyone seeking information about

---

[3] The ABELL does, however, cite the TTHA site more than once.
[4] http://www.scholars.nus.sg/landow/victorian
[5] http://listserv.indiana.edu/archives.victoria.html

Hardy. The most important is Michael Millgate's[6] *Thomas Hardy's Library at Max Gate: Catalogue of an Attempted Reconstruction.*[7] This is a fully searchable catalogue of great potential value for anyone investigating Hardy's reading. As of December of 2003, Millgate's resource has not appeared in the other major current bibliographies.

Hence the title of this brief report: four years after its inception, TTHA's "Checklist of Recent Hardy Publications" has emerged as a treasure not only for its currency but, quite unexpectedly, for the richness of its annotations and for its extraordinary thoroughness.

For TTHA Checklist team,
Robert Schweik
<Schweik@fredonia.edu>

AN ADDENDUM TO "AN OVERVIEW OF TTHA CHECKLIST"

THE following section provides a few further details about *Thomas Hardy's Library*. This is an extraordinarily rich resource not only offering important details about individual books but also providing information on and guidance to the present location of the books themselves. In addition, gathering and collating items from many miscellaneous sources – libraries, private collections worldwide, and a mass of sometimes recondite dealers' and auctioneers' catalogues – the *Library* provides information that could otherwise take (and has, in Michael Millgate's case, already taken) a lifetime of travelling and delving.

The importance of maintaining the *Library*'s state-of-the-art currency cannot be over-emphasised; it is imperative that its resources be constantly corrected, amplified, and kept up to date by its users. Any relevant information will be gladly welcomed and acknowledged by Michael Millgate.

The opening page of *Thomas Hardy's Library at Max Gate: Catalogue of an Attempted Reconstruction* launches the project with these words:

---

[6] michael.millgate@utoronto.ca
[7] http://www.library.utoronto.ca/fisher/hardy/

> The aim of this project has been to reconstruct as fully as possible the contents of Thomas Hardy's library at Max Gate, his Dorchester home, at the time of his death in January 1928. In so doing it seeks to provide an accessible resource for scholars and general readers interested in the specific books that Hardy owned, in the overall character of his library, and in the somewhat melancholy story of that library's dispersal.

Appropriately enough, in this instance, a little "melancholy" is also how Hardy looks in the *Library's* opening page (below).[8]

This image originally appeared in the magazine *Black and White*, 27 (August 1892, 238). The name printed in lower right-hand corner, G. Grenville Manton, is presumably the artist. The portrait shows Hardy in his *Tess* study – not the study at the back of Max Gate (now on show in reconstructed form at the Dorset County Museum).

One of the most intriguing parts of the collection is Millgate's analysis of the evidence of the Hardy bookplates – or, rather, often *spurious* bookplates – affixed to books after Hardy's death. As Millgate describes it:

---

[8] Western cultural representations of the public face have changed over the past 100 years. As in Japan, today, Victorians at all times presented a serious, even lofty, expression to the world; equally, smiling into the camera was not favoured. Indiscriminate smiling signified insincerity, affectation, doltishness, idiocy.

Hardy himself did not have any bookplates printed or inserted – the crudely printed 'Thomas Hardy' labels found in one or two early volumes could well have been his father's – and the earliest and most significant of the Max Gate labels were those inserted by Sydney Cockerell immediately after Hardy's death (*Thomas Hardy's Library*).

And from this point on, following Hardy's death, there appears to have been quite a free-for-all with Max Gate bookplates – with their acquisition, their application and not least, with their tendency to become roaming gnomes, with occasional ignominy.

Finally, here's a small sample of contents, listed in *Library* by A-Z. Since "Q" suggests itself as a good contender for paucity readers can judge for themselves the kind of bibliographical Aladdin's Cave lurking in the remaining A-Z.

Quayle, Thomas. See Walter de la Mare

Quiller-Couch, A. T. (later Sir Arthur). *On the Art of Writing: Lectures Delivered in the University of Cambridge 1913-1914.* Cambridge: Cambridge University Press, 1916.

Bookplate; pres. ins. from author. (*Collected Letters*, v. 150-1; MG Sale/253; Heffer 532/1996) **[Nigel Williams Rare Books 53/509]**

---, ed. *The Oxford Book of English Prose.* Oxford: Clarendon Press, 1925. Includes selections from TH. (Purdy purchase at MG Sale) [Yale: Purdy]

---, ed. *The Oxford Book of English Verse 1250-1900.* Oxford: at the Clarendon Press, 1900.
Marked, annotated, and with insertions. (*Collected Letters*, ii. 277; MG Sale/221; Adams) **[Sotheby's 6-7 Nov. 2001/502; seen at Adams]**

---, ed. *The Oxford Book of Victorian Verse.* Oxford: at the Clarendon Press, 1912.
Red SCC **bookplate**; TH signature; v. lightly annotated, but FEH's inserted letter of gift to TH's friend Dorothy Allhusen, April 1930, refers to bookmarks (at pp. 126-7 and 712-13) as indicating poems TH particularly liked. (*Collected Letters*, iv. 227)

Vol. contains four poems by TH. [DCM]

---. *The Sacred Way.* Reprints from *The Cambridge Magazine*, no. 3 (1918).

[*Collected Letters*, v 193]

* * * * * * * * * * * * *

For the TTHA Checklist team,
Rosemarie Morgan
<rosemarie.morgan@yale.edu>

THE THOMAS HARDY ASSOCIATION MEMBERS' RESEARCH RESOURCES

– II –

AN OVERVIEW OF TTHA REVIEWS PAGE

SINCE its unveiling two years ago, the TTHA *Reviews* Page has been steadily evolving into a comprehensive resource for Hardy scholars. One of the more exciting features of the page is its immediacy. Because the page is web-based, there are no print delays from reviewer to reader. The page is also becoming increasingly dynamic, featuring not only multiple reviews of the same book, but also a growing number of responses from reviewed authors: this fosters a type of scholarly dialogue that is essentially impossible in a print journal. To add to the more than 30 reviews already published, the *Reviews* Page is beginning to broaden its focus to include media other than books, including CD-Rom/Hardy resources and film versions of his work.

In the coming weeks we will have reviews of Ralph Pite's *Hardy's Geography*, T.R. Wright's *Hardy and His Readers*, the recent A&E production of *The Mayor of Casterbridge*, and Andrew Radford's *Thomas Hardy and the Survivals of Time*, to name just a few. The wealth of recent scholarly activity concerning Hardy promises that there will be ample opportunity for more critical reviews as well as lively discussions both on the Forum and on the *Reviews* Page itself.

Shannon Rogers
Reviews Page Director
<srogers@sju.edu>

THE following small sample of reviews from TTHA's *Reviews* page has been selected for diversity and variety. Topically speaking, the books reviewed encompass an exceptionally broad range. From biographical material generated by the great bard himself and edited by his greatest biographer down to the simplest of "student" beginner's guides, and then from the most suppositional study on Hardy to the least hypothetical – critical theory and

bibliography respectively – the work reviewed here exemplifies the richness and diversity of current Hardy studies. It also represents but a tiny proportion of the critical essays available on TTHA's *Reviews* page. For TTHA's *Members' Research & Resources* team,
Rosemarie Morgan

Please note: these reviews were written for online publication. I have made some minor editorial changes to fit them to book publication.

MILLGATE, MICHAEL, ed. *Thomas Hardy's Public Voice: The Essays, Speeches and Miscellaneous Prose* (Oxford and New York: Oxford University Press, 2001), 500   ISBN 019818526X, Cl, $110/£70.

By editing this comprehensive collection of Hardy's non-fictional public utterances, Michael Millgate has done yet another great service for Hardy scholarship and put us all more than ever in his debt. His *Thomas Hardy: His Career as a Novelist*, first published thirty years ago, remains a lucid and informative guide to the novels. *Thomas Hardy: A Biography* followed in 1982 and has rightly been called 'the standard biography'. Described when it was first published as 'by far the most detailed and comprehensive account of Hardy's personal and literary life now available' it is still so.

Then, during the decade of 1978-1988, in collaboration to some extent with Professor R. L. Purdy, he edited the seven volumes of *The Collected Letters of Thomas Hardy* which provided a great deal more information about Hardy's life and work. Although dismissed by some of what Dr. Leavis used to call the 'Sunday reviewers' as dull and uninteresting the letters are, in fact, full of interest, and Volume 7 has a 120 page index which is a valuable source of information. For example, if you want to know whether Hardy knew or ever wrote anything about G. B. Shaw, the index will enlighten you. Desmond Hawkins saw the *Letters* as among the highest achievements of literary scholarship and how right he was!

Next came Millgate's much-needed re-editing of what was mistakenly called *The Life of Thomas Hardy* by Florence Hardy but was written almost entirely by Hardy himself with posthumous interference by Florence. In allowing Florence to claim that she was the author Hardy has been accused of excessive secretness, but was he doing more than allow a wife, desperate to be a writer, to be so in the eyes of the public? Millgate's recension of the text with its new title of *The Life and Work of Thomas Hardy by Thomas Hardy* gives us the text as Hardy intended. If you haven't read it, do so. It is a fascinating mixture of comments on his life and his writings, and of anecdotes and stories some tragic, some comic but always interesting.

And now Millgate gives us *Thomas Hardy's Public Voice*, a volume of Hardy's essays, speeches, and miscellaneous prose. It is a massive book of 500 pages. In his introduction Millgate writes,

> what the present edition reveals is that Hardy's public utterances were not only more numerous than previously assumed but took many different forms and addressed a wide variety of literary, social and political issues.

If ever evidence were needed of Hardy's astonishing range of interests it is here and may be seen in the 400 or so items which are listed at the beginning of the book. Here are a few of them selected consecutively but at random:

- Mr. Hardy's Poems
- The Moral Rights of Animals
- Nature's Indifference to Justice
- Edited Article on His 70th Birthday
- Letter to the *Freethinker*
- Lloyd's Sixpenny Dickens
- On retiring as President of the Dorset Men in London
- Speech on Receiving the Freedom of the Borough
- Some Old-Fashioned Psalm-Tunes Associated with the County of Dorset

There is not one of these which is without interest to the serious student of Hardy's life and thought, and many of them are a joy to read.

Here is part of his obituary of Lucy Baxter, the daughter of William Barnes:

> The information that I can give concerning the life and personality of this accomplished woman will, I fear, be of the most meagre description; for since her girlhood I have caught only passing glimpses of her ... just as one may discern through trees a bird in flight, now here, now there, now a long way off, ere lost beyond the horizon ... I can first remember (her) as an attractive girl of nineteen or twenty, living at the house of her father ... At that time of her life she was of sweet disposition, but provokingly shy, with plenty of brown hair, a tripping walk, a face pretty rather than handsome, and extremely piquant to a casual observer, having a nose tip-tilted to that slight Tennysonian degree which is indispensable to a countour of such character. When she grew nervous she showed a momentary hesitation of speech

> ... like that of an embarrassed child, which to myself and to many others was not the least of her attractive qualities. Her appearance, gracefulness and marked gentleness, made her a typical 'Lucy', from whom the numerous Lucys in the novels of that date seemed to be drawn.

Hardy wrote this in 1902 for the *Dorset County Chronicle* and it was published simultaneously in *The Times* and subsequently in several journals. Millgate's notes about the history of such items, and there are many of them, are comprehensive and reveal scholarship and research of the highest quality.

There is some slight overlap with Hal Orel's *Thomas Hardy's Personal Writings* which has been such a useful book to many of us since its publication in 1966. Both books, for example, include Hardy's literary essays, 'Candour in English Fiction', 'The Dorsetshire Labourer', and 'The Profitable Reading of Fiction', but most of Millgate's items are new and Orel includes 'Prefaces To Hardy's Writings' which do not come within Millgate's terms of reference.

It is sad that the Oxford Press finds it necessary to charge £70 for this latest monumental Millgate work and, thus, rules out many a 'common reader' who would wish to buy it. Of course, the publishers know that every library of any standing will have to buy a copy no matter what the price, and they would rather sell 1,000 copies at £70 than 5,000 copies at £35. I think that they are wrong and it is this attitude which to some extent has brought about the present crisis in academic publishing. But if you can possibly afford it, *Thomas Hardy's Public Voice* is a book to buy.

JAMES GIBSON

ABBOTT, ROB & CHARLIE BELL. *Thomas Hardy: A Beginner's Guide* (London: Hodder and Stoughton, 2001). 88,

ISBN 0340800364, paper, £5.99.

Thomas Hardy: A Beginner's Guide is just that – a guide for the student or adult reader who knows little to nothing about Hardy and is approaching his works for the very first time. With simple, easy to read prose, this handy little guide – more substantial and broader in scope than the perennially popular *Cliff's Notes*[9] – provides an overview of Hardy's major themes (or "obsessions" as the authors call them) as well as a few fairly in-depth explorations of major works. In the margins, as well as at the end of the book, there are definitions of

---

[9] *York Notes* in the UK.

unfamiliar terms, and each chapter closes with a summary of main points. In addition, cute illustrations accompany the text, much in the vein of the "90 Minute Philosophers" series, providing a touch of humor and the visual cues that are so important to students in our "post literary" age. There is also well-placed advice to switch off modern sensibilities before reading Hardy. While cautioning the reader not to take biographical connections too much to heart, Abbott and Bell provide relevant details about Hardy's life and background. After all, we all crave human faces for our authors. And many issues and events in Hardy's work are obviously connected to his life. The authors do an admirable job of explaining, in a short space, Hardy's historical relevance in recording the passing of rural traditions, the impact of the spread of railways, and other issues.

The book is mostly concerned with the novels, although discussion of "The Withered Arm" is included as well as a chapter on the poems. The authors' obvious preference for *Tess* (a preference I share) is apparent in numerous references to the novel as well as in the section specifically devoted to it. While the discussion of *Tess* is perceptive it raises some issues of problems in her character that could perplex the novice rather than lead to further and deeper understanding. In particular, a reference to Claridge's assertion that Tess "chooses her sexual initiation" seems out of place and could lead to students' failure to see the events in the Chase as more than simple seduction. That said, the discussion of the novel's visual impact and the role of landscape is helpful to the beginning reader, opening doors to possibilities in interpretation rather than leading the reader to a particular passageway.

The authors use *A Pair of Blue Eyes* as an entry into most of Hardy's major themes, which seems an innovative way to encourage readers to try out one of his "lesser" works. The handling of *The Mayor of Casterbridge*, on the other hand, seems reductive, focusing on the role of secrets in the book and little more. The discussion of *Jude* includes a well-constructed explanation of the dichotomies inherent in Jude's and Sue's characters and provides a useful overview of the major themes of the book.

In the poetry chapter, there is an explication of "The Oxen" and a brief discussion of the Emma poems in their context. Both are useful and encourage a novice reader to look further. There is also a good explanation of modernism, Hardy's tentative entry into that realm, and the under-appreciation of his poetry by some of the modernists themselves who failed to see Hardy's essential radicalism.

My chief complaints with these sections lie mainly in an over reliance on secondary works for details not found in the novels and poems themselves. For instance, when quoting Dr. Acton, the source is Boumelha, not Acton (16); Seymour-Smith, whose questionable reliability was the focus of a recent lively TTHA Forum discussion, is mentioned several times including as a source for a quotation from Hardy's own letters. How about Millgate and Purdy? In the section "Hardy as a Victorian Thinker," Darwin and Mill are cited as influences upon Hardy's thought, but only Darwin is explored at any length (17-18).

A Beginner's Guide closes with details of further sources for learning about Hardy. The discussion of feminist responses and their various shifts will be especially helpful to a student attempting to decipher diametrically opposed feminist interpretations. I found the explanations of structuralism and post-structuralism – complete with examples – particularly useful to the non-literary critic. Suggestions are also included not just for explicating the texts but for enhancing appreciation of Hardy. Holding place of prominent interest are TTHA and the Thomas Hardy Society: mail and web addresses are included. **SHANNON ROGERS**

PURDY, RICHARD LITTLE, *Thomas Hardy: A Bibliographical Study*. Ed. Charles P. C. Pettit (Oak Knoll Press & the British Library: Delaware & London, 2002), 432, Cl., illustrated. ISBN 1-58456-070-3, $65.00

For some unaccountable reason Richard Little Purdy's *A Bibliographical Study* has been out of print for about 20 years despite the fact that for all of that time it has been regarded as the authoritative Hardy bibliography – universally acclaimed for its comprehensiveness and accuracy and holding a unique place in the world of Hardy scholarship. "Unique" because Purdy not only had unrestricted access to Hardy's books and private papers but, shortly after the great man's death, also learned, directly, a good deal from his acquaintance with Florence Hardy and such solid family friends as Sydney Cockerell and Harold Child.

The outcome of this unique confluence of events – "the right scholar in the right place at the right time"[10] – is a remarkable work in which bibliographical expertise meets biographical erudition under the auspices of formidable scholarship. You can almost hear the

---

[10] See "Supplement," p1, to *Thomas Hardy: A Bibliographical Study* – hereafter *Supplement*.

breathless admiration in Charles Pettit's narrative voice as he reflects on Purdy's "unique ... influence," his "authoritative ... bibliography," "biographical work of enormous significance," "painstaking research," "meticulous control of detail," "clarity of concept and exposition."[11] This is, in fact, pure editorial generosity. Purdy scarcely needs such promotional *hype*. His name is legendary among Hardy scholars and not solely because it accompanies that of Michael Millgate on their magisterial 7 volume edition of Hardy's *Collected Letters*.

Back in the land of bibliophiles, expanding the scope of the bibliographical study to "its accounts of composition as well as publication history"[12] Purdy pioneered a system of descriptive bibliography outmatched in only one area: Robert Schweik's *Checklist* on TTHA's "Members' Research Page" (the *Checklist* is not restricted by selectivity nor confined to printed publications – and it is constantly updated). And while we are still among the bibliophiles, as all book collectors will vouch, the "Not-in-Purdy" tag in booksellers' catalogues usually sets the heart beating faster despite the fact that Purdy's is a selective bibliography and that such a tag adds nothing, in reality, to the index of rarities unless there happens to be an item which he had unwittingly missed.

The achievement of Pettit's book is threefold. First, and most important, it re-issues Purdy's 1979 impress and, most commendably, reproduces it photographically. Perhaps it takes a scholar of Pettit's high standing to perceive the importance of this manner of preserving precision and accuracy, but it also requires of a publishing house – in this instance, Oak Knoll Press and the British Library – no mean vision for this is an expensive undertaking. Second, in going some way to opening up the question (which for Purdy, has a single answer only), of the textual importance of the first editions and, by extension, the manuscript versions of Hardy's novels, Pettit offers his modern readers a very necessary reassurance: Hardyans, for far too long, have followed blindly in Purdy's footsteps regarding the "Wessex Edition [as] in every sense the definitive edition of Hardy's work and the last authority in questions of text." As Pettit stresses, however, few would make this statement without qualification today. Today, there is a greater awareness, and wariness, of the influence of editors and compositors on Victorian texts. This makes it difficult to accept as truly 'definitive' even an edition which bears the stamp of Hardy's final close and comprehensive scrutiny and which he himself described as 'definitive.' Indeed the very concept of

---

[11] *Supplement*, 1.
[12] These are the words of bibliographical scholar, G. Thomas Tanselle: *Supplement*, 4.

the definitive text, *per se*, and more particularly the definitive edition of all Hardy's works, would now be held to be highly questionable.[13] This contestation is, to my mind, a critically important point. Claims, such as Purdy's, that there is, in Hardy, a 'definitive' text and, even more problematically, that this definitive text is the Wessex Edition queers the solid pitch of the authoritative text which, in all pragmatic wisdom, should surely be authorised solely by the author. In truth, the Wessex Edition remains to this day "authorised" by a host of editors and this includes those works Hardy "corrected" and "revised" himself.

There seems to be a curious literary double-standard at large here. Had Hardy's editors suggested changes and revisions to his poetic texts he would have been outraged. But when they pushed him in this direction with the novels he complied, although, towards the end of his novel-writing he was more inclined to rebel. But not at the outset. When submitting his very first novel, *The Poor Man and the Lady*, for publication, he was advised by editors that those selfsame editors knew best what readers wanted. It is significant, in the case of the puritanical Leslie Stephen, that the *Cornhill* lost so many readers under his editorship that he was forced, eventually, to resign. One wonders how well editors did in fact know what was best for their readers.

This brings me to the third consideration – and this, inadvertently, reflects well on Pettit. In correcting the errors in Purdy, and providing an invaluable Corrigenda of additional information, he notes that in their very shortness the errors stand "as an implicit tribute to the meticulousness of Purdy's work."[14] Inevitably, "meticulousness" now transfers to Pettit, if only for picking out Purdy's errors. At the same time he is also shown to be a good deal more modest and unassuming than the subject of his study. My sense, in reading Purdy's *Bibliography*, is that this august compiler and annotator lacks this one quality of greatness – intellectual humility. A great mind is more aware than most of its own shortcomings. Moreover, those who genuinely possess power do not need to prove it. Bearing all this in mind, I suspect something about Purdy's Preface to his *Bibliographical Study* fails to fulfil expectations of these qualities. Is it that he is too quick to expose the "inadequate and incomplete" bibliographies that have preceded his own? Or is it that he is a little too hasty in claiming that Hardy was not "equipped" to provide bibliographical material

---

[13] See *Supplement* 7.
[14] New Preface, *Supplement*, vii.

for the *Life*?[15] How would Purdy know this – from Florence, from colleagues? No – this, for a scholar, would not suffice. The truth is that Purdy did not "know." Hardy, in fact, was approached by John Lane about producing a bibliography of his works as early as 1891: he offered to assist "with pleasure." On the basis of this Lane subsequently contributed a bibliography of Hardy's first editions to Lionel Johnson's *The Art of Thomas Hardy*.[16] In 1916 Hardy, in like vein, fully cooperated with Henry Danielson's *The First Editions of the writings of Thomas Hardy and Their Values* and was sufficiently well "equipped" to annotate the entries extensively (now in the DCM). Harold Child, in 1914, was similarly blessed by Hardy's detailed listings when producing his *Thomas Hardy* in 1916.

In Hardy's eyes the very notion of a bibliography seemed at first and possibly for some time to come, self-aggrandising. Indeed, he implored Lane not to make his bibliography "eulogistic" but rather a "cool honest analysis."[17] Richard Little Purdy may disdain Lane and Hardy's other bibliographers as "inadequate" but to malign Hardy's intellectual equipment itself seems inappropriate to say the least. Nor does it particularly endear him to his reader that in his second paragraph he is bound to relate that the notes he has added to Hardy's poems "may easily prove the most useful thing I have done." Standing alone, this little vanity might be overlooked but there is also the cavalier way he assures his reader that he has "singled out" only works of "textual significance" – the "many reprintings in authorized and pirated editions" being "of no special value." And so it goes. As fortune has it, pirated editions like forgeries in the art world do have a very special value – but perhaps Purdy is trying to make a moral point here.

These value judgements are, in themselves, of small account, perhaps, in the face of so substantial a work. Nevertheless, it strikes this particular reader that taken in the aggregate, including a slighting observation that Hardy had "no sufficient command of any foreign language" to be able to judge the quality of the translations of his books (but he did insist on sending them to language specialists to have them evaluated), they offer an epistemology at some expense of largeness of soul.

The only quibble I have concerning Pettit's own superb Introduction – aside from the inevitable fact that his "textual development"

---

[15] Florence Emily Hardy, *The Life of Thomas Hardy, 1840-1928* (London and Basingstoke: Macmillan Press, 1962.).
[16] Elkin Mathews and John Lane, 1894.
[17] *Collected Letters*, Vol I, 239, 256.

section is already outdated[18]– is his slant on Hardy's pseudonymous writing of the *Life*. Pettit opens the topic by saying "a number of people in Hardy's circle had already suspected that the *Life* had been essentially written by himself."[19] He then goes on to speak, at length, of Purdy's "revelations" in making the "fiction" of Florence's authorship known to the public. This (sadly typical) slant on Hardy's pseudonymous authorship completely misses the point and, in turn, misleads readers. It "misses the point" because pseudonymous authorship had, for Victorians, a long and respectable history. It was not reserved only for women writers wishing to gain a foothold in a male-dominated profession and thus being obliged to adopt a male persona. Nor was it reserved for male essayists practising the reverse when writing "advice columns" in the national periodicals for which they would often adopt a female pseudonym; nor for authors wishing to produce very different kinds of books – one nom-de-plume for the poet, say, and another for the horticulturist writing a gardener's column. Pseudonyms, cross-sexual or otherwise, were ubiquitous and not in the least "suspect." Moroever, adopting the name of Florence Hardy allowed Hardy a vision in self-writing in which the traps of autobiography were minimised. For the painfully shy Hardy the pseudonym would also have spelled liberty and self-invention – the kind of liberty and invention, at a more complex level of artistic creation, that the speaker of the poems enjoys in so many of his dramatic monologues. In this post-Victorian age it appears that the adoption of literary "masks" – as Parson Brontë advised his famous daughters, if they were to become effective writers – is not fully understood. The adoption of a pseudonym, in literary history, has never been uncommon and certainly has never been taken to be in any sense suspect. It is a convention, a device, pure and simple. To make it out to be other than that is to impose a false interpretation and limited understanding upon what was respectable writing practice in the nineteenth century, and earlier.

At another level of comprehension, Hardy became, in fact, a veritable expert on autobiography. I would go so far as to say that the Life-and-Letters genre of Victorian literature formed the bulk of his daily reading material during his last years. He read autobiographies copiously – by the dozen. Thus, when he started on his own letter-sorting years (1917-1919) and the beginnings of the *Life*, with Florence Hardy busily typing out his manuscript versions at his side,

---

[18] Oxford World Classics editions have already been superseded by Penguin World Classics.
[19] *Supplement*, 10.

he had become one of the best-versed readers in autobiography of his time. And several of his friends knew of his self-writing of the *Life* – "knew" as opposed to "suspecting," as Pettit puts it (which instantly taints Hardy's practices and motives). Contrary to Purdy's assertion of "secrecy" (267-8), as early as 1907 Hardy had told Gosse, when discussing the issue of autobiography, that he had been "compelled often to put into handbooks &c. personal details that I detest printing, solely to give ... gossip the lie."[20] And where T. E. Lawrence and James Barrie not only knew he was writing the *Life* pseudonymously but were even implicated in the process there was little concealment from publisher Macmillan who was aware as early as 1919 that Hardy wished to remain an autobiographical nonentity: "I am glad [Florence] mentioned to you what she is doing," he wrote Macmillan, "which I should never have done myself, though I don't mind her doing it."[21] Taken at face value, and given his intense sense of privacy, a third-person narrator would preserve Hardy from the excruciating exposure of the autobiographical "I" while, at the same time allowing him a certain poetic license in governing the text.

The whole purpose of pseudonymity is to organise the reader's responses in a specific manner. This act was and still is considered valuable for its psychological function. One other aspect of pseudonymity which might well have appealed to Hardy is the implication of non-verifiability. For example, the third-person narrator could (theoretically) write that "he used to say he did this or that..." thus placing the truth-value of the statement at one step removed from the statement which could have said "I did this or that." This last retains only a relative truth-value depending on the established veracity (or otherwise) of the speaker, but the first, third-person statement is effectively "hearsay" and as such it is inadmissible testimony.[22] The modernist in Hardy who so highly valued the indeterminate and the irrational might well have favoured the pseudoonymous mode with these considerations in mind.

That apart – and to be sure we should now leave it apart – what follows, in the 352 pages of *A Bibliographical Study* is an annotated bibliography complete with 20 odd pages of comprehensive indexing (a scholar's dream!), which stands alone as a great monument to Purdy's workmanship. Each and every poem and each and every novel is described carefully, from end-papers to bindings to design

---

[20] *Letters*, Vol III, 282.
[21] See Hardy's letter to Frederick Macmillan, October 17th, 1919: *Letters*, Vol V, 331.
[22] Autobiography is not of course legal documentation but the manner in which Hardy gets "accused" (in the context of his *Life* writing) may mislead inexperienced readers into thinking in those terms.

blocks and, on the interior, from collations of each volume to notes on composition and publication and variant editions. How many readers know, for instance, that shortly after *Far From the Madding Crowd* Hardy tried his hand at a dramatisation (of *FFMC*) called *The Mistress of the Farm* (1879). In this version Boldwood is eliminated and, with the collaboration of J Comyns Carr and wife (who, in passing, plagiarised Hardy's play for a Pinero version), the play was finally produced at the Prince of Wales Theatre in Liverpool and subsequently at the Globe Theatre London where it ran from April to July – 114 performances in all. Hardy, evidently, hated the whole commercial venture (which was very messy) but that didn't stop him from trying his hand at yet more dramatisations throughout his entire life.

Purdy has an investigative journalist's eye. He manages to find the cutest headliner effect for many Hardy publications. The scholarship is there but so is the showmanship. This doesn't, of course, diminish the value of *Thomas Hardy: A Bibliographical Study*. Without doubt this is a book that should be on every Hardy-scholar's bookshelf. Students can do without it if they use the Penguin World Classics issue of Hardy's first editions in which they will find all the bibliographical information necessary for that particular novel and an updated set of notes and research information that Purdy can't be expected to provide. Pettit correctly cites TTHA and its Checklist for up-to-the minute data "Not-in-Purdy" – as Jeanie Smith says in the May, 2003 *Hardy Journal*, nothing beats TTHA for currency and comprehensiveness. Likewise, for historical data, nothing beats Purdy.

ROSEMARIE MORGAN

G. GLEN WICKENS. *Thomas Hardy, Monism, and the Carnival Tradition: The One and the Many in **The Dynasts*** (Toronto: University of Toronto Press, 2002). xix + 255.   ISBN 0-8020-4864-1, Cl, $60.

The Dynasts can be a stumbling block to the Hardy enthusiast; many would rather commend it than read it. After a quarter of a century, another full-length study of the work is overdue. The focus of *Thomas Hardy, Monism, and the Carnival Tradition* raises two key questions: does this book tell us more about Hardy's relations to the thought of his day? Does a reassessment of the genre of *The Dynasts* help us to appreciate Hardy's unique Napoleonic drama more fully? The answer to both is a qualified 'yes'. The argument falls into two parts, with a synthesising conclusion. The first three chapters explore links between the metaphysical framework of *The Dynasts* and thinkers like Eduard

Von Hartmann in whom Hardy either demonstrably did or plausibly could have taken an interest. Readers will find the broad content of this section familiar from the brief outline in F. B. Pinion's *A Hardy Companion* or the detail in J. O. Bailey's *Thomas Hardy and the Cosmic Mind*, but Wickens discusses the phrasing and implications of the philosophical texts in far greater detail. In spite of Hardy's reluctance to present himself as a philosopher, his engagement with contemporary theoretical debate about whether the structure of the universe is based on one sole principle (monism) or is dualistic or pluralistic is clearly an active one.

After brief and accessible introductory passages, each of these chapters is very densely textured, and the ideal reader is probably a specialist cultural historian. Others are likely to be uncomfortably conscious of the imminent undermining of the scientific basis for the philosophical systems referred to by the new physics of relativity.

With a Hardyan irony, the views quoted here look like self-exposing whistling in the dark, and Hardy seems all the more creditably human for his empirical insistence on the significance of suffering; as he complains, mere idealising rationalism 'doesn't help much' (75). As far as *The Dynasts* is concerned, the most enlightening message of this section is that Hardy is dramatising the debate between conflicting concepts of monism, and creating tensions not only between the spirits but within the positions adopted by individual spirits, particularly the Spirit of the Years.

Chapters 4 to 8 read *The Dynasts* in relation to Bakhtin's theories of dialogism and carnival. They are much easier to read and generate a far lighter burden of notes. However, they still seem somewhat clotted, for two reasons. First, Wickens has chosen (throughout the book) to locate nearly all his references parenthetically within the text. In order to distinguish at a glance between the words of Hardy himself and those of his sources, analogues and critics, this is essential. Wickens's method involves the intricate and detailed weaving together of large numbers of short textual quotations from a variety of sources (often away from their immediate contexts). Secondly, there are times when Wickens seems determined to quote every section of *The Dynasts* rather than just the most significant examples, so these latter chapters have a high proportion of content summary.

The differing effects of these two parts of the book illustrate a structural problem over the linkage of the history of ideas with the application of Bakhtinian theory. To some extent this reflects Hardy's difficulties in integrating the world and the Overworld. Wickens certainly addresses this issue, in his introduction and in the thought-provoking but rather brief conclusion. In between, however, the argument hangs in the air, in spite of cross-references to Bakhtin woven into the early chapters. For those who have not read Bailey's book, or Von Hartmann or Bakhtin, it might have been more helpful to present some more information and contextualising material in the introduction. Similarly, for those who have read some Bakhtin, it would be worth directly addressing the difficulties caused by inconsistencies and changes in Bakhtin's own thinking at an earlier point rather than summarising them after they have emerged from the discussion.

The major thesis here is that *The Dynasts* should be relocated 'within the serio-comical genres' and redefined as a novel (xi). Wickens establishes a firm case that Hardy's constant use of reversals of fortune and the folk humour in the working-class sections of the work (and in Hardy's novels) are carnivalesque in effect, and he recognizes the need to accommodate the overall non-comic tone of *The Dynasts*. His claim that it is Menippean in its inclusion of discourses from a huge variety of genres is convincing. However, this need not in itself leads us to redefine the work as a novel, in spite of Wickens's neat and correct insistence that Hardy himself explored such a redefinition (3-4, 67). An alternative to seeing every work that is dialogic and carnivalesque as a novel is to revise Bakhtin's generic boundaries to see heteroglossia as characteristic in some degree of all forms of discourse. Wickens is ready to rethink Bakhtin by readdressing 'some of the problems of Bakhtinian carnival, especially its relation to history and violence' (216) but sticks by his challenge to our notion of genre. It is not his purpose here to develop this argument through extensive comparisons with other novels (though Tolstoy receives several references).

However, a literary critic might object that, for example, Thackeray's part-Napoleonic *Vanity Fair* is palpably serio-comic, dialogic, heteroglossic, and in places carnivalesque. It is also clearly a novel. If *The Dynasts* is a novel, where are its descendants and multigeneric analogues? If we want to retain any useful specificity in the term 'novel', it might be better to see Hardy's work as a magnificent anomaly largely unclassifiable in modern generic terms.

To the first-time reader of *The Dynasts* who wants to grapple with Hardy's thought and with the dramatic effect of the whole, this reviewer would still be inclined to recommend Bailey or Susan Dean's *Hardy's Poetic Vision in* **The Dynasts**. Both deal, in varying degrees, with questions of genre and intellectual influence, although both reflect the critical assumptions of their times[23] and neither displays the

---

[23] 1956 and 1977 respectively.

recognition of the complexities of discourse which Wickens offers. Nevertheless, *Thomas Hardy, Monism, and the Critical Tradition* is welcome as a serious, provocative study that will encourage readers to revisit *The Dynasts*. May it not be another quarter century before the next such book. **C.M.JACKSON-HOULSTON**

Programme cover from ***The Dynasts.***
Adapted by H. Granville Barker and Thomas Hardy, **The Dynasts** opened at the Kingsway Theatre, London, 25 November 1914.

"THE CAMERA'S EYE POEMS"
January-August, 2003

William W. Morgan
wwmorgan@ilstu.edu

Winter Night in Woodland
(Old Time)

The bark of a fox rings, sonorous and long: —
Three barks, and then silentness; 'wong, wong, wong!'
In quality horn-like, yet melancholy,
As from teachings of years; for an old one is he.
The hand of all men is against him, he knows; and yet, why?
That he knows not, — will never know, down to his death-halloo cry.

With clap-nets and lanterns off start the bird-baiters,
In trim to make raids on the roosts in the copse,
Where they beat the boughs artfully, while their awaiters
Grow heavy at home over divers warm drops.
The poachers, with swingels, and matches of brimstone, outcreep
To steal upon pheasants and drowse them a-perch and asleep.

Out there, on the verge, where a path wavers through,
Dark figures, filed singly, thrid quickly the view,
Yet heavily laden: land-carriers are they
In the hire of the smugglers from some nearest bay.
Each bears his two 'tubs', slung across, one in front, one behind,
To a further snug hiding, which none but themselves are to find.

And then, when the night has turned twelve the air brings
From dim distance, a rhythm of voices and strings:
'Tis the quire, just afoot on their long yearly rounds,
To rouse by worn carols each house in their bounds;
Robert Penny, the Dewys, Mail, Voss, and the rest; till anon
Tired and thirsty, but cheerful, they home to their beds in the dawn.

WINTER NIGHT IN WOODLAND[1]

TTHA's "Camera's Eye" Poem of the Month: January 2003 [Read 120 times]

WILLIAM W. MORGAN
wwmorgan@ilstu.edu

IN my dozens of readings of Hardy's *Complete Poems* over the years, I have come back repeatedly and with pleasure to a small cluster of poems, almost all of which appear in *Human Shows* (1925), and all of which seem to aspire to an impersonal, value-free, camera-like narrration. I have in mind "The Sheep-Boy," "Life and Death at Sunrise," "A Light Snow-Fall After Frost," "Last Week in October," "A Sheep Fair," "Last Look Round St. Martin's Fair," "Shortening Days at the Homestead," "An East-End Curate," "A Backward Spring" (the exception, being published in *Moments of Vision* in 1917), "Ice on the Highway," "No Buyers," and this month's poem, "Winter Night in Woodland."

Most of these poems, though undated, were probably written between 1922 (the date of *Late Lyrics*) and 1925 (*Human Shows*); can we draw any inferences from the probable date of "Winter Night in Woodland" and the others? Clearly this poem is not value-free (nor, probably, is any of the others); but what do the poems gain from their reaching after something like neutrality? – Bill.

Thursday, January 02, 2003 10:33 PM
PHILIP ALLINGHAM <apalling@tbaytel.net>
Topic: "Winter Night in Woodland."

This is not the purely pastoral world of Shakespeare's Forest of Arden, for negative elements are present: obscuring fog in "The Sheep-Boy" and a drenching downpour in "A Sheep Fair." In "Winter Night in Woodland (Old Time)," such an element is the presence of night-time predators and outlaws: foxes, bird-baiters, poachers, and smugglers ... Hardy (although a detached observer rather than an engaged commentator) permits us to hear (stanza one) and see (stanzas two and three) the interaction of the animals and the humans

---

[1] See *The Variorum Edition of the Complete Poems of Thomas Hardy*, ed. James Gibson (London: Macmillan, 1979) – hereafter *VECP* -- and *The Complete Poetical Works of Thomas Hardy*, III, ed. Samuel Hynes (Oxford: Clarendon, 1985) – hereafter *CPW*. Hynes, following the holograph and some separate, non-volume publications, includes a comma after the word "twelve" in line 19, whereas Gibson, following *Collected Poems*, shows no internal punctuation in the line subsequent to the comma after "then."

attuned to this green world, and then both to see and hear once again those cherished figures from the Mellstock Quire, "Robert Penny, the Dewys, Mail, Voss, and the rest," who have just completed their seasonal tromp around the cottages to sing the old songs of Hardy's youth ... There is nothing impersonal (despite the absence of the narrator), about the lovingly chosen details that accumulate to produce this appreciation of the Green World, for despair and satire both are absent. Lines that seem "value-free" are in fact an assertion of the value of observation without intrusion, of simply letting the natural rhythm of things be without overt comment or criticism. – P.A.

Friday, January 03, 2003 09:53 AM
PHILIP IRWIN <philip.irwin@btinternet.com>
Topic: "Winter Night in Woodland"

I find this a dark poem, and far from value-free. All four stanzas depict humans satisfying their desires without regard to the harm that ensues. Thus they hunt foxes to the death, steal game birds, act as mules in the distribution of contraband, and disturb their neighbours in the middle of the night and (it is presumed) beg from them. We have but one character giving us a view in this poem, and that is the fox in the first stanza who, in spite of his long experience, finds no logic in human activities. Hardy does not need to give the human rationale: the fox is hunted because it is a thief. Yet this poem shows that nocturnal man is no better. Are we meant to observe a contrast between the hackneyed and disruptive melodies of the revelling carollers and the bewildered but pure howl of the future victim? – P.I

Ice on the Highway

Seven buxom women abreast, and arm in arm,
   Trudge down the hill, tip-toed,
     And breathing warm;
They must perforce trudge thus, to keep upright
   On the glassy ice-bound road,
And they must get to market whether or no,
   Provisions running low
     With the nearing Saturday night,
While the lumbering van wherein they mostly ride
     Can nowise go:
Yet loud their laughter as they stagger and slide!

Yell'ham Hill.

ICE ON THE HIGHWAY[2]
TTHA's "Camera's Eye" Poem of the Month: February 2003: [Read 86 times]

WILLIAM W. MORGAN

"Ice on the Highway" appears just after "Winter Night in Woodland" in *Human Shows* and would seem to be a slighter, less ambitious piece – more of a sketch than a full-blown rhetorical and artistic statement. Is that slightness, however, perhaps strategic, given the poem's placement among the several winter-and-snow poems that make up an informal grouping in this, Hardy's 1925 volume?[3] Are there thematic links between last month's poem and this one? And to what degree is it accurate or useful to talk about this poem's narration as neutral, camera-like? – Bill.

Sunday, February 02, 2003 03:39 PM
PHILIP ALLINGHAM <apalling@tbaytel.net>
Topic: "Ice on the Highway."

Hardy's portrait of "Seven buxom women" making the best of what the weather has made of their lifeline to town is full of the exuberance of a clear day after a winter storm ... "Glassy" suggests that the road has been polished by previous traffic so that the "van" cannot get down "Yell'ham Hill" safely with the women aboard. They make the best of the inconvenience of staggering and sliding by sharing their laughter in momentary release from domestic duties and the privation implied by "Provisions running low." The final words of the poem, "stagger and slide," are keys to the form of the verse itself: eleven lines contain five rhymes (two of a, b, c, and e; three of d) and are made up of five long lines (varying between hexameter and pentameter) and six shorter lines of varying syllables (as few as four in lines 3 and 4, as many as eight in line 8). The scansion, metre, and rhyme scheme are all literally "all over the place," like the slipping, sliding, laughing women on the Dorset high road.

That nature is our adversary and that we must make the best of whatever it imposes upon us is perhaps the link between this lighthearted winter lyric and last month's more ambiguous, darker-tinged verse. Here, too, are the natural backdrop, implied suffering (deprivation, low supplies), and sharp necessity ("they must get to market

---

[2] See *VECP* and *CPW*: there are no discrepancies.
[3] See the introduction (above) to "Winter Night in Woodland."

whether or no"), and the counter note – in "Winter Night in Woodland" struck by the jolly voices of the Mellstock Quire, in "Ice on the Highway," the merry laughter of the momentarily-liberated women. – P. A.

Sunday, February 02, 2003 03:22 PM
PHILIP IRWIN philip.irwin@btinternet.com
Topic: "Ice on the Highway"

As someone who took the day off last week rather than stagger and slide over country roads, I am full of admiration for the determination of this septet to get to market! 'Seven' – albeit a fairy-tale like number – is well chosen. It is just low enough not to make the reader completely disbelieve that such a thing could ever be seen. It is high enough for the line of women completely to dominate the road, and also to be filled with the awareness of how ridiculous they must appear, leading to their hilarity. (Incidentally, by 'buxom' did Hardy mean 'full-bosomed', and if so, is the proximity to 'abreast' intended to be humorous?)

I feel that I am coming at this poem from a different direction to that of Philip Allingham (again!). I don't see privation here – for my part, I never have any food left on a Saturday morning either, since that is my shopping day. Indeed, the fact that these women are off to market, yet are carrying nothing to trade, indicates that they have money in their purses. But what I do agree with is Philip Allingham's remark on the 'exuberance' of this charming poem.

I have an image of dancing. These women are arm in arm, in a line, as at a dance. They are on tiptoe. They are laughing loudly, they are breathless. They stagger, they slide. And I suspect that they will be doing it all again later, for it will soon be Saturday night. – P.I.

Sunday, February 16, 2003 05:39 PM
JASON JONES <mailto:jason.jones@lcc.gatech.edu>
Topic: "Ice on the Highway"

I wonder about the dance-like "exuberance" of this poem, which seems an effect largely produced by the opening and closing lines. But what of lines 2-4, in which the women "Trudge down the hill, tip-toed, / And breathing warm; / They must perforce trudge thus"? That second line is startling: It is extraordinarily hard to "trudge" "tip-toed" – my arches ache just thinking about it. And yet they must "perforce trudge thus." "Perforce" twice over: the ice forcibly requires them to tiptoe this way, and their bare cupboards require them to make this trip today and not another. These lines repeating "trudge," to me, carry a minor undercurrent of privation.

Physically speaking, then, anytime that they "slide" might offer a brief relief from the tip-toed trudging — a relief both bodily and emotional. (This relief is congruent with Philip's observation about making the best of whatever adversarial nature deals us.) I suspect that if we wanted to speak of Hardy's narration here as "neutral," then it is only ostensibly so.

All the best, Jason (who happily lives below the snow).

Sunday, February 23, 2003 06:59 PM
COLIN: <cgame@kalnet.com.au>
Topic: "Ice on the Highway"

A cheerful poem, although it does express the physical hardship of the women: "tip-toed and breathing warm" expresses the earthy pleaure of being pitted against the elements; and again the concluding line expresses the elation of physical exerction and companionship. – C.

A Light Snow-Fall after Frost

On the flat road a man at last appears:
    How much his whitening hairs
Owe to the settling snow's mute anchorage,
And how much to a life's rough pilgrimage,
    One cannot certify.

    The frost is on the wane,
And cobwebs hanging close outside the pane
Pose as festoons of thick white worsted there,
Of their pale presence no eye being aware
    Till the rime made them plain.

    A second man comes by;
His ruddy beard brings fire to the pallid scene:
    His coat is faded green;
    Hence seems it that his mien
    Wears something of the dye
Of the berried holm-trees that he passes nigh.

> The snow-feathers so gently swoop that though
>   But half an hour ago
> The road was brown, and now is starkly white,
> A watcher would have failed defining quite
>   When it transformed it so.
>
> Near Surbiton.

A LIGHT SNOW-FALL AFTER FROST[4]

TTHA's "Camera's Eye" Poem of the Month: March 2003: Read 120 times

WILLIAM W. MORGAN

In last month's poem the ice on the roadway was one among several constraints imposed upon the characters; in this poem the snow seems benign, perhaps even affirmative because aesthetically elegant. Can we draw any conclusions about winter weather and human life from "A Light Snow-Fall after Frost"? The voice in the poem deflects responsibility for his observations onto "One" (line 5) and "a watcher" (line 20); do those gestures allow the poem to maintain a filmic detachment or do they introduce an element of the personal? If the poem were filmed how much would the director have to add to the existing script to make it interesting to a viewer? And, finally, a question about the poem's form: why is the third stanza 6 lines long, while the other three are all 5 lines long? – Bill.

Sunday, March 02, 2003 03:39 PM
PHILIP ALLINGHAM <apalling@tbaytel.net>
Topic: "A Light Snow-Fall after Frost."

Two-and-a-half hours of snow on the 1st of March followed by a thermometer plunge to -31 Celsius or -21 Fahrenheit seems to accord well with the physical dimension of Hardy's lyric. And realists will probably insist that the late winter poem has no other dimension, that the two solitary walkers, the frozen cobwebs, and "the berried holm-trees" possess no particular significance beyond the fact that they are what the first-person commentator sees "outside the pane" of his window (dare we add "at Max Gate"?) ... However, the third stanza is emphasized by a difference in its scansion, there being only two long lines (12 and 16), namely those that introduce the ruddy-bearded man and the "berried holm-trees that he passes nigh."

---

[4] See *VECP* and *CPW*. There are no discrepancies.

Furthermore, the "C" rhyme of line 11 is connected to an earlier stanza (the first), so that it is pivotal, throwing us back to the introduction of the first walker and moving us ahead to the "dye" of the holm berries .... The "watcher" in the poem is curiously detached and objective, a virtual camera, observing but refraining from drawing conclusions; he or she is ungendered and almost unlocated (behind a window pane in a house or office or institution), so that the action is almost unprocessed by a consciousness until the snow-flake image of the last stanza. The emphasis, then, remains on the road, the landscape, the snow, and the two contrasting walkers.

But these elements are not enough to make an interesting film. Somehow, the filmmaker will have to suggest the difference in the two walkers by establishing their very different contexts. What sort of life has each led? What awaits each man at the end of the "pilgrimage"? What interior has each left to venture out into a snow-storm, and with what compelling motive? ... If we need the holm tree to be an image of natural regeneration or of eternal life, so be it, says the lyricist – or perhaps it is, after all, just another species of tree lining the highway and not a cosmic axis or corner-pillar of the earth and sky. – P.A.

Sunday, November 02, 2003 04:18 AM
CAROLYN McGRATH <carolynedwardsuk@yahoo.co.uk>
Topic: Introducing "Light Snow-Fall after Frost"

Just a brief note really, to Philip, about the location. It can't be Max Gate as it says it was written near Surbiton, which today is a part of Greater London (south west of the Thames) and synonymous with the most suburban of suburbia. In Hardy's day it would have been way "out in the sticks" and relatively rural, although not isolated to the extent he was accustomed to. I think this adds to the sense of detachment as the figures would more likely to have been unknown to him and, in the same way, the watcher remains undefined and anonymous – big city life for you!

Thinking of the film idea as more of an impressionistic "short" rather than a blockbuster (it fails miserably on action, motive, development of character – and no car chase) –- I was thinking of something along the lines of Bunuel with an interminably long view of the road with nothing much happening at all. Then at last a human figure appears, only to walk slowly past the window (giving us time to consider the whiteness of hair – appropriate flashes of hard times an option maybe), and slowly disappear along the road. Then another interminable wait followed by a refocus of lens into detail of frozen cobweb (this must be a pub and slow drinking of cider is taking place, if not other substances — reminiscent of bubbles in a glass as in "Taxi Driver"). Slowly, we become aware of a figure approaching and again, with great sense of anticipation, the lens refocuses on the face (first sense of colour with redness of beard/berries and greenness of coat/leaves). Appropriate flashes of Bacchanalian/Celtic delights possibly an option here. Then the man disappears in the opposite direction (interminable wait). Double image of un-snowy road/snowy road to highlight change and then (really corny ending), an aerial view that ascends and ascends until scene is realised as inside one of those snow-scene shaker things and the hand of an Unseen Watcher places it down! Blackout! (It's OK, you don't need to tell me: I'll stick to the day job!) – Carolyn

The Sheep-Boy

A yawning, sunned concave
Of purple, spread as an ocean wave
Entroughed on a morning of swell and sway
After a night when wind-fiends have been heard to rave:
Thus was the Heath called 'Draäts', on an August day.

Suddenly there intunes a hum:
This side, that side, it seems to come.
From the purple in myriads rise the bees
With consternation mid their rapt employ.
So headstrongly each speeds him past, and flees,
As to strike the face of the shepherd-boy.
Awhile he waits, and wonders what they mean;
Till none is left upon the shagged demesne.

To learn what ails, the sheep-boy looks around;
Behind him, out of the sea in swirls
Flexuous and solid, clammy vapour-curls
Are rolling over Pokeswell Hills to the inland ground.
Into the heath they sail,
And travel up the vale
Like the moving pillar of cloud raised by the Israelite: –
In a trice the lonely sheep-boy seen so late ago,
Draäts'-Hollow in gorgeous blow,
And Kite-Hill's regal glow,
Are viewless – folded into those creeping scrolls of white.

On Rainbarrows

THE SHEEP-BOY[5]
TTHA's "Camera's Eyes" Poem of the Month: April 2003: Read 106 times

WILLIAM W. MORGAN

If we believe that Hardy's narrators in these "camera's-eye" poems are not wholly neutral, then perhaps it is worthwhile to ask what specific values such narrators as the one who speaks "The Sheep-Boy" may be said to hold. What features of the poem, in other words, mark the narrator's axiological stance?

The narrator knows the look of the sea, the name of the hills over which the fog is rolling, several other local names, and even the story of the daytime pillar of cloud that led the children of Israel out of captivity. But does he or she reveal any core values by which the experience may be evaluated?

Neutral or not, these poems all induce us to look intently at their scenes: is it part of their strategy that they also are all arranged on the page in such a way as to induce us to look at their shapes? — in other words, do they make themselves into visual objects as their narrators make the poems' scenes into visual objects?

And finally, do we feel a tension in the poem between the personal and local (Draäts'-Hollow, Kite-Hill, Rainbarrows, and Pokeswell Hills – normally spelled Poxwell, by the way), and the universal (the human attempt to understand the behavior of the natural world)?

– Bill.

Monday, April 21, 2003 07:14 PM
KIM OVRUTSKY < ktovrutsky@aol.com>
Topic: Introducing "The Sheep-Boy"

I am puzzled by the biblical reference "like the moving pillar of cloud raised by the Israelite:-"In *Exodus* it is God (through an angel) who creates the pillar of cloud to enable the Israelites to escape the pursuing Egyptians. It is referred to as God's angel and acts as both a guide and protector (a smoke screen).

In "The Sheep-Boy" the cloud is described as being raised by the Israelite(s), not by divine intervention. What is the significance of this? – Kim.

---

[5] See *VECP* and *CPW*: the pattern of indentation differs in the two editions. Hynes's indentations have been followed.

Sunday, April 06, 2003 04:13 PM
ROY BUCKLE <erb@segr.demon.co.uk>
Topic: "The Sheep-Boy"

Neglecting, if I may, who or what I suppose myself to be when reading this poem, the sense of the uncanny conveyed by the description of its lonely scene is associated in my mind with several things. The wonderfully evocative, ancient name of Draäts',[6] possibly denoting ownership of the parcel of land containing the hollow, reminds one of Vagg's Hollow, that other Hardean location (of ill repute). The poem's title is suggestive as well as puzzling. Thinking of the situation of the lonely boy one imagines him perhaps whistling awhile to keep his spirits up (until the bees sound the alarm, of course).

A strange little tune in Debussy's piano suite "Children's Corner" is entitled "The Little Shepherd".[7] This has subtle variations of notional tonality (key) that convey different moods of tranquillity and apprehension not unlike the Hardy poem. But why "The Sheep-Boy" for the title and variously "sheep-boy" and "shepherd-boy" in the somewhat irregular metre of the text? Is this just an instance of the use of "elegant variation"? – Roy.

Thursday, April 10, 2003 03:38 PM
BETTY CORTUS < hardycor@owl.csusm.edu>
Topic: Action in the Poem

"Camera's eye" is an apt epithet for this poem given the fact that its appeal is primarily visual. However, the recording eye must belong to a movie camera because the scene depicted is no still life, but one alive with kinetic energy. First, the undulations of the heath's vegetation gently mimics the nearby ocean waves. Then the action is accelerted as the agitated bees rise in bellicose alarm, speeding hither and thither as if to augur the impending natural disturbance. Finally, the awe-inspiring approach of the fog culminates the action, and the poem ends with total visual white-out of the scene. Likening the approaching fog bank to the biblical "pillar of cloud" is not an overdramatization. I have watched spellbound as a similar dense fog bank, appearing as out of nowhere on a perfectly clear, calm day, rolled in ominously from the Pacific, with jittery sea birds fleeing before it. What a memorable sight! – Betty.

---

[6] "Draäts Hollow" is taken from the Dorset dialect word "draäts" meaning drafts or moist winds (Jim Gibson).

[7] Listen to the Debussy on < www.segr-music.net>. RB

A Sheep Fair

The day arrives of the autumn fair,
    And torrents fall,
Though sheep in throngs are gathered there,
    Ten thousand all,
Sodden, with hurdles round them reared:
And, lot by lot, the pens are cleared,
And the auctioneer wrings out his beard,
And wipes his book, bedrenched and smeared,
And rakes the rain from his face with the edge of his hand,
    As torrents fall.

The wool of the ewes is like a sponge
    With the daylong rain:
Jammed tight, to turn, or lie, or lunge,
    They strive in vain.
Their horns are soft as finger-nails,
Their shepherds reek against the rails,
The tied dogs soak with tucked-in tails,
The buyers' hat-brims fill like pails,
Which spill small cascades when they shift their stand.
    In the daylong rain.

POSTSCRIPT

Time has trailed lengthily since met
    At Pummery Fair
Those panting thousands in their wet
    And woolly wear:
And every flock long since has bled,
And all the dripping buyers have sped,
And the hoarse auctioneer is dead,
Who 'Going--going!' so often said,
As he consigned to doom each meek, mewed band
    At Pummery Fair.

Last Look round St. Martin's Fair

The sun is like an open furnace door,
Whose round revealed retort confines the roar
    Of fires beyond terrene;
The moon presents the luster-lacking face
    Of a brass dial gone green,

Whose hours no eye can trace.
The unsold heathcroppers are driven home
To the shades of the Great Forest whence they come
By men with long cord-waistcoats in brown monochrome.
The stars break out, and flicker in the breeze,
    It seems, that twitches the trees. –
    From its hot idol soon
The fickle unresting earth has turned to a fresh patroon--
    The cold, now brighter, moon.
The woman in red, at the nut-stall with the gun,
    Lights up, and still goes on:
She's redder in the flare-lamp than the sun
    Showed it ere it was gone.
Her hands are black with loading all the day,
And yet she treats her labour as 'twere play,
Tosses her ear-rings, and talks ribaldry
To the young men around as natural gaiety,
And not a weary work she'd readily stay,
    And never again nut-shooting see,
    Though crying, 'Fire away!'

A SHEEP FAIR & LAST LOOK ROUND ST. MARTIN'S FAIR[8]

TTHA's "Camera's Eye" Poems of the Month: May 2003: Read 56 times

WILLIAM W. MORGAN

Like several of the poems in this series (that is, poems with narrators who seek to function as neutral observers), these two appear to be carefully shaped as visual objects on the page; notice, for example, the symmetry of the three stanzas of "A Sheep Fair" and the movement among the various line-lengths in "Last Look round St. Martin's Fair": is there some relationship between the poems' camera-like neutrality and their formal "stillness" as objects on the page? Do we prefer to read "Last Look round St. Martin's Fair" with a stanza break after line 14 (see note below) as Hardy left it in the holograph or without the break as he revised it for *Human Shows*, *Collected Poems* and the Wessex Edition? What can we say about fairs in Hardy's work – remembering, besides these two poems, the

---

[8] See *VECP* and *CPW*. There are no discrepancies although Hynes, following the holograph, gives a stanza break after line 14, whereas Gibson, following *Human Shows* and the Wessex edition, gives no stanza break. Gibson is followed in this matter.

important scenes in *Far From the Madding Crowd* and *The Mayor of Casterbridge*? – Bill.

Sunday, May 04, 2003 04:18 PM
PHILIP ALLINGHAM <apalling@tbaytel.net>
Topic: "A Sheep Fair" & "Last Look round St. Martin's Fair."

The rain, in "A Sheep Fair," is an objective correlative for one aspect of the natural rhythm of things, the autumn of all natural cycles. The dreary mood and depressing weather are established by a montage of still-shots against the wide pan of ten thousand sheep. That the rain is life-giving hardly occurs to us as we experience a thorough drenching through identification with the auctioneer who, frustrated with the situation, must wring out his beard and wipe his book – the buyers' "hat-brims fill[ed] like pails." Such telling details as the auctioneer's using the edge of his hand to clear the rain-water, the ewes' fleeces being "like a sponge" and the sweating shepherds "reek[ing] against the rails" convince us of the miserable nature of this fall fair. The "Postscript" adds the pensive note, the application of the scene's inner meaning to human life: man is as a grass.

The "allegro" tempo of "Last Look round St. Martin's Fair" hinges upon the representative of the life force ... The moon ....which governs the tides and is associated with the hours of the night, is green and pale here; the sun is in the ascendant. Although this, too, is a working fair, and she is but a working woman, "The woman in red" takes joy in her labour, which is the very opposite of work: amusement, entertainment, "ribaldry." Although undoubtedly her customers are of all ages, the camera-like poet's eye notes "the young men" who respond to the phallic call of the summer siren: "Fire away!"– P.

Sunday, May 04, 2003 09:15 AM
PHILIP IRWIN < philip.irwin@btinternet.com>
Topic: "A Sheep Fair" & "Last Look round St. Martin's Fair."

The fairs in both of these poems are dominated at first by a single character – the auctioneer and the sun – each of whom loses his grip in consequence of the natural order of the universe, one through sunset and the other through death. The blistering sun at St Martin's Fair washes out the brightness of other objects, be it the moon, the clothes of the pony drivers, or the lamp at the nut stall. The observer presents the fair as being more amenable at night. The colour of the lamp is now inviting, and, with the crowd at the nut stall, we are provided for the first time with a sense of the thronging that should be part of a fair. At first the setting of the sun seems to have had a liberating effect. The earth has changed her lord. The ponies, presumably tethered in the sun during the day, are now freely roaming the shadows of the forest. The young men are flirting with the red-illuminated woman, and all are being invited to 'fire away', without restriction. Yet the woman herself is not so free. She would rather 'never again nut-shooting see', but must appear playful in this laborious job. (Hardy means to suggest that the 'natural gaiety' is contrived in order to encourage custom).

At Pummery Fair, just as at St Martin's Fair, the weather makes things uncomfortable. And at both, the animal traders are prepared to endure the conditions. But the fate of the auctioneer and the sheep may prompt a wry smile at such endurance, as futile as the lunges of the immobilised ewes. The humour crafted by the four successive rhymes in each stanza builds up to the ghastly irony of the auctioneer's life: that the phrase 'going, going' applies equally to him, and his time will end with the unspoken 'gone'. God-like with his beard and book, he despatches the flocks to their doom ('doom' here also carrying the connotations of its older meaning, 'judgement'). Yet, as for the sheep who will be slaughtered no matter where they go from the auction, so for him: both he and those whose fate he seemingly managed will end up no more than an observer's memory of a scene on a rain-soaked day. – Philip Irwin

A Backward Spring

The trees are afraid to put forth buds,
And there is timidity in the grass;
The plots lie gray where gouged by spuds,
    And whether next week will pass
Free of sly sour winds is the fret of each bush
    Of barberry waiting to bloom.

Yet the snowdrop's face betrays no gloom,
And the primrose pants in its heedless push,
Though the myrtle asks if it's worth the fight
    This year with frost and rime
    To venture one more time
On delicate leaves and buttons of white
From the selfsame bough as at last year's prime,
And never to ruminate on or remember
What happened to it in mid-December.

April 1917

Shortening Days at the Homestead

The first fire since the summer is lit, and is smoking into the room:
    The sun-rays thread it through, like woof-lines in a loom.
    Sparrows spurt from the hedge, whom misgivings appal
That winter did not leave last year for ever, after all.
    Like shock-headed urchins, spiny-haired,
    Stand pollard willows, their twigs just bared.

Who is this coming with pondering pace,
Black and ruddy, with white embossed,
His eyes being black, and ruddy his face,
And the marge of his hair like morning frost?
    It's the cider-maker,
    And appletree-shaker,
And behind him on wheels, in readiness,
His mill, and tubs, and vat, and press.

Last Week in October

    The trees are undressing, and fling in many places –
    On the gray road, the roof, the window-sill –
    Their radiant robes and ribbons and yellow laces;
    A leaf each second so is flung at will,
Here, there, another and another, still and still.

    A spider's web has caught one while downcoming,
    That stays there dangling when the rest pass on;
    Like a suspended criminal hangs he, mumming
    In golden garb, while one yet green, high yon,
Trembles, as fearing such a fate for himself anon.

A BACKWARD SPRING, SHORTENING DAYS AT THE HOMESTEAD & LAST WEEK IN OCTOBER.[9]

TTHA's "Camera's Eye" Poems of the Month: June 2003: Read 42 times

WILLIAM W. MORGAN

All three poems are about the transition between the seasons – from winter into spring in the first and from autumn into winter in the

---

[9] See *VECP* and *CPW*: there are no discrepancies.

other two – and all three of them cast winter as the persistent threat to natural life. But in "Shortening Days at the Homestead," it would appear that the arrival of the cider-maker can give a kind of pleasure to humans, despite the coming season's hardships; is it claiming too much to suggest that Hardy in this piece gives humanity an exemption from winter's threat – an exemption based, perhaps, on our knowledge of the cyclical pattern of the seasons? Although these three are in the same general family with the other "camera-eye" poems we have been looking at, they do just hint at a narrating consciousness in a way we haven't seen before in this series: they all project consciousness onto plants, leaves, and birds (thereby suggesting a narrative presence capable of doing the projecting), and the last one gives weight and value to its narrator by introducing the question "Who is this coming?" with its attendant tone of welcome (or at least I think I detect welcome – in the two short lines in particular). Are these faintly drawn narrators effective devices, or would we prefer the more nearly objective camera-eye of, say, "A Light Snow-Fall after Frost"? – Bill.

Thursday, June 05, 2003 20.34
PHILIP ALLINGHAM <philip allingham apalling@tbaytel.net>
Topic: Imposing Persona in Seasonal Lyrics

Despite the effectiveness of the metaphor, is winter for flora and fauna, per se, the equivalent of death for human beings? The cider-maker, despite the frost in his hair, maintains a healthy, cheerful disposition despite his age, bringing the promise of momentary forgetfulness of Adam's curse to those who will consume the product of his labour. Throughout the three poems, these pessimistic plants and animals fear the oblivion of winter and never consider the possibility of rebirth in the following spring; this attitude seems to be a projection of the narrator's mental state rather than what they really "feel." The narrating consciousness infuses the birds, leaves, and trees not merely with self-awareness but also with a defeatist attitude that seems inconsistent with the possibility of physical renewal. – PA

Saturday, June 07, 2003 01:45 AM
ROSEMARIE MORGAN rosemarie.morgan@yale.edu
Topic: "A Backward Spring," "Shortening Days ..." "Last Week ..."

The narrative consciousness in these three poems seems to me to be far too subjective – interior, even – to fulfil that impartial exteriority we might expect of a "camera's eye." To start with, each one of the poems points to a temporal sense of expectation – an awareness of something about to happen, and as far as we know the inanimate observer (camera lens) does not possess or express sensory experience. "A Backward Spring" not only glances at things to come which have not yet arrived but also to a past as well as a memory of that past: "What happened ... in mid-December." This implies a human presence and a partial consciousness – or I should say a consciousness which is partial (and therefore selective). The partiality resides in the projection of specific feelings (anxiety, despair) on to a natural world (first stanza) to which that world is oblivious (second stanza). The element of temporality, or consciousness of time, is strongly marked: there is an awareness of "next week," "this year," "last year," and of course, of rumination and remembering.

Something similar occurs in "Shortening Days at the Homestead." The temporal sense is palpable – acute enough to convey that profound, contented sense of a deep rhythmic, if unconscious, response to the seasons; there is the reassurance of recurrence and repetition; there is the comforting idea of the lighting of that "first fire since the summer." And that *frisson* of expectation, of awaiting with pleasant anticipation all that the winter season might bring, is made manifest with the arrival of the cider-maker. The narrator's eagerness here banishes any sense of the camera's-eye. This is no impartial framing. There is first a questioning intelligence afoot: "Who is this coming"? Curiosity is aroused. The narrator then intensifies this by "seeing" at a distance the gait, the pace, and then shortly afterwards a blur of colours "Black and ruddy," and the graying hair. Then comes the satisfaction of recognition: this is indeed the cider-maker.

This long-shot to close-up could of course be performed by the "camera's eye" but no artifical lens is capable of conveying the question and subsequent emotional anticipation inherent in "Who is coming"? At this point in the poem, with a sense of imminent completion, we are given the season's blessing, the knowledge of a well-prepared-for winter – all is as it should be: there is good cheer in expectations fulfilled, in "readiness."

For a finely developed "interior" consciousness of greater psychological complexity, "Last Week in October" invokes a sensuality not uncommon to the highly imaginative mind in a state of reverie. It is not that the trees are shedding their leaves but that they are "undressing." And as they do so they "fling" their "radiant robes" about in wild abandon: there is no ambiguity to the sexual overtones. Some of the "garments" are (traditional) feminine attire – they sport "ribbons and yellow laces." A predator (spider) enters the scene and lays a trap. At this point the mood changes. There is now a sense of menace as a leaf is caught in the web: "Like a suspended criminal hangs he." Notice the gender. The erotic action is over (as gestured in the "dangling" male?). The time of reckoning has come. Possibly the act of shedding in such wild abandon is fateful; why else does each remaining leaf fear "such a fate for himself"? Interestingly the word "leaf" is mentioned only once in the entire poem. Whatever it triggers in the mind of the narrator the arboreal, by the time the poem concludes, is far more remote to the reader's mind than are the sensual and the psychological implications. – R.M.

Saturday, June 07, 2003 12:33 PM
BETTY CORTUS <hardycor@owl.csusm.edu>
Topic: "A Backward Spring," "Last Week ..." "Shortening Days..."

Although "Last Week in October" is superficially one of those "camera's-eye" poems simply depicting a scene in nature, the subtextual message that autumn's falling leaves symbolize human mortality cannot be entirely dismissed. The metaphor of the trees "undressing" is reminiscent of Hopkins' lines: "Margaret are you grieving / Over Goldengrove unleaving?" Here the realization that the subconscious knowledge of her own mortality is the deeper cause for the child's regret over the autumnal leaf-shedding is much more explicitly delineated than in Hardy's poem: "It is the blight man was born for / It is Margaret you mourn for" (Spring and Fall). Hardy's rather macabre likening of the fallen leaf dangling on a spider's web to "a suspended criminal" hanged for his misdeeds is a blunter, and more circuitous way of linking the seasonal death of nature to human mortality. If the comparison between these two poems can be extended to view Hopkins' Margaret as analogous to Hardy's still-green, unfallen leaf, the child's grief suggests a poignancy of feeling that the leaf's, near-comic, trembling fear does not. However, grief and fear are both emotions integral to thoughts of death. But Hardy's poem manages to conceal this darker human tragedy under a maquillage of arresting figurative language and vivid pictorial imagery. – B.C.

June 26, 2003 10:34 AM
JOAN SHESKI <harrys@cnetco.com >
Topic: "A Backward Spring," "Last Week..." "Shortening Days..."

The last two lines, "And never to remember, What happened to it in December," suggest to me a 'natural order' or fundamental axiom without which life could not begin anew; the balm of denial and forgetfulness of death. This is underscored when one compares nature's December to humankind's constructions at that time – solstice lights and fires, celebrating the birth of Jesus, using blood red and leaf green colors — we fling life symbols at December, yet its stone-grey cold death continues to surround us. Thus the lines minimize human consciousness and volition. We, just as the myrtle, are subject to nature's laws, and one of them is "never to remember" death when we need so very much energy for new life. – Joan Sheski

Wednesday, July 02, 2003 06:07 AM
MICHALINA PAWLIKOWSKA <michalina_maria@poczta.onet.pl>
Topic: Melancholy vs joy. Hanging scene.

The interplay of melancholy and joy is visible in all three poems. "Shortening Days in a Homestead", however, is written in a much lighter tone than the two other poems. There's an air of mischief about it. The sparrows are described as "shock-headed urchins" deliberating in a mock-serious manner over why winter didn't depart last year for ever. "Backward Spring" seems enveloped in a darker mood. I'd like to point to the musical quality of its last 2 lines. They seem to flow on, quickening, echoing with an ominous ring. The idea of fate comes to mind. The myrtle is shown as a passive victim manipulated by forces beyond its control (things "happen" to it).

Winter is indeed presented as a threat. Such words as "fret" "tremble", "fearing", "misgivings", "appal", emphasize the feeling of fear. On the other hand, there's no "gloom" in the "snowdrop's face". The primrose seems very eager to grow; it "pants", in a "push" (words reminding one of the process of childbirth). In "A Last Week in October", the vigorous motions of the undressing trees in stanza 1 stand in contrast to the gloomy hanging scene in stanza 2. The trees seem as eager to shed their garments as the primrose in the previous poem was to grow. They undress speedily ("a leaf" falling "each second") and emphasis is placed on their "will". The preparation for winter is presented as a necessary stage in the cyclic movement of the seasons. It is as important as the preparation for spring.

In "Shortening Days in a Homestead" the melancholy image of smoke interwoven with sun-rays is followed by the boisterous, invigorating image of the "cider-maker". The compact lines presenting him ("It's the cider-maker / And appletree-shaker") suggest that he "shakes" the trees with force. He reminds me of Winterborne, described as "autumn's very brother", an image of force, vigor and life.

The contrast between the hanging golden leaf caught in the spider-web and the green leaf on the tree is reminiscent of the closing scene in *Tess*, where, symbolized by the "black flag" (signifying her hanging) Tess is contrasted to the "spiritualized image of Tess", Liza-Lu. One has already experienced life's tragedy, while the other is still fresh, "green" ("She has all the best of me without the bad of me"). Perhaps, while watching the execution, Liza-Lu experiences a fear similar to that of the leaf.

An ever-surprising feature of Hardy's poetry is the freshness of his descriptions. Such expressions as "buttons of white" or the comparison of sun rays to woof lines testify to the fresh, imaginative quality of his observations. The interlacing of sun rays and tendrils of smoke suggests a union of autumn (sun) and winter (fire, smoke). Another interesting thing is Hardy's use of alliteration: "sly sour winds", "radiant robes and ribbons", "golden garb, while one yet green" – they add to the musical quality of his verse. – Misia.

Wednesday, November 12, 2003 06:19 PM
CAROLYN McGRATH < carolynedwardsuk@yahoo.co.uk>
Topic: "Backward Spring", "Last Week ...", " Shortening Days ..."

I'll add my comments to Joan's as I would also like to limit myself, in this posting, to 'A Backward Spring'. It interested me in its distinct tone which, as Michalina has already noted, is darker than the other two. It was written earlier than the others, which were written, I think, in the 1920s. The significance of April 1917 leaps out as being the end of the third year of The Great War when the promise of being 'over by Christmas' had not only failed miserably to materialize in 1914, but seemed just as unlikely in the coming year. The previous year the horrors of trench warfare had plumbed new depths and so it seems little wonder that Hardy should view the delayed spring of '17 so pensively.

The reason I think the poem is a reflection of the social and political context is not merely due to the dating of the poem, although Hardy is drawing our attention to the significance of time rather than place by doing so, but also to the structure and content of the poem. The poem seems more 'philosophical' in the logical development of its argument than the other poems. The first stanza is a quatrain, although interestingly the rhyme scheme pushes across to the first two lines of the second stanza – ababcd(dc)effefgg – is it a sort of sonnet, stretched by an extra line? And would the extra line be the additional rhyme, "From the selfsame bough as at last year's prime"? This stanza describes the lateness of spring that year by attributing human characteristics to the trees, grass, potato fields and barberry (blackberry?)[10] bushes which are apprehensive about risking their

---

[10] Barberry, common in ornamental hedges, is a thorny shrub (*Berberis*), bearing yellow flowers and red (occasionally black) berries.

buds and blooms to an uncertain, potentially hostile, future. These plants are common and wide-spread; it seems to be the generally held opinion of nature to err on the side of caution when faced with the risk of "sly sour winds".

The second stanza, linked by the rhyme scheme to the first stanza, is logically separated from it by the contrasting idea introduced by "Yet". There follow only two lines which give two examples – the snowdrop and the primrose – whose life force urges them on to grow despite the risks. I can't quite put my finger on Hardy's attitude to this, but he doesn't seem to be neutrally recording the power of these natural impulses as the word "betrays" suggests the snowdrop is not oblivious to the dangers and the primrose, being 'heedless', is powerless to act with reason.

The third line, on the other hand, poses an alternative point of view, that of the myrtle (and the Hardyan 'speaker'), who questions the value of persisting in this seemingly futile battle to survive. Why the myrtle? Is it coincidence that the myrtle is associated with Aphrodite who, as it says in my dictionary of world mythology, is "not only a deity of sexual love but also of affection and all the impulses that underpin social life"? The myrtle seems to be a lone voice in Nature who not only questions whether it is "worth the fight / This year../ To venture one more time," but the emphasis lies on that extra line, "From the selfsame bough as at last year's prime," and it is the myrtle who must knowingly suspend its consciousness or memory of "What happened to it in mid-December" to be able to continue to make further sacrifices. [11]

I am not arguing that this limits the poem to any literal connection like "last year's prime" = the dead of 1916 or that "December" = the 12th month or that "snowdrop" = warmonger! I am suggesting that the context of the war and the late spring provoked a rumination on Hardy's part on the connections between the adversity and cruelty faced by nature year on year and that of the seemingly endless repetition of human history destroying itself, an affliction we are sadly not free of today. – Carolyn.

---

[11] There are a variety of "myrtle" connotations. Myrrh is obtained from the Arabian myrtle (*Balsamodendrun myrrha*). *Myrtle* is associated with turtledoves, Cupid's bow, Cupid's dart, love tokens. A leaf of *myrtle*, viewed in a strong light, shows innumerable tiny punctures. **Fable**: 1. Phaedra fell in love with her stepson, Hippolytus, and hid in a *myrtle* tree to await his return from the hunt, meantime she pierced the leaves with a hairpin. He rejected her love and she then plotted his death. 2. In *Orlando Furioso* Astolpho is changed into a *myrtle* tree by Acrisia. 3. Myrrha, mother of Adonis, had an incestuous love for her own father, and was changed into a *myrtle* tree. 4. Ancient Jewish tradition holds that eating *myrtle* leaves confers the power of detecting witches; also, that if the leaves crackle in the hands of a beloved that s/he would prove faithful.

No Buyers
A Street Scene

A load of brushes and baskets and cradles and chairs
    Labours along the street in the rain:
With it a man, a woman, a pony with whiteybrown hairs, –
    The man foots in front of the horse with a shambling sway
        At a slower tread than a funeral train,
    While to a dirge-like tune he chants his wares,
Swinging a Turk's-head brush (in a drum-major's way
        When the bandsmen march and play).

A yard from the back of the man is the whiteybrown pony's nose:
He mirrors his master in every item of pace and pose:
    He stops when the man stops, without being told,
    And seems to be eased by a pause; too plainly he's old,
        Indeed, not strength enough shows
    To steer the disjointed wagon straight,
Which wriggles left and right in a rambling line,
Deflected thus by its own warp and weight,
And pushing the pony with it in each incline.

    The woman walks on the pavement verge,
        Parallel to the man:
    She wears an apron white and wide in span,
And carries a like Turk's-head, but more in nursing-wise:
        Now and then she joins in his dirge,
        But as if her thoughts were on distant things.
        The rain clams her apron till it clings. –
So, step by step, they move with their merchandize,
        And nobody buys.

An East-End Curate

A small blind street off East Commercial Road;
    Window, door; window, door;
    Every house like the one before,
Is where the curate, Mr Dowle, has found a pinched abode.
Spectacled, pale, moustache straw-coloured, and with a long thin face,
Day or dark his lodgings' narrow doorstep does he pace.

A bleached pianoforte, with its drawn silk plaitings faded,
Stands in his room, its keys much yellowed, cyphering, and abraded,
'Novello's Anthems' lie at hand, and also a few glees,
And 'Laws of Heaven for Earth' in a frame upon the wall one sees.

He goes through his neighbours' houses as his own, and none regards,
And opens their back-doors off-hand, to look for them in their yards:
A man is threatening his wife on the other side of the wall,
But the curate lets it pass as knowing the history of it all.

Freely within his hearing the children skip and laugh and say:
    'There's Mister Dow-well! There's Mister Dow-well! in their play;
    And the long, pallid, devoted face notes not,
But stoops along abstractedly, for good, or in vain, God wot!

NO BUYERS & AN EAST-END CURATE[12]
TTHA's "Camera's Eye" Poems of the Month: July 2003: Read 40 times

WILLIAM W. MORGAN

Like several other poems in this series of "camera-eye" poems, both present street scenes with people immersed in their work lives in a fairly routine – perhaps even mechanical – manner. But "No Buyers" is probably a rural or small town scene, whereas "An East-End Curate" is explicitly urban (unusual in Hardy's canon); the former presents work as a labor of self-directed sustenance and survival, whereas the latter describes a kind of work that consists of service to others. My lead-off question, therefore, is this: does the distant, impersonal stance of the narrator in the two poems work equally well with the two settings and with the two kinds of work? And, following up on the idea of work as service, is it useful to compare the donkey in the first poem with the curate in the second?

Finally, I wonder once more what we can say about the arrangement of these poems on the page. It's clear to me, for instance, that lines 2 & 3 and 16 & 17 of "An East-End Curate" are indented the same in order to suggest an aural and thematic kinship between them (both sound like skip-rope rhymes, and both present a kind of mindless repetition); can we say more about the logic of Hardy's indentation and visual shaping in the poems? – Bill.

---

[12] See *VECP* & *CPW*. There are no discrepancies.

Wednesday, July 02, 2003 11:31 AM
ROBERT SCHWEIK <schweik@fredonia.edu>
Topic: Introducing "No Buyers" and "An East-End Curate"

With respect to "No Buyers," I'd like to call attention to a recent comment on that poem in McSweeney, L. "J. Stanyan Bigg's 'An Irish Picture.'" *Victorian Poetry*, 39.3 (Fall, 2001): 407-11. The comment is on what John Hollander has called "notional ecphrasis" (or ekphrasis).[13] The idea is that certain poems, including J. Stanyan Bigg's and Hardy's, have a resemblance to ekphrastic poetry in that, although they do not purport to provide a description of a piece of visual art, they have qualities characteristic of that kind of poetic description.

In this respect, it seems to me, "No Buyers" differs from "An East-End Curate" in its far greater reliance on spatial references – e.g., "in front," "a yard in back," "left and right," "parallel" – as well as far more detailed physical description. – Bob.

Sunday, July 20, 2003 04:22 PM
BETTY CORTUS <:hardycor@owl.csusm.edu>
Topic: "No Buyers" and "An East-End Curate."

One element that the characters in "No Buyers" share with Mr Dowle, the East-End curate, is the painful futility of their chosen occupations. Yet while all are fruitless in their attempts to sell their wares, whether mundane or spiritual, to an uninterested public, it is the plodding persistence of the hapless street vendors and their geriatric pony that engage my sympathies more readily than do the aimless dodderings of the absent-minded curate.

I am not sure why this is. Perhaps it is the dogged willingness of the hawkers to carry on in the face of total discouragement that indicates a stubborn fortitude and a commitment to life that the curate lacks. Although equally indigent as they, he appears to have given up trying to pursue his ineffectual ministry. Ignored by adults and jeered at by children, he lets life pass him by, inured to the poverty and domestic violence around him, he is as one who has seen "the history of it all" and whose crusading days are long past. So while he seems

---

[13] "*Ekphrasis*, when used as a literary term, refers to a verbal description of a painting or other work of visual art. John Hollander uses the term "notional *ekphrasis*" to refer to a poem or other verbal work, which, although there is no explicit reference to a painting or other work of visual art has, nevertheless, the qualities of *ekphrasis*.."

to be too far sunken in apathy to elicit a great deal of sympathy from this reader, I still cherish a feeble hope that the vendors' luck might eventually change for the better. – Betty.

Wednesday, December 17, 2003 09:58 AM
CAROLYN McGRATH carolynmcgrathuk@yahoo.co.uk
Topic: "No Buyers" and "An East-End Curate."

A few words in defence of the hapless Mr Dowle:

I agreed with Betty regarding the ease with which our compassion is aroused by the three figures in "No Buyer", and that Mr Dowle, the "East End Curate", appears to provoke our irritation in equal measure, which modifies our empathy. However, it irked me somehow that I felt critical of this man and, as my response to that poem seemed more complex, I kept going back to both and have gradually altered my view.

"East End Curate" is gritty, black and white, kitchen-sink, social realism. Whereas, it seems to me, the picture painted by "No Buyers" is an Old Masters in oils. "No Buyers" seems picturesque despite the alienation it portrays. Rather than fleshed out human beings, the three figures remain symbolic of the human/working class under the 'weight and warp' of market forces. The goods 'labour' and the living creatures are driven in absentminded pursuit of a non-sale. Their passivity is dispiriting yet their stoicism, as they plod on in the rain, stirs our respect. The horse 'mirrors his master' and survives the hardship of his life despite his obvious age. The human figures may also be elderly, but there is an abstract timelessness about them. The man's slow, fervourless progress is an image of wasted 'male energy'; the funereal march and dirge-like chant incongruously contrast with the vigour of a military band; the woman, nursing the Turk's head brush in her empty arms, is an image of maternal potential. Their enervation is due, in part maybe, to their age, but ultimately to the deadening hand of futility/capitalism/fate sapping their life force. Despite their passivity, it is the survival of this potential that we respond so warmly to.

Why then doesn't poor Mr Dowle evoke similar sympathy? We know so much more about him than the figures of "No Buyers"yet, or therefore, are far more critical of him. He lives in a dead-end road off East Commercial Road and serves a very impoverished parish. In Hardy's day, this would have been the gateway to and from the Empire, yet for those who lived and worked there, the riches offered were denied and many on the docks survived on very irregular and unreliable sources of income. Yet it is here that Mr Dowle "has found a pinched abode". It is the adjectives throughout the poem that paint such a paltry picture of the man and his life: "small blind street", "pinched abode", "spectacled", "pale", "straw-coloured", "long thin face", "narrow doorstep", "bleached", "faded", "yellowed", "abraded", "long, pallid". They accumulate to emphasise the shrunken, insipid and ineffectual aspects of his existence. Which is why the word "devoted" suddenly shines out. What is this man devoted to?

On re-reading the poem I discovered more energy, however futile and ineffective it be spent, than in "No Buyers". No slow tread for this man, "Day or dark his lodgings' narrow doorstep does he pace". To what end is never quite clear but therein lies the tragedy. Within his room, the aging pianoforte appears much used and his current musical interests lie at hand. The loneliness of his existence is suggested by the reference to "glees", apparently unaccompanied male solos. (What does cyphering mean here? Is it much as my annotations of Hardy's poems?) The fact that he can go "'through his neighbours' houses as his own" is as much a tribute to his being part of the community he lives in as a source of condemnation for not being regarded as different, in respect to his being a man of the cloth.

This side of the twentieth century, we read his non-interference in the domestic dispute as collusion with domestic violence. In a community where, "Window, door, window, door" people live in close proximity to each other, he would know "the history of it all". It is true, isn't it, that sometimes the 'threatening' of violence is understandable, even forgivable? Sometimes that can be said of violence itself. That Mr Dowle "lets it pass" suggests that, in other circumstances, he would step in but considers it inappropriate here. Is he wrong?

Neither can I condemn him for allowing the children "Freely within his hearing" to "skip and laugh" and mockingly call his name. His "long, pallid, devoted face" must look quite kindly on these, his young parishioners, as he "stoops along abstractedly". He may be a figure of fun but he's our figure of fun. He neither condemns nor colludes, he is part of yet remains apart from the community he serves. That he does so "for good, or in vain", Hardy does not resolve, but the character of Mr Dowle is not a ne'er-do-well and, although we may have greater aspirations for those who would spiritually lead in our communities, I cannot judge him harshly.

Carolyn McGrath

Life and Death at Sunrise

(Near Dogbury Gate, 1867)

The hills uncap their tops
Of woodland, pasture, copse,
And look on the layers of mist
At their foot that still persist:
They are like awakened sleepers on one elbow lifted,
Who gaze around to learn if things during night have shifted.

A waggon creaks up from the fog
With a laboured leisurely jog;
Then a horseman from off the hill-tip
Comes clapping down into the dip;
While woodlarks, finches, sparrows, try to entune at one time,
And cocks and hens and cows and bulls take up the chime.

With a shouldered basket and flagon
A man meets the one with the waggon,
And both the men halt of long use.
'Well,' the waggoner says, 'what's the news?'
' – 'Tis a boy this time. You've just met the doctor trotting back.
She's doing very well. And we think we shall call him "Jack".

'And what have you got covered there?'
He nods to the waggon and mare.
'Oh, a coffin for old John Thinn:
We are just going to put him in.'
' – So he's gone at last. He always had a good constitution.'
' – He was ninety-odd. He could call up the French Revolution.'

LIFE AND DEATH AT SUNRISE[14]

TTHA's "Camera's Eye" Poem of the Month: August 2003: Read 89 times

WILLIAM W. MORGAN

I hope that we will be able to use this poem, the last in the series on Hardy's "camera-eye" poems, as a chance not only to become more familiar with "Life and Death at Sunrise" but also as a chance to attempt to draw some conclusions about these poems as a group. As I

---

[14] See *VECP* & *CPW*. There are no discrepancies.

mentioned in my first introduction to this series, for "Winter Night in Woodland", all but one of the "camera-eye" poems first appeared in Hardy's 1925 volume, *Human Shows, Far Phantasies, Songs, and Trifles*. The exception is "A Backward Spring," first published in *Moments of Vision* (1917). If we assume that the bulk of these poems was written between 1922 (the date of *Late Lyrics*) and 1925, two hypotheses occur to me about Hardy's writing life during those three years: he may have set out deliberately to write some poems in which he meant to keep his narrators at some distance from the matter they narrated; or he may have been, without consciously choosing his technique, psychologically drawn to narrative distance for the coolness, even the ego-lessness it might offer. In either case I'm glad he did it, and my curiosity is piqued by the question of why he might have done it. Can we make any useful connections between what is known about the life of Hardy the citizen in the period 1922-5 and this feature of the poetic practice of Hardy the writer in the same period?

Some questions about this poem: where does the narrator (or camera?) stand in order to be able to see everything that happens in the poem? The poem's title and its matter-of-fact reporting of a simultaneous birth and death suggest an ongoing natural cycle of beginnings and endings – the man who has died is John Thinn, the new baby is "Jack": are we to read the young one as a kind of continuation of the old man's life? Does the four-stanza structure support this theme or possibly compete with it? – Bill.

Tuesday, August 12, 2003 08:21 AM
PHILIP ALLINGHAM apalling@tbaytel.net
Topic: "Life and Death at Sunrise"

In "Life and Death at Sunrise" the visual and auditory elements are subtly presented so that the effect is like that of a roving sound-camera: "A waggon creaks up from the fog," for instance. Is Hardy, then, extending the technique of the moving picture, or is he merely continuing to use detailism – telling sounds and images – as he has always done in order to establish the scene more palpably in the mind's eye? – P. A.

Wednesday, August 13, 2003 08:01 AM
RICHARD MINTZ < jhexam7563@aol.com>
Topic: "Life and Death at Sunrise."

A comment in passing: the word copse reminds me of something I read of woodland economy. The practice was to cut down a tree from the stump of which new sprouts would grow. I'm not sure how that fits in – old Thinn was not cut down in the prime of life, but in any case, new sprouts will come forth. The "camera" can't take in all the details. – Richard

Tuesday, August 19, 2003 04:44 AM
PHILIP IRWIN < philip.irwin@btinternet.com>
Topic: Introducing "Life and Death at Sunrise."

This poem shows a contrast between the revealed and concealed, the former associated with life, the latter with its absence. The coffin is carried out of the invisible part of the world, which is also the place to which the doctor returns. The sharpened hills are the witnesses of all that is passing – how many times have they seen dawns and deaths among those who inhabit their slopes? Is the "chime" from the animal world a funereal one for all on the hill that morning, the baby included?

For there is an uneasy connection between the new-born and the deceased, in the coincidence of birth and death dates, in the meetings between coffin-bearer, doctor and father on the hill, and in the name that has been chosen ('Jack" being a hypocoristic form of the name of the dead man, John). Like John Thinn – and indeed, like all of us – the baby is born to die, and when the time comes even the doctor will be of no help, just as old John Thinn's lifelong good constitution availed him nothing.

How soon will the baby leave the visible, light part of the world? one might speculate that perhaps he is to enjoy it only in his youth – we may note that the father, bearing his dinner, the mark of a day labourer, is on his way into the fog-covered parts, since he must support his young family. I wonder if Hardy had in mind how the French Revolution gave rise to the optimism of another young man – 'Bliss it was in that dawn to be alive / But to be young was very heaven!' (Wordsworth). Did John Thinn, recalling his earliest memories, find that the dawn cast into shadow all that came later? – Philip Irwin.

Monday, August 25, 2003 08:18 AM
MICHALINA PAWLIKOWSKA <michalina_maria@poczta.onet.pl>
Topic: Introducing "Life and Death at Sunrise."

Where does the narrator / camera stand? A panoramic view of the hills around Blackmore Vale is offered, followed by a close look at the two speaking acquaintances (a miniature). This may indeed be a cinematic technique, but it also resembles painting. Panorama /

miniature – Hardy often uses this contrast. It appears in the opening scenes of *The Return of the Native*, where the description of the grim, awe-inspiring heath is followed by the meeting of Diggory Venn and Captain Vye.[15] In this context it's interesting to note the title of the chapter in which this meeting occurs: "Humanity Appears Upon The Scene, Hand In Hand With Trouble" (ch. 2). Hardy developed a two-sided attitude towards humanity. On the one hand humanity is a disturbance of the natural scenery, bringing misconceptions, chaos and trouble. On the other hand it's curiously blended with the landscape, belonging to it as its natural element.

In this poem both perspectives seem to be present. There is a contrast between the haunting beauty of the description in stanza 1 and the more homely words in the following stanzas. The layers of mist delicately lifting from the woodlands and pastures have a certain elegance in contrast to the "laboured leisurely jog" and the common "clapping" of the wagon. At the same time the use of couplets unifies the whole structure of the poem. Thanks to this unity humanity is established as an integral element of nature. The narrator seems objective, yet certain traits of the romantic observer are discernable in the choice of scenery in stanza 1. The cloudy, dreamy vision of mist-covered hills and the touching comparison of the hills to "awakened sleepers", hinting at a certain privacy and informality, point to the romantic inclination of the observer.

The four-stanza structure does support the theme of ongoing life and death. The theme is carefully developed, step by step; consecutive levels of existence are revealed. In stanza 1 inanimate nature is introduced, in stanza 2 animals (first wild birds, then tamed – beasts of the field), finally people appear in stanzas 3 and 4.

The poem establishes the human being firmly in the landscape first, and then introduces the opposition of life and death. But perhaps it doesn't really matter whether this is done in four stanzas or not (the number four has certain connotations – the four ages of men, for instance).

One can also trace a certain resemblance to the days of creation in the order of elements introduced. It's interesting that conversation appears so late in the poem, only after the contours of the painting

---

[15] Hardy's fascination with vision and perception (which is connected with the camera-eye technique) is visible in his choice of strange standpoints from which the characters observe the scenes in his novels – e.g. in *Far from the Madding Crowd* when Troy watches Bathsheba through a hole in the tent the scene gains a strange intensity (ch. 50). Or, earlier in the novel, when Bathsheba is seen by Gabriel from above in the cowshed, in a bird's-eye view (ch. 2). Another instance of Hardy's concern with vision is the habit of often referring to paintings in his novels. – M.. P.

are clearly delineated. The picture comes first, the word only afterwards.

About camera-eye poems: even though these poems may belong to one group in their "objective" approach to description, it's possible to discern certain sub-categories within this group.

1. In "A Light Snow-Fall After Frost" the persona of an observer is established. Such expressions as "one" (line 5), "no eye" (line 9), "a watcher"(line 19) point to a person observing the scene.
2. In other poems there are no direct references to an observer. The scenes are presented directly. Most of the other poems in this group fall into this category. Examples are "Ice on the Highway" and "A Light Snow Fall after Frost".
3. Sometimes elements of nature are endowed with consciousness. In "A Backward Spring" the trees "are afraid" and the plants in general are hesitant to grow. In "Last Week in October" the trees are very active, undressing and flinging their clothes. In "Shortening Days at the Homestead" the sparrows wonder why winter didn't leave forever. In "Life and Death at Sunrise" the hills "uncap their tops" and check what has changed during the night.
4. Several of these poems are not fully objective or neutral: they are permeated with a spirit of compassion. There seems to exist some feeling of consciousness commenting on the state of affairs and asking: "Why? Why is it so? Is all this suffering really necessary?" The compassionate comments often seem uttered only half-consciously, a mere slip of the tongue. In "Winter Night in Woodland" an air of deep pathos and pity is established through the question "and yet, why?" following the description of the fox's awareness that "the hand of all men is against him".[16] In "A Sheep-Fair" this compassion is revealed in the expression "And every flock long since has bled", and the mention of the "doom" of the ewes. The phrase "to doom each meek mewed band" certainly isn't neutral or objective. In "No Buyers" it's the expression "too plainly", added to the age of the pony that reveals the compassionate feelings of the observer. In "Last Look Round St.Martin's Fair" we may catch a glimpse of an inner suffering reality, at odds with the outer show of things when we realize that the smiling "woman in red" is actually tired and would gladly "never again nut-shooting see." There seems to be compassion behind this phrase. In "An East End Curate" the

---

[16] This is similar to Tess's exclamation when putting to death the mangled pheasants: "Poor darlings – to suppose myself the most miserable being on earth in the sight of such misery as yours!" (*TD*, ch.41). – M. P.

evils of an unfeeling life are visible in the curate's behavior. He ignores the "man ... threatening his wife" and demonstrates a shocking lack of compassion.

Hardy might have been drawn to this technique in a belief that seeing the world and observing it closely one can gain a deeper knowledge, a wisdom absent from words. It's the idea of seeing to the core of things and of looking at objects in all their bareness, uncompromisingly. Concentration on the visual is an important feature of Hardy's work. He achieves a great intensity thanks to this concentration. Close observation results in detailed descriptions of natural phenomena. Hardy is always at pains to describe every natural element with great precision, as it reveals itself step-by-step during the process of observation. For example, in "A Light Snow-Fall after Frost" he describes how the frost reveals the presence of the cobwebs; the observer must be looking very closely to notice such a fragile detail as the cobwebs and he must be observing all the minute changes in the scenery to note that only after the arrival of the rime did the cobwebs become visible. This looking out for even the smallest of changes recurs in the last stanza of this poem, where "But half an hour ago / The road was brown, and now is starkly white." It's as if the observer is trying to catch the exact moment when the change occurred, to lift nature's mask and discover her secret. Another example of close observation is the comparison of intertwining sun-rays and tendrils of smoke to "woof-lines in a loom". A striking comparison, it describes the visual effect quite accurately.

I believe that Hardy set out to compose these poems because he was psychologically drawn to the objective technique. He often used this technique earlier, especially in his novels, e.g. in the harvesting scene in *Tess*. The idea of concentration and meditation comes to mind. Observation is a means of purification. It allows one to see one's thoughts clearly and not to identify with them. This would be in accordance with seeking an inner stoic balance, a state of mind that Hardy often desired to reach. It's no coincidence that he referred to Marcus Aurelius's phrase: "Be not perturbed." – Michalina.

NOTES AND QUERIES

AMONG the dozens of different topics which crop up on TTHA's *Forum* every month there are many which remain largely unexplored on the List-serve as the stream of developing conversations evolve into escalating threads. I have selected, for publication in this edition of *The Hardy Review*, a tiny sample of those singular instances – hundreds more can be found in the *Forum Archives*, an extensive resource superbly managed by archivist John Cortus. I should add that in recent months, the *Forum Archives* have been equipped with a sophisticated Search Engine for ease of access and research. This can be found at:

www.yale.edu/hardysoc/Welcome/Forum/Searchable%20Archives.htm

Rosemarie Morgan,
for the *Forum* team

CANFORD MANOR FRIEZE

THERE is an interesting story of the discovery of a marble frieze from ancient Assyria at Canford Manor school in Dorset, and its sale for $11.8 million here, at:

http://www.columbia.edu/cu/record/record2005.24.html

Chene Manor in Hardy's story "Barbara of the House of Grebe" was, I believe, based on Canford Manor which I understand Hardy had visited from time to time when it was the home of Lord Wimborne[1] (aka Sir John Guest) and he may therefore have been familiar with the frieze. I am sure its current appearance in the news would have inspired another of his stories or poems.

Patrick Roper,
patrick@prassociates.co.uk

**If you follow Patrick Roper's link at:
http://www.columbia.edu/cu/record/record2005.24.html
You'll find the following:**

---

[1] Montague John Guest (1839-1909), wrote to Hardy in May 1892 inquiring about place-names and fictional locations in *Tess*. Guest was M.P. for Wareham 1880-5 and a younger brother of the first Lord Wimborne (*Letters*, Vol VII, 122).

Professor Finds Ancient Frieze in Students' "Sweet Shop."

A **COLUMBIA** art history professor's recent sleuthing resulted in the discovery of a 3,000-year-old carved stone panel from the throne room of Assyrian King Assurnasirpal II (883-859 B.C.). This summer the rare find was sold at auction for a record $11.8 million. John Russell, an associate professor of art history, found the slab in the sweet shop of the Canford School, an English boarding school, in 1992. The stone carving was covered with several thick coats of whitewash, and hung between a dart board and a candy machine.

British Museum's Confirmation

"At first, the school didn't believe it was true," said Russell, who is beginning his eighth year at Columbia. "They didn't do anything for a year because they were between headmasters." The antiquity wasn't removed by conservators until one of the school's trustees was told that the British Museum had confirmed the piece's authenticity.

Russell visited the Canford School when he was in England completing research on a book about Sir Henry Layard, the discoverer of the "lost city" of Nineveh, an ancient Assyrian city located in what is now modern Iraq.

The school originally housed an extensive private collection of Assyrian antiquities held by Sir John Guest, a friend and patron of Layard's. The school's sweet shop, nicknamed "The Grubber" by the students, was designed by Charles Barry, the architect of the Houses of Parliament. The small brick and stone building, which has a Gothic facade but an Assyrian interior, drew Russell's interest. "We knew that most of the collection was sold in 1919 and ended up in the New York Metropolitan Museum of Art," said Russell. "Seven remaining pieces had been discovered and sold at auction in 1959. There was no indication that anything remained of the collection." However, a large Assyrian frieze was just inside the door of "The Grubber," across from a Coke machine and a pizza counter. "We thought we wouldn't find any antiquities and we weren't looking. And since we weren't looking, we didn't see it at first," said Russell. "What we saw were plaster casts – reproductions – of Assyrian sculptures." Covered with paint the original slab was positioned between two reproductions. All three were covered with several thick coats of paint, obscuring any detailed carving.

It wasn't until Russell returned to his research at the British Museum that he uncovered an inventory list of the entire collection of Assyrian art housed at Canford. The list showed that the piece, depicting a royal attendant and a bearded, winged figure, was unaccounted for. With the help of Julian Reade, a curator at the British Museum, Russell documented the stone carving's authenticity.

PHOTO CREDIT: CHRISTIES

Except for a few pinpoint holes from thrown darts – two show up clearly on the attendant's forearm and cheek – the 72 x 42" stone carving is considered to be in better shape than those housed in many museum collections. Christie's, the auction house, estimated that the carving would bring $1.5 million. In a fierce four-minute bidding war, however, a well-known Japanese art dealer successfully bid $11.8 million. The Canford headmaster said the windfall will fund several new scholarships and the construction of a theater and gymnasium.

ST JULIOT

THE dedication of a Hardy memorial window – designed and engraved by Simon Whistler[2] – at St Juliot's church on July 5th 2003, sparked some roving excursions on the Forum. – R.M.

PHOTOCREDIT ANGELA BELL

---

[2] Funds for Simon Whistler's work were raised by the Hardy Society and TTHA..

THERE are 3 panels and 2 small lights above. In one of the latter is depicted the sun and in the other the moon and night sky. The top of the centre panel shows St Juliot church with Hardy's name above and below it, and at the top of the side panels are the tools of his trades, on the left – items from his writing desk, and on the right – the measuring rules etc of architecture – the birth date being on the left and the death date to the right.

The centre panel tells the story of the journey from Dorset to Cornwall, depicting the hills and valleys, rivers, railways and roads leading to trees and an open gate. Below – in an uncannily good representation of Hardy's handwriting – are lines from 'When I set out for Lyonnesse'. The left panel shows the rolling Cornish landscape, with the Vallency valley and its many waterfalls, leading to lines from 'Under the Waterfall', and the right panel shows most delicately 'the phantom horsewoman' silhouetted in clear glass on Beeny Cliff with, in Hardy's hand, 'O the opal and the sapphire of that wandering western sea....'

Helen Gibson
helen.gibson@ukgateway.net

FIRST, I was planning to go and see the new window at St Juliot's while I'm staying nearby soon and then I got to thinking about the dedication. After digging around a bit I found in my book of Celtic Saints that Juliot (aka Juliana) was a daughter of the king of the area around the Brecon beacons. As well as St Juliot's, she also had a chapel dedicated to her as St Juliet at Tintagel. All so far quite simple, but the dedication of Luxulyan church is to SS Julitta and Cyr. These are a mother-and-son pair of saints and definitely non-Celtic, being Turkish (although of course Galatia had Celtic connections). And some people seem to have assumed that Juliot and Julitta of Luxulyan are one and the same — there are references to a (Celtic) Juliot of Luxulyan. Apparently the total number of sons and daughters attributed to the aforementioned king (Brychan) runs well into the twenties or thirties, so maybe Juliot's parentage was invented to give a Celtic heritage to a Turkish saint. Anyway, the reason I bring all this up is the presence in *A Pair of Blue Eyes* of Lord Luxellian. Did the coincidence of the dedications of the two churches inspire Hardy to give that nobleman his name? He visited that area, so probably knew the dedication and may have put two and two together.

Second, did Hardy ever meet Hawker of Morwenstow? There is a brief reference to Hawker in *Early Life*,[3] but a few things struck me

---

[3] See Florence Emily Hardy, *The Life of Thomas Hardy, 1840-1928* (Macmillan & Co, Ltd, 1962)

while reading over Hawker's life (staying just outside the parish); like Mr Swancourt, Hawker was highly intolerant of Dissenters; like Lord Luxellian he was apparently dissatisfied with his (second) wife's producing only daughters. And like Elfride, he had an interest in Arthurian legend. Also, if Hardy had visited Morwenstow, it might explain the way that Endelstow church is much closer to the ocean in *A Pair of Blue Eyes* than St Juliot is in reality. SS Morwenna and John the Baptist church is in a really dramatic location next to the cliffs; if its tower fell, the view out to sea would be remarkably like the scene in where Knight and Elfride have a disagreement in the church.

On the other hand, the most striking of Hawker's interests seems to have been burying shipwrecked sailors (not the survivors), and one would have expected Hardy, if they had met, to have borrowed the material for use at some point. Hawker was a good friend of Emma's brother-in-law, Mr Holder, the vicar of St Juliot, according to *Early Life*. Nectan himself has a church dedicated to him at Welcombe in Devon, about 15 miles up the coast from St Juliot.

Gary Alderson,
Gary.Alderson@btinternet.com

THANKS for that Gary; the whole story of the one or more early medieval Nectan(s) is complicated and still not properly understood. 'Nectan' is, for example, generally thought to be a Pictish name. There is a good deal of information on St Nectan in Cornwall and Devon, including the various fantasies concocted by Robert Hawker, Vicar of Morwenstow (fantasies he later admitted to[4]). A "Nectan" also seems to have had some sort of cult in the Cheddar area and connected with Glastonbury.

A St. Nectan appears to have been Juliot's sister and he supposedly gave his name to St. Nectan's Kieve near Tintagel, another place and person known to Hardy. Much of the story of Nectan and goings on in the Kieve were invented by Hawker who was, I believe, known to the Gifford family at St. Juliot. Despite this 19th century fantasy, one or more St Nectans do appear to have exisited in the Dark Ages. Hardy, of course, mentions Nectan and his Kieve in *The Famous Tragedy of the Queen of Cornwall* (as Neitan, or similar – there are several spellings).

---

[4] See *St Nectan's Glen. Its History & Legends*, edited by Kelvin I. Jones (Oakmagic Books, Penzance 2001). He draws in this on material from 'The Cultus of Nectan' by Charles Henderson in *St. Nectan, St Keyne & The Children of Brychan in Cornwall* by G. H. Doble (1925) and 'St Nectan' also by G. H. Doble (The Devonshire Press, Torquay, 1940).

What it would be good to know is what knowledge and interest Hardy and/or Emma and her relatives had of Cornish history and language. The so-called Celtic Revival that had got going in Scotland at the end of the 18th century and had been boosted in the mid-19th by Lady Charlotte Guest's translation of the Welsh 'Mabinogion' reached Cornwall in a substantial way with Henry Jenner who did much research into Cornish language and history in the 1870s when Hardy was frequently visiting St Juliot and writing *A Pair of Blue Eyes*. Also Robert Hunt had, in 1865, published his *Popular Romances of the West of England; or The Drolls, Traditions and Superstitions of Old Cornwall* which demonstrated that the Duchy shared many stories and tale types with other Celtic areas. One wonders if this had any influence on Hardy or Emma.

Hardy and Emma might also have had some knowledge of the meaning of various Cornish placenames. Craig Weatherhill in his *Cornish Place Names and Language* (1995) says Luxulyan comes from Middle Cornish 'lok Sulyen', "Sulyan's chapel/cell". He adds "The personal name is an ancient one, from Brythonic 'sulo-genos', 'sun-born'". To me that seems to fit quite well with *PBE*. Another speculation is that Hardy might have known of the idea that 'Lanivet' (according to Weatherhill) comes from Old Cornish 'lan neved' meaning 'church site on a pagan sacred site'. My knowing this adds an interesting dimension to my reading of Hardy's poem 'Near Lanivet 1872'.

Trouble is I don't know if Hardy and/or Emma knew any of this Cornish stuff, so my ramblings are all in the speculative area.

Patrick Roper,
patrick@prassociates.co.uk

THE other day I wrote:
> Another speculation is that Hardy might have known of the idea that 'Lanivet'... comes from Old Cornish 'lan neved' meaning 'church site on a pagan sacred site'.

I have today discovered an interesting extra dimension relating to this. .First, the linguists seem to be agreed that the 'nivet/neved' part of 'Lanivet' comes from pre-Saxon Brittonic and is cognate with 'nymet' (found in places like King's Nympton in Devon) and 'nemeton', a word found widely in the pre-Christian Celtic-speaking world and meaning 'a sacred grove' or similar. As many will know, one of Hardy's closest friends was Edward Clodd who was president of the Folk-Lore Society in the late 19th century. In 1896 he asserted that

> many medieval churches had been built on or near former pagan shrines, providing 'unbroken evidence of the pagan

foundation which, itself resting upon barbaric bedrock, upholds the structures of classical and Christian faiths.'

Clodd may have known of the origin of 'Lanivet' and I am sure this was one of the sorts of things he would have talked about with Hardy as he knew of both his interest in folk-lore and in Cornwall. It is clearly likely that some of Clodd's ideas were absorbed and remembered by Hardy and, since 'Near Lanivet 1872' was written (I think) after 1896,[5] one wonders if Clodd had mentioned to Hardy this was a place that illustrated his theory. Patrick Roper.

I AM not sure how far we can accept that the second element in the place-name 'Lanivet' is cognate with the pan-Celtic nymet/ nemed/neved etc. First, the general (though not universal) rule of Lan/Llan ('church') place-names is that the second element refers to the saint(s) to whom the church was dedicated. While the current Oxford Dictionary of English Place-Names, an authoritative work not to be ignored, interprets the second element as 'pagan sacred place', Ekwall's magisterial (though earlier) dictionary considers this etymology but prefers to regard the second element as the name of a St 'Nivet'. Secondly, the Celtic Christians, like the Anglo-Saxons after conversion, lacked any historical or sentimental attachment to the vestiges of pre-Christian religion – they were of course much closer to paganism, and considered it both uncivilised and diabolical: it was not something to be deliberately recalled in a place-name. Therefore, if the English Place-Names etymology is correct, then by the time the name 'Lanivet' came into being, the pagan connotations of the word must have vanished for the Cornish. I would conjecture that by this point it may have just meant the more neutral 'shrine'.

None of this, of course, is likely to have had any bearing on Hardy's view of the place name! Philip Irwin

IT does seem that there were a number of nemetons in the West Country whose presence has persisted in placenames regardless of any Celtic-Christian attitude towards their earlier paganism.

---

[5] The dating of this poem is unclear: Hardy writes (*Letters*, VI, 246), that the idea for the poem was based on an event in 1872 and that "owing to lack of time, through the necessity of novel-writing for magazines, many of the poems were temporarily jotted down to the extent of a stanza or two when the ideas occurred, and put aside till time should serve for finishing them -- often not till years after".

There is, for example, a fascinating map in Nora Chadwick's *The Druids*,[6] a map which I think she got from Anne Ross, which shows many 'nemeton' place names in the Taw Valley area of Devon. These include King's Nympton, Bishop's Nympton, Nymet House, the Nymet Mole river and more. The possibility that they are derived from the 'nemeton' word is strengthened by the fact that there is a Roman marching station in the southern part of this area called 'Nemetostatio'. This was rather off the beaten track for the Romans and one cannot help wondering if there was some troublesome Celtic power-centre in the Taw Valley, much as there was on Anglesey. Interestingly, Nemetostatio was close to what is the A30 trunk road through to Cornwall today and Lanivet is on this same road.

I do agree, however, that the meaning of the names of all these places may well have been forgotten by the time they reached their modern form. As with ourselves though, there could have been some interesting conversations between Hardy and his friends as research of various kinds started to bring the distant past of the country into sharper focus.

Patrick Roper

THE WORDSWORTH EDITION

I RECENTLY saw a volume of what appears to be the complete Hardy poems, published by Wordsworth, at a friend's home. I only glanced at it so don't have the full documentation. It is in paperback, and resembles the Gibson edition, but the poems are not numbered, and I didn't see any notes. The title was different as well – and misleading – something like *The Works of Thomas Hardy*. I was told it was very inexpensive. Do any of you know how reliable – or otherwise – this edition might be? Thanks in Advance – Betty Cortus.

THOMAS Hardy's *Collected Poems* was first published in 1919. Hardy, whom we all know always wanted to be recognized as a poet rather than a novelist, had by that time had five books of verse published and for some time he had been suggesting to Macmillan that they should be collected into one volume. It sold very well and his last three books of verse were added to it, one by one, until the book reached its final form in 1930. It was a big book of over

---

[6] University of Wales Press, Cardiff, 1997.

900 poems and it is sad that Hardy was never to see it in its final form.

It sold and sold and was reprinted again and again until by the time of the final printing in 1968 the printing plates had deteriorated badly. Full-stops had disappeared, semi-colons become colons, and the printed text could only be described as 'poor'. For example in the poem "A Man"[7] the word 'backed' had mysteriously become 'packed'. As there is no authority for this, and 'backed' is the far better word, one can only guess that the letter 'b' had fallen out and been replaced as a 'p' by someone in the printing-house.

As one of Macmillan's English advisers in the Sixties and Seventies, I warned them that the Hardy copyright was coming to an end, and that the time had come to think anew. This led to the New Wessex Edition and which is not as good as it should have been because it was proof-read 'in house'. It also resulted in my editing of the new *Complete Poems*, a job which was given to me because I had been working on the text of the poems for several years for the Variorum Edition. For my work on *Complete Poems* which involved a complete recension of the text and took many months, Macmillan rewarded me with the magnificent sum of £300 and they failed to take my advice that to call the book *Complete Poems* was unwise, as it assumed that no more poems would turn up. In fact, in the 2nd edition I have added one more poem.

When Hardy came out of copyright the firm Wordsworth, realizing that the copyright on the actual printing lasted for only twenty-five years (a fact not generally known), took advantage of this, and were free to reproduce the last edition of *Collected Poems* with all its sins upon it, and this they did.

I don't know whether the 1968 printing is still being used by them or whether they have done some tidying up themselves. However, I tell my students that if they can't afford £15 for the present paperback, they can use the old *Collected Poems* or the Wordsworth edition. They will, however, not have approximately 40 poems added to *Complete Poems*.

Kind regards,
Jim Gibson
James.Gibson@ukgateway.net

---

[7] Thomas Hardy, *The Complete Poems*, edited by James Gibson (Macmillan, 1976) 153-4.

A HARDY HYMN

HARDY, the iconoclast who experimented with verse form at every opportunity and for whom the sacred and the profane often walked hand in hand, once published a hymn in *Songs of Praise*.[1] The publishing date of the first edition is 1925. This shows that the "hymn," which is, in truth, but a copy – with altered accidentals – of a segment from *The Dynasts*,[2] was included in *Songs of Praise* in his lifetime yet there is no extant correspondence to indicate that he knew of the event or ever gave his permission for Oxford University Press to use *The Dynasts'* verses in their *Songs of Praise*.

Some eight days after Hardy's death, one of the editors, Percy Dearmer, made a statement in *The Times* (January 18th 1928), to the effect that:

> Mr Thomas Hardy gave permission to the Oxford University Press to include his great hymn from *The Dynasts*, "To Thee, Whose eye all nature owns," in the hymn-book, *Songs of Praise*, and [it] is now sung in church as No. 389 in that book.[3]

From 1911 and onward for fifteen years Hardy had been in close communication with Oxford University Press over several different projects. His commissioning editor for educational books was Vere Henry Gratz Collins. Previously his contact at O.U.P had been Henry Frowde. In 1911, Collins, as editor, had gained Hardy's permission to publish, in *Poems of War and Battle* (1914), the poem "Embarcation," an extract from *The Dynasts, Part Third*, and three other poems. In 1921, Collins approached Hardy again. He was hoping to persuade

---

[1] *Songs of Praise, Enlarged Edition*, edited by Percy Dearmer, Ralph Vaughan Williams, Martin Shaw (Oxford University Press, London: Humphrey Milford, 1931), 824 : Hymn Number 684. I am indebted to James Gibson for the hymn's provenance.

[2] Thomas Hardy, *The Dynasts, An Epic Drama of the War With Napoleon, in Three Parts, Nineteen Acts, & One Hundred & Thirty Scenes* (Macmillan & Co, Ltd, 1910), Part Third, After Scene.

[3] See Peter Coxon, "Hardy's Favourite Hymns," *The Thomas Hardy Journal*, Vol XIII, May 1997, 42-55.

him to write a Preface for a new O.U.P series to be called *The Poets' Shakespeare*. Hardy declined. He said he was now too old for critical writing. In 1924, Collins tried again: this time he sought permission to publish three more Hardy poems in *A Book of Modern Verse*, to be edited by J. C. Smith (1925). Hardy agreed, this time, adding that he was sure his publishers (Macmillan) would also approve. The three poems were: "Friends Beyond," "Weathers,"and "When I set out for Lyonnesse."

But then, in 1925, the climate changed: some confusion had arisen (with O.U.P) over song settings. Macmillan wrote inquiring into the matter and found Hardy had earlier received a request for permission from one Mr Foss

> to perform a musical setting of "The Sergeant's Song", which I granted, and that he might publish his setting on payment of a fee of two guineas. He later wrote: "I have now completed a cycle of seven songs to poems of yours" (naming those you have named) "which I want to have performed at a Concert .... I should be very grateful if you would grant me permission to have these performed on the same conditions as before. I shall offer these songs for publication by the Oxford University Press".[4]

Hardy was dismayed, feeling that he might have misled Foss about permission; consequently he didn't want Macmillan to press too hard for royalties. He told Macmillan that he had not known Mr Foss was Musical Editor to Oxford University Press.

The point of all of this is – where is Hardy's permission (sought and gained) to publish a portion of *The Dynasts* as a "hymn" in *Songs of Praise*? Among the three editors, Percy Dearmer, Ralph Vaughan Williams, and Martin Shaw, there are extant letters addressed to one person only: Vaughan Williams. Vaughan Williams had been keen to create a setting to "A Soldier's Song" from *The Dynasts*. Hardy (an admirer) was agreeable and, on his own part, intensely keen to have *The Dynasts* promoted. Twice he reminded Vaughan Williams to make sure he named *The Dynasts* as his literary source.[5]

So that was the extent of Hardy's *Dynasts* written agreement with Vaughan Williams. No mention of *Songs of Praise* – not with Vaughan Williams, not with any other of the three editors, not in his

---

[4] See *Letters*, Vol. VI, 334.
[5] Hardy was so keen to promote *The Dynasts* at this time that, under the title of "Chorus of the Pities," he included the After Scene set of eight verses in *Selected Poems of Thomas Hardy* (1916). See also, *Complete Poems*, 942-3. "Chorus of the Pities" keeps closer to the original After Scene verses than does the *Songs of Praise* version.

autobiographical *Life*, not in Millgate. And his personal library[6] holds no edition of *Songs of Praise*. Surely he would have owned a copy had he contributed to the making of it?

Indeed, had the agnostic-hymn-loving Hardy known of his contribution to the 1925 edition of *Songs of Praise* he might have relished the prospect, if N. Temperley is to be believed. *Songs of Praise*, he writes,

> drew on a wide variety of religious poetry of the kind that Victorians would not have considered solemn enough for church ... For the music recourse was had to English folk songs, and other tunes of homely, cheerful rhythm were provided.[7]

"Homely" and "cheerful rhythms" would have done little to redeem Hardy's cruelly-violent deity of *The Dynasts*. In his richly ironic lines the divinity (now of *Songs of Praise*) "hurlest" and "shak'st" humanity while turning its customary deaf ear to the "suffering sobs" of mankind – at the same time as it metes out "purges as by wounds to heal."

Solemnity there is, as well as a concerted effort on Hardy's part to celebrate humanity's faith and hope in what remains, essentially, an Immanent Will lightly masked as the orthodox Christian God.[8] A triumphal ending to *The Dynasts* is, after all, a dramatic necessity.

However, would the lines have been "solemn" enough for church-going Victorians? Well – although Hardy conceived the idea for his epic drama way back in the 1870s *The Dynasts* (1910) was not written for a Victorian audience. Moreover, the 1925 publication of *Songs of Praise* arrived on the scene within a decade of the First World War. It was reprinted in 1931 as the Second World War was fast approaching.

In both cases – *The Dynasts* and *Songs of Praise* – Victorians, in solemnity or otherwise, were, at this point, irrelevant.

Rosemarie Morgan

---

[6] See http://www.library.utoronto.ca/fisher/hardy/

[7] N. Temperley, *The Making of the English Parish Church*, Vol I. (Cambridge University Press, 1979) 339. Cited by Coxon., "Hardy's Favourite Hymns," *The Thomas Hardy Journal*, Vol XIII, May 1997, 42-55.

[8] In *The Dynasts* Hardy's capitalization of "Nature" (omitted in *Songs of Praise*) in the first stanza points not only to a personification but also to an ironic edge to the verses: for instance, is the deity's "eye" owned by Nature? The reading could go either way. However, the last line of the stanza which refers to "her men" is less ambiguous: "her men" are clearly Nature's men, not God's. And again "Her" is capitalized in *The Dynasts* but not in *Songs of Praise*. If irony is not yet apparent and a lurking Immanent Will not at the heart of it, then what do we make of the arrival, in stanza 4, of an ameliorative "Prescience" (not capitalized/personified in *Songs of Praise*), who, "for final hope" may "lull" the deity's "unscanted scope"?

GENERAL

684 DEO GRACIAS. (L.M.)
In moderate time, dignified. Unison.

English Melody, 15th cent.

[This hymn may also be sung to ILLSLEY, 610.]

Magnificat.

Thomas Hardy, 1840-1928.

1 TO thee whose eye all nature owns,
Who hurlest dynasts from their thrones
And liftest those of low estate,
We sing, with her men consecrate!

2 Yea, Great and Good, thee, thee, we hail,
Who shak'st the strong, who shield'st the frail,
Who hadst not shaped such souls as we
If tender mercy lacked in thee.

3 Though times be when the mortal moan
Seems unascending to thy throne;
Though seers do not as yet explain
Why suffering sobs to thee in vain;

4 We hold that thy unscanted scope
Affords a food for final hope,
That mild-eyed Prescience ponders nigh
Life's loom, to lull it by and by.

5 Therefore we quire to highest height
The Wellwiller, the kindly Might
That balances the Vast for weal,
That purges as by wounds to heal.

6*The systemed suns the skies enscroll
Obey thee in their rhythmic roll,
Ride radiantly at thy command,
Are darkened by thy master-hand.

7*And these pale panting multitudes
Seen surging here, their moils, their moods,
All shall fulfil their joy in thee,
In thee abide eternally.

8. Exultant adoration give
The Alone, through whom all living live,
The Alone, in whom all dying die,
Whose means the End shall justify!

---

[9] I apologise for the inferior quality of this copy from *Songs of Praise*. See Note 1.

SEA CREATURES

Sea creatures we,
With spiraled shells enclosing
Dim and cryptic chambers.

Cool salt water
Of our primeval cradle
Still pulses through warm blood.

We are spiked, crab-like,
Our vulnerability encased,
Our helplessness encrusted,
Transparent squid
Oozing ink to hide our frailty.

Like sea anemones,
Our predatory petals trailing, seeking –
Wanting to touch,
But each chance touching
Evokes a timeless reflex . . .

And the flower flattens inward
In a tight knot
Against rejection.

AESCHYNOMENE

We are not one flesh,
No interfused amalgam,
We're braided separates, life partner mine.
Like two adjacent plants whose roots entwine,
Whose leaves share glancing kisses,
Passing pedestrian hours in loose embrace.
Yet should one of us be pruned
The other would shudder, shiver.
Should one be weeded out
The other would wilt, then wither . . .
Then whither?

Betty Cortus,
Oceanside, 2003

BEEN THERE, DONNE THAT

John Donne said one evening, to God,
"I'm a lustful and lecherous clod.
Though I'm Dean of Saint Pauls,
Still the Devil enthralls
Me. Pray batter him out with Thy rod!"

Said God, "Doctor Donne, you engage in
Excesses of imagination.
Thy sins are forgiven.
Get up, man, you're shriven,
Now let us get on with Creation!"

Isobel Robin
Heathmont, Victoria, 2003

WINTER JOURNAL

12/18: Snow With Hard Freeze

    Glassy crystals in sunlight –
    transparent stars lounging
    on banks of still, brittle air.

    Days menacingly short;
    nighttime earth holding its breath
    under blue-white sheets.

1/20: January Thaw

    Silver water in rivulets;
    slush, bordered with ice;
    mud and pale brown grass.

    Wet fur of raccoon searching in gutter-
    grey streams; earth exhaling
    upward through a soggy mask.

2/22: Ice-in

    Cardinal flash, scatter
    of powder dusted off
    snow-crusted limb.

    Sundown: blood and air
    locked in; the pale world shuts
    down tight, chest motionless again.

Bill Morgan,
Illinois, 2003

THE BODLEIAN MANUSCRIPT
of

Poems of the Past and the Present

MARTIN RAY

THIS ARTICLE is a comparison of Thomas Hardy's manuscript of *Poems of the Past and the Present*[1] and Samuel Hynes's edition of the volume, which is contained in *The Complete Poetical Works of Thomas Hardy*.[2] I record what appear to be Professor Hynes's occasional inaccurate transcriptions of variant readings in the manuscript, and I also note variants which are outside the scope of the criteria for the edition which Hynes laid down: for instance, unlike Professor Hynes, I have reported all of those cancellations where the deleted word in the manuscript was later restored, as I think it is significant to see Hardy's initial doubts over the choice of a word.

Richard Little Purdy describes the manuscript thus:

> The MS. of *Poems of the Past and the Present* is written on 163 leaves of fine paper, measuring 8" × 10" and numbered i–vi (Contents, &c.) and 1–157 by Hardy. Like all Hardy's poetical MSS., this is a fair copy with late revisions and agrees closely with the printed text. [...]
>
> The MS., still in its rough brown paper covers, is bound in three-quarters blue morocco and was given to the Bodleian Library, Oxford, in October 1911, when Hardy, through Sydney Cockerell, was distributing his MSS. among various public collections (*Thomas Hardy: A Bibliographical Study* [Oxford University Press, 1954], pp. 117–8).

TEXTUAL NOTES: I have adopted Hynes's system of notation, which he describes thus:

> Textual notes are keyed to the text by a line number and, when necessary for clarity of reference, by a keyword. When

---

[1] *Poems of the Past and the Present* is Bodleian Ms Eng. poet d 18, and I am grateful to the Carnegie Trust for the Universities of Scotland for funding my research visit to Oxford in January 2003.

[2] Vol. I, Oxford: Clarendon Press, 1982.

the variant is a single word, the word as it appears in the established text is quoted, followed by a closing square bracket [...]. When the variation is in punctuation only, the word or words that precede the variant mark of punctuation are indicated by a tilde (pp. xxvi–xxvii).

Words which Hardy deleted in the holograph manuscript ('*Hol.*') are enclosed within angle brackets. When I have thought it necessary for clarification, I have added an explanatory note within square brackets at the end of the entry. Page references are to Hynes's edition and indicate only those pages where the variants which I am recording occur.

Preface   **p. 113**

    8 And that] <That> Moreover, that ['That' had its first character altered to lower case]

V. R 1819–1901 **p. 115**

    Date in *Hol.* reads: Sunday night, 27 January 1901.

Embarcation   **p. 116**

    Headnote Docks:] ~,

Departure   **pp. 116–7**

    3 sea-line] sea line [no hyphen in *Hol.*]

    11 polities] <enquiries> <polities> [i.e. 'polities' was deleted then re-inserted after 'enquiries' in *Hol.*]

The Colonel's Soliloquy **p. 117**

    7 again!] < ~; > [*Hol.* originally read 'again;' but the semi-colon was altered to an exclamation mark]

The Going of the Battery **pp. 119–20**

    7 readily!] < ~ > [the exclamation mark seems to have been inserted at a later stage]

    28 fulness] fullness

A Wife in London **p. 123**

    Subtitles in *Hol.* read

    <Overnight> The <Eve> Tragedy ['The' was not deleted in *Hol.*]

    11 The *Hol.* has a semi-colon after 'morning'. The semi-colon after 'morrow' in Hynes's annotation should be deleted, since it suggests that it was not in *Hol.*

The Souls of the Slain **pp. 124–6**

    Footnote to l. 3 in *Hol.* reads thus:

    The "Race" is the turbulent sea-area off the Bill of Portland, where contrary tides meet.

    [see Hynes, p. 370. Hynes omits to note the words 'of

Portland' in the *Hol.* and subsequent publications.]

17 well-nigh] wellnigh [one word in *Hol.*: no hyphen]

35 hearth-ward] hearthward [one word in *Hol.*: no hyphen]

53 And] <And had> Had [the lower case 'h' was capitalized after the deletion of 'And']

Song of the Soldiers' Wives and Sweethearts **p. 128**

2 again;] ~, [comma, not semi-colon, after 'again'].

13 do] Do [definitely upper case in *Hol.*]

15 Loves!] < ~, > [comma altered to exclamation mark in *Hol.*]

The Sick Battle-God **p. 130**

14 sheen] <mien> <sheen> ['mien' possibly has dotted underlining in *Hol.* to indicate retention]

15 glimpsed] <glimpsed> <eyed> ['glimpsed' has dotted underlining in *Hol.* to indicate retention]

25 crescent] <crescent> crescive [the final three letters of 'crescent' in *Hol.* were altered to read 'crescive']

30 many-sidedness] manysidedness [no hyphen in *Hol.*]

Rome: The Vatican: Sala delle Muse **p. 136**

Title Sala] <Sall>

14 Tune:] <Song:> <Sound:> Tune; ['Sound' is followed by a colon in *Hol.*]

Rome: At the Pyramid of Cestius Near the Graves of Shelley and Keats **p. 137**

17 pilgrim feet] pilgrim-feet [hyphen in *Hol.*]

Lausanne: In Gibbon's Old Garden **p. 138**

Headnote: completion] <completion> Completion [the opening character of the word was initially lower case and was then capitalized]

1 spirit] Spirit

Zermatt: To the Matterhorn **pp. 138–9**

Headnote: -July,] ~:

1 Thirty-two] Thirty two [no hyphen in *Hol.*]

10 Thou didst behold] <Thou'st watched each <<night>> <year>> night> Thou watch'dst each night [Hardy originally wrote 'watched' and not 'watch'd' in *Hol.*]

The Bridge of Lodi **pp. 139–40**

Headnote [in the *Hol.* version of the headnote, 'Visited' was a later insertion, probably to indicate that the date was not that of composition]

17 sunlit] sun-lit [hyphen in *Hol.*]

The Mother Mourns **p. 145**

   37 mind-sight] mindsight [no hyphen in *Hol.*]
   46 Night-queen] \<Sky-queen\> \<sky-queen\> [double underlining beneath initial letter of 'Sky' was later deleted]
   51 lure] \<lie\> \<?\> [this deleted reading is difficult to decipher]

'I Said to Love' **pp. 147–8**
   18 dove] ~,
   23 –Man's] Man's
   threatenest] dost threaten

A Commonplace Day **p. 148**
   15 Days] [It is impossible to tell whether 'Days' was originally lower case, or whether the double underlining beneath the initial letter was present before the revision of 'flat-pitched'. It is possible that 'Days' was capitalized later to be consistent with 'Day's' in line 18]

At a Lunar Eclipse **p. 150**
   12 gauge] guage [sic]
   13 teem] \<teem\> teem

The Lacking Sense **pp. 150–2**
   Headnote sad-coloured] sad coloured [no hyphen in *Hol.*]
   29 dead-reckoning] deadreckoning [no hyphen in *Hol.*]

To Life **p. 152**
   16 feign,] \<mumm\> [there is no comma after 'mumm' in *Hol.*, as Hynes's notation implies]

Doom and She **pp. 153–4**
   13 clay-made] claymade [no hyphen in *Hol.*]
   31 World-weaver!] ~, [comma, not exclamation mark, in *Hol.*]
   36 –Unanswered] Unanswered

The Sleep-Worker **p. 156**
   11 surprise] surprize

The Bullfinches **pp. 156–7**
   10 well known] well-known
   29 to-day's] the days [*sic*: no apostrophe in *Hol.*]

To an Unborn Pauper Child **p. 163**
   Title Pauper Child] Pauper-Child

To Lizbie Browne **p. 166**
   11 glance-giving] glancegiving [no hyphen in *Hol.*]

'I Need Not Go' **p. 174**
   28 no! –] \< ~!!\> [the second exclamation mark was deleted and replaced with a dash]

His Immortality p. 180

>The date is given in *Hol.* as 'Feb. 1899.'

The To-Be-Forgotten pp. 181–2

>**13** count] bide [not 'bid']
>
>Date <Feb. 9. <<?1889?>> 1899.?> [there is a full stop immediately after '1899', perhaps indicating that Hardy added the question mark later]

The Caged Thrush Freed and Home Again p. 185

>**19** be.'] be. [*Hol.* accidentally omits closing quotation mark]

The Puzzled Game-Birds p. 186

>**5** For did we then cry, they would heed us.] <And would, at least, fair terms concede us. – > [i.e. one should remove question mark from Hynes's notation, since it was added when the line was revised]

The Darkling Thrush p. 188

>**25** carolings] carollings
>
>**30** good-night] goodnight [no hyphen in *Hol.*]

The Comet at Yell'ham p. 188

>Title The Comet at Yell'ham] The Comet at Yalbury, or Yell'ham [comma after 'Yalbury' in *Hol.*]

Mad Judy p. 189

>**3** christening mirth] christening-mirth [hyphen in *Hol.*]

A Wasted Illness p. 190

>**12** Death] Death [*Hol.* appears to be upper case]

A Man p. 192

>**26** whiled.] <passed.> wore.

The Dame of Athelhall p. 192

>**1** 'Dear!] "Soul! [not caps in *Hol.*]
>
>**8** predesigned] pre<->designed [hyphen is deleted in *Hol.*]
>
>**37** came, at] <came. At> came; at

The Milkmaid p. 196

>**14** tear;] tear:

The Ruined Maid p. 198

>**17** – 'You] "You
>
>**24** ain't] aint [no apostrophe in *Hol.*]

The Respectable Burgher on 'The Higher Criticism' p. 199

>**30** Malchus'] Malchu's
>
>**32–3** [*Hol.* indicates "white line" between these two lines]

The King's Experiment p. 201

>**2** lane] Lane

The Tree   **pp. 202–4**
>**3** south-wester's] Southwester's [no hyphen in *Hol.*]
>**21** *Hol.* reads: Meant not for me," <to her> at length said I; [double quotation mark after 'me']
>**22** I] "I
>**33** lovecraft] Lovecraft

Her Late Husband   **p. 205**
>Headnote: no full stop after '182–' in *Hol.*

In Tenebris II   **p. 208**
>**9** sweet;] sweet; [semi-colon is present in *Hol.*]

In Tenebris III   **p. 209**
>*Hol.* originally read: <Witless that fruits of this life show them bitter, and <<black>> black, and untoward,> ['black' was deleted twice]

The Church-Builder   **pp. 210–3**
>**1** <flings forth> in *Hol.* is dot underlined for retention.
>**78** one] <me>

The Lost Pyx   **p. 213**
>**8** choir).] choir.)

Tess's Lament   **p. 217**
>**36** A standing] A-standing [hyphen in *Hol.*]

The Supplanter   **p. 218**
>**7** gravestone] <grave-stone> [hyphen is deleted in *Hol.*]

Sapphic Fragment   **p. 222**
>**5** fellow-thralls] fellow thralls [no hyphen in *Hol.*]

Catullus: XXXI   **p. 222**
>Headnote: *Hol.* reads: Sirmione. [full stop, not comma, in *Hol.*]

After Schiller   **p. 223**
>**1** sister-love] sisterlove [no hyphen in *Hol.*]

[*Retrospect*   **p. 224**]
>'Retrospect' replaces the deleted 'Conclusion'

'I Have Lived with Shades'   **pp. 225–6**
>**12** shapeless] shapless [error in *Hol.*]
>**29** dim] Dim [possibly upper case in *Hol.*]
>Date in *Hol.* is: Feb 2. 1899.

'ΑΓΝΩΣΤΩΙ ΘΕΩΙ   **p. 228**
>**4** *Hol.* reads: By labouring all-unknowingly, <may be> maybe.

CHESS AND SOCIAL GAME PLAYING
in
A Pair of Blue Eyes

GLEN R. DOWNEY

> Game, sport, art, science, passion, madness, recreation, obsession--chess is no one thing but all of these things: It is a world ... Chess, like love, like music, has the power to let us see ourselves. — Burt Hochburg

IN *A Pair of Blue Eyes*, the chess games which Elfride Swancourt plays against Stephen Smith and Henry Knight serve as cogent prefaces to her relationships with these men. Elfride's profound confusion about whether to admire or admonish Stephen's lack of skill, and the tactical miscues which inform her chess games with the more experienced Henry, are replayed during the course of her failed romantic involvements. A close scrutiny of the parallel chess episodes in *A Pair of Blue Eyes* suggests that these matches are part of a larger conceptual scheme in which the patterns of chess take on a compelling presence in the narrative. Elfride, the chess-playing aspirant to polite society, is at the centre of a game contested for the stakes of social power against the chequered backdrop of Hardy's Wessex landscape.[1] In this game she assumes roles both as the principal player and quintessential plaything, the engineer of subtle combinations and positional sacrifices, and the overprotected but isolated piece striving to find its place on the field of social combat. Elfride's approach to the game is informed by a controlling father who tries to teach her the importance of playing for position. However, the social power she craves lies not in the get-rich-quick schemes of her pretentious teacher or his desperate forays into the realm of privilege, but in a liberation from such concerns through the ability to play not simply for the slow accumulation of positional advantages, but for a mate, with all the implications that this term connotes.

---

[1] See Appendix

Elfride is forced to learn the rules of social game playing from Swancourt, who painstakingly leads his daughter through every phase, from the importance of book knowledge in the opening stages to the principles of playing for position and eventually, to conducting an end-game when the situation deems it necessary. However, since Elfride and her father play for radically different stakes, she can only confound his game and therefore ultimately, her own. In portraying a world where Fate thwarts the carefully planned moves of his characters, Hardy explores what happens when an individual's bid for liberation ultimately traps her within the very combination she plays to free herself. Although the novel's chess episodes have value as allegorical constructs, the motif manages to exceed these limitations in revealing to the reader how the Wessex universe operates as its own evolving game environment. Hardy not only explores the symmetry and ordered logic that many earlier writers perceived as the essence of the chess game, but further exploits its intricacy and complexity. In so doing, he presents an unfolding fictional gameworld replete with conflicts and cross-purposed goals that chess in its complexity has the capacity to illuminate, but in its ordered logic ultimately lacks the power to replace.

Although a great deal of criticism has been written about *A Pair of Blue Eyes*, very little has been said about the novel's parallel chess episodes. Several critics have acknowledged how the chess games function as a literary device in the novel, mirroring Elfride's romantic involvements with Stephen and Henry, but they have seldom pursued any deeper investigation of how the game takes on a metaphorical presence in the narrative as a whole. Pamela Jekel is perhaps the first critic to spend more than a couple of sentences in discussing the novel's parallel chess episodes. She argues that Elfride's game with Knight is "a prelude to the swordplay of Sergeant Troy in *Far From the Madding Crowd* (1874), and Bathsheba's obsession with her soldier is similar to Elfride's for Knight."[2] Not only does Jekel recognize the implicit sexuality of the chess game, but shows how it is underscored by Elfride's reaction to it when she is bested by Knight:

> Elfride was lying full-dressed on the bed, her face hot and red, her arms thrown abroad. At intervals of a minute she tossed restlessly from side to side, and indistinctly moaned words used in the game of chess.[3]

---

[2] Pamela Jekel, *Thomas Hardy's Heroines: A Chorus of Priorities* (Troy NY: Whitston, 1986), 58.

[3] Thomas Hardy, *A Pair of Blue Eyes*, edited by Pamela Dalziel (Penguin World Classics, 1998), 172-3. Hereafter *PBE*.

However, once Jekel ends her discussion of the chess motif she puts it aside and does not use it to address some of the arguments she raises later in her article.

Swancourt and Knight are fated to be unhappy because each of them tries to control his affairs from a position that lacks objectivity. They attempt to regulate the game from within, which is impossible as Hardy well understood, because they always lack important pieces of information. However, Elfride is also destined to fail in her bid for liberation because her education in social game-playing has confusingly taught her both to strive for control and to relinquish it, a process which wears her down and ends in her premature death. Jekel is consistent with earlier critics in not connecting this feature of Hardy's plot with the fact that the queen is ultimately an expendable piece in the chess game.

A comprehensive analysis of Hardy's chess motif can be found in Mary Rimmer's "Club Laws: Chess and the Construction of Gender in *A Pair of Blue Eyes*."[4] Rimmer not only recognizes that the parallel chess episodes "structure, develop, and symbolize the currents of social and sexual dominance that define Elfride's relations with her two suitors," but also acknowledges the game's more subtle implications for Hardy's novel, such as the relationship between Elfride and the expendable queen piece, and the game of interpretation between the author and his readers. One of Rimmer's arguments is that Elfride has a certain degree of autonomy in the early part of the story and that her chess matches chart its decline:

> In the early chapters of the novel she has considerable autonomy and without consciously rebelling violates many of the decorums of femininity. She rides her horse bareheaded, unattended and recklessly through the countryside, and exploits her unladylike equestrian habits to elope with Stephen, the distinctly ineligible son of the local stonemason.[5]

However, my interpretation of Hardy's chess motif proposes that Elfride only has a very superficial autonomy, and that because she learns the rules of social game-playing from her father — an incompetent teacher who only serves to confuse his pupil — she is forced to play out her relationships with Stephen and Henry like a novice chess player struggling to negotiate the tangled web of choices and decisions on a chessboard.

---

[4] Mary Rimmer, "Club Laws: Chess and the Construction of Gender in *A Pair of Blue Eyes*," *The Sense of Sex: Feminist Perspectives on Hardy*. Ed. Margaret R. Higonnet (Urbana: U of Illinois Press, 1993), 203-20.

[5] Rimmer, 208.

The manner in which Elfride is taught the art of social game playing by her father is more richly understood in light of an intertextual connection that the text establishes with Shakespeare's *The Tempest*. At the novel's outset, the narrator makes an overt allusion to the play by drawing a comparison between Elfride's first encounter with Stephen and Miranda's discovery of Ferdinand:

> The point in Elfride Swancourt's life at which a deeper current may be said to have permanently set in, was one winter afternoon when she found herself standing, in the character of a hostess, face to face with a man she had never seen before – moreover, looking at him with a Miranda-like curiosity and interest that she had never yet bestowed on a mortal.[6]

A more subtle allusion takes place a bit further on when Swancourt's complaint to Stephen of existing in "absolute solitude" is greeted by the young architect with what appears to be another reference to the play: "You have your studies, your books, and your – daughter." Like Shakespeare's Prospero, Swancourt has a profound sense of his own isolation, not in being segregated from the rest of humanity, but from those whom he considers his social equals. Furthermore, his demonstrated faith in Hewby's letter and Burke's *Peerage* recalls Prospero's obsession with his magic tomes.

At the same time, however, Swancourt is much more a comic figure than Shakespeare's reclusive mage, his penchant for scheming not unlike that of Stephano, Trinculo, and Caliban, who bumblingly plot against Prospero. Indeed, by drawing a correlation between *A Pair of Blue Eyes* and *The Tempest* – works in which chess takes on an often subtle but important metaphorical presence – Hardy examines what happens when a conspicuously fallible patriarch is responsible for the education in social game-playing of a strong-willed and rather unpredictable daughter.

Although a critical juxtaposition of Swancourt and Prospero provides a clear sketch of the former's pronounced fallibility in the matter of his daughter's education, Hardy evidently recognizes that these characters share some peculiar similarities. Both endure a form of segregation: Prospero isolates himself from his dukedom and is in turn banished into physical isolation by Antonio, while Swancourt sees himself as inheriting a position that isolates him from those he would be friends with and necessitates a self-imposed isolation from those who would be friends with him. Both men yearn for the position they have lost: Prospero has been stripped of his Dukedom by

---

[6] *PBE*, 8-9.

heedlessly immersing himself in his arcane studies, while Swancourt sees himself as the product of a noble family that has systematically relinquished its former prestige through unfortunate circumstances and eccentric overindulgence. Both men pursue a course to regain what they consider to be rightfully theirs: Prospero orchestrates the shipwreck of his enemies to bring them under his control, and encourages the relationship between Ferdinand and Miranda that will bring his daughter to the throne of Naples, while Swancourt seizes upon Mrs. Troyton in a marriage designed essentially to bring her finances under his control, and quietly encourages Elfride's relationships with men who, he believes, are of a respectable social class.

But in suggesting these affinities to the reader, Hardy's novel also recognizes that they serve as the starting point for a critical investigation into the very real differences between how Swancourt and Prospero play chess on a human scale for the stakes of social power, and how they instruct their daughters to this end. Although Prospero is forced to endure physical isolation from his dukedom through his brother's duplicitous dealings, he acknowledges some responsibility for his own banishment because of his immersion in private studies and his willingness to leave the affairs of state to Antonio: "The government I cast upon my brother / And to my state grew stranger, being transported / And rapt in secret studies" (I.ii 75-77). Prospero's admission demonstrates an awareness that his banishment is the product of a previous self-imposed isolation. This knowledge empowers him to assume responsibility for righting not only his suffferings at the hands of Antonio and Alonso, but what his neglect has brought upon Miranda, "his only heir / And princess" (I.ii. 58-59).

In contrast, Swancourt seems to have an acute awareness that his social isolation is the product of those who have gone before him: an inherited condition that must be both vigorously prevented from further decline and systematically improved. Swancourt does not seem to recognize, or perhaps does not relish admitting, that the various get-rich-quick schemes in which he has previously invested capital have considerably diminished his fortune. Unlike Prospero, who recognizes that eccentricity and neglect have cost him in the past, Swancourt recklessly schemes in the name of familial duty. This is evident in his eager but veiled description of the plan to get control of his future wife's finances:

> 'Elfride,' said her father with rough friendliness, 'I have an excellent scheme on hand, which I cannot tell you of now. A scheme to benefit you and me. It has been thrust upon me for some little time – yes, thrust upon me – but I didn't

dream of its value till this afternoon, when the revelation came. I should be most unwise to refuse to entertain it.'

'I don't like that word,' she returned wearily. 'You have lost so much already by schemes.'[7]

Coupled with his failing to acknowledge the dangers associated with his own scheming, his tendency to assign blame places a great deal of stress on his relationship with Elfride because she not only serves as a symbol of his own isolation, but carries with her the potential for immortalizing him in the sacred annals of genealogical history as the one who irreparably humiliated the Swancourt name.

But although Swancourt's numerous misgivings can neither be dismissed nor ignored, Hardy's allusion to *The Tempest* is crucial in helping the reader to recognize that Elfride's father is bereft of those powers to which Prospero has been granted access. Indeed, the latter is as much the grand-master of events on his sheltered isle as Swancourt is a piece struggling for understanding from within the Wessex game universe. Critics have traditionally recognized that Prospero is in many ways the character of Shakespeare himself, taking the stage in his final play to comment on the relationship between nature and art, and on the artistic process. In contrast, Swancourt, like each of the characters in *A Pair of Blue Eyes,* is little more than an isolated piece on the cosmic chessboard, controlled to a certain extent by the hand of Fate.

Shakespeare's scene depicting Miranda and Ferdinand at chess carries with it the implication that his characters are players as well as pieces, but Hardy explores what happens when pieces – deprived of a beneficent controlling presence to correct mistakes and maintain order – attempt to control the game from within as a player would from without. Indeed, Hardy shows us that the reason Swancourt is a *patzer*[8] when it comes to social game playing is in no small part because of this very limitation. In some ways, Swancourt is no more in control of things than Caliban; like Shakespeare's character, he greedily takes to those who can assist him out of his current predicament. When Swancourt meets Stephen for the first time and tries to make him into something he is not, his actions are not unlike those of Caliban when the latter deifies Stephano upon their first meeting:

Caliban: Hast thou not dropped from heaven?
Stephano: Out o'th'moon, I do assure thee. I was the Man

---

[7] *PBE*, 88.

[8] A poor or amateurish chess player.

                i"th'moon when time was.
Caliban: I have seen thee in her, and I do adore thee.[9]

One of the problems that plagues Swancourt's ambitious attempts to control the progress of the "game" is his inability – and fundamental disinclination – to be present at important moments in the novel. There is little question that the absence or presence of the father figure as patriarchal overseer provides a telling contrast between the parallel chess matches in Hardy's novel and the chess scene in Shakespeare's play. Prospero reveals the lovers to Alonso and the others, and is present when Miranda initiates what appears to be a playful accusation of duplicity directed at Ferdinand:

Miranda: Sweet Lord, you play me false.
Ferdinand: No my dearest love, I would not for the world.
Miranda: Yes, for a score of kingdoms you should wrangle,
           And I would call it fair play. [10]

Prospero has previously warned Ferdinand about the importance of Miranda's chastity and thus makes himself present at this moment when the pair is engaged in a game replete with sublimated sexuality. Prospero recognizes Miranda's vulnerability in light of the traditional notion that women at chess are susceptible to the romantic advances of their male counterparts. His presence during this scene serves as one of the many examples of his controlling presence throughout the play. Swancourt, on the other hand, is absent during critical moments of his daughter's chess encounters. During her games with Stephen he is initially present, but being so preoccupied with his own, as yet unrevealed, affairs concerning Mrs. Troyton, he is unaware that Elfride is letting her opponent win out of pity: when the moment comes for Stephen's realization that Elfride has been letting him win, the narrator remarks that Swancourt has left the room. He is not present to prevent Stephen's passionate admission of love for Elfride, an admission that is brought about by competitive tension and the recognition of being the object of another person's play:

> 'Ah, you are cleverer than I. You can do everything – I can do nothing! O Miss Swancourt!' he burst out wildly, his heart swelling in his throat, 'I must tell you how I love you! All these months of my absence I have worshipped you.' [11]

---

[9] II.ii.134-37.
[10] V.i. 171-74
[11] *PBE*, 54.

The sublimated hostility and sexual symbolism that chess embodies, with its eradication of enemy forces climaxing in "mate," is not tempered here by the presence of a controlling father-figure.

The same is true of Elfride's match with Knight. Swancourt is present when the two decide to play and boasts that Elfride "plays very well for a lady", but he once again fails to see the significance of his daughter playing chess against a male visitor:

> Mr. Swancourt had forgotten a similar performance with Stephen Smith the year before. Elfride had not; but she had begun to take for her maxim the undoubted truth that the necessity of continuing faithful to Stephen without suspicion, dictated a fickle behaviour almost as imperatively as fickleness itself; a fact, however, which would give a startling advantage to the latter quality, should it ever appear.[12]

Swancourt does not stay to watch the succession of games and indeed is not heard from again until the next morning. As such, he is unable to control his daughter's growing anxiety over the series of defeats she suffers against Knight, defeats which cause her to be both increasingly attracted to, and repulsed by, her opponent. Swancourt is also not present for Elfride's final game with Knight, during which she feels so humiliated that she is forced to leave the room. He scolds his daughter for slavishly playing so soon after her troubled sleep was filled with "armies of bishops and knights", but he is ineffective in dissuading her. Just as Prospero's presence during the discovery of Ferdinand and Miranda at chess reinforces his controlling presence throughout the course of the play, Swancourt's absence during Elfride's matches with Stephen and Henry accentuates his recurring absence throughout the novel. After Stephen leaves in humiliation, Swancourt tells Elfride that he recognized the possibility of her romantic attachment with Stephen, but in so admitting demonstrates a fundamental lack of interest in his daughter's emotional well-being:

> I know – since you press me so – I know I did guess some childish attachment might arise between you; I own I did not take much trouble to prevent it; but I have not particularly countenanced it.[13]

Swancourt's attempt at absolution rings hollow in that he claims no responsibility for circumstances perpetrated largely by his equivocating silence.

Apart from his disappearance during Elfride's chess matches, Swancourt is physically absent at other key moments. His journey to

---

[12] *PBE*, 167.
[13] *PBE*, 84-85

Stratleigh to be married allows Elfride the opportunity to run off with Stephen to London. Similarly, his absence upon her return – he only travels as far as Wadcombe and returns the following day – prevents him from discovering Elfride's deception. Such a discovery could well result in Elfride's marriage with Stephen to prevent scandal: in an earlier conversation with his daughter Swancourt is forced to admit: "If he were allied to us irretrievably, of course I, or any sensible man, should accept conditions that could not be altered; certainly not be hopelessly melancholy about it."[14] Once again, Swancourt demonstrates his emotional distance from Elfride – an acute lack of understanding as it concerns her reckless intentions – as if their discussion about her hypothetical marriage to Stephen could not have any ramifications.

Hardy's allusion to *The Tempest* juxtaposes a series of binary oppositions – fate and will, presence and absence, denial and accountability, player and plaything – in suggesting how Swancourt, an exceedingly fallible Prospero, educates his daughter, a dutiful but free-spirited Miranda, in a chessic class game played for the stakes of social power. In making these connections with Shakespeare's play, *A Pair of Blue Eyes* suggests both the limitations of its characters in their ability to negotiate the fictional gameworld of the text as well as the richness of their inherent complexity in being so limited. Swancourt does not have the means to work magic when it comes to teaching his daughter the art of social game playing; rather, his own tendencies to conceal, manipulate, misinterpret, and scheme teach Elfride that he is not to be trusted with her confidence and that she herself must use the same kind of deception that ultimately checkmates her.

Swancourt's initial miscalculation in educating Elfride is his use of unsuitable texts to instruct her in the art of social game playing. He oversimplifies the game in assuming that success ultimately derives from handling a complicated situation as though it has an uncomplicated solution, and then attempts to impart this knowledge to his daughter by teaching her moves without properly explaining the principles behind them. Indeed, a consideration of Swancourt's conduct in light of the novel's prevailing chess motif suggests that his correspondence with Hewby and the genealogical contents of Burke's *Peerage* prove to be dangerously unreliable rule books for instructing Elfride about how to negotiate the Wessex game-board.

As a seasoned social player, Swancourt makes clear to his young protégée his firm belief that the ability to deal with unfavourable situations can only be accomplished if one learns the art of social game

---

[14] *PBE*, 107.

playing from the proper texts. Swancourt holds Elfride's novels responsible for the threat they pose to her development as a player, and when he complains that she "gets all kinds of stuff" into her head from reading these romances, he is objecting to the fact that this sort of literature threatens to leave her with an inappropriate strategy for dealing with real-life situations. In a sense, Swancourt sees the novel as a set of unreliable instructions: a guide to playing a fictional game.

One of the misconceptions that Swancourt surely suspects Elfride of having formed from her steady diet of romance novels is that Hewby's assistant will not come because of the inclement weather, and he is quick to inform her that such logic is nonsensical: "Wind! What ideas you have Elfride! Who ever heard of wind stopping a man from doing his business."[15] Swancourt recognizes a danger in letting such preconceptions go unchecked because they threaten to expose his pupil as an unprepared player while at the same time drawing attention to her instructor's incompetence. Thus, he corrects her on a number of points, not only on the ridiculousness of assuming that the weather will prevent their guest from arriving, but on what sort of meal to serve Hewby's assistant (Elfride apparently gets it wrong twice), and on how a young woman should conduct herself in the presence of a visitor – Elfride claims to be uncomfortable engaging in conversation with someone to whom she has not been formally introduced, which her father finds ludicrous in light of his conviction that anyone travelling such a great distance will "hardly be inclined to talk and air courtesies." Naturally, his conviction is altogether fallacious as Stephen proves to be more than inclined.

Swancourt tells his daughter to read the correspondence between himself and Hewby to learn more about their impending visitor because such information – unlike the matter contained in her "contemptible" novels – is likely to give Elfride a good indication about how to receive their guest. Like a chess player who prizes the texts from which he derives an opening repertoire, Swancourt treats the letters as a collective treatise on the theory of how to begin a game of social exchange, and he tells Elfride that if she wants to learn more about the nature of their visitor, she can consult the account of the moves that have been played to this point.

Unlike Elfride and her suitors who face off directly against one another in over-the-board play, Swancourt and Hewby are engaged in a game of social correspondence in which the letters act as a record of the moves that have been played to this point. However, a correspondence game involves adversaries who examine their positions

---

[15] *PBE*, 9.

without the benefit of sharing a common board, and who must further rely on interpreting each other's notation for recording their moves. Unfortunately, Swancourt is not inquisitive enough about the implications of Hewby's use of the term "assistant" to describe Stephen; instead, he defines the term himself to mean "partner" and even in retrospect accepts this as the only logical interpretation:

> 'Here's what he said to me .... "My assistant, Mr. Stephen Smith" – assistant, you see he called him, and naturally I understood him to mean a sort of partner. Why didn't he say "clerk"?'
>
> 'They never call them clerks in that profession, because they do not write. Stephen – Mr. Smith – told me so. So that Mr. Hewby simply used the accepted word.'
>
> 'Let me speak, please, Elfride! "My assistant, Mr. Stephen Smith, will leave London by the early train tomorrow morning ... *many thanks for your proposal to accommodate him ... you may put every confidence in him,* and may rely on his discernment in the matter of church architecture." Well, I repeat that Hewby ought to be ashamed of himself for making so much of a poor lad of that sort.'[16]

Swancourt errs in his interpretation because of his own peculiar brand of egotistical logic: he assumes that Hewby's priorities are identical with his own, and that the architect would naturally make class consciousness a higher priority than professional considerations. Thus, he misinterprets the game of correspondence with Hewby in assuming that Stephen is the sort of person whom he would want dealing with his family on a social level, and falls victim to the very kind of opening trap from which he is striving to protect his daughter. Swancourt is prone to such traps because of his tendency to interpret situations in which he interacts with "gentlemen" as necessarily favourable to his family's fortunes. Because he acutely recognizes his own isolation, he greedily takes to any individual who might potentially liberate him from his social stalemate.

The book in which Swancourt places absolute trust regarding the high stakes game of social advancement is John Burke's *A Genealogical and Heraldic Dictionary of the Landed Gentry of Great Britain and Ireland.* Here, Swancourt traces his own ancestral history and justifies his position as a blue-blooded social player. When Stephen comes to Endelstow for the first time, Swancourt is quick to establish his guest's ties to "a well-known ancient country family – not ordinary Smiths in the least." Stephen protests, but Swancourt's fidelity to his own self-

---

[16] *PBE*, 87.

aggrandizing assumptions easily wins out over his guest's puzzled objections:

> 'Here in this book is a genealogical tree of the Stephen Fitzmaurice Smiths of Caxbury Manor. You may be only a family of professional men now ... [but] Mr. Smith, I congratulate you upon your blood; blue blood, sir; and, upon my life, a very desirable colour, as the world goes.'[17]

Swancourt is frustrated with being essentially cut off from more polite society – in one sense like the king in a chess game, deprived of mobility and dependent upon the sacrifices of others (the Luxellians for instance, who allow him their acquaintance), and in another sense like the bishop, fated to travel only half of the social playing field, separated from those who won't be friends with him and incessantly colliding with those whom he feels himself to be above.[18] His cursory, albeit enthusiastic, research into Stephen's genealogy is not for the benefit of his guest so much as for his own need to find himself in the company of a fellow gentleman and not in the hands of yet another pretentious pawn. This becomes readily apparent when having once established Stephen's ancestry, Swancourt then immediately embarks upon a description of his own:

> 'Now look – see how far back in the mists of antiquity my own family of Swancourt have a root. Here, you see,' he continued, turning to the page, 'is Geoffrey, the one among my ancestors who lost a barony because he would cut his joke.'[19]

Swancourt's feelings of isolation cause him to have this pretentious attachment with the past and impart it to his impressionable daughter. He firmly believes that by a close study of the appropriate texts, coupled with a clever and careful manoeuvring, the Swancourt family can climb out of its social stalemate and recapture its lost position.

Swancourt's abnormal confidence in the powers of Burke's text is illuminated by considering the topological relationship between a genealogical tree and the algorithmic web of decisions that underlie both the prevailing chess motif and the social game playing in which Elfride's father engages. Swancourt believes that proving the validity of one's pretensions to a higher class is no more difficult than tracing his family's lineage through the pages of Burke's *Peerage*. His perceiveed right to privilege derives from the absurd belief that as part of a genealogical tree, his family is legitimately entitled to the status held

---

[17] *PBE*, 20.
[18] See Appendix.
[19] *PBE*, 20.

by its most successful ascendant. Therefore, in his social game playing, Swancourt is prone to overestimate those whose social position he envies and, consequently, underestimate anyone whose origins could threaten his cherished class ascension. In effect, Swancourt plays chess with his social ambitions; having knowledge of a formerly favourable position or past victory dictates that the course of play must see his current position improve to that previous standard. Naturally, this line of reasoning gets him into trouble because an understanding of position – whether it be contained in a genealogical tree or within the confines of a chess board – is the recognition and appreciation of numerous factors, and not simply the acknowledgement of a relationship between two unrelated points.

Because a favourable marriage by Elfride could resurrect her family's fallen prestige, Swancourt endeavours to instill in his daughter his concept of playing for position. He believes that Elfride needs instruction to this end, discouraged as he is by the patterns of behaviour established by her female relatives:

> [T]he family history sets her the example of unorthodox behaviour: her mother eloped with Mr. Swancourt in defiance of her family, and her grandmother's romantic elopement with a musician is a matter of local legend.[20]

Because of the faith Swancourt places in Burke's *Peerage* as irrefutable proof of his blue-blooded ancestry, he decides that the solution to his class crisis lies in suppressing the possibility of his daughter's romantic attachment to a member of the working class, while at the same time doing nothing to discourage her relationships with men who appear to move in the appropriate social circles. For Swancourt, Elfride is not simply a pawn to be manipulated towards promotion, but a potentially mad queen in need of a controlling hand.

The latter idea is critical in understanding Swancourt's inability to instruct his young daughter judiciously in the art of social game playing. Swancourt's faith in the notion that affluence through social ascension is the direct result of traversing a very specific course finds itself undermined by his attempt to use Elfride as a pawn in controlling her capabilities as a queen. In so doing, Swancourt is unable to teach Elfride about herself; he wants to take advantage of her ability to bring the family out of bankruptcy without allowing her to realize her full potential as an autonomous individual, simply because there is no room for this in his clever scheming. This has a controlling influence on the manner in which Elfride becomes trapped within her search to be free of the problems that plague her romantic involvements. At

---

[20] Rimmer, 208.

those moments in the novel when it is imperative that she look upon herself as having the self-directing powers of a queen, she can only manage to see herself as an isolated pawn.

Swancourt naturally views the bettering of social position as the only stake worth playing for, and endeavours to convince Elfride of this in explaining his dispassionate marriage of convenience with Mrs. Troyton:

> Elfride, I am past love, you know, and I honestly confess that I married her for your sake. Why a woman of her standing should have thrown herself away upon me, God knows. But I suppose her age and plainness were too pronounced for a town man. With your good looks, if you now play your cards well, you may marry anybody.[21]

Swancourt is unable to recognize that Elfride is not past love, and that her choice of a husband might be influenced by such "unprofitable" considerations as romantic affection and sexual attraction. As the somewhat feeble king, Swancourt is comfortable with getting Mrs. Troyton to resign, but Elfride's search for autonomy encourages her to play for a mate. Swancourt tries to instruct by example, but it is one riddled with inconsistencies and alien to a daughter who understands the concept of a relationship as involving a complex of emotions rather than a simple set of economic exchanges.

If an inability to comprehend her father's attitude towards marriage impairs Elfride's positional play, it is further marred by the fact that he teaches her the art of making precarious assumptions about others and then hastily forming fixed opinions about them. Swancourt is immediately convinced of Stephen's blue blood – blood which turns out to run through the veins of an ancestor who practised the art of assistant gardening – and subsequently decides within a few minutes of meeting his guest that it is as though he has known him for five or six years. But the instant Swancourt learns of Stephen's humble beginnings, he immediately converts all positive assessments of the young man's character into negative ones, and forges a new image of Elfride's suitor in his own mind. He even manages to disparage those qualities in Stephen with which it seems impossible to find fault: "Uniform pleasantness is rather a defect than a faculty. It shows that a man hasn't sense enough to know whom to despise."[22]

Swancourt also sets a poor precedent for his daughter in the various schemes he devises to bring his family out of its present

---

[21] *PBE*, 122.
[22] *PBE*, 87.

situation. His errant investments in mines and railways serve to reinforce his mistaken belief that "desperate" financial situations can somehow be remedied by spending large amounts of capital, and that position is ultimately subject to tactical considerations.[23] Like the false and speculative lines of play found amid the network of choices and decisions on the chess board, the symbolism of the mine and the railway is crucial in illustrating how Swancourt either buries his money in the earth or places it on a pair of infinite rails leading nowhere. He tries to escape his problems rather than confront them because the latter would force him to acknowledge that a more complex solution is required than he is willing to admit. Indeed, this logic helps to inform and convolute many of Elfride's own decisions in the novel.

Elfride's game commences like the opening stages of a chess game upon Stephen's unexpected arrival: "Her start of amazement at the sight of the visitor coming forth from under the stairs proved that she had not been expecting this surprising flank movement.[24]

The narrative adopts the terms of an ambush to characterize this first encounter between Stephen and Elfride. The latter is immediately caught off guard because her expectations of being engaged in a more direct manner are thrown into disarray by Worm's decision to lead Stephen in through what is presumably the servant's entrance. Although Elfride has studied her father's correspondence with Hewby, there is nothing in the contents of either letter to prepare her for such an opening. The irony of this seemingly innocuous scene becomes readily apparent when we later learn of Stephen's humble origins. Not only does he enter the rectory by the back door, but he enters into the Swancourts' social circle in the very same fashion. Stephen accepts the fact that the front door is stuck fast and that the "Turk can't open [it]," and indicates by his willingness to follow Worm that he is an individual of modest origins.

Elfride is further caught off guard because instead of confronting a seasoned opponent –

> the dark, taciturn, sharp, elderly man of business who had lurked in her imagination – a man with clothes smelling of city smoke, skin sallow from want of sun, and talk flavoured with epigram –

she finds herself standing before someone not unlike herself in appearance:

---

[23] This is very much the antithesis of the principle that is fundamental to a strategic game like chess, where tactics must always be undertaken with positional onsiderations in mind.
[24] *PBE*, 15

> Judging from his look, London was the last place in the world that one would have imagined to be the scene of his activities: such a face surely could not be nourished amid the smoke and mud and fog and dust ...
>
> His complexion was as fine as Elfride's own; the pink of his cheeks as delicate. His mouth as perfect as Cupid's bow in form, and as cherry red in colour as hers.[25]

Elfride is put at ease by the fact that Stephen is not what she had expected, and like her father, appears to abandon any sense of caution or reserve. She finds relief in the physical similarities she shares with her guest as proof of a shared affinity, much in the same way that Swancourt delves into Stephen's genealogy to establish a connection between himself and his guest. Thus, Elfride becomes a casualty of her own penchant for formulating hasty opinions about others based on faulty assumptions. This tendency causes her to let down her guard at critical moments, as when she allows Stephen a kind of intimacy by singing to him "airs" that she only half knows, because he impresses her as one who is not "critical, or experienced, or – much to mind." She allows this guard to drop further when she makes the admission that most men think her life "a dreadful bore in its normal state" with the implication that she yearns for more than the isolation of the parish community.

During the scene in which she tells Stephen about writing Swancourt's sermons for him, Elfride demonstrates her proclivity for being too familiar, only to regret it and attempt immediate rectification:

> after this childish burst of confidence, she was frightened, being warned by womanly instinct, which for the moment her ardour had outrun, that she had been too forward towards a comparative stranger.[26]

Indeed, this awkward feature of Elfride's character is a recurrent one. In yearning to sever her dependence on Swancourt and gain a measure of freedom, Elfride is prone to rash action, but in the performance of that action she is frequently checked by the principles she has been taught to uphold. One of the manifestations of this longing to take back moves is found in her predisposition for telling secrets, and the present scene subtly captures how the telling of secrets works to paralyze Elfride's progress in her search to be free of certain constraints. Elfride reveals to Stephen the secret that she writes her father's sermons for him, but in so doing must ask Stephen to keep

---

[25] *PBE*, 15-16.
[26] *PBE*, 30

this information secret. When Elfride says, "he talks to people and to me about what he said in his sermon today, and forgets that I wrote it for him," she unburdens herself from the anxiety she feels in not taking any of the credit for what she writes; however, she can only do this by establishing another secret. In this case there appears to be little harm done because she confides a rather innocuous bit of information in the trustworthy Stephen, but this sort of game becomes deadly when fate allows a character like Mrs. Jethway to get hold of Elfride's most intimate secrets.[27]

A related source of frustration for Elfride in her efforts to be free of social constraints is that she has difficulty in ascertaining whether Stephen is an appropriate partner in helping her to achieve this goal. Should she despise Stephen's awkward deficiencies or admire his attempts to overcome them? This confusion manifests itself most tellingly in the chess match they play, and because of the game's symbolic parallels with their romantic involvement, it informs their entire relationship. When Elfride plays chess against Stephen, she perceives that he is a beginner and has "a very odd way of handling the pieces when castling or taking a man." The narrative discloses that this is a source of great consternation for Elfride:

> Antecedently she would have supposed that the same performance must be gone through by all players in the same manner; she was taught by his differing action that all ordinary players, who learn the game by sight, unconsciously touch the men in a stereotyped way.[28]

Stephen's actions are consistent with those of a chess novice. Experienced players remove the captured piece before placing their own on the square in question. Rimmer convincingly argues that Stephen's difficulty in manipulating the chess pieces has serious class implications:

> Stephen, who has taught himself the game from a book, regards chess as one of his passports to middle-class status. He knows that his unorthodox handling of the chess pieces threatens to identify him as an interloper, just as his peculiar Latin pronunciation does.[29]

Another implication of Stephen's awkward use of the pieces is that he will prove inadequate in "handling" Elfride once he has won her heart. In addition, his clumsy castling manoeuvre foreshadows both

---

[27] Elfride plays her greatest tactical miscue in the presence of her most dangerous opponent, and is then forced to hope in vain that Mrs. Jethway will not take advantage of the secret weakness she has learned.
[28] *PBE*, 51.
[29] Rimmer, 206

his failure to secure her as a wife and his further inability to protect her from her own mistaken perceptions of herself.

Elfride's feelings of "indescribable oddness" towards her guest are not simply the result of his lack of familiarity with practical play, but the product of her own assumptions about class difference which she has, in part, inherited from Swancourt. She is alerted to her opponent's ineptitude by Stephen's admission that his theoretical knowledge has never been tested by practical experience. His mediocre abilities are then confirmed by his subsequent play which Elfride recognizes to be that of a novice. However, instead of approaching Stephen as an opponent to be objectively contested against, Elfride determines that he both requires and deserves special treatment. Elfride's heart tells her to let Stephen win because his labour and perseverance deserve reward, but in so doing she finds herself gripped by the need to show that his winning is nothing more than a game on her part.

Hence, while Elfride is said to be "absolutely indifferent as to the result," she is quick to make up for the two defeats by crushing Stephen in the third game. Although the narrative does not comment on the matter, Elfride's sudden improvement betrays the actions of a player who, in letting an opponent get the better of her to a certain point, now decides that she must assert her superiority in a swift and decisive manner: "'You have been trifling with me till now!' [Stephen] exclaimed, his face flushing. 'You did not play your best in the first two games?'"[30]

Elfride's decisions in the chess game are based on her confusion about whether to feel admiration or disdain for her adversary. She perceives that Stephen is not an ordinary opponent and, confronted with the choice of speaking out or keeping silent, proceeds to embarrass him by commenting on his handling of the pieces. However, she then allows Stephen to win undeservedly by having compassion for his fighting "at such a disadvantage and so manfully." Confronted with a final choice, she humiliates and lessens him in asserting her dominance at the game. The result is that she both embarrasses her opponent, making him "the picture of vexation and sadness", and experiences her own feelings of guilt and regret.

Elfride's difficulty in coming to terms with Stephen's character problematizes her relationship with him. Because Swancourt principally sees others as valuable pieces or expendable pawns, he can admire Stephen and then all at once dismiss him. However, Elfride is unable to do this because she sees that the revelation of her lover's

---

[30] *PBE*, 53.

humble origins does not nullify his positive qualities or somehow solve the existing complexity of his character. Swancourt can redefine Stephen's actions as essentially dishonourable in light of the new information he learns about him, but Elfride recognizes that such a rigid reinterpretation oversimplifies things. Thus, whereas her father finds liberation in trapping himself within the confines of never really understanding the people around him, Elfride imprisons herself within the cycle of trying desperately to understand. Both have radically different approaches in attempting to control the game from within: Swancourt assumes that his knowledge of the rules is accurate and that he is firmly in control, but Elfride is aware that there is much she does not know and that control is something for which she must constantly strive.

As Elfride's decisions in the chess match with Stephen are constructed around both her diminishing and elevating him as a player, further investigation shows that this behaviour is identical with her approach to Stephen in the larger context of their relationship. On the day following the play at chess, Mr. Swancourt proposes a drive to the cliffs beyond Targan Bay, but the actual journey must be made on horseback when the carriage axle unexpectedly breaks. Elfride learns that Stephen lacks equestrian skills and she shows her disappointment in a manner that recalls the chess game: "Fancy a gentleman not able to ride!" Elfride's class-based criticism questions Stephen's manhood by positing that his inability to ride is vulgar and unnatural. Her words demean him to such an extent that Swancourt is forced to come to his defence: "That's common enough; he has had other lessons to learn."[31]

However, this defence is laden with bitter irony; Swancourt eventually rejects Stephen because he is common. As in their chess match, Elfride both rewards and penalizes Stephen throughout the early part of their relationship by allowing him to assume seemingly important roles, only to humiliate him when he eventually blunders. Elfride mingles airs of dependency and superiority in using Stephen as she would a servant to watch her favourite earrings. While Stephen feels empowered in being entrusted with such a responsibility, Elfride's pretentious authority betrays that she is ordering him about as Swancourt might order her. And because we learn that she has already used her parlour-maid Unity to assist in rediscovering her lost earrings on a number of previous occasions, Stephen is symbolically brought down to the level of a mere servant. How fitting it is that as soon as she is through with her recollections, Elfride allows Stephen

---

[31] *PBE*, 55-56.

to lift her onto her horse, a moment of erotic contact that physically and symbolically raises her as it lowers him, but which ultimately brings her tumbling down when Stephen can not get her properly seated. When Swancourt advises Stephen to try again, Elfride will have no part of it, and confers upon her suitor the lowest possible place by assigning his duties to the workhand Worm.

The symbolism of this episode reinforces the theme of Elfride's frustrated progress, of being trapped within the cycle of trying to free herself of social constraints. In failing to perform the simple task of getting Elfride properly seated, Stephen is revealed to be inadequate as a partner in her bid for liberation. His awkward Latin pronunciation, clumsy manoeuvring of chess pieces, and ungraceful manipulation of Elfride herself, all look forward to his mishandling of the marriage license and their aborted plans to be together. Therefore, just as Swancourt fails his daughter in being too rigid in his control, Stephen fails her in being too passive.

As Stephen walks beside Elfride – who by this point has managed to get herself properly seated – their relative positions suggest a symbolic distance that she augments by all at once galloping off and leaving him behind:

> Stephen beheld her light figure contracting to the dimensions of a bird as she sank into the distance – her hair flowing behind. He walked on in the same direction, and for a considerable time could see no signs of her returning.[32]

Elfride appears to abandon Stephen in the same cruel manner that she crushes him in their final chess game after giving him the illusion that he is an equal opponent. And although this looks forward in symbolic fashion to her eventual rejection of Stephen in favour of Knight, the whole concept of Elfride rejecting Stephen is illusory – a kind of sham sacrifice – because Mrs. Jethway's knowledge of their elopement binds them inseparably.

Elfride's confusion in the opening stages of her relationship with Stephen is again underscored during the scene in which she blushingly consents to look into Stephen's eyes, but then forbids him to express his affection for her romantically. The illusion that she fully accepts Stephen as an equal by allowing him to look at her is dispelled by her insistence that he kiss her in the manner that a subject shows fidelity to his mistress, or a pawn to its Queen:

> He expressed by a look that to kiss a hand through a glove, and that a riding-glove, was not a great treat in the circumstances. 'There, then; I'll take my glove off. Isn't it a pretty

---

[32] *PBE*, 58.

white hand? Ah, you don't want to kiss it, and you shall not now!'[33]

However, Elfride adopts not only the role of a queen bestowing royal favour, but that of a pawn subjecting herself to the will of her king, and it is little wonder that Stephen regards her as both the object of his sexual passion and as the "queen" for whom he would give anything.

Elfride continually chides Stephen for his improper conduct, suggesting that he forces her to "behave in not a nice way at all" and the reader wonders whether this is the same attitude that prompts her to cheat for him during the chess match. When he sits across from her as an opponent in the chess game, Stephen is mildly scolded for his awkward handling of the pieces. When he takes his place as Elfride's suitor, he is either perceived as the bumbling fool who can not get her properly seated on her horse, the too-familiar lover who struggles for her hand, or the coarse suitor who has the unmitigated temerity to plunk himself down beside her in a manner that is hardly proper.[34]

Her consistent devaluation of him culminates with a moment of triumph which recalls her emotion when she seriously undertakes to defeat Stephen in their final game of chess: "What a proud moment it was for Elfride then! She was ruling a heart with absolute despotism for the first time in her life."[35] But the complexity of Elfride's relationship with Stephen derives from the fact that although she has a tendency to patronize and humiliate him, she is nonetheless in love, even though she is often unable to express this love without emasculating him:

> 'I know, I think, what I love you for. You are nice-looking, of course; but I didn't mean for that. It is because you are so docile and gentle.'
>
> 'Those are not quite the correct qualities for a man to be loved for,' said Stephen, in a rather dissatisfied tone of self-criticism.[36]

During the first two chess games, the narrator mentions that Elfride is "absolutely indifferent as to the result," although we learn this to be not wholly true when she crushes Stephen in the final game. This

---

[33] *PBE*, 58.
[34] Rimmer sees Stephen's knowledge of chess as representative of his aspirations to middle-class status. Not wanting to be seen as common, he nevertheless recognizes that his inability to ride jeopardizes his situation in the same way that "his handling of the chess pieces threatens to identify him as an interloper" (206).
[34] *PBE*, 58.
[35] *PBE*, 58.
[36] *PBE*, 64

has its parallel in the game of indifference that Elfride plays with her suitor when she becomes displeased about his constant mention of Knight during their return from the cliffs beyond Targan Bay:

> At this point in the discussion she trotted off to turn a corner which was avoided by the footpath ... On again making her appearance she continually managed to look in a direction away from him, and left him in the cool shade of her displeasure. Stephen was soon beaten at this game of indifference.[37]

Just as in the final chess game, Elfride consciously chooses a path that leaves Stephen feeling beaten and insecure. She takes advantage of his docility and gentleness – the qualities for which she claims to love him – by forcing him to admit that his affection for her outweighs his respect for Knight.

When Elfride uses the Muzio Gambit to defeat Stephen in the third game of their match, the opening system she employs acts as a metaphor of the events that are to follow. The Muzio Gambit is a variation of the King's Gambit, a romantic opening popular in the nineteenth century.[38] Hardy's reference to the Muzio Gambit invites the reader to draw important parallels between the representative pieces of that particular opening system and the characters involved in the social game playing of the novel. It is a simple matter to see Stephen as a sacrificed pawn, adored by Elfride but ultimately given up for the chance of maintaining her present position (by aborting the elopement) or possibly improving it (through her relationship with Knight). Elfride makes the decision to sacrifice Stephen rather than hold onto him because this would mean subjecting her own position to serious jeopardy, both from the unrelenting verbal attacks of her father and the general disapproval of polite society.

If Hardy's novel has a Black Queen who is eager to deliver a "check" it is Mrs. Jethway, whose knowledge of Stephen's sacrifice provides her the means to attack Elfride where the damage will be

---

[37] *PBE*, 66-67.

[38] Characterized by the moves 1. e4 e5, 2. f4 exf4, 3. Nf3 g5, 4. Bc4 g4, 5. O-O gxf3, 6. Qxf3, the Muzio Gambit has the White player sacrificing first a pawn and then a knight both for the sake of development and a natural attack along the semi-open f-file. The crux of this opening system lies in whether or not White can succeed in delivering checkmate before the material sacrificed unbalances the game in Black's favour. The symbolism of the Muzio Gambit suggests that Stephen corresponds to White's f-pawn, and this carries with it a number of additional implications. However, one of the dangers of advancing the f-pawn at such an early stage in the game is that it exposes the e1-h4 diagonal, a line available for the Black Queen to deliver check. With a further weakening of the White King's field taking place, the results of such a check can prove devastating.

most acute. Just as the movement of the Black King's pawn allows the Black Queen access for attack, so does the premature death of Mrs. Jethway's son provide her the impetus to ruin Elfride and lay waste to her social position.

It would be foolish to think that once Stephen is sacrificed for the sake of Elfride's development and she becomes involved with Knight there is no more to be said about this sacrificed pawn. However, Hardy understands that in life, as in chess, what is gained must be weighed against what is given up, and that if Stephen's sacrifice can not be brought to good account then his loss will reveal itself in the most damning way. The Muzio Gambit is a fitting metaphor for Elfride's tragic progression because so much is sacrificed or lost that the resulting imbalance proves to have fatal consequences.

The novel's transition to the "middlegame" begins with the misreported account of John Smith's hand being "squashed ... to a pummy,"[39] and Stephen's revelation to Swancourt that his family is not descended from the Smiths of Caxbury Manor. Elfride now embarks on a long-term strategy for marrying secretly while deceiving her father into thinking that she can give up Stephen as easily as she might relinquish a sacrificed pawn. However, a consideration of the novel's recurring chess motif reveals that those factors which have plagued Elfride's relationship with Stephen from the beginning – her penchant for making hasty decisions and then changing her mind, his self-deprecation and inability to take control of matters, and their shared need to be secretive about their romantic involvement – will prove most damaging in the dangerous game that has now been undertaken.

Although he never lacks praise for Elfride's moderate chess skills, Swancourt has hypocritically ingrained in his daughter that she is rather a poor judge of things and prone to confuse "future probabilities with present facts." Indeed, by making unsound financial investments in attempting to recapture his family's fallen prestige, Swancourt teaches Elfride by his own example to make the same kinds of rash decisions from which he otherwise attempts to dissuade her. Ultimately, both characters encounter severe setbacks because they think the games in which they are involved have solutions, and that they are winnable rather than simply playable.[40]

---

[39] *PBE*, 80: pummy: apple pulp as in preparation for cider-making.

[40] This is a common theme in nineteenth and twentieth century novels that feature a controlling chess motif. Carroll's Alice believes that becoming a Queen will win her the game by bringing her the social power she yearns for; Nabokov's Luzhin thinks that he can find a defense to the irresistible combination that life plays against him; and

The chess motif exposes that Elfride's penchant for self-contradiction makes her a poor tactician in the social game playing in which she is presently engaged. Elfride's unsound tactical ability, influenced by Swancourt's numerous precedents, never fails to create weaknesses in her social position, and this reveals itself most tellingly in her aborted elopement. Her decision to marry Stephen and bring him into the family by secret means is a plan that requires tactical play beginning with a positional sacrifice on her part, but the problem is that instead of making the sacrifice and seeing it through to the end, or declining it and calling off the elopement, Elfride sacrifices only to then fall back, without the realization that Mrs. Jethway's scheming will ensure her deteriorating position is devoid of compensation.

Hardy carefully prepares the reader for the disaster of the aborted elopement in preceding scenes where Elfride takes various risks involving her physical safety. Such episodes show how often Elfride's efforts to demonstrate her autonomy are undercut by the circumstances in which she finds herself. One such scene occurs when Elfride and Stephen are returning from their visit to the Luxellian mansion:

> There was no absolute necessity for either of them to alight, but as it was the rector's custom after a long journey to humour the horse in making this winding ascent, Elfride, moved by an imitative instinct, suddenly jumped out when Pleasant had just begun to adopt the deliberate stalk he associated with this portion of the road.
>
> The young man seemed glad of any excuse for breaking the silence. 'Why, Miss Swancourt, what a risky thing to do.'[41]

The explicit irony of Elfride's bold and deliberate move is that it is made in imitation of Swancourt, the source of her tactical knowledge. The symbolic value afforded by the image of her leaping down from the carriage and rendering herself different from Stephen is undercut by the very real danger she is forced to assume. This suggests that on some level she associates autonomy with self-injury. Furthermore, Elfride's action is immediately followed by Stephen's offer to take her hand as they continue walking, and although she puts him off temporarily – "No, thank you, Mr. Smith; I can get along better by myself" – she rationalizes a way to avoid resisting the proposal for very long:

---

even Beckett's Clov – resigned as he is to a perpetual endgame – briefly places his hopes on the boy he sees near the close of the play.

[41] *PBE*, 45. A parallel incident is Elfride's precarious and seemingly foolhardy walk upon the parapet of the church tower in the presence of Henry Knight.

> It was Elfride's first fragile attempt at browbeating a lover. Fearing more the issue of such an undertaking than what a gentle young man might think of her waywardness, she immediately afterwards determined to please herself by reversing her statement.[42]

In this scene as in others, Elfride's desperate act of achieving some semblance of autonomy through hazardous means only brings her back into the literal and figurative control of the novel's patriarchal representatives.

The chess motif helps us to see in general terms that because Elfride acts rashly and is prone to retract moves, she is liable to fare poorly in the secretive game of marrying herself to Stephen. However, an understanding of the specific principles involved in opening and "middlegame" play can illuminate how Elfride's micarried flight with Stephen provides for the permanent collapse of her entire game. One of the most important elements in a chess opening or early "middlegame" is time, and whichever side is said to have the most *tempi*[43] is often the one with the advantage, especially if this is accompanied with similar advantages in force and space. When Elfride arrives in London with Stephen and all at once decides to return, she appears to make the mistake of a novice player who thinks that there is nothing wrong with moving a piece and then returning it to its initial position on a subsequent move: "'Will you allow me to go home?' she implored. 'I won't trouble you to go with me .... It is better that I should return again; indeed it is, Stephen.'"[44]

The problem with making a move and then returning the moved piece to its original square on the next turn is that the player doing so allows the opponent time to marshall his or her forces. Elfride recognizes this only after she has returned from London, and the terms in which she summarizes her position could well be applied to a chess game in which her rash movements have proven costly:

> 'I did not see all the consequences,' she said. 'Appearances are wofully [sic] against me .... It was my only safe defence. I see more things now than I did yesterday. My only remaining chance is not to be discovered; and that we must fight for most desperately.'[45]

Of course, these words are no sooner spoken than Mrs. Jethway's "glistening eyes" spot the couple and discern their terrible secret.

---

[42] *PBE*, 46.
[43] *Tempi*: unit of time measured by piece development.
[44] *PBE*, 113.
[45] *PBE*, 115.

The manner in which Elfride plays with Stephen while she plays against him during their chess match suggests that although he is representative of the patriarchal system that imprisons Elfride within her discouraging search for liberation, his passivity and equivocation allow her to transgress the established norms of Wessex society. As Rimmer observes, Elfride

> disrupts the social order more seriously than her rebellious forbears; her mother's and grandmother's clandestine marriages allow them to be accepted back into their families, but Elfride's anomalous position after her abortive elopement with Stephen resists conventional definition and leaves her without firm connections to either Stephen or her father.[46]

Stephen proves to be not only a weak opponent, but an equally ineffectual partner, and his play brings out his passivity and willingness to compromise, like a chess player only too willing to accept a draw or stalemate in a superior position. Elfride endangers her social position by making hasty assumptions and rash decisions, and Stephen is ineffective in preventing this from happening. He watches the game being played out before him and can offer a limited amount of counsel to a player like Elfride, but when it comes to interfering directly he inevitably abstains. Indeed, he is frequently ineffectual in dissuading Elfride from embarking upon a rash course of action:

> 'O Stephen,' she exclaimed, 'I am so miserable! I must go home again – I must – I must! Forgive my wretched vacillation. I don't like it here – nor myself – nor you!' Stephen looked bewildered, and did not speak.[47]

Stephen's skill at handling Elfride is equivalent to his deficient chess skill: although he has a theoretical appreciation of the dangers to which Elfride will expose herself by returning home unmarried, he lacks the practical experience to prevent her from doing so. By partaking in the conspiracy to keep their plans a secret from Swancourt, he undercuts his ability to prevent Elfride from subjecting herself to the possibility of domestic ruin.

A consideration of the novel's chess motif demonstrates that Elfride's reliance on the element of secrecy in carrying out her plan to marry Stephen is riddled with logical defects which she unconsciously acknowledges during one of their private conversations:

---

[46] Rimmer, 208.
[47] *PBE*, 113.

'All we want is to render it absolutely impossible for any future circumstance to upset our future intention of being happy together; not to begin being happy now.'[48]

Like her father, who believes in his ability to control social game playing from his position within the game, Elfride betrays her conviction that through a process of careful manoeuvring, she and Stephen can convince their opponent to resign: "'He would then believe that hearts could not be played with; love encouraged be ready to grow, love discouraged be ready to die, at a moment's notice.'"[49]

However, the logical fallacy in this is that Elfride and Stephen make the mistake of assuming that they are playing together against a single opponent, and subsequently look upon their careful deception of Swancourt as proof of a flawless scheme. But in chess, as in social game playing, there is no element of secrecy; the moves of the pieces and the ever-changing position of the board are there for all to see. Who is to say that a quiet bystander like Mrs. Jethway is not potentially as much a player as one who purports to be handling the pieces? Elfride and Stephen are not merely carrying out a plan to deceive her father as they believe, but to deceive the very social system that stands in judgment when their plans go awry. By carrying the desire for secrecy to the point where the marriage plans are mis-carried and the discovered mate is not played, Elfride leaves herself vulnerable to opponents from every portion of the social chessboard.

Another problem with Elfride's brief discourse on secrecy is her admission that while she ultimately wants to be happy, she does not necessarily "want to begin being happy now." Elfride traps herself within a frustrated cycle in assuming that she can achieve happiness by enduring a series of trials that make her essentially unhappy. Regardless of the fact that she is making one precarious move after another, Elfride hopes to arrive at a position in which she attains the control she has been seeking, but this is no less ludicrous than Swancourt's conviction that by thoughtlessly investing his money he can set his family on the road to economic independence. Elfride initially thinks that marrying Stephen will allow them to win the game they are secretly contesting, but she does not feel the sense of liberation she expected upon arriving in London, the exit to the "maze of rails over which they traced their way." Rather, she is overcome with the gloom of finding herself on an alien square of the chessboard, where she sees "only the lamps, which had just been lit, blinking in the wet atmosphere, and rows of hideous zinc chimney-pipes in dim

---

[48] *PBE*, 98.
[49] *PBE*, 99

relief against the sky. She writhed uneasily."[50] Confronted with the confusion of being on "strange ground," Elfride immediately makes her decision to choose the safety of returning home over seeing her sacrifice through to the end. However, in determining that marriage to Stephen is no longer the key to achieving victory, she cannot possibly know that aborting the elopement will make her a pawn in the hands of the vengeful Mrs. Jethway.

Although Elfride is bound to Stephen through Mrs. Jethway's knowledge of their trip to London, his relocation to India provides her with the opportunity to overcome any lingering feelings of dependency.[51] Indeed, she eventually finds herself becoming increasingly more attracted to the "nice voice [and] singular temper" of Henry Knight, the middle-aged book reviewer who scathingly critiques her novel.

Once again, Elfride engages in a series of chess games with a male visitor, although this time she is unable to manipulate her opponent as she would like. This second chess match demonstrates her acute concern with defeating Knight and proving that if he does not respect her abilities as a writer, he has no choice but to respect her abilities as a player. However, Elfride's ruthlessness in seizing the advantage, her desperate but futile attempts to manipulate Knight when she has blundered, and the building emotion with which she experiences her successive defeats all serve to mirror not only her inability to realize some measure of autonomy, but her gradual forfeiture of the illusion that this autonomy is possible.

When Knight blunders his rook in the first game, Elfride seizes the opportunity without hesitation: "It was her first advantage. She looked triumphant – even ruthless." Elfride does not take pity on Knight for his oversight as she did with Stephen, but instead reminds him of "Club Laws" and the importance of playing by the strictest of rules.[52] This comes in the wake of Knight permitting her to take back previous moves: he "had two or three times allowed her to replace a man on her religiously assuring him that such a move was an absolute blunder."[53] By insisting upon the adoption of these new rules, Elfride indicates that this is no disinterested affair but a serious intellectual contest.

However, this fundamental interest betrays the fact that she is not in control of things. Elfride subverts the game as a game because she

---

[50] *PBE*, 113.
[51] It is interesting that Stephen accepts a position in India, the birthplace of chess.
[52] The rules of competitive chess have long dictated that a move is considered complete once the player has released the piece onto a square.
[53] *PBE*, 168.

plays for a stake contained outside the parameters of the game itself. She derives a feeling of control over Stephen by being indifferent as to whether or not she wins (although the reader learns that this is only a half-truth in light of her conduct during the final game of that match), but she can only feel in control against Knight by defeating him and being acknowledged as superior in at least one area of their shared acquaintance.

When the advantage passes to Knight in the first game and Elfride grows "flurried" and blunders her queen, she humiliates herself in taking every step possible to have her move retracted. First, she claims that only a fool would have made such a move knowingly, the implication being that she is not a fool and that she should be allowed to retract it. When this does not work, she implies that Knight is being unpleasant in taking advantage of her mistake. This failing, she denigrates the very "Club Laws" she promoted only moments before.[54]

As Elfride is defeated again and again, she goes from being merely flushed, to being distracted, to being overcome with bitter weeping.[55] It was a simple matter to manipulate Stephen and to have him win and lose as she pleased, but Knight is mechanical and disinterested; he allows her to establish the rules and then simply defeats her in adhering to them. When she finds herself losing the match to him, any illusions she holds with respect to her ability to derive some measure of control are painfully dispelled. Because Knight is a better player and able to defeat Elfride rather easily, she can only win his respect by being gracious in defeat, but since admitting defeat is for her a sign of not being in control, she finds herself in the same sort of frustrated cycle that informs her progress throughout the novel. That Elfride forfeits control after losing this latest series of games both harks back to the failure of the aborted marriage plans and looks forward to her eventual collapse when Knight rejects her.[56]

The principal quality in Elfride's chess play that informs her relationship with Knight is her tendency to miscalculate. She makes profound errors of judgment in the various games she plays with him, and these cause her to experience feelings of dejection and humiliation. On the morning after their final chess game, Elfride asks to look

---

[54] Elfride's appeals to Knight foreshadow her encounter with Mrs. Jethway, in which she will again prove ineffective in manipulating her opponent.

[55] "Although her father and the narrator both call Elfride a good player, they assume that she cannot genuinely compete at chess, and that the limits on her skill derive from her womanhood ... Good enough to beat the men in her small provincial circle, Elfride is expected to lose to any male player (short of a beginner like Stephen) from the metropolis" (Rimmer 207-8).

[56] Her loss of control also recalls Stephen's passionate outburst after Elfride crushes him in the final game of their match.

at a book in which Knight is making notations, only to discover that it contains a passage in which she is rather pompously critiqued:

> Girl gets into her teens, and her self-consciousness is born. After a certain interval passed in infantine helplessness, it begins to act. Simple, young, and inexperienced at first. Persons of observation can tell to a nicety how old this consciousness is by the skill it has acquired in the art necessary to its success – the art of hiding itself. Generally begins career by actions which are popularly termed showing-off. [57]

Elfride is desperate for validation and the sense of control and security it engenders, even if these things come from someone whose opinions concerning young women have their basis in theoretical assumptions that have not been adequately tested by practical experience.

Elfride constructs a game in which she attempts to control Knight's responses to a series of questions designed to flatter her, but his consistent failure to fall in with her scheme symbolically reinforces the gradual breakdown of the larger game in which she participates. After Knight makes an incorrect guess at Elfride's age, he is asked if he prefers women who seem older or younger than they really are. Of course, he plays a move she was not expecting by responding: "Off-hand I should be inclined to say those who seem older". Elfride miscalculates yet again when she asks Knight to tell her his favourite colour of hair and he admits to favouring dark:

> It was impossible for any man not to know the colour of Elfride's hair …. You saw her hair as far as you could see her sex, and knew that it was the palest brown. She knew instantly that Knight, being perfectly aware of this, had an independent standard of admiration in the matter.[58]

Elfride's miscalculation not only stems from Knight's inability to respond correctly, but in her own willingness to break herself down into disembodied parts for him to fetishize and critique simultaneously:

> Elfride was thoroughly vexed. She could not but be struck with the honesty of his opinions, and the worst of it was, that the more they went against her, the more she respected them. And now like a reckless gambler, she hazarded her last and best treasure. Her eyes: they were her all now.
>
> 'What coloured eyes do you like best, Mr. Knight?' she said slowly.
>
> 'Honestly, or as a compliment?'

---

[57] *PBE*, 176.
[58] *PBE*, 177-78

> 'Of course honestly; I don't want anybody's compliment!"
>
> And yet Elfride knew otherwise: that a compliment or word of approval from that man then would have been like a well to a famished Arab.
>
> 'I prefer hazel,' he said serenely.
>
> She had played and lost again.[59]

The image of Elfride as a gambler is an appropriate one, and points to an acute problem both in her ability to play chess and to apply this strategic knowledge in her relationships with men. Gambling in a chess game is regarded as foolish unless it can be justified by a consideration of the position, but Elfride is desperate to know whether or not she can win the respect of someone as intelligent and indifferent as Henry.

The game of indifference which Elfride herself played during her courtship with Stephen, and of which Henry now shows himself to be her master, continues during their walk after one of Swancourt's services. Elfride wants him to describe the difference between "women with something and women with nothing in them," but once again the straightforwardness of his answer confounds her and throws her on the defensive:

> 'I knew a man who had a young friend he was much interested in; in fact, they were going to be married. She was seemingly poetical, and he offered her a choice of two editions of the British poets, which she pretended to want badly. He said, "Which of them would you like best for me to send?" She said, "A pair of the prettiest ear-rings in Bond-Street, if you don't mind, would be nicer than either." Now I call her a girl with not much in her but vanity; and so do you I daresay.'
>
> 'O yes,' replied Elfride with an effort.[60]

Elfride believes that she finally has Knight in a position to admit his admiration for her feminine qualities, not simply for her enjoyment of music which indeed he compliments, but what this implies about her inner nature. However, when Knight brings up the subject of the earrings, it is as though Elfride once again finds herself sitting across a chessboard from him and watching as he slowly reveals to her the instability of her position:

> 'No, no, no, no!' she cried petulantly; 'I didn't mean what you think. I like the music best, only I like – '

---

[59] *PBE*, 178-79.
[60] *PBE*, 183.

> 'Ear-rings better – own it!' he said in a teasing tone. 'Well, I think I should have had the moral courage to own it at once, without pretending to an elevation I could not reach.'[61]

Perhaps the most powerful scene in the novel, and one which further helps us to understand the importance of Hardy's chess motif, is Knight's near death upon the Cliff Without a Name and Elfride's ingenious rescue of him using a rope fashioned out of her own undergarments.[62] In the early moments of their predicament, Elfride claims that she anticipated this calamity while on the church tower, revealing her psychic ability to recognize the future repetition of events but not to prevent these events from taking place. Furthermore, her penchant for miscalculation, which is fatal to her play at chess with Henry, nearly proves fatal to him when she fails to secure every link in the rope she fashions to save him:

> 'Now,' said Knight, who, watching the proceedings intently, had by this time not only grasped her scheme, but reasoned further on, 'I can hold three minutes longer yet. And do you use the time in testing the strength of the knots, one by one.'
>
> She at once obeyed, tested each singly by putting her foot on the rope between each knot, and pulling with her hands. One of the knots slipped.
>
> 'O, think! It would have broken but for your forethought,' Elfride exclaimed apprehensively.[63]

The calamities which befall the male characters typically pose an even more serious threat to Elfride, and here as in her chess games it is she who is the most vulnerable. Although Knight appears to face certain death upon the cliff, it is Elfride who must physically and symbolically render herself vulnerable if she is to save him:

> An overwhelming rush of exultation at having delivered the man she revered from one of the most terrible forms of death, shook the gentle girl to the centre of her soul .... Perhaps he was only grateful, and did not love her. No matter; it was infinitely more to be even the slave of the greater than the queen of the less.[64]

Elfride's seemingly autonomous action of using her own clothes to rescue Knight is undercut both by her failure to secure the rope

---

[61] *PBE*, 184.
[62] Perhaps nowhere else in literature has a writer more graphically depicted the chess adage that "A Knight on the rim is grim."
[63] *PBE*, 219.
[64] *PBE*, 220.

properly without his assistance and the sexually vulnerable position in which she leaves herself:

> 'I must leave you now,' she said, her face doubling its red, with an expression between gladness and shame .... Elfride had absolutely nothing between her and the weather but her exterior robe or 'costume.'[65]

Like a queen forced to defend her king, Elfride is able to perform the task admirably, but not without ultimately assuming the greatest risk.

The episode that marks the transition to the novel's endgame and acutely foreshadows its grim denouement is the meeting that takes place among Stephen, Henry, and Elfride in the Luxellian tomb. This scene has a great deal of symbolic value because it represents the one and only meeting of all three central characters; they are reunited in this very tomb at the end of the novel, but Elfride is of course dead. Her recitation from the book of Psalms in the tomb episode is most telling: "My days, just hastening to their end, / Are like an evening shade; / My beauty doth, like wither'd grass, / With waning lustre fade."[66] This scene also demonstrates both Elfride's ability to deceive Knight and his own penchant for self-deception, and thus it serves to reveal why Elfride is able to maintain her destructive cycle of secrecy. Knight is convinced that the sight of death in the Luxellian tomb has turned Elfride pale, and she is content in allowing him to assume this:

> His obtuseness to the cause of her indisposition, by evidencing his entire freedom from the suspicion of anything behind the scenes, showed how incapable Knight was of deception himself, rather than any inherent dulness in him regarding human nature. [67]

Knight may be incapable of intentionally deceiving others, but he deceives himself rather easily, trusting that odd behaviour on Elfride's part can not have any sinister implications because of the faith he places in her sexual innocence. His manner in dealing with others is straightforward; in chess terms, he seems more the rook than a knight, since among chess pieces the last is by far the most deceptive. However, like the knight, he unwittingly manages to leap over Stephen and "wriggle" into his romantic affairs. During his encounter with Stephen in the Luxellian tomb, Knight lands on a square directly between his Queen and her pawn:

---

[65] *PBE*, 221. Hardy later adds the suggestive word "diaphanous' to 'exterior robe.'
[66] *PBE*, 261. The Psalm quoted by Elfride is taken from the Tate and Brady metrical version of Psalm 102.
[67] *PBE*, 265.

> It was a scene which was remembered by all three as an indelible mark in their history. Knight, with an abstracted face, was standing between his companions, though a little in advance of them, Elfride being on his right hand, and Stephen Smith on his left.[68]

Rimmer observes that

> Knight's name, in its connections with knighthood and with chess, emphasizes his position as an insider in a world that excludes Stephen, and that Elfride can enter only as the passive "lady" whom the knight defends against others and himself besieges for sexual favours.[69]

However, Knight is not only the stuffy modernized version of the chivalrous and trustworthy knight, but also a self-deceiving interloper who manages to come between others and their games because he expects them to be playing by the same set of rules he religiously follows.

Although Knight cannot help Elfride to break out of the frustrating cycle that prevents her happiness because of his penchant for self-deception and inability to see past his rigid convictions, Elfride herself is paralyzed by a constant need to hide the truth from him. For instance, although Elfride's experience inside the Luxellian tomb and the "intense agony of reproach in Stephen's eye" when she leaves with Knight prompt her to reveal the previous attachment to her new lover, she is ultimately unable to go through with it:

> The moment had been too much for her. Now that the crisis had come, no qualms of conscience, no love of honesty, no yearning to make a confidence and obtain forgiveness with a kiss, could string Elfride up to the venture. Her dread lest he should be unforgiving was heightened by the thought of yesterday's artifice, which might possibly add disgust to his disappointment. The certainty of one more day's affection, which she gained by silence, outvalued the hope of a perpetuity combined with the risk of all.[70]

Like a chess player who feels forced into distracting her opponent from a weakness rather than rectifying it, only to see the weakness become irreparable, Elfride declines revealing the truth to Knight because she fails to recognize that her secret is not a static thing, and that it grows over time into something over which she has no control.

---

[68] *PBE*, 260.
[69] Rimmer, 207.
[70] *PBE*, 269-70.

Not surprisingly, Elfride soon runs into Mrs. Jethway, the enemy Queen, and wants nothing more than a quick exchange to remove herself from the game:

> 'I defy you!' cried Elfride tempestuously. 'Do and say all you can to ruin me; try; put your tongue at work; I invite it! I defy you as a slanderous woman! Look, there he comes.'
> .... 'Not now,' said the woman, and disappeared down the path. [71]

The narrator understands that a "queen exchange" is not necessarily to Jethway's benefit, and that more damage can be done to Elfride by keeping the secret hidden from Knight until the proper moment.[72]

A similar scene is replayed soon after when Henry and Elfride travel with her family by boat from London to Plymouth and the mysterious Mrs. Jethway apparently comes aboard. Elfride's sleep is haunted on two separate occasions by the threats of her nemesis and she makes every effort to stay out of the dark lady's path. Once again, Knight fails to recognize the source of Elfride's moments of disquiet, assuming that they result from the manner of travel rather than any sort of emotional upset. However, while the previous episode shows how Elfride's problems continue to develop because of her deception, the current scene shows what happens when she is plagued by all of the strategic weaknesses that inform her play at chess, most specifically her tendencies to overestimate and miscalculate. Just as Elfride makes serious errors of judgment in her chess games with Knight and then symbolically repeats them when she tries to have him admit his admiration for her physical beauty, she repeats them yet again in questioning Knight about his previous romantic involvements:

> 'I wanted to ask you,' she went on, 'if – you had ever been engaged before.' She added tremulously, 'I hope you have – I mean, I don't mind at all if you have.'
>
> 'No, I never was,' Knight instantly and heartily replied. 'Elfride' – and there was a certain happy pride in his tone – 'I am twelve years older than you, and I have been about the world, and into society, and you have not.'

---

[71] *PBE*, 273-74.

[72] A rule of thumb in chess is that a player who is on the attack does not want to exchange pieces, especially queens, because he or she thereby reduces the number of pieces that can be brought to bear on the opponent's position. Similarly, a defender welcomes exchanges since they tend to make the position less complicated. Mrs. Jethway could reveal the secret to Knight during this scene, and effectively remove both herself and Elfride from the "game," but she wants to do more than spoil Elfride's relationship – she wants to inflict injury on her opponent – and so she holds off on an exchange until the last possible opportunity.

> .... Elfride shivered .... The belief which had been her sheet-anchor in hoping for forgiveness had proved false.[73]

Elfride thinks that she can best Knight at chess during their match, and now she believes that reducing him to her level by making him admit to previous indiscretions will provide her with the opportunity to reveal the truth about her past: "Whenever I find you have done a foolish thing I am glad, because it seems to bring you a little nearer to me, who have done many." Naturally, her strategy backfires because Knight is a romantic novice. Perhaps most importantly, however, tied in with Elfride's penchant for secrecy and tendency to miscalculate is a combination of hero-worship and self-loathing that ultimately prevents her from ever recognizing herself as anything but Knight's pawn.

As in the gradual exchange of pieces on a chessboard leading to the bare bones of an endgame, Knight eventually begins the arduous process of removing the layers of guilt and deception that clothe Elfride's secret about her previous romantic involvement with Stephen. Knight may be able to defeat Elfride time and time again at chess, but his ability to uncover her strategies quickly over the board does not manifest itself in the context of their relationship. Not only does it take Knight a considerable time to learn the extent to which Elfride will go in playing her game of secrecy, he also misjudges her honesty and guilt when he assumes she is not a virgin.

Elfride's journey with Stephen to the cliffs beyond Targan Bay is now repeated with Knight as her new travel partner; however, the chess-like repetition of events reinforces not so much how these parallel episodes are the same, but rather how much circumstances have altered. Once again the pair travels to Windy Beak, with Elfride riding her horse while her lover walks beside her, but as the narrator remarks:

> how different the mood from that of the former time! She had, indeed, given up her position as queen of the less to be vassal of the greater. Here was no showing off now; no scampering out of sight with Pansy, to perplex and tire her companion; no saucy remarks on *La Belle Dame sans Merci*. Elfride was burdened with the very intensity of her love.[74]

Elfride finds herself in the predicament of a chess player who recognizes that although a series of moves has brought about a position similar to one which previously existed, certain subtle differences in the new position render it unplayable.

---

[73] *PBE*, 291.
[74] *PBE*, 308.

The novel's endgame is signalled by the elimination of the Black Queen when the Church Tower comes crashing down on Mrs. Jethway. Hardy marks the transition by colouring the scene with chessic tones, not only in the symbolic capture of Rook (Tower) takes Queen and in the latter's removal from the "board," but in the description of Mrs. Jethway's house: "The fire was out, but the moonlight entered the quarried window, and made patterns upon the floor." Knight's initial discovery of the body is ironic on a number of levels and serves as a kind of symbolic reenactment of how he uncovers things (like Elfride's secret elopement) slowly by degrees:

> 'It is a tressy species of moss or lichen,' he said to himself.
> But it lay loosely over the stone.
> 'It is a tuft of grass,' he said.
> But it lacked the roughness and humidity of the finest grass.
> 'It is a mason's whitewash-brush.'
> Such brushes, he remembered, were more bristly; and however much used in repairing a structure would not be required in pulling one down.
> He said, 'It must be a thready silk fringe.'
> He felt further in. It was somewhat warm. Knight instantly felt somewhat cold.[75]

Knight has a theoretical knowledge about certain matters which has never adequately been tested by practical experience, and here he must actually touch Mrs. Jethway in order to convince himself that a human being lies pinned underneath the Tower.

Now that this major piece is removed from the field of play, the game enters its final stages presumably with a distinct edge for the "White pieces." After all, Mrs. Jethway's death prompts Knight to think about his state of affairs with Elfride and to consider an immediate union instead of continued procrastination:

> The unutterable melancholy of the whole scene, as he waited on, silent and alone, did not altogether clash with the mood of Knight, even though he was the affianced of a fair and winning girl, and though so lately he had been in her company .... the lengthened course of inaction he had lately been indulging in on Elfride's account might probably not be good for him as a man who had work to do. It could quickly be put an end to by hastening on his marriage with her.[76]

---

[75] *PBE*, 323.
[76] *PBE*, 328.

However, in typical Hardyan fashion, the episode provides the means by which Knight gains access to Mrs. Jethway's residence and discovers that she has been earnestly endeavouring to compose an important letter. Thus, on the following day when he receives by post both this letter and Elfride's self-incriminating one, Knight is emotionally devastated.

When Henry discovers the "truth" about Elfride's past and concludes that his affections have been trifled with, his protective layer of self-deception is dispelled. Like Swancourt who performs an immediate about-face when he learns of Stephen's humble origins, Knight's conviction about Elfride's innocence transforms itself into an even stronger conviction of her guilt:

> It is a melancholy thought that men who at first will not allow the verdict of perfection they pronounce upon their sweethearts or wives to be disturbed by God's own testimony to the contrary, will, once suspecting their purity, morally hang them upon evidence they would be ashamed to admit in judging a dog.[77]

Knight finds himself in the same kind of position that Stephen does after his humiliating loss to Elfride in the final game of their chess match, when his previous wins against her are revealed to be nothing more than games of pity on her part. Knight's violent reaction can be understood in chess terms, for when a player believes that a particular position is favourable, only to have this belief shattered by an unexpected move from the opponent, the player's perception of the resulting position is often far more negative than it ought to be.

Literary scholars have frequently criticized the fact that Elfride disappears from the last six chapters of the novel (she undergoes a kind of promotion by castling with the novel's resident rook, Lord Luxellian) and that Hardy's narrative turns to an examination of what happens to Knight after he leaves Endelstow. They argue that Elfride's premature death makes the story anticlimactic, and occasionally suggest that it constitutes a disturbing kind of practical joke on Hardy's part. However, as Rimmer has noted, Elfride's early death is consistent with the novel's controlling chess motif, because if she is associated with the queen in the game, Elfride is as expendable as any other piece excepting the king: "Her relations with Knight and with Stephen …have progressively reduced her … and like a captured queen in chess, she is put aside while the game she has seemed central to goes on without her."[78]

---

[77] *PBE*, 335.
[78] Rimmer, 215.

The King is the only piece that can not be sacrificed or otherwise given up because it must remain on the board throughout the entire game. Thus it is not surprising that in the final scene, Stephen, Henry, and Lord Luxellian – men of differing social classes who have nonetheless been at one time or another the "king" in Elfride's life – are left to look on at their sacrificed queen.

In *A Pair of Blue Eyes*, Hardy incorporates his chess motif in such a way that he shows his novel to be a complex and evolving game universe replete with conflicts and cross-purposed goals which the metaphorical implications of orthodox chess illuminate rather than simply replace. The world of the novel is not merely an elaborate chess game, but a disturbing mix of order and disorder, strategy and tactics, growth and decay, winning and losing, fate and circumstance, which all combine to simulate an unorthodox game involving not only human characters but non-human entities as well. Hardy's characters are much more developed than, for example, Middleton's allegorical chess pieces in *A Game at Chess*, and although a character like Mrs. Jethway is for the most part a one-dimensional combination of grief, vengeance, and malevolence, other characters are not so easy to classify. Stephen is Elfride's pawn, but being first in her heart he is also to some degree her king. Knight is the chivalrous knight, the straight-dealing medieval rook, the romantic pawn of Elfride's game of deception and the king of her affections. Even the consistently characterized Swancourt is at once a pawn, a king, and a bad bishop struggling to become better.

At the centre of all of this is Elfride, a character whose efforts to find happiness are frustrated because the means she uses to free herself from the forces that keep her in check are the ones that ultimately paralyze her. Hardy's use of the chess motif reminds us that although Elfride is brought down by her deceptions, she is a product of her education in social game-playing at the hands of Swancourt, and of the unspoken but understood social conventions that limit and devalue her as a Victorian woman. Hardy carefully traces Elfride's history in terms of the forces that strive to define and control her, and expresses through the chess metaphor the idea that her struggle against this control is as noble as it is ultimately futile.

WORKS CITED AND CONSULTED

Abercrombie, Lascelles. *Thomas Hardy: A Critical Study.* New York: Russell, 1964.

Blunden, Edmund. *Thomas Hardy.* London: Macmillan, 1962.

Braybrooke, Patrick. *Thomas Hardy and His Philosophy.* 1928. New York: Russell, 1969.

Bullen, J. B. *The Expressive Eye: Fiction and Perception in the Work of Thomas Hardy.* Oxford: Clarendon, 1986.

Casagrande, Peter J. *Unity in Hardy's Novels: 'Repetitive Symmetries'.* Lawrence: Regents Press of Kansas, 1982.

Devereux, Jo. "Thomas Hardy';s *A Pair of Blue Eyes*: The Heroine as Text." *The Victorian Newsletter* 81 (1992): 20-22.

Fleissner, R. F. "The Endgame in *The Tempest*." *Papers on Language and Literature* 21 (1985): 331-35.

Gittings, Robert. *Young Thomas Hardy.* Heinemann: London, 1975.

Goode, John. *Thomas Hardy: The Offensive Truth.* Oxford: Basil Blackwell, 1988.

Grimsditch, Herbert B. *Character and Environment in the Novels of Thomas Hardy.* New York: Russell, 1962.

Hardy, Thomas. *A Pair of Blue Eyes.* Ed. Pamela Dalziel. Harmondsworth, Middx: Penguin Books, 1998.

Hornback, Bert G. *The Metaphor of Chance: Vision and Technique in the Works of Thomas Hardy.* Athens: Ohio UP, 1971.

Hyman, Virginia R. *Ethical Perspective in the Novels of Thomas Hardy.* Port Washington: Kennikat P, 1975.

Jekel, Pamela L. *Thomas Hardy's Heroines: A Chorus of Priorities.* Troy NY: Whitston, 1986.

---. "Jonson and Shakespeare at Chess." *Shakespeare Quarterly* 34 (1983): 440-48.

---. "Ferdinand and Miranda at Chess." *Shakespeare Survey: An Annual Survey of Shakespeare Studies and Production* 35 (1982): 113-18.

Morgan, Rosemarie. *Women and Sexuality in the Novels of Thomas Hardy.* London: Routledge, 1988.

Rimmer, Mary. "Club Laws: Chess and the Construction of Gender in *A Pair of Blue Eyes*." *The Sense of Sex: Feminist Perspectives on Hardy.* Ed. Margaret R. Higonnet. Urbana: U of Illinois P, 1993. 203-20.

Schmidgall, Gary. "The Discovery at Chess in *The Tempest.*" *English Language Notes* 23 (1986): 11-16.

Seymour-Smith, Martin. *Hardy.* London: Bloomsbury, 1994.

Shakespeare, William. *The Tempest.* Ed. Anne Barton. London: Penguin, 1988.

Southerington, F. R. *Thomas Hardy's Vision of Man.* New York: Barnes and Noble, 1971.

Springer, Marlene. *Hardy's Use of Allusion.* Lawrence: UP of Kansas, 1983.

Stave, Shirley A. *The Decline of the Goddess: Nature, Culture and Women in Thomas Hardy's Fiction.* Westport: Greenwood, 1995.

Stewart, J. I. M. *Thomas Hardy: A Critical Biography.* London: Longman, 1971.

Sumner, Rosemary. *Thomas Hardy: Psychological Novelist.* London: Macmillan, 1981.

Taylor, Richard H. *The Neglected Hardy: Thomas Hardy's Lesser Novels.* London: Macmillan, 1982.

Thurley, Geoffrey. *The Psychology of Hardy's Novel's: The Nervous and the Statuesque.* St. Lucia, Queensland: U of Queensland P, 1975.

Tristam, Philippa. "Stories in Stones." *The Novels of Thomas Hardy.* Ed. Anne Smith. London: Vision P, 1979.

APPENDIX
ADDITIONAL CHESS MOTIFS

In *A Pair of Blue Eyes*, Hardy frequently paints the Wessex landscape in chequered tones. When the reader is first introduced to Stephen Smith on his way to Endelstow rectory, the scene of the dusk "thickening" into darkness is captured in the depiction of Lord Luxellian's mansion as a transforming chessboard (ch. II). The image is particularly provocative because it comes in the wake of our learning from Robert Lickpan about Hedger Luxellian's promotion to a lord at the hands of the mysterious King Charles III. In this early scene, Hardy introduces several images that are suggestive of pieces littering the chessboard landscape: the silhouettes of Robert and Stephen travelling "along the whole dreary distance of open country," in the manner of hanging pawns; the Rook-like twin lighthouses "reposing on the horizon with a calm lustre of benignity"; and the Endelstow rectory, representative of the resident "bishop" and built on the site of an old quarry, suggesting its replacement of a piece now lost. These kinds of images reappear throughhout the novel, especially with the depiction of chequered patterns formed by the sharp contrasts between light and dark, as in the scene where Henry, Stephen, and Elfride meet in the Luxellian tomb: "The blackened coffins ...the whitened walls" (II. xiv).

One indication that the chess motif is not simply an allegorical tool for Hardy is that a strict one-to-one correspondence between characters and chess pieces is undercut by the numerous associations which suggest themselves throughout the novel. For instance, Swancourt is not only a kind of slow moving King, but also an acutely restricted bad Bishop.[79]

This frustrating sense of confinement in which a bad Bishop becomes hampered by its own pawn is established by Hardy in the novel's opening scene: "'Ugh-h-h!...'Od plague you, you young scamp!' .... she withdrew from the room, and retired again downstairs" (I.i.). Swancourt's ailment prevents him from moving at all and Elfride herself appears confined within the limits of the staircase which she perpetually ascends and descends. Elfride is worried that while it is "plainly a case of necessity" Hewby's assistant might think their position odd, but the "bad bishop" recognizes that their situation is such that they have little choice in the matter.

Swancourt forms judgments about people strictly on the basis of class; Stephen plays manfully enough to deserve reward, humanly enough to deserve compassion, and badly enough to deserve punishment. Elfride recognizes that although the men in her life occupy different social classes, their worth is not determined on this basis alone. Like a chess player, she recognizes the importance of the relative values of her men. Smith might only be a pawn, but he has a great potential to become passed – and, of course, this is precisely what happens when he accepts the position in India. Knight (knight) and Swancourt (bishop) are essentially equal but in certain situations they dominate over one another and over Elfride. Knight replaces Swancourt as Elfride's "lord" during their courtship, but after the break-up

---

[79] See Brace, 26.

when Elfride goes to Knight and is followed by Swancourt, Knight has no choice but to let himself be dominated by the oblivious bishop (III. viii).

On the cliffs

Illustration to the serialisation of *A Pair of Blue Eyes*, T*insleys' Magazine* (September 1872 – July 1873), by James Abbott Pasquier.

NOTES ON CONTRIBUTORS

The Thomas Hardy Association is deeply indebted to all contributors, whether named here or not, especially those participating in our debating groups – the *Poem of the Month*, and the *Forum* discussion group. Whereas each and every contribution is valued and *all* are archived we regret that due to the limitations of space only a selected sample of our debates can be published in *The Hardy Review*.

- ❖ **BETTY CORTUS** received her Ph.D. from the City University of New York: her major area of concentration was on Hardy's poetry. In retirement she continues to research and write as an independent scholar. She volunteers her time to teach literature in a Learning-in-Retirement Program at Mira Costa College in Oceanside, California. She is a Vice President of **The Thomas Hardy Association** and directs its on-line Discussion Group, the ***Forum***.

- ❖ **GLEN DOWNEY** received his Ph.D. from the University of Victoria in 1998, and is currently co-chair of the English department at Appleby College, Ontario. He has taught at UBC, where he was awarded the Ian Fairclough Prize for Teaching in 2000. His publications include *The Fifty Fatal Flaws of Essay Writing* (Althouse Press, 2002); he appears in the PBS Telecourse, English Composition: Writing for an Audience. He is also a member of the Chess Federation of Canada and has been a Candidate Master since 1996.

- ❖ **ROSEMARIE MORGAN**, editor and publisher of *The Hardy Review*, has taught at Yale University since 1984 and is currently holding a research position. She is President of **The Thomas Hardy Association** and Vice President /Symposium Chair of the Thomas Hardy Society (UK). Her publications include *Women and Sexuality in the Novels of Thomas Hardy* (Routledge, 1988), *Cancelled Words* (Routledge, 1992), also essays on Charlotte Brontë, Mary Chesnut, Toni Morrison and women writers of the American Frontier. Her edition of the holograph manuscript version of *Far From the Madding Crowd* (Penguin World Classics) came out in 2000; she is "Year's Work" essayist for *Victorian Poetry*, author of "Women" and "Marriage" in *The Oxford Reader's Companion to Hardy* (2002), "Hardy and his Editors" in *The Palgrave Guide to Hardy Studies* (2004) – and work in progress includes a book on *Editing Hardy*.

- **WILLIAM W. MORGAN** is Executive Vice President (TTHA) and Director of **The Thomas Hardy Association's Poetry** page (& ***POTM.***) He is Professor Emeritus at Illinois State University, where he taught courses in Victorian Literature, Poetry as a Genre, English as a Field of Study and, occasionally, Women's Studies. He has published essays on Hardy in *PMLA*, *JEGP*, *Victorian Poetry*, *The Hardy Review*, and other journals. In 1998 he published his first chapbook of poems, *Trackings: The Body's Memory, The Heart's Fiction* (Boulder: Dead Metaphor Press). He is co-editor with Rosemarie Morgan of TTHA's *Occasional Series, Volume* II: *The Emma Poems* (2000) and is the driving force behind the Hardy Associations's Collection of Early Hardy Criticism held at Milner Library.

- **RICHARD NEMESVARI** is Associate Professor and Chair of the Department of English at St. Francis Xavier University. He is a Vice President of **The Thomas Hardy Association** and Director of the Association's ***Life*** page. His edition of Hardy's *The Trumpet-Major* was published by Oxford University Press in its World's Classics series, and his edition of Charlotte Brontë's *Jane Eyre* was published by Broadview Press in its Literary Texts series. Along with articles on Hardy he has published essays on Emily Brontë, Wilkie Collins, Mary Elizabeth Braddon, and Joseph Conrad. His latest piece, "Hardy and his Readers," will appear in *The Palgrave Guide to Hardy Studies* (2004).

- **MARTIN RAY** teaches at the University of Aberdeen, Scotland. He is a Vice President of **The Thomas Hardy Association**, Director of the ***Short Stories*** page and editor of *The Thomas Hardy Journal*. His publications include, *Thomas Hardy: A Textual Study of the Short Stories* (1997), *Thomas Hardy: An Annotated Critical Biography* (co-author, Ronald Draper, 1989), *Joseph Conrad* (1993), and has edited several works on Conrad. He has recently compiled and produced a Thomas Hardy Poetry Concordance on CD Rom (free to TTHA members), a *Dynasts* Concordance and concordances for the four volumes of short stories. His *Thomas Hardy Remembered* (Ashgate) and *The Poetry of Thomas Hardy: Contemporary Reviews* (Palgrave Macmillan), will be out in 2004.

- **ISOBEL ROBIN** embarked, late in retirement, on her M. A. thesis on Hardy, entitled "Devolutions of Power in *The Dynasts* and Other Works of Thomas Hardy." She was first published in *The Hardy Review*, Vol. I, in 1998; she has since produced her first book of poetry, *Freud's Back-Yard* (Five Islands Press, 2002). She has recently been commissioned by her publishers to produce new poems. Isobel Robin is a life member of **TTHA.**

❖ **SHANNON ROGERS** received her Ph.D. in European history from Penn State University and teaches in the History department at Saint Joseph's University. She is a Vice President of **The Thomas Hardy Association** and General Editor of the *Reviews* page. Her publications include "'The Historian of Wessex': Thomas Hardy's Contribution to History" (*Rethinking History*, 2001, 5: 2), "Medievalism in the Last Novels of Thomas Hardy: New Wine in Old Bottles" (*English Literature in Transition*, 1999, 42: 3), "'The Past is a Dream': The Neo-Feudalism of Benjamin Disraeli" (*Victorian Review*, 2002, 28:2). She is also Newsletter Editor for the William Morris Society and has published several articles on Welsh history. She is currently finishing a book on 19th century historical fiction and its role in shaping the writing of scholarly history. She has recently been commissioned to write *All Things Chaucer* about Geoffrey Chaucer and his medieval milieu (Greenwood, 2006).

❖ **ROBERT SCHWEIK** is University Distinguished Teaching Professor, Emeritus, of the State University of New York. He is editor of the Norton Critical Edition of *Far from the Madding Crowd*, and author of *Hart Crane: A Descriptive Bibliography* (University of Pittsburg Press) and of *Reference Sources in English and American Literature* (Norton), along with parts of sixteen other books, as well as numerous articles on Hardy, Tennyson, Browning, J. S. Mill, analytic bibliography, rhetoric, and cultural history in the nineteenth and early twentieth centuries. He is a Vice-President of both the Thomas Hardy Society and **The Thomas Hardy Association** where he directs **TTHA's** *Checklist*, *Links* and *Syllabus* pages. Bob is also co-chair of the International Thomas Hardy Conference Symposium.

.

ADVERTISEMENTS
As featured on **TTHA PROMOTIONS** www.yale.edu/hardysoc

Advertising rates for *The Hardy Review*
Up to 3 lines: $45 (£25)   Half Page: $60 (£45)   Full page: $90 (£70), if predesigned
For advertising copy designed by TTHA there is an added charge of $50 (£30).
Copy and payment to be sent to the editor on floppy disk or e-attachment
Rosemarie Morgan, 124 Bishop St, New Haven, CT 06511

THE THOMAS HARDY ASSOCIATION
MEMBERSHIP INFORMATION
Membership form can be accessed at :
http://www.yale.edu/hardysoc/Welcome/memform.htm

A. **INDIVIDUALS APPLYING FOR MEMBERSHIP OF TTHA** ....$35.00/£25.00
B. **COUPLES APPLYING FOR MEMBERSHIP OF TTHA.**............$45.00/£35.00
C. **STUDENT** (please state affiliation) **FOR MEMBERSHIP OF TTHA.** .... $25.50/£20.00

TTHA MEMBERSHIP OFFERS THE FOLLOWING TO ALL

➢ **Free** copy of annual publication: *The Hardy Review*

➢ Membership option to purchase earlier editions of *The Review*: at half price (plus postage) & *Occasional Series*: $7.50/£5.00

➢ **Free CD-Rom** of the *Thomas Hardy Poetry Concordance*. Please apply direct to Martin Ray giving your membership #
www.yale.edu/hardysoc/Order Form

➢ **Free** UK snailmail service: see Martin Ray:
< http://www.yale.edu/hardysoc >- VP BOX

➢ Reduced advertising fees on TTHA Promotions
➢ See PROMOTIONS page on www.yale.edu/hardysoc

➢ **Access to TTHA Members Research Resources**, featuring:
  1. **CHECKLIST**: the most comprehensive and up-to-date literary Checklist in existence online: updated twice monthly by a team of 20 scholars and professors world-wide.
  2. **REVIEWS Page**: book reviews of recent works on Hardy.
  3. *The Complete Poems* (under construction—currently holds *Time's Laughingstocks*)
  4. **OTTAKAR'S BOOKLIST**.
  5. **JEANIE'S BIBLIOGRAPHY:** a complete checklist of works on Hardy published through the 1990s – the perfect complement to the **CHECKLIST.**
  6. **COMPLETE POEMS**

For further informations contact: rosemarie.morgan@yale.edu

THE THOMAS HARDY ASSOCIATION PUBLICATIONS

TTHA publications can be ordered by copying & returning this form with payment cheque *made out to:*

Rosemarie Morgan,
124 Bishop Street, New Haven, CT 06511, USA

Title ....
Qty ....

The Hardy Review, Vol I, (1998) ISBN: 0-9669176-0-X	£18/$25
The Hardy Review Vol II, (1999) ISBN: 0-9669176-3-4	£18/$25
The Hardy Review Vol III, (2000) ISBN: 0-9669176-5-0	£18/$25
The Hardy Review Vol IV, (2001) ISBN: 0-9669176-7-7	£18/$25
The Hardy Review, Vol V, (2002) ISBN: 0-9669176-8-5	£18/$25
The Hardy Review, Vol VI, (2003) ISBN: 0-9669176-9-3	£18/$25
Days to Recollect: Essays in Honour of Robert Schweik ISBN:0-9669176-4-2	£25/ $36
Human Shows: Essays in Honour of Michael Millgate ISBN: 0-9669176-2-6	£25/$36
Occasional Series, Vol I: Editing Hardy (1999) ISBN: 0-9669176-1-8	£10/$15
Occasional Series, Vol II: Emma Poems (2001) ISBN: 0-9669176-6-9	£10/$15
Postage & Packing per volume:	£4.50/$5.50

Grand Total .... _____

Title/First Name: ....   Last Name: ....
Department: ....   Position: ....
Establishment:
Address:...Town................................
Zip/Postcode: ....   Country ....
Telephone: ....
Date: ....   Signature: ....

DISCOUNT to TTHA Members: 50% off all TTHA publications

THE THOMAS HARDY ASSOCIATION
TTHA Vice Presidents and Board of Directors

Gillian Beer: VP

Elena Carp: VP: *News From Romania*

Betty Cortus: VP: *Forum* Director
<Hardycor@owl.csusm.edu>

Shanta Dutta: VP: *News From India*
< shanta_dutta16@yahoo.com>

Ralph Elliott: VP
<Ralph.elliott@anu.edu.au>

James Gibson: VP: *Poetry Consultant*
<JamesGibson@ukgateway.net>

Sumiko Inoue: VP: *News from Japan* <ks-inoue@mx2.nisiq.net>

Yasushi Kamiyama: VP

Suzanne Keen:VP: *Elections* Director <Skeen@wlu.edu>

Rosemarie Morgan: *President/The Hardy Review* Ed/*Resources* Page Dir./*Maps* Page Dir./*News Updates* Dir./*Bibliography* Page Dir/ *Promotions* Page Dir.
<Rm82@pantheon.yale.edu>

William Morgan: VP:
Executive Vice President/ Poetry Page Director
<wwmorgan@mail.ilstu.edu>

Richard Nemesvari: VP
Life Page Director
<rnemesva@stfx.ca>

Linda Peterson: VP
<Linda.peterson@yale.edu>

Birgit Plietzsch: VP: *Novels* Page Director/*Network Consultant*
<bp10@st-andrews.ac.uk>

Martin Ray: VP:*Short Stories* Page Director
<Enl090@abdn.ac.uk>

Shannon Rogers: VP: *Book Reviews* Page Director
<srogers@sju.edu >

Robert Schweik: VP: *Syllabi* Page Director/ MRR – *Checklist* Page Director
<schweik@fredonia.edu>

Rosemary Sumner: VP:

Dennis Taylor: VP: *Poetry Consultant*<Taylor@bc.edu>

Keith Wilson: VP: *Drama* Page Director
<Kgwilson@uottawa.ca>

Ling Zhang: VP
China Consultant